Studies in Church History

16

THE CHURCH IN TOWN AND COUNTRYSIDE

THE CHURCH IN TOWN AND COUNTRYSIDE

PAPERS READ AT
THE SEVENTEENTH SUMMER MEETING AND
THE EIGHTEENTH WINTER MEETING
OF THE
ECCLESIASTICAL HISTORY SOCIETY

EDITED BY
DEREK BAKER

PUBLISHED FOR
THE ECCLESIASTICAL HISTORY SOCIETY
BY
BASIL BLACKWELL · OXFORD
1979

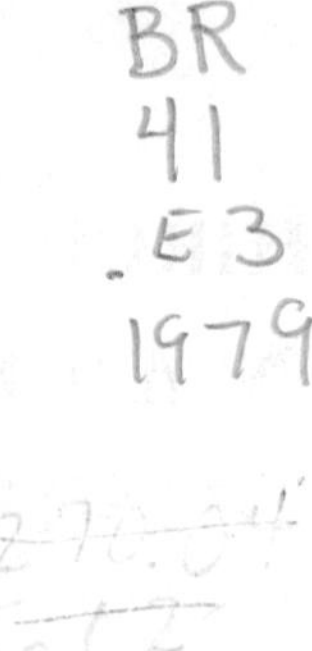

ISBN 0 631 11421 1

Printed in Great Britain
by Crampton & Sons Ltd, Sawston, Cambridge

PREFACE

The present volume of *Studies in Church History* is the sixteenth to be produced by the Ecclesiastical History Society and the seventh to be published by the Society itself in collaboration with Basil Blackwell. 'The church in town and countryside' was the theme of the seventeenth summer meeting of the Society, held at the University of Sheffield, and of the eighteenth winter meeting. The thirty-four papers included in this volume are a selection from those read at these two meetings.

The Society is grateful to the British Academy and Twenty-Seven Foundation for generous financial assistance in the production of this volume.

Derek Baker

PREFACE

CONTENTS

Preface *page* v

List of contributors xi

Introduction xv

Country bishops in Byzantine Africa (*Presidential Address*) 1
R. A. MARKUS

Problems arising from the conversion of Syria 17
W. LIEBESCHUETZ

Town and countryside in early Christianity 25
W. H. C. FREND

From town to country: the Christianisation of the Touraine 370–600 43
C. E. STANCLIFFE

Early Merovingian devotion in town and country 61
I. N. WOOD

The work of Audoenus of Rouen and Eligius of Noyon in extending episcopal influence from the town to the country in seventh-century Neustria 77
PAUL FOURACRE

Town and monastery in the Carolingian period 93
ROSAMOND MCKITTERICK

Charles the Bald and the church in town and countryside 103
JANET L. NELSON

The church in Anglo-Saxon towns 119
J. CAMPBELL

Crossroads and crises in the religious life of the later eleventh century 137
DEREK BAKER

CONTENTS

Urbanitas–rusticitas: linguistic aspects of a medieval dichotomy 149
MICHAEL RICHTER

A medieval urban church: the case of the crusader states 159
BERNARD HAMILTON

'A truth universally acknowledged' 171
EMMA MASON

Sermons to the upper bourgeoisie by a thirteenth-century Franciscan 187
D. L. d'AVRAY

Town mice and country mice in the province of York 1317–40 201
ROSALIND M. T. HILL

The secular clergy of the diocese of Carlisle in the fourteenth century 207
RICHARD ROSE

The late Byzantine monastery in town and countryside 219
ANTHONY BRYER

Penitence and peace-making in city and contado: the *Bianchi* of 1399 243
DIANA M. WEBB

The town in church history: general presuppositions of the reformation in Germany 257
BERND MOELLER

Parochial structure and the dissemination of protestantism in sixteenth-century England: a tale of two cities 269
CLAIRE CROSS

Church and chapelry in sixteenth-century England 279
CHRISTOPHER KITCHING

Factionalism in town and countryside: the significance of puritanism and Arminianism 291
ANTHONY FLETCHER

Thomas Fuller as royalist country parson during the interregnum 301
W. B. PATTERSON

CONTENTS

'A practice of a very hurtful tendency' 315
W. M. JACOB

Perpetual curacies in eighteenth-century South Wales 327
JOHN R. GUY

When city speaks for county: the emergence of the town as a focus for religious activity in the nineteenth century 335
ALAN ROGERS

The Victorian town parish: a rural vision and urban mission 361
DAVID E. H. MOLE

Thomas Chamberlain – a forgotten tractarian 373
PETER G. COBB

Urban church attendance and the use of statistical evidence, 1850–1900 389
NIGEL YATES

Between town and countryside: contrasting patterns of churchgoing in the early Victorian Black Country 401
GEOFFREY ROBSON

The city, the countryside and the social gospel in late Victorian nonconformity 415
D. W. BEBBINGTON

Church extension in town and countryside in later nineteenth-century Leicestershire 427
DAVID M. THOMPSON

Ideals in urban mission: episcopalians in twentieth-century Glasgow 441
GAVIN WHITE

Urban problems and rural solutions: drink and disestablishment in the first world war 449
STUART P. MEWS

Abbreviations 477

CONTRIBUTORS

R. A. MARKUS (*President*)
Professor of Medieval History, University of Nottingham

A. A. M. BRYER
Reader in Byzantine Studies and Director of the Centre for Byzantine Studies, University of Birmingham

JAMES CAMPBELL
Fellow and tutor in Modern History, Worcester College, Oxford

W. H. C. FREND
Professor of Ecclesiastical History, University of Glasgow

STUART P. MEWS
Lecturer in Department of Religious Studies, University of Lancaster

BERND MOELLER
Professor of Church History, University of Göttingen

ALAN ROGERS
Reader in Local History, University of Nottingham

DEREK BAKER
Lecturer in History, University of Edinburgh

D. W. BEBBINGTON
Lecturer in History, University of Stirling

PETER G. COBB
Librarian, Pusey House, Oxford

CLAIRE CROSS
Senior Lecturer in History, University of York

D. L. d'AVRAY
Lecturer in Medieval History, University of London, University College

ANTHONY FLETCHER
Senior Lecturer in History, University of Sheffield

CONTRIBUTORS

PAUL FOURACRE
University of London, King's College

JOHN R. GUY
Rector of Wolvesnewton

BERNARD HAMILTON
Senior Lecturer in Medieval History, University of Nottingham

ROSALIND M. T. HILL
Emeritus Professor of Medieval History, University of London, Westfield College

W. M. JACOB
Vice-principal, Salisbury and Wells Theological College

CHRISTOPHER KITCHING
Assistant Keeper, Public Record Office, London

J. H. W. G. LIEBESCHUETZ
Reader in Ancient History, University of Leicester

ROSAMOND McKITTERICK
Fellow, Newnham College, Cambridge

EMMA MASON
Lecturer in History, University of London, Birkbeck College

DAVID E. H. MOLE
Tutor, College of the Ascension, Selly Oak Colleges, Birmingham

JANET L. NELSON
Lecturer in Medieval History, University of London, King's College

W. B. PATTERSON
Professor of History, Davidson College, North Carolina

MICHAEL RICHTER
Lecturer in Medieval History, University College, Dublin

CONTRIBUTORS

GEOFFREY ROBSON
Senior Lecturer in Religious Education, Westhill College, Selly Oak Colleges, Birmingham

RICHARD ROSE
University of Edinburgh

C. E. STANCLIFFE
University of Newcastle-upon-Tyne

DAVID M. THOMPSON
Lecturer in Modern Church History, University of Cambridge

DIANA M. WEBB
University of London, King's College

GAVIN WHITE
Lecturer in Ecclesiastical History, University of Glasgow

I. N. WOOD
Lecturer in Medieval History, University of Leeds

NIGEL YATES
City Archivist, Portsmouth

INTRODUCTION

The questions posed in the consideration of the church in town and countryside are varied and ramifying: how different were the problems faced by churchmen in these two environments? What problems, and what solutions, were created by changing relationships between town and countryside? What effect did urban development have upon established ecclesiastical attitudes and institutions? How far do sociological differences between urban and rural life determine the patterns of the Christian life, and its roles, in societies differing historically, geographically and culturally, as well as sociologically? Whatever its pastoral message, Christianity was in origin predominantly an urban religion—a fact overshadowing its early development. How far was the organisation of the church determined by its urban origins? What effect did these exercise in its later development? How did the urban background affect ecclesiastical culture, values and outlook? And when it moved to 'the winning of the countryside' what problems were posed for the urban, organised church? How far were traditional and accepted values, precepts and positions modified in practice to adapt to these new circumstances?

This is the perspective for Professor Dickens' assertion that 'the German Reformation was an urban event', and Professor Moeller's 'no towns, no reformation'. It is the context, on the one hand, for Dr Liebeschuetz's remarks on the decline of the city and development of the village in late antiquity, and, on the other, for Victorian concern for 'the breath and blandness of a village economy'[1] in the face of the isolation of 'the masses . . . of our large and growing towns . . . a world apart, a nation by themselves; divided almost as effectively from the rest as if they spoke another language or inhabited another land'.[2] It may seem a far cry from the 'heathenism' of Victorian towns to the paganism of the countryside in later antiquity, but the essential distinction between town and countryside is present in both, and the problems under discussion are largely explained in terms of this fundamental dichotomy.

It must, however, be asked whether such distinctions are useful, or even valid. Professor Markus, referring to 'a nexus of urban and rural churches', remarks upon that 'synthesis of local and cosmopolitan in

[1] See below p 367.
[2] Below p 402.

which urban and rural tradition had coalesced to form a remarkably vital and tenacious religious culture'.[3] If Athonite monasteries are walled towns[4] for Dr Chitty the desert was a city, while Dr Stancliffe seeks a subtler, multi-classified approach to the simple categories of town and countryside[5] – an attitude reinforced at numerous points by Dr Bryer, who emphasises the 'unequivocably urban' character of Trapezuntine St Sabbas,[6] demonstrates the practical absurdity of regarding thirteenth-century Lampsakos as a *polis* in anything other than legal definition,[7] and declares that 'the Byzantine city is a concept which scarcely survived the seventh century'.[8] There is a direct connection between the late medieval Byzantine world where 'the distinction between town and countryside is almost meaningless'[9] and Dr Mews' twentieth-century society[10] where matters political and ecclesiastical can be made to combine tangentially in a socio-spiritual Charleston. Complexity rather than simplicity is the principle of ecclesiastical inter-relationships in urban and non-urban contexts throughout the ages. As with institutions, so with men: there is no clear line to be drawn between Auden's 'rootless tribe from windblown states' and his 'artistic souls that lie out in the weed and pollen belt'. The problems are all too often problems of definition – or over-definition – in a readiness to fix the fugitive phenomena of urban and non-urban pieties. But if these are practical cautions against oversimple categorisation of complex realities it remains nonetheless true that the city is at the centre of Christian cosmological discussion, for here

The choice of patterns is made clear
What the machine imposes, what
Is possible and what is not,
To what conditions we most bow
In building the Just City now.[11]

[3] Below pp 2, 15.
[4] Below p 241.
[5] Below p 45.
[6] Below p 223.
[7] Below p 221.
[8] *Ibid.*
[9] Below p 223.
[10] Below pp 449–76.
[11] W. H. Auden, 'The promise of American Life', *New Year Letter* (London 1941) pp 67–9.

COUNTRY BISHOPS IN BYZANTINE AFRICA (PRESIDENTIAL ADDRESS)

by R. A. MARKUS

TOWN and countryside are contrasting, even opposed ideas: one of those doublets which have dominated European thought since antiquity. Our vocabulary of 'politics' and 'civilization' bears ample testimony to the deep hold that the prejudices of the townsmen of antiquity have established over our language and our thinking. Sometimes, even in antiquity, those prejudices would be turned on their head: the town, the exclusive milieu of culture, refinement and rational human behaviour, could become, as for instance in the eyes of a Jewish rabbi of the third century[1] the seat of iniquity, set up to extort and to oppress. Whatever the attitude one took to the town, the dichotomy of town and countryside became almost a category in the Kantian sense in terms of which modern Europeans have come to perceive the world around them. With Max Weber it became a fundamental category of sociological understanding, with Rostovtzeff of historical analysis, especially of the ancient world in its decline; and in the hands of William Frend—the Rostovtzeff of ecclesiastical history—it showed its power to illuminate, even to transform, the study of ancient heresy and schism. 'The church in town and countryside' might be thought to extend the franchise of a notion which has already had too wide and at times, as some would have it, perhaps even a baleful, influence. But both the value of the notion of town and country as an interpretative tool for the ecclesiastical historian, and its limitations, its liability to obscure and to distort, will, I hope, become clearer in the course of discussion.

The subject of this paper, country-bishops in Byzantine Africa, must seem to lead into a remote by-way of ecclesiastical history. Even that could be a profitable path to explore if it turned out to lead to a better appreciation of the part played by both the links and the

[1] Compare D. Sperber, 'Angaria in rabbinic literature,' *Antiquité classique* 38 (Brussels 1969) pp 164–8, at p 166, n 15. I owe the reference to R. MacMullen, *Roman government's response to crisis* (New Haven 1976) p 164 n 48 where it is, however, wrongly given.

divisions between town and country in the life of the church—especially in an area where the two worlds of town and country are notoriously hard to separate, even to define.[2] But it is not only methodological questions and problems about our interpretative concepts and their appropriateness to the facts that I want to explore; indeed I intend to leave questions of this kind in the margins of my enquiry, and to welcome any light that may get thrown on them as an extra bonus. What I should like to investigate is the nexus of urban and rural churches in that brief interlude of something a little more than a century and a half between the Byzantine reconquest of Africa and the Moslem conquest.

I will not need to stress the enormous part played by the dichotomy of town to countryside in attempts to explain the great African schism, reaching back into the time of Constantine, between the two African Christian communities which became known as Catholic and Donatist respectively. The Donatist movement is the classic instance of a religious movement whose roots have been traced to pre-existent tensions in society. It has been seen as the religious expression of a dissent non-religious in origin. Among the non-religious origins claimed for the movement the opposition of town and countryside has been combined with other tensions, regional, ethnic, social or cultural.[3] To be sure, some of these tensions are hard to disentangle, and I do not intend to raise, once again, the grand old question whether ancient heresies were really social or national protest movements in disguise. But we need at least to begin with the reminder that Donatism has been seen as the religion of the rural poor, the under-privileged and the under-Romanised. The last phase in the African church's history before its eclipse under moslem rule has been seen as manifesting these same tensions; even to the extent of representing Donatism as a kind of *praeparatio Korani*. 'If the Islamic conquest was the final act in the division of Rome and Carthage,' Frend concludes his book on Donatism '. . . then the Donatists and the dissenting sects contributed powerfully to that result. Donatism was

[2] P. A. Février, 'Toujours le Donatisme: à quand l'Afrique?', *Rivista di storia e letteratura religiosa* 2 (Florence 1966) pp 228–40; C. Courtois, 'De Rome à l'Islam,' *Revue africaine* 86 (Algiers 1942) pp 25–55, esp at pp 28–9; G. Charles-Picard, *La civilisation de l'Afrique romaine* (Paris 1959) pp 6, 43–4, 160–3. For a general survey of recent work, see R. Chevallier, 'Cité et territoire,' *Aufstieg und Niedergang der römischen Welt*, ed H. Temporini (Berlin 1972–) 2/1 (1974) pp 649-788; for North Africa, pp 719-22, 778-9.

[3] See my paper 'Christianity and dissent [in Roman Africa: changing perspectives in recent work'], *SCH* 9 (1972) pp 21–36 for a survey and discussion.

not merely a schism, it was part of a revolution'.[4] Like Rostovtzeff's backward rural masses, unassimilated to the civilization of Roman townsmen, it is Frend's Donatists, unreconciled to the urban religion of the Roman governing classes, who are the agents of destruction.

The formula has come to dominate our vision of the end of Roman rule and the extinction of Christianity in Africa. It is a hypothesis of great and simplifying power; and we have still only woefully fragmentary evidence to reveal to us the nature of Christianity in Africa during the last century before the Moslem conquest. Fifteen years ago I questioned the ability of Frend's explanation to make sense of the scraps of evidence we possess about Christianity in Byzantine Africa.[5] I would now like, more constructively, to scrutinize some of that evidence and attempt a reconstruction of the nature of rural Christianity in Africa and its relation to the urban church of the empire.

The African church's organisation had developed over the centuries along lines which produced a structure very different from the pattern of dioceses grouped into metropolitan provinces which had become standard throughout the territory of the empire. In Africa, there was only one metropolitan province, that of Carthage; the other ecclesiastical provinces, as they emerged one by one by the early fifth century, had their own primates. These were not, however, the bishops of metropolitan sees for, except in the proconsular province, there were no metropolitan bishoprics. Instead of having a fixed primatial see located in the metropolis of the civil province, as would be usual, each of the African provinces appears to have had a rule of succession to the office of primate by seniority among the bishops of the province. The provincial primates all recognised a somewhat undefined pre-eminence over them held by the bishop of Carthage. This anomalous organization was restored at the time of the Byzantine reconquest of the African provinces in the 530s, and remained in force during the whole history of the African church so far as it can be traced.[6]

The African church always cherished its own individuality, and when pope Pelagius II tried in the 580s to get it to come into line with the arrangements generally followed elsewhere, he encountered resistance. His successor, Gregory the Great, had to come to terms—

[4] [W. H. C.] Frend, [*The*] *Donatist church* (Oxford 1952) pp 334–6; quotation from p 336.

[5] 'Donatism: [the last phase'], *SCH* 1 (1964) pp 118–26.

[6] On the attempt by Justinian to change the state of affairs, and the tensions engendered, see my paper 'Carthage, [Prima Justiniana, Ravenna: an aspect of Justinian's *Kirchenpolitik*'], *Byzantion* (forthcoming).

as had more than one of his predecessors—with the tenacity of African traditions. In a letter written in the first year of his pontificate, concluding the affair begun under Pelagius, he conceded to the province of Numidia the free observance of their peculiar customs, with one proviso: that 'those who have come to the episcopate from the ranks of the Donatists' be debarred from the additional dignity of the provincial primacy.[7] There is nothing odd about the exclusion of Donatists, nor about the conflict between Roman love of uniformity and African jealousy of ancient peculiarities, nor about Gregory's pastoral flexibility and readiness to withdraw gracefully. But there are two striking further demands that he addressed to the Numidian bishops at the same time: first that the traditional succession rule to the primacy should be modified: let the primate not succeed automatically by seniority, but let him be elected by his fellow bishops in consideration of his merits; Donatists being, of course, *ipso facto* assumed to be disqualified. Gregory's second curious demand (addressed in a letter written at the same time to the exarch of Africa)[8] was that the elected primate was not to reside in the countryside—*per villis*—but in a city, according to the bishops' choice. In other words, country bishops were either not to be elected to the primacy, or, alternatively, were to cease being country bishops on election.

Who and what were these country bishops, and why were they required to move to a city? Country bishops had a long history. With the different forms of the institution, its past and its future, we need happily not concern ourselves.[9] In Africa many small places, villages, *castella* and rural settlements had their bishops at the end of the fourth century. In its closing years, and during the first decade of the fifth century, catholics and Donatists were both multiplying bishoprics

[7] Gregory I, *Ep* I 75, [ed Ewald & Hartmann], *MGH Epp* 1 and 2 (1887–99) 1 p 95 especially lines 17–19. The phrase quoted in the text is usually interpreted to refer to bishops who have been converted from Donatism rather than to Donatist bishops who have managed, somehow, to 'aggregate' themselves to the body of the Numidian episcopate, as for example by L. Duchesne, *L'Église au sixième siècle* (Paris 1925) p 649 n 1. As I go on to show, however, there is no reason to reject the literal sense of the words, which make perfectly good sense in the context properly understood.

[8] *Ep* I 72, 1 p 92 lines 15–17; compare R. Aigrain's comment in 'La fin de l'Afrique chrétienne,' *FM* 5 (1947) p 215 n 1.

[9] On the chorepiscopate, see F. Gillmann, *Das Institut der Chorbischöfe im Orient* (Munich 1903); T. Gottlob, 'Der abendländische Chorepiskopat,' *Kanonistische Studien und Texte* 1 (Bonn 1928) (who does not, in fact, discuss Africa); E. Kirsten, 'Chorbischof' in *RAC* 2 (1954) cols 1105–14; and the excellent summary by H. Hess, *The canons of the council of Sardica* (Oxford 1958) pp 100–3. Compare Leo I, *Ep* 12.10 for an attempt to phase out the chorepiscopate in Africa (Mauretania Caesariensis) in the 440s.

in a race to keep up with each other. But there was more to Gregory's dislike of these rural bishoprics than a Roman town-dweller's prejudice against the countryside; more even, than the church's canonical tradition which had, since the council of Nicaea, set into an urban mould and frowned upon country-bishoprics. Gregory tells us his reasons: his demands for reforming primatial elections and his rules for residence are designed to enhance their potential in resisting the Donatists.[10] It is clear that Gregory's—and, we may assume, his predecessor's—worries about the African episcopate and primacy sprang from the conviction that the bishops of Numidia, at any rate, were too favourably inclined towards Donatism. If we scrutinise the evidence at close quarters, it becomes clear that the pope had good reasons for his worries, even if they sprang from misunderstandings. He thought that there was a Donatist revival in full swing, and that the heresy was 'spreading daily.'[11]

There appears to be ample basis for the pope's continual worry over the lack of concern shown by the clergy about the spread of the heresy and over the failure of his moves to get the state of affairs remedied by a council.[12] The two churches which had, two hundred years before, faced each other across a gulf of bitter mutual hostility, seem now to have settled down into a comfortable partnership. Catholics, and what is worse devout catholics (*religiosi*) allow their families, slaves and other dependants to be given Donatist baptism;[13] Donatists are being put in charge of churches by catholic bishops and, apparently, promoted over the heads of catholic clergy.[14] The Numidian episcopate had no objection certainly to ex-Donatists, and probably [15] to Donatists among its ranks and, as we have seen, taking their turn in the normal provincial succession to the primacy. The Donatist wolves were ravaging the Lord's sheepfold as if 'unrestrained by any shepherd's protection.'[16]

How the African situation was understood in Italy can be seen reflected in a formula which has survived in the formulary book of the papal writing office. It contains, among other instructions given to

[10] *Ep* 1 72, 1 p 92 lines 16–17.

[11] *Ep* 2 46, 1 p 147 lines 23–4. Other letters concerned with this: *Epp* 1 72, 75, 82; 2 46; 4 32, 35, 41(?); 5 3; 6 34, 59, 61; (7 2).

[12] *Ep* 4 7, 1 p 239 lines 3–4.

[13] *Ep* 6 34, 1 p 413 lines 6–8.

[14] *Ep* 1 82, 1 p 100 lines 13–15.

[15] See above n 7.

[16] *Ep* 4 35, 1 p 271 line 7.

newly consecrated Italian bishops, a prohibition of accepting Africans 'who dare to apply for admission to ecclesiastical orders, in any circumstances, for they frequently turn out to be Manichees or *rebaptizati*'.[17] Frend has taken the use of this formula in a letter of pope Gregory II's to Boniface[18] as 'formal evidence for the survival of Donatism up to the very end of African Christianity'[19]. It is nothing of the kind; what we have is the fossilised remnants of notions enshrined in the practice of the papal *scrinium*, which sheds light only on an institution noted for its conservatism: it was still churning out the same formula in the middle of the eleventh century.[20] In any case the assumption that *rebaptizati* in the formula refers to Donatists[21] is mistaken: the formula in fact originated in the time of pope Gelasius I around 490 [22] and must be read in the light of the provisions made at the Roman synod of 487[23] for the treatment of African *rebaptizati*. These are clearly people who apostatised during the Vandal persecutions, particularly under Huneric in 484; we know that many catholics underwent Arian rebaptism at this time.[24] We may readily admit that in the 590s the *rebaptizati* were assumed to be Donatists; but all that use of the formula tells us about is Italian habits of mind. What it tells us is that Africans who might have been perfectly acceptable, perhaps even unnoticed and un-labelled as 'Donatists' in their own African churches, were suspect in Italy, for no better reason than that they came from Africa and you never know what you are buying when you buy African. Gregory the Great, and other popes, evidently read the African situation in terms of ancient and familiar concepts which the practice of papal notaries had helped to fossilise, but which had, in reality, lost their original meaning and their application to the

[17] *Liber diurnus*, 6, ed T. E. von Sickel (Vienna 1889) pp 5–6; ed E. de Rozière (Paris 1869) pp 22–9.

[18] *Ep* 18, *MGH Epp* 3 (1892) p 267; *MGH Epp Sel* (2 ed 1955) 1 pp 31–2.

[19] Frend, *Donatist church*, p 313; it is true that Frend prefaces this statement with the qualifying 'If this interpretation is true;' but it has never been questioned, so far as I know, except in my papers 'Donatism' p 124 n 1; and 'Reflections [on religious dissent in North Africa in the Byzantine period'], *SCH* 3 (1966), p 145 n 1, where, however I failed to arrive at an adequate reconstruction of its history.

[20] Nicholas II, *Ep* 25, *PL* 143 (1882) col 1347.

[21] Defended by L. Godard, 'Quels sont les Africains que le pape Grégoire II défendit en 723 d'élever au sacerdoce?', *Revue africaine* (1861) pp 49–53.

[22] Jaffé 675, *PL* 59 (1862) cols 137–8.

[23] Jaffé 609, *PL* 58 (1862) col 924.

[24] For example Victor of Vita, *Historia persecutionis africanae provinciae*, I. 33, II. 29, III. 46–8, ed M. Petschenig, *CSEL* 7 (1881) pp 15, 34–5, 94–6; Ferrandus, *Vita Fulgentii* 21.45, *PL* 65 (1861) col 140).

contemporary situation in Africa. All the evidence suggests that the division between orthodoxy and heresy, so sharp as seen from Rome, was much blurred in Numidia, the stronghold of Donatism in its heyday. It would be curious, if there really had been a revival of the ancient heresy after nearly two hundred years during which we hear nothing of it, that such a revival should produce two ecclesiastical communities living comfortably together. Sects have longer memories than the proverbial elephant, and one would expect a revival to have deepened rather than closed the rift between them.

Can we get any further in re-interpreting the evidence, making allowance for the systematic distortion due to mis-applied concepts? It is instructive to take a closer look at Gregory the Great's objection to the African arrangements for provincial primacies, and especially, to his suspicion of country-bishops. We have seen that his suspicion was related to a notion that only respectable city-bishops could be effective in combatting Donatism. There is one very revealing case which came up about a year after Gregory's attempts to lay down new lines for the Numidian church which shows that his rule for the residence of primates may have been part of a wider attack on country-bishops, and also allows us to glimpse the likely reason. One Maximian, bishop of an unidentified Numidian see called Pudentiana[25] had given permission for the consecration of a Donatist bishop in his place of residence (*in loco quo deget*). The language strongly suggests that Maximian was not residing in the *civitas* of his see, but somewhere outside it, presumably *per villis*; what he had allowed was the appointment of a new Donatist bishop in the neighbourhood of the existing catholic bishopric. Maximian, it was alleged, had been bribed[26] to allow this. The darkness is only further deepened by Gregory's remark that although 'this' had been permitted by previous custom (*anterior usus*), its continuance was now prohibited by the 'catholic faith'.[27] But what exactly had been sanctioned by previous custom

[25] At the conference of Carthage in 411 the Donatist bishop of Pudentiana claimed that there were no catholics in his diocese; the catholic bishop of Macomades replied that there had been catholic bishops who had died and would be replaced. It seems therefore that Pudentiana was in the neighbourhood of Macomades—*Gesta Coll Carth,* 1, 201, ed S. Laurel, *CSEL* 149A (1974) p 148 lines 58–69. Compare St Gsell, *Atlas archéologique de l'Algérie* (Paris 1911) note to map 28 n 3. In the *Notitia provinciarum et civitatum Africae,* ed M. Petschenig, *CSEL* 7, p 121 line 44 the church of Pudentiana occurs only with a presbyter against its name. This does not, however, necessarily mean that it was not a bishopric in the 480s.

[26] *Ep* 2 46, 1 p 147 line 8.

[27] *Ibid* lines 9–10.

that has now been abrogated? It cannot have been the bribery; it must be either the making of a new country-bishop, or allowing a Donatist to be made a bishop, and it could be both these things *if* they amounted to the same thing in the writer's mind. It seems very likely that what Gregory had in mind were his prohibitions, issued only in the preceding year, of primates residing in the countryside and Donatists being promoted to the primacy. The only difference is that he now seems to be extending the application of those prohibitions to other bishops, not only primates of provinces. The situation at Pudentiana is clearly related to Gregory's suspicion of country bishops and of their links with Donatism: the two things were closely associated in the pope's mind.

And not without reason. What had happened in the case we have just examined was that a catholic bishop had given way to a Donatist pressure-group within his diocese to allow the consecration of a bishop for them; the bishop's see was not, however, to be in the *civitas* where the catholic bishop had his see, but somewhere in the surrounding countryside. If this case at Pudentiana was at all typical, one could easily understand the grounds for the assumption that country bishoprics and Donatism were apt to go together, and the disapproval of country-bishoprics and the attempt to outlaw them in Africa would make good sense.

The clue to the real nature of the relations between catholic and Donatist communities is to be found in the fact that this particular case was of a type which had until recently been normal and sanctioned by custom. The papal objection to the custom is based on the likelihood that the equation of 'Donatist' with 'country bishop' will frequently hold. This is where we come upon the crucial difference between the 590s and the fourth and fifth centuries. In that classic age of the schism each catholic bishop, by and large, had his Donatist opposite number, as revealed, for instance, in the roll-call at the Carthage conference in 411, when Donatist bishops were queuing up to recognize in the catholic bishop of their locality their rival, their 'persecutor,' as some of them liked to say. What we lack now at the end of the sixth century, is precisely that set up of two churches each with its own hierarchy, altar against altar and church against church, divided by bitter hostility and intolerance. The situation now appears to be that something that can still be called 'Donatism' exists in the interstices of the network of a single episcopate, in a very peaceful co-existence disturbed only when local tensions, perhaps sparked off by clerical rivalries, difficulties over promotion and the like, flared into occasional conflict which brought papal intervention in its train.

Just what distinguished a Donatist from a catholic community it is impossible to say. In Italy, at any rate, it was thought, or perhaps only assumed, that re-baptism was still being practised.[28] We must not conclude too much from that, but it may well be that there were communities in the African church, and especially in Numidia, which still preserved peculiarities originally associated with the schismatic church. The historical development of the two churches since the time of the Vandal conquest could easily have led to such a situation. At the time of the conference held at Carthage in 411 catholic and Donatist bishops were more or less evenly balanced in towns, and many rural bishoprics had both a catholic and a Donatist bishop. But the Donatist certainly had a majority in the countryside, where there were many Donatist bishops without a catholic opposite number; in Numidia the Donatists' majority in rural sees was 'massive.'[29] The fate of the Donatist church under the Vandal occupation is obscure, but it does not seem to have been too clearly distinguished from its ancient rival by their common Arian conquerors, and was probably treated with like severity. In the church which emerged into the era of the Byzantine reconquest the old divisions were little more than a memory, and quite different tensions came to eclipse the schism between Donatist and catholic. But it is not at all unlikely that within a single ecclesiastical structure some communities maintained Donatist traditions. This could have come about in various ways, such as the disappearance of the catholic bishop or clergy in places which had had both catholic and Donatist communities at the time of the Vandal conquest; but it is especially likely to have happened in places which had had only Donatist churches in the early fifth century. Such places, as we know, were concentrated in the countryside of Numidia: and it is to this province that all our evidence for Donatism at the end of the sixth century relates.[30] Along lines such as these we can understand the symbiosis of communities contained in a single ecclesiastical

[28] *Epp* 4 32, 1 p 267 and 4 35, 1 p 271.

[29] Compare *Actes de la conférence de Carthage en* 411, ed S. Lancel (Paris 1972–) 1 pp 134–43 and 154–64. For the 'massive' superiority of churches in the unchallenged grip of Donatists in the Numidian countryside, see p 161.

[30] The exact locations can, unfortunately, only be identified in the case of Lamiggiga (?) (*Ep* 1 82) and Nicivibus, which was almost certainly the see of bishop Columbus, Gregory's *confidant* in the province; Compare H. Jaubert cited by Frend, *Donatist church*, pp 309–10. For Pudentiana, see n 25 above.

structure without duplicate hierarchies but with divergent traditions, catholic and Donatist in their origins, as the result of a natural development of some one hundred and fifty years.[31]

The papal correspondence of the 590s does, however, suggest that there was more to arouse disquiet in Rome than the peaceful survival of local traditions in pockets of rural Numidia. It may even be that Gregory had come to see the inappropriateness of his notions to African realities: for after 596 Donatism is never again mentioned in his letters, although his worries about the African church continued. He may have learnt to be on guard against the assumption which modern historians have been only too ready to make, that 'Donatist' is a label with a clear and invariable meaning. It had certainly had such a meaning originally; and that meaning may well have survived during at least some part of the Vandal occupation of Africa. But in Justinian's time it had already become something not unlike the label 'Communist' in McCarthy's America: the staunchest defenders of Chalcedonian orthodoxy, such as Augustine's faithful disciple Facundus, had earned themselves the label of 'Donatist' from others more ready to comply with imperial policy.[32] If sheer orthodox intransigence in the face of official pressure could be called 'Donatism' around 550, it is unlikely that many of the movements other features were still in the forefront of contemporary minds. The well-known case of a Numidian bishop called Paul very strongly suggests that in Gregory the Great's time 'Donatist' was a label attached to people not so much in virtue of their belonging to a schismatic group, but in virtue of a certain *Autonomiegefühl*[33] towards both the government and the Roman see.

This bishop Paul had arrived in Rome probably in the early summer of 596, after having been prevented from sailing for at least two years by the local civil administration.[34] When he finally did get to Rome,

[31] S. A. Morcelli, *Africa christiana* (Brixiae 1816) 3 pp 339–40 confessed himself astonished that Donatism survived longer in Africa than Arianism, and conjectured that the sect had been able to lurk in small villages and remote places by clinging to its traditions and refraining from proselytism.

[32] Facundus, *Contra Mocianum, PL* 67 (1865) cols 855–8; Compare Markus, 'Reflections' pp 143–7.

[33] Compare E. Caspar, *Geschichte* [*des Papsttums*], 2 vols (Tübingen 1933) 2 p 446.

[34] The case has been well summarised by F. H. Dudden, *Gregory the Great,* 2 vols (London 1905) 1 pp 424–6 and in my paper 'Donatism' pp 121–2. On the government's delaying tactics: *Ep* 4 32, 1 p 268 lines 2–5, of July 594. Three years before this Gregory had already urged the exarch of Africa not to delay Numidian bishops wishing to travel to Rome: *Ep* 1 72, 1 p 92 lines 17–19.

Paul complained that he had 'suffered the annoyance of persecution by Donatists;[35] and, as he went on to amplify his grievance—after a letter from the exarch had been read out to him, presumably with a very different version of the events, to which Paul was required to reply—he explained that he was put out not so much by the resentment he had incurred among some people, presumably 'Donatists,' on account of his campaign of repression against them, but rather 'by the general ingratitude shown by many people for his defence of the catholic faith'.[36] What was this 'ingratitude' Paul complained of? The answer, as we learn, a few lines further on, is that he had been excommunicated by a synod of his province. It is significant that the excommunication had been notified to the pope—to his pained surprise—not by the primate of the province, but the exarch of Africa.[37] In Rome Paul seemed a zealous and long-suffering defender of orthodoxy. In Numidia he had evidently been a troublesome busybody, a nuisance both to his fellow clergy and the local administration.

This one example speaks volumes, and confirms the impression given by all the other evidence we have discussed. 'Donatism', if the word figured at all in the vocabulary of the Numidian church, certainly did not mean a schismatic church with its own hierarchy duplicating that of the catholics. The division we see in its ranks is between those who, like the majority of the Numidian bishops who excommunicated Paul, wished to keep the papacy at arm's length; and their opponents, channels of papal influence, like Paul himself. 'Donatism' seems here to be merging into the majority party among Numidian churchmen, those intent on maintaining local autonomy in the province. Bishop Paul's case is all of a piece with the wealth of evidence[38] which indicates the tenacity of African traditions of independence in relation to the Roman see and interventions from 'across the sea.'

In the 590s this resistance to Roman influence seems to have been concentrated in the province of Numidia. Though there are hints of a similar sense of alienation from the Roman see in Byzacena,[39] it would be hazardous to generalise from the single incident which is the only one we have any information about. And in the case of the proconsular

[35] *Ep* 6 59, 1 p 434 line 8.
[36] *Ibid* lines 15–16.
[37] *Ibid* lines 28–30.
[38] Surveyed in my paper 'Donatism' esp pp 122–3.
[39] *Epp* 9 24, 27; 12 12.

province and its metropolitan church of Carthage there appears to be a sharp contast with the Numidian situation. There the metropolitan bishop, Dominicus, of Carthage, was a friend of Gregory's and they corresponded regularly over nine years. Their relations were cordial, and Gregory, far from having to seek every opportunity to assert the authority and to exert the influence of Rome, could here set the keynote of the correspondence by insisting on the rights and privileges of the church of Carthage.[40] Here the pope could count on support, and though personal friendship no doubt played its part, the reason is clear: Carthage had Rome's support in the claims to privileges over the other African provinces which it was advancing.[41] But it is also clear that the situation in its province was very different from that which obtained in Numidia. We learn this from a revealing incident in 594. The 'African province'[42] had held a council, in response to imperial directives, and had enacted very severe penalties against those who were negligent in hunting down heretics. On receiving notification of the council's decisions, Gregory was horrified by the savagery of their measures, and he was clearly apprehensive about the possibility that they might provoke a schism between the Carthaginian and other African churches. The province of Carthage was evidently very differently placed from the Numidian (and perhaps the Byzacenian) and much more readily aligned with the outlook of Rome, and more compliant with the commands of Constantinople. If there were country-bishops in the province, they were clearly not suspect as were their Numidian colleagues, and Carthage could afford to deal with problems remote from its concern with a zeal which closer proximity might have inhibited.

The reasons for the difference between the alignments of the Numidian and the Carthaginian churches can only be a matter of conjecture. Perhaps the strong sense of autonomy in the former province is a relic of the Donatist ethos which may have survived more actively there, especially in some rural communities. It may

[40] *Ep* 2 52, 1 p 156 lines 36–41.

[41] On this see my forthcoming paper 'Carthage'.

[42] *Ep* 5 3, 1 p 283 line 11. The status of this council is hard to decide: was it one of the proconsular province, or was it one for all the African provinces? If it was the former, it is hard to understand why its decisions should be expected to give rise to objections in other provinces. If, however, it was an African council, it is difficult to understand how it could enact decisions seen even in Rome to be unrealistic and possibly dangerous if applied in the other provinces. I think the likeliest explanation is that it was intended to be a council for all the African provinces but actually attended by bishops of *Proconsularis* only, or to a dominant extent.

also be related to the Christianisation of the resurgent Berber kingdoms especially in the regions of the Hodna and Aurès mountains; or it may be that in the aftermath of the collapse of the opposition to the condemnation of the Three Chapters the proconsular province was more completely brought into line with the officially imposed imperial and papal orthodoxy than the more remote areas of rural Numidia. Whatever the reasons, there is no doubt that Carthage was closer to both Rome and Constantinople than to Numidia and perhaps the rest of Africa: and its pretensions to supremacy over the other African provinces, promoted by Justinian and supported by the popes[43] certainly accentuated any tensions there were between Carthage and the rest of Africa.

The full significance of African country-bishoprics appears only in the context of such tensions introduced into the African church through its relations with the government. It is striking that the attitude adopted in Constantinople towards Donatists in Africa was very different from the tolerance shown towards, for instance, Istrian schismatics. There, urgent papal entreaties for the adoption of a policy of coercion were firmly resisted, for very sound political reasons. In Africa, though the orders made by the emperor Maurice have not survived, we have good clues to their nature: they caused the pope to be overjoyed at the emperor's zeal, amid all his other cares, for the religious orthodoxy of his subjects; Gregory complimented him on having turned 'against the wicked depravity of the Donatists, moved by a sense of righteousness and zeal for the purity of religion,'[44] which he found evinced by the tenor of the edicts. In Africa, the court had evidently given its support to the papacy's drive against Donatism; and, as we have seen, Carthage responded eagerly at a council held in accordance with the imperial *iussiones.*[45] But it was very different in Numidia. Here the imperial edicts were a dead letter, and when a council was eventually held (it seems unlikely to have been one in response to the government orders, as the Carthage council was) it was far from satisfactory, and the pope had to ask the exarch of Africa—with what results we cannot know—to get its 'uncanonical' decisions reversed.[46] Gregory repeatedly complained about the indulgence shown by the administration to heretics, and generally

[43] see n 41 above.

[44] *Ep* 6 61, 1 p 436 lines 29–31.

[45] *Ep* 5 3, 1 p 283 lines 7–8 and in n 42 above.

[46] *Ep* 4 7, 1 p 239 lines 3–4, 7–11.

attributed their lack of rigour in enforcing the imperial directives to bribery—'the catholic faith is being publicly sold,' he once wrote.[47] The case of the bishop Paul we examined above reveals that many African officials were not only failing to give solid support to the policies of the government, but were actively resisting them and undermining their effectiveness. The exarch and his officials had been detaining Numidian bishops wishing to travel to Rome; they had placed every possible obstacle in the path of the bishop Paul; and they were darkly charged with other crimes never specified.[48] It is significant that Gregory thought it wise to refer the case of Paul to the emperor's judgement, on account, as he said, of the involvement of the secular authorities in it.[49] Neither pope Gregory nor the unhappy Paul can have derived much comfort from the case being referred back after eighteen months, for trial in Africa. The lesson was not lost on Gregory: when another appeal reached him, this time from Byzacena, it was once more an African official who frustrated the pope's attempts to get the case properly settled, despite the emperor's express wish that he should settle it.[50] It is scarcely surprising that Gregory should have suspected the orthodoxy of some senior African officials.[51] An air of resignation hangs heavily about Gregory's later dealings with Africa.[52] Far from suggesting that 'unity, concord and ecclesiastical discipline' had been re-established, that the African church was 'turning towards Rome'[53] it appears that Gregory had come to see the situation more realistically and accepted the inevitable limitations on the exercise here of papal, or, for that matter, of imperial, authority.

What we catch a glimpse of in the 590s is a closing of the ranks in Africa. The administration in Africa had come to identify itself with the local, indigenous church: government officials were promoting its interests in defiance of court, emperor and pope. Ranks had also

[47] *Ep* 6 61, 1 p 437 line 2; Compare *Ep* 4 32.

[48] *Ep* 6 59, 1 p 434 lines 17–18 and n 34 above.

[49] *Ep* 8 13, 15. Caspar, *Geschichte*, p 445, seems certainly right in inferring that the case was referred back to be decided by a synod in Africa.

[50] *Epp* 9 24, 27; 12 12.

[51] *Ep* 4 41.

[52] Compare above n 50, and Markus 'Donatism,' p 123.

[53] C. Diehl, *L'Afrique Byzantine* (Paris 1896) pp 510–11. Diehl's account is largely plagiarised (with errors introduced) by J. Ferron and G. Lapeyre in their 'remarkable article' (description by P. Goubert, *Byzance avant l'Islam*, 2/II: *Rome, Byzance et Carthage* (Paris 1965) p 235) in *DHGE* 11 cols 1208–9. Much the same line is taken by C. A. Julien, *Histoire de l'Afrique du Nord*, 2 vols (2 ed Paris 1961) 1 pp 273–4 and Frend, *Donatist church*, p 314. But see A. Schindler, 'Africa I: Das kirchliche Nordafrika,' *Theologische Realenzyclopädie*, 1 (Berlin 1977) pp 640–700, especially at p 661.

closed within the African church: Donatist traditions surviving in remote pockets of rural Numidia were an accepted part of the African church's life, jealous, as it always was, of its native peculiarities. The only dissonant note in this African harmony was the distinctly 'trans-marine' voice of Carthage. Seen from Numidia or Byzacena, Carthage was the mouthpiece of a distant government and an equally distant papacy.

But even this one rift was to be closed before long. In the course of the fifty years or so following Gregory the Great's pontificate, secular and ecclesiastical politics conspired to thrust Carthage firmly back into the African orbit. In 608–10 Africa was in the lead in the revolt against the tyranny of Phocas. Rallying behind its exarch, Heraclius, Africa was to be the empire's salvation. Forty years later it was another exarch of Africa who again led the revolt, this time against Heraclius's great-grandson, the emperor Constans II. Africans saw themselves as the champions of orthodoxy, and were acclaimed as such by the pope.[54] Once again the African church and the African administration were fighting side by side, against the heresy and tyranny of the court; and the fierce loyalty of Christianised Berber tribesmen enlisted behind their Roman leaders and catholic bishops is a measure of the extent to which the African church had succeeded in assimilating its backward countryside, the rural poor and the half-Romanised native.

The fleeting glimpse which is all we can catch of African Christianity on the eve of the Moslem conquest shows us a church as united as it had perhaps never before been united. And now, in its championship of ancient orthodoxy, it was aligned with the see of Rome in its resistance to a distant government and its new heresy. But fifty years later Carthage was in moslem hands. The curtain which descended on African Christianity descended on a church which had been singularly successful in achieving a synthesis of local and cosmopolitan, in which urban and rural traditions had coalesced to form a remarkably vital and tenacious religious culture. The history of the eclipse of African Christianity cannot be written in terms of a catholicism which, in Frend's words, 'had no appeal for the masses of the native population.'[55]

University of Nottingham

[54] Martin I, *Ep. ad ecclesiam Carthaginensem, PL* 87 (1863) cols 145–50.
[55] Frend, *Donatist church* p 334.

PROBLEMS ARISING FROM THE CONVERSION OF SYRIA

by W. LIEBESCHUETZ

IT is the aim of this paper to ask questions rather than to answer them. The area with which I am concerned is a strip of central Syria extending from the Euphrates in the north to Baalbek (ancient Heliopolis) in the south. This region has a large number of village-remains from late antiquity, some of them exceptionally well preserved. These remains have yielded a large number of inscriptions, of which a significant proportion bears a date. They are being collected in the volumes of the *Inscriptions grecques et latines de la Syrie*. Seven volumes have appeared.[1]

The inscriptions start in the early empire and continue to the end of the sixth century. They thus start in pagan times and cover the whole development of Syrian Christianity.[2] Only a few of the Christian inscriptions come from the great cities of Syria, for example Antioch, Aleppo [Beroea], the ancient Apamea, or Homs [Emesa]. They do not therefore throw light on the development of urban Christianity, which at Antioch especially was of great importance, and of long standing. The development reflected by the inscriptions is the conversion of the countryside.

The first conclusion suggested by this material is that there was very little rural Christianity in this area before Constantine. In the territory of Antioch the flow of Christian inscriptions starts, with only a few isolated exceptions,[3] after 324, the year Constantine gained control of the east.[4] Contrary to the opinion of Harnack[5] it would seem that

[1] *IGLS.*

[2] See list of dated inscriptions *IGLS* 4, pp 375–8.

[3] Isolated early Christian inscriptions from territory of Antioch: *IGLS* nos 393–5 (272/3), from Aradus: *ibid* no 4042 (287).

[4] Start of the Christian series after Constantine's conquest: *IGLS* nos 594 (326), 600 (335), 443 (336/7), 518 (341/2), 596 (349), 396 (349/50), 542–3 (351). The series continues without break until *c*600.

[5] In my opinion the negative evidence of inscriptions outweighs the plausible inferences from a few literary passages on the basis of which A. von Harnack concluded that rural Christianity was significant even before Constantine. See *Mission und Ausbreitung des Christentums*, 2 (Leipzig 1906) p 279.

pre-Constantinian Christianity in Syria was largely an urban phenomenon.[6] We are once again reminded of the importance of the conversion of the emperor for the expansion of Christianity in the Roman empire.[7]

The evidence of inscriptions suggests that Christianity spread from north to south. Christianisation of the territory of Apamea was fifty years or so behind that of the territory of Antioch. Further south, in the territories of Hama [Epiphania], Homs [Emesa] and Baalbek [Heliopolis] conversion to Christianity would appear to have been later still, as late as the middle, or even the end, of the fifth century. Eventually Christianity prevailed everywhere, but when the Mohammedan Arabs broke into Syria in 634 many Syrian villages would have been Christian for one hundred and fifty years or less.[8] The Arabs conquered an area in which Christianity was not yet deeply rooted.[9]

The inscriptions do not tell us how Christianity was spread, but they do suggest that there was a relationship—at least in northern Syria—between the settlement of hermits and monks and the expansion of Christianity in the countryside. The main area of early Christian inscriptions in the territory of Antioch lies on both sides of the Antioch-Aleppo [Beroea] road. Communications from villages on each side of the road converge on the plain of Dana. It is surely not a coincidence that the hillsides surrounding that plain were thronged by hermits, and that some of the earliest monasteries of Syria were founded there. This is the region where saint Symeon Stylites was to spend some forty two years (417–59) on the top of pillars, and where his memory has been preserved by a great monastery and pilgrimage centre whose remains are impressive even today.[10] That monks played an essential part in the conversion of Syria is confirmed

[6] Some evidence on urban Christianity in R. Devréese, *Le patriarcat de Antioche depuis la paix de l'église jusqu'à la conquête Arabe* (Paris 1945) caps 8, 11.

[7] A. H. M. Jones, *Constantine and the Conversion of Europe* (London 1949) pp 237–9.

[8] For the evidence see my paper 'Epigraphic Evidence [on the Christianisation of Syria'], *Akten des XI internationalen LimesKongresses, Székesfehérvar*, ed J. Fitz (Budapest 1978) pp 485–505.

[9] Paradoxically the Maronites seem to have been comparatively late arrivals in the territory in which they have maintained their identity so vigorously ever since. Their early history is still very obscure. See article 'Maron', *DACL* 10, cols 2188–202; S. Vailhé, 'Les origines religieuses des Maronites,' *EO* 4 (Paris 1900) pp 96–103, 154–62; K. S. Salibi, 'The Maronites of Lebanon under Frankish and Mamluk Rule (1099–1516)', *Arabica* (Leiden 1957) pp 288–303.

[10] A. J. Festugière, *Antioche païenne et chrétienne* (Paris 1959) pp 311–13. [G.] Tchalenko, *Villages [antiques de la Syrie du nord]*, 3 vols (Paris 1953–8) 1, pp 145–82.

by the contemporary testimony of the Antiochene orator Libanius writing around 380,[11] and of Sozomen, the ecclesiastical historian, a native of Gaza, writing after 440.[12]

In the territory of Apamea, and in areas further south, the history of monasticism is much more obscure. The location of the famous monastery of Nicerta is being currently sought by archaeologists.[13] There is however no reason to doubt that the monks played an important role there also.

The preceding paragraphs summarise the conclusions of an earlier paper of mine where more detailed references to the inscriptional evidence can be found.[14] Some problems arise from it. First there is a problem of method: is the approach valid? If this question is answered affirmatively, there arises the further question of how far the method can profitably be applied to other parts of the empire.[15] There are very few areas where so large a proportion of inscriptions bear a date, or where they have been so conveniently collected. On the other hand other areas have produced more extensive literary evidence to provide a check on the conclusions derived from epigraphy. North Africa and Asia Minor [16] are areas which have produced large numbers of early Christian inscriptions.

The Christianisation of Syria touches on a wider historical problem: that of the interrelation of religious and economic change. It is a fact that the area of northern Syria where Christianisation started was undergoing economic development. G. Tchalenko has examined the remains of villages on the limestone plateau between Antioch and Aleppo and traced the development of a prosperous rural society, whose livelihood depended on steadily expanding olive plantations.[17]

[11] Libanius, *Or.* 30, *Pro Templis.* See also G. Fowden, 'Bishops and Temples in the Eastern Empire,' *JTS* 29 (1978) pp 53–78.

[12] Sozomen, *HE* 6, 34.

[13] [P. H. E.] Voûte, ['Chronique de fouilles et prospections en Syrie de 1965 à 1970'], *Anatolica* 14 (Istanbul 1971–2) pp 83–137, relevant pp 92–3.

[14] For references see my 'Epigraphic Evidence'.

[15] D. I. Pallas, 'Investigation sur les monuments chrétiens de Grèce avant Constantin,' *Cahiers Archéologiques* 24 (Paris 1975) pp 1–19. The pre-Constantinian evidence is very thin. M. Leglay, *Saturne Africain* (Paris 1966) is very informative on the epigraphic evidence for the last stages of paganism and the beginnings of Christianity.

[16] F. Cumon, *Les inscriptions chrétiennes de l'Asie Mineure* (Rome 1895). [W. M.] Calder, 'Early Christian Epitaphs from Phrygia,' *Anatolian Studies* 5 (London 1955) pp 27–38; Calder, 'Philadelphia and Montanism,' *BJRL* 8 (1923) pp 309–54.

[17] Tchalenko, *Villages* 1, esp pp 404–21. D. Bowder, *The Age of Constantine and Julian* (London 1978) p 144 stresses that the economy of the plateau involved its population in close contact with the Christian population of Antioch.

It is a plausible hypothesis that the dissolution of an older order, dominated by large landowners, favoured conversion to Christianity.[18]

The areas further south, which were converted later were also undergoing economic development. They too have provided extensive late-ancient remains[19] but the period of rural building like that of conversion was delayed. South of the limestone plateau expansion was presumably not based on monoculture of olive trees. Perhaps there was a settlement of previously nomadic tribesmen, and an advance of agriculture at the expense of nomadism.[20] Village development was in fact a characteristic of many frontier areas in late antiquity. It can be observed in Syria, Palestine,[21] Arabia,[22] Cyrene, Tripolitania and perhaps even Egypt.[23] It is a phenomenon the scale of which has not been fully taken into account in A. H. M. Jones's gloomy portrayal of the condition of the late-Roman peasantry.[24] It has still to be fully explained.

It is conceivable that Christianisation favoured village development. As we have seen Christianity was spread by monks. The process of conversion was preceded and accompanied by the settlement of hermits, and later by the foundation of an enormous number of monasteries. Hermits and abbots were men of authority. They were influential locally, and they were also heard with respect by members of the imperial administration.[25] I would suggest that by their presence in villages these men changed the balance of power between city and countryside. They were effective patrons, who could protect men

[18] In North Africa too rural conversion took place in combination with economic development based on the production of olive oil. Both happened earlier in Africa. See W. H. C. Frend, *The Donatist Church* (Oxford 1952) pp 42–8.

[19] J. Lassus, *Inventaire archéologique de la région au nord-est de Hama* (Beirut 1935).

[20] H. Seyrig, 'Caractère de l'histoire d'Émèse, *Syria* 36 (Paris 1959) pp 184–92. R. Sullivan, 'The dynasty of Emesa,' in H. Temporini, *Aufstieg und Niedergang der römischen Welt*, 2, pt 8 (Berlin 1978) pp 198–219 is pure political and military history but cites literature.

[21] M. Avi Yonah, 'The Economics of Byzantine Palestine,' *Israel Exploration Journal* 8 (Jerusalem 1958) pp 39–51. S. A. M. Gichon, 'Roman Frontier Cities in the Negev,' *Acts of the 6th International Congress of Limes Studies* (Zagreb 1961) pp 195–207. R. Paret, 'Les villes de Syrie du sud et les routes commerciales d'Arabie à la fin du VIe siècle,' *Akten des XI internationalen Byzantinisten Kongresses* (Munich 1960) pp 438–44.

[22] G. M. Harper, 'Village Administration in the Roman Province of Syria,' *Yale Classical Studies* 1 (1928) pp 103–68.

[23] R. Goodchild, *Libyan Studies* (London 1977) pp 8–9, 92, 255–6. A. C. Johnson and L. C. West, *Byzantine Egypt: Economic Studies* (Princeton 1949) p 32 concluded that Egypt was prosperous.

[24] A. H. M. Jones, *The Later Roman Empire* (Oxford 1964) 2, p 823.

[25] P. Brown, 'The Rise and Function of the Holy Man in Late Antiquity,' *JRS* 61 (1971) pp 80–101. Interference with tax collection: Theodoret *Hist Rel* 17 *PG* 82 (1864) col 1413.

from the demands of landlords, creditors or tax collectors. They were in a position to mitigate the effect of debt, that perpetual threat to the existence, or at least freedom, of small peasants. They could settle disputes between villagers. Henceforth there would be less need to visit the city for the sake of justice. Again, wealthy villagers might leave legacies to a local monastery or church,[26] with the result that the countryside retained resources which in earlier times might have been diverted to conspicuous public expenditure in the city. It is at least arguable that such development contributed both to the flourishing condition of villages and to the decline of cities which happened in the east no less than in the west, even if the decline of the eastern cities was considerably delayed.[27]

I would like to mention now some problems of narrower scope. According to Tchalenko there is a distinction between the layout of monasteries in the territory of Apamea and those in the territory of Antioch. Antiochene monasteries seem to be open to the world, Apamean ones shut-off. The distinction is particularly obvious in the planning of churches. In the territory of Antioch we find large separate churches which seem to have been open to the villagers. Around Apamea, monasteries have small chapels, tightly tied into the layout of the rest of the buildings.[28] Tchalenko's book is based on a more thorough study of Antiochene than of Apamean remains.[29] If his observation is nevertheless valid it raises the question: how can we account for the coexistence of two plans in adjacent areas? In the monophysite schism Syria I, the province of which Antioch was the capital, was largely monophysite while Syria II, the province of Apamea, was on the whole Chalcedonian.[30] While the religious division did not correspond precisely to the administrative one we are left with the possibility that the planning of the monasteries reflects the religious allegiance of their monks.[31]

[26] E. Wipsycka, *Les resources et les activités économiques des églises en Égypte du IVe au VIIIe siècle* (Brussels 1972) p 37.

[27] D. Claude, *Die byzantinische Stadt* (Munich 1969). E. Kirsten, *Die byzantinische Stadt, Berichte zum XI internationalen Byzantinisten Kongress 1958* (Munich 1958).

[28] Tchalenko, *Villages* 1, p 178; 2, plate 51.

[29] He is extending his survey year by year though the material has not yet been published. See Voûte p 85.

[30] W. H. C. Frend, *The Rise of the Monophysite Movement* (Cambridge 1972) pp 223–9 and map on pp 250–1. In the city of Antioch itself monophysites were never a majority. See G. Downey, *A History of Antioch in Syria* (Princeton 1961) p 510.

[31] Passages like Theophanes, *sa* 6003, pp 153.29–154.2; Evagrius, *HE* 3, 32; Mansi, 8, pp 425–9, 1130–8; *Collectio Avellana* (*CSEL* 35) esp p 139; Michael the Syrian, 1,

A final problem. Among the Christian inscriptions of Syria there are a large number bearing the formula εἷς θεός 'One God' or 'God is unique', or longer phrases including this formula.[32] The inscriptions derive from tombs, churches and private houses. The majority come from the lintels of doorways. One is inevitably reminded of *Deut* 6, 14: 'Hear O Israel, the Lord is our God, the Lord is one. And these words which I command you this day you shall write them on the door-posts and on your gates.' Jews have of course always obeyed this commandment literally.[33] Inevitably one asks whether the Christianity of the Syrian countryside was strongly influenced by Jewish Christianity. One thinks of the Nazaraeans of Beroea [Aleppo], among whom Jerome claimed to have seen a gospel according to saint Matthew written in Hebrew.[34] One also recalls that the Christianity of Edessa is said to have been strongly influenced by Judaism.[35]

The εἷς θεός inscriptions are not evenly distributed over Syria. The area south of the limestone plateau, that is most of Syria II, has produced very few of them.[36] In the Arabian and Palestinian provinces it seems to be restricted to particular areas, and even there the number of inscriptions is small. A few come from the territory around Damascus.[37] Some more have been found in the Hauran and Batanaea around Bostra.[38] This is another region where Jewish-Christians emigrated at the time of the sack of Jerusalem.[39] Some

---

cols 270–4 show that the monasteries of Syria II acting collectively were Chalcedonian. But Tchalenko, *Villages* 2, plate 153 shows that at least some of the monasteries on the Apamean side of the limestone plateau were monophysite.

[32] A mass εἷς ις θεός material, mainly Christian, but also pagan and Jewish, has been assembled in [E.] Peterson, ΕΙΣ ΘΕΟΣ, *Forschungen zur Religion und Literatur des alten und neuen Testaments*, NF 24 (Göttingen 1926). See also the indices of the volumes of *IGLS*.

[33] W. O. E. Oesterley and G. E. Box, *The Religion and Worship of the Synagogue* (London 1911) pp 447–9, 454 *seq*. On the Shema prayer see *ibid* pp 364 *seq*, 432, 477 *seq*.

[34] Jerome *Vir Illustr* 3; J. N. D. Kelly, *Jerome His Life Writings and Controversies* (London 1975) p 65.

[35] J. B. Segal, *Edessa, the Blessed City* (Oxford 1970) p 100; H. J. W. Drijvers, 'Edessa und das jüdische Christentum,' *Vigiliae Christianae* 24 (Amsterdam 1970) pp 4–33.

[36] *IGLS* 4 (regions of Apamea and Laodicca) has twenty-five inscriptions; *IGLS* 5 (Hama and Homs) has six. *IGLS* 6 (Baalbek) has none; *IGLS* 7 (Aradus) has one.

[37] Peterson p 27 nos 70–1, no 72 is in the Golan.

[38] *Ibid* pp 28–37, nos 74–85.

[39] For the date see W. H. C. Frend, *Martyrdom and Persecution in the Early Church* (Oxford 1965) p 177 n 116. Eusebius *HE* 3, 5. Epiphanius *Haer* 18, 1; 29.7. Origen debated the pre-existence and independent hypostasis of the Son with bishops at Bostra: Eusebius, *HE* 6, 33. See J. E. Coulton and H. Chadwick, *Alexandrine Christianity*, (London 1954) p 430.

inscriptions derive from the neighbourhood of Jerusalem itself.[40] The oldest of the 'Syrian' inscriptions come from Dura Europos on the Euphrates, and must therefore be earlier than 256.[41] The bulk of the inscriptions date from the fourth and first half of the fifth century. They fade out in the second half of the century, and almost cease in the sixth.[42]

The second large group of εἷς θεός inscriptions has been found in middle and upper Egypt. Over a hundred are known. The great majority of them are on tombstones. In Egypt the forumula has not been found on lintels and surprisingly, on only one papyrus.[43] Most of the inscriptions are undated or only dated with reference to the indiction, which does not provide an absolute date. But the tombstones continue into the period of Arab rule.[44] In addition to the Greek inscriptions there are numerous Coptic ones bearing the formula.[45] It would therefore seem that the phrase continued to be popular in Egypt, or at least in parts of Egypt, long after it had ceased to be so in Syria. A few isolated inscriptions have been found outside Syria (using the term in its widest sense) and Egypt. But it looks as if Syria and Egypt were the areas where the formula had special importance for Christians.[46]

The εἷς θεός inscriptions raise many problems. How did this slightly adapted[47] Jewish formula come to be used almost as a proclamation of religious identity[48] by so many Christian villagers? Why was the popularity of the phraise limited to some areas only? Why did the use of the phrase fade out in Syria when it did? Did the

[40] Peterson, pp 37–40, nos 86–91.

[41] C. H. Kraeling, *Dura Europos: Final Report,* 8, pt 2 (Yale 1956) p 95; P. V. C. Baur, M. I. Rostovtzeff, A. R. Bellinger, *Dura Europos: Preliminary Report* 4 (Yale 1923) p 150 nos 291–2.

[42] Peterson has only two sixth century inscriptions from the Syrian area: nos 6 and 30.

[43] Peterson p 275.

[44] G. L. Lefebure, *Recueil des inscriptions grècques chrétiennes d'Égypte* (Cairo 1907).

[45] Peterson p 76.

[46] Peterson has also assembled a good deal of non epigraphic material including evidence bearing on the Jewish and pagan use of the formula.

[47] The formula was used in popular acclamations against bishop Ibas at Edessa: J. Flemming, *Akten der ephesinischen Synode vom Jahre 449, AAWG,* PhK, ns 15 (1917) pp 15, 17, 41. It was used by bishops in acclamation at the council of Constantinople: Mansi 8, pp 49a, 1083; also at Chalcedon: *ibid* 7 pp 49, 1087, 1091.

[48] [M.] Simon, [*Verus Israel*] (Paris 1948) p 357, n 2 cites Epiphanius, *Haer* 1, 30, 12 where the defeat of Jewish magic by the name of Jesus and the sign of the cross is acclaimed:

εἷς θεός ὁ βοηθῶν τοίς Χριστιανοῖς

On the use of the formula in apocryphal Acts of apostles and in hagiography to acclaim the marvellous divine power revealed by a miracle see Peterson pp 183–8.

use of the phrase derive from Jewish Christianity or did it perhaps arise in the course of the continuous competition between Judaism and Christianity in Syria?[49] Should the rise and fall of the formula be linked with that of the Antiochene theology? Or is it perhaps part of the prehistory of so-called monophysitism? Thanks to Peterson we have a great deal of material—and some interesting suggestions.[50] But the answers still have to be worked out.

University of Leicester

[49] See Simon pp 220, 356–93.

[50] See also his interesting suggestions in εἶς θεός in der sepulkralen Epigraphik,' *Zeitschrift für Katholische Theologie* 58 (Vienna 1934) pp 400–2 and 'Jüdisches und christliches Morgengebeet in Syrien,' *ibid* pp 110–43. The latter, based on a passage in the Acts of the martyr Romanus, ed H. Delehaye, *An Bol* 50 (1932) pp 241 *seq*, see esp p 256, suggests that our formula was part of a morning prayer in use in Syria.

TOWN AND COUNTRYSIDE IN EARLY CHRISTIANITY

by W. H. C. FREND

A VISITOR to the Greco-Roman world about the year 350 AD would have found himself confronted by one of the great 'sea changes' in the lives of its peoples. The structure of city, farm and village that had persisted for centuries would appear to be intact. The market-places of the towns would be lined with altars and statues of long-dead benefactors. Temples to the gods of Rome and perhaps to a native deity duly Romanised, would dominate the scene. Wherever one stood in the city the temples in the forum would be the landmark. Nearby, would be the amphitheatre and great bath-building, the social centres of the old community, and near the entrance to the town the triumphal arch, marking perhaps the unification of Roman citizen and native inhabitant into one community.

By 350, however, this civilisation was passing away. In the west, for every Bordeaux with its fine classical schools and antiquarian interests, the home of the poet and politician, Ausonius, there was an Aventicum, a one-time *colonia* and cantonal town of the Helvetii described by the historian, Ammianus Marcellinus as abandoned and full of half-ruined buildings.[1] In the east, Antioch could live up to Libanius's description of its magnificence, its wealth based on its customs dues and busy trade, and could afford to supply lavish amusements,[2] but many other once famous cities, even Diocletian's capital, Nicomedia, and Carnuntum, the one-time Danube citadel, were impoverished, their walls 'a heap of ashes'.[3] Moreover, such rebuilding as there was going on, was mainly of a different type. Big new halls of assembly and worship were springing out of the ground. At the dedication of one, the church of the Golden Dome at Antioch, the emperor Constantius had held a council attended by nearly one hundred

[1] A[mmianus] M[arcellinus, *Res Gestae*], ed J. C. Rolfe (London/Cambridge, Mass., 1935) bk 15 cap 11 para 12.

[2] Libanius, *Antiochikos, Orationes* 11, 196, ed R. Förster (Leipzig 1903) 1 p 504, and compare A. J. Festugière, *Antioche païenne et chrétienne, Bibliothèque des écoles françaises d'Athènes et Rome* 194 (Paris 1959) pp 23–7.

[3] AM bk 22 cap 9 para 4 (Nicomedia) and bk 30 cap 5 para 2 (Carnuntum).

bishops in 341[4] At Aquileia at the nothern end of the Adriatic, Athanasius had watched another large church being built in 345.[5] Even more impressive, outside some of the old towns entire quarters dedicated to the needs of the new all-conquering Christian religion were making their appearance. At Djemila and Timgad in north Africa and at Salona in Dalmatia these were the new centres of urban life.[6] The leaders of this new civilisation, the bishops, presbyters and the host of administrative underlings had supplanted the old city councils in all but name as the rulers of the community. Theirs was the power and the wealth. The magistrates merely administered the law and paid the taxes. Our visitor would have seen the Mediterranean in a state of transition, when the old cities, their fierce local patriotism, and their religion based on the traditional gods of the locality were giving way to a world-wide faith whose leaders could impose a common teaching on their believers from one end of the Mediterranean to the other.

In the countryside a similar transition was taking place, but in a different form. Our visitor, if he was a bishop and had been provided with a diploma to use the public posting service[7] to travel, let us say, from Constantine to Timgad in Numidia, would have encountered a distinctive form of Christianity as he would have found a different style of life. In the dry climate that prevailed in an inhospitable landscape, he would have seen fewer towns until he reached the zone of military cantonments that guarded the Aures passes. His journey would have taken him through villages, thickly but untidily spaced and he would have noticed how each family had its olive press and silo for storing grain and, above all, the numerous small whitewashed churches that could be found at every corner. If he had stopped to enter, he would have perceived a similarity in design, a raised apse at the east end, and in front a roughly constructed square enclosure for the altar, beneath which would lie the sacred relics of the martyrs.[8] An inscription proclaiming that here 'the just shall enter',[9] or a snatch

[4] Sozomen, *HE* bk 3 cap 5 para 2, ed J. Bidez and G. C. Hansen, *GCS* (Berlin 1960) p 105.

[5] By bishop Fortunatianus. See H. Leclercq, 'Aquilée', *DACL* 1.2 col 2661. For Athanasius's presence with Fortunatianus at Aquileia see *Apologia ad Constantium* 3, *PG* 25 (1884) col 599B.

[6] See J. Lassus, 'Les edifices du culte autour de la basilique', *Atti del 6 Congresso Internazionale di archeologia cristiana, Ravenna* 1962 (Rome 1965) pp 581–610.

[7] Compare AM bk 21 cap 16 para 18.

[8] These churches are described by A. Berthier and his colleagues in his *Le christianisme antique dans la Numidie centrale* (Algiers 1942) pp 39 *seq.*

[9] For example, see P. Monceaux, *Histoire littéraire de l'Afrique chrétienne* (Paris 1912) pp 444–84.

from the Psalms, 'Praise ye the Lord and rejoice, ye righteous, and let us glory in the Lord with a true heart' (Ps 30.12), or merely the expressive, 'Praise to God' (*Deo Laudes*) would have caught his attention,[10] and perhaps, too, the traditional native geometric designs, based on the wood-carver's art cut on the pillars that supported the roof either side of the apse. Outside, his attention could have been attracted to a group of men carrying clubs, whose language amongst themselves he might not have understood, ostensibly on pilgrimage from one martyr's shrine to another but (if he could understand Berber) expressing contempt for the church in the city,[11] and vowing that if they saw one of the local landowners riding in his carriage, they would pitch him out, put a slave in his place and give him a taste of what servitude meant.[12] These were the 'saints', the circumcellions for whom Christianity involved dramatic reversal of fortunes of this world and the glory reserved for the martyr in the next. Our friend would have reached Timgad a puzzled but a wiser man.

In Egypt and Syria he would have found similar differences between Christianity in town and countryside, but without some of the violence of sentiment against the institutions of the empire and the personalities of the urban bishops. Monasticism, however, in both these areas was largely a native movement. In Egypt, its founder, *c*270 had been Antony (251–356) who, despite his Greek name, was the son of a relatively wealthy Coptic farmer. In contrast to the urban episcopate, the vast majority of whose members were Greek, or Jewish-Christian by origin,[13] Antony's colleagues and imitators were Egyptians such as Amoun and Pachomius, men who struggled with Greek as a second language. Moreover, the way they understood scripture differed from that of their urban and Greek-speaking superiors. 'If thou wilt be perfect, go, sell all that thou hast', and other similar Domenical commands were to be taken literally and not allegorised away into moral

[10] See [W. H. C.] Frend, [*The Donatist Church*] (Oxford 1952) p 318.

[11] On the circumcellions see Frend pp 172–7; Frend, 'Circumcellions and monks', *JTS*, ns 20 (1969) pp 542–9; and for their contempt even for Donatist bishops see Optatus, [*De Schismate*], bk 3 cap 4, ed C. Ziwsa, *CSEL* 26 (1893)—'Dicuntur [episcopi] huiusmodi homines in ecclesia corrigi non posse'.

[12] Optatus p 82, and in the early fifth century see Augustine *Ep* 185.4.15, ed A. Goldbacher, *CSEL* 57 (1911) p 14.

[13] See A. Martin, 'L'Eglise et la Khora egyptienne au IVe siècle', *Les Transformations dans la société chrétienne au IVe siècle, Actes du Congrès à Varsovie du CIHEC*, 1978 (to be published).

platitudes.[14] Antony's monks accepted 'the whole yoke of the Lord'. They 'took no thought for the morrow' (Mt 6.34).[15] They believed in solitary prayer and fasting. In the deserts, beyond the boundaries of city and village, they fought the demons with the weapon of asceticism, self mortification, martyrdom in intent if not in deed. They were, like the circumcellions, men of the bible. For up to twenty years, between 284–304 while living in an abandoned fort on the east side of the Nile, Antony and his followers could not have received eucharist from the hands of a priest.[16] The communal, or coenobitic monastic movement, inspired and organised by Pachomius, a generation later, was scarcely less un-hierarchic. Pachomius resisted strenuously Athanasius's wishes to ordain him presbyter,[17] and though his monastic settlements were eventually under episcopal control, the emphasis of his teaching lay on the ascetic life, on work with one's hands, literal application of the bible, and alleviation of all forms of suffering and distress in the community on an individual basis. His outlook recalled the spirit of the gospel rather than that of the ordered churches that had established themselves in the Egyptian towns. In Syria, the monastic movement was even more given to extremes of individual asceticism. The *boskoi*, or grass-eaters, symbolised their rejection of urban civilization.[18]

One major aspect of Egyptian and Syrian monasticism differed from the rural Christianity of the north African circumcellions. Though they disliked judges and tax-collectors,[19] and confronted economic and social conditions as bad as those prevailing in north Africa, they were not even implicitly revolutionaries against secular authority.[20] By superb tact, Constantine had won the allegiance of the native Egyptian confessors at Nicaea.[21] A few years later, Athanasius

[14] Such as by Clement of Alexandria in *Quis dives salvetur?*, ed G. W. Butterworth (London/Cambridge, Mass., 1953).

[15] See [*Athanasius, Life of*] *Antony* cap 3 *PG* 26 (1887) col 844, and compare *ibid* cap 20.

[16] The point made by L. Duchesne, *The History of the Early Church* (Eng trans London 1931) 2, p 390.

[17] Theodore, *Vita Pachomii* cap 28, ed T. Lefort, *CSCO, Scriptores Coptici*, III.7 (Paris 1924, Louvain 1936).

[18] On the *boskoi* see Sozomen, *HE*, bk 6 cap 33, also A. Vööbus, 'A History of Asceticism in the Syrian Orient', *CSCO Subsidia* 17 (1960) pp 24–5.

[19] *Antony* cap 44, col 907B.

[20] For instance, see John Chrysostom, *Homilia in Matt* 61.3, *PG* 58 (1862) col 591. Syrian landowners were described as 'more cruel than the barbarians because they imposed intolerable and unending taxes and corvées on the working population on their lands'.

[21] His reception of Paphnutius who had been terribly mutilated in the persecution, for instance; see Socrates *HE* bk 1 cap 11, *PG* 67 (1864) col 101C.

was to begin a series of tours and visitations that consolidated the friendship of the Coptic monastic leaders into a lasting loyalty. From that time on the monks were the staunch allies of the see of Alexandria. In Syria they acted as God-inspired intermediaries between people and authorities.[22] They were never to be a destructive force within the eastern Roman empire.

Yet for all that, Christianity in town and countryside in east and west was developing on different lines, separate in one part of the empire, complementary in the other. Our friend bumping along the uneven roadways from one *mansio* to the next might well be asking himself why this should be so.

Even to sketch an answer for him, one must go back to two different elements in the background of the history of the early church. First, there are the contrasts that existed within Israelite society which affected the earliest Christian message, and secondly, the structure of society that confronted the Christian mission in the Greco-Roman world.

As is well known, the old testament tells the social as well as the religious history of the Jewish people. From the earliest moment in creation there were to be conflicts of interests. The story of Cain and Abel, the one 'the tiller of the ground', the other, 'the keeper of sheep' (Gen 4.2) reflects the age-old rivalry between the two basic communities in the evolution of primitive society. Later, one can detect the thinly disguised tensions between the priestly and the prophetic parties in Israel. The priests served the temple of the Lord in an orderly, urbanised environment. The prophets, as Elijah and Elisha or Amos, were countrymen (see 1 Kings 19.19 on Elisha), often itinerant, moving from place to place, even living in caves (1 Kings 19.9), warning kings against backsliding from the strict worship of the Lord, or denouncing the crimes of the rich. And grave were the penalties for ignoring the commands of 'the sons of the prophets', even if these seemed ridiculous (see 1 Kings 20.35–7). The wilderness and the heroic age of Israel rather than Jerusalem and Solomon's temple inspired them. Wandering about 'in sheepskins and goatskins' in deserts, persecuted by those who thought they knew better, was how romantics of the time of Christ depicted them (Hebs 11.37–8).

The prophetic tradition hardened and steeled the Jews against possible absorption into surrounding alien cultures. In the growing

[22] See the excellent study by P. R. L. Brown, 'The Rise and function of the Holy Man in Late Antiquity', *JRS* 61 (1971) pp 80–101.

crisis that followed the annexation of Judaea by Antiochus III after the battle of Raphia in 198 BC, the country districts stood firm for uncompromising Judaism whereas the high priests and Jewish aristocracy in Jerusalem were prepared to move a long way towards hellenisation. In the great war against the Seleucids that lasted between 165 and 141 BC, the Maccabees triumphed. They represented the conservative country areas and enforced their will on Jerusalem. Their successful revolt was aimed as much against apostate Jews—mainly in Jerusalem—as against the Seleucids.[23]

Another century passed in which the pattern of events tended to repeat itself. The Hasmonaean, that is, the dynasty of Judas Maccabaeus, was a bad neighbour to surrounding states, but it also imitated many of their ways. The court of Alexander Jannaeus resembled that of a Syrian princeling and his aggressive wars were fought with mercenaries like those employed by his neighbours. At some point, a group of pious Jews accepted the leadership of one whom they called 'The Righteous Teacher' and went out into the wilderness with the set intention of separating themselves 'from the abode of perverse men' and from the Temple itself.[24] As in the great days of Israel, they prepared themselves to fight the final war of Jahwe, and expected his kingdom to descend, not in Jerusalem, but in the wilderness, as prophesied in Is. 40.3. In the monastery established at Q'mran, the Dead Sea covenanters maintained themselves, observing the letter of the law and separating completely from idolatrous society, including that of Jerusalem itself. Property they regarded as sin. Some of the aims of the sect expressed in unity through the Spirit—love for one's fellows in the brotherhood, and the breakdown of all social barriers—foreshadowed those of the primitive church.

There can be little doubt that John the Baptist had some affinity with these covenanters,[25] even if the supposition that his aged parents committed him to the sect instead of the Temple, can never be proved. The baptism he proclaimed, however, was not a proselyte baptism but a ceremony of purification such as those undertaken by the

[23] See the short but invaluable account of the decisive years 167–4 BC, by Fergus Millar, 'The Background to the Maccabaean Revolution; Reflections on Martin Hengel's "Judaism and Hellenism",' *Journal of Jewish Studies* 29, 1 (Oxford 1978) pp 1–21.

[24] The Sectarian Rule of the Community from Q' mran, Cave 1 (= IQS) 8, 12–13. See also J. T. Milik, *Ten years of Discovery in the Wilderness of Judaea* (London 1959) pp 115–16, and F. Moore Cross, *The Ancient Library of Q'mran* (London 1958) p 55.

[25] I accept the view put forward by [J. A. T.] Robinson ['The Baptism of John and the Q'mran community'], *HTR* 50(July 1957) pp 175–90, (references to work by Brownlee, Bo Reicke and A. S. Geyser).

covenanters. For our purpose, however, one should notice that John's message was that of a prophet who emerged from the desert. He proclaimed in fearsome terms the imminent arrival of the kingdom of God, and, like the covenanters, he believed it would arrive 'in the wilderness'. 'Prepare ye the way of the Lord: make his paths straight', found in all four gospels (Mt 3.3, Mk 1.3, Lk 3.4 and Jn 1.23), are probably his own words. He, too, has severe things to say to the representatives of the urban religion associated with the Temple, who visited him. 'You viper's brood', he addressed the pharisees and sadducees, 'who warned you to escape from the coming retribution? Then prove your repentance by the fruit it bears, and do not presume to say to yourselves, "We have Abraham for our father", for I tell you, God is able to raise up from these stones children to Abraham' (Mt 3.2–9). The end was near; the fire would purge thoroughly and drastically. John's irruption from the desert boded ill for even the nationally minded pharisees and indeed, to all Jews who believed that Jahwe could best be served through the Temple cult.[26]

Jesus accepted John's baptism and His first mission was carried out —I can see no reason to disbelieve the fourth gospel here—in association with his cousin in the Jordan valley (Jn 3.22–3, 4.2).[27] Though Jesus frequently visited and had a deep affection for Jerusalem, the main area of His mission was rural Palestine. It was among the villages of Galilee that the lepers were cleansed, the blind received their sight, and the sick were healed (see Mt 11.5). Satan's kingdom was attacked there in the first place. Towns he seems to have avoided. There is no evidence he went to Sepphoris, Antipas's capital a bare four miles from Nazareth, and it was to the villages round about Caesarea Philippi, not to that centre itself, that he took his disciples after the end of the Galilean ministry (Mk 8.27). Though Jesus did not dress or behave like an ascetic prophet—the pharisees pointed out early in His mission (Luke 6.1 *seq*) that John's disciples fasted often but 'yours do not fast' (Mt 9.14), the way of life that he demanded of his followers was rigorous in the extreme. 'Foxes have holes and the birds of the air have nests, but the Son of Man hath not where to lay his head' (Lk 9.58). The tradition which he allowed those who heard him to believe he represented, was that of the prophet. The crowds in Jerusalem hailed

[26] On the eschatological character of John's ministry, see Robinson p 189. 'The purpose of John's baptism, we may say, was precisely to force the eschatological issue.'

[27] See C. H. Dodd, *Historical Tradition in the Fourth Gospel* (Cambridge 1963) compare pp 279 *seq*, 300–1.

him as 'the prophet from Nazareth' (Mt 21.10). Earlier, at the outset of his mission, Jesus had opened his sermon in the town of his upbringing, with the words of Second Isaiah (61.1–2) and when roused by the growing hostility of his audience reminded them of the words of the great prophets of the past, Elijah and Elisha (Lk 4.25–8). His message that blessed poverty and equated piety with humility, that preached the practical impossibility of the salvation of the rich, and associated wealth or Mammon with unrighteousness, stood within the prophetic tradition of Israel. The question he posed to his generation was whether he was the prophet who would be 'raised up from among you' who must be heeded (Deut 18.15) or a false prophet 'who presumes to speak a word in my name which I have not commanded him to speak', and so be worthy of death (Deut 18.20). Jesus's complete reversal of current values and absolute commands for purity, self-sacrifice and selfless love for one's neighbour were too much for the Jewish high-priesthood in Jerusalem.

Jesus's mission had been rural and his parables and examples of conduct worthy of the kingdom of God were drawn mainly from rural life. Within a very short time from the crucifixion, however, His followers were giving a different emphasis to his message. Long before Paul appeared on the scene, Christianity had concentrated on the towns of Palestine, on Caesarea, Joppa, Damascus and distant Antioch. These centres and even Samaria rather than Galilee became the focus of the first Christian mission.

The point is worth making, for the contrast is too often drawn as simply one between Jesus and Paul. In fact, Paul merely continued the work, with brilliant success, that had already been begun by the disciples themselves. With Paul, of course, the Christian message was transformed from a rural Palestinian to an urban Jewish dispersion setting with incalculable results. Only with reservations can Paul be called the interpreter of Jesus's religion. Like his Master, he believed that the end was approaching, but he preached no gospel of repentance, nor did he attempt to explain Jesus's teaching to his urban audiences. He did not disavow Jesus 'born of woman' (Gal 4.4), but for him and his hearers the heavenly being, the Lord Christ had replaced the prophet of Nazareth.[28] His medium was Greek and not Aramaic. For Jews and proselytes in the towns of Asia Minor and the Aegean coasts his message was, that the first-born of creation familiar to them in their

[28] See W. L. Knox, *St Paul and the Church of the Gentiles* (Cambridge 1961) pp 163 *seq* for the development in Paul of the equation of Jesus with the heavenly Wisdom of God.

reading of Proverbs and the Book of Wisdom had indeed come in flesh, and that through the cross salvation was available to all believers. Paul's mission was not to the outcasts of the highways and byeways outside the cities but to town-dwellers who already knew their septuagint and debated the law. Just as he himself moved easily among the upper reaches of provincial society, so his audience was drawn from the urban middle classes, not from the rural multitudes to whom Jesus had spoken. Indeed, his words would have meant nothing to the Lycaonians who if they had understood them (Acts 14.11–17), might have retorted, 'Why should this benevolent God you preach want to destroy his creation?'.[29] A God of Jewish history was hardly intelligible to those who looked for a saving god in nature.

To the God-fearers, however, who heard him, Paul was a deliverer. There can be no doubt that in city after city of Asia Minor and Greece, Paul's message was heard with rapture.[30] This was a revolutionary religion based on personal commitment to Christ, a new exodus based on a new torah. In ten years, between 47 and 57 Paul turned the Jewish dispersion upside down. The Jewish communities were irretrievably split and never returned to unity.

Paul's revolution, however, was religious, not social. Himself respectful to the authorities, loyal to the empire, he was not the man to draw out the implications of Jesus's social teaching. Relations between Christian and Christian were indeed to be characterised by 'love towards the brethren', but the institutions of the empire were sacrosanct. Slavery remained unassailable. There is no word of sympathy for the lot of the scarcely less unfree cultivator.[31]

In 70 AD Jerusalem fell and with it the link that bound Pauline to Palestinian Christianity. For the next three centuries, Christianity was to be primarily a western, a Greek-speaking, religion. Its organisation was based on the urban community, led first by presbyter-bishops and after the end of the first century by bishops, who were assisted by presbyters and deacons. It was the organisation of the hellenistic synagogue adapted to the needs of Christianity. Prophets and teachers gradually faded out of reckoning as the Coming with which their message was primarily concerned was even further delayed.

[29] See M. Dibelius, *Studies in the Acts of the Apostles* (Eng trans London 1956) p 71 n; E. Haenchen, *The Acts of the Apostles: a Commentary* (Eng trans London 1971) pp 431–4.

[30] For instance, the Galatians, 'received me as an angel of God, as Jesus Christ', Gal 4.15.

[31] For Paul's social teaching see G. E. M. de Ste. Croix, 'Early Christian attitudes towards Property and Slavery', *SCH* 12 (1975) p 19.

Moreover, though the lordship of Jesus was assumed and the gospels were increasingly read alongside the septuagint, the prevailing interpretation of His teaching was either Pauline or a Christianised pharisaism which emerged towards the end of the first century.[32] It has often been noted that the writer of 1 Clement quotes Paul without appearing to discuss specific Pauline doctrines. It seems that the dispersion communities, including Rome, grafted the personality of Jesus on to what they had accepted in Judaism, namely, the predominantly pharisaic religion of the last two centuries BC and a Judaised stoic ethic. It is interesting that even in the *Didache*, that owes much to Matthew's gospel, the writer does not insist that the way of life was marked through carrying out the precepts of the sermon on the mount, but rather by a generalised formula of benevolence towards one's neighbour.[33] Not surprisingly, the Christian communities of the first half of the second century, such as Polycarp's at Smyrna, were small, self-contained and introspective. Being 'blameless before the Gentiles' was more important than going out to convert them.[34]

The church's progress during the second century committed it even further to an urban environment. The first great intellectual movement within Christianity, namely gnosticism, could not have been more city-based. Though still accepting many of the pre-suppositions of Judaism, the gnostics attempted to fuse all current religious knowledge whether pagan, Jewish or Christian, round the person of Christ portrayed as the divine saviour.[35] Though they failed, their orthodox rivals found in their turn that they could not express themselves adequately without recourse to the language of philosophy. It was part of the church's strength at this time, that it could absorb philosophical ideas without abandoning its uncompromising opposition to idolatry. Sect and great church alike were finding a place for the active and inquiring gentile mind dissatisfied with the inability of philosophers to find answers to religious questions. Justin Martyr, Tatian, and for a short time Proteus Peregrinus were typical recruits. To the outside observer, Christianity was an opposition urban cult, whose members

[32] I refer in particular, to the long moralising passages in 1 *Clement* which have no reference either to the gospels or Paul and yet reflect Christian teaching of the day.

[33] Thus *Didache* 1 and 4, with the emphasis on selective almsgiving rather than drastic self-denial.

[34] Polycarp to the *Philippians* 10.2, with the emphasis also on general philanthropy and good works as the Christian's task.

[35] See Hans Jonas's fine work, *The Gnostic Religion* (Boston 1963); John Dart, *The Laughing Saviour*, (The Discovery and significance of the Nag Hammadi Library) (San Francisco 1976) part 2.

having 'rejected the Greek gods', formed an 'illegal association' bound together by oaths, who sought to subvert tradition and family for the sake of the deluded worship of the 'crucified sophis'.[36] With few exceptions, the Christian groups in the second century were found in cities where Judaism was strong, as in Sardes in the east, or among merchant colonies, such as at Lyon. Traders and artisans made up their numbers.[37]

Episcopal government, too, was based on the city. This put its bishops and clergy willy-nilly among the privileged orders of ancient society. The persecutions of the Christians in the second century related to their status and influence within that society. We hear of no organisation of country parishes at this time, and certainly no rejection of urban institutions. The church had settled down as a radically-minded Judaistic sect, whose members believed that the world had been created for their sake, and who debated lengthily who amongst them would be most worthy to be saved from its coming destruction.[38] Their heroes were recognisably urban, like Attalus, the Phrygian physician and stalwart among the martyrs of Lyon in 177, and Justin Martyr himself. Their enemies were local philosophers who feared Christian rivalry[39] or urban mobs always ready to lay local disasters at their door.

There was one major exception, however, to this second century urban Christianity. Parts of Phrygia may have been a 'special case'. Certainly, there were many Jewish inhabitants, including, it would seem, Jews on the land, the descendants of colonists given land there by Antiochus III. There may have been something that could be termed a rural Dispersion, but whatever the causes, Christianity there retained a prophetic basis, which burst into the open in 172 with the preaching of a converted priest of Cybele, Montanus and his two female companions, Priscilla and Maximilla. Their message was dynamic and uncompromising. They claimed to be inspired by the Holy Spirit and announced the Coming was at hand and would take place near the villages of Tymion and Pepuza some fifteen miles west of the city of Philadelphia. This was a revival of the wilderness doctrine

[36] The accusations of Celsus in [Origen], *C[contra]* *C[elsum]* 1.1 and 3.55; for 'rejection of the gods' see Lucian, *On the Death of Peregrinus* 13.

[37] Note, for instance, the immigrant merchant character of the community of Lyon as shown by the account of the martyrs of Lyon, preserved by Eusebius, *HE* bk 5 caps 1–2.

[38] Celsus, in Origen, *CC* bk 4 cap 23.

[39] Such as the Cynic Crescens, who appears to have denounced Justin to the authorities in Rome. See Justin 2 *Apologia* 2.2.

of the Coming. People summoned by the prophets to attend the inauguration of the millenium abandoned their families and work to stream into the countryside. Wars, rumours of wars, and other messianic woes were prophesied, and death by martyrdom prepared for by fasting and continence was enjoined on Montanus's followers as the command of the Spirit.[40]

Originally, Montanus found support in the cities of Asia Minor as well as in the countryside, but his movement was resisted strongly by the urban episcopate who tried to convict him and his prophetesses of being false prophets.[41] The women in particular were persecuted. Montanism remained primarily a rural movement, its most lasting influence was in up-country Phrygia, in the Tembris valley for instance, in the north of the province. Inscriptions from the imperial estate that included a large part of the area, dated 249–79 proclaim an open confession of 'Christians to Christians', shunning 'neutral' or 'concealed' Christian formulae used by urban congregations at the time and rejoicing in the title of 'soldier of Christ'.[42]

So, where we have evidence for a rural Christianity in the late second and early third century, we find its characteristics much different from those of its urban contemporary. Its basis is prophecy, and its hope is eschatological: its emphasis is on martyrdom. There is no tendency to compromise with secular society. The faith is not to be concealed but to be proclaimed from the roof tops. Here, the second factor which was mentioned at the beginning of this paper may be taken into account. The ancient world was a severely hierarchical and structured society. The towns were the exclusive organs of government, taxation, policing and culture. The village had no identity of its own apart from its existence within the territory of a city. Romans, Greeks and Jews might contest for supremacy in the cities, but beyond the city walls was barbarism, represented by a succession of conquering and conquered races, retaining their own customs, crafts and languages, but all now subservient to the rulers in the towns, supported if needed by the authorities of the empire itself. The persistence of languages, such as Phrygian, Lycaonian, Aramaic, Coptic, Neo-Punic, Berber, and Celtic remind us that the Roman empire in the first two centuries was divided

[40] Eusebius's account based on anti-Montanist sources, *HE* bk 5 caps 16–18. For assessments of the evidence, see P. de Labriolle's classic, *La Crise Montaniste* (Paris 1913); J. Massingberd Ford, 'Montanism a Jewish-Christian Heresy?' *JEH* 17.2 (1966) pp 145–58.

[41] Eusebius, *HE* bk 5 cap 16, 12–16.

[42] See W. M. Calder, 'Philadelphia and Montanism', *BJRL* 8 (1923) pp 309–46.

by class and caste, and that these divisions had often resulted from military conquest and/or economic dispossession. Between town and countryside, citizen and barbarian, there was little love lost. If the countryside was to be converted to Christianity, it was likely to be to the uncompromising religion of Jesus and not the salvation-theology of Paul. Montanism was a warning of things to come.

The third century continued developments already discernible in the late-second. In the first half of the century, the church emerged from the shadows of Judaistic cult to become one of the major religions of the Greco-Roman world. Its urban character, however, was emphasised to an even greater degree than before. The bishop was the head of an urban community, with a staff of clergy resembling a civil service with a career structure based on service, experience and age. Presbyters, at least in Carthage, were paid a monthly stipend.[43] The congregations over which they presided were becoming as institutional as themselves; people were seeking office, Origen tells us *c*240, for 'the sake of a little prestige'.[44] A major reason why the Decian persecution of 250 so nearly succeeeded was that it fell on almost exclusively urban communities, which, when put to the test of obeying either church or empire, still instinctively obeyed the orders of the emperor.

Nonetheless, protest and opposition, within the framework of urban society was maintained by Christians. One has only to read the story of Perpetua and her companions at Carthage in 202/3, to realise how deep could be the sense of alienation from pagan society in the Severan era and how attractive the martyr ideal. Perpetua had everything in life, wealth, good Carthaginian family, well educated, fluent in Greek and Latin and married with a child and her own establishment.[45] Yet she turned her back on all this, defied her father and the provincial authorities alike, strode into the amphitheatre as though she owned it, and after one encounter with a heifer had the strength to summon catchumens together and tell them, 'You must all stand fast in the faith, and love one another, and do not be weakened by what we have gone through'.[46]

There were martyrdoms in this period in other parts of the empire, notably in Rome, Antioch and Alexandria. Behind a common bravery and devotion to Christianity there were beginning to emerge

[43] Cyprian, *Ep* 34.2, ed [W.] Hartel, *CSEL* 3, 2 (1881) p 571.
[44] Origen, *CC* bk 3 cap 9, Eng trans H. Chadwick (Cambridge 1953) p 134.
[45] See the *Passio Perpetuae* 2, ed and Eng trans [H.] Musurillo (Oxford 1972).
[46] *Ibid* 20.10.

differences in interpreting this aspect of the faith. Perpetua's stance would not have been praised universally. In Alexandria, her contemporary, Clement, compared voluntary martyrdom, such as hers had been, with the suicidal activities attributed to the devotees of Indian religion.[47] He accepted Christianity as the true philosophy, the climax of human endeavour, to which the individual attained gradually through study, ascetic practices, and subjugation of the passions leading to moral and spiritual perfection. This was to be the monastic ideal, and the Coptic monks were to accept this lead from the Christian intellectuals in Alexandria.

For Perpetua and her companions, however, the world, its philosophy and ways of life stood starkly contrasted with the church. The Holy Spirit who entered the prison with the confessor convicted the world of sin. Baptism was the sign of the convert's rejection of his pagan past and foreshadowed even his second baptism, that of martyrdom.[48] In this respect, the north African radical was to influence the attitudes of the rural Christian in the next century. Donatism was to be the religion of puritanical (as well as purely self-seeking) Carthaginian Christians as well as the Numidian villagers. In east and west, therefore, the interpretation given to the most drastic of all Christian witness, namely, martyrdom played its part in forming lasting relationships between urban and rural Christianities, and also the relationship between church and empire.

Meantime, however, common interests and common factors affecting their daily lives were tending to draw most urban Christians into relative harmony with their pagan neighbours. Between 250 and 300 the churches or Christian meeting places became part of the landscape of many of the larger cities, especially in the east. At Nicomedia, Diocletian's capital, the cathedral stood in full view of the palace[49]—anticipating the future relations between church and empire in the east. The church itself had become a property-holding corporation, with its buildings and movable assets.[50] Its members were an identifiable community, enjoying a sort of rudimentary *millet* status. Their leaders were respected by the authorities and, like Dionysius

[47] Clement, *Stromateis*, bk 4 cap 17 paras 1–4, ed O. Stählin and L. Früchtel, *GCS* (Berlin 1960) p 256.

[48] Thus, *Passio Perpetuae* 3.5 and Tertullian, *Apologia* 50.16.

[49] Lactantius, *De Morte Persecutorum* 13.3, ed J. Moreau, *SC* 39 (1954).

[50] A typical late third-century example is provided by the controversy over the ownership of the bishop's house at Antioch after Paul of Samosata had been deposed by a council in 268. See Eusebius *HE* bk 7 cap 30 para 19.

of Alexandria (247–64), liable even to be used as intermediaries in important negotiations.[51] The urban Christian either in east or west was far from being a revolutionary. He was concerned with his own salvation, not in changing society according to the precepts of the gospel. Tobit, the example of the upright pharisee who was generous with his alms-giving and punctilious in charitable duties was also the Christian's ideal.[52] The lot of the Christian slave might be alleviated, but slavery itself was never challenged as an institution. Cruel punishments of slaves, and even their murder by their owners could be absolved by penance.[53] One of the features of the council of Elvira in south-eastern Spain, *c*300/10, is that adultery and sexual misdemeanours seem to take pride of place against other forms of wanton and unsocial behaviour.[54] The persecution of Diocletian and his colleagues 303–12, was an interruption, but no more than an interruption, in the process of growing together by church and secular authorities in the Mediterranean cities.

The last twenty years of the third century, however, saw the beginnings of the Christianisation of some important rural areas in the Roman empire. For reasons still obscure, the traditional deities that had watched over cultivators for centuries, even millenia, began to lose their hold, to be replaced by Christianity. In Numidia, the numbers of bishoprics in small centres increased considerably between 260 and 300.[55] The rural population around Cirta, the capital, in the time of Valerian (253–60) hostile to Christian confessors was in 300 enthusastically Christian.[56] For Eusebius of Caesarea, north Africa was second only to Egypt in its toll of martyrs,[57] and not for nothing does the Coptic era open with the accession of Diocletian, the reign

[51] Recounted by Eusebius, *HE* bk 7 cap 21. Dionysius of Alexandria was a supporter of Gallienus against the rebel Macrianus. See C. Andresen, 'Der Erlass des Gallienus an die Bischöfe Aegyptens', *Studia Patristica* 12 (Berlin 1975) pp 385–98.

[52] Thus, Cyprian, *De Dominica oratione* 33, Hartel, p 290; and *De Mortalitate* 10, Hartel p 302.

[53] Thus, canon 5 of the council of Elvira. Seven years penance was decreed against a mistress who murdered her slave, five years for the equivalent of culpable homicide.

[54] See canons 7 (life excommunication for the repeated offence of adultery), 13, 14, 17, 35, 47, 63–5.

[55] See A. von Harnack, *The Mission and Expansion of Christianity in the First three Centuries,* Eng trans, *Theological Translation Library,* publ Williams and Norgate (London 1905) 2 pp 422–4.

[56] Contrast, *Passio Mariani et Jacobi* 2, ed Musurillo (Oxford 1972) p 195, with *Gesta apud Zenophilum* (= Optatus of Milevis, *De Schismate,* app 1, p 186).

[57] Eusebius, *HE* bk 8 cap 6 para 10.

that witnessed the triumph of the native Egyptian martyrs over the pagan empire.

The biblical ideal was being recovered. Antony's followers 'put on the whole armour of Christ', and like their Master before them, sought to destroy Satan's kingdom by combat with demons and powers of evil that had their abode in desert places. In North Africa, the communities in remoter parts of proconsular Africa were attracting young enthusiasts from Carthage, for that was where the true ideal of Christian brotherhood was to be found. 'These are my brethren who keep the commandments of God', were the words of the wealthy Carthaginian 'confessor', Victoria, regarding the martyrs of Abitina with whom she had been arrested at the end of 303.[58]

Yet there was a difference of emphasis between Egyptian monk and north African confessor. Antony did not seek martyrdom during the great persecution. He offered encouragement to those who did,[59] but clearly for him the ascetic ideal did not necessitate the martyr's witness. In north Africa on the other hand martyrdom was the ideal. One finds the same spirit of defiance among rural Christians as had existed among the Christians of Carthage at the beginning of the third century. Listen to this scrap of dialogue between Maximilian, brought to Theveste (Tebessa) probably from the surrounding Numidian countryside by his father as an army recruit, and the proconsul, Dion. He has refused to receive the military seal (*signaculum*) at the hands of Dion. The date is 295.

> *Dion*: 'You must serve, and accept the seal—otherwise you will die miserably.'
>
> *Maximilian*: 'I shall not perish. My name is already before my Lord. I may not serve.'
>
> *Dion*: 'Have regard for your youth. Serve. That is what a young man should do.'
>
> *Maximilian*: 'My service is for the Lord. I cannot serve the world. I have already told you. I am a Christian.'[60]

In vain, the proconsul told him that there were Christians serving in the imperial bodyguard. He would not be moved and went to his death.

[58] *Acta Saturnini* 5 and 14 – 'et illi sunt fratres qui Dei praecepta custodiant' – *PL* 8 (1844) cols 693, 698.

[59] *Antony* cap 46, col 909C. He was 'unwilling to give himself up, but aided the confessors in the mines and in prisons'.

[60] *Acta Maximiliani*, ed Musurillo, p 247.

This was the spirit that survived among the rural Christians in north Africa and united them with many of their urban contemporaries in the Donatist movement. Between church and world and their respective institutions no dealings and no compromise was possible. The devil was always active. When persecution failed in its aim, he would use other means to destroy Christians and other agents to further his plans. From Satan in the imperial authorities to Satan in extortionate landowners as well, demanded no great imagination.[61] The circumcellion was the successor to the spirit of the martyrs of the great persecution. So, too, was the Egyptian monk, but in a different way. As heir to a tradition in which Christianity marked progress from superstition to illumination and truth, he would be a reluctant rebel, once the emperor had himself espoused the true religion. Constantine, by repudiating the pagan past of the empire, completely won the loyalty of both urban and rural Christian in the east.

A generation has passed. Our visitor has seen society in transformation. He would also have become wary of drawing too absolute distinctions. Gnostic sects and Marcionites, pre-eminently urban in the second century, included both town and country congregations in the fourth century. Sects in Syria and Egypt were tending to be village-based. The Nag-Hammadi gnostic library provides an obvious example. In the east, however, Christians whether heretical or orthodox were beginning to feel a common sense of identity, as belonging to 'the race of Christians', that marked them off from pagans and the Persian enemy. One Syrian Christian leader would have told our friend, 'Their[the Romans'] empire will never be conquered. Never fear, for the hero whose name is Jesus will come with power, and his might will sustain the army of the empire'.[62] Incidental defeats by the Persians were due to sin, punished by God accordingly, but final victory would be theirs. Ephrem Syrus and Aphraat spoke for the native provincials on the Persian frontier. Constantius II, even if of doubtful orthodoxy, was infinitely preferable to the Persians.

In the west, however, few would have displayed such a spirit of patriotism and unity. There were many cross currents. In north Africa,

[61] For the Roman authorities denounced as mouthpieces of Satan, see *Acta Saturnini* 6 – 'Quid agis hoc in loco, Diabole' – addressed by the confessor, Dativus, to the prosecuting advocate, *PL* 8 col 694A.

[62] Aphraates, *Demonstratio* bk 5 cap 24, ed G. Lafontaine, *CSCO, Scriptores Armenici* 7 (1977) p 59 of Latin translation.
For similar sentiments of jubilation at the defeat of the Persians in 350, see Ephrem Syrus, *Carmina Nisibena* 3, *CSCO, Scriptores Syria*, 92–3, ed E. Beck (1961) pp 11–15.

the Donatists, whether urban or rural, maintained the pre-Constantinian tradition of protest against idolatry in all its forms. Augustine, on the other hand, accepted a society still based on the superiority of town over countryside. He was aware of the inequalities of wealth between the inhabitants of the two, and knew of the rising tensions because of these, but he had no remedy.[63] Peasant risings, especially as part of the circumcellion movement he abominated, as contrary to apostolic precept.[64] As we know, between 427 and 439, African catholicism was shattered by a combination of revolt by African tribes and the Vandal invasion. Catholic clergy, admitted Augustine's biographer Possidius, were hated 'because of their lands'.[65] In the west as a whole, the contradictions between town and countryside, the ordered episcopal government and the sectarian, prophetic movement continued to exist into the middle ages. Indeed, the religious outlook of urban master and peasant servant are not to be reconciled easily through a common Christianity, even down to our own day.

University of Glasgow

[63] Augustine, *Enarratio in Ps* 39.7, *PL* 36 (1865) col 438; and *In Ps* 48.8, *ibid* cols 561–2.
[64] Augustine, *Ep* 108.5.18, ed A. Goldbacher, *CSEL* 34.2 (1895) p 632.
[65] Possidius, *Vita Sancti Augustini*, cap 28, *PL* 32 (1877) col 58.

FROM TOWN TO COUNTRY: THE CHRISTIANISATION OF THE TOURAINE 370–600

by C. E. STANCLIFFE

WHEN Martin became bishop of Tours *c*370, Christianity had already taken root in the town; but the surrounding countryside was still untouched by the new religion. Although it was over fifty years since Constantine had first recognised Christianity, and thirty-three years since Tours had had a permanent bishop,[1] the attention of the Gallic bishops had been distracted first by the Arian heresy, and latterly by Julian's revival of paganism. Martin was therefore the first bishop of Tours to concern himself with the conversion of the countryside, and this work was continued by his successors in the fifth and sixth centuries.

We are lucky in our sources for this period. Gregory, bishop of Tours *c*573–94, gives us a list of all his predecessors, and includes not only the lengths of their episcopates, but also the names of the churches they founded in the *vici*.[2] A wholly different slant on the process is provided by Sulpicius Severus's writings about Martin, which date from *c*400.[3] Here, we see Martin preaching to the peasants, and destroying pagan temples by force. We are also fortunate in the work of the French archaeologist and historian, Jacques Boussard, whose publications include a gazeteer of all Roman archaeological finds in the Touraine,[4] and a study of how settlement patterns there altered between the Roman and the Merovingian periods.[5] The subject thus promises well.

[1] Gregory [of Tours] *Hist*[*oriae*] 10, 31, ii; ed B. Krusch and W. Levison, *MGH SRM* I.1 (new ed 1951) pp 526–7.

[2] *Ibid* 10, 31.

[3] [Sulpicius Severus] *V*[*ita*] *M*[*artini*] (*c*396); *D*[*ialogi*] (*c*404–6); ed C. Halm, *CSEL* 1 (1866).

[4] [*Forma Orbis Romani: Carte archéologique de la Gaule romaine*], directed by A. Grenier and P. M. Duval, 13: [J.] Boussard, *Carte* [*et Texte du département d'Indre-et-Loire*] (Paris 1960). It is on this that the archaeological information in fig 1 is based, although the map and the classification of material are my own.

[5] '[Essai sur] le peuplement [de la Touraine du Ier au viiie siècle]', *Moyen Age* 60 (1954) pp 261–91. This has provided me with the settlement evidence indicated on fig 4, although the map is my own.

However, when we consider the general theme 'the church in town and countryside' the prospect grows darker. For, first, we have to ask whether we can make a meaningful division between town and countryside, *tout simple*; and then we have to consider whether such a division remains as valid for the year 600 as for 370. I shall therefore begin with a brief analysis of settlement patterns in the Touraine during this period.

I

From a geographical point-of-view, the Touraine falls into two main divisions. On the one hand there are the raised plateaux, typically formed of limestone, where the soil is thin and would have supported only a rather sparse vegetation. On the other hand there are the great river valleys of the Loire, Cher, Indre and Indrois, Vienne and Creuse, where the soil is rich, being composed in part of alluvium. It was in these fertile valleys that the Romans settled in their villas, their main agricultural concerns probably being cereals and viticulture.[6] Tours itself was a Roman foundation which grew up at the meeting-point of many roads;[7] and alongside these same roads smaller settlements, *vici*, would have sprung up. I think, for instance, of Amboise, Luynes, Langeais and Candes in the Loire valley, and there would have been many others. We should probably think of these *vici*, with their tradesmen and often their temples, as serving the rural population for some distance around them.[8]

Here, we reach a much discussed topic: that is, whether there were independent peasant farmers coexisting with the large estates farmed by the *coloni*; and, if there were, how the two worlds meshed with each other. We are not in a position to give a definite answer for the Touraine, but evidence from elsewhere in France suggests that where the land was most fertile, it was divided up between large estates, farmed by *coloni*; while on poorer land, independent peasants living

[6] Boussard, 'le peuplement' pp 264 *seq*, 287–9; P. Vidal de la Blache, *Tableau de la Géographie de la France* (Paris 1908) pp 163–70.

[7] See J. Boussard, 'Étude sur la ville de Tours du Ier au IVe siècle', *Revue des études anciennes*, 4 ser, 50 (Bordeaux 1948) pp 313–29.

[8] [A.] Grenier, *Manuel [d'archéologie gallo-romaine]*, 4 parts in 7 vols (Paris 1931–60) part 2, 2 (1934) pp 695–726, esp 719 *seq*. [W.] Seston, 'Note [sur les origines religieuses des paroisses rurales]', *Revue d'Histoire et de Philosophie religieuses* 15 (Strasbourg 1935) pp 244–6.

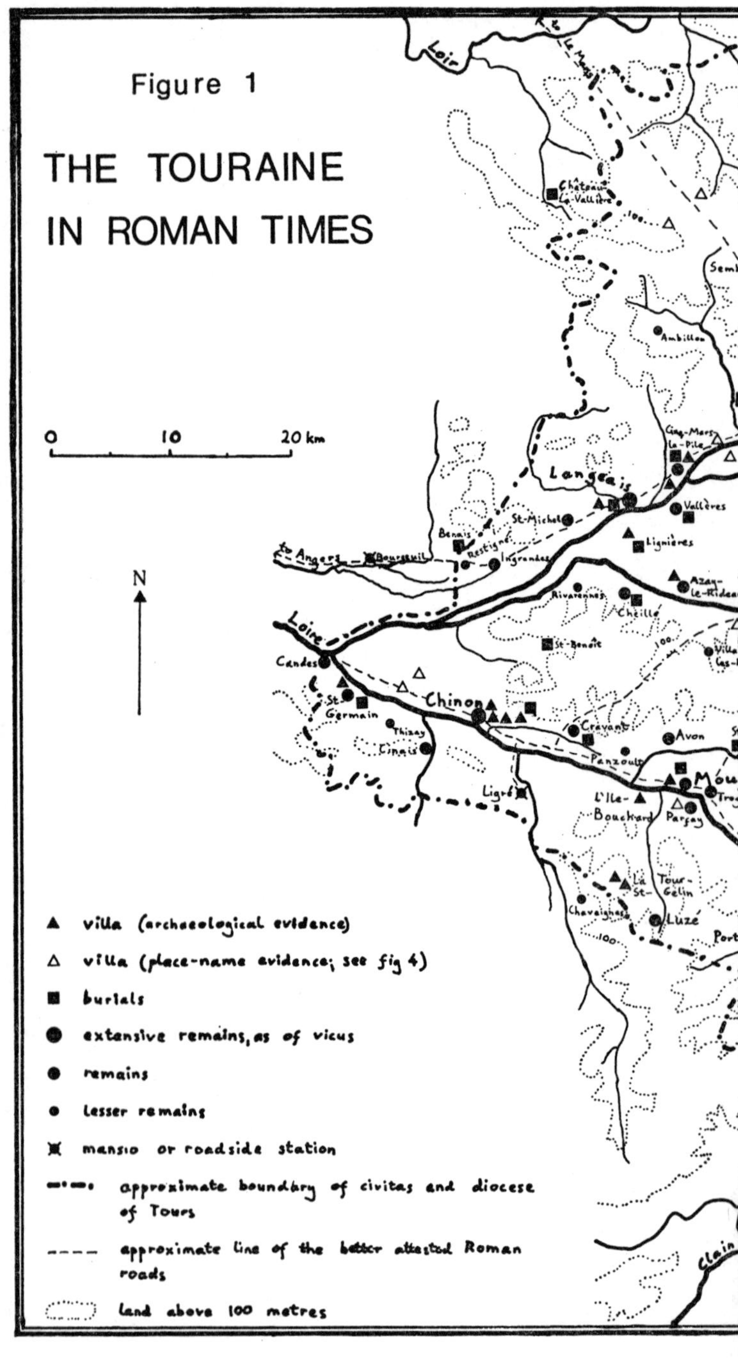

Figure 1
THE TOURAINE IN ROMAN TIMES
0 10 20 km
N
Loir
to Le Mans
Château-la-Vallière
100
Ambillou
Cinq-Mars-la-Pile
Langeais
St-Michel
Vallères
Benais
Restigné
Ingrandes
Lignières
to Angers
Bourgueil
Azay-le-Rideau
Rivarennes
Cheillé
Loire
Candes
St-Benoît
St Germain
Chinon
Thizay
Cinais
Cravant
Avon
Panzoult
Ligré
L'Ile-Bouchard
Parçay
La Tour-St-Gelin
Chaveignes
Luzé
Ports
Clain
villa (archaeological evidence)
villa (place-name evidence; see fig 4)
burials
extensive remains, as of vicus
remains
lesser remains
mansio or roadside station
approximate boundary of civitas and diocese of Tours
approximate line of the better attested Roman roads
land above 100 metres

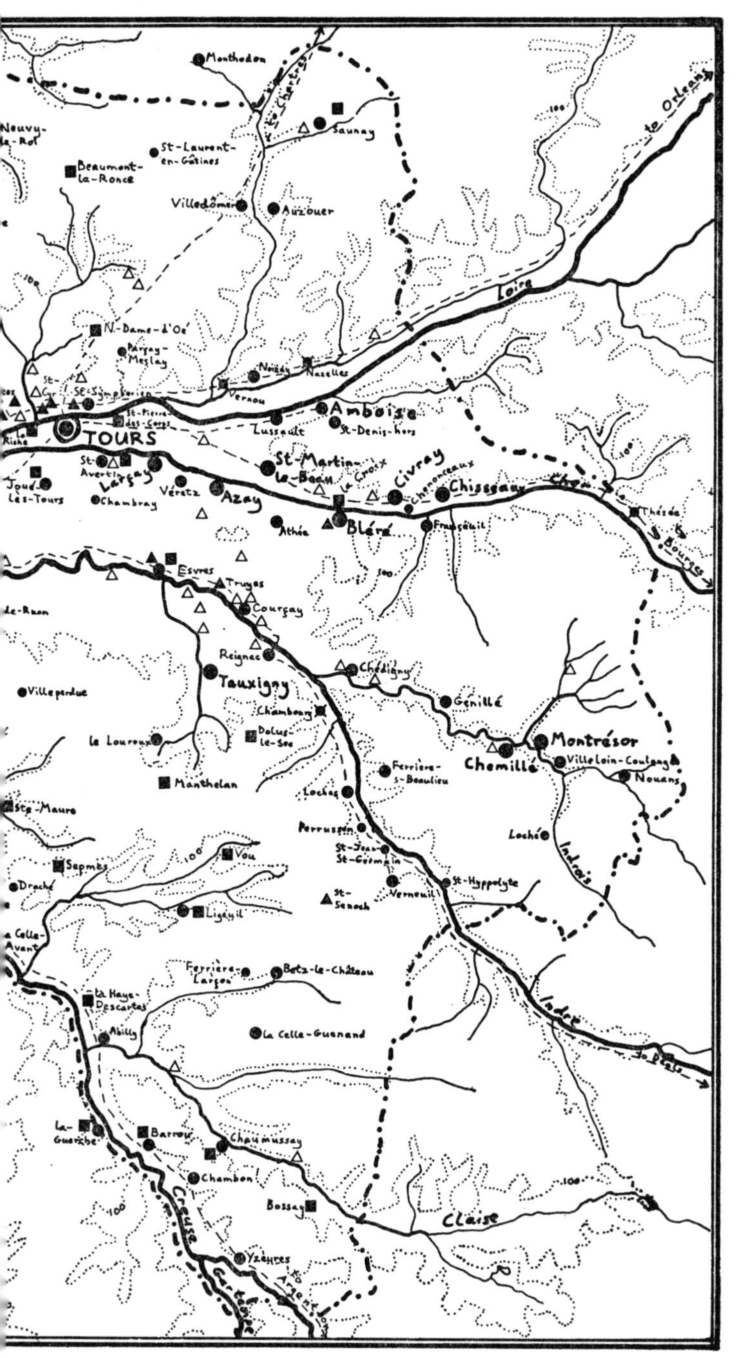

in villages or hamlets could still be found.[9] Figure 1 shows that, in the Touraine, Roman villas were restricted to the fertile river valleys; so there would have been plenty of room for independent peasants, particularly on the plateaux. Their settlements are hard to locate because, where the inhabitants did not adopt a Roman style of building or culture, there is little chance of our finding archaeological evidence of their existence which can be securely dated to the Roman period. However, I think it is worth pondering the fact that Martin founded *vicus* churches not only in places which have yielded considerable Roman remains, such as Amboise and Langeais, but also at Ciran-la-Latte and at Tournon. At Ciran itself, no traces of any Roman buildings have been found, though several coins have been picked up in the commune, and there is some evidence of Roman occupation a few kilometres away.[10] Tournon is even more interesting, as there is no evidence at all of any occupation of that area in Roman times. My own suggestion would be that both churches were founded to serve a scattered rural population.

This brief discussion of settlement patterns in the Touraine leads me to suggest that instead of making a twofold distinction, between town and countryside, we should adopt a subtler approach, recognising that different classifications may be appropriate for different purposes. Thus, if we seek to classify buildings and agglomerations of buildings, I would propose a fourfold distinction. First, there is the city of Tours itself, together with its suburbs.[11] Secondly, there are the villas, which may have dependent settlements nearby where their agricultural workers were housed. Thirdly, there are the *vici*, with their tradesmen and temples; and fourthly, the settlements of independent peasant farmers. If, on the other hand, we were to classify *people* according to their social class, culture and occupation, then we might make a three-fold distinction between, first, the senatorial aristocracy, who were well-educated and lived much of their time on their country estates; secondly, the urban middle classes and petty bourgeoisie, which would

[9] The whole question of rural settlement in Gaul is much discussed at the moment. See E. M. Wightman, 'The pattern of rural settlement in Roman Gaul', *Aufstieg und Niedergang der römischen Welt* (1974– in progress) 2, 4, ed H. Temporini and W. Haase (Berlin/New York 1975) pp 584–657, esp 646–54; [R.] Agache, 'La campagne [à l'époque romaine dans les grandes plaines du Nord de la France d'après les photographies aériennes]' *ibid* pp 658–713, esp 700–2; J. Percival, *The Roman Villa* (London 1976) cap 6; Grenier *Manuel* pp 733–5.

[10] Boussard *Carte* pp 25–26.

[11] Compare Gregory *Hist* 5, 4, 'civitatem et omnia suburbana eius'; see also R. Latouche, *The Birth of Western Economy* (Eng tr London 1961) pp 109 *seq.*

include both those of Tours itself and their counterparts in the *vici*; and finally, the peasants, whether they were *coloni* on a villa owner's estate, or independent farmers cultivating their own land.

In its broad outlines, and with some modifications, I think that this picture remains valid for the whole period under discussion. The evidence of archaeology, in fact, points to the real break with Roman prosperity coming with the Germanic invasions of *c*270, before this study begins.[12] This is not to deny that the invasions, the violence and the plague which ravaged the Touraine in the fifth and sixth centuries took their toll: some villas and *vici* went under. However, some survived, and some new ones were founded.[13] The most important physical change was probably that the population became further dispersed. In the Frankish period we find settlements not only in the fertile valleys which had attracted the Romans, but also on the upland plateaux.[14] It is also likely that the same period saw a change in the life of the *vici*. Originally, these had been peopled by artisans and petty traders; but with invasions and sporadic warfare disrupting communications, it is likely that their inhabitants had to turn to agriculture to eke out a living. On the whole, however, we can continue to think in terms of my fourfold and threefold classifications throughout the period under discussion.

If we now consider the question of conversion to Christianity, my reason for discussing these other matters will become apparent. As space is limited, I propose to concentrate on those characteristics of the rural population which presented new challenges for an urban-based church, and to look at the church's response to these. This means that I shall not be considering every aspect of the conversion of the countryside, but only those that posed problems which did not arise in the conversion of cities. Three areas of investigation spring to mind. First, there is the geographical aspect. As soon as the population is scattered over the countryside, not concentrated within a small space, there arises the problem of having to provide sufficient churches and priests to enable everyone to hear the gospel and to attend church regularly. Here, the fourfold classification of town, villa, *vicus* and hamlet/farmstead is the relevant one. Secondly, there is the question of whether differing degrees of Romanisation would have affected people's readiness to accept Christianity, with its Latin bible. Roman civilisation

[12] Boussard 'le peuplement' pp 273–5; *Carte* pp 11–12.
[13] Compare the settlement evidence on figs 1 and 4.
[14] Boussard 'le peuplement' pp 278–91.

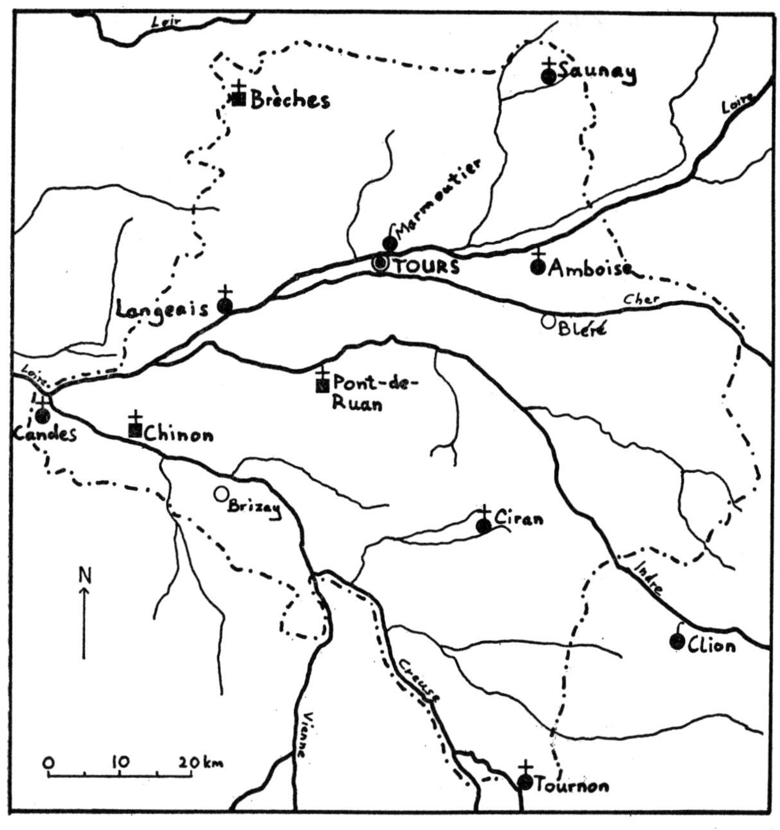

vicus church founded by Martin (c370–97)

monastery, convent, founded by Martin

vicus church founded by Brice (397–c444)

approximate boundary of diocese of Tours

Fig 2.
TOURAINE CHURCHES FOUNDED 3705444

radiated from the towns and the smaller settlements, strung out along the Roman roads; but peasants in the remoter parts of the Touraine were still speaking Celtic in the year 400.[15] Thirdly, we should consider whether differences in environment and occupation are likely to have made people more or less receptive towards Christianity. For instance, we would expect the religious needs and outlook of the petty bourgeoisie in Tours and the *vici* to have been different from those of peasant farmers, rooted in the soil; and both would have differed from those of the aristocracy. For both the second and the third questions, the threefold distinction into wealthy landowner, petty bourgeoisie and peasant farmer is the relevant one.

The issues I have posed are broad ones, and here I can do no more than touch on two of them: first, I shall take the purely geographical question of how the church set about meeting the needs of a scattered population; and, secondly, I shall consider briefly why the peasantry, in particular, may have been loth to exchange their old gods for the new religion.

II

The stages whereby Christianity was implanted in the countryside around Tours can best be shown in maps.[16] Figure 2 shows that Martin founded six *vicus* churches, scattered throughout the diocese of Tours. He also destroyed pagan temples and founded churches outside his own diocese, and I have included the convent of Clion on this map, as it is only just in the diocese of Bourges.[17]

Martin's successor, Brice, founded five *vicus* churches. In locating three of them at the modern villages of Brèches, Chinon, and Pont-de-Ruan, there is no disagreement. However, rival theories have been propounded for Gregory's *vicus Briotreidis*, with some arguing for Brizay on the Vienne;[18] others for Bléré on the Cher.[19] I am not

[15] This is implicit in Sulpicius, *D*, 1, 27, 4.

[16] The source is Gregory *Hist* 10, 31. Unless otherwise indicated, I have followed the identifications of [A.] Longnon, *Géographie* [*de la Gaule au VI*e *siècle*] (Paris 1878) pp 260 *seq*.

[17] 'in confinio Biturigum adque Turonorum', Sulpicius, *D*, 2, 8, 7.

[18] Longnon *Géographie* pp 264–6, followed by [M.] Vieillard-Troiekouroff, [*Les monuments religieux de la Gaule d'après les oeuvres de Grégoire de Tours*] (Paris 1976) p 72.

[19] Notably Mabille, who points to a tenth-century charter which designates Bléré as *villa Bidrada*. See Longnon *Géographie* p 265, and E. Mabille, 'Notice sur les divisions territoriales et la topographie de l'ancienne province de la Touraine', *BEC* 25, 5 ser, 5 (1864) p 248. Mabille is followed by Boussard 'le peuplement' p 276; and by [E.] Griffe [*La Gaule chrétienne à l'époque romaine*], 3 vols (Paris 1947–65) 3 p 282.

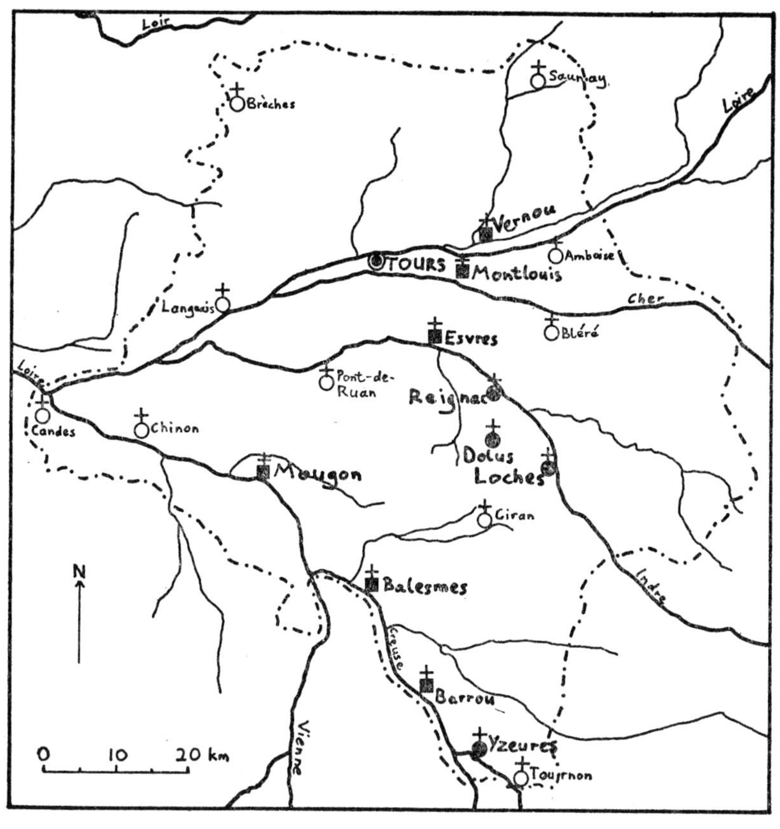

vicus church already in existence by 444

vicus church founded by Eustochius (c 444–61)

vicus church founded by Perpetuus (c 461–91)

approximate boundary of diocese of Tours

Fig 3.
TOURAINE CHURCHES FOUNDED 444–91

competent to adjudicate on philological grounds; as a historian, I would only say that Bléré seems a far more likely choice. It was an important centre in Roman times, and remained so under the Merovingians, becoming the centre of a *vicaria*. The same cannot be said of Brizay: the only real evidence of Roman settlement near there is the remains of a villa a couple of kilometres away, at l'Île-Bouchard. Further, Mougon, where Perpetuus founded a church, is only just the other side of the river Vienne; and when churches were still so scarce, it would have been a little odd to place two of them so close together. On the other hand, the lower Cher valley was thickly settled, and if we disallow a church at Bléré, then it would still have had no church between Mareuil and the plain of Tours itself, even in the time of Gregory. Provisionally, therefore, I accept the identification of *vicus Briotreidis* with Bléré. As for the fifth church that Brice founded, that was at *vicus Calatonnus*. Most scholars feel too uncertain to volunteer any identification, though Griffe suggests Saint-Julien-de-Chedon, some fifteen kilometres further up the Cher from Bléré.[20]

Brice was succeeded by Eustochius (*c*444–61), who founded four churches; and Eustochius was followed by Perpetuus, who founded six. These are shown on figure 3. After Perpetuus's death *c*491, the foundation of *vicus* churches appears to have lapsed: whether because of political disturbances, or because the existing churches sufficed for the present, we do not know.[21] It is only with Gregory's predecessor, Eufronius (*c*556–73), that the work was taken up again, and three more *vici* were given their own churches (figure 4). Finally, we come to Gregory himself. He writes that he has dedicated many churches and oratories within the diocese of Tours: too many for him to list them all.[22] For the historian, that is a pity; however, his own writings afford much incidental information, and I have shown this on figure 4.

A few general points can be made about the foundation of *vicus* churches as shown on these maps. One striking fact is the large number of churches located on or near the border of the Tours diocese. This may be because they were founded on the sites of pagan temples.[23] Aerial surveys of Artois and Picardy confirm that, while the small pagan sanctuaries stood in the open countryside, large sanctuaries with a theatre were always placed in frontier areas, and on Roman

[20] *Ibid* p 282.

[21] Both Perpetuus's successor, Volusianus, and the next bishop, Virus, were exiled by the Visigoths; but compare also below p 51.

[22] Gregory *Hist* 10, 31, xviii.

[23] Compare Seston 'Note' pp 245–9.

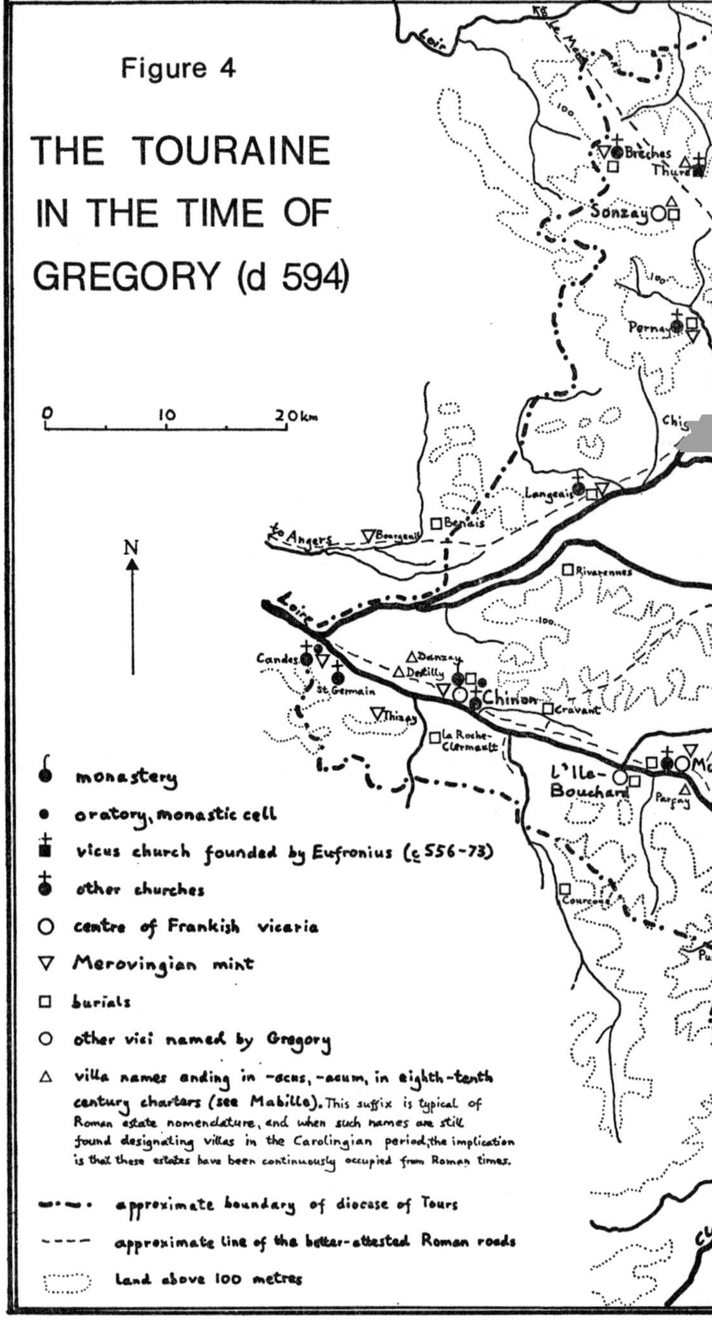

Figure 4
THE TOURAINE IN THE TIME OF GREGORY (d 594)
0 10 20km
N
Loir
Brèches
Thuré
Sonzay
Pernay
Langeais
Benais
to Angers
Bourgueil
Rivarennes
Loire
Candes
St Germain
Danzay
Détilly
Chinon
Cravant
Thizay
La Roche-Clermault
L'Ile-Bouchard
Parçay
Courçoué
monastery
oratory, monastic cell
vicus church founded by Eufronius (c 556–73)
other churches
centre of Frankish vicaria
Merovingian mint
burials
other vici named by Gregory
villa names ending in -acus, -acum, in eighth–tenth century charters (see Mabille). This suffix is typical of Roman estate nomenclature, and when such names are still found designating villas in the Carolingian period, the implication is that these estates have been continuously occupied from Roman times.
approximate boundary of diocese of Tours
approximate line of the better-attested Roman roads
land above 100 metres

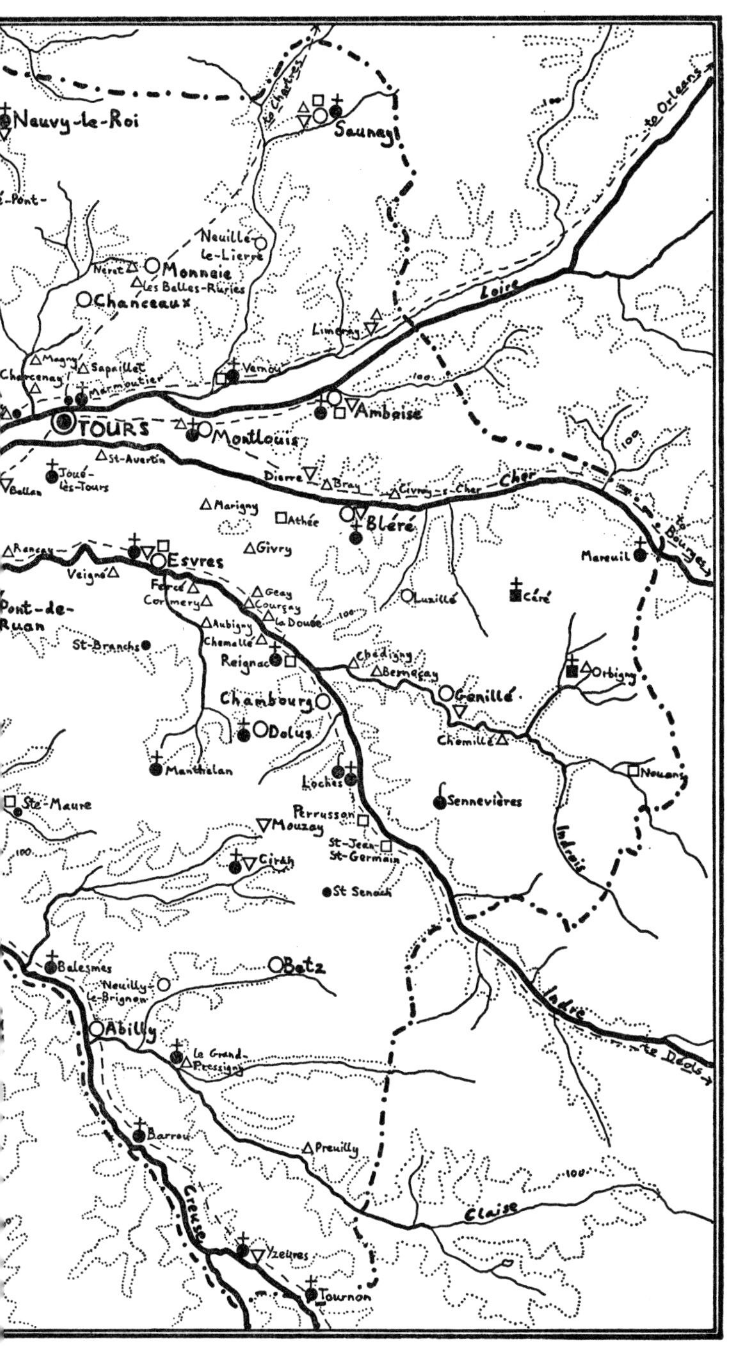

Neuvy-le-Roi
Saunay
to Chartres
to Orleans
Pont-
Neuillé-le-Lierre
Nérat
Monnaie
Les Belles-Ruries
Chanceaux
Loire
Limeray
Magny
Sapaillet
Charcenay
Marmoutier
Vernou
Ambóise
TOURS
Montlouis
St-Avertin
Joué-lès-Tours
Ballan
Dierre
Bray
Civray-s-Cher
Cher
Marigny
Athée
Bléré
to Bourges
Mareuil
Givry
Esvres
Veigné
Fercé
Cormery
Geay
Coursay
La Douée
Aubigny
Luzillé
Céré
Pont-de-Ruan
St-Branchs
Chemillé
Reignac
Chédigny
Bemeçay
Orbigny
Chambourg
Genillé
Dolus
Chemillé
Manthelan
Loches
Nouans
Sennevières
Ste-Maure
Perrusson
Mouzay
St-Jean-St-Germain
Indrois
Cirân
St Senoch
Balesmes
Betz
Neuilly-le-Brignon
Indre
Abilly
Le Grand-Pressigny
to Déols
Barrou
Preuilly
Creuse
Claise
Yzeures
Tournon
100

roads.[24] We know that Martin's general policy was to destroy pagan temples, and replace them with either a church or a monastery.[25] He certainly did this at Amboise,[26] and he may have done likewise at Candes.[27] We also know that the church at Yzeures replaced a great temple dedicated to Minerva,[28] which suggests that his successors carried on the same policy.

Secondly, it is interesting to look at the patterning of church foundations. Initially, they were widely spaced out throughout the diocese, suggesting that the impetus for their foundation came from the centre, from the bishop himself.[29] However, a different pattern emerges with the churches dedicated by Eustochius and Perpetuus. These were founded within striking distance of existing churches, as with the string of churches down the Indre, from Loches to Dolus to Reignac, and then on to Esvres; or with those along the Creuse valley, downstream from Tournon. First, a church was founded at Yzeures; then ones at Barrou and Balesmes. Although in the absence of literary evidence we cannot be certain, it looks very much as though the missionary impulse in these cases came from the older *vicus* churches of Ciran and Tournon, which founded new missionary centres as Christianity gradually spread further down the valleys.

Thirdly, it is worth considering how well the churches served the population. To facilitate this, I have indicated evidence of habitation on the maps.[30] However, there is one respect in which these maps, with the partial exception of figure 4, are highly misleading: they mark only churches founded in *vici*, whereas there must also have been many churches and oratories on private estates throughout the diocese.[31] The problem is that we only hear of the latter category incidentally, if they happen to come up in the course of Gregory's narrative.[32] In this predicament it is worth citing Chaume's estimates

[24] Agache 'La campagne' p 697.

[25] *VM* 13, 9.

[26] *D* 3, 8, 4–7.

[27] The extensive archaeological remains at Candes may indicate a temple: see Boussard *Carte* p 38. Martin definitely founded a church there: Sulpicius *epp* 3, 6, 9.

[28] Sculptured stones from this temple were found in the Merovingian foundations of the twelfth-century church: see Boussard, *Carte* p 15.

[29] This was certainly so in the case of Martin: *VM* caps 13–15.

[30] This may be misleading in individual cases, as some sites marked as Roman may have been abandoned by the fifth century, while other sites of our period may await discovery. However, the general picture is reasonably clear.

[31] On this see Griffe pp 291–6.

[32] As, for instance, in Gregory's *de [passione et] virt[utibus Sancti] Jul[iani martyris]* cap 50; ed B. Krusch, *MGH SRM* 1, 2 (new ed 1969) pp 133–4.

for the diocese of Auxerre to give some idea of the likely number of estate churches involved. Chaume reckons that, *c*500, the Auxerre diocese contained eight *vicus* churches and twelve villa churches; and that by *c*600 the number had risen to thirteen *vicus* churches and twenty-four villa churches.[33] While I do not feel very happy about Chaume's methods of dating the churches he discusses,[34] his findings do suggest that estate churches were quite numerous, even to the point of out-numbering *vicus* churches. However, when all this has been said, the fact remains that sixth-century church councils banned the celebration of Christmas, easter and whitsun in estate churches;[35] nor would they have allowed baptism to have been conferred in them.[36] This means that they were unable to fulfil all the necessary functions for the neighbouring population, who would have been compelled to seek out their nearest *vicus* church for all important occasions.[37] Thus, even allowing for the existence of many estate churches, there is still some point in seeing how adequately the *vicus* churches served the rural population.

A *vicus* church would have had quite a large number of clergy attached to it. A council held at Tours in 567 implies that each *vicus* church was controlled by an archpriest, who had priests, deacons, subdeacons and readers in his *familia*.[38] Although some in lower orders may have been children or part-timers, this sort of scale would enable each church to cover quite a large area satisfactorily; and the idea of grouping clerics together under an archpriest, rather than scattering them, one to each hamlet, would have been beneficial from the point-of-view of upholding religious, moral and educational standards amongst illiterate peasants. Now, figure 3 shows that, by the end of the fifth century, most people would have had a church within ten kilometres of their homes.[39] Given the large staff, I think this

[33] M. Chaume, 'Le mode de constitution et de délimitation des paroisses rurales aux temps mérovingiens et carolingiens', *Revue Mabillon* 27 (Ligugé 1937) pp 61–73 at p 65.

[34] He appears to rely entirely on the evidence of church dedications: *ibid* p 65, n 1.

[35] For example, Orleans (AD 511) §25; *Concilia Galliae 511–695*, ed C. de Clercq, *CC* 148A (1963) p 11.

[36] Compare [H. G. J.] Beck, [*The*] *Pastoral Care* [*of Souls in south-east France during the sixth century*], *Analecta Gregoriana* 51 (Rome 1950) p 74; J. D. C. Fisher, *Christian Initiation: Baptism in the Medieval West, Alcuin Club Coll*, no 47 (London 1965) pp 72–4.

[37] In time, of course, this changed, and the estate churches became full parish churches. In southern Gaul this development began in the sixth century: Beck, *Pastoral Care*, pp 75–6; Griffe pp 295–6.

[38] § 20; *CC* 148 A pp 183–4; Compare Beck, *Pastoral Care*, p 79; [P.] Riché, *Education* [*et Culture dans l'Occident barbare, vi*e*- viii*e *siècles*] (3 ed Paris 1962) pp 170–1.

[39] Assuming that we accept the identification of *Briotreidis* with Bléré.

would have been adequate. It is also worth comparing this situation with that in Gregory's days, a century later (figure 4): the most notable additions occur on the higher ground, away from the great river valleys where the majority of churches had been founded hitherto. I would connect this phenomenon with the expansion of the population up onto the plateaux in the Frankish period.[40] In other words, more churches may have been founded in the sixth century primarily because the population had shifted, not because fifth century provision had never been adequate.

Another way of evaluating the provision of churches in the Touraine is by comparing the number of churches in the countryside with those in Tours itself: by 500, there were approximately four churches in the city of Tours, compared with twenty in the *vici*; by 600, there were approximately sixteen churches, oratories and monasteries in Tours, compared with forty-two in the countryside that we know of.[41] I think that these figures sum up all I wish to say about the provision of churches in the countryside around Tours in the fifth and sixth centuries:—the country areas were tolerably provided for; but the numerous religious foundations in Tours itself show that the church continued to centre on the city.[42]

III

I wish now to turn to the question of whether the environment and the preoccupations of the Touraine peasantry are likely to have affected their receptivity towards Christianity;[43] and to see how the church accommodated itself to their needs.

I shall begin by looking at Nock's distinction between natural and prophetic religions. Nock points out that man has no control over certain basic processes which affect him closely, such as birth and death, or good luck in fishing and hunting; but that, nonetheless, he has from time immemorial sought to influence them, that is, to influence

[40] Above p 46.

[41] Details are given by Gregory *Hist* 10, 31. These are interpreted slightly differently by Longnon, *Géographie* pp 245–60, and by Vieillard-Troiekouroff pp 304–29.

[42] Note that Gregory gives us details of his work on the churches in Tours itself, while not finding space to record the names of those he has dedicated in the countryside: *Hist* 10, 31, xviii.

[43] I do not think that sociological analysis on its own can 'explain' religious conversion; but it can usefully throw light upon the sort of social conditions in which people are more likely to respond to the call of a prophetic religion. It can analyse the soil in which the word of God falls, and predict whether it has a high or low chance of taking.

nature; and this comprises natural religion. 'Such a religion is part of the whole scheme of life which each man inherits.' It goes with the society into which he is born, and the locality in which he lives. Nock then contrasts this type of religion with the prophetic religions: whereas natural religion seeks to satisfy a number of basic human needs, a prophetic religion has to create in man the deeper needs it claims to fulfil. It demands man's complete allegiance; and, in return, it offers him salvation. Whereas natural religion requires of man only certain actions, a prophetic religion requires faith.[44]

Bearing this distinction in mind, let us briefly consider the position of the Touraine in the wider context of the religious situation of the late empire. The Roman empire had linked distant places through its roads and trade, through its government and army; and it seems likely that we should connect this tremendous widening of men's horizons with the changes in religious life that occurred in the second and third centuries AD.[45] Many people in the great Mediterranean cities felt that the old gods no longer sufficed: they could not provide them with a sense of personal belonging in a world that had grown frighteningly large. This was the seedbed for a great number of conversions, both to Christianity and to the oriental mystery religions. However, such changes were little felt in the Touraine, which lay away from the great urban centres of international trade.[46] Here, life carried on much as before, and there was no falling away from the old Celtic deities, whose popularity survived intact all through the Roman period. This indigenous Gallic paganism was primarily a natural religion: its festivals were related to the seasons, its mother-goddesses were fertility goddesses, and sacred springs, trees and rocks long continued to be venerated, despite the church's prohibitions.[47] Thus, in the Touraine, natural religion remained strong and continued to satisfy the needs of its inhabitants. Their basic concerns would have been health and prosperity, which, for a farming community, meant freedom from disease and from famine, fertility of beast and of soil, and good luck with the weather. This was the purpose of religion

[44] A. D. Nock, *Conversion* (Oxford 1933) pp 1–10.

[45] Peter Brown, *The World of Late Antiquity* (paperback ed London 1971) cap 2, esp pp 60 *seq*.

[46] In Tours itself, it was the hostility of pagans which prevented the city from having a permanent bishop till *c*333: Gregory *Hist* 1, 48 and 10, 31, ii.

[47] T. G. E. Powell, *The Celts* (paperback ed London 1963) pp 116–20; C. Jullian, *Histoire de la Gaule*, 8 vols (Paris 1908–20) 6, cap 1, esp pp 53–64; H. Leclercq, art 'Paganisme', § xxix, *DACL* 13, 1, cols 311–29.

as they saw it; and, if God would not oblige, they would turn against him.[48]

How would such people respond to the call to forsake their pagan deities, and instead to accept Christ as Lord? From the peasants' point-of-view, both propositions would appear dubious. To start with, they were unwilling to forsake their ancestral religion for something as new-fangled as Christianity; for, if they neglected the customary rituals, how could they be sure that their crops would flourish, and that the weather would remain temperate?[49] It would be safer to continue with the customary rituals, as their ancestors had done before them. A second set of doubts might assail them in connection with the positive aspect, the call to accept Christianity; for what appeal had Christianity for the likes of them? Certainly, it claimed the power to free men from disease; for Jesus's example had been followed by his disciples, and Tours itself contained the shrine of St Martin, a potent healer in death, as in life. However, as regards the peasants' other, agricultural, concerns, Christianity had little to offer. The distinctively Jewish concept of Yahweh had been forged during the Israelites' wanderings in the desert under Moses, when they were nomads, not agriculturists; and although, once settled in Palestine, the Canaanite fertility religions exerted a pull, the Jewish God remained pre-eminently a God who intervened at specific times in history, not a God of the annually recurrent seasons which made up the farmer's calendar.

Christianity developed out of Judaism; and its most distinctive teaching was that God had, at a particular time and place in history, become man: Jesus had been born in Judaea in the reign of Augustus, and executed in the governorship of Pontius Pilate. The great Christian festivals celebrated by the church of Tours in the fifth century consisted of Christmas, epiphany, easter, ascension and whitsun; the feasts of John the Baptist, Peter and Paul; and those of six local bishops.[50] All these festivals commemorated specific events or people of the past, bound up either with Jesus's life on earth and the sending of the Holy Spirit, or with the exemplary lives (or deaths) of his

[48] Gregory *Hist* 6, 44.

[49] These are the objections which Arnobius and Prudentius sought to answer. See F. J. Dölger, 'Christliche Grundbesitzer und heidnische Landarbeiter', *Antike und Christentum*, 6 vols (Münster im Westfalen 1929–50) 6 pp 297–320, esp 298–300.

[50] Gregory *Hist* 10, 31, 6. It is true that some feast days were fixed on pagan festivals (for example, Christmas on the day of *Sol invictus*); but even here, the accommodation was more to the oriental mystery religions.

followers. There is no mention of special services for fine weather, or for any other of the farmer's specific concerns.[51] What is more, the Christian life of the diocese revolved around the city of Tours: the *vicus* churches were dependent upon the bishop, who would do the rounds of them but once a year;[52] and the estate oratories, which may have been the most numerous type of church in the countryside, were shut for the central feasts of the Christian year, easter, whitsun and Christmas. To a farmer who was accustomed, for instance, to carrying images of the gods round his very own fields in order to ensure the success of his crops,[53] Christianity could all too easily have appeared distant and irrelevant. One might characterise the situation by saying that there was, at best, a certain lack of co-incidence between a pagan peasant's expectations of religion on the one hand, and Christianity on the other.

Given this situation, there seem to me to be theoretically two approaches to the task of converting the countryside. One option would be to continue to preach the gospel as a prophetic religion; to insist that Christianity is essentially about entering into a relationship with God, and that becoming a Christian necessitates making an absolute break with one's pagan past. One would teach that the purpose of Christianity is not to ensure physical health and material prosperity; on the contrary, its acceptance might well involve toil and tribulation in this life, but all this should be gladly borne for the sake of a God who is so concerned with the world he has made that he himself has been born into the world as a man, taken upon himself the burden of man's sins, and thus, through his death and resurrection, reconciled man with God. The alternative to this forthright proclamation of the gospel would be to try and build a bridge between religion as a pagan peasant understood it, and Christianity. Here, the Christian God would be presented as the true source of the health and prosperity for which the peasant had formerly looked to pagan deities. In such

[51] This does not necessarily mean that none whatever were held, even in the countryside; but it does reveal which feasts the bishop regarded as of major importance. The origins of the 'Major Rogations' to protect crops (distinguish from the 'Minor Rogations', to protect people from pestilence) are obscure; but they seem to have been celebrated in Rome under Gregory I (*DACL* 9, 2, col 1551). Note also that the synod of Riez in 439 mentions blessings 'per familias, per agros, per privatas domos' (can 4; *CC* 148, p 68); while later Gallic liturgical books contain at least some readings and prayers suitable for farmers, for example, *The Bobbio Missal,* ed E. A. Lowe, *HBS* 58 (1920) pp 88–90.

[52] Griffe pp 289–90.

[53] Note the revealing mistake made by Martin, *VM* 12, 2.

ways one would try and widen the church's reach to embrace everyone, on the grounds that once they had become members of the church, there would be greater opportunities for educating them gradually in the true nature of Christianity.

Which approach was taken in the conversion of the Touraine? As far as Martin is concerned, we know only that he was accustomed to preach to the peasants with great effect;[54] we do not know the content of his sermons. However, I would guess that it was a prophetic type of Christianity which Martin preached; for, as a monk, Martin bore living witness to the contrast between the ways of secular society, and the life to which Christians are called; and he was not one willingly to compromise the demanding requirements of following Christ.[55] Nonetheless, Martin was far from typical of the Gallo-Roman bishops of his day; and his successor, Brice, conformed more to their pattern of compromise with secular society, than to that of Martin, who stood out against it.[56] I suspect, therefore, that after Martin's death the emphasis in converting the Touraine went more upon trying to accommodate Christianity to the people; and this tendency would have been strengthened by the imperial legislation which prohibited paganism altogether, and sought to compel all within the empire to accept Christianity. Certainly, it is in this direction of accommodation to embrace all within the church that our later sources point: both the Martinian miracle-stories redacted *c*462–4[57] and those recorded by Gregory a century later use miracles to attest the supernatural powers of Christianity in a fairly crude way, impressing upon the people the importance of conformity to Christian teaching.[58] Further, the picture of the Gallic church as a whole which we get from the writings of Gregory of Tours is one of accommodation, where possible, to prevailing religious and social customs. The classic example of this in relation to the Christianisation of the countryside is the story of how the bishop of Mende found the peasants in his diocese making offerings

[54] *VM* 15, 4; compare *D* 2, 4, 4–9.

[55] For example *ibid* 2, 11.

[56] C. E. Stancliffe, *Sulpicius' Saint Martin*, unpubl Oxford D Phil thesis (1978) p 435 and cap 12, esp pp 348–50. On Brice compare *D* 3, 15, 2 and 1, 21, 3–5.

[57] Bishop Perpetuus commissioned Paulinus of Périgueux to versify Sulpicius's Martinian writings; and to conclude this work he transmitted to Paulinus accounts of miracles wrought recently by Martin's *virtus*. These form the sixth book of Paulinus's poem, *de vita Martini*, composed *c*462–4. It is edited by M. Petschenig, *CSEL* 16 (1888).

[58] Paulinus concludes, 'Haec . . . signavi indoctus populo relegenda fideli' (*ibid* 6, lines 500–1); and he tells stories with an obvious moralising intent: for example 6 lines 67–8; 6 lines 165–214. For Gregory, see below.

to a lake. He preached against this practice; but with no effect, until he hit upon the idea of building a church containing relics of St Hilary next to the lake, and getting the peasants to transfer their offerings from the lake to St Hilary. This worked.[59]

This story illustrates what I suspect was a fairly common phenomenon: that is, the role assigned by churchmen to saints and their relics in the process of trying to adapt Christianity to the understanding of the people.[60] Relics were a *locus* of the holy that could be seen and touched, while at the same time they performed miracles which were held up to the public as visible authentication of the church's preaching. This appeal to the *virtus* of saints as manifested in miracles began in the post-Constantinian period, and continued in the following centuries. It is in this context that I suggest we take a closer look at Gregory of Tours.

From Gregory s own writings, it is clear that he was very much concerned to build up the church; and that he saw himself fulfilling this aim not in travelling around the diocese dedicating new churches, but, rather, in recording miracles wrought by the saints.[61] We may note with interest that when Gregory encountered a Jew or an Arian, he would seize the opportunity to try and argue him into accepting catholic Christianity;[62] for this reveals Gregory's genuine concern to make converts, and also his ability to engage in theological discussion to this end. Nonetheless, Gregory chose to write not theological treatises, but book upon book of miracle-stories; and I suspect that his motives were much the same as those which prompted him to write in the way that people talked: it was in order to get through to ordinary people.[63] For him, a saint like Martin who continued to work miracles was a *praedicator*, a proclaimer of the gospel.[64] Miracles *were* preaching.

Thus, when we read Gregory's miracle-stories, we see him at work in trying to teach people, trying to wean them away from their pagan practices, and turn them to Christianity. So we read how a man out hunting was struck senseless by fear, and all the soothsayers' remedies

[59] Gregory, *In gloria confessorum*, cap 2; ed Krusch, *MGH SRM* 1, 1 pp 299–300.
[60] Of course, this was not the only way the church sought to reach people; but it is all I have the space to consider here. Compare Riché *Education* pp 536–47.
[61] *In gloria martyrum*, pref; *Vita patrum*, pref; both ed by Krusch, *MGH SRM* 1, 2 pp 37, 212.
[62] *Hist* 6, 5; 6, 40.
[63] Compare *de virt*[*utibus beati*] *Mart*[*ini episcopi*] pref, ed Krusch, *MGH SRM* 1, 2 p 136.
[64] *Ibid* 2, 40.

were of no avail; but a sojourn at St Martin's basilica healed him. Another man was cured after spending a year at the church, and Gregory drew the conclusion: a little dust from Martin's basilica was worth far more than the potions of soothsayers.[65] In this way, Gregory is showing how Christianity can fulfil the requirements for which people had formerly looked to paganism.

By far the greatest number of Gregory's miracle-stories are those where the saints bring healing to a sufferer. These would be equally applicable to men from the city of Tours or to those from the surrounding countryside. However, we can pick out a few examples where the saints help peasant farmers with their own particular problems: they will halt cattle disease, or help catch a swarm of bees.[66] However, perhaps the best example of all lies in their aid with the weather. This poses one of the perennial problems for the farmer, and in central Gaul hail storms appear as the worst menace of all. Paganism had had its own remedies: a law of 321 explicitly allowed *suffragia* in order to protect the grape-harvest from hail storms.[67] However, from an early date, saints took over this task from the pagan deities. So, in his lifetime, Martin was able to afford protection to one region near Sens, which had formerly been gravely affected by hail storms.[68] In this particular instance, the protection lapsed with the saint's death; but by Gregory of Tours' day, an alternative had been found: wax candles from the saint's tomb proved just as efficacious.[69]

Perhaps the most telling weather story of all comes not from the Touraine, but from Brioude, where St Julian lay buried.[70] Near the martyr's tomb there was a great pagan shrine, with statues of Mars and Mercury on the top of a high column. At a pagan festival there, a fight broke out between two lads. The one who was getting the worst of it took refuge in the little cell which had been built over the martyr's tomb, and the other lad got badly hurt in trying to force him out. His parents solicited St Julian's forgiveness with gifts; and a priest, who happened to be passing, assured them that their son would be healed, if only they would renounce their paganism. However, when another pagan festival came four days later, the whole populace again went

65 *Ibid* 1, 26 & 27.

66 *Ibid* 3, 18; 4, 15.

67 *Theodosian Code* 9, 16, 3; ed T. Mommsen and P. M. Meyer, *Theodosiani libri xvi*, 2 vols (Berlin 1905) 1.

68 Sulpicius *D* 3, 7.

69 Gregory *de virt Mart* 1, 34.

70 Gregory *de virt Jul* caps 5, 6.

off to their idols. When he saw this, the priest prostrated himself on the martyr's tomb, and prayed that divine power would put an end to this idolatry. At this, a great thunderstorm broke, lightning flashed, and rain, mixed with fire and hail, poured down upon them. In terror, the people rushed to the martyr's cell and begged for God's mercy: if the hail storm would go away, they promised they would abandon their heathen idols. In their place they would accept St Julian as their patron, and his God as their God. The storm receded; the boy and his parents believed, and he was healed; and the whole village was baptised, and remained Christian from then onwards.

It was in ways such as these that the church tried to fit Christianity to the sort of religious demands which peasants would make on it: notably, it stressed the efficacy of Christian saints and their relics to achieve those results for which peasants had formerly looked to their pagan gods. Yet, one cannot but wonder how successful a compromise this was, either from the point-of-view of the peasant, or of Christianity. The major local saint was, of course, St Martin, who was buried at Tours. But Tours itself would have been a long way away for most country-dwellers, whereas paganism offered them holy springs, holy trees, and holy stones, in their own localities. In other words, even the cult of the saints was focused in cities, and in a few other shrines at lesser places, such as Brioude. It was not spread out all through the countryside, where the peasants and their problems were.

When reading through the miracles wrought by St Martin at Tours, one cannot but be struck by the preponderance of healing miracles, and the paucity of those which relate to the specific needs of farmers. There are two possible reasons for this:—one is, that farmers carried off home with them *brandea* or other holy relics, but that Gregory was not well informed about the miracles they wrought. The second is that peasants continued to look to their pagan traditions for help with that side of life, at the same time as they were attending church on Sundays. I suspect that this remained a common practice in the countryside throughout our period.

As for the question of how successful the conversion of the countryside had been from the point-of-view of the church: I suspect that here also, the results were far from ideal. The point is, that if one seeks to embrace everyone within the church, and does not demand too great a reorientation of life and attitudes of those who come seeking baptism, then one must attempt to teach them gradually the true meaning of the religious commitment they have taken upon themselves; otherwise, there is little point in pretending that they are Christians.

It was here that the Merovingian church failed so dismally. One searches through the sixth-century synods in vain for demands that priests should teach the people about Christianity. Instead, the major preoccupations seem to be with church property, and with the rights of bishops. There is surprisingly little interest shown in the Christianisation of the countryside, and the few rulings that are made consist mostly of prohibitions: for instance, against agricultural work on a Sunday. It is here that we see the limitations of the fifth and sixth century attempts to convert the countryside; and it throws the attitudes and achievements of the Carolingian period into strong relief.

University of Newcastle upon Tyne

EARLY MEROVINGIAN DEVOTION IN TOWN AND COUNTRY

by I. N. WOOD

ALTHOUGH Merovingian cities were not prepossessing they were important. Physically they straggled outside the Roman walls of the third century and divided increasingly into suburbs dependant on the great basilicas.[1] Dijon, technically a *castrum*, was thought to be worthy of higher status, but its aspect was one of walls, fields, streams and mills.[2] To be fair, urban centres throughout the middle ages possessed equally bucolic attributes.[3] More important, the *civitates* were secular and ecclesiastical centres. The greatest of them could boast strong associations with the royal court,[4] but even those with no such cachet were distinguished by the presence of a bishop. This last figure has attained considerable eminence in the eyes of historians and perhaps his authority has been exaggerated,[5] nevertheless if his position was weaker than we have been taught, it was because of the strength and vigour of urban society; the reputation of the cities is not diminished. Not surprisingly they provided the backcloth for many of the dramas of sanctity and martyrdom recorded by the hagiographers.[6]

Outside the *civitas* capitals lay the rural lands of the diocese; the two were inseparable both for the government and for the church. The social, economic and ecclesiastical bonds of the cities and their

[1] J. Lestocquoy, 'De l'unité à la pluralité; le paysage urbain en Gaule du Ve au IXe siècle,' *Annales* 8 (1953) pp 159–72.

[2] Gregory [of Tours], [*Decem Libri*] *Hist* [*oriarum*], ed [B.] Krusch and [W.] Levison *MGH SRM* 11 (1951) bk 3 cap 19.

[3] For example London, *London Assize of Nuisance 1301–1431*, ed H. M. Chew and W. Kellaway, *London Record Society* 10 (1973) for example pp 177–8. I owe this comparison to Dr W. R. Childs.

[4] [E.] Ewig, 'Residence et capitale pendant le haut moyen âge', *RH* 230 (1963) pp 25–72; [C. R.] Brühl, 'Remarques sur les notions de "capitale" et de "résidence" pendant le haut Moyen Age', *Journal des Savants* (Paris 1967) pp 193–215; Brühl, *Palatium und Civitas* (Cologne 1975).

[5] F. Prinz, 'Die bischöfliche Stadtherrschaft im Frankenreich' *HZ* 217 (1973) pp 1–35 and the criticisms by [P. R. L.] Brown, 'Relics [and Social Status in the Age of Gregory of Tours]', *Stenton Lecture* 1976 (Reading 1977) pp 19–20.

[6] Especially *Passiones Leudegarii* and *Passio Praeiecti*, ed Krusch and Levison, *MGH SRM* 5 (1910) pp 282–356, 225–48.

territories have been studied in surveys of individual districts.[7] This relationship of town and country is equally well illustrated by a consideration of some aspects of religious devotion. It is possible to examine the point by looking first at Sunday observance and at the popularity of the major liturgical festivals, and second at the supervision of relics and the relationship between a city and its saints. From these the dominant position of the cathedral city in the piety of the diocese can be emphasised. Before concluding it will be necessary to examine two exceptional cases where the *civitas* capital seems not to have been the major cult centre.

Information on the observance of holy days is to be found primarily in the *Miracula* of Gregory of Tours.[8] Some twenty anecdotes record the dire effect of working on Sundays or other festivals of the church. The geographical background of these tales is not significant in this context, because although the stories relate to Angers, Bourges, Brioude, Châlons-sur-Marne, Dijon, Evaux, Le Mans, Langeais, Mayenne, Orleans, Poitou and the Touraine, their distribution reflects Gregory's sources and not any local hagiographic peculiarity. The chronology of these anecdotes, on the other hand, may have greater significance, as we shall see.

The evidence in question consists of a series of miraculous cures for injuries sustained during work on holy days. Thus ploughing, hedging, baking, key-making, indeed any sort of work, as well as drinking during matins (*mos gentium*), combing one's hair and sexual intercourse on Sunday, led to the withering of a hand, lameness, blindness and the begetting of deformed children.[9] Individual holy days which are specified include easter, when mending fences and baking excited divine wrath;[10] Good Friday, when Vitalina temporarily excluded herself from heaven by washing her face;[11] St John's day, when the hand of a lady who was hoeing was burnt by divine fire,[12] St

[7] Ewig, *Trier im Merowingerreich* (Trier 1954); R. Kaiser, *Untersuchungen zur Geschichte der Civitas und Diözese Soissons in Römischer und Merowingischer Zeit* (Bonn 1973); M. Roblin, *Le Terroir de Paris* (2 ed Paris 1971).

[8] *MGH SRM* 1 (2), ed W. Arndt and Krusch (1885); [Gregory of Tours] *L*[*iber in*] G[*loria*] *M*[*artyrum*]; *L*[*iber de Passione et*] *V*[*irtutibus sancti*] *J*[*uliani Martyris*]; *L*[*ibri de*] *V*[*irtutibus sancti*] *M*[*artini episcopi*]; *L*[*iber*] *V*[*itae*] *P*[*atrum*]; *L*[*iber in*] G[*loria*] *C*[*onfessorum*].

[9] Gregory *LGM* 15; *LVJ* 11; *LVM* bk 2 cap 24; *LVM* bk 3 caps 7, 29, 31, 38, 45, 55; *LVM* bk 4 cap 45; *LVP* bk 7 cap 5. Also the slightly different case of Sisulfus, *LVM* bk 2 cap 40.

[10] *LVM* bk 2 cap 13; *LVM* bk 3 caps 3, 56; *LVP* bk 15 cap 3.

[11] *LGC* 5.

[12] *LVM* bk 2 cap 57.

Marianus's day when a man burnt down his house while drying corn, and St Avitus's day, when another twisted his neck while digging his vineyard.[13]

The denouement of these stories comes not with the deformity but with the maimed sinner seeking a cure at the shrine of Avitus of Orleans, John the Baptist, Julian of Brioude, Gregory of Langres or, especially, Martin of Tours. One injury was healed by the living hermit Senoch. In several cases the cure was accompanied by a public admission of guilt and a vow not to break the sanctity of a holy day again.[14] The open acknowledgement of sin may reflect on the social structures of the groups in which these miracles took place, for on one occasion Gregory does stress the fact that secret deeds were being made public and it is possible that the villagers who did observe the taboos on Sunday work felt that those who broke them were acting in an underhand manner and this feeling might well have been stronger for those saint's days only observed by local consensus. But whilst village jealousies might have been engendered by working on holy days, it is less likely that anything more than a delight in scandal would have been excited by confessions of sexual intercourse on a Sunday. For this reason it is fair to assume that the stories reflect the professional concerns of Gregory himself even more than they reflect the thought-world of the villages.

This assumption is made more plausible by closer consideration of the last mentioned incident. The woman of Bourges admitted to Sunday intercourse because her child was deformed. But since it is highly unlikely that she could remember the night of conception, there is a strong probability that she admitted to Sunday intercourse in order to explain the deformity.[15] Moreover the clergy would have been delighted to support her in this deduction, for it provided a marvellous instance of the effect of breaking the canons. That Gregory was mindful of church law when he recorded these anecdotes is clear from his attack on work *quam in die illo fieri patrum inhibebat auctoritas.*[16]

The canons of the Gallic councils do condemn work on Sundays. The councils of Agde (506), Orleans (538), Mâcon (585) and Chalon (647–53) all uphold the sacrosanct nature of the *dies dominica*, as does

[13] *LGC* 80, 97.

[14] *LGM* 15; *LVM* bk 2 caps 24, 40, 57; *LVM* bk 3 caps 7, 29, 55.

[15] *LVM* 2, 24. L. Theis, 'Saints sans famille?', *RH* 255 (1976) p 15. Compare the English tradition that redheads are conceived on Sundays.

[16] Gregory *LVM* bk 3 cap 55.

the diocesan synod of Auxerre (561–605).[17] Of these, the most interesting in the present discussion is the council of Mâcon, for it is contemporary with the writings of Gregory of Tours. This point, however, requires careful handling, since although he was aware of the council, neither Gregory nor the bishops of most of the sees for which he recorded a Sunday miracle attended.[18] Further some of the miracles definitely antedate the year 585, thus making it certain that Gregory's attention was not directed by conciliar legislation. Despite this, the correlation between the Sunday miracles and the council of Mâcon is too striking to ignore, for a great proportion of the incidents are recorded in the third book of the *De Virtutibus Sancti Martini*, which was being compiled between 582 and 587.[19] Thus the council of Mâcon and the miracles recorded by Gregory both belong to a period of considerable concern over Sunday observance on the part of churchmen.

This concern can be seen in other ways, but nowhere else so strongly. It appears in the account of the resurrection in the *Decem Libri Historiarum* where Gregory stressed that Christ rose again on a Sunday, in opposition to those who regarded easter day as the sabbath.[20] The distinction between the sabbath and the *dies dominica* was also emphasised in the church canons concerned with fasting.[21] There was, however, an additional catch in that the sabbath ended at sunset.[22] One facet of this legislation is its deliberate anti-semitism.[23]

The evidence for Sunday observance can be interpreted in the following way; although the majority of the population revered the holy day, there were dissidents. The church authorities in the 580s were concerned to stamp out such lukewarm piety and to this end they legislated in the canons; they also took note of any occurrence which might illustrate the divine punishment meted out to those who disobeyed church law, for the examples recorded provided first-rate

[17] *Concilia Galliae*, *CC* 148, ed C. Munier, and *CC* 148A, ed C. de Clercq (1963); Agde (596) 47, Orleans (538) 31, Mâcon (585) 1, Chalon-sur-Saône (647–53) 18, Auxerre (561–605) 16.

[18] Gregory, *Hist* bk 8 caps 12, 20 and less certainly bk 8 cap 7.

[19] For this dating G. Monod 'Études Critiques sur les sources de l'histoire mérovingienne', 1, *BEHE* 8 (1872) pp 41–5 and more precisely J. Schlick, 'Composition et chronologie des *De virtutibus sancti Martini* de Grégoire de Tours', *TU* (1966) = *Studia Patristica* 7, pp 278–86, esp p 286. I owe this referenceto Dr R. Van Dam.

[20] Gregory, *Hist* bk 1 cap 23.

[21] *S*[*tatuta*] *E*[*cclesiae*] *A*[*ntiqua*] 77 (*CC* 148), Agde (506) 12, Orleans (541) 2, Mâcon (581–3) 9.

[22] *LVM* bk 3 cap 31.

[23] Gregory, *Hist* bk 6 cap 17.

admonitory material. But a further point can be made; many of the anecdotes in Gregory's *Miracula* relate specifically or by implication to the villages and the countryside; scarcely any of the contexts are urban. From a rural point of view, on the other hand, the canons could be destructive; a man had to make sure that his fences were effective, even on a Sunday; this was not just a matter of common sense, it was a point of secular law.[24] Thus at one level the promotion of the *dies dominica* in sixth-century Gaul was a reflection of urban and perhaps upper-class interests, so that a peasant farmer might have objected with some justice that the sabbath was made for man, not man for the sabbath.[25]

But for the most part the evidence for religious observance does not suggest general antipathy. Certainly there is little to reveal popular attitudes towards Sunday[26]; the festivals of the saints, however, are well documented, especially at the great shrines of St Martin and St Julian.[27] The celebration of any saint's day was a complex affair, though from the bishop's point of view it probably revolved around the liturgy.[28] That the church offices were highly charged affairs can be seen from the activity of the possessed, who were then at their most vociferous.[29] But what made their prophesies so significant on these occasions was the crowd of the faithful. Naturally the local populace attended and in some cases they were provided with free wine, which must have added to the spirit of the gathering.[30] Members of the local aristocracy of the region would also have been present; the family of Gregory of Tours regularly attended the festival of St Julian.[31] In addition there were the pilgrims, especially if the saint was of more than local repute,[32] and also those who had travelled in

[24] *Pactus Legis Salicae* 9, ed [K. A.] Eckhardt *MGH LNG* 4 (1) (1962); *Lex Salica* 10, ed Eckhardt *MGH LNG* 4 (2) (1969).

[25] Mark 2, 27.

[26] The story of the two boys and the witches of Voultegon (*LVM* 2, 45) suggests regular attendance from childhood onwards.

[27] Festivals of saints Julian and Martin can be deduced for the following; *LVJ* 10, 16, 18, 20, 23–5, 28, 34. *LVM* bk 2 caps 12, 14, 15, 29, 31, 34, 35, 44, 46, 47, 49, 50, 54–6; *LVM* bk 3 caps 4, 5, 14, 19, 24, 39, 41, 48–50, 57, 58; *LVM* bk 4 caps 4–6, 13, 17–19, 22, 23, 27, 38, 41, 45. Doubtless there are other cases and often when there is no such indication the occasion was probably a festival.

[28] The laity might have a different view, Sidonius Apollinaris, *Epistulae* 5, 17.

[29] Brown, 'Relics' p 13.

[30] *LVP* bk 3 cap 1.

[31] *LVJ* 16, 23–5, 34. Does *LVJ* 46a suggest that Gregory's family had a house there?

[32] The journeys of Aridius of Limoges to Brioude and Tours provide an illustration. Gregory *LVJ* 28, 41; *LVM* bk 2 cap 30; *LVM* bk 3 cap 24; *LVM* bk 4 cap 6.

search of a cure from the neighbouring countryside or beyond; some maimed as a result of Sunday work fell into this category.[33]

These holy days also had an importance outside the purely religious sphere. They were occasions for exchanging greetings directly or by letter and thus for strengthening the bonds of friendship between bishops and aristocrats.[34] At an even higher level they were days when it was advantageous to entertain the king, for royal generosity and magnanimity was occasionally vouchsafed in such circumstances.[35] There is also a rare hint of economic activity which might be taken as an indication of a small fair.[36] All in all the major festivals attracted considerable attention and turned the towns into genuine centres of social activity, if only for a day.

Saint's days were genuinely happy occasions, but the calendar of most major churches also included liturgies of penance, most notably the rogation ceremonies. How popular these were is a moot point. Mamertus of Vienne, the founder of the *Litaniae Minores* canvassed senatorial support for his processions and planned as attractive a penitential route as possible.[37] He was regarded by contemporaries as astonishingly successful[38] and thirty years later many still attended the ceremonies in Vienne.[39] Sidonius Apollinaris, Mamertus's exact contemporary, on the other hand, seems to have had difficulty in popularising rogation. He too desired senatorial support and even encouraged one aristocrat, who had retired to the country, to return for the processions.[40] Nevertheless the penitential tradition survived in Clermont and was thought efficacious enough to produce an additional rogation pilgrimage during a plague scare.[41]

In general, therefore, church observance seems to have been respectable, although in the south Caesarius of Arles was not impressed by the lackadaisical approach of his congregation.[42] The

[33] *LVJ* 11; *LVM* bk 2 caps 24, 40; *LVM* bk 3 caps 3, 7, 31, 38, 45; *LGM* bk 4 cap 45.

[34] Avitus of Vienne, ed R. Peiper *MGH AA* 6 (2) (1883) *epp* 32, 59, 60, 61, 62, 79–85.

[35] *Lex Burgundionum* 52 (4), ed L. R. de Salis *MGH LNG* 2, 1 (1892).

[36] *LGM* 36. [37] Avitus Homily 6.

[38] Sidonius Apollinaris *ep* 7, 1.

[39] Avitus Homily 7, *Ecce hodie ad ecclesiam conveniunt multi.*

[40] Sidonius *ep* 7, 1 (2) for a comparison of Clermont and Vienne; *ep* 5, 14 for his request to Aper.

[41] For the *Litaniae minores* at Clermont in the sixth century *LVP* bk 4 cap 4; for Gallus's lenten rogations, *LVP* bk 5 cap 6; *Hist* bk 4 cap 5. For *Litaniae minores* in Paris *Hist* 9, 6, compare Orleans (511) 27; Lyons (567–70) 6; for occasional rogations bk 9 cap 21 (ordered by Guntram), bk 10 cap 30.

[42] Caesarius Sermons 55, 74, ed D. G. Morin, *CC* 103 (1953), compare Gregory asleep in a service *LGM* 86.

high-points of the church year were undoubtedly the major festivals, which were primarily urban occasions. Indeed certain church councils went some way to make this inevitable, for they legislated on the devotional practices of those people whose lives were most likely to revolve round an oratory; the priest who officiated and the aristocrat. The bishops present at Agde in 506 forbade mass in private chapels at easter, Christmas, epiphany, ascension, pentecost and on the feast of St John the Baptist. On these days worship should take place in the city (*civitas*) or parish.[43] At Clermont in 535 it was decreed that priests and deacons who officiated only in oratories should attend their bishop at easter, Christmas and pentecost.[44] As for the aristocrats themselves, at Orleans in 511 they were forbidden to celebrate easter, Christmas and pentecost in their *villae*, whilst the council of Epaon in 517 forced the leading citizens to seek episcopal blessing on Christmas and easter and one is left to understand that the bishop would usually have attended his cathedral church on the great feasts of the year.[45] Other canons of this type were enacted during the sixth century.[46] But the concern that major festivals should be celebrated in the *civitates* was not new; Ausonius had grumbled about leaving his estate for easter long before.[47]

One result of this legislation must have been to emphasise the liturgical importance of the cities. Other evidence suggests a similar pattern. For instance, granted the infrequency of baptistries, the insistence on easter baptism at Mâcon in 585 is likely to have drawn some to celebrate the chief festival of the church year at the diocesan capital.[48] Similarly the command that priests should seek the chrism from their bishops during lent must have brought many of the clergy to the episcopal church.[49] More rarely, church councils, especially the diocesan ones which were supposed to take place annually, would have

[43] Agde (506) 21.

[44] Clermont (535) 15.

[45] Orleans (511) 25; Epaon (517) 35; Orleans (511) 31 merely tells us that a bishop had to attend the nearest church on Sunday. Avitus *epp* 27, 63, 78 shows bishops attending festivals outside their own *civitates* on major festivals. It is not clear from Epaon 35 whether the citizens or the bishops are referred to in *nec interest in quibus civitatibus positos*. For a later example of this tradition compare *The Chartulary of the High Church of Chichester*, ed W. D. Peckham, *Sussex Record Society*, 46 (Lewes 1942–3) p 20. I owe this reference to Mr J. W. Cox.

[46] Orleans (541) 3.

[47] Ausonius Epistulae 4 6 See R. Van Dam *Heretics, Bishops and Bandits*, unpublished Cambridge PhD thesis (1977) pp 20–1.

[48] Mâcon (585) 3; Auxerre (561–605) 18.

[49] *SEA* 87; Auxerre (561–605) 6.

had the same effect.[50] Thus church attendance, which we have seen to be respectable, would have emphasised the importance of the city in devotional matters.

Before turning to the importance of relics and their cults it is worth emphasising the fact that not every holy man was respected and that not every saint cult prospered. Sometimes this was because of the rivalry of cults, although at Lyons both Nicetius and Priscus were revered in time.[51] Elsewhere saints were forgotten because no *Passio* existed, even if others were remembered despite the lack of any martyr acts.[52] By contrast Liminius of Clermont was not the focus of a cult, despite the existence of such a document.[53] The reasons for this variety cannot be traced here, for they lie in local circumstances. In addition the early middle ages had a dose of irreverence; the locals laughed at the living Friardus. Similarly a native of Evaux scoffed at St Marianus who was found dead, probably after falling out of a tree.[54] As for St Eutropius of Saintes, he appeared in a vision to explain that the scar on his head was the result of his martyrdom, thus stifling any wild rumours.[55] In addition there were the professional sceptics, the lawless shrine robbers and the political sanctuary breakers. But despite this negative picture, belief in saints was certainly not mere credulity.[56]

It has recently been shown that relics were central to the social structures of Merovingian Gaul, notably in the faction fighting which affected towns and their bishops.[57] Associated with this issue is the slightly surprising fact that major relics were not easy to obtain.

[50] *SEA* 9; Agde (506) 49; Orleans (533) 2; Orleans (538) 1; Orleans (549) 18. Most sixth-century councils took place in diocesan centres; Epaon is an exception.

[51] Brown, 'Relics' pp 18–19.

[52] No cult and no *vita;* Gregory *LVP* bk 2; *LGC* 29. Cult, no *vita; LGM* 52. *Vita* discovered after cult starts; *LGM* 50.

[53] *LGC* 35. By contrast, cults starting after *Passio* discovered, *LGM* 63, after inscription read *LGC* 103. Gregory also mentions documents or lack of them *LGM* 39, 43, 56, 57, 73, 85, 103, 104; *LVM* bk 2 cap 49, *LVM* bk 3 cap 42, *LVP* bk 8; *LGC* 76, 93, 94. See also [M.] Vieillard-Troiekouroff, [*Les Monuments Religieux de la Gaule d'après les oeuvres de Gregoire de Tours*] (Paris 1976) p 17 n 58.

[54] *LGC* 80; *LVP* bk 10 cap 1; Brown 'Relics' p 10.

[55] *LGM* 55.

[56] Brown, 'Relics' pp 3, 8, 15. Evidence of robbers in Gregory's *Miracula; LGM* 43, 58, 65, 71, 89, 91, 96; *LVJ* 7, 8, 20, 44; *LVM* bk 1 cap 2; *LGC* 61; of men acting irreverently against a church and its possessions; *LGM* 60, 78, 84; *LVJ* 14, 15, 17, 31; *LVM* bk 1 cap 29; *LVP* bk 8 cap 11; bk 14 cap 2; bk 18 cap 2; *LGC* 3, 62, 64, 78, 81; irreverence towards clergy or saints; *LVP* bk 6 cap 4; bk 8 cap 5; bk 19 cap 1; *LGC* 6, 12, 26, 79; compare *Hist* bk 2 caps 23, 37; perjurers *LGM* 19, 52, 102; *LVM* bk 1 cap 31; *LVP* bk 8 cap 9; *LGC* 67, 70, 91, 92; sanctuary breakers; *LGM* 104; *LVJ* 10, 13, *LVM* bk 1 cap 23; *LVM* bk 2 caps 27, 58.

[57] Brown, 'Relics' passim.

Anyone could gather up the dust or scrape the candle grease off a tomb and these provided phylacteries and medicines for the pious who sought them; but a genuine cult object was something different. Unfortunately the most plentiful evidence on relics concerns their diffusion; there is much less material relating to the way in which a relic was obtained and kept, but these are the topics which are of concern here.

Gregory of Tours occasionally comments on the merit of men who obtained relics. Thus a lady of Maurienne who prayed for two years and seven days at Bazas was rewarded with a relic of St John the Baptist, as she deserved. An archdeacon of Turin, who tried to remove her acquisition from Maurienne, died.[58] A similar story is told of a *devotus* who did merit a relic of saints Timothy and Apollinaris from Rheims, distributed by the bishop, and of an *indigna* who gained nothing.[59] Undoubtedly worthiness had much to do with reverence; Mummulus, who hacked off part of the finger-bone of St Sergius, received his just deserts—or at least Gregory was prepared to see this irreverent act as one of the factors in his downfall.[60]

But possession of a relic was not the end of the problem; keeping it reverently was also difficult. Thus one of Gregory's men failed to keep a splinter from the chancel of St Martins' church in an appropriate style; his master, who was then a deacon was divinely appointed as the new guardian of the relic.[61] The rich were better equipped to provide a suitable home for a holy object, while status and influence gave them other advantages. The *matrona* of Trezelle, who seized the corpse of Lupicinus, seems to have been of local importance.[62] When Nunninus, an Auvergnat tribune, was caught cutting a jewel off the shrine of St Germanus at Auxerre by some little boys, he extricated himself by vowing to place the relic in his basilica and to celebrate the saint's feast day regularly.[63] It is difficult to believe that a lesser man would have got off so lightly.

But there were occasions when aristocrats and even churchmen angered the saints. Thus, when Quintianus moved the body of St Amantius of Rodez, he was rewarded with exile;[64] when Alcima and Placidina, the sister and wife of bishop Apollinaris of Clermont, moved that of St Antolianus they unwittingly alienated the other holy men

[58] *LGM* 13. Brown, 'Relics' p 15.

[59] *LGM* 54.

[60] Gregory, *Hist* bk 7 cap 31. Brown, 'Relics' pp 10–12.

[61] *LVM* bk 1 cap 35.

[62] *LVP* bk 13 cap 13.

[63] *LGC* 40. [64] *LVP* bk 4 cap 1.

whose bones they moved; as a result they never completed the church they were building.[65] In both these cases an act displeasing to the saints is being cited retrospectively as a cause of failure. Indeed the interpretation is determined by the assumed consequences. On the other hand when the relics of St Illidius brought to Tours by Gregory went mouldy there was no fearsome divine intervention, indeed the episode was concluded by a miracle, for the holy object was hung over a fire on a piece of string until it dried.[66]

All these stories are of course subjective records; the role of the relic varies according to the situation and also according to the interpretation of Gregory himself. The misfortunes of the family of Apollinaris might have passed unnoticed were it not for the author's dislike of that family. But on the whole the nobility suffered less than did the poor when direct contact with the holy was involved. Thus catastrophe struck the peasant of Brioude who was forced to give up his house because it had housed relics of St Saturninus for one night.[67] A similar story in which a man of Embrun refused to hand over his pear tree which grew by the tomb of saints Nazarius and Celsus ended with a great basilica being built on the site.[68] Thus in the *Miracula* the anecdotes concerning the acquisition and possession of relics are related from the point of view of the church and more precisely of an aristocratic family of bishops. But this bias may well reflect the reality of the situation; relics were more easily obtained by families such as that of Gregory of Tours than by any other group.

The evidence of the canons of the Gallic church on the subject of relics is negligible but one canon of the council of Epaon (517) is relevant. The bishops of Burgundy legislated against the placing of relics in oratories unless a cleric was near at hand to sing psalms regularly.[69] Similar as this is to those canons already cited which concern religious observance in private chapels, its intention must have been to keep holy objects as firmly as possible under the eye of the church. Whether this was achieved cannot be known. To some extent the fact that some individuals carried relics with them must have undermined the power of the church.[70] But it is unlikely that cult

[65] *LGM* 64. Compare Gregory's other comments on these ladies, *Hist* bk 3 caps 2, 12.
[66] *LVP* bk 2 cap 3.
[67] *LGM* 47 but compare *LGM* 89.
[68] *LGM* 46. [69] Epaon (517) 25.
[70] Gregory's family in particular collected relics *LGM* 83 and *LVM* bk 3 cap 17 *licet temerario ordine*. Some when they travelled with relics did place them on an altar overnight; *LGC* 38.

centres could long escape the vigilance of the bishop even if it was possible to keep relics out of his hands, as the monks of Gourdon originally kept the body of St Desideratus from bishop Agricola of Chalon-sur-Saône.[71] Thus although Gregory of Tours does not provide confirmation of the efficacy of the canon of Epaon, he does reveal a world in which the church managed to supervise the handling of holy objects, albeit in a rather more haphazard and personal way than the church fathers would have desired. One aspect of this was the tendency to stress the importance of the parish and particularly the city festivals and cults at the expense of devotion centred on oratories, which for the most part are likely to have been rural. But the cities themselves were *foci* of devotion simply because of the numbers of relics they possessed and the number of festivals they celebrated. To this we may now turn.

First it should be stressed that the major cult churches were not necessarily cathedrals. When Balthildis decided to remove the most important shrines from the hands of the bishops in the seventh century, she was not interfering in the episcopal churches.[72] For the most part cult centres lay outside the old Roman walls in the cemeterial suburbs, where saints could still be discovered far into the Merovingian period; Eligius's credibility as a bishop depended on just such a discovery.[73] Others with rather less at stake visited these cities of the dead, but such activity was the mark of a pious man and is not indicative of the attitudes of the average town-dweller.[74] For the latter the great cults already in existence would have provided adequate opportunities for piety.

Many cities associated themselves with particular patrons, though such associations were still very fluid in this period. Nevertheless Honoratus was seen as protector of Arles immediately after his death, his patronage possibly being recognised sooner than that of Martin or

[71] *LGC* 85. Compare St Patroclus, whom the *archipresbiter* of Néris failed to snatch; *LVP* bk 9 can 3.

[72] *Vita Balthildis* 9 ed Krusch *MGH SRM* 2 (1888) p 493. On this text see Ewig, 'Das Privileg des Bischofs Berthefrid von Amiens für Corbie von 664 und die Klosterpolitik der Königin Balthild', *Francia* 1 (Munich 1973) pp 62–114 esp pp 106 *seq* and Janet L. Nelson 'Queens as Jezebels: the careers of Brunhild and Balthild in Merovingian history', *Medieval Women, SCH subsidia* 1 (1978) pp 34–77.

[73] *Vita Eligii* bk 2 cap 6, ed Krusch *MGH SRM* 4 (1902) p 697. But see Gregory *LGC* 72.

[74] Apart from those seeking cures, *LVJ* 2; *LVP* bk 6 caps 4, 7; *LVP* bk 17 cap 4; *LGC* 4, 5, 58, 61, 72 shows pious men visiting the holy places, to these should be added the pilgrim. But for Theodebert and the holy sites of Trier, *LGC* 91. See Vieillard-Troiekouroff pp 387–9.

Germanus.[75] Another quickly made reputation was that of Remigius at Rheims.[76] In Paris the rise of saints Genevieve and Denis is almost impossible to date,[77] whilst at Chalon-sur-Saône the local cult of St Marcellus seems to have overtaken that of Vincent of Saragossa, perhaps in Guntram's reign.[78] One of the best recorded of these tutelary saints is the less familiar Eutropius of Orange, whose *vita* commissioned by bishop Stephanus of Lyons must reflect what a bishop expected to hear of an older contemporary and it certainly reveals what the townsmen wanted from their patron: protection.[79]

But it would be wrong to place too much emphasis on the outstanding cults of the period; many cities had no single guardian. Lyons was one such yet it was the city with the greatest Christian past in Gaul and could boast martyrs galore, including the apostolic figures Pothinus and possibly Irenaeus. Even at the end of the century, when Gregory of Tours might have argued for the importance of Nicetius, many would have championed his old enemy Priscus. Eusebius Gallicanus, however, announced that St Blandina's relics protected the city.[80] Probably every saint whose cult was observed was expected to intervene in cases of emergency, especially in the days of Visigothic expansion. Nor is Lyons likely to have been exceptional; in a homily fragment

[75] Hilary of Arles Sermon, *De Vita Sancti Honorati*, caps 31, 39, *PL* 50 (1865) cols 1266, 1272. Martin's patronage of Tours becomes most apparent in Paulinus of Perigueux, *De Vita Sancti Martini Episcopi* bk 6 1. 506, ed M. Petschenig, *CSEL* 16 (1888) pp 17–159 and later in *LVM* bk 2 cap 25. It may be significant that Sulpicius Severus wrote much of his work before 406 but he was not writing primarily from the point of view of Tours. Constantius's *Vita Germani*, ed Levison, *MGH SRM* 7 (1920) pp 247–83 was commissioned by Patiens of Lyons and paints Germanus as a patron of the whole of Gaul (cap 46) and therefore it does not illuminate the origins of the saint's patronage of Auxerre.

[76] *LGC* 78.

[77] W. Wattenbach-Levison, *Deutschlands Geschichtquellen im Mittelalter* (1952) p 113 n 254; also *LGC* 89.

[78] For the cult of Vincent of Saragossa, Avitus of Vienne *epp* 76, 79. On Guntram and Chalon-sur-Saône, Fredegar bk 4 cap 1, ed Krusch, *MGH SRM* 2 p 124. One of the *Passiones Marcelli ASB* September 2 (1868) pp 196–200 (4 September) might easily belong to the sixth century, especially when taken together with the *Passio Valeriani ASB* September 5 (1866) pp 26–7 (15 September). There are several other examples of parallel *vitae* originating in the fifth and sixth centuries, relating to the evangelisation of the Rhône-Saône complex during the early persecutions; J. van der Straeten 'Les actes des martyrs d'Aurelien en Bourgogne. Étude littéraire', *An Bol* 79 (1961) pp 115–44. The cult of saints Marcellus and Valerian however, is certainly older; see the Bagnols inscription, *ASB* September 2 p 191; 5 p 21.

[79] *Vita Eutropii, Bulletin du Comité Historique des Monuments Écrits de l'Histoire de France* 1 (Paris 1849) pp 52–64. See J. M. Wallace-Hadrill, *Early Medieval History* (Oxford 1975) p 3.

[80] *Eusebius Gallicanus,* ed J. Leroy and F. Glorie, *CC* 101 (1970) Homily 11 (2).

relating to an unidentifiable town Avitus of Vienne pointed out that the great basilicas of the place acted as sentinels, as indeed they were, both physically, standing outside the walls, and spiritually, because of the power of the saints.[81] For Avitus the heavenly Jerusalem was an apt comparison.[82] And indeed his association of supernatural protection and the walls of the city was almost a common-place at the time.[83]

Dependence on a single patron was not the norm; Vienne itself seems never to have placed overwhelming emphasis on the cult of its own Ferreolus.[84] Promotion of a number of saints was possibly an advantage and certainly feasible, since considerable variety of relics was something that differentiated any town of size from the surrounding countryside. This in its turn made urban centres especial *foci* of devotion. The only rural cult which might have upset this balance both from its importance and from the number of saints involved was that of the Theban legion at Agaune, but this was sterilised within a monastic foundation.[85]

The high points of the church year thus emphasised the importance of the urban shrines and for the most part these were to be found in diocesan capitals. There are, however, two exceptions to this equation of episcopal city and devotional centre which require consideration; Dijon and Brioude. In both cases these are southern centres, whilst the capitals, Langres and Clermont, lay in the north of the *civitas*, but this apart their importance demands separate consideration.

There can be no question that the cult of St Julian was the greatest in the Auvergne. Gregory of Tours pleaded that the cathedral city had numerous relics and there is good evidence to support his contention.[86] But no cult equalled that of the Brioude martyr of whom

[81] Contra the identification by C. Perrat and A. Audin, '*Alcimi Ecdicii Aviti Viennensis Episcopi Homilia dicta in dedicatione superioris basilicae*', *Studi in Onore di A. Calderini e R. Paribeni* (Milan 1957) 2 pp 533–46. Avitus Homilies 24 (p 145), 28–9 (p 150). Compare *LVP* bk 4 cap 2. See Vieillard-Troiekouroff pp 143, 369.

[82] Avitus Homily 24.

[83] *Eusebius Gallicanus* Homily 11; Ennodius *Vita Epifani* 110, ed F. Vogel, *MGH AA* 7 (1885) p 98; *LVP* bk 17 cap 4; *LGC* 78; and by implication *LGM* 59. *Passio Marcelli Altera* 1, *ASB* 2 September p 199.

[84] Mamertus showed interest in the cult, Sidonius Apollinaris *ep* 7 1 (7); Avitus appears not to have done so. Gregory of Tours's interest was based on the fact that Ferreolus was the master of Julian, Gregory's own patron saint; *LVJ* 2.

[85] For the episcopal forces behind Sigismund's foundation at Agaune, *Vita Abbatum Acaunensium* 3, ed Krusch, *MGH SRM* 3 (1896) p 176.

[86] *LGC* 31–6; for a much later list of cults in Clermont, most of which have their origins in this period, *Libellus de ecclesiis Claromontanis*, ed Levison, *MGH SRM* 7 pp 456–67.

Gregory was himself an *alumnus.*[87] The reasons for the high standing of Julian are not hard to seek; first his *Passio* was early and rested on good traditions.[88] Second, although the cult site was outside the Roman *vicus*, this settlement was a place of some importance with a pagan temple, whose cult animals seem to have been transferred to the Christian shrine.[89] Third, Brioude's geographical position worked to its advantage; at the southern end of the Limagne, it was also on the edge of the mountain pastures, where its own flocks of sheep could graze.[90]

The Auvergne is significantly the region about which the historian knows most during this period. For this reason, while it may be unique, it could equally well be a better reflection of the norm than the evidence suggests. In either case two centres dominated the diocese, Clermont and Brioude. These two centres, however, were not rivals for influence and one point in the liturgical year united them both, for the rogation pilgrimage inaugurated by Gallus was a trek from the cathedral city to the basilica of the martyr.[91]

The cult of St Julian refines the relation of town and country as I have described it. It was not a city cult, although the bishop was to be found often at the shrine and he probably led the rogation pilgrimage. The cult also provided the diocese with a patron saint, though outsiders, especially, one may guess, the inhabitants of the neighbouring *civitas Gabalitensium*, attended the festival.[92] Dijon complicates the picture further.

Dijon was a *castrum* though Gregory of Tours could not understand why it was not a *civitas.*[93] Within the town there was an episcopal residence, although this does not prove that Langres had none, nor that the bishops regarded Dijon as the ecclesiastical centre of the diocese.[94] As for the great shrine of St Benignus, this was only a

[87] *LVJ* 2; Venantius Fortunatus *Carm* 5, 3, ed F. Leo, *MGH AA* 4, 1 (1881) pp 106–7.

[88] *MGH SRM* 1, 2 pp 428–31.

[89] For Brioude, G. Fournier, *Le Peuplement Rural en Basse Auvergne durant le Haut Moyen Age* (Clermont-Ferrand 1962) pp 160–9. *LVJ* 31.

[90] *LVJ* 17. The Limagne was a corn producing region; it is possible that St Julian's day, 28 August, fell conveniently close to the harvest.

[91] *LVP* bk 5 cap 6; Gregory, *Hist* bk 4 caps 5, 13.

[92] *LVJ* 30 suggests this.

[93] Gregory, *Hist* bk 3 cap 19. What Gregory means by *civitas* here is unclear; he might have felt that Dijon should become a cathedral or administrative city instead of or in addition to Langres.

[94] *LVP* bk 7 cap 2; that Gregory travelled to Langres for epiphany (*LVP* bk 7 cap 3) might suggest that he still regarded Langres as the liturgical centre of the diocese. The

development of the pontificate of Gregory (*c*506–540).[95] And whilst it later overshadowed the cult of the Tergemini of Langres the latter was probably older and did not lose its popularity in the early medieval period.[96] Thus it is not possible to argue that Dijon had become the ecclesiastical capital by the end of the sixth century. Indeed the very fact that Langres continued to be recognised as the centre of the *civitas* in an age when episcopal seats were moved suggests that its importance continued,[97] whilst the fact that Dijon did not become the centre of a diocese until 1731 may mean that we overestimate the place because we see it through partial eyes.

But what Dijon does reveal is first the importance of the bishop and second the need to harness local devotional practices. It was not Gregory of Langres, but the *rustici* who ensured the survival of the Benignus cult.[98] Its expansion, however, lay in the bishop's hands and ultimately he, like other bishops of Langres, was buried in the Dijon church of St John.[99] These factors of local devotion and episcopal control are also present in much of the other evidence that we have considered.

To conclude, the bishop clearly dominated or wished to dominate the religion of sixth-century Gaul. This domination resulted in part in an emphasis on the city as a focus for devotion. This is not surprising, for the great occasions of a bishop's career were urban. It was in the city that he was elected, provided that simony and the royal court did not intervene. His principal residence would have been near one of the urban churches, probably in the episcopal complex. His major acts of munificence whether religious or secular would usually have had the same context. Finally his burial confirmed the whole pattern of his life and if he was well enough esteemed he might join the protectors of the city.

But the bishop was also the touchstone of orthodoxy and places outside his purview might easily slip into heresy, which does not

---

evidence for the importance of Dijon is overstated by P. Lejay, 'Saint-Benigne de Dijon', *Revue d'Histoire et de littérature religieuses*, 7 (Paris 1902) pp 71–96.

[95] *LGM* 50.

[96] *Historia Abbatum auctore Baeda* cap 23; *Historia Abbatum auctore anonymo* cap 36, ed C. Plummer, *Baedae Opera Historica* (Oxford 1896) pp 386, 402.

[97] The Classic case is Windisch-Avenches-Lausanne. L. Duchesne, *Fastes Épiscopaux de l'Ancienne Gaule*, 3 (Paris 1915) pp 21–2. For a new see, Maurienne, *Vita Tigris* 3, *MGH SRM* 3 pp 533–4. For change in a town's secular status, see the addition of Mâcon to the *Notitia Galliarum*, ed T. Mommsen, *MGH AA* 9 (1892) p 585.

[98] *LGM* 50.

[99] *LVP* bk 7 cap 3.

simply mean doctrinal deviation. To step outside episcopal surveillance was to offer a challenge; at the upper end of the scale it might have appeared as a new Priscillianism, at the lower end it could have meant a reversion to local paganism or the appearance of some self-proclaimed messiah.[100] Heresy or *rusticitas* could emerge all too easily and against these the city was a bastion of true religion.[101]

University of Leeds

[100] Brown, 'Relics' p 9 and n 40.

[101] See the discussion of *rusticitas* in *ibid* pp 8–9, though it should be remembered that Gregory still used the word in its stylistic sense as well; *LVM* bk 1 *Praefatio; De Miraculis B Andreae Apostoli* 38; *Hist* bk 9 cap 6. The importance of cities as centres of orthodoxy would have been emphasised by the urban canon-collections; H. Mordek, *Kirchenrecht und Reform im Frankenreich, Beiträge zur Geschichte und Quellenkunde des Mittelalters* 1 (Berlin 1975) pp 70–9.

THE WORK OF AUDOENUS OF ROUEN AND ELIGIUS OF NOYON IN EXTENDING EPISCOPAL INFLUENCE FROM THE TOWN TO THE COUNTRY IN SEVENTH-CENTURY NEUSTRIA

by PAUL FOURACRE

HELD almost as an article of faith amongst Merovingian historians is a belief in the strength of the bishops' position in the town in early Frankish society.[1] Passages from the life of bishop Desiderius of Cahors are often used to illustrate the busy bishop at work in his town, responsible, it seems, for maintaining the town's defences.[2] The assumption of secular duties by the bishop has been charted by a German scholar—Claude[3]—who shows how in many cases the crown's principal representative in the town—the count—began to reside outside the town, having been deprived of his specifically urban functions by the bishop. The interest shown in the bishops in the town has, however, led to a rather unbalanced picture of the bishop as an urban creature. In contrast, the Merovingian church councils of the sixth and seventh centuries show that the bishops were very much concerned with rural work, and from the legislation which applies to both town and country[4] it could be argued that the distinctions between the two are less clear-cut than a concept such as *bischöfliche Stadtherrschaft* implies.

The biographies of two figures at work in the mid seventh century—saint Audoenus and saint Eligius—illustrate well the problems faced by the church in the country in the later Merovingian period, as both bishops were extremely active in rural work. Luckily, near-

[1] The most recent expression of this view is to be found in [F.] Prinz, 'Die Bischöfliche Stadtherrschaft', *HZ* (1973) pp 1–35, an important article, but marred by Prinz's failure to distinguish between fact and fancy in the life of saint Eligius – bk 1 cap 32 – where it is claimed that the bishop of Tours gained the right to appoint the town's count. For a summary of earlier secondary material on bishops and towns, see E. Ewig, 'Kirche und Civitas in der Merowingerzeit', *SSSpoleto* 7 (1960) 1 pp 47–71.

[2] *Vita Desiderii* caps 16–18, ed [B.] Krusch, *MGH SRM* 4 (1902) pp 574–7.

[3] D. Claude, 'Untersuchungen zum frühfränkischen Comitat,' *ZRG GAbt* 81 (1964) pp 1–79.

[4] For a summary of Merovingian conciliar legislation see [C.] de Clercq, *La legislation religieuse Franque de Clovis à Charlemagne* (Louvain/Paris 1936) cap 6 pp 89–103.

contemporary accounts of their work[5] have survived. Both men were functionaries at the courts of kings Clothar II and Dagobert I. Held in high esteem at the court and members of an élite circle of powerful men dedicated to the support of Columbanian monasticism,[6] they were consecrated bishops on the same day in the year 641—saint Audoenus to the see of Rouen, saint Eligius to that of Noyon-Tournai. The two were also very close friends, which is reflected in the similarity of their aims, and in a common attitude towards the Merovingian dynasty—this being one of close co-operation and support.[7] The general problems Audoenus and Eligius faced in trying to extend their influence as bishops into the countryside can be seen in the canons of the council of Chalon-sur-Saône,[8] the only council at which their attendance is recorded, and held sometime between 649 and 653. The basic principle expressed in this council is of safeguarding the bishops' right of jurisdiction from encroachment by secular officers or individuals and does not differ from that expressed in earlier councils,[9]

[5] The *Vita Audoeni*, ed [W.] Levison, *MGH SRM* 5 (1910) pp 536–67, and the *Vita Eligii*, ed Krusch, *MGH SRM* 4 pp 663–741. The *Vita Audoeni* consists of a base which shows contemporary witness but which was revised in the Carolingian period. [E.] Vacandard, *Vie* [*de Saint Ouen*] (Paris 1902) p xiii emphasizes the *caractère sérieux d'historicité* of the source – a view with which Levison agrees, [W. Wattenbach-W. Levison], [*Deutschlands*] *Geschichtsquellen* [*im Mittelalter*, 1, *Vorzeit und Karolingern*] (Weimar 1952) p 128. Saint Audoenus, in a letter to Chrodbert bishop of either Tours or Paris, *MGH SRM* 4 p 741, says that he himself composed a life of Eligius. This work is unidentifiable in the surviving version of the source, but the *Vita Eligii* is used by the author of the *Vita Landiberti*, ed Krusch, *MGH SRM* 6 (1913) pp 299–384, which, in turn, can be more surely dated to the first quarter of the eighth century. For details of the dating of the *Vita Eligii* and the *Vita Landiberti* see [L.] Van der Essen, *Étude critique* [*et littéraire sur les vitae des Saints Merovingiens de l'ancienne Belgique*] (Louvain/Paris 1907) pp 329–36 and 25–33.

[6] For an account of the growth of Columbanian monasticism and the contribution of its court patrons see Prinz, *Frühes Mönchtum* [*im Frankenreich*] (Munich/Vienna 1965) pp 124–41.

[7] The close personal ties between the two bishops are reflected in their respective *Vitae*: *Vita Audoeni* cap 4 p 556, *Vita Eligii* bk 1 cap 12 p 679. The same sources show their close cooperation with the Merovingian house, but this is shown in a more concise manner in the *Vita Amandi*, ed Krusch, *MGH SRM* 5 pp 428–49, cap 17 p 440, where bishop Amand has refused to baptise king Dagobert's son to punish the king for his licentious behaviour. Eligius and Audoenus are sent by Dagobert to get Amand to change his mind.

[8] The edition of Frankish church councils used here is: *Concilia* [*Galliae 511–695*], ed [C.] de Clercq, *CC, Series Latina* 148 A (1963). See pp 302–10 for the council of Chalon-sur-Saône.

[9] The principle is expressed as early as 541 at the council of Orleans. De Clercq *Concilia* p 137 canon 20: 'Ut nullus saecularium personarum praetermissa pontifice seu praeposito ecclesiae quemquam clericorum pro sua protestate constringere, discutere audeat aut damnare.'

applying equally to town and country. There are provisions from Chalon, however, extending this principle to specifically rural problems. Canon five states that laymen should not interfere with the property and control of rural parishes. Canon eleven complains that the *iudices publices*—surely meaning the counts—have infringed the bishops' rights in touring the *parrochias* and *monasteria* and in trying to impose their authority on the clergy and on the abbots. Canon fourteen says that several bishops have complained that the powerful (*potentes*) were contradicting episcopal orders by not allowing the clergy who served in their private churches on their estates to be subject to the authority of the archdeacon.[10]

None of these canons is entirely original in subject matter, but they do represent fresh and intensified complaints concerning rural abuses. That such abuses themselves had actually increased is less sure. One could argue, as Aigrain has done,[11] that as the parish churches grew in wealth and independence, the office of *archipresbyter* became more attractive to laymen, who could then use the office to control the income of the church. The complaints about this particular evil do indeed grow with the development of the office of *archipresbyter*[12] starting in the early seventh century. On the other hand, the tendency of the powerful to regard the clergy of their private churches as under their control alone goes back a long time, and the canon itself acknowledges that such churches have been *iam longum constructa tempore*. Likewise, complaints about comital abuses go back as far as the council of Orléans held in the year 541.[13] So it is not the abuse and rejection of episcopal authority which has grown to merit such a response from the council of Chalon. Rather, the complaints are symptomatic of attempts to extend that authority into areas previously beyond episcopal influence. How did saint Audoenus and saint Eligius tackle these problems in their own diocesan areas?

Firstly, it must be stated that the two areas did not face exactly similar problems.[14] The see of Noyon-Tournai contained a far greater

[10] De Clercq, *Concilia* pp 304, 305, 306. [11] In FM 5 (1938) p 554.

[12] The fullest account of the development of the office of *archipresbyter* remains that by Imbart de la Tour, 'Les Paroisses Rurales dans l'Ancienne France', *RH* (May/August 1896) pp 24–9.

[13] For the council of Orléans, see note 9. The clergy of the private churches are first mentioned in 517, when it is stated that holy relics should not be placed in such churches unless there were parish clergy near enough to make sure that the correct liturgical duties were carried out. De Clercq *Concilia* p 30.

[14] Vacandard, *Vie* cap 6 pp 119–54, and Van der Essen, *Étude Critique* pp 327–9 describe the diocesan areas of Rouen and Noyon-Tournai respectively.

pagan element than that of Rouen, and so much of saint Eligius's work was missionary in nature. Noyon-Tournai can, though, almost be divided into two areas along an east-west axis. To the north of a rough line from present day Lille to the North Sea coast at a point approximately on the modern French-Belgian border lived groups of pagan Sueves, Frisians and other unnamed *barbari*.[15] To the south of this line the conditions were very similar to those in the area of Rouen. In the countryside in these areas the centres of religion were to be found in the larger rural communities, the *vici*, sometimes called *vici publici* served by a network of priests, led by the *archipresbyter* and with their own churches. The aristocracy, as mentioned earlier, worshipped in private churches—*oraturia*—on their estates *villae*.[16] Lastly, there were the monasteries, increasing in number throughout the period, often supported by the aristocracy but in co-operation with the episcopacy.[17]

The biographies of Eligius and Audoenus show that their first moves after consecration were to make their influence felt in the capitals of their sees. Both Eligius and Audoenus were extremely powerful men in the political sphere (for which, in fact, they are chiefly remembered), and being royal appointees to important sees,[18] it is interesting to note that they too had to build up their local prestige before tackling other problems. The *Vita Audoeni* says that saint Audoenus endowed his cathedral church with more lands, riches and treasures than any of his predecessors had done. He also paid special attention to the clergy of Rouen, encouraging them in discipline, and being a *largus procurator* for their more material needs. For the rest of the town he built hospitals—*exenodochia*—and poor houses—*matriculas*—generously endowing them.[19] The *Vita Eligii* has less to say of Eligius's work in Noyon, but it is significant that soon after his accession to the see he founded and endowed a convent in the town.[20]

In their work outside Noyon and Rouen a general pattern can be seen. Episcopal influence could be extended in two ways. Firstly, by

[15] *Vita Eligii* bk 2 cap 3 p 696.

[16] See note 13.

[17] Prinz, *Frühes Mönchtum*, pp 124–41.

[18] This is clearly stated in the *Vita Audoeni* cap 7 p 558: 'ad honus pontificalem iusso regalis insedisset.' Both Eligius and Audoenus were made bishops whilst still laymen. They therefore spent a year in learning the trade, as it were, before taking up their appointments.

[19] *Vita Audoeni* bk 2 cap 24 p 557.

[20] *Vita Eligii* bk 2 cap 5 p 697.

frequent visits to rural communities, and secondly by the establishment of cult centres under the control of the bishop. The first method is seen in the complaint against the counts in the council of Chalon, where the counts are accused of making visits to the rural religious centres. Monasteries are also mentioned here, so the counts can be seen to be threatening cult-centres as well. It is the creation of cult-centres, either as monasteries or as shrines or churches built over the body of the holy which is a key factor in Merovingian religious life. They were built in towns, in the suburbs, and in the countryside, and do much to confound modern distinctions between 'town' and 'countryside'. It is hardly accurate to call Merovingian Christianity an 'urban' religion—a 'cult' religion would be a better term. As for Eligius's missionary work in Flanders, his biography refers to it in such general terms, culled mainly from Rufinius's *History of the Church*, that the accounts are of very little use.[21]

Saint Audoenus's biography goes into less detail on his rural work than that of saint Eligius; the former is, anyway, very much shorter than the latter. There is enough information, however, to show the direction of his work. As with Eligius, much emphasis is laid on his abilities as a preacher—he is a *praedicator egregius.* The spoken word was obviously the main tool, to be used for making an impression on the rural populations.[22] Apart from preaching, saint Audoenus used his visits to found new churches in those rural communities which lacked them, or if the communities had churches, he made sure they were in good repair. His general attitude towards the *vicos publicos* and the *plebeias ecclesias* is expressed in his biography as *cura et diligentia.*[23]

These general statements are much amplified in the account of saint Eligius's work in the countryside. Saint Audoenus, it seems, never met any opposition to his preaching. Eligius had a much tougher task. One episode[24] gives a very fine picture of the sheer physical problems of trying to maintain ecclesiastical discipline in a Merovingian rural community. One of Eligius's visits is to a *vicus* where, for a reason unspecified, he excommunicates the village priest. The priest's

[21] *Ibid* cap 3 p 696, cap 8 pp 700–1.

[22] *Vita Audoeni* cap 4 p 556 and cap 10 p 559: 'Sicque vir sanctus per diversas parrochias virtutum semina atque verborum acumina spargebat.'

[23] *Vita Audoeni* bk 2 cap 24 p 557.

[24] *Vita Eligii* bk 2 cap 21 p 713. The *Vita Eligii* neatly divides such episodes into separate chapters, in contrast to the *Vita Audoeni* in which differences in time and space are often concealed in the same chapter.

response is simply to wait until he thinks that the bishop is out of earshot before ringing the church bell for the next service. The bell, bound by divine intervention, refuses to ring. It is then that several villagers actually remember the excommunication and hurry off after Eligius, asking him to rescind the order. He refuses and will not do so until, significantly, certain *optimates* and *seniores* ask him to free the bell. It was no easy task, then, to get episcopal authority accepted in the remoter areas.

Who these *seniores* and *optimates* are here it is impossible to tell. Another passage, however, is far more specific concerning the interference of the aristocracy in the bishop's struggle to bring the rural communities under control.[25] Eligius visits a *vicus* near Noyon to preach against what his biographer calls 'diabiolical games', 'wicked dancing' and 'other superstitions'. His audience reacts violently to his words, and the most prominent men, the *praestantiores*, accuse him of trying to despoil them of customs and privileges which were theirs by right. The leaders of the community are followers of Erchinoald, at that time the *major domus* of the Neustrian palace,[26] and are so incensed by Eligius's attitude that they threaten to lynch him. The bishop, unintimidated, carries on upbraiding them for being in the grip of the devil, and their response is this little speech:

> *Roman that you are,*[27] *although you are always bothering us, you will never uproot our customs, but we will go on with our rites as we have always done, and we will go on doing so always and forever. There will never exist the man who will be able to stop us holding our time-honoured and most dear games.*

Eligius, however, with divine help, is able to bring the village to heel, causing his main opponents to dance for a year—this being the time elapsed before he next visits the village.

It is hardly likely that these villagers really were indulging in superstitious practices to a greater extent than the vast majority of their contemporaries. There is a *basilica* in the village, the village is

[25] *Vita Eligii* bk 2 cap 20 pp 711–12.

[26] *Ibid.* Erchinoald: 'qui erat eo tempore praepositus palatii.'

[27] *Ibid.* The vocative use of *Romanus* is interesting. Eligius came from the region of Limoges, as bk 1 cap 1 of his life says. That this should mark him out as a 'Roman' in the Noyon region suggests that racial fusion between the Gallo-Roman and Frankish elements in the area had not taken place to the extent that it had elsewhere in the kingdom. The title also seems to indicate contempt, hinting at racial tensions. Van der Essen, *Étude critique,* p 333 argues that the author of the *Vita* was a German. If so, it would follow that it is his racial outlook expressed here, rather than that of the people of the Noyon region.

near the important religious centre of Noyon, and the followers of Erchinoald would surely not be outside the mainstream of Neustrian religious activity. Erchinoald was involved in supporting Columbanian monasticism,[28] and, as *major domus* was closely involved in the religious affairs of the kingdom. The accusation of pagan affinities is here a subjective concept, hurled at the subjects to 'explain' Eligius's differences with them. More significant is the information that the *praestantiores* believed that their *legitimas consuetudines* were being threatened. The *Romanus* title given to Eligius is perhaps meant to show their contempt for an outsider. The speech shows a complete refusal to contemplate change. What, then, was at stake? It looks as if it is the bishop trying to impose his authority on a rural community formerly under the influence of a local magnate—in this case, Erchinoald. Although the passage mentions a *basilica* there seems to be no priest attached to it, so perhaps the church had been taken over by laymen—an example of the abuse mentioned in canon five of the council of Chalon. The violence of the response caused by Eligius's presence hints at the lucrative profits to be had from controlling such a *vicus*, and finally, the fact that the community is *haud procul a noviomense oppido* suggests that the extent of the problem was very great indeed.

Cult-centres, too, were coming under the influence of the aristocracy in this period, as the richest and most powerful families founded monasteries in the countryside. Prinz has shown how the burial places of the founders of such monasteries became centres of cults based on the founding family.[29] The area of Rouen, far more than the region of Noyon, attracted such foundations, and saint Audoenus was energetic in touring the monasteries of his diocese maintaining a strict episcopal control over them. This seems surprising if one considers his active role in creating special privileges of immunity from episcopal interference in the monasteries outside his diocese, and especially in his plea for immunity for his own foundation of Rebais.[30] But one could argue that the only occasions on which saint Audoenus actually interferes in monastic affairs is when there is a crisis in the monastery.

[28] Erchinoald helped found the abbey of Lagny near Paris, helped saint Audoenus in the foundation of St Wandrille, and built the monastery of Peronne Scottorum over the body of saint Fursey. For the details of this work, see Prinz, *Frühes Mönchtum*, pp 128–9.

[29] *Ibid.* pp 492–504 on *Selbstheiligung der adeligen Gründerfamilien.*

[30] *Ibid.* The Rebais privilege is in *Diplomata, Chartae, Epistolae, Leges* 2, ed J. Pardessu (Paris 1849) pp 39–41. For a detailed account of the origins and nature of immunity privileges see E. Ewig, 'Beobachtungen zu den Klosterpriviligien des 7 und frühen 8 Jahrhunderts pp 52–66', *Adel und Kirche – Gerd Tellenbach zum 65 Geburtstag dargebracht von Freunden und Schülern,* ed K. Schmid (Freiburg/Basel/Vienna 1968).

At other times his interest is more fraternal than coercive, some of the abbots of the monasteries being personal friends of the bishop before their appointment!

Monastic life in the area of Rouen centred on the foundations of St Germer (or Penitale), Jumièges, St Wandrille, Fécamp, and Pavilly, the latter being a convent. In the literature stemming from these centres, saint Audoenus is treated with a special respect.[31] This is partly due to the fact that much of this literature is from a later date and is thus influenced by the posthumous reputation of the bishop, which grew to be very large. Certain episodes, though, stripped of their more fanciful embellishments, do show the basic attitude of the bishop to the monasteries under his care. The life of saint Geremar tells of how Geremar was appointed abbot of Penitale by Audoenus[32] and of how he was rejected by members of the monastery.[33] Audeonus persevered with his protégé and helped him found a new monastery, that of St Germer.[34] In the convent which became that of Pavilly, again a protégé of the bishop was rejected,[35] and again the solution was to move the convent—to the site at Pavilly.[36]

The life of saint Lantbert—a more trustworthy source than most in the context of Rouen monasticism,[37] tells of how the king Childeric II on his accession to the Neustrian throne gave lands to the abbey of St Wandrille.[38] Saint Audoenus was absent from the area at the time,

[31] This literature includes: *Vita Geremari,* ed Krusch, *MGH SRM* 4 pp 626–33 – a ninth century work and *wenig glaubwürdig* according to Levison in *Geschichtsquellen* p 139 n 343; *Vita Lantberti,* ed Levison, *MGH SRM* 5 pp 606–12, composed around the year 800, in Levison's view also expressed in *Geschichtsquellen* p 139; *Vita Filiberti,* ed Levison, *MGH SRM* 5 pp 568–606, a work of the later eighth century, again this is Levison's view in *Geschichtsquellen* p 138; *Vita Waningi,* ed [J.] Mabillon, *ASOSB* 3 (1669) pp 971–4. This work survives only in fragments dating from the Norman period; *Vita Austrebertae,* ed Mabillon, *ASOSB* 3 (1672) pp 27–9, again fragmented and from a later period.

[32] *Vita Geremari* cap 8 p 630. Though the work is *wenig glaubwürdig* one is inclined to believe the author when he treats with the central subject of Geremar's appointment – and especially when he describes the revolt of the monks against him – for why include an untruth which belittles the hero's stature? The same argument can be applied to the *Vita Austrebertae* in the description of Austreberta's troubles.

[33] *Ibid* cap 10.

[34] *Ibid* cap 18.

[35] *Vita Austrebertae* cap 12.

[36] *Ibid* cap 11.

[37] More trustworthy than the *Vitae Geremari, Austrebertae* and *Waningi.* Most of the source unfortunately has been lost. What remains is very detailed and contains important information on the supporters of king Childeric II.

[38] *Vita Lantberti* cap 3 p 610, an example of the detail to be found in this source – the petitioners in this grant are all named, as are all the properties granted.

and when he returned, he questioned this grant and went to court over it on the grounds that it adversely affected the monastery of Jumièges.[39] It seems that what had happened was that Childeric had taken advantage of Audoenus's absence to try and weaken the bishop's hold over one of the most important monasteries in his diocese. Such an attitude stresses the degree of influence saint Audoenus had over these monasteries. The events at Penitale and Pavilly show how such influence came to be exercised as Geremar and Austreberta became dependent upon his help. The early history of the foundation at Fécamp is an illustration of how a family institution came to be used for other purposes. Count Waning founded Fécamp on his own lands, and on the site of an oratory.[40] It is saint Audoenus and his colleague saint Wandrille who consecrate and open the institution, and not long after its opening, it is being used by the *major domus* Ebroin, ally of Audoenus, as a prison for his main political opponent saint Leudegar.[41] Significantly, none of Waning's family ever held office at Fécamp, and although the source for Fécamp explains this fact away as the express wish of the family,[42] it is more likely that the reason lies in the failure of Waning and his family to establish Fécamp as a strictly familial cult-centre.

Saint Audoenus's intervention in the affairs of the monastery of Jumièges was less benign. Again the intervention is connected with his relationship with Ebroin. Saint Filibert had refused to come to terms with Ebroin after the latter had returned from exile to the control of the Neustrian palace in the year 675.[43] Filibert was not only imprisoned by Audoenus, but also deposed from his position as abbot, the bishop appointing one of his own men to the vacant position.[44] Although this

[39] *Ibid* cap 4 pp 611–2. Saint Audoenus's initiative in bringing the case to court is seen in his request to king Childeric II for written permission to judge it: 'Audoenus una cum sua auctoritate simulque prefati regis epistola eadem re sibi directa ad verae pacis concordiam revocavit.' Theoretically, the case should have been within Audoenus's competence as bishop – it was an ecclesiastical matter. That he needed the king's permission to hear it reflects upon the fact that he was trying to alter a royal grant.

[40] *Vita Waningi* cap 5 p 972.

[41] *Ibid* cap 7 p 973, the source here merely copies the *Passio Leudagarii* bk 2, ed Krusch, *MGH SRM* 5 pp 324–56. For this source there is a surer tradition and an established reliability on the point of Leudegar's imprisonment at Fécamp.

[42] *Vita Waningi* cap 1 p 974. The wish that: 'de sua stirpe nulli ad regendum committeret.'

[43] The *Liber Historiae Francorum*, ed Krusch, *MGH SRM* 2 (1888) pp 213–328, a Neustrian chronicle, has the account of Ebroin's return to Neustria and tells of how saint Audoenus advised him to attack Leudesius, his rival as *major domus* – cap 45 pp 318, 319. The *Vita Filiberti* cap 24 p 596 tells of Filibert's rejection of Ebroin.

[44] *Vita Filiberti* cap 25 p 597 on Filibert's imprisonment. The source has great difficulty in explaining how it was that Filibert came to be punished by a bishop of such a spotless

affair has more significance for the political, rather than the religious history of Neustria, it does help to show the power of the bishop in this area. The legacy of such power passed to saint Audoenus's successor as bishop of Rouen, Ansbert, formerly abbot of St Wandrille, and yet another of saint Audoenus's protégés.[45] Under Ansbert, however, with the eclipse of Neustrian power after the battle of Tertry, conditions did not favour a continuation of saint Audoenus's policy and Ansbert was soon sent into exile by the Austrasian leader, Pepin.[46]

Saint Eligius's attitude towards cult-centres was based on the same principle as that of saint Audoenus, but expressed in a different context. His problem was not to bring existing centres under control, but to create new centres. The antipathy between Eligius and Erchinoald, expressed in the episode mentioned earlier, seems to have stemmed from Eligius's attempts to stop Erchinoald building a centre and monastic community over the body of saint Fursey, an Irish saint.[47] The diocese of Noyon-Tournai appears to have been somewhat short of marked burial places of saints before Eligius's arrival, and this is why the body of saint Fursey became a literal 'bone' of contention. The bishop's solution to the problem was to track down and bring to light the remains of saints known to be somewhere in the diocese. How exactly this was done his biography does not say, beyond the statement that it was done, 'with a great and burning faith'.[48]

---

reputation. Ebroin is very much the devil's man in the *Vitae* of this period, and so his relationship with saint Audoenus is never mentioned, and must be reconstructed from the tangle of circumstantial evidence. Here, for instance, the clergy of Rouen are put between Ebroin and Audoenus – it being more acceptable for the latter to take heed of his clergy than of Ebroin: '[Ebroin] incitans quosdam urbis Rodomagensium clericus, coepit discordiam ingerere et malivola verba sancto Audoeno pontifice de Filiberto viro Domini incantare.' When Audoenus actually deposes Filibert the source turns its venom on his replacement 'quidam miser homuncolus' (cap 26 p 598) – surely a unique, if indirect, criticism of Audoenus who chose the replacement.

[45] *Vita Ansberti*, ed Levison, *MGH SRM* 5 pp 613–41 – composed early ninth century, according to Levison in his introduction to the work p 615, cap 2 p 261 for Ansbert's early relationship with Audoenus, cap 15 p 628 on the death of Audoenus and Ansbert's succession as bishop of Rouen.

[46] *Ibid* cap 21 p 634: 'Quo tempore incusatus apud ipsum principem (Pepin) praefatus pontifex sanctus iussu eiusdem exilio deportatur in Altummontem monasterium.'

[47] *Vita Fursei*, ed Krusch, *MGH SRM* 4 pp 423–40, a very early source, the traditions of which are reflected in Bede. For the treatment of saint Fursey's body, see cap 10 p 439. Eligius failed to stop Erchinoald building over the body, but after four years, with the help of bishop Audebert of Cambrai managed to get the body moved.

[48] Two consecutive chapters from the *Vita Eligii* bk 2 deal with the bishop's recovery of the saint's remains. They are caps 6 and 7.

Significantly, this detective work was begun at the beginning of his episcopate. The source gives the impression that relic-worship in the area was in a state of chaos before Eligius took office. People were arbitrarily venerating places simply rumoured to contain the bones of saints.

It is surely no accident that the first body to be found was that of saint Quentin, the most renowned of the saints of the diocese. The body was found near Vermand, significantly the official *metropolis urbs* of the diocese,[49] and Eligius *promovit palam in publicum*—'put it on show'—in the place where it was found. Interestingly, the bishop had a rival in the search for saint Quentin's remains, one Maurinus, a singer, and companion of the king. Whether Maurinus's intention was to add saint Quentin to the relics held by the palace we cannot tell, for his pride led him to destruction before the body came to light. The next body to be found was that of the martyr Piato, found in the *vicus* of Sacilinio (the present day town of Séclin), to the south of Lille. Fitting the need to instruct the rural folk about what a treasure they had in their midst, Eligius extracts the very long nails with which Piato was tortured and shows them *in argumentum* to the community. The body is left in the *vicus* and a mausoleum built over it.[50]

The *civitas* of Soissons is next on the list. There the bodies of the martyrs and brothers Crispin and Crispian were found, and again put on show in a finely decorated memorial building. Finally, the *municipium* of Beauvais is the site of the discovery of the body of the martyr Lucian, one time colleague of saint Quentin. Lucian's body is, like the others, put on show in a finely decorated setting. The account goes on to say that a great number of other saints got similar treatment, but since they are not named, one would tend to doubt such a claim. The emphasis throughout is on putting the relics on show to the ordinary people, to provide a focus for their religious life. The memorial buildings would also serve to remind them of their bishop's existence. Eligius's work in building up cult-centres prefigures a far greater but similar enterprise undertaken by the Merovingian house itself.[51] The first hint we have of this is a report in the *Liber Historiae Francorum*

[49] *Vita Eligii* bk 2 cap 2 p 695. Eligius is given *custodem* of 'Vemandensi scilicet, quae est matropolis urbs. . . .'

[50] *Ibid* cap 7 p 700. The mausoleum is described as *urbane* – fit for a town, to give emphasis to the fact that it was built in a mere *vicus*.

[51] The similarity here concerns the aims of the respective exercises, the control of the cult-centres.

of king Clovis II breaking off one of the arms of saint Denis.[52] The movement gathered strength after saint Eligius's death in the year 660 under Clovis's widow Balthildis, and is commonly referred to as Balthildis's *Klosterpolitik*.[53] Saint Eligius was a member of the regency council governing the kingdom under Balthildis for the short period between the death of Clovis in 657 and his own in 660. It may well be that he helped Bathildis to plan this policy,[54] drawing on his own experience of building up cult-sites as focal points of influence.

Audoenus and Eligius, as we have seen, conducted their rural work in accordance with the consensus of episcopal opinion as expressed at the council of Chalon-sur-Saône. It seems a little surprising, then, that hardly any of their contemporaries as bishops had similar rural interests. The *Lives* of the bishops Desiderius of Cahors,[55] Sulpicius of Bourges,[56] Nivard of Rheims,[57] Leudegar of Autun,[58] and Praejectus of Clermont[59] all stress the urban role of their subjects and say nothing of regular visits to rural communities. In two cases, those of Leudegar and Praejectus, the episcopal appointments were made after periods of civil strife in their respective towns and so a significant part of their pastoral energy was diverted into keeping civil order.[60] All of these sees lay in the more heavily Romanised areas of the Frankish kingdom, with a stronger urban tradition. Consequently, the focal points of religious life in these areas were in the towns and in the suburbs which housed many monasteries.[61] In the north of the

[52] *Liber Historiae Francorum* cap 44 p 316: 'Eo tempore Chlodoveus brachium beati Dionisii martyris abscidit, instigante diabulo.'

[53] [E.] Ewig is the authority on this 'Klosterpolitik'. See [Das Privileg des Bischofs Berthefrid von Amiens für Corbie von 664 und die Klosterpolitik der Königin Balthild] *Francia* 1 (Paris 1973) for his latest work.

[54] Ewig certainly thinks so, see p 107.

[55] *Vita Desiderii*, ed Krusch, *MGH SRM* 4 pp 547–602, written at the end of the eighth century at the earliest according to Levison, *Geschichtsquellen* p 127.

[56] *Vita Sulpicii*, ed Krusch, *MGH SRM* 4 pp 364–80, put together from contemporary traditions sometime in the eighth century – Levison, *Geschichtsquellen* p 127.

[57] *Vita Nivardi*, ed Levison, *MGH SRM* 5 pp 157–71, a ninth century work – Levison, *Geschichtsquellen* p 128.

[58] *Passiones Leudegarii*, ed Krusch, *MGH SRM* 5 pp 249–356. *Passio* 1 has a near contemporary base, detailed by Krusch.

[59] *Passio Praejecti*, ed Krusch, *MGH SRM* 5 pp 212–48. More surely a contemporary work, some have argued, by Jonas of Bobbio; see *Geschichtsquellen* p 129.

[60] *Passio Leudegarii* bk 1 cap 2 p 248: Leudegar, a *strinuus* man is chosen by Balthildis to bring peace to Autun. *Passio Praejecti* cap 4 p 228 – feuding amongst the clergy of Clermont.

[61] A certain level of rural activity in these areas must be presumed, however, if only from the legislation concerning rural problems drawn up at the councils held in them. This can be seen as early as 511 in the council of Orleans, canon 15, De Clercq, *Concilia* p 9.

kingdom the picture was rather different, the towns being less prominent apart from such centres as Paris and Rheims. In the north, the energetic bishop had little choice but to attend to the rural areas. The *Life* of saint Amand, bishop of Tongres-Maastricht illustrates this well.[62] Saint Amand is remembered for his missionary work amongst the pagans of the Scheldt region. But for a period of three years he devoted himself to the more mundane tasks of pastoral care amongst the already Christianised people of his diocese, eventually returning to missionary work in disgust at the apathy of his clergy.[63] In this period saint Amand's work centred on the *vicos* and *castra*—there were simply no *urbes* for him to visit.[64]

Apart from such regional considerations, another factor has a bearing on the ability of a bishop to undertake rural work. As is clear from the account of saint Eligius's visit to the *vicus* near Noyon, the bishop at work in the countryside put himself at considerable personal risk if he chose to disagree with the sentiments of the local population. Conversely, the bishop behind the walls of his town was in an almost impregnable position.[65] In another sphere, the bishop was vulnerable as he personified the church in its role as a landowner and was liable to attack from rival local landed interests. The death of Praejectus of Clermont shows how a bishop, caught outside his town, could easily fall under knives drawn to settle a land dispute.[66]

[62] *Vita Amandi*, ed Krusch, *MGH SRM* 5 pp 395–449 – written sometime in the first half of the eighth century. For the dating and evaluation of the source see E. de Moreau 'La plus ancienne biographie de saint Amand', *RHE* 22 (1926) pp 30–67.

[63] *Vita Amandi* cap 18 p 443: 'sicque per triennium fere vicos vel castra verbum Domini constanter omnibus praedicavit. Multi etiam . . . sacerdotes atque feritae praedicationem illius respuentes, audire contempserunt.'

[64] On the settlement patterns in the Flanders and Maastricht regions see A. Bergengruen, 'Adel und Grundherrschaft im Merowingerreich,' *Vierteljahrschrift für Sozial und Wirtschaftgeschichte* 41 (Wiesbaden 1958). This work has come under attack from many scholars because of the conclusions that Bergengruen draws from his research – namely that the Franks had no aristocracy in the invasion period, and that the basis of the development of the aristocracy was service to the king. The research itself – on the northern areas – is sound, and Bergengruen gives details of the expansion of settlements out from the *castra*, creating new *villae* in the seventh century, pp 109–17.

[65] A good example of this is the case of bishop Leudegar of Autun. When the *major domus* Ebroin wished to take him into custody, he was forced to lay siege to his episcopal town. *Passio Leudegarii* bk 1 cap 21 p 302.

[66] *Passio Praejecti* cap 29 p 242 on the death of the bishop, *ibid* cap 23 p 239 on the origins of the land dispute. This was over land left to the church of Clermont by a wealthy Auvergnate widow (Claudia) but appropriated by Hector, the ruler of Provence. Hector was put to death after resisting a royal judgement on the case. Two of his supporters then took vengeance on Praejectus.

There is an account of a land dispute in the life of saint Eligius.[67] An unnamed man demands of Eligius a wood belonging to the church of Noyon. When Eligius refuses the request, the man threatens to take the property by force, but Eligius literally strikes him down with a pronouncement of excommunication. Clearly, Eligius possessed powers which Praejectus lacked, and the source of these powers seems to have been more political than divine. Eligius, was able to take on Erchinoald and win. It seems that saint Audoenus was never challenged, or even had any opponents. These two bishops were in a very strong political position, being close to the court and the ruling family. At a later date, after the death of Eligius, when the value of royal support rapidly declined, Audoenus maintained a close relationship with the major power in the land, Ebroin,[68] and so maintained his own position in the Rouen area. It is not hard to understand the necessity of political power (meaning: wealth, followers, and royal support) to the bishop who wished to extend his influence into the countryside. The demand that the *vici* and *villae* should come under episcopal jurisdiction in religious affairs, amounts to a demand that the inhabitants of such places should divide their loyalties between the bishop and their secular lord.[69] For it to be feasible to make such a demand, the bishop had to be powerful enough to be worth following. This, Eligius and Audoenus certainly were.

The conciliar history of the Merovingian church shows that its bishops were not disinterested in the religious affairs of the rural communities. Few bishops, however, found themselves able to convert this interest into a more practical approach. Saint Audoenus and saint Eligius were given diocesan areas which made a certain amount of rural work necessary, and luckily they were of the political stature to undertake it. The pressure of the aristocracy on the rural communities meant that there was competition for the loyalties of the rural folk. This pressure could be countered by making frequent visits to the communities and by making sure that cult-centres had an episcopal rather than aristocratic significance. The work of Eligius and Audoenus in this direction seems to have had no permanent effect, as the

[67] *Vita Eligii* bk 2 cap 19 p 710: 'Quidam itaque vir infaustus . . . volens ecclesiae eius silvam quandam valde optimam pertinaciter praeripere suaeque ditioni mancipare.'

[68] On the relationship between Audoenus and Ebroin, see nn 43, 44.

[69] Though the *vici* as rural centres were generally inhabited by people free in status, such centres were under pressure from neighbouring magnates throughout the period. A concise statement on their position is given by G. Fourquin, *Histoire de la France Rurale*, 1, ed G. Duby (Seuil 1975) cap 3 pp 310–2.

pressure of the aristocracy led to a secularisation of the episcopacy in the later seventh century, and royal power, essential in monitoring episcopal appointments, declined. The church councils for this period show problems far greater than those of rural abuses, in that there seems to be a general collapse of ecclesiastical discipline.[70] Saint Audoenus and saint Eligius were the last survivors of the circle of bishops who had trained at the court of Dagobert. With them died much of the drive and energy of the Merovingian church, a lull left unbroken until the age of Boniface.

University of London, King's College

[70] This is stated clearly in the preamble to an Aquitanian council held under king Childeric II, De Clercq *Concilia* pp 311–3: '. . . multa contraria statuta patrum vel canonica auctoritate inventa sunt, eo quod clerici per contumacia propriis episcopis dispicerint et adhuc, quod peius est, amplius quam saecularis diversa contraria agerent.'

TOWN AND MONASTERY IN THE CAROLINGIAN PERIOD

by ROSAMOND MCKITTERICK

ALTHOUGH there were both urban and rural monastic communities in the Frankish kingdoms in the Carolingian period, far more is known about the landed monasteries in the countryside regarding both their internal organisation and the relationship between them and the rural community in which they lived and over which they were the lords. The statutes of Adalhard of Corbie for example provide information concerning the monastery both within the monastic community and on its estates, and show us the abbey as the centre of an agricultural region.[1] The monasteries in the towns on the other hand are much less well-documented and the evidence for Carolingian towns themselves is both sparse and difficult to interpret. If a town is understood to be 'a concentration of population larger than the neighbouring agricultural settlements in which there is a substantial non-agricultural population which may be concerned with defence, administration, religion, commerce or industry',[2] there are not very many Carolingian centres for which enough evidence survives to justify their being called towns. Valenciennes for example, described recently as *une ville carolingienne*, is mentioned in the sources occasionally as a *portus* and seems to have succeeded Farrars in importance in the region sometime in the eighth century. In the time of Charles the Bald it had a mint, and Charlemagne, Charles the Bald, Lothar I and Lothar II are all known to have issued charters from a royal *palatium* at Valenciennes. There were several churches and the abbey of St Salvius in the settlement, and it is likely that some trading activity went on. But other than that Valenciennes was a settlement which carried on some sort of economic activity, very little is known.[3] The abbey of St Amand, a rural monastery nine miles from Valen-

[1] L. Levillain, 'Les statuts d'Adalhard', *Moyen Age* (1900) pp 333–86, and A. Verhulst and J. Semmler, 'Les statuts d'Adalhard de Corbie de l'an 822', *Moyen Age* (1962) pp 90–123, 233–69. J. Godard, 'La place de la ville et l'abbaye de Corbie dans l'économie du moyen âge', and P. Doubliez, 'Le monnayage de l'abbaye Saint-Pierre de Corbie', *Corbie, Abbaye Royale* (Lille 1963) pp 311–7, 283–310.

[2] C. T. Smith, *An Historical Geography of Western Europe before 1800* (London 1967) p 299.

[3] F. Deissen-Nagels, 'Valenciennes, ville carolingienne', *Moyen Age* (1962) pp 51–90.

ciennes, achieved a far more influential and important position in the kingdom than the town of Valenciennes ever did.

Carolingian towns and their churches and monasteries have to be seen in the context of, on the one hand, the possible continuity with the towns of late Roman Gaul, and on the other, the new types of urban settlement which developed in the aftermath of the barbarian invasions. The invasions considerably altered the economic structure of Gaul. There seems to be a consensus of opinion that the barbarian, particularly Frankish, settlements in Gaul involved a redistribution of land already occupied rather than a fresh colonisation of new areas.[4] Urbanisation in late Roman Gaul had been according to the Roman pattern, and Gallo-Roman towns have been divided, very generally, into three distinct types. Towns like Arles were constructed on a grid plan with amphitheatre, forum and baths, and were founded for army veterans and their families. The population of these was quite small in contrast to cities such as Aix, Vienne, Nîmes and Trier, which were established primarily to resettle people from rural Italy but which included a large proportion of indigenous population. Thirdly there were the indigenous centres such as Rheims or Tours, reestablished as Roman capitals by Augustus.[5] After the barbarian invasions these towns, which had usually been built on a large open plan, contracted into smaller, walled, towns, and many of the cities seem to have become largely depopulated, albeit it should be remembered that the social structure of Gaul in the late Roman period had already begun to change, with more people leaving the cities to live on the land.[6] For the Franks the land, and the demesne manor on it, was the centre of economic and social life, so that rural settlements acquired a new importance. The Frankish kings for example came to live much more in *palatia* in the countryside such as St Denis or Ingelheim rather than in the semi-urban settlements of Cambrai or Tournai, and these *palatia* became in their turn the nuclei for further settlement. The emphasis of town life also changed. Hitherto the town had acted as the focal point of a region, its food needs served by the surrounding rural areas. With the coming of the barbarians it was the nobles and ecclesiastics who assumed prominence in the life of the towns, and in many cases from Sidonius Apollinaris onwards, it was the bishop who

[4] P. Bonnard, 'Peopling and the origins of settlement', in [H. D.] Clout, [*Themes in the historical geography of France*] (London 1977) pp 42–54 at p 45.

[5] Clout p 78; see also P. MacKendrick, *Roman France* (London 1971).

[6] E. Ennen, 'Die Entwicklung des Städtewesen an Rhein und Mosel vom 6. bis 9. Jahrhundert', *SS Spoleto* 6 (1959) pp 419–52.

emerged as the leader of his city.[7] It was sometimes only as a diocesan centre that a town continued to exist, so that apart from the episcopal towns there were hardly any towns to merit the name before the eighth century.[8]

Ecclesiastical buildings played a crucial role in the topographical and social evolution of towns in Frankish society. The process of alteration of the function and structure of Gallo-Roman towns has been described by Böhner as the 'disintegration of the late Roman town into private domestic units', the best examples of which are Mainz and Trier, in which the creation of Frankish manors completely transformed the inner structure of the towns.[9] At Mainz the churches indicate the spread of settlement in the town area and the private churches attached to the Frankish manors further altered the town structure. Oratories by the cemeteries outside the old Roman walls of Trier developed into important abbey churches, but inside the city it was the cathedral and its precinct which was the centre of the town. The bishop in this case also determined the site of the town market and succeeded ultimately in gaining power over the other ecclesiastical and lay magnates. Franks often established manors in the immediate vicinity of a Roman walled town and the settlement which developed round it eventually superseded the older settlement, a development Böhner has noted at Alzey and Kreuznach. A further type of Frankish settlement was that associated with the shrine of a saint or martyr. Bonn for example became part of the Frankish royal domain, and the martyrs' chapel in what had been the civilian cemetery of the Gallo-Roman settlement became the cathedral of saints Cassius and Florentinus. The enlargement of the cathedral building in the Carolingian period has been associated with the establishment of a monastery to which a settlement was attached. At Tours too, a new community grew up round the shrine of St Martin. Roman forts such as those at Nijmegen and Utrecht could also form the nuclei of Merovingian and Carolingian towns.[10]

[7] Gregory of Tours comments on the power of the bishops in their cities, *Historia Francorum*, bk 6 chap 46, *MGH SRM* 1, p 320.

[8] [F.] Vercauteren, ['La vie urbaine entre Meuse et Loire du VIe au IXe siècle'], *SS Spoleto* 6 (1959) pp 453–84.

[9] K. Böhner, 'Urban and rural settlement in the Frankish kingdom', *European Towns. Their Archaeology and Early History*, ed M. W. Barley (London 1977) pp 185–201. See too [E. M.] Wightman, ['The towns of Gaul with special reference to the North East'], *ibid* pp 303–14.

[10] H. Safratij, 'Archaeology and the town in the Netherlands', *ibid* pp 203–17. Gregory

Continued settlement of towns from the late Roman into the Merovingian and Carolingian periods was thus encouraged in some instances by the existence of fortifications or economic activity, and in almost every instance by the church. Cemeteries, chapels, shrines and the cathedral church with its bishop could each act as a new nucleus of urban settlement.[11] The bishop in his city also kept alive the concept of administration proceeding outwards from a centre.[12] All these developments continued very gradually into the Carolingian period, but it is only in the tenth century that the evidence for mercantile activity in a number of towns and for a greater density of urban population increases appreciably. A slight decline of town life has been noted in the eighth century and in Neustria Vercauteren has remarked on the relative decadence of the material structure of some cities, such as Rouen or Rheims. Between 817 and 825, the bishop of Rheims obtained the permission of Louis the Pious to demolish part of the old town wall in order to obtain building material for his churches, and some Carolingian capitularies reiterate the need to repair roads and bridges and public buildings.[13] In the second half of the ninth century moreover, urban development was interrupted in many towns due to the incursions of the Northmen.[14] Many town walls were restored and abbeys in the *suburbia* such as St Remigius at Rheims, St Vaast at Arras, St Medard at Soissons and St Gery at Cambrai, were also fortified.

Towns in the Carolingian period therefore were very different from the Gallo-Roman cities before the invasions, and it was their ecclesiastical character in particular which increased considerably in the eighth and ninth centuries. Ganshof has suggested furthermore that the economic life of the towns in the Frankish kingdoms revived

---

of Tours provides a great deal of incidental information concerning towns in the Merovingian period and some of this has been discussed by Vercauteren.

[11] F. L. Ganshof, *Étude sur le développement des villes entre Loire et Rhin au Moyen Age* (Paris 1943) discusses Liège in this context. See too [D. A.] Bullough, ['Social and economic structure and topography of the early medieval city'], *SS Spoleto* 21 (1974) pp 351–99 and the articles by [J.] Hubert, 'Évolution [de la topographie et de l'aspect des villes de Gaule du Ve au Xe siècle'], *SS Spoleto* 6 (1959) pp 529–58 and 'La Renaissance Carolingienne et la topographie des cités épiscopales', *SS Spoleto* 1 (1954) pp 218–25.

[12] Wightman. p. 309.

[13] Flodoard, *Historia Remensis ecclesiae,* bk 2 chap 19. *MGH SS* 13, p 469, and see [F.] Vercauteren, *Étude [sur les civitates de la Belgique Seconde]* (Brussels 1934). For legislation on repairs see *MGH Cap* 1, p 288, chap 8; 2, p 64 chap 7.

[14] Hubert, 'Évolution' pp 556–7.

largely because of ecclesiastical interest.[15] Both abbeys and cathedrals possessed urban rights and property, but it is for the bishops and cathedrals that there are details concerning their relations with the townspeople in spheres other than that of the exercise of political power or judicial rights. From the list of stational churches at Metz found in an early ninth-century Gospel book, now BN MS lat 268, we know that there were station days during the liturgical year on which the bishop of Metz celebrated mass in one of the thirty-five churches of Metz, and that there were processions of clergy and people from church to church with litanies and prayers being chanted on the way. Preaching to the people of the city is also mentioned; the people were to receive a sermon on lent before the season of fasting began.[16] In Lyons too there were liturgical processions of the people and pilgrims to the various shrines of the city, and a large proportion of the population consisted of priests and monks.[17] It is necessary to distinguish between the activities of the secular clergy, bishops and priests and the function of the churches in the town, and the activity and function of the monks and their monasteries, but about the monastery's relationship with the townspeople relatively little is known. Many have stressed how 'important' monasteries were in the towns but for the Carolingian period at least there is little unequivocal evidence concerning the way in which they exerted an influence on town and bishop. One obvious function of the monastery, and of the secular clergy as well, was in the sphere of social welfare, for the monastic (and episcopal) *hospitia* and *xenodochia* were designed to care for the poor and the sick, and for the pilgrim, and were an essential part of the life of the town as well as of the countryside.[18]

A town monastery was however in rather a different position from that of the rural landowning monasteries, and this was due to the differences in the aims of their foundations. The rural monasteries

[15] F. L. Ganshof, 'A propos du tonlieu à l'époque carolingienne', *SS Spoleto* 6 (1959) pp 485–508.

[16] T. Klauser, 'Eine Stationslist der Metzer Kirche aus dem 8. Jahrhundert, wahrscheinlich ein Werk Chrodegangs', *Ephemerides Liturgicae* 44 (Rome 1930) pp 162–93. The pastoral role of the clergy of Metz was also emphasized in Chrodegang of Metz's *Rule*. See too R. Folz, 'Metz dans la monarchie franque du temps de Saint Chrodegang', *Saint Chrodegang* (Metz 1967) pp 11–24.

[17] A. Kleinclausz, *Histoire de Lyon* 1 (Lyons 1939) pp 90–101.

[18] W. Schönfeld, 'Die Xenodochien in Italien und Frankreich im frühen Mittelalter', *ZRG KAbt* 43 (1922) pp 1–54 and W. Ullmann, 'Public welfare and social legislation in the early medieval councils', *SCH* 7 (1971) pp 1–39. J. M. Besse, *Les Moines de l'ancienne France* (Paris 1906) is still useful.

were the descendants of the establishments of groups of holy men and women who had retreated from society into a form of collective solitude in the 'wilderness' and separated themselves physically from the world.[19] Whether or not the increase in the foundation and endowment of landowning and land-cultivating monasteries from the early seventh century was related, as has been suggested by Prinz in a recent paper, to the arrival of Columbanus and the activities of his followers is not clear,[20] but the greater number of Carolingian monasteries were certainly based on the land, many with large estates and with a virtually closed economy. The self-sufficient monastery established in a remote place moreover remained an important aspect of the ascetic life.[21] Town monasteries on the other hand were the descendants of the coenobitic communities John Cassian and his disciples had founded in Marseilles and the towns of southern Gaul, which stressed spiritual solitude within society rather than physical separation from it. Even within the city however, the groups of men and women who had dedicated themselves to a life of purity and piety set themselves apart from the town community and the parish; they used their own church and oratory and practised their own forms of discipline and worship. This withdrawal must have decreased the influence such communities may have exerted in the life of a parish.

The increase in barbarian raids certainly affected the development of urban monasticism: a canon of the council of Vannes of 465 for example refers to monastic communities being driven inside the town walls by barbarian raids,[22] and most of the urban monasteries of the Carolingian period were in the episcopal towns. In Lyons for example were the monasteries of St Nizier, St Peter, St Martin and the Île Barbe, and in Rheims there were the monasteries of saints Remigius, Thierry, Nicasius and Denis, and outside the town, Hautvillers. It was rare however that a monastery in an episcopal town exerted as much influence as the bishop over the town and its inhabitants, and in practice they tended to enhance the bishop's power and prestige. It was more likely that a monastery in a non-episcopal town would

[19] On the development of monasticism in early medieval Gaul see C. Courtois, 'L'évolution du monachisme en Gaule de St Martin à St Columban', *SS Spoleto* 4 (1957) pp 47–72 and F. Prinz, *Frühes Mönchtum im Frankenreich* (Munich 1965).

[20] F. Prinz, 'Columbanus, the Frankish nobility and the lands east of the Rhine', paper presented to the colloquy on *Ireland and the Continent 500–750*, Dublin, May 1977.

[21] See for example the account of the foundation of Fulda, Eigil, *Vita sancti Sturmi*, ed Pertz, *MGH SS* 2, pp 366–77.

[22] *CC* 148, p 153.

possess a clearly defined relationship with the town populace. The abbey of Centula-St Riquier is the most obvious, albeit not the most typical, example of such a monastery in the Carolingian kingdoms. Although St Riquier's position is well known, it is useful to include a brief account of it here as it represents by far the best documented instance of a monastery's relationship with the town with which it was associated.

The main source for the history of St Riquier is the late eleventh-century chronicle of Hariulf, monk of St Riquier and later abbot of Oldenbourg, which covers the history of the abbey from the fifth century to 1104.[23] The chronicle incorporated a number of royal privileges concerning the abbey, two important works of Angilbert, abbot of St Riquier, the *Libellus* and the *Institutio de diversitate officiorum*, and an invaluable inventory of the property, books, possessions and vassals of St Riquier, presented to Louis the Pious in 831.

The town of Centula-St Riquier is an example of a settlement which developed in relation both to the manor of a Frankish lord and to the monastery founded there in the seventh century by Richarius. By the late eighth century when Angilbert, the Homer of the palace school of Charlemagne, came there to restore the monastery and build the great Carolingian abbey, Centula-St Riquier was a fairly thriving urban settlement.[24] The new abbey was dedicated in 799, and the expense of its extensive and impressive buildings was largely provided for by a large gift of silver made by Charlemagne. Charlemagne is also said to have provided the craftsmen to work in stone, glass, marble, stucco and wood and to have ordered bases, columns and mouldings from Rome.[25] There were three churches in the cloister of the monastery, arranged as if on the points of a triangle, and intended to symbolise the Trinity. The main church contained two large chapels, one dedicated to the Saviour and all the saints, the other dedicated to Richarius or St Riquier. The other two churches were dedicated to Mary the Virgin and all the apostles, and to Benedict and all the holy abbots. Each church contained many altars dedicated to different saints, and many of them also contained their relics. The list of relics made by

[23] Hariulf, [*Gesta ecclesiae Centulensis*], ed F. Lot, *Hariulf, Chronique de l'abbaye de Saint-Riquier* (Paris 1894).

[24] On the history of St Riquier see the old-fashioned but useful account by l'Abbé Henocque, *Histoire de l'abbaye et de la ville de Saint-Riquier* (Amiens 1880).

[25] Hariulf gives an account of the contruction, bk 2, chap 7. See too K. Conant, *Carolingian and Romanesque Architecture 800–1200* (Harmondsworth 1966) pp 43–6.

Angilbert is impressive: it included relics of the True Cross, of the Virgin Mary, and of the saints Peter, John the Baptist, Stephen, Dionysius, Rusticus, Eleutherius, Richarius, Laurence and Martin.[26] The importance of these relics and the magnificence of the altars as objects of pilgrimage should be emphasized.

Angilbert informs us that there were five chapels in the town of Centula-St Riquier in addition to the abbey churches. The western sanctuary of the abbey church, dedicated to the Saviour, however, acted as the parish church, for it contained a baptismal font.[27] The town was thus in a sense spiritually dependent upon the abbey. It was also so much involved economically in the abbey that the abbey complex together with the town has been called a 'holy town'.[28] The extent of the town is not known, but a census recorded in 831, and preserved on fol 84^{v} of Vatican MS reg lat 235 in a thirteenth-century copy, attests that there were two thousand five hundred houses in the town, so that there may have been as many as seven thousand inhabitants.[29] There were also four mills and thirteen ovens. All the houses belonged to the abbey, and rents for them had to be paid, mostly in kind. Every year each dwelling paid a rent of twelve deniers, four chickens, thirty eggs, one 'bag' of wheat, one 'bag' of oats and one 'bag' of beans to the abbey.[30] The census gives further information about the occupation of the inhabitants and how they rendered their dues to the abbey apart from the house rent. The town was divided into a number of *vici*, streets or quarters, in which those who followed a particular profession lived. Thus there was the soldiers' quarter, and the soldiers rendered military service to the abbey and provided horses, equipment and weapons. Other *vici* were occupied by the smiths, saddlers, dyers, fullers, skindressers, cobblers, butchers, bakers and vintners (who provided both wine and oil), merchants and innkeepers. These paid the abbey either in money or in kind. The chapel of the nobles gave incense and perfume, and the four other chapels of the town also had to pay some sort of tribute. The relations between abbey and town were not just based on extortion; the abbot observed his obligations towards the poor and

[26] Hariulf bk 2, chaps 8–10.

[27] Lack of a font limited the autonomy of a city church, see Bullough p 362.

[28] J. Hubert, 'Saint-Riquier et le monachisme benedictin en Gaule à l'époque carolingienne', *SS Spoleto* 4 (1957) pp 293–309.

[29] The text is included as appendix 7 in Lot's edition of Hariulf, pp 306–8.

[30] The wheat, oats and beans may have been received from a different type of dwelling. The text does not make it clear.

needy, and was supposed every day to provide for three hundred of the poor, one hundred and fifty widows and sixty clerics. There was too the impressive ceremonial participation of town and monastery in the liturgy of certain feast-day processions. The festivals are described very fully and enthusiastically by Angilbert in his *Institutio de diversitate officiorum*, preserved on fols 78-82 of Vatican MS reg lat 235.[31] The processions, if they really took place as Angilbert describes them, were on a grand scale. The column was seven people abreast, and Angilbert tells us proudly that had the column been as narrow as two or three persons, the procession of brethren alone would have been a mile long. Seven crosses and the priests led the procession, followed by the deacons, subdeacons, acolytes, exorcists, lectors, ostiarii and the monks. Then came the boys of the lay school and of the abbey school, then the noblemen and noblewomen, followed by the seven crosses of the churches of the villages outside St Riquier and the boys and girls of the villages, 'who rustics as they are know how to sing the Lord's Prayer and Creed and other things which they have been taught with the help of our Lord.' After them came the men and women of the town and of the neighbouring villages, then the lower orders of each and finally the old and the feeble. Those too old or weak to walk closed the procession on horseback. The procession sang prayers and antiphons as they went, the creeds and the Lord's Prayer and the general litany. The monks and boys sang the Gallic, Italic and Roman litanies and the long litany of saints. A final Te Deum was sung as the procession returned to the monastery. The liturgical importance of this ritual by Angilbert will be obvious, but the text also proffers a fascinating glimpse of the religious life of a town dominated by its monastery.

Why the abbey of St Riquier came to exert such control over the town of Centula is not entirely clear. St Riquier or Richarius was according to legend a count of Ponthieu and great-nephew of Clovis, who inherited the comital palace at Centula, was converted to the Christian faith by Irish missionaries and consequently founded the abbey of St Riquier. Richarius however was active in the seventh century rather than the sixth; yet there may be an element of truth in the story, in that Richarius may have been the Frankish lord whose manor acted as the nucleus of the settlement which grew into the town of Centula. If the original inhabitants of the town had been vassals and tenants of the Merovingian lord it would perhaps account for

[31] Hariulf appendix 6, pp 296–306.

the interdependent relationship between monastery and town which had developed by the ninth century. The ruin of the monastery in 881 by the northmen in the great raids of that year in the northeast was also that of the town, and Centula gradually decreased in importance until in the twelfth century it was surpassed by Abbeville. There are many questions one would wish to ask concerning St Riquier and the other Carolingian monasteries in the towns, particularly with regard to the quality of their spiritual and ascetic life within the community, what pastoral influence they exerted on the urban population, what particular problems their impact on each other created and how the monasteries reacted, but unfortunately the sources extant cannot provide the answers. There is a greater possibility of such questions being answered for later centuries, when the towns had evolved more as urban institutions and the town monastery's aims and position were more clearly defined.

Newnham College, Cambridge

CHARLES THE BALD AND THE CHURCH IN TOWN AND COUNTRYSIDE

by JANET L. NELSON

'THE CHURCH in town and countryside' is a fruitful theme. But for early medievalists it is an especially challenging one. We first have to establish our right to participate at all. There is a classic tradition of interpreting western history, and the history of western Christianity too, in terms of an opposition between town and countryside:[1] but according to exponents of this tradition, from Marx and Engels through Weber and Troeltsch to some contemporary historians, the early middle ages present a dull, townless void between antiquity and the eleventh or twelfth century. We have to begin then, by affirming that there were towns in the early middle ages. To justify this, we must do more than point out continuity in the terminology used by late classical and early medieval writers. We need to show that places existed which functioned as towns. Biddle[2] has given a useful archaeologist's list of functional criteria: defences, a planned street-system, a market, a mint, legal autonomy, a role as a central place, a relatively large and dense population, a diversified economic base, plots and houses of 'urban' type, social differentiation, complex religious organisation, a judicial centre.

Biddle suggests that if a place fulfils three or four at least of these criteria, it merits serious consideration as a town. At this point, the early medieval ecclesiastical historian can rub his or her hands: not only are we qualified to join actively in discussion, but we have a particularly good qualification to do so—simply because in the early middle ages it was churches, episcopal and monastic, which provided the major, if not quite the only, *foci* for town life on the criteria

[1] See for example K. Marx, *Pre-capitalist Economic Formations,* ed E. Hobsbawm (London 1964) pp 35–6, 77–8, 127 *seq*; F. Engels, *The Peasant War in Germany,* ed L. Krieger (Chicago/London 1967) pp 33 *seq*; [M.] Weber, *Economy* [*and Society*], ed G. Roth and C. Wittich, 3 vols (New York 1968) 3, cap 16, pp 1212–62; E. Troeltsch, *The Social Teaching of the Christian Churches,* 2 vols (London 1931) 1, pp 254 *seq*; C. Haase, 'Die mittelalterliche Stadt als Festung', *Die Stadt des Mittelalters,* ed C. Haase, 3 vols (Darmstadt 1969) 1, pp 377–408, and other essays in the same collection.

[2] 'Towns', *The Archaeology of Anglo-Saxon England,* ed D. M. Wilson (London 1976) pp 99–150 at p 100.

specified above.[3] If 'a role as a central place' and 'complex religious organisation' go without saying, the defensive, economic, and governmental functions of ecclesiastical centres seem to me equally characteristic and peculiar—certainly for ninth-century west Francia on which I propose to concentrate.

But by way of preliminary, I want to make two points, one specific, one general. The first concerns the economic features of our ecclesiastical towns: they are centres not primarily of production but of consumption and, to a lesser but increasingly significant extent, of exchange. As consumers of rural products, the town-dwellers—religious specialists and those who service them—clearly exist in intimate dependence on the countryside. But those who produce for or supply the urban élite are also its dependants. There is no merchant class, no bourgeoisie: only agents and servitors of churchmen. This explains why there is no qualitative distinction between the religiosity of town and countryside such as Weber and Troeltsch posited for later medieval Christendom and Gellner for north African Islam.[4] My second, general, introductory point is this: that compared with any other society I can think of since urban civilisation began at all, the differentiation of town and countryside in the early medieval west had quite peculiar implications. Elsewhere towns were the locations of political power. And if political and religious institutions were structurally differentiated, it was the religious ones, if any, which shifted to the countryside.[5] The growth of the Christian church within the Roman empire, and especially during 'the birth of the Middle Ages', had consequences specific to the early medieval west: institutional continuity of the church in old urban centres; the transformation of those old centres and the growth of new ones under ecclesiastical direction or at least strong influence; the disappearance or attenuation of certain urban functions in these centres as barbarian lay political power was established in the countryside; and a spatial

[3] [J.] Hubert, 'Évolution [de la topographie et de l'aspect des villes de Gaule du Ve au Xe siècle]', *SS Spoleto* 6 (1959) pp 529–58 at 540 *seq*; [R.] Latouche, [*The*] *Birth* [*of Western Economy*] (London 1967) pp 97 *seq*; E. Ennen, *Die europäische Stadt des Mittlelalters* (Göttingen 1972) caps 1, 2; [G.] Duby, [*The*] *Early Growth* [*of the European Economy*] (London 1974) pp 97 *seq*, esp p 106.

[4] [E.] Gellner, '[A pendulum swing theory of] Islam', *Annales Sociologiques* (Paris 1968) pp 5–14.

[5] For pioneering attempts at a comparative approach, see Weber, *Economy* 3, pp 1226 *seq*, 1236 *seq*, 1260–2, and Gellner, 'Islam'. But the uniqueness of developments in the early medieval west remains to be explored.

dislocation between lay and ecclesiastical power which meant that kings, though based in the countryside, had to find some mode of access to the towns through relations with the church. Balthild's interference with urban and sub-urban cult-sites throughout her Neustro-Burgundian realm shows the interaction of all these themes[6]. In the ninth century, that interaction took other forms—arising from the terms on which the early Carolingians had set about the reconstruction of ecclesiastical culture and institutions after the disintegration of the late seventh and early eighth centuries.[7] Reform depended, as in the eleventh century, on maximising material resources: no scriptoria without sheep and cows! Carolingian royal and aristocratic piety ensured that the reformed church had its riches. Herlihy[8] has calculated that church lands over western Christendom as a whole tripled in area between 751 and 825, rising from ten to over thirty per cent of the total of land cultivated. No contemporary power-holder could neglect such a trend, and kings especially were bound to claim some benefits from it. I start from the assumption that this royal exploitation could be, not wanton plundering, but a highly discriminating exercise the pattern of which may be clearer if we apply the distinction between town and countryside. And since Charles the Bald has the reputation of an arch-exploiter, his activities seem worth closer examination.

First then, what was the interest of the church in the countryside to Charles the Bald? Following an ancestral tradition which may well predate the Carolingians,[9] Charles used church lands to reward, and secure the loyalty of, his vassals and his counts. In his father's reign, clerical protests against this practice had become noisy; but though Louis the Pious probably tried to stop making new appropriations, he did not revoke those of his ancestors.[10] During the wars of 840–3, further spoliations, royal and otherwise, had been made. Charles the Bald therefore began his effective reign under intensified pressure to restore ecclesiastical property. He did so, as twenty-four surviving

[6] See my 'Queens as Jezebels: the careers of Brunhild and Balthild in Merovingian History', *Medieval Women, SCH Subsidia* 1 (1978) pp 31–77.

[7] E. Ewig gives a fine survey in *Handbook of Church History*, ed H. Jedin and J. Dolan 3 (London 1969) sections 1, 3 and 4.

[8] 'Church property on the European Continent, 701–1200', *Speculum* 36 (1961) pp 81–105.

[9] [É.] Lesne, [*Histoire de la*] *Propriété* [*ecclésiastique en France*], 6 vols (Lille 1910–43) 1, pp 446–50; 2, pp 1–9.

[10] Lesne, *Propriété*, 2, ii (1922) pp 148 *seq*.

charters testify.[11] But did this mean that he was having to 'despoil his own domains to buy off revolt'?[12] Can we infer from such acts of restitution increased royal weakness, measured in terms of loss of control of lands? Let us look at a case where we know what actually happened next. In 845, with Hincmar at his elbow, Charles restored substantial properties to the church of Rheims.[13] But his vassals were not thrown off their estates. They now became, instead, vassals of the archbishop[14] and were told by the king to pay their due rents (*nonae et decimae*)[15] to the church. In practice, though, what mattered was that Charles's men retained their benefices and through them their personal link with the royal benefactor; so that, when one such vassal wished to pass on his benefice to his son, he applied not to Hincmar but to Charles.[16] Where is the alleged loss of royal political control?

It is true that ninth-century churchmen had successfully vindicated their exclusive rights—in principle—to the disposition of church property.[17] A vassal holding such property no longer held it from the king (*verbo regis*) but from an ecclesiastical *rector*.[18] Churchmen recognised, nevertheless, that in practice royal needs had still to be met in the interests of the realm as a whole. Paschasius Radbertus, writing in 852, attributed a shrewd assessment of the situation to Wala of Corbie a generation before: 'If the state (*respublica*) cannot survive without the help of church property, a procedure and a system (*modus et ordo*) must be sought' so that laymen could receive such property without damage to the church.[19] New rules were found. But as Southern said in another context:[20] '... though the system had its ... philosophers, it was also, as practical men knew, capable of being

[11] [G.] Tessier, [*Receuil des Actes de Charles II le Chauve*], 3 vols (Paris 1943–55) 3, pp 213–15.

[12] [J. M.] Wallace-Hadrill, [*Early Germanic*] *Kingship* [*in England and on the Continent*] (Oxford 1971) p 127.

[13] Tessier, 1, no 75, pp 210–13.

[14] Tessier, 1, no 99, pp 262–5.

[15] G. Constable, 'Nona et decima', *Speculum* 35 (1960) pp 224–50.

[16] Hincmar of Rheims, *De villa Noviliaco, PL* 125 (1879) col 112.

[17] [W.] Goffart, [*The Le Mans*] *Forgeries* (Cambridge, Mass. 1966).

[18] Lesne, *Propriété*, 2, i, pp 164 *seq*.

[19] *MGH SS* 2, ed G. H. Pertz (Hanover 1829) p 549. On this passage, see W. Wehlen, *Geschichtsschreibung und Staatsauffassung im Zeitalter Ludwigs des Frommen, Historische Studien* 418 (Lübeck/Hamburg 1970) p 114, and for the meaning of *respublica* (in some ninth-century contexts equivalent to *Staatsgut*) pp 33 *seq*, 53–4. It is worth stressing that Paschasius was writing this in the context of the reign of Charles the Bald, not Louis the Pious.

[20] *The Making of the Middle Ages* (London 1959) p 140.

manipulated to give much the same results as had been obtained in a . . . cruder age. The whole secret lay in knowing the ropes, and in sensing how far one could go.' Charles the Bald knew the ropes. On the lands of the church of Laon he confided so many vassals to the bishop that the lands of the see were hardly adequate to support them and additional royal grants had to be promised.[21] Given the loyalty and the effective generalship of the bishop in question, Charles had nothing to lose by having his vassals become the bishop's: service to church and realm were then perfectly congruent. Moreover, those vassals persisted in regarding the king as the real source of their benefices, appealing to him against the bishop when the latter tried to evict them. But in that case it was not the king or his men but the bishop himself who could be depicted as despoiling church property, and at the same time betraying his king.[22]

Continuing effective royal disposition of the lands of churches (whatever theory might say) could in fact work to the benefit of those churches as corporate institutions. Individual bishops or abbots sometimes presided over the despoiling of their own churches' lands.[23] In such circumstances royal protection could mean what it said. It was to protect the abbey's lands against abbots who might 'make grants to laymen more inordinately than was fitting' that the monks of Fleury sought the king's help.[24] Charles dispatched four *missi* to establish the true extent of the abbey lands, and in a diploma recording the findings of the inquiry he commanded '. . . that no future abbot . . . should presume to subtract to any degree from the named manors, but from them should both strenuously perform our [military] service . . . and take care to provide adequately for the monks', whom Charles naturally expected to pray for himself, his family and the stability of the realm.[25] Charles' candour is refreshing: in his view the

[21] Hincmar of Laon, *PL* 124 (1879) col 1029.

[22] *PL* 126 (1879) cols 495, 583, Mansi 16, cols 649–50. See Lesne, *Propriété,* 2, i, pp 278 *seq*; [J.] Devisse, *Hincmar,* [*Archevêque de Reims 845–882*], 3 vols (Geneva 1975–6) 2, pp 738–85, esp p 775, n 402, where it becomes clear that the central issue is not legal but political.

[23] Lesne, *L'Origine des Menses dans le temporel des églises et des monastères de France au IXe siecle* (Lille 1910) pp 63 *seq*; but the comments on pp 59–60 need modifying in the light of [F.] Felten, 'Laienäbte [in der Karolingerzeit'], *Mönchtum, Episkopat und Adel zur Gründungszeit des Klosters Reichenau,* ed A. Borst (Sigmaringen 1974) pp 397–431.

[24] Tessier, 1, no 177, pp 465–9 at 467: '. . . propter rerum diminutionem quas praeteriti praelati ejusdem monasterii inordinatius quam decuit saecularibus attribuerunt. . . .'

[25] *Ibid* p 468: '. . . ut nullus abbas futurus de eodem momasterio eligendus secundum nostram indulgentiam et sanctorum episcoporum privilegium de nominatis villis vel locis aliquid diminuere praesumat, sed de ipsis et nostrum servitium strenue peragat,

interests of *servitium nostrum* and of the monastic community went hand in hand, and both had to be defended against the arbitrary action of self-interested abbots. Interestingly, the passage referring to secularisations of Fleury lands by abbots (*praelati*) caused two respectable nineteenth-century editors[26] to treat this diploma as 'suspicious': abbots, they declared, did not do that sort of thing.

Charles the Bald exercised a special control over the lands of royal abbeys, especially in Neustria. Like his immediate predecessors, he could grant abbacies, with their appurtenant vast estates, to able clerics who made their careers in the royal service.[27] More often than those predecessors, Charles sometimes granted abbacies to laymen.[28] The disposition of St. Martin's at Tours, for instance, successively to well-connected clerics and powerful laymen, played a key part in the king's policy in western Neustria.[29] Lay abbacies tended to lead to dismemberment of monastic holdings, they were uncanonical and aroused episcopal protest;[30] but they continued to provide Charles with a useful fund of lands for distribution. Alternatively, he could keep royal abbeys for himself or for members of his own family, in which case royal agents ran the monastic estates directly. Abbey lands became, in other words, an extension of the royal domain. Thus in 864 Charles commanded his counts 'that the manors of our royal domain and also the manors of the monasteries which we hold conceded and granted to our wife and our sons and daughters, and which are under the royal immunity, shall maintain their existence within the counties and be preserved intact with due respect paid [to their

---

adjunctis vassallorum annuis donis et aedificiis monasterii et munitione, consueto adjutorio, et ipsis servis Dei in eodem loco habitantibus congrua stipendia ministrare studeat' and a few lines above: '. . . quatenus et praesentes et secuturi ejusdem loci monachi absque ulla penuria stipendiorum valerent Domnino libere militare, et delectaret eos pro nobis et stabilitate regni nostri uxorisque ac prolis Dominum exorare'. The military service owed from monastic lands and by abbots in person is discussed by [F.] Prinz, *Klerus und Krieg* (Stuttgart 1971) pp 105 *seq*, 120–2.

[26] M. Prou and A. Vidier, cited by Tessier, 1, p 466.

[27] [K.] Voigt, [*Die Karolingische*] *Klosterpolitik* [*und der Niedergang des westfränkischen Königtums*] (Stuttgart 1917); Lesne, *Propriété*, 2, ii, bks 1 and 2; Ewig, 'Descriptio Franciae', *Karl der Grosse*, ed W. Braunfels, 4 vols (Düsseldorf 1965–8) 1, pp 160 *seq*.

[28] This development and its significance have been ably demonstrated by Felten, 'Laienäbte', esp 408 *seq*, 421 *seq*.

[29] J. Boussard, 'Les destinées de la Neustrie du IXe au XIe siècle', *Cahiers de Civilisation Medievale* 11 (Poitiers 1968) pp 15 *seq*.

[30] See Hincmar's comments in *Ann* [*ales*] *Bert* [*iniani*], *sa* 866, ed F. Grat, J. Vielliard and S. Clemencet (Paris 1964) pp 126; 131; 132 (here the culprit is Charles himself).

special status].'[31] In 867 Charles himself assumed the abbacy of St. Denis, consigning its economic management to provost, dean and treasurer, and the organisation of its military service (*cura militiae*) to a *maior domus*.[32] The monks themselves seem to have collaborated willingly in these arrangements:[33] after all they stood to benefit from the king's attention. This was a case of mutual advantage. Hence the lack of any clerical criticism of Charles' action.

Of further significance was the use to which Charles put his *Klosterpolitik* in providing for two of his four sons who reached maturity.[34] It may seem only a short step from setting up your daughters as abbesses, as Charles' predecessors had done, to making oblates and in due course abbots of your legitimate sons. But this latter, Charles's innovation,[35] had large political implications. It enabled Charles to break with the Frankish royal tradition, so assiduously followed by Charlemagne and Louis the Pious and continued also by east Frankish kings down to the 880s, of partitioning the realm between all of a king's legitimate sons. No doubt the spur was shortage of sub-kingdoms: Charles only had two.[36] But the availability of royal monasteries provided an alternative to dismembering the fisc, or more dangerously, disinheriting his younger sons. Like appanages, rich abbeys might with luck keep princes happy, and unlike appanages, they did not carry the risk of heritability, for Charles's sons were properly professed monks. From the king's standpoint, it was also potentially very useful to have such important

[31] *MGH Cap* 2, ed A. Boretius and V. Krause (Hanover 1897) no 272 (edict of Pîtres) cap 5, p 313: 'Volumus et expresse comitibus nostris mandamus, ut villae nostrae indominicatae, sed et villae de monasteriis, quae et coniugi nostrae et filiis ac filiabus nostris concessa atque donata habemus, quaeque sub immunitate consistunt, cum salvamento et debita reverentia in comitatibus illorum consistant'.

[32] *Ann Bert sa,* pp 134–5. See further Voigt, *Klosterpolitik,* pp 87 *seq.*

[33] Tessier, 2, no 379, pp 347–50 (an original), where, p 350, Charles calls himself abbot *fratrum electione.* On royal abbacies, see Lesne, *Propriété,* 2, ii, pp 172–84.

[34] For the abbacies held by Lothar (St Germain at Auxerre and perhaps St Jean at Réome) and Carloman (St Amand, St Riquier, Lobbes, St Médard at Soissons and St Arnulf at Metz) see Voigt, *Klosterpolitik,* pp 38 *seq.* Two younger boys may also have been destined for the church: sent for education to St Amand, they died there in 865 or 866. See *MGH Poet* 3, ed L. Traube (Berlin 1896) pp 677–8. For this and other dealings of Charles the Bald with St Amand, see now the important forthcoming article of Rosamond McKitterick in *EHR* (1979). I am very grateful to her for letting me see this in advance of publication.

[35] I had thought this point hitherto neglected until I found that Lesne, as usual, had already seen it: *Propriété,* 2, ii, pp 167–8.

[36] See Boussard, 'Neustrie'; and W. Kienast, *Studien über die französischen Volksstämme des Frühmittelalters* (Stuttgart 1968).

abbeys as those of St. Medard (Soissons), St. Amand, St. Riquier, and St. Germain (Auxerre) firmly in filial hands. The system worked well until 870 when the abbot of St. Medard, having seen one of his two elder brothers die and his father then acquire part of Lotharingia, made a desperate bid for a realm of his own and was ruthlessly suppressed.[37] But Charles had set a precedent: later monarchs from the Ottonians onwards would dispose of surplus princes by dedicating them to the service of God—a strategy which of course presupposed effective (if indirect) control of churches and their lands.

I turn now to Charles's dealings with the church in the towns: what specifically urban services could the church offer? Despite its rural bases, Frankish royal power had always had important links with *civitates*.[38] But relations that had been quite informal and personalised under the Merovingians became rather less so under the Carolingians. Not that churchmen now occupied permanent posts in royal government, though they did act very frequently on special commissions, for example as *missi dominici* sitting alongside counts in public courts held in *civitates*.[39] But in general terms, it was because permanent, thus urban, central places came to play a more conspicuous part in ninth-century administration that more, and more varied, governmental activity was required of churchmen, especially bishops.[40] On the supply side, the workings of the Carolingian renaissance produced more experts capable of drafting complex legislative documents or compiling estate surveys. On the demand side, growing defence problems created new needs. As an initial response individual churchmen, like the bishops of Orleans and Chartres, led local resistance to the Vikings from their *civitates*.[41] When Charles implemented something like a defence policy for the realm (at any rate those regions worst affected) he looked to the church not merely to contribute but to bear the main burden. Fortification was largely an urban task, in that whole cities or monasteries were enclosed in walls.[42] Danegeld, the alternative method

[37] *Ann Bert sa* 870, 871, 873, pp 178–9, 194.

[38] F. Prinz, 'Die bischöfliche Stadtherrschaft im Frankenreich vom 5. bis zum 7. Jht', *HZ* 217 (1974) pp 1–35; see further my comments in *SCH Subsidia* 1 (1978).

[39] For example *MGH Cap* 2, no 261, p 278.

[40] F. Ganshof, *The Carolingians and the Frankish Monarchy* (London 1971) pp 206–7; W. Ullmann, 'Public welfare and social legislation in the early medieval councils', *SCH* 7 (1971) pp 1–39.

[41] *Ann Bert sa* 854, p 69. See also Prinz, *Klerus und Krieg*, pp 124 *seq.*

[42] F. Vercauteren, 'Comment s'est-on défendu, au IXe siècle, dans l'empire franc, contre les invasions normandes?', *Annales du XXXe Congres de la Fédération archéologique et*

of defence, meant urban and episcopal organisation.[43] Bishops had to contribute from their own treasuries; they also had to collect the sums due from other ecclesiastical contributors throughout their dioceses. Like the Merovingians' tax-system, that of Charles the Bald was run in and from *civitates*—which explains why the famous Danegeld edict of 877, after specifying the central role of bishops, ended by requiring contributions also from 'traders and people living in *civitates* . . . in proportion to their resources'.[44]

Since Lot showed that the church was effectively the sole bearer of this financial burden, we have learnt more about the sources of the church's wealth in the ninth century.[45] It is not just a matter of dethesaurisation. When bishops like those of Rheims and Orleans, or the monks of St. Riquier and St. Bertin, could undertake large and often long-term building programmes, when successive bishops of Auxerre could disburse quantities of silver and cash for the adornment of every parish church in the diocese,[46] it looks as if urban ecclesiastical centres, episcopal and monastic, were able to dispose of increasing cash incomes deriving not only from increased revenues from vast, well-managed estates, but also from the growth of the markets they controlled. It is in this context of ninth-century economic growth—not universal, by any means, but concentrated precisely in those centres with which I am now concerned—that we can look at Charles the Bald's new exploitation of what was for him surely the most important of the church's urban services: hospitality. Charles's itinerary, compared with those of his predecessors, shows a striking increase in the frequency of stays at *civitates*.[47] Only rarely was an ancient royal palace available: Charles restored the one

historique de Belgique (Brussels 1936) pp 117–32; Hubert, 'Évolution', pp 550–7, with figs 15, 16.

[43] F. Lot, 'Les tributs aux Normands et l'Église de France au IXe siècle', *BEC* 85 (1924) pp 58–78.

[44] *MGH Capit* 2, no 280, p 354.

[45] The fundamental work is Lesne, *Propriété*, esp vols 2 (1936) and 6 (1943). See further, works cited above p 104 n 3; and Duby, *Rural Economy and Country Life in the Medieval West*, trans C. Postan (London 1968).

[46] Rheims: *MGH SS* 13, ed G. Waitz (Hanover 1881) pp 478–9; Orleans: *MGH SS* 15, ed W. Wattenbach, 2 parts (Hanover 1887/8) p 497; St Riquier: Hariulf, *Chronicon Centulense*, ed F. Lot (Paris 1894) pp 53–4; St Bertin: *Cartulaire de l'abbaye de St Bertin*, ed B. Guerard (Paris 1841) p 109, and *MGH SS* 15, pp 513–44; Auxerre: *MGH SS* 13, pp 396–7. See also Lesne, *Propriété*, 3, pp. 91 *seq*; 6, pp 425 *seq*.

[47] [C.-R.] Brühl, *Fodrum*, [*Gistum, Servitium Regis*] (Cologne 1968) pp 39 *seq*. It would be misleading to neglect the continuing preponderance of Charles's stays on royal manors, though even here the overwhelming preference for two of them, Quiersy

at Senlis *c*860.[48] Early in his reign, he had got into the habit of visiting himself and his court on the bishop's own residence, the *episcopium*. Later Charles more often chose to say in the palaces built within royal or episcopal monasteries and what needs stressing here is the urban, or more precisely sub-urban, character of these monasteries: St. Denis near Paris, St. Medard at Soissons, St. Martin at Tours, St. Sernin at Toulouse, St. Germain at Auxerre, St. Remi at Rheims, St. Mesmin at Orleans.[49] How is this new royal practice to be explained? Brühl who first drew attention to it explained it mainly in terms of dwindling royal land resources[50]—in particular of the famous 'squandering of the fisc' for which every scholar who has read his Dhondt (and every student his Barraclough) knows Charles the Bald was responsible.[51] Given political pressures which forced him to travel rapidly and continuously about his realm moving far more frequently than any previous or later Carolingian (he seldom spent more than a few weeks, or even days, in one place), Charles found his remaining fisc lands inadequate to sustain his court. Instead the burden had to be imposed on a reluctant church. Of course, all this is partly true, though I think the alleged squandering of the fisc by Charles has been much exaggerated.[52] But I would suggest a positive as well as a negative reason for his changed choice of residence. Why could he not have solved his accommodation problem by staying frequently on rural episcopal or monastic manors (something he in fact did, but rarely)?[53] One obvious reason for choosing urban ecclesiastical sites was veneration for the saints who rested there. But Charles's motivation for visiting a place, as expressed in his own charters, was

---

and Compiègne, is strikingly suggestive of new possibilities for the concentration of supplies. But what concerns me here is the nonetheless notable increase in the urban component in Charles's itinerary.

[48] Brühl, 'Königspfalz [und Bischofsstadt]', *Rheinische Vierteljahrsblätter* 23 (Bonn 1958) pp 206–7.

[49] On all these monasteries, the last two controlled respectively by the bishops of Rheims and Orleans, see Brühl, 'Königspfalz'. There is little additional information, for present purposes, to be found in Brühl's recent work, *Palatium und Civitas* 1 (Cologne 1975).

[50] 'Königspfalz', pp 269–74; *Fodrum*, pp 50–2.

[51] J. Dhondt, *Études sur la naissance des principautés territoriales en France IXe–Xe siècle* (Bruges 1948), pp 264–6, 272–4; G. Barraclough, *The Crucible of Europe* (London 1976) pp 88–9.

[52] I hope to defend this view at length elsewhere.

[53] For example *Ann Bert sa* 846, p 52, Épernay, a manor of the church of Rheims restored in 845, Tessier, 1, no 75; Hincmar, *MGH Epp* 8, i, ed E. Perels (Berlin 1939) p 72, Neauphles, a manor of the church of Rouen.

surprisingly pragmatic: he might come 'for the sake of prayer (*orationis causa*)' but he might equally well come 'to make arrangements for other affairs of our realm'.[54] Another likely reason for staying in *civitates* was the partial survival of the Roman road system that linked them.[55] But the main reason surely was that the *civitates* and monastic urban centres were becoming wealthier, and the churches which could tap that wealth by controlling markets were therefore in a good position to sustain the new royal demands—sustain, and perhaps also to benefit from them. The bishops at the synod of Meaux-Paris in 845 registered a famous complaint which is conventionally cited to show their rooted opposition to Charles's new impositions. This is what the bishops said:

> It should be suggested to [the king] that . . . he should enter the episopal residence . . . in a respectful manner whenever he may stay in a *civitas* to claim his due hospitality, and should not allow women in . . . Also the immunities granted by previous emperors and kings prohibit excessively long visits from kings, their magnates and their secular followings . . . [From now on] when your journeying brings you to *civitates*, let your majesty give orders that the houses within a *civitas* be free from the exactions of plunderers; because [what is happening now is that] all who used to bring their goods to the *civitates*, both to keep them in safe storage and to sell them more peacefully there, are refraining from doing so, existing immunities are being infringed, and the citizens are being . . . not just oppressed but plundered by the visitors [that is, the king's entourage] and prevented from selling their goods . . .[56]

[54] Tessier, 1, no 18, p 44 (for Corbie); 2, no 240, pp 43, 44 (St Martin, Tours). References to *orationis causa* belong only to the early part of the reign. See Brühl, *Fodrum,* pp 45–6, 104.

[55] Brühl, *Fodrum,* pp 62 *seq*. For the realm of Charles the Bald, this topic is in need of further study.

[56] *MGH Capit* 2, caps 26, 27, p 405: 'Suggerendum est . . . regiae dignitati, ut episcopium . . . reverenter introeat, et . . . quando orationis et debitae susceptionis gratia in transitu convenienti civitatem ingressus fuerit, habitaculis episcopalibus reverenter inhabitet, et non diversoria feminarum magnificentia sua et religio venerabilis ibidem fieri permittat. . . . Sed et inmunitates praecedentium imperatorum ac regum ab huiusmodi longiori et diuturna conversatione et commoratione regum et quorumcumque potentium ac secularium personarum in episcopio prohibent. . . . Vestra studebit magnitudo obnixius observare, ut, quando transitus vester iuxta civitates acciderit, inmunes et liberas vestra dominatio iubeat a depraedationum exactionibus fieri mansiones intra civitatem, quia omnes, qui sua ad civitates deferebant, ut et salva quaeque ibi haberent et illa plus pacifice venderent, iam et hoc refugiunt et pristinae inmunitates et confir-

This protest is interesting because it is equivocal. The complaint is not about royal visits as such: had the 'citizens' and the suppliers of the urban market been able to rent out lodgings and sell their wares, instead of having them appropriated, would not everyone have been happy? We know that Charles subsequently imposed many times upon ecclesiastical hospitality; but there is a notable absence of subsequent complaints.[57] Rheims was visited more often than any other *civitas*, but there is no sign at all that it was ruined[58]—rather its flourishing scriptoria and new buildings indicate the contrary. When Charles visited Auxerre in September 861, his court occupied all the available accommodation in and around the *civitas*.[59] But no clerical complaint is recorded: perhaps women were kept out of the churchmen's way. Is it possible that Charles's urban subjects, both ecclesiastical governors and the citizens for whom they were responsible, had begun to appreciate the benefits of increased consumer demand? Charles himself, after all, was highly sensitive to commercial considerations. He husbanded his revenues from tolls;[60] and in the enormous capitulary of 864 he provided for a sophisticated coinage reform, including a *renovatio monetae*, and for a firm royal control of mints (all but one of them in *civitates*).[61] Charles granted land to churches surprisingly rarely (surprisingly, that is, if you think of him an inveterate fisc-squanderer) but he did have other valuable things to give: to Corbie, a bridge and rights to tolls thereon;[62] to the bishop of Paris, the Grand Pont with its mills, and later, the right to dispose of some newly-built houses;[63] to the monks of St. Denis control of a weekly market at

---

mationes infringuntur, dum et cives ab hospitibus opprimuntur et ab his, a quibus non solum opprimuntur, verum et diripiuntur, sua non solum vendere prohibentur, sed et propter direptionem post eos cum gemitu clamare coguntur'.

[57] The ravaging of the countryside by the king's troops was occasionally complained of, but is hardly relevant in the present context.

[58] Hincmar's only complaints about royal demands for hospitality occur in a thoroughly disingenuous letter to pope Hadrian II, *PL* 126, col 183, in which Hincmar affects to exculpate himself from complicity in Charles's invasion of Lotharingia! Even M. Devisse, *Hincmar*, 1, p 458, n 596, is moved to observe: 'la sincérité de l'argumentation, cette fois, n'est pas éclatante'. In the very same letter, Hincmar affirms the king's rights to hospitality at bishops' expense.

[59] Lupus of Ferrières, *ep* 115, *Correspondance*, ed L. Levillain, 2 vols (Paris 1935) 2, p 162.

[60] Ganshof, 'A propos de tonlieu à l'époque carolingienne', in *SS Spol* 6, ii (1959) pp 485–508 at 496–7.

[61] *MGH Capit* 2, no 273, pp 310–32, at 314–20 (caps 8–24). See M. van Rey, 'Die Münzprägung Karls des Kahlen', *Die Stadt in der europäischen Geschichte. Festschrift E. Ennen,* ed W. Besch and others (Bonn 1972) pp 153–84.

[62] Tessier, 1, no 18, pp 42–4.

[63] Tessier, 1, no 186, pp 491–2; 2, no 391, pp 374–5.

Cormeilles;[64] to the bishop of Châlons-sur-Marne a mint and (carefully specified) the profits thereof.[65] It seems that from about 860 onwards, Charles was trying to establish regalian rights over the foundation of markets as well as over the profits of trade.[66] Certainly he knew how to invest in, as well as to exploit, the urban wealth of churches.

So far I have surveyed in a general way Charles the Bald's use of ecclesiastical resources first in the countryside, then in towns. Now I want briefly to bring these strands together by looking at royal policy in action at a particular place and time: Auxerre and Burgundy in 858–9. This was the great crisis-point of Charles's reign, when his realm was invaded by his half-brother Louis the German and most of the aristocracy deserted him. So did the archbisop of Sens, whose treachery represented a major military loss for Charles. But fortunately for him, the rest of the episcopate stayed loyal and explained why, in terms both of principle and of self-interest, in the famous Quiersy letter addressed to Louis the German. That the church 'saved Charles's kingdom' in this sense is well-known.[67] Less well-known is the church's contribution to Charles's political come-back. In late September 858, hearing of Louis' long-threatened invasion, Charles made for Burgundy.[68] To the monk Heiric writing a generation later, it was clear that Charles came to Auxerre 'having lost all hope of earthly help' to commit his cause to God and St. Germain.[69] No doubt. But Auxerre had other attractions too. Charles had two powerful friends there: the bishop, Abbo, who had close connexions with the court and whose brother and uncle had been bishops of Auxerre before him, and the abbot of St. Germain's, Charles's cousin Hugh who already held this office in 853.[70] The church in Auxerre was wealthy, whether we measure that by the silver it could distribute, the marble it could buy or the school it could support.[71] Charles's political influence

[64] Tessier, 2, no 323, pp 210–12.

[65] Tessier, 2, no 277, pp 120–1.

[66] T. Endemann, *Markturkunden und Markt in Frankreich und Burgund vom 9. bis 11 Jhdt.* (Constance 1964) pp 27–34; 40–8; 98 *seq;* 210–11.

[67] On all this see [J.] Calmette, [*La*] *Diplomatie* [*carolingienne*] (Paris 1901, repr 1977) pp 34 *seq,* 51 *seq.*

[68] *Ann Bert sa* 858, pp 78–9.

[69] *MGH SS* 13, pp 403–4.

[70] Abbo: *MGH SS* 13, p 398, and Lupus, *Correspondance,* 2, nos 95, 96, pp 108–115; Hugh: Calmette, *Diplomatie,* pp 42, 60.

[71] *MGH SS* 13, pp 396–8, 403–4; E. Jeauneau, 'Les écoles de Laon et d'Auxerre au IXe siècle', *SS Spol* 19 (1972) pp 495–522.

there, attested by episcopal and abbatial appointments before 858, was further shown when his cousin Conrad became count in that year.[72] It was from Auxerre, after staying in the palace he himself had probably had built in the precincts of St. Germain's,[73] that Charles set out soon after 9 January 859, to mobilise resistance to the invaders in Burgundy. With the recently-appointed young bishop of Laon at his side, Charles rallied his vassals from church lands in the region, and by the end of January had marshalled enough troops to cause the invader's support to wane and Louis himself to withdraw.[74] There are frustrating gaps in our information but the outlines of the picture are clear. When Charles to survive had to use every instrument at his disposal, from family connexions to saintly intercession, what really tipped the scales was his ability to exploit the carefully-husbanded resources of the church in town and countryside. A last point worth noting is that Burgundy was a conspicuous area of economic activity in the ninth century and later, activity of which Charles himself was among the early sponsors.[75]

My conclusion is two-fold. First, I am sure Émile Lesne was right to focus on ecclesiastical property as a crucial determinant of the relations between the king and the church in ninth-century Francia. Lesne's approach was criticised fairly recently on the grounds that it was 'too narrowly material' and took insufficient account of 'changes in the law' during the early Carolingian period.[76] I cannot share such reservations; and if I must plead guilty to narrowness, I can only find solace in the company of a materialist monseigneur. Of course Wallace-Hadrill is right to stress how much books (produced in

[72] L. Auzias, *L'Aquitaine carolingienne* (Paris 1937) p 295, n 58 (where, however, the grant of the abbacy of St Germain to Hugh is misdated). See also Calmette, *Diplomatie,* pp 42, 58 (but the reference to Heiric, *MGH SS* 13, pp 401–2, seems misplaced: Heiric praises the generosity to St Germain of Conrad senior, father of the man made count in 858 – which only goes to show the longstanding Welf connexion with Auxerre).

[73] Brühl, 'Königspfalz', pp 171–2.

[74] *MGH Epp* 8, no 126 p 52; *Ann Bert sa* 859, p 80. See Calmette, *Diplomatie,* pp 58–9.

[75] The map at the end of Endemann, *Markturkunden,* is suggestive. For evidence of Charles's interest in the region, see Tessier 2, no 326, pp 218–23; no 354, pp 287–8; no 365, pp 315–17; no 378, pp 342–7. See also Latouche, *Birth,* p 221, and Duby, *Early Growth,* pp 104–5. No doubt an influx of refugees had an effect on economic growth in Burgundy. But it would be premature to claim a direct connexion between that growth and relative freedom from Viking raids. Notwithstanding the arguments of Wallace-Hadrill, 'The Vikings in Francia', Stenton Lecture for 1974 (University of Reading 1975) pp 13–18, the question of the Vikings' impact on economic developments in western and, especially, northern Francia seems to me still open.

[76] Goffart, *Forgeries,* p 6.

ecclesiastical centres) meant to Charles the Bald;[77] but I think that land and money, bed and breakfast meant even more.[78] It is probably true that Charles had little alternative to exploiting the church. But that does not mean that such exploitation was bad policy. When Wallace-Hadrill points out that for the monks of St. Calais in dispute with the bishop of Le Mans, 'the only escape' from episcopal domination was 'into the arms of the king',[79] he has put his finger on the vulnerability of the church. The need of churches for royal protection (*tuitio*) was greater, in the end, than the king's for ecclesiastical support (*suffragium*)—which makes me unable to follow Wallace-Hadrill when he claims that Charles's 'unprecedented and unwelcome reliance on bishops and abbots for hospitality and the upkeep of his court was bound in the long run to play into their hands'.[80]

This brings me to my second conclusion: that it is false to see Charles's exploitation of the church as, in Brühl's word, *rücksichtslos*[81]—wanton, ill-considered—and ultimately self-defeating, a view which seems currently to be widely shared. It was not Charles, after all, who created the vulnerability of the church. Ecclesiastical property-holding was always, and inevitably, at the mercy of lay politics. I have tried to show that Charles, far from ruining the churches' material base, generally sought to strengthen it when he could; and was able to do so, and exploit it at the same time, because he worked within an economy which, however tentatively and patchily, was showing the first signs of expansion. The analogy I would like to evoke is not that of a cake which, though its slices may vary, has fixed limits of total size, but that of a healthy cow which you can not only milk without killing, but whose production you can greatly increase if you improve its feed. Charles the Bald was no cynic: he seriously meant to protect the church, and on the whole contemporaries believed that he did so.

[77] Wallace-Hadrill, 'A Carolingian Renaissance Prince: the Emperor Charles the Bald', Sixtieth Raleigh Lecture on History, given at the British Academy, 18 May 1978. There is much valuable information on books written for Charles the Bald in the forthcoming article by McKitterick cited above n 34.

[78] Compare the presentation of the Ottonians by J. Gillingham, *The Kingdom of Germany in the High Middle Ages*, Historical Association (London 1973). Brühl, 'Königspfalz', p 274, n 703, contrasts Charles's 'system' with that of the Ottonians, whereas I am more impressed by the similarities.

[79] Wallace-Hadrill, *Kingship*, p 126: by implication, royal arms are preferable to aristocratic ones.

[80] *Ibid* p 127.

[81] Brühl, *Fodrum*, p 52.

Hincmar and others held up hard standards for the king to meet. They obeyed him because Charles, despite his many problems, did not fall so far short of the model *minister Dei*. In the end, I hope that my view of the relation of political practice to clerical ideology is not incompatible with the views of Wallace-Hadrill and Ullman; for if, as Wood recently wrote,[82] they move in the same world, it is surely one roomy enough to contain political, social and economic historians too.

University of London
Kings College

[82] *Early Medieval Kingship* (University of Leeds 1978). If there is currently something of a 'Carolingian Renaissance' amongst younger British medievalists, this is largely due to the influence, direct and indirect, of these two scholars.

THE CHURCH IN ANGLO-SAXON TOWNS

by J. CAMPBELL

TO BEGIN, as is natural, by considering the *sedes episcopales* of early England is to realise how little we know of its significant places—even to use the word 'town' is to beg a question. It is certain that some *sedes* were established at major centres of authority. Bede used *metropolis* to describe London and Canterbury and by that he meant the capital of a kingdom.[1] Gregory the Great was probably wise in selecting London as the seat of an archbishop, an intention in which he seems to have persisted even after he was informed of English conditions.[2] Not only was it the capital of a kingdom but it had geographical advantages which Canterbury could not rival. Even though Canterbury was established as the archbishops' *sedes* there are indications that already from the seventh century they were using London as a meeting place, and perhaps as a dwelling place, at least on occasion.[3] No major council of the early English church was held at or near Canterbury.[4] York's position in the north probably resembled that of London in the south. Our view of it has been transformed by Phillips's excavations, which have shown that the great headquarters building of the legionary fortress was maintained and used, at least in part, until well after the conversion period.[5] This discovery is a reminder of how much *Romanitas* may have remained and fits with what used to seem odd, that according to Bede Paulinus was able to start building a fine stone church at York (as also

[1] [Ed C. Plummer,] *Opera Historica*, 2 vols (Oxford 1896) 1 pp 46, 85.

[2] D. Whitelock, *Some Anglo-Saxon Bishops of London* (London 1974) p 4 n 3.

[3] *Ibid* p 9 n 4 for archbishops of Canterbury consecrating bishops at London in 676 and 838–9 and for ninth-century councils there. Some eighth century councils were held at Chelsea, nearby. Boniface thought Augustine had held a synod at London, *Die Briefe des Heiligen Bonifatius und Lullus*, ed M. Tangl (Berlin 1955) p 84. However suspect Eddius's account of Theodore's summoning Wilfrid and Eorconweald to him it is significant that it is to London he says they were summoned, *Eddius* [*Stephanus. Het Leven van Sint Wilfrid*, ed H. Moonen] ('S-Hertogenbosch 1946) cap 43 p 148.

[4] Unless some unidentified meeting place or places was in that area.

[5] This derives from a paper read by Mr Phillips to an Anglo-German archaeological colloquium at York in September 1977.

at Lincoln), which implies he found masons.[6] Other excavations, those of Biddle, have done much to illuminate one further *sedes*, Winchester, which appears to have survived as a centre of authority, but not of population (though the presence of something in the nature of a palace there in the early period remains to be demonstrated).[7] It is likely that others of the fifteen *sedes* of before 900 which have been definitely located were similarly centres of authority for wide areas. Worcester was described in the eighth century as the *metropolis* of the *Hwicce*;[8] such a place as Leicester may have had the same kind of significance.

But the location of *sedes* was not necessarily at major centres with a Roman past. Bede gives a clue to why this was so when he complains that kings have given so much land away that *non facile locus vacans ubi sedes episcopalis nova fieri debeat inveniri valeat.*[9] It seems that to him a *sedes episcopalis* meant something like an estate sufficient to sustain a bishop. This agrees with Eddius's account of how Lichfield came to be the *sedes* of the Mercian bishopric in 669. It was, he said, a *locus* which Wulfhere had given to Wilfrid to be a *sedes* for himself or someone else and which Wilfrid gave to Chad.[10] What made Lichfield suitable may be guessed from Domesday Book which shows it as the centre of a vast multiple estate.[11] Similarly with Selsey, which was a royal vill to which eighty seven hides were attached.[12] Such *sedes* as Sherborne and Hexham were not improbably of the same type.

Recent research has emphasised the importance in early England not so much of towns as of centres of authority for units of government of the 'small shire' or lathe type or for multiple estates.[13] It is becoming increasingly clear that all or most of England had a network of such places. They were not towns but significant places. Their relationship to the church is important; for it was at such places that minsters tended to be built. For example Miss Deanesly showed the relationship

[6] *Opera Historica* 1 pp 114, 117. The Lincoln church is now thought to have been discovered, *The Times* (26 July 1978) pp 1, 2.

[7] M. Biddle, '*Felix Urbs Winthonia*', *Tenth Century Studies*, [ed D. Parsons] (London/Chichester 1975) pp 125–7.

[8] *CS* 1 no 166.

[9] *Opera Historica* 1 p 413 (Letter to Egbert).

[10] Eddius cap 15 p 92.

[11] *VCH Staffordshire* 4 pp 8–10 (though the estate may have been enlarged after the eighth century).

[12] Eddius cap 41 p 144.

[13] G. R. J. Jones, 'Multiple Estates and Early Settlement', *Medieval Settlement, Continuity and Change*, ed P. H. Sawyer (London 1976) pp 15–40; G. W. S. Barrow, *The Kingdom of the Scots* (London 1973) pp 7–27.

between the minsters and the lathes of early Kent, and a relationship with governmental arrangements (sometimes very old) is apparent in the minster system as it appears in partial decline in Domesday Book.[14] Bede mentions the construction of a major church at a local centre of royal authority as early as the time of Edwin when at his *villa regia* of Campodonum the king built a *basilica*.[15] The late ninth-century translator of Bede rendered his description of Aidan's journeyings *per cuncta et urbana et rustica loca* as *þurh mynsterstowe ge þurh folcstowe*.[16] He is indicating the distinction which seemed important to him, not so much one between town and country, as between important local centres of the kind where minsters were built and ordinary places. His distinction is important in the history of the early church in England. It could not be an urban church but, as it developed under the aegis of kings, so its pattern of authority echoed theirs and where the *villa regis*, the royal *tun*, was, there, more often than not, the minster was; and there often enough, in later centuries a real town grew up.

It is a question how far in the early period the church helped to create towns. It may have been that in a sense some of the communities most resembling towns were major monasteries. When Ceolfrith left Monkwearmouth-Jarrow in 716 there were over six hundred *milites Christi* there apart from those he took with him.[17] For many centuries a population of three hundred would have been enough for a small town and no secular settlement in the early period can be proved to have been so populous (though doubtless at least a handful were so). A monastery such as Whitby, with its numerous buildings, its crafts and its maritime contacts must have been considerably more like a town than were most places.[18]

An important meeting-place for the urban and the ecclesiastical historian is the graveside of the great. The importance attached to burial in particular places throughout the Anglo-Saxon period enables us both to identify significant centres and to see means whereby piety

[14] M. Deanesly, 'Early English and Gallic Minsters', *TRHS* 4 ser 23 (1941) pp 15–40; [W.] Page ['Some Remarks on the Churches of the Domesday Survey'], *Archaeologia* 66 (London 1914–5) pp 61–102; [F.] Barlow, [*The English Church 1000–1066*] (London 1966) p 184.

[15] *Opera Historica* 1 p 115.

[16] *The Old English Version of Bede's Ecclesiastical History*, ed T. Miller, pt 1, *EETS* 95 (1895) p 161.

[17] *Opera Historica* 1 pp 400–1 (anonymous life of Ceolfrith).

[18] R. J. Cramp, 'Monastic Sites', *The Archaeology of Anglo-Saxon England*, [ed D. M. Wilson] (London 1976) pp 223–9, 453–7, 459–62.

could attract population to them. The Anglo-Saxon Chronicle shows a steady interest in places of burial, and that bodies were often taken a long way. Thus after the fight between Cynewulf and Cyneheard in 757 the former was taken to Winchester for burial, the latter to Axminster.[19] In 871 the body of an ealdorman who was killed at Reading was transported to Derby to be buried.[20] The gilds of the late period provided for the transport of deceased members' bodies to their chosen burial places; at Abbotsbury there was a distance limit, sixty miles.[21] It was customary to make a substantial legacy to one's burial-place. With this often went provision for the poor. The earliest evidence is a grant by the ealdorman Oswulf to Christ Church, Canterbury, *c*810. He provides for 1,120 loaves to be distributed annually on the anniversary of his death 'as is done on the anniversaries of lords'.[22] About twenty years later a priest called Waher made similar provision for the anniversary of his death. One thousand two hundred poor men were to be fed, each was to be given bread with cheese or bacon and a penny.[23] Such practices continued in the later period. For example, in 1015 Athelstan provided for a hundred poor men to be fed at Ely on the anniversary of his death.[24] If, as is likely, there were many such benefactions a great religious centre must have had considerable power to attract population, perhaps especially the poor such as we find crowding round Oswald, or huddled at a monastery door.[25] The prestige of a sanctuary could attract the less deserving. Cuthbert feared that his burial at Lindisfarne would lead to *incursionem profugorum vel noxiorum.*[26]

Waher's provision for the distribution of pennies to twelve hundred men is an important indication of the early circulation of coin and of the extent to which the economy developed before 850. Much greater development took place in the next two centuries. It is strikingly demonstrated in the extensive growth of towns. By 1066 probably

[19] *Two of the Saxon Chronicles Parallel*, ed J. Earle and C. Plummer, 2 vols (Oxford 1899) I p 48.

[20] *The Chronicle of Aethelweard*, ed A. Campbell (London 1962) p 37.

[21] *Diplomatarium* [*Anglicum Aevi Saxonici*, ed B. Thorpe] (London 1865) pp 607, 611.

[22] *Select English Historical Documents of the Ninth and Tenth Centuries*, ed F. E. Harmer (Cambridge 1914) pp 1–2, 39–40; cheese or something of the sort was to go with the loaves.

[23] *CS* I no 402.

[24] D. Whitelock, *Anglo-Saxon Wills* (Cambridge 1930) no xx.

[25] Bede, *Opera Historica* I p 138; Aethelwulf, *De Abbatibus*, ed A. Campbell (Oxford 1967) p 38.

[26] *Two Lives of Saint Cuthbert*, ed B. Colgrave (Cambridge 1940) p 278.

about a tenth of the population lived in towns. The major provincial towns were of the same order of size as in the later middle ages. Urban manufactures flourished in an economy in which silver coin circulated abundantly. The last Anglo-Saxon centuries probably saw economic changes on a scale not paralleled till the eighteenth.[27]

The transformation of the church in the towns in the late Anglo-Saxon period was as notable as the economic changes which accompanied and influenced it. The impact on towns of reformed monasticism was various but often of a second order kind. At Winchester not only did the West Saxon kings create a real and prosperous town where previously there may have been only a centre of government, they also created a holy city within it, where the New Minster stood just beside the Old Minster, the one grandly built, the other grandly rebuilt, with a west work probably over a hundred feet high; immediately opposite stood a royal nunnery.[28] Canterbury remained what it had been, a church town, and one to which kings went but rarely. It must have depended very largely on the wealth of its two great monasteries; and by the end of the Anglo-Saxon period that was great indeed, together their landed incomes were of the order of a quarter of that of the crown.[29] Bury Saint Edmund's was by 1086 certainly a considerable, perhaps a major, town; a major addition had been made to it since 1065 by abbot Baldwin.[30] Winchester, Canterbury and Bury were extreme cases. Worcester and Gloucester were the only other towns of much note which had Benedictine abbeys at the Conquest. Some other abbeys, notably Saint Alban's had attempted to stimulate urban growth beside the abbey but without Bury's success.[31] The chief connection between urban growth and monastic reform was probably this, that reformed monasteries were very expensive. They required rich patronage. That it was available probably owed much to a prosperity in which towns played a large part. It may be significant that much of what Ethelwold

[27] M. Biddle, 'Towns', *The Archaeology of Anglo-Saxon England*, pp 120–41; H. R. Loyn, 'Towns in Late Anglo-Saxon England', *England before the Conquest: Studies in Primary Sources presented to Dorothy Whitelock*, ed P. Clemoes and K. Hughes (Cambridge 1971) pp 115–28; [J.] Campbell, 'Norwich', [*The Atlas of Historic Towns*, ed M. D. Lobel] 2 (London 1975) pp 5, 7–8; J. C. Russell, *British Medieval Population* (Albuquerque 1948) p 305.

[28] Biddle, '*Felix Urbs Winthonia*', *Tenth Century Studies* pp 127–38.

[29] Knowles, *MO* pp 702–3; F. Barlow, *Edward the Confessor* (London 1970) pp 153–4.

[30] [M. D.] Lobel, [*Bury St Edmunds*] (Oxford 1935) pp 4–13, 12.

[31] *VCH Hertfordshire* 4 p 67.

received seems not to have been land, but rather gold and silver with which he bought land.[32]

The important religious communities in most towns were not Benedictine monasteries, but minsters of secular priests. Though important, they are not well-documented. The surviving sources generally amount to a handful of enigmas, separated by large empty spaces. The evidence for Saint Frideswide's at Oxford is unusually rich: two charcoal burials (probably ninth century), a reference in an early eleventh-century tract, a charter of Ethelred II indicating fairly extensive land-holdings round Oxford, mention of the canons in Domesday and a cock-and-bull origin story from William of Malmesbury which may retain a faint residue of fact.[33] That is all, until Saint Frideswide's was made over to Augustinian canons under Henry I. Yet, as Stenton argued, the community may indeed have had a very long history and considerable importance; its tithe claims suggest a connection with the big royal manor at Headington nearby.[34] In considering the growth and development of Oxford in the tenth century it is impossible to tell whether or when Saint Frideswide's was a focus or on the contrary a backwater. More characteristic, because less well-evidenced, is Cirencester. A major and very ancient demesne centre, one would expect there to have been an important minster there. There is no mention of any such thing in any pre-Conquest source. Yet there was one; it has been found under the remains of the Norman church and was a hundred and seventy nine feet long.[35] Often our first reference to a minster comes in Domesday. It is, however, nearly demonstrable that minster communities could be omitted from the survey.[36] This makes Hill's argument that Saint Mary's, Lincoln, was a major minster with extensive rights in the late Saxon period the more plausible;[37] and imposes a certain caution in deducing too much from Domesday's failure to mention a minster

[32] *Liber Eliensis,* [ed E. O. Blake] *CSer,* 3 ser 92 (1962) pp 75, 80, 82, 84, 89, 91.

[33] F. M. Stenton, 'St Frideswide and her Times', *Oxoniensia* 1 (Oxford 1936) pp 103–12; T. G. Hassall, *Oxoniensia* 28 (1973) pp 270–4.

[34] The authenticity of the clause in the charter of 1004 relating to tithe is questioned: D. Whitelock, *EHD* 1 p 546.

[35] [H. M.] Taylor, *Anglo-Saxon Architecture,* 3 (Cambridge, 1978) p 751.

[36] Domesday Book does not mention canons at, for example, Great Paxton or Worksop but there is evidence for them somewhat later: C. A. R. Radford, 'Pre-Conquest Minster Churches', *Arch[aeological] J[ournal]* 130 (London 1973) p 133; C. Brown, 'Foundation Charter of Worksop Priory', *Thoroton Society* 9 (Nottingham 1905) p 85.

[37] [J. W. F.] Hill, *Medieval Lincoln* (Cambridge 1965) pp 64–73.

community at, for example, Norwich. As often in Anglo-Saxon history we know enough to realise there was more than we know.

Still, we do know that urban minsters were numerous. Some, as was probably the case with Saint Frideswide's, were old and antedated the town with which they were associated. Others were new. The most obvious example was the New Minster at Winchester, though there the canons were not allowed many generations in which to enjoy their comforts. Saint Oswald's, Gloucester, was probably founded early in the tenth century by Ethelred and Aethelflaed, who moved the body of Saint Oswald to it from Bardney.[38] It is not certain how far the burh building of Alfred and Edward was accompanied by the foundation of new minsters. In Ethelred II's reign the fortification and occupation of South Cadbury for no more than ten years was accompanied by preparation for the erection of what may have been intended to be an impressive church.[39] The appearance of minsters in such a Danelaw town as Derby suggests foundation or refoundation in the tenth century, though the discovery of a splendid ninth century coffin at one of them, Saint Alkmund's, indicates at least continuity of site.[40] A considerable number of northern and Midland churches later claimed a tenth-century founder.[41] There are instances of towns with more minsters than one: for example Derby, Shrewsbury, Chester, Gloucester (where besides Saint Oswald's there was Saint Peter's, which was not monastic until the eleventh century); Hereford, beside the cathedral minster of Saint Ethelbert, had another, Saint Guthlac's.

The urban minsters of late Anglo-Saxon England were numerous and diverse. Many had formed part of fairly orderly systems of ecclesiastical authority corresponding to those of secular government. Some retained some of what this had given them (Saint Mary's Derby is a case in point)[42] but many must have lost much of what they once held. Some were small and poor, others large, rich and nobly built. For example recent work indicates that Saint Oswald's at Gloucester

[38] *VCH Gloucestershire* 2 p 84.

[39] L. Alcock, '*By South Cadbury is that Camelot . . .*' (London 1972) pp 198–200.

[40] *VCH Derbyshire* 1 pp 87–8; R. A. Hall, 'The Pre-Conquest Burh at Derby', *D*[*erbyshire*] *A*[*rchaeological*] *J*[*ournal*] 94 (Kendal 1974) p 18.

[41] [A.] Hamilton Thompson ['Notes on Secular Colleges of Canons in England', *ArchJ* 74 (1917)] p 142.

[42] *VCH Derbyshire* 1 p 310; *The Cartulary of Darley Abbey*, ed R. R. Darlington, Derbyshire Archaeological and Natural History Society (Derby 1945) 1 p liv; A. Saltman, 'The History of the Foundation of Dale Abbey', *DAJ* 87 (1967) p 25.

had very considerable buildings.[43] It would have been very much a shrine to West Saxon success. That no source earlier than Wendover even professes to record where Offa was buried is an indication of Mercian failure and of how that failure must have carried minsters down with it.[44] Wherever Offa actually was buried it must have been in what was at the time a powerful minster. Many minsters may have had residual rights and residual memories from regimes long toppled.[45] Others were new; and that they continued to be founded is a warning against accepting too easily that they were institutions without a future. It is true that they were threatened in various ways. Monastic reformers cast pious and greedy eyes on lax ways and substantial estates. Minster property was coming to be exploited to maintain great royal servants. In the towns, even more than in the country, the proliferation of parishes threatened the substance of 'old minster' rights. Still, relatively few were monasticised. A number survived the middle ages with the select status of royal free chapels.[46] Some survived as ordinary secular colleges. A considerable number were made over into houses of Augustinian canons in the twelfth century. In Edward the Confessor's England communities of priests, doubtless often married and often hereditary, were very important in some towns. The thirteen *canonici prebendarii*, alias *presbyteri de burgo* of Saint Mary's Stafford must, if resident (and certainly they had been intended to be, for Domesday shows them with a messuage each) have formed a conspicuous element in a small town.[47] In very many towns such bodies if they did not weigh as once they had must still have counted for something.

The most remarkable thing in the church in towns before the Conquest is the multiplication of parishes. This growth was recent, probably reaching its peak in the eleventh century, and ceasing in the twelfth; and it was on the largest scale.[48] Norwich, the only major

[43] Taylor, *Anglo-Saxon Architecture*, 3 p 1073.

[44] R. Vaughan, *Mathew Paris* (Cambridge 1958) p 191.

[45] Blythburgh in Suffolk could be a case in point if there was substance in the twelfth-century contention that Anna king of the East Angles was buried and still venerated there, *Liber Eliensis* p 18.

[46] J. H. Denton, *English Royal Free Chapels* (Manchester 1970).

[47] *VCH Staffordshire* 4 pp 22–3. The recorded population of the town was a hundred and sixty six. If this figure was accurate one household in thirteen was that of a canon.

[48] [C. N. L.] Brooke, ['The Church in the Towns, 1000–1250'], *SCH* 6 (1970) pp 59–83; [C. N. L.] Brooke and [G.] Keir, [*London 800–1216: the Shaping of a City*] (London 1975) pp 128–48; [A.] Rogers, ['Parish Boundaries and Urban History'], *Journal of the British Archaeological Association*, 3 ser 35 (London 1972) pp 46–64 are the most im portant recent studies.

town for which Domesday provides a comprehensive figure had a minimum of forty nine churches and chapels by 1086.[49] London must have had more and some other major towns cannot have been far, if at all, behind. It is certain that many of these urban churches were, or had originated as, private chapels and that many, but not all, were very small.[50] Why was it that in the towns, and in particular (though by no means only) in the great eastern towns, of England there was a church on every corner?

First, as Brooke points out, this is the urban aspect of something more general. The proliferation of churches in the East Anglian countryside was as marked. It is unlikely that there was any rural area in medieval Europe where parishes were so small as in parts of Norfolk. By the time of Domesday East Anglian village churches were very numerous; some villages had more than one.[51] It is interesting that the contemporary Adam of Bremen describes something similar in Denmark: there were, he says, three hundred wooden churches in Scania alone.[52] One simple explanation for the proliferation of churches is important. People needed space to go to church in. The smallest urban churches were tiny: one at Winchester was thirteen feet by sixteen and the average size cannot have been high.[53] Even fifty churches may have been hardly enough for such a place as Norwich, where more, perhaps many more, than five thousand people lived. As, again, Brooke, to whom I owe much, points out, the founding of new churches was the fruit not only of an impulse from below but a failure of authority above in that one church can be created only at the expense of another.[54] Brooke suggests that the failure was to some extent personal, by the default of absent or negligent bishops, and to some extent institutional. One cannot be totally happy about the hypothesis that Stigand's deficiencies extended to a neglect

[49] *D[omesday] B[ook seu Liber Censualis Willelmi Primi Regis Angliae*, ed A. Farley], 2 vols (London 1783) 1 pp 117–18; Campbell, 'Norwich' pp 3, 23–4.

[50] [M.] Biddle and [D. J.] Keene, ['Winchester in the Eleventh and Twelfth Centuries', *Winchester in the Early Middle Ages: an Edition and Discussion of the Winton Domesday*, ed F. Barlow, M. Biddle, O. von Feilitzen and D. J. Keene] (Oxford 1976) pp 329–35, 498–9.

[51] Page pp 85–6.

[52] L. Musset, *Les Peuples Scandinaves au Moyen Age* (Paris 1951) p 144.

[53] Biddle and Keene p 334; *Medieval Archaeology* 18 (London 1974) for a church in York little larger; T. G. Hassall, *Oxoniensia* 39 (1974) for a church in Oxford converted from a domestic building. In a Suffolk village the construction of a chapel beside the cemetery of the mother church was explained on the ground that the latter could not hold the whole parish, *DB* 1 p 281.

[54] Brooke pp 76–7.

of his own interests; as the proprietor of two churches in Norwich he must have been well-acquainted with the problems.[55] That there were institutional reasons is probable. The institutions which had most to lose by the proliferation of new parishes were the head minsters. It is probable that the most likely explanation for the dearth of early charters from East Anglia will serve also to explain in part the abundance of late churches there; that the minsters had been destroyed or weakened by the Danish invasions.[56] Thus, that Domesday shows much fainter traces of an orderly minster system in the east as against the west would indicate as much the cause as the consequence of extensive church foundation. There were, of course, very numerous churches in some western towns. But at least in Winchester they seem generally to have lacked rights of burial and sometimes even of baptism.[57] Third, Brooke emphasises simple devotion and the extent to which pious groups of craftsmen clubbed together to build themselves a neighbourhood church. One has only to look at the surviving gild regulations to see how devout late Anglo-Saxons could be. Some of the Winchester churches were associated with gilds and gild halls. Attempts to stop eating and drinking in churches suggest that the churches themselves may sometimes have fulfilled the functions of halls, perhaps in particular for funeral feasts.[58]

They had other public functions also. Certain kinds of ordeal were held in churches; and a post-Conquest tract says that a man accused of theft was to be kept in a church from the Tuesday before the Sunday when he took the ordeal.[59] It is a question how far churches were used as courts and meeting-places. There is abundant evidence for their being so used in the medieval period. Earlier it is harder to find. Eadmer says that the south porch of Canterbury cathedral was used as a court 'where pleas were settled which could get no solution in hundred or shire or the royal court'.[60] A reference in the *Leges Edwardi* to *proprinquiorem ecclesiam ubi iudicium regis erit* is

[55] *DB* 2 p 116. Stigand may possibly have been a Norwich man, Barlow p 78 n 1.

[56] Though there are indications in Norwich that Edgar's law on the division of tithe between an old minster and a new church may have been applied, Barlow p 195; Campbell, 'Norwich' p 4 n 12.

[57] Biddle and Keene p 332.

[58] *Ancient Laws* [*and Institutes*, ed B. Thorpe] (London 1840) p 397; *Die Hirtenbriefe Ælfrics*, ed B. Fehr (Hamburg 1914) pp 24–5.

[59] M. Deanesly, *The Pre-Conquest Church in England* (London 1961) pp 332–3; [F. Liebermann, *Die*] *Gesetze* [*der Angelsachsen*], 3 vols (Halle 1898–1916) 1 p 417 (dated by him to 1066–*c*1150).

[60] R. W. Southern, *Saint Anselm and his Biographer* (Cambridge 1963) p 242.

suggestive of a connection between churches and justice.[61] Certainly in the early twelfth century the joint county court of Norfolk and Suffolk sometimes met in one of the churches of the French borough.[62]

Churches had a part to play at the point where commercial transactions met the law. Bishops were supposed to have a responsibility for weights and measures.[63] It is understandable that manumissions of the unfree should take place in church 'on the altar' but when slaves are sold 'at the church door' that is another matter and probably indicates a connection between the church and proper legal form.[64] A connection between priests, churches, trade and public order appears particularly clear in a passage in the *Leges Edwardi* relating what is to happen when anyone claims to have found cattle or property. He is to bring it before the church and then to summon the priest and the reeve.[65] This was a society in which the priest is a natural link between authority and his flock. The priest who was summoned to come with the reeve and six men from each vill to give evidence in the Domesday inquiry was fulfilling one of his normal roles.[66] There may have been much such work for him to do in towns.

But he had, of course, his living to make. Some urban priests received tithes and it was at least hoped that 'shipmen' would pay a tithe on their gains.[67] Others had livings which were virtually unendowed. One manuscript of the taxation of 1254 lists not only 29 churches in Norwich which were taxed but adds that there are other churches in Norwich not taxed *propter beneficiorum exilitatem* and goes on to list twenty-eight of them.[68] Many priests, if their church had burial rights, must have depended heavily on funeral dues. The image of ravens swooping on a corpse was one which twice occurred to Aelfric in this connection.[69] Wulfstan of Worcester's biography tells

[61] *Gesetze* I p 633 (earlier twelfth century but probably often reflecting pre-Conquest law).

[62] *Saint Benet of Holme*, ed J. R. West, Norfolk Record Society (Norwich 1932) nos 120, 178, 217.

[63] *Ancient Laws* pp 426–7.

[64] *Diplomatarium* pp 642–9, 628.

[65] *Gesetze* I p 649.

[66] W. Stubbs, *Select Charters* (9 ed Oxford 1951) p 101.

[67] Brooke and Kerr pp 126–7; Rogers p 50 n 1; *Ancient Laws* p 484 (an Old English version of the *Capitula* of Theodulf of Orleans).

[68] W. Hudson, 'The Norwich Taxation of 1254', *Norfolk Archaeology* 17 (Norwich 1910) p 106.

[69] *Ancient Laws* p 462; K. Jost, *Die 'Institutes of Polity Civil and Ecclesiastical'* (Berne 1959) pp 97–9.

of those who would not christen a child without payment.[70] We do not know how far being a parish priest was normally a full-time job. They were forbidden to act as traders or reeves, which suggests that they did.[71] This was a society which would probably have seen nothing remarkable in a priest undertaking ordinary work; for the compatibility of orders and marriage may have ensured not only that most clergy were married but that some men were clergy who had no intention of being ministers. There almost certainly were far more clerics than there were benefices. In Bury St. Edmunds in 1086 thirty priests, deacons and clerks were among the inhabitants of the three hundred and forty two new houses in the recently built extension to the town.[72]

Most town churches, like most other churches, were property which could be bought and sold.[73] Churches seemed quite often to have been owned by priests and they may often have been in the nature of family businesses. One extremely interesting passage in the Domesday account of Lincoln shows an intention, perhaps a system, for keeping ownership within the community. A Lincoln man had given the church of All Saints to the abbey of Peterborough on becoming a monk there. All the burgesses of Lincoln declared that such a grant could not be made outside the city or the family without royal consent.[74]

This concern to exclude outsiders contrasts with the appearance of a marked tendency in the latest Anglo-Saxon period towards the use of churches as sources of profit not simply by landowners but by distant pluralists. In a degree there was nothing new about this; great religious houses had long owned far-off churches and minsters. What may well be new is the appearance of such a figure as Regenbald, whom Round called 'the first great pluralist'. Regenbald is well enough known, not least because of the controversy as to whether he was the Confessor's chancellor. He was in any case a very important clerk in Edward's service, so important that he was granted some of the status of a bishop. He swiftly attached himself to the Conqueror, receiving writs in 1067 which secured his property and gained him more. We know the extent of what he was given before and after the Conquest chiefly because Henry I used his possessions to endow a

[70] *The Vita Wulfstani of William of Malmesbury*, ed R. R. Darlington, *CSer* 3 ser 40 (1928) pp 12–3.

[71] *Ancient Laws* p 462.

[72] Lobel p 12.

[73] For example p 131 n 80 below.

[74] Barlow p 193.

house of Augustinian canons at Cirencester in 1133.[75] A high proportion consisted of churches. Regenbald held twenty churches, all, like the rest of his property, in the south and west. Thirteen of these were sufficiently important to have one or more subordinate chapels. Several were at places of note: Cirencester itself (where he was almost certainly head of the college of secular canons),[76] the market towns of Frome and Milborne Port in Somerset, both important demesne centres, and Cookham and Bray, similarly important centres. At two of the places where he held benefices, Cookham and Cirencester, Domesday says there was a new market.[77] At Cirencester there was a college of canons; Cookham and Cheltenham had at one time been the seat of monastic houses of some kind and so possibly had Frome.[78] In short, what the prospering Regenbald had been given was to a large extent churches associated with the royal demesne, often minsters, and naturally often at centres of local importance. Other royal clerks were similarly endowed, though none apparently on quite the scale of Regenbald.[79] Such clerks were prominent at court from the middle generations of the eleventh century as they never seem to have been before. Probably they were the men who ran Edward's administration, and their rewards were commensurate with its not inconsiderable virtues. The active nature of their interest in ecclesiastical property is brought home in the Domesday entry which shows a royal chamberlain buying the church at Huntingdon from two of the king's priests and then selling it again.[80] Thus in the Confessor's England among the currents in the distribution and creation of ecclesiastical property there were two which were in a degree opposite. While old churches at centres of royal authority (often places which, if they were not towns were not ordinary villages either) were passing into the hands of distant pluralists, the new churches which were being created in

[75] [C.] Ross, [*The*] *Cartulary* [*of Cirencester Abbey*],/(Oxford 1964) prints (no 28/1) the foundation charter and refers (pp xix, xxi–xxii, xxv–xxviii) to the literature on Regenbald. J. H. Round, 'Regenbald the Chancellor', *Feudal England* (London 1909) pp 421–30 is fundamental.

[76] Ross, *Cartulary* no 575 and Round's article on him in *DNB*.

[77] *The Domesday Geography of South West England*, ed H. C. Darby and R. Welldon Finn (Cambridge 1967) pp 200–1, 204, 209; *The Domesday Geography of South East England*, ed H. C. Darby and E. M. J. Campbell (Cambridge 1962) p 281; *The Domesday Geography of Midland England*, ed H. C. Darby and I. B. Terrett (Cambridge 1954) pp 20, 49.

[78] *MRHEW* pp 470,471, 473.

[79] Barlow pp 129–37; J. H. Round, 'Ingelric the Priest and Albert of Lotharingia', *The Commune of London and other Studies* (London 1889) pp 28–38.

[80] Barlow pp 192–3.

major towns, especially in the east, seem chiefly to have been held by local men.

Such currents could frequently change their directions. Minster communities probably found Edward the Confessor's and William I's new clerks as much of a threat as Edgar's new abbots had been. One might have supposed that such institutions as Cirencester (in which Roger of Salisbury had an interest after Regenbald), Christchurch (Twyneham) and Saint Martin's, Dover (in both of which Flambard had his claws) would have faded away. In fact all three were transformed into Augustinian houses.[81] So too were a number of other secular communities, not least in towns. The urban parishes, whose extensive creation had been an indication of burgess independence, also went in a new direction from the early twelfth century. To a large extent they passed into ecclesiastical ownership: for example, by 1200, the bishops of Lincoln and of Norwich held a high proportion of the churches which once had belonged to the priests and burgesses of those cities.[82]

In the Confessor's time there had been no bishop in either Norwich or Lincoln. It is an important question why so many of the Anglo-Saxon *sedes* remained in minor places. Only one of their pre-Conquest moves was to an important town: that from Crediton to Exeter.[83] A partial explanation for so many sees remaining in places which by 1066 were relatively unimportant was that the urban growth which made major towns very different from lesser had often been fairly recent. Norwich may well have been much more like North Elmham in 950 than it had become by 1050. Another is that it was not necessarily inconvenient for a bishop to live in the country: at their country manors was precisely where many medieval bishops spent most of their time. Perhaps above all, a move of the kind which was made to Norwich or Lincoln could not have been accomplished without powerful royal support expressed in ways which might have seemed difficult or inconceivable to an Anglo-Saxon king. To construct

[81] *DB* I fols 1–2, H. H. E. Craster, 'A Contemporary Record of the Pontificate of Ranulf Flambard', *Archaeologia Aeliana,* 4 ser 7 (Newcastle-upon-Tyne 1930) p 47, *MRHEW* pp 154, 470, *VCH Hampshire* I p 152. For valuable remarks on the conversion of minster communities to Augustinian, [M.] Brett, [*The English Church under Henry I*] (Oxford 1975) pp 138–40.

[82] Hill, *Medieval Lincoln* pp 141–5; F. Blomefield and C. Parkin, *An Essay towards a Topographical History of the County of Norfolk,* 11 vols (London 1805–11) 2 pp 75, 91, 105, 116, 118, 126, 137, 145, 238, 255, 272, 299, 353, 367, 423, 429, 438, 439, 443, 466, 475 (2), 484.

[83] Barlow pp 208–31 gives a most thorough account of the sees and their moves.

the equivalent of a continental *cité episcopale* at Norwich Herbert Losinga had to clear a substantial part of the town. To support a cathedral monastery on the scale he envisaged endowments exceeding those of the see of Elmham were essential.[84] Similarly the new see and cathedral of Lincoln were extensively endowed by means which involved the gift of a good deal of ecclesiastical property and a willingness to treat burgesses high-handedly.[85] Particularly interesting is Henry I's gift to bishop Robert of all the, apparently numerous, churches which the burgesses held of the king.[86] Such moves of *sedes* as these were not just a matter of deciding to take a sensible practical step. They involved heavy expenditure, royal support, and the transformation of the cathedral establishment.

They also involved the building of enormous new churches. The problem of how far these were needed, apart from being thought appropriate, raises other questions about the relationship in Anglo-Saxon times between bishops and towns, and between mother churches and their dioceses. The first lively glimpse we get of life in Norwich comes from the life of Saint William of Norwich and relates to Stephen's reign. It mentions two events in 1144 relating to the connection between the cathedral and the diocese. One is a diocesan synod, treated as if it were a matter of course.[87] The medieval diocese of Norwich contained more than one thousand three hundred parishes. It is a fair guess that a very high proportion of them were there by 1100. If Æthelmaer, the last Saxon bishop of Elmham, had thought fit to hold a diocesan synod (as some of his contemporaries did), and all his clergy had come, where could he have put them? The other regular diocesan event mentioned in 1144 is Absolution Sunday when 'the penitents of the whole diocese were accustomed to assemble in crowds in the mother church'. The streets were said to have been packed with them.[88] This event may well have been a Norman innovation.[89] It is a question how far the religious life of men living at some distance was involved with their cathedral church in the Anglo-Saxon period. There are indications at Exeter that it could be. The

[84] Campbell, 'Norwich' pp 8–9 and the works there cited.

[85] For example, *VCH Bedfordshire* 1 pp 196–7; *VCH Buckinghamshire* 1 pp 223–4, 281, 311–2; *VCH Derbyshire* 2 pp 87–8; Hamilton Thompson pp 155–6.

[86] Hill, *Medieval Lincoln* pp 144–5.

[87] *The Life and Miracles of Saint William of Norwich*, ed A. Jessopp and M. R. James (Cambridge 1896) p 43.

[88] *Ibid* p 26.

[89] Brett pp 162–4.

records of the Devonshire village gilds associated with the cathedral are of 1072–1103, but they may very well describe pre-Conquest institutions. As far away as Bideford men had been adopted into association by the bishop and canons, were making small annual payments to them and were rewarded by the canons 'performing such service as they ought to perform'.[90] (It may be significant that this was a cathedral which had been moved to a major town and whose chapter had been reformed before the Conquest.) Those looking to a cathedral in such a way are likely to have wanted to come to it. The piety of the day may have expressed itself in devotion to, and in, great churches as well as small. Indeed, the more home churches became very local and so very small, the more people may have felt the need at least occasionally to attend grander establishments. Small churches may well, as Brooke suggests, have led to an intimate relationship between priest and people, but one defect of a church sixteen feet by thirteen is that you cannot put on much of an ecclesiastical show in it.[91] So, perhaps the gigantic nave of Norwich cathedral and the swarms of new small parish churches in East Anglia were complementary.

The relationship between the English church and English towns was affected for many centuries afterwards by what had happened in the Anglo-Saxon period. Many early arrangements and rights were long perpetuated, largely thanks to twelfth-century developments in canon law and to the reformation, which long preserved the *ecclesia anglicana* from Roman rationalisers. The effects of the distant past are to be seen in large towns and in small. For example the famous ministry of W. F. Hook in Leeds was possible because when he was presented in 1837 almost the whole of the city comprised one vast parish. The great size of the parish was probably due to Leeds having been a major ecclesiastical centre at a very early date; it has recently been convincingly argued that it was the Campodunum where Edwin built the *basilica*.[92] That it was not divided reflects the great difficulty found in creating new parishes in England between the twelfth century and the nineteenth. A curious instance of the effect of the Anglo-Saxon past on the history of a small town is that of Hadleigh in Suffolk. Hadleigh has a modestly conspicuous role in Anglican history: Rowland Taylor, the martyr was its rector (1544–55); so too was

[90] *Diplomatarium* pp 608–10; Barlow pp 196–8.
[91] Brooke (1970) pp 80–1.
[92] See p 121 above. I owe this identification with Campodunum to a so far unpublished paper by Miss Margaret Fell.

David Wilkins of the *Concilia* (1719–45); and so too was Hugh Rose who in July 1833 held there the 'conference' which had some significance in the rise of the Oxford movement.[93] That there was something very remarkable about Hadleigh can be seen from its revenues. In the early nineteenth century its tithes were commuted for an annual charge of £1,325.[94] It was not only a very rich living, but a Canterbury peculiar which formed part of the exempt jurisdiction of the deanery of Bocking. The association with Canterbury antedates the Conquest and may go back to a grant from Byrhtnoth the hero of the battle of Maldon.[95] Its ecclesiastical history may be taken back further yet. One of the few valuable fragments in the twelfth-century *Annals of Saint Neot's* records that Guthrum, the Danish king of East Anglia, was buried in 890 at the *villa regia* of Hadleigh.[96] The importance of Hadleigh in the history of the church derives in the end almost certainly from its having been an important royal church under the East Anglian kings; with its revenues being preserved and coming into the gift of the archbishops of Canterbury. When one considers the threads which link the Saxon church with later centuries there is a certain symbolic weight in the fact that among the churches held by Regenbald, who served the Confessor so profitably and came so quickly and effectively to terms with the Conqueror, was Bray.

University of Oxford
Worcester College

[93] H. Pigot, 'Hadleigh', *Proceedings of the Suffolk Institute of Archaeology* (Ipswich 1863) pp 30–81.

[94] *Ibid* p 79.

[95] *HMC Eighth Report* p 322.

[96] *Asser's Life of King Alfred together with the Annals of Saint Neot's*, ed W. H. Stevenson (new impr Oxford 1959) p 140.

CROSSROADS AND CRISES IN THE RELIGIOUS LIFE OF THE LATER ELEVENTH CENTURY

by DEREK BAKER

IT IS fifty years since Germain Morin, in an article in the *Revue Bénédictine*[1] articulated discussion of the tensions and developments in eleventh and early twelfth-century regular, and para-regular, life around a central 'crisis of cenobitism', and twenty years since Leclercq stabilised the debate in a wide ranging article which has become the basis of all subsequent comment.[2] This crisis in the cenobitic life is now a commonplace, expressed in Leclercq's terms as 'the crisis of prosperity'[3] and answered by the resurgence of rural monasticism, eremitical in character, in reaction to the elaborate structures and relationships of an established monasticism resident in the urban centres of population and influence. The individual austerities and renunciations of Romuald stand at the beginning of a proliferating development in western Christendom, and may, in a general sense, be taken to characterise these new initiatives. The direct influence of Romualdine ideas and practices, whether through his foundations or through his self-proclaimed spiritual heir Damian, which is sometimes alleged is difficult to prove,[4] but there is an obvious consonance between the Italian experiments and those elsewhere in the west, a compatibility of outlook and attitude between Romuald and Damian, and men like Bruno, Stephen Harding, Robert of Arbrissel. All, in one sense or another, in their lives and in their words, express a profound unease within the old dispensations of established Benedictinism, the victim of its own reform and resurgence in the tenth

[1] Germain Morin, 'Rainaud l'Ermite et Ives de Chartres: un épisode de la crise du cenobitisme au XIe–XII siècles', *RB* 40 (1928) pp 99–115.

[2] [Jean] Leclercq, 'La crise du monachisme aux XIe et XIIe siècles', *BISIMEAN* 70 (1958) pp 19–41, trans Noreen Hunt, *Cluniac Monasticism in the Central Middle Ages* (London 1971) pp 217–37. For more recent comment, with bibliography, see, for example, [Bede] Lackner, ['The Crisis of Cenobitism'], [*The Eleventh-century background of*] *Cîteaux* (Washington, D.C., 1972) pp 92–112.

[3] Leclercq p 222.

[4] For a brief examination of the careers of Romuald and Damian see my '*Fortissimum genus:* élitist attitudes to religious life in the late tenth and eleventh centuries' (forthcoming Warsaw/Louvain 1979) and the bibliography there given.

century. In the simplest terms, for contemporaries as for modern writers, the reaction was against Cluny, and the way of life and spiritual attitudes it represented: the future was symbolised in the frontier communities of white monks, intent upon following Benedict to the letter in his primitive simplicity and seclusion—though here, as in many another case, eternal truths were apt to undergo a contemporary translation. The confrontation has a natural appeal: subsequent developments the melancholy fascination of all seemingly inevitable betrayals. Within twenty years Cîteaux had become an order, and less than a century separates the ideals of Robert of Molesme's New Monastery from the criticism and invective of Walter Map and Gerald of Wales.[5] The process by which these individual initiatives and vocations were submerged and transformed by the pressures of patrons, eccelesiastical authority, and social expectation and need has often been discussed and examined, and the individual agonies of men like Gervase of Louth Park, overtaken and overwhelmed by the social success of the movements with which they were associated, viewed as unfortunate, but inescapable, incidents in the tidal sequence of reform and decay,[6] with the process repeating itself in the surge and ebb of the mendicant ideal in the next century.

Yet for all its basic simplicity this presentation and identification of a crisis in cenobitism, its resolution by the adoption of the poverty and isolation of the country for the affluence and involvement of the town, and the rapid reshaping of these initiatives by Christian society into conformity with its expectations, is not wholly convincing. If the temper of the times was so strongly critical of established monastic values as to induce a 'crisis of cenobitism' is it realistic to portray the attitudes of Christian society—of people, patrons and ecclesiastics—as so divergent that they progressively forced the new initiatives into a procrustean traditionalism almost indistinguishable from the old?[7] What are we to make of the leaders who led the way from the

[5] See Knowles *MO* pp 662–78.

[6] See, for example, my 'Desert in the North', *NH* 5 (1970) pp 1–11, and 'San Bernardo e l'elezione di York', *Studi su S. Bernardo di Chiaravalle* (Rome 1975) pp 115–80, and the references there given.

[7] See, for example, the various studies of monastic patronage in *Religious Motivation: sociological and biographical problems for the church historian, SCH* 15 (1978); [Derek] Baker, 'Legend and Reality: the case of Waldef of Melrose', *SCH* 12 (1975) pp 59–82; Baker, 'Patronage in the early twelfth-century church: Walter Espec, Kirkham and Rievaulx', *Traditio, Krisis, Renovatio aus theologischer Sicht*, ed B. Jaspert and R. Mohr (Marburg 1976) pp 92–100.

hermitages to the communities of the new orders? For the most part demonstrably men of position and status, men of the establishment, were they, for all their ascetic example and profound spirituality, essentially organisers, legislators, leaders rather than solitaries? Should the crisis itself perhaps be viewed simply as a spasm of the sedentary body spiritual adjusting to the more intense and active life of the eleventh century, and soon past? What is plain is that by the later twelfth century, except in points of detail, and in location, the new foundations are indistinguishable from the old, variations upon a continuing tradition of regular life which may for a time have been superficially obscured, but which was never superseded.[8] For all the rhetoric and activity of the eleventh and early twelfth century the predominant impression is one of continuity not crisis, and a careful reading of Leclercq's article suggests that he himself is not unaware of this, nor wholly comfortable within his own interpretation.

For all this it remains true that the eleventh century was a period of widespread revival of eremitical life and ascetic practices in the west, of revulsion from the elaborate life and liturgy of established and reformed Benedictinism, and of a return to 'the desert', however understood. The temptation to seek a general explanation for such phenomena is strong, but it may be more instructive in the short term, to examine a particular instance, and I propose to scrutinise, briefly and superficially, the well-known and frequently described process by which Molesme spawned Cîteaux.

The story is, of course, clearly and attractively outlined from the Cistercian viewpoint, in the various *Exordia*.[9] Probably in the autumn of 1097 Robert, abbot and founder of Molesme, sought and gained

[8] See Leclercq's comments on Damian's 'new and original form of monasticism – a new Benedictine tradition, differentiated from that of the past by its eremitic trend' (p 226), and his remark that 'innovators and traditionalists, solitaries and protagonists of community life alike were bringing against one another the same accusations, and to some extent justifiably' (p 228).

[9] Discussion of the precedence and validity of the fundamental Cistercian documents – Exordium, Carta Caritatis, Instituta – is not necessary to my purposes here, but it should be said that in the continued absence of properly established critical texts few of the problems indicated by Lefèvre have been finally settled. An outline, and full bibliography, of the controversies is given by Knowles in *Great Historical Enterprises* (London 1963) pp 197–222, and more recently by [L. J.] Lekai, [*The Cistercians, ideals and reality*] (Kent State University Press 1977), and Lackner. The latter's heroic struggle to make coherent sense of the early history of both Molesme and Cîteaux is itself an indication of the continued confusion in the evidence for both houses: any account of these events can be challenged and qualified at almost every point, though without seriously amending the significance of the story.

authorisation from the papal legate, Hugh of Lyons, to found and to join a new monastery in order to follow the Benedictine Rule 'more strictly and more perfectly' than at Molesme where the observance was 'lukewarm and negligent'.[10] Returning to Molesme he recruited some twenty-one monks for the new foundation, and early in 1098, traditionally on March 21, the feast of St Benedict, and Palm Sunday in that year, the new monastery was founded on its first site—*locus horroris et vastae solitudinis*.[11] An initial calm was broken by Molesme's realisation of the material loss resulting from Robert's departure, and its appeal to Urban II for Robert's return. Delegated to the legate by the pope the appeal was heard probably in late June 1099, and with the bishop of Langres supporting the community of Molesme the legate decreed Robert's return. He was accompanied, if William of Malmesbury, writing some twenty-five years later, is to be believed, by all but eight of the monks who had founded Cîteaux.[12] Alberic, the former prior of Molesme, succeeded Robert as second abbot of Cîteaux, and on his death on 26 January 1109, the Englishman Stephen Harding was elected, to rule for twenty-six years, and to be the effective creator of the Cistercian order, the first daughter house being founded at La Ferté-sur-Grosne in May 1113.[13] In Cistercian propaganda the early years at Cîteaux were ones of heroic hardship, austerity and

[10] *Exordium Parvum* cap 2. See Lackner pp 261–2; J. Lefèvre, 'Que savons-nous du Cîteaux primitif?', *RHE* 51 (1956) pp 5–41; and [J.] Marilier, [*Chartes et Documents concernant l'Abbaye de Cîteaux 1098–1182*], *Bibliotheca Cisterciensis* 1 (Rome 1961) for discussion of these events.

[11] Deuteronomy 32.10. The phrase is a topos for monastic foundations. It comes to be applied particularly to Cistercian foundations, but though it is present in both the Exordium Cistercii and the Exordium Magnum it does not appear in the Exordium Parvum. The Exordium Parvum (cap 1) is explicit that it was in 1098 that Robert approached Hugh of Lyons, returning immediately to Molesme, and leaving with his augmented party to found the New Monastery on March 21. Though this date is generally agreed to be symbolic rather than accurate this outline calendar of events has secured general acceptance. Lefèvre has been almost alone in maintaining that Robert's approach to the legate was made in 1097 (at some point after Robert's last recorded act at Molesme on 5 April 1097). More recently Lekai (p 13) has recorded the approach to the legate as occurring 'perhaps in the fall of 1097' and Lackner (pp 261–2) has outlined the controversy without seeking to resolve it. Marilier (p 34) has placed the beginnings of the Cistercian initiative, without comment, in 1097–8, and ascribed no date to the legate's letter (pp 34–5). Marilier's remark elsewhere (p 22, see also pp 23–6) – 'Le point de départ de notre discussion sera une manière de postulat: Cîteaux fut fondé en 1098' – may be left to speak for itself.

[12] See Lekai pp 15–6.

[13] *Ibid* p 19. See A. H. Bredero, 'Études sur la *Vita prima* de Saint Bernard', *ASOC* 17 (1961) pp 60–2 for discussion of the date of Bernard's arrival at Cîteaux and its relationship to the foundation of La Ferté.

achievement in a context of continuing hostility from Molesme and other monasteries, faced with this 'exceptional and new kind of monks',[14] and suffering by comparison. Other evidence may lead us to modify this impression of the early Cistercian years,[15] but the essentials of the story remain the same: the austerity and simplicity of the life of these white monks in their savage solitude diverted the attention and patronage of the neighbourhood towards them, making of them and their order the new *divites Christi* while Molesme and houses like it ceased to command the attention and respect that they had previously enjoyed.

Pride in the spectacular success of the order in the first half of the twelfth century has much to do with this triumphant and circumstantial account of Cistercian origins, but there were other reasons, too, why the white monks should lay great stress upon legality and justification in the foundation of Cîteaux. At the most obvious level the legality of the move from Molesme to Cîteaux could be, and was, questioned.[16] Further, the relationship of Cîteaux to its mother house Molesme could, as in the later case of Byland and Furness,[17] pose serious problems, not least in the light of other earlier ill-defined sorties and foundations from Molesme. Placed in the context of Bruno of Cologne's brief residence at the dependent hermitage of Sèche-Fontaine, Robert's own departure to the hermitage of Aux (?1090–3) without relinquishing his position as abbot, the possible exodus for some years to the hermitage of Vivicus by Alberic, Stephen and two others, the departure of Guido and Guarinus to the alpine hermitage of Aulps *c*1090 and its later elevation (1097) at their request to the status of dependent abbey,[18] the precise position of the new monastery at Cîteaux, the intentions underlying its establishment, and the actions and standing of the principal participants seem less certain, and perhaps less obviously respectable than they generally appear.

Similar qualifications must be entered about the actual foundation at Cîteaux itself. Deserts and forests, savage solitudes, are of course stock terms, and should not be taken too explicitly: both Molesme

[14] Lackner p 272, quoting from the probably spurious letter of Hugh of Lyons to Paschal II – see Lekai pp 16–7; Marilier p 47.

[15] See Lekai pp 16–9.

[16] See the discussion in Lackner pp 262–6.

[17] See R. H. C. Davis, *King Stephen* (London 1967) pp 101–4.

[18] For extended discussion of these much-discussed incidents see Lackner pp 228–40, and the references there given.

and Muret—founded it would seem almost simultaneously—were established on sites claimed to be better suited to wild beasts than to men: both were adjacent to long-established main roads. But even in the context of such literary convention the case of Cîteaux is striking. Situated, as the name may imply, on the line of the Roman road from Langres to Chalon it is in fact directly adjacent to the intersection of two Roman roads.[19] Its first site was adequate; its second a mere kilometre away, to which it made an early move, is superbly placed beside the Vouge, and close to the point where the road from Dijon crosses the river. That it was already inhabited seems beyond doubt, and it appears likely that there was a chapel there.[20] As its early benefactions emphasise it lay close to the old road from Dijon to Beaune under the slopes of the Côte d'Or, and less than five miles from the important Roman road junction at Vidubia (St. Bernard). The site itself was donated by Raynald, viscount of Beaune, already a benefactor of Robert, and his kinsman. It is plain that Robert benefited as much from his relatives at Cîteaux as he had at Collan and Molesme,[21] and it is difficult to accept the *Exordium Cisterii*'s claim that it was only 'after many labours and extreme difficulties' that they reached their goal'.

It was not the viscount of Beaune, however, who became the principal patron of Cîteaux, but the dukes of Burgundy—Odo, until his death in the holy land in 1102, and his son Hugh thereafter.[22] The list of ducal and noble benefactions supply a significant gloss upon the earliest regulations for the receipt of benefactions at Cîteaux,[23] and the prohibition, in the penultimate chapter of the *Exordium Parvum*, of the keeping of the ducal court at Cîteaux on great feast days is a further indication of the close ducal interest in Cîteaux, which made of it *le Saint-Denis de Bourgogne*.[24] Perhaps the clearest indication, however, of the position of the new house in the feudal and

[19] *Voies Romaines* [*du département de la Côte d'Or et Répertoire archéologique des arrondissements de Dijon et de Beaune*], Commision des antiquités du département de la Côte d'Or (Dijon/Paris 1872). See Marilier p 53; Lekai pp 13–4; J. Richard, 'Passages de Saône au XIIe et XIIIe siècles', *Annales de Bourgogne* 22 (Dijon 1950) pp 249–52.

[20] See Lekai pp 14, 16 (though he places the first site to the south of the present location); Marilier p 53. See also [G.] Duby, [*Rural Economy and Country Life in the Medieval West*], trans C. Postan (London 1968); G. Roupnell, *Histoire de la campagne française* (Paris 1932) p 129.

[21] See Lackner pp 221–4; Marilier p 36 no 4, and the references there given.

[22] See Lekai p 16; Marilier pp 35–8, 49–53.

[23] Compare *Exordium Parvum* cap 15.

[24] *Voies Romaines* p lxix.

ecclesiastical world of Burgundy, and in the monastic ambiance of Cluny, can be found in its early and local foundations—Maizières founded in 1132 upon, and to administer, Cîteaux's rich properties in the neighbourhood of Mersault; La Bussière, in 1131, on a rich site in the valley of the Ouche to the west of Dijon, conveniently close to the main road north from Dijon to Tonnerre, and early patronised by the court and nobility of Burgundy, as its church and surviving buildings demonstrate.[25] Above all, however, there is La Ferté founded in May 1113, the first daughter house of Cîteaux, established upon a fine site overlooking the valley of the Grosne not far from its junction with the Saône, and beside the main valley road. Scarcely a remote solitude, but perhaps of more significance is its position downstream from Cluny itself, flanked by the heartland granges and priories of the great abbey, close to the pilgrimage route to Cluny. It is difficult to think of a more provocative and assertive act: clearly it is not necessary to wait for a Bernardine *Apologia* to characterise the Cistercian posture towards Cluny.[26]

In all this it is the customary rather than the revolutionary which is most striking. For all the changed colour of their habits, the majestic starkness of their twelfth-century churches—based largely, as Dimier has shown, upon the plan of Clairvaux[27]—and the pharasaical stridency of their later claims and assertions, these white monks, this new monastery, belong within the general revival of the monastic life in Burgundy and Champagne, and must be related to the social, political and economic changes, as well as the ecclesiastical, taking place in this area. In particular the continuity with Molesme is striking. Taking its origins from the original hermitage at Collan,[28] Molesme became the permanent home of an enterprise established, like Cîteaux, in a

[25] The site of the abbey is in a side valley, close to the main Ouche valley. The church is said to date from 1172, and there are substantial remains of the domestic buildings, much remodelled. More generally see *Les débuts des abbayes cisterciennes dans les ancien pays bourguignons comtois et romands* (Dijon 1953).

[26] In spite of excellent regional studies on Cluny and the Mâconnais the physical extent of Cluny's influence in the region, its range of interests and investment, well-represented in surviving churches and buildings, can only really be appreciated on the ground. Amid all this La Ferté, even in its eighteenth-century form remains a striking intrusion. See Duby pp 73–4 for a comment on the site of La Ferté; Duby, *La Societé aux XIe et XIIe siècles dans la région mâconnaise* (Paris 1953); and *Recueil des pancartes de l'abbaye de la Ferté-sur-Grosne (1113–1178)*, ed Duby, *Annales de la Faculté des lettres*, 3 (Aix-en-Provence 1953).

[27] A. Dimier, *l'Art Cistercien*, 1 (2 ed 1974) pp 46 *seq*.

[28] See Lackner pp 220–31. Collan lies some forty kilometres to the west of Molesme, and not far from Tonnerre.

wooded and savage region. Its success was spectacular, the first dependencies being established in the diocese of Sens within four years of the foundation, and by 1100, it would seem, there were some forty dependent communities spread over thirteen dioceses, from Thérouanne to Geneva. The growth is chronicled and discussed in Laurent's edition of the cartularies of Molesme,[29] a work more acknowledged than consulted I suspect, and it is not without reason that he calls Molesme the first monastic order. With Molesme, the final decade of the eleventh century is particularly productive, and in the light of these benefactions and this expansion it is easy to understand the community's apprehension and dismay at the apparent effect of Robert's departure upon their patrons, and their eagerness to get him back. Robert's family connections had been important in establishing first Collan and then Molesme, and they continued to be influential in attracting benefactors to Molesme itself, and in prompting the establishment of the outlying dependencies: Cîteaux itself is a case in point. Amongst the patrons of Molesme the bishop of Langres was of particular importance, not only for his own benefactions, but for the encouragement of secular support. His appeal of 1083 to his own vassals, and to the lords of his diocese, marks an important stage in the development of Molesme,[30] but for the most part it was the backing of the magnates, their involvement in every aspect of the life of Molesme and their adoption of the house which was most significant.[31] Molesme, it was alleged, came virtually to monopolise the alms of the region,[32] and as Laurent remarked, 'in the first half century of its existence, but above all from 1075 to 1111, there was no baronial house in southern Champagne, in the episcopal lordship of Langres, and in northern Burgundy, which did not shower benefactions on Molesme'.[33] Prominent amongst these benefactors throughout this period are the dukes of Burgundy, and the lords of the duchy are associated with the house from the start: the foundation charter[34] bears the names of Achard of Châtillon, seneschal of Burgundy, and Tescelin the Red, lord of Fontaines-lès-Dijon, and father of the future St Bernard.

[29] [*Cartulaires de l'Abbaye de Molesme, ancien diocèse de Langres 916–1215. Recueil de documents sur le nord de le Bourgogne et le midi de la Champagne,* ed J.] Laurent, 2 vols (Paris 1907) – the edition was of only 250 copies.

[30] See Lackner pp 225–6.

[31] *Ibid* pp 224–33; Laurent 1 pp 112–14, 121–5, 127–8.

[32] Laurent 1 p 127. [33] *Ibid* 1 p 113.

[34] See Lackner pp 223–4; Laurent 1 pp 115–16.

Clearly here, as with many other foundations, family and feudal inter-relationships played a large part in guaranteeing and sustaining the house, but two points may be emphasised. First, the house did not depend solely on secular self-interest and concern for a substantial spiritual investment for its continuing growth and prosperity. Whatever the ambiguities and confusions about the conduct and nature of life at Molesme—and they are many—it is clear that it contained and continued to attract men of a high spiritual and ascetic vocation. The departure of Bruno to the Chartreuse, of Guido and Guarinus to Aulps, the peregrinations of Alberic, Stephen, and others may seem to demonstrate the inadequacies of life at Molesme, but Bruno was attracted to Molesme at a period of high prosperity,[35] Guido and Guaranus sought the elevation of their hermitage into an abbey from Robert, and when Robert departed to found Cîteaux he led a substantial party of twenty-one monks. In all this the key figure, for all the later Cistercian criticism, is that of Robert. However much he might vacillate his ascetic reputation and spiritual appeal throughout his life are undeniable, and his formal canonisation followed a century after his death.[36] As the cartulary of Molesme indicates there was no falling off in the level of benefactions during his final years at Molesme, after his return from Cîteaux.[37] What might have happened had Robert

[35] See Laurent I pp 125–6. According to his biographer Bruno sought 'a place of perfect solitude and proper for the eremitical life' – see the Bollandist comments, *PL* 152 (1880) cols 251–2, and see the *Life* of St Hugh of Grenoble, *PL* 153 (1879) col 769 – and he remained in confraternity with the community of Molesme even after his departure to Calabria. See Laurent I pp 125–6, (*PL* 152 col 567) for Molesme's reaction to Bruno's death.

Tempore dispositio migrat de corpore Bruno
cuius, dum fixit, vita Deo placuit.
Subveniat illi, quibus est permissa potestas
Ut sit ei requies et sine fine dies.

Nostris versiculis, qui habitamus Molernium, addentes vobis, qui estis Turris, innotescimus, quod pro domino Brunone, patrono vestro, nostro autem familiarissimo, Missarum solemnia diebus triginta celebravimus, eius etiam obitus anniversarium diem in catalogo fratrum nostrorum conscripsimus,

and compare Marilier pp 51–2 (*PL* 152 cols 565–6) for the Cistercian response.

[36] In 1220. Two years later, in 1222, the Cistercian calendar designated 29 April as his feast day.

[37] According to Laurent there may have been a pause in the flow of donations coincident with Robert's absence at Cîteaux, though it is difficult to be precise about this. What is clear is that donations continued to be abundant during the years up to his death, in 1111, as abbot of Molesme. Under his successor as abbot, Guy de Châtel-Censoir (died 1132), Laurent asserts that 'les acquisitions à titre gratuit devinrent fort rares' (p 128), and ended totally after his death. Whether this decline should be set against Cistercian expansion in the area in precisely this period, whether it should be related

stayed at Cîteaux is, of course, another question, but it may, I think, be suggested that lay patrons and benefactors saw no need to choose between Robert's two foundations, and that the divisions between the houses have been exaggerated. St Bernard's father had been an early benefactor of Molesme: with Bernard himself, and the companions he took with him in 1113, the family interest would seem to have switched to the new ascetic community at Cîteaux, but Bernard's uncle, Gaudry de Montbard, lord of Touillon, and it is claimed, Bernard's earliest associate in the intention to enter Cîteaux,[38] continued to support Molesme, granting the church of Saint-Germain de Crais to Robert, and being the first founder of Molesme's dependency at Touillon in the Auxois. The foundation was consolidated by his eldest son Walter in a series of benefactions associated with the tonsuring of his brother at Molesme, his own entry into the regular life, and the adoption by his mother of the religious life—at Molesme.[39] Such intermingling of interests can be paralleled in other families, and whatever the later developments it may be suggested that both Molesme and Cîteaux should be placed in the context of a rapidly developing and expanding society in Champagne and Burgundy. For Burgundy itself the eleventh century is the period which sees the effective creation of the duchy. From the Capetian Robert's reacquisition of the duchy proceed the establishment of ducal centres at Dijon and Beaune, the revival of religious life in Dijon[40]—at St Benigne, St Philibert, Notre Dame and la Sainte Chapelle—and at Beaune with the ducal foundation of Notre Dame de Beaune. It is the period when Burgundy emerges from a relative obscurity[41] and backwardness to rival the developments taking place in Anjou, Normandy and elsewhere, and of these developments Cîteaux was in a real sense part.

Such an examination may lead us to question not Leclercq's crisis, but its characterisation—at least in this local context. In Burgundy,

---

to changing attitudes to monastic possession of churches and performance of pastoral functions, or whether it is to be explained simply by Robert's death it is impossible to say.

[38] See Watkin Williams, *Saint Bernard of Clairvaux* (Manchester 1935) pp 10–12.

[39] See Laurent 1 pp 124, 240–1, though the ramifications of the family are not entirely clear from Laurent's accounts. See also S. Thompson, *SCH Subsidia* 1 (1978) pp 229–30.

[40] For a survey of William of Volpiano's activities at Dijon and elsewhere in the region see Watkin Williams, 'William of Dijon', *Monastic Studies* (Manchester 1938) pp 99–120.

[41] For comment on these developments, see Jean Richard, *Les Ducs de Bourgogne et la formation du duché au XIe au XIVe siècle* (Paris 1954), and on the lack of real urban centres in the area in Roman times see *Voies Romaines*.

and elsewhere, there was a crisis in society. Endemic unrest—to which the peace movements testified in seeking to control it—war, the tensions and disturbance attendant upon state-building, the dispossession arising from the establishment of succession by promogeniture, the aggressive activity of the reforming church sharply defining the area of the sacred and excluding laymen from it, all tended to produce what some have called 'limital', frontier, conditions—Christopher Holdworth's placing of English post-Conquest eremiticism in such a context comes to mind here[42]—and there are the material frontiers of cultivation and culture. In Burgundy, no less than on the eastern frontiers of Germany, or the northern and western borders of England, all this applies. The eleventh and early twelfth century is the period when central Burgundy, stretching across from the hills of the Côte d'Or to the valley of the Saône is being colonised.[43] Leclercq reminded us at the beginning of his article that the 'social and economic aspects of the crisis deserve more careful and perhaps more objective study than they have hitherto had',[44] and nowhere is this more apparent than with the Burgundian context of Cistercian origins. The crisis is in society, and in the Christian life as a whole, with an increasingly sacralised and clericalised church holding ordinary Christians at a distance. There was not, in any determinant sense, a crisis of prosperity, nor do we need to adopt a simplistic town to country transition as our overview of these monastic developments—even if it were possible to arrive at a more coherent definition of 'country' than it is for eremiticism.[45] The celtic monasteries of non-urban Ireland, the complex communities of Nubia[46] and the Syrian desert,[47] and Cluny itself remind us that the rural community is frequently a town in its own right. Continuity, community of attitude and

[42] See, for example, his study of Christina of Markyate, *Medieval Women, SCH Subsidia* 1 (1978) pp 185–204.

[43] See Duby pp 69, 81; A. Déléage, *La Vie rurale en Bourgogne jusqu'au début du XIe siècle,* 2 vols (Mâcon 1941); P. de Saint-Jacob, 'La Bourgogne rurale au haut Moyen Age. A propos d'un ouvrage récent', *RH* 195 (1945). See too the comments of I. N. Wood and Janet L. Nelson (above pp 74–5, nn 93–5, and 112–16), though the latter's discussion of developments in the Auxerrois should not be too readily applied to the very different circumstances of the southern part of the region.

[44] Leclercq p 219.

[45] See Leclercq's comments on the ambiguities of the term eremitic, *ibid* p 217 n 2.

[46] See, for example, the complex community revealed in the reports on the excavations at Faras, listed in the Polish National Museum's handbook to its permanent display of the Faras frescoes (Warsaw 1974).

[47] On the Syrian monasteries see the classic account of G. Tchalenko, *Villages antiques de la Syrie du Nord,* 3 vols (Paris 1953–8).

interest, whatever the particular differences, inter-relationships are the prime characteristics, and the simple tides of reform and decline cease to flow, to be replaced by more complex currents. We should perhaps concur in Henry Miller's judgement that 'every Middle Age is good, whether in man or history. It is full sunlight and the roads extend in every direction, and all the roads are downhill'.[48]

University of Edinburgh

[48] From *Black Spring*, quoted in *The Best of Henry Miller* (London 1960) p 19.

URBANITAS-RUSTICITAS: LINGUISTIC ASPECTS OF A MEDIEVAL DICHOTOMY

by MICHAEL RICHTER

CHRISTIAN teaching places man's origin in paradise, a rural setting, and the end of mankind in the celestial city of Jerusalem. Thus both town and country have potentially positive connotations to the believer. Yet just as the angel could fall to become satan, so town and country could acquire evil reputations, depending on the behaviour of human beings in these settings (after all, the fall of man took place in paradise).

Christian writings draw in many respects on human experience, including the setting of man in society. At times in history town and country were experienced as different settings of life. Certainly there existed a notion of a superiority of urban over rural existence in classical Greek times; in contrast, Roman civilisation was more geared towards rural life. Both Hellenic and Roman thought contributed a great deal to the shaping of early Christianity. I am concerned here primarily with medieval attitudes towards town and country, but it is a fact that these were, partly at least, based on earlier tradition.

What medieval Christians felt towards town and country can be investigated by studying the works in which they refer, directly or indirectly, to their own experiences and attitudes. So far as I know, there is no systematic investigation of this subject. A thorough analysis of the connotations associated with town and country will eventually help to deepen our understanding of the Christian religion as a social force in medieval society.

I here present a trial investigation which may prove helpful in a later, more comprehensive, study. In analysing some works by medieval authors, I shall concentrate on the vocabularies associated with town and country life, be it allegorically or realistically. There is no need to define town life, as we shall see, but country life requires some elucidation. It may be understood here in a rather loose sense as the association of man with nature, more precisely with the plants and animals that feed him.

I am dealing with some works of the medieval period, particularly from the fifth and sixth centuries and from later times, mainly from the twelfth century. This offers the possibility of comparison and contrast. The presentation of the material will be followed by more general considerations which may be of help in further investigations of what looks like a complex and rewarding line of research.

A key concept in St Augustine's *De catechizandis rudibus*[1] is that of *civitas* and *cives*. It occurs in concrete and allegorical usage. In concrete usage, the attitude towards *civitas* may be described as one of reservation if not open hostility. The city is the place of distraction and entertainment, as such preventing man from attaining his inner peace (XVI, 25). Christ was born in a city, but this was the small city of Bethlehem, so small in fact that in Augustine's time it was rather more like a village. Obviously, the terrestrial status of *cives* was not desirable (XVII, 40).

For a full appreciation we have to turn to the allegorical dimension of the *civitas*. Augustine distinguishes two cities, Babylon, the place glossed as *confusio*, symbol of man the sinner, on the one hand, and the celestial city of Jerusalem, glossed as *visio pacis* and described as the community of saints, on the other. In earthly society both are present and shape man (XI, XXI, 37). He is faced with a choice between two different cities, and he should aspire to Jerusalem. A separation of the two cities, Jerusalem and Babylon, will occur at the last judgment when Christ presides over his *civitas* as king (XX, 36; XXIV, 45).

With regard to man as creature, St Augustine states that there is a qualitative difference between man and animal: man even as sinner is superior to the beast (XVIII, 30).

Jerusalem supernae pacis visio, is the *civitas* which figures prominently in pope Gregory the Great's *Cura Pastoralis*.[2] In this work, the *civitas* is referred to merely in an allegorical sense. Yet the description of it is done in concrete terms. The *civitas* emerges as a place of fortification and defence, as is evident from a glance at the vocabulary he uses: *adversitas, circumdare, defensio, destruere, iacula, impugnare, munita civitas, murus, obsidio, penetrare*. The use of the pair *intra/foras* (III, 25) betrays the city as a rather circumscribed place.

[1] *CC* 46 (1969) pp 121–78. Augustine's *De Civitate Dei* (where *civitas* equals 'society') requires separate analysis, see Etienne Gilson, 'Église et Cité de Dieu chez St Augustin', *Archives d'Histoire Doctrinale et Littéraire du Moyen-Age*, 20 (Paris 1954) pp 5–23 with further references.

[2] *PL* 77 (1896) cols 13–149.

Contextual analysis shows that the city occurs in various functions, negatively and positively. On the one hand, it symbolises the enclosed human mind, enclosed against God's truth—*veritatis ad se iacula non admittunt* (III, 1). This city will be destroyed on the day of reckoning, the *dies irae.* On the other hand, the walls of Jerusalem, the archetypal city, are the virtues which are erected to protect man against *luxuria* (III, 19, on Jer 39, 9; 4 Kings 25, 10). Finally, there is the image of the *civitas* as the place where man obtains divine virtue which will equip him to leave the city in order to instruct his fellow men (III, 25).

Turning to the country in this work in the same manner we may present the rural vocabulary as classified functionally. Gregory refers to domesticated animals and such animals as are beneficial to man who appears in his function as pastor: *grex/gregis custodia, bos, pecus, sus, gallus, canis.* In addition, there are *irrationalia animalia, bruta animalia, bestiae agri*; we read of the *mola asinaria* and the *lupus.*

Contextual analysis reveals the following functions. The burden of the ass is worldly toil (I, 2). Those who fail to protect their flock are compared to the dumb dogs that do not bark (Is. 56, 10; II, 4). The oxen appear as water containers at the entrance to the Temple where the believers wash their hands before entering (II, 5). The cock is compared to the good preacher (III, 40). Here the domesticated animals are introduced allegorically to represent the people in charge of Christians. The intruders and those who threaten the safety are the untamed animals. Gregory even goes a step further and becomes more specific. He reminds his audience that in ancient times leaders of society had in fact been the pastors of the flock; in his own times this function seems to be transferred to the kings who ruled over man. He feels called, however, to emphasise that the functions of the rulers of men are different from those of the pastors, for man should dominate animals, but according to nature there is no justification for man having to fear those men who are set above him (II, 6). Gregory stresses that according to natural order there is no difference between lord and servant (III, 5).

Otfrid of Weissenburg, in the mid-ninth century, in his letter to archbishop Liutbert of Mainz in which he explains the purpose of his writing the *Liber Evangeliorum* in the vernacular, makes some comparisons between Latin and the German vernacular. He speaks of the vernacular in the following terms: *Huius enim linguae barbaries, ut est inculta et indisciplinabilis atque insueta capi regulari freno grammaticae artis,* and again: *nam dum agrestis linguae inculta verba inseruntur*

Latinitatis planitiae, cachinnum legentibus prebent. Lingua enim haec velut agrestis habetur.[3] Here we meet a clear concept of a qualitative difference between Latin and the vernacular, the latter being called *barbarus, incultus, agrestis*. Nature as well as the cultivated countryside is presented as inferior to the discipline associated with the tamed Latin, and the wildness is somewhat ridiculous.

Three centuries later, Otto of Freising reports the civilising influence of Latin which changed the barbarous Lombards. Latin represents the higher level of civilisation: *Latini sermonis elegantiam morumque retinent urbanitatem.*[4] Elegance is associated with town life (*urbanitas*), with a more refined lifestyle.

In a similar vein, Peter of Blois praises the elegance and sweet urbanity of the Latin style of his teacher Hildebert of Lavardin: *Profuit mihi, quod epistolas Hildeberti Cenomanensis episcopi styli elegantia et suavi urbanitate praecipuas firmare et corde tenus reddere adolescentulus compellebar.*[5] A complementary attitude can be perceived in the work of William of Newburgh when he describes the arrival in England of heretics in 1160. They are called people *sine literis et idiotae, homines plane impoliti et rustici.*[6] His choice of vocabulary gives the impression of country people being regarded as unlearned and uncouth.

Let us close with a brief look at Alain de Lille. In one of his sermons, he describes the Christian community as a fortified city, yet more concretely than Gregory the Great: *In hac civitate, murus fuit constantia, caementum temperantia, fortitudo propugnaculum, prudentia vallum. Orientalis porta fides, per quam sol iustitiae in ea illuxit; meridiana porta charitas, per quam in ea spiritus sancti ardor incaluit; septentrionalis porta virginitas, per quam in ea concupiscentia carnalis exstincta est; occidentalis porta humilitas, per quam in ea mundanae tentationes propulsatae sunt.*[7] Finally, in a passage on luxury Alain reveals his attitude towards country life: *O homo, haec est luxuria quae hominem in pecudem mutat; imo, homo per eam infra pecudem degenerat.*[8]

We now turn to an analysis of the material. Plainly the concept of *civitas* in St Augustine's work is different from that in the works of Gregory the Great and Alain de Lille. Augustine's allegorical *civitas*

[3] *MGH Epp* 6 (1925) p 167 lines 34–5; p 168 lines 27–9. The medieval attitudes towards Latin and the vernacular languages respectively deserve a full investigation.

[4] *Gesta Friderici Imperatoris* bk 2 cap 13, *MGH SRG* 46 (1912) p 116.

[5] *PL* 207 (1904) col 314.

[6] *Historia Rerum Anglicarum*, ed R. Howlett *RS* 82.1 (1884) pp 132 *seq*.

[7] *PL* 210 (1855) cols 200–1.

[8] *Ibid* col 123.

is the community of people who are held together by a special status. They are the chosen people of Christ, and they are individually characterised by their perception and experience of peace. In contrast, the *civitas* in Gregory and Alain is a fortified place (thus potentially a place of peace as well), isolated physically and set off against the surrounding area.

We notice an important semantic shift in the term *civitas* from the meaning of 'a group of people' to that of 'a place'. In Gregory the Great, the shift emerges, while Alain presents the end of its development. This semantic change must have occurred gradually, and a quotation from Isidore of Seville's *Etymologies* throws some light on this change: *Cives vocati quod in unum coeuntes vivant, ut vita communis et ornatior fiat et tutior.*[9] Again: *Civitas est hominum multitudo societatis vinculo adunata, dicta a civibus, id est ab ipsis incolis urbis ... Nam urbs ipsa moenia sunt, civitas autem non saxa, sed habitatores vocantur.*[10]

In contrasting the language use of the fifth and the twelfth century the full shift in the meaning of *civitas* becomes apparent. Augustine's use of *civitas* is close to the meaning in classical Latin, to the sense of community[11] (in the later Roman empire, the *civis Romanus* included the country dweller). We have seen that this sense is also still familiar to Isidore—possibly indicating the retarded evolution of Latin in Spain compared to the dynamism of Latin in Italy. By the twelfth century, the *civitas* had become the nucleated settlement with fortifications, the walled town. By then the term generally used for the territorial diocese (still known as *civitas* to Gregory of Tours) was *provincia*.

The way of life associated with towns in the twelfth century is described by *urbanitas*, a term derived, according to Isidore of Seville, from the most prominent feature of the medieval town, the wall. We met the concept of *urbanitas* as one of elegance and refinement.

It may well be that an increased appreciation of town life was required in order to associate rural life with negative connotations. In the examples given above, such a negative attitude is not yet perceptible in the works of Augustine and of Gregory the Great, but it appears in Otfrid as well as in William of Newburgh and Alain. Augustine and Alain also represent the opposite views of animals. To

[9] *PL* 82 (1830) col 348.

[10] *Ibid* col 536.

[11] See Carlo Battisti, 'La terminologia urbana nel Latino dell' alto medioevo con particolare riguarda all'Italia', *La Città nell'Alto Medioevo, SS Spoleto* 6 (1959) pp 647–77.

Augustine, man as sinner is superior to the beast, while Alain maintains that *luxuria* makes man lower than the animal. Thus by the twelfth century, town and country were experienced as contrasts, and life in town and country stamped its own quality onto man.

The way of life associated with the opposite of towns in the twelfth century is not invariably seen in a negative light,[12] but the connotations of *rusticitas* are generally negative. It appears, however, that not every person living in the country was a *rusticus* but only the lower classes which did the dirty work, the peasants. Their lack of education manifested itself in lack of refinement.[13] After all, schools that offered education to the interested secular person were associated with the cathedrals, situated in the *civitates*.[14]

In order to understand the evolving attitudes towards town and country in the middle ages we have to look at the development of society at large during that period. Augustine witnessed the invasion of the Roman empire by the barbarians, and he experienced the crumbling of a society in which *civitas* and community were identical. In the Roman empire, the cities were important, but their existence was related functionally to the provinces in which they were situated. Cities as administrative and military centres could not be separated from the country. Both formed one organic unit.

With the collapse of the Roman empire, the city lost this function in the areas of the *romanitas*. To people like Gregory the Great the city became the embattled isle in a sea of destruction. Whatever may be said about the decline of the cities in the dark ages, there is no convincing evidence that the barbarians themselves had a viable concept of towns. Where they were dominant, no new towns were established although it is true that the barbarians gradually settled in the towns already existing.

Positive urban growth in western Europe did not occur on a large scale before the eleventh century. From then onwards a great

[12] Here the concept of nature will have to be further analysed. Compare Bernard of Clairvaux, *Opera* 4 (Rome 1969) p 172: *In hac igitur ove duo reperies, naturam dulcem, naturam bonam, et bonam valde, tanquam butyrum et peccati corruptionem, ut caseum;* again p 173: *Virgo flos campi est, et non horti.*

[13] Compare the statement by Salvian that *malos esse servos ac detestabiles satis certum est,* quoted in J. Le Goff, 'Les paysans et le monde rural dans la littérature du haut moyen-âge (V–VI siècles),' *Agricoltura e mondo rurale in Occidente nell'Alto Medioevo, SS Spoleto* 13 (1966) pp 723–41.

[14] A revealing statement from the late thirteenth-century treatise 'De commendatione cleri' runs: *Qui facultatem deridet artium aut rusticus est quia litteras non novit aut uterum detestatur in quo formatus est,* Vat MS Pal Lat 1252 fol 104^{v}.

number of towns were founded. These towns became places of relative economic prosperity and of greater security for the individual. They were, or were being, fortified, and their inhabitants enjoyed special privileges which set them apart from the rural population and may have given rise to a feeling of superiority of the townspeople over the *rustici*. It is true that the medieval town was economically dependent on the country, but it is important that life in towns showed substantial differences from life in the country with regard to the occupation of the people. Townspeople had appreciably less daily contact with animals and plants than the inhabitants of the village, the hamlet or the farmstead.

It appears that the changes in attitude towards town and country between the fifth and the twelfth century are paralleled by changes in society as far as towns are concerned. There was general agreement that even after paradise man led originally a rural existence where pastor and king were identical. Urbanisation was not necessarily an indication of progress but it was an indication of change in society.

In the present discussion, I have taken several factors for granted which will have to be discussed in any detailed analysis of the subject. Only some of these can be indicated here. Christian writing draws heavily on biblical stories, and therefore a discussion of medieval attitudes towards town and country must be preceded by a discussion of town and country in the old and the new testament. In addition, we have to be aware that the bible was studied in western Europe in Latin translations, the septuagint and the vulgate. These two versions may contain different attitudes towards town and country. We thus have to face the problems posed by the Latin language itself. By the time the biblical translations were made, this language had already had a long history of its own. The Latin language originated in a rural setting, and it retained clear traces of this origin. Augustine, for example, was very conscious of it.[15] The Latin language had a particularly rural slant; the medium may have shaped the message.

We have come across this phenomenon in our discussion of the semantic change of *civitas*. An originally secular term gradually

[15] Compare 'De Disciplina Christiana' 6, 6, *CC* 46 (1969) p 213: *Totum enim quidquid homines possident in terra, omnia quorum domini sunt, pecunia vocatur. Servus sit, vas, ager, arbor, pecus; quidquid horum est, pecunia dicitur. Et unde sit primum vocata pecunia. Ideo pecunia, quia antiqui totum quod habebant, in pecoribus habebant. A pecore pecunia vocatur. Legimus antiquos patres divites fuisse pastores.* On the rural background of the Latin language see J. Marouzeau, *Lexique de la terminologie linguistique* (2 ed Paris 1943).

assumed a new meaning, it became a Christian technical term. We must mention another term where the development is different. *Paganus*, indicating the non-believer, is a term newly coined by the western Christians and apparently originating in the fourth century. From the seventh century onwards, it was believed that this term denoted the country people and thus showed that they had been the non-Christians, witness Isidore of Seville: *Pagani ex pagis Atheniensium dicti ubi exorti sunt. Ibi enim in locis agrestibus et pagis gentiles lucos idolaque statuerunt, et a tali initio vocabulum pagani sortiti sunt.*[16] Much research has been done on the term *paganus* in recent times, and there is general agreement now that *paganus* originally indicated the non-Christian in the sense of *alienus*, a person not belonging to the community.[17] It corresponds thus nicely to the concept of *civitas* as it is used by Augustine,[18] while the later associations of *paganus* with country people could possibly be associated with the gradually developing differentiation of town and country when the town dwellers believed themselves to be superior to the country people just as the Christians felt superior to the pagans.

Town and country are important concepts in the history of Christianity. They can be studied in many different ways, and I think that the analysis of the vocabulary is one of many fruitful approaches to the study of this subject. It is necessary to be aware of the social environment in which Christianity grew. Not surprisingly, there emerge points of contact between concepts and social reality. Christian concepts are to an appreciable extent influenced by general social factors in which Christianity lives. In this way an analysis of the attitude of the church towards town and country becomes a vital chapter in the history of human development more generally. The line of research outlined here promises particularly interesting results for the period I have chosen, for the early middle ages, a period for which the extent and degree of urbanisation in western Europe are

[16] *PL* 82 col 314.

[17] So Orosius, *Historia*, prologue 1, 9, quoted by Christine Mohrmann, 'Encore une fois: paganus', *Vigiliae Christianae* 6 (1952) pp 109–21; compare also Michel Roblin, 'Paganisme et rusticité', *Annales* 8 (1953) pp 173–83; [Ilona] Opelt, [Griechische und lateinische Bezeichnungen der Nichtchristen. Ein terminologischer Versuch'], *Vigiliae Christianae* 19 (1965) pp 1–22. An alternative to *paganus* is the most common new testament term *gentilis*, which is used in the non-urbanised early medieval Irish society.

[18] The new testament term closest to Augustine's *civitas* to designate the non-Christian is οἱ ἔξω compare Opelt p 11.

at present debated vigorously among historians and archaeologists.[19] Sociolinguistic studies can make a valuable independent contribution to this debate.

University College
Dublin

[19] Compare most recently *Topografia urbana e vita cittadina nell' Alto Medioevo in Occidente, SS Spoleto* 21 (1974); *Vor- und Frühformen der europäischen Stadt im Mittelalter,* ed Walter Schlesinger and Heiko Stever, 2 vols (2 ed Göttingen 1975); Susan Reynolds, *An Introduction to the History of English Medieval Towns* (Oxford 1977).

A MEDIEVAL URBAN CHURCH: THE CASE OF THE CRUSADER STATES

by BERNARD HAMILTON

ALTHOUGH the great majority of first-generation western settlers in the crusader states must have come from rural areas, most of them lived in towns when they reached the levant. This presented no problem: there was plenty of space in the towns of Outremer, for the Franks either slaughtered their Moslem inhabitants[1] or, more commonly, expelled them.[2] Initially, therefore, the towns of Frankish Syria were inhabited only by Franks and native Christians. The crusaders did not pursue a similar policy in the countryside because they were conscious of the need to keep an adequate labour-force. Native Christian peasants presented no problem in any case, while the Moslem peasants, who were probably the more numerous, were left undisturbed by their new rulers.[3]

Western forms of land tenure were introduced in Syria by the crusaders, but manorialism was not. The new Frankish landlords had very few demesne lands, and normally lived from the dues which their peasants paid them, which were usually a percentage of the crops.[4] Some of the Frankish lords lived in cities, but others lived in castles around which small townships often grew up. The only other forms of primary Frankish settlement outside the towns were a few fortified administrative centres and a few fortified churches and

This paper is a report on work in progress on a book which I am writing on the Latin church in the crusader states. In it I intend to substantiate more fully some of the controversial generalisations I have made here, which cannot be more fully treated in an article of this length.

[1] At Antioch in 1098, Jerusalem in 1099, Caesaraea in 1101.

[2] For example at Arsuf in 1101, Acre in 1104.

[3] In 1184, for example, most of the villages between Toron and Acre were inhabited by Moslem peasants. [*The Travels of*] *Ibn Jubayr,* [trans R. J. C. Broadhurst] (London 1952) pp 316–17.

[4] Some examples of fortified Frankish manor houses dating from the twelfth century have been discovered. Their function is not clear. Possibly they were collecting centres for Frankish landlords. M. Benvenisti, *The Crusaders in the Holy Land* (Jerusalem 1970), pp 233–45. On the rural organisation of Frankish Syria see J. Riley-Smith, *The Feudal Nobility and the Kingdom of Jerusalem, 1174–1277* (London 1973) cap 3, 'The Domain in the Countryside', pp 40–61.

monasteries which served important shrines.[5] Only slowly were Franks persuaded to settle in villages under the patronage of the church or of the crown, and such settlements were rare: less than a dozen of them are known, and their inhabitants were all Franks.[6]

The crusaders were very tolerant of the religion of their native subjects. Moslems were allowed the free practice of their faith, and as the twelfth century wore on were even permitted to open mosques in some of the cities from which they had at first been expelled.[7] Few attempts were made to convert them to Christianity,[8] although there were some Moslems who voluntarily became Christians.[9]

Except in Jerusalem, where exotic sects like the Saint Thomas's Christians and the Ethiopian Copts were found,[10] the native Christian population of the crusader states belonged mainly to four confessions. Armenians and Syrian Jacobites were found in large numbers in Edessa and Antioch, with a few congregations in some of the cities of the south; while the Maronites formed a close-knit community in the mountains of the county of Tripoli. In the view of the western church members of all three of these communions were heretics; but, to the surprise of some of the native Christian prelates, the crusaders made no attempt to force these dissident groups into union with the Roman see, but allowed them to keep their property and granted them complete religious freedom.[11]

[5] The *casale* of Saint Gilles to the north of Jerusalem is an example of a rural administrative centre; the mount Thabor monastery in Galilee and the convent of Bethany in Judaea are examples of fortified shrines.

[6] Darum was founded as a royal Frankish village by Amalric I, W[illiam of] T[yre, *Historia rerum in partibus transmarinis gestarum*,] bk 20 cap 19, *RHC Occ* 1, p 975; Beth-Gibelin was a Frankish village founded by the Hospitallers in 1168, *CGOH* p 399.

[7] There were mosques at Acre and Tyre in 1184, Ibn Jubayr pp 318, 321.

[8] An exception was the Praemonstratensian house of Saint Habacuc at Ramleh whose first abbot, Amalric, was commissioned by Innocent II to preach to the pagans in the holy land, N. Backmund, *Monasticon Praemonstratense*, (Straubing 1949–) 1, pp 397–9.

[9] For example, Abu 'l-Durr of the Mahgrib who became a Christian monk in Syria, Ibn Jubayr p 323. He seems to have been motivated by religious conviction, but many Moslem converts were deserters and, even at the time, Christians were sceptical about their sincerity. *Itinerarium Peregrinorum et Gesta Regis Ricardi auctore ut videtur Ricardo, canonico S. Trinitatis Londonensis*, bk 3 cap 16, ed W. Stubbs, *Chronicles and Memorials of the Reign of Richard I*, 1, *RS* 38, 1 (1864) p 230.

[10] *Description of the Holy Land by John of Würzburg, A.D. 1160–1170*, trans C. W. Wilson, *PPTS* 14 (1890) p 69.

[11] 'The Franks never raised any difficulties about matters of faith, nor [sought] to reach a single definition [of belief] among the Christians of different races. . . . They accepted as a Christian anybody who venerated the Cross, without [further] . . . examination.' [*Chronique de*] *M*[*ichel le*] *S*[*yrien, patriarche jacobite d'Antioche* (*1166–99*),] bk 16 cap 1, [ed with French translation J. B.] Chabot, 4 vols (Paris 1899–1924) 3, p 222.

The fourth group of native Christians were the Orthodox, who in the sources are sometimes called Greeks and sometimes Syrians, depending on which liturgical language they used.[12] The majority of the native Christians in the kingdom of Jerusalem were of this faith and there were substantial groups of them also in the cities of the northern states. In the eyes of the crusaders the Orthodox formed part of the one, holy, catholic church to which they themselves belonged. Unlike the separated eastern Christians, the Orthodox were required by the Franks to recognise the authority of the holy see, but if they did so they were allowed to keep their own churches and monasteries and to use their own rites. Indeed, they were allowed considerable latitude in matters of usage and doctrine when those diverged from western norms.[13] However, one consequence of the crusaders' belief in the unity of Catholics and Orthodox was that only one bishop could exercise authority over both communities in each diocese. In places where Orthodox bishops held office the crusaders initially expelled them and replaced them by Latins.[14] But the need to provide for the spiritual oversight of Orthodox clergy led the Franks during the twelfth century to modify their ecclesiastical system and to appoint Orthodox co-adjutor bishops to assist the Latin bishops. This practice had certainly been adopted by Amalric I's reign[15] and it may well have come into being at an earlier date, for when ratifying a similar settlement for the church of Cyprus in 1223, Honorius III affirmed that it was modelled on the traditional practice

[12] When the sources speak of Greeks they clearly mean Orthodox. Syrian is an imprecise term which could mean either Orthodox or Jacobite unless it is qualified – for example, 'Suriens de la loy de Grèce', *Chronique du Templier de Tyr (1242–1309), Les Gestes des Chiprois,* ed G. Raynaud, *Publications de la Société de l'Orient Latin, série historique* 5 (Geneva 1887) pp 151, 239. From the context it is clear that most references to Syrians in the kingdom of Jerusalem relate to Orthodox. This has been convincingly argued by G. Every, 'Syrian Christians in Palestine in the early Middle Ages', *Eastern Churches Quarterly* 6 (Ramsgate 1945–6) pp 363–72.

[13] For example, at a time when feelings ran high between Rome and Constantinople on the subject of the *Filioque* clause, Greek artists commissioned by the Byzantine emperor Manuel I executed a mosaic illustrating the council of Constantinople of 381 in the Latin cathedral of Bethlehem in which belief in the Holy Spirit is formulated in the Orthodox way without the addition of the *Filioque.* H. Stern, 'Les réprésentations des Conciles dans l'Église de la Nativité à Bethléem', *B* 11 (1936) pp 101–54; 13 (1938) pp 415–59; text of the mosaic *ibid* 13, p 421, see also p 437.

[14] This was the situation in north Syria, *MS* bk 14 cap 9, Chabot 3, p 191. There is no information known to me about initial crusader treatment of Orthodox bishops in the patriarchate of Jerusalem.

[15] A document of 1173 mentions an Orthodox 'archbishop of all the Syrians and Greeks living in Gaza and Jabin' who was in communion with the Latin church. Gaza and Jabin were in the Latin diocese of Hebron. *CGOH,* p 443.

of the kingdom of Jerusalem.[16] As a result of this modification the Orthodox in the crusader states came to form a virtually self-governing community under the authority of Latin bishops.

Therefore, the Latin church which the crusaders established in their territories ministered solely to western settlers, who formed only a fraction of the total population. At the head of the Latin establishment were the patriarchs of Antioch and Jerusalem and they were assisted by a varying number of bishops of whom, at the period of maximum Frankish territorial expansion, there were thirty.[17] Each bishop had his own household officials, and was assisted by an archdeacon who was responsible for the judicial and administrative business of the see. Each Latin cathedral was administered by a dean and chapter of canons, who were sometimes regulars, but more often seculars, and whose numbers varied from twelve to eighteen. The diocesan structure or Frankish Syria resembled that of western Europe and compared favourably with it: there were, for example, fourteen dioceses in the twelfth-century kingdom of Jerusalem and only seventeen in the far larger Angevin kingdom of England. On a parish level, however, there was no parity between the Syrian and western churches.

In the twelfth century there was normally one Latin parish in each crusader town. In towns which were episcopal sees the cathedral fulfilled this function, but in other towns a church of the Latin rite was built and given parish status.[18] Only in cases where the town grew beyond the walls was a new parish set up to serve the *faubourg*.[19] Most Frankish castles had chapels, and chaplains were appointed by the castellans,[20] but such chapels did not usually enjoy parochial rights.

[16] '. . . quatuor . . . episcopi graeci, qui de consensu nostro . . . semper remanebunt in Cypro, oboedientes erunt Romanae Ecclesiae et archiepiscopo et episcopis Latinis, secundum consuetudinem regni Hierosolymitani.' *Pontificia Commissio ad redigendum codicem iuris canonici Orientalis, Fontes,* 3 series, 3, ed A. L. Tautu, *Acta Honorii III et Gregorii IX* (Vatican City 1950) pp 144–8, no 108.

[17] Patriarchate of Antioch, Latin sees at Antioch, Mamistra, Tarsus, Edessa, Coricium, Hierapolis, Apamea, Marasch, Keiçoun, Artah, Raphaniah, Laodicea, Tortosa, Tripoli, Biblos, Jabala. Patriarchate of Jerusalem, Latin sees at Jerusalem, Tyre, Petra, Nazareth, Caesaraea, Bethlehem, Hebron, Lydda, Sebaste, Tiberias, Banias, Acre, Sidon, Beirut.

[18] For example, Saint Peter's, Jaffa, [*Cartulaire de l'Église du St-Sépulcre de Jérusalem,* ed E.] de Rozière, *Collection des documents inédits sur l'histoire de France,* 1 series, 5 (Paris 1849) pp 15–17, no 14; Saint Paul's, Ascalon, WT bk 17 cap 30, *RHC Occ* 1, p 812.

[19] For example, Saint Nicholas, built to serve the *faubourg* of Jaffa, de Rozière, pp 289–90, no 161.

[20] See Baldwin IV's letter of appointment of William Lovell as chaplain of the royal castle of Jaffa, [H.-F.] Delaborde, [*Chartes de la Terre Sainte provenant de l'Abbaye de Notre-Dame de Josaphat*], *BEFAR* 19 (1880) pp 85–6, no 38.

If a township grew up around the castle a separate church was customarily built to serve the Frankish inhabitants.[21] The few Frankish villages had their own parish churches[22] and there were a few other rural churches of the Latin rite in important administrative centres.[23] But, overall, rural parishes were exceptional in Outremer and town parishes not numerous, so that Latin bishops had comparatively few subordinate clergy.

The Latin clergy drew their income from various sources of which the most important was the tithe payable by all Frankish landowners, but not levied on lands owned by eastern-rite Christians before the fourth Lateran council.[24] Bishops and chapters also took over any endowments which had formerly belonged to Orthodox dioceses,[25] while the churches of Jerusalem, Bethlehem and Nazareth, because of the esteem in which they were held, received landed endowments from the faithful in Outremer and throughout the west.[26] In marked contrast to western Europe, laymen in the crusader states in the twelfth century did not own tithes,[27] although some of them attempted to evade payment of tithe by nominally conveyancing land to eastern Christians who were not liable to pay tithe.[28]

The few Latin clergy of Outremer should therefore have been

[21] For example Nostre-Dame du Bourg in the Hospitaller castle of Krak des Chevaliers, J. Delaville Le Roulx, 'Inventaire des pièces de Terre Sainte de l'Ordre de l'Hôpital', *R*[*evue de l'*] *O*[*rient*] *L*[*atin*] 3 (Paris 1895) p 87, no 267.

[22] For example those built by the canons of the Holy Sepulchre in villages which they founded, de Rozière, pp 233–8, no 128.

[23] For example the church *cum iure parrochiali* in the royal *casale* of Saint Gilles, de Rozière, pp 258–60, no 142.

[24] The consequences of this ruling are explained in a letter of Innocent IV to the abbot of Sainte Margarite de Agros, in the archdiocese of Nicosia, L. de Mas Latrie, *Histoire de l'Ile de Chypre sous le règne des princes de la maison de Lusignan,* 3 vols (Paris 1852–61) 3 pp 643–4.

[25] For example, in 1140 the prior of the Holy Sepulchre successfully laid claim to property at Antioch which had belonged to his cathedral *temporibus antiquorum Grecorum,* de Rozière pp 178–80, no 90.

[26] For example, Eugenius III's confirmation of the lands of the Holy Sepulchre, de Rozière pp 36–41, no 23; Gregory IX's confirmation of the lands of the church of Bethlehem, [P.] Riant, [*Études sur l'Église de Bethléem*], 2 vols (Genoa 1889, Paris 1896) 1, pp 140–7, no 11; and documents relating to the property of the church of Nazareth in Italy, *Società di Storia Patria per la Puglia, Codice diplomatico Barese,* 18 vols (Bari 1897–1950) 8, pp 123–4 no 85, pp 155–6 no 110, p 170 no 125, pp 178–9 no 134, p 210 no 164, pp 244–5 no 190, pp 342–3 no 269, pp 337–8 no 267, pp 343–4 no 270, pp 346–7 no 273, pp 359–60 no 279, pp 360–1 no 280.

[27] [G.] Constable, [*Monastic Tithes from their origins to the Twelfth Century*] (Cambridge 1964) p 85, n 2.

[28] [*Les Régistres de Grégoire IX,* ed L.] Auvray, 3 vols, *BEFAR,* 2 series (Paris 1896–1955) no 4474.

affluent and episcopal authority should have been strong. This was not so, because the Frankish secular clergy had to share their resources and their authority with other groups of western churchmen. First there were the monks. The chief shrines of the holy land, which were the official *raison d'être* of the crusading movement, were entrusted to communities of monks and nuns who built and served churches on those sites. In some ways they were of help to the secular clergy, for they ministered to the large, but seasonal, influx of western pilgrims who came to Syria each year, but in other ways they proved something of a mixed blessing to their secular colleagues. For these communities received endowments throughout the crusader states and founded priories in some of the cities to act as administrative centres for their lands.[29] The mother houses and each of their priories had their own chapels which, while not enjoying parochial status, tended to attract some Franks away from their parish churches. The secular clergy were particularly concerned when their parishioners were buried in monastic churches and left legacies to those communities which would otherwise have been made to their parish churches.[30] Conflicts also arose at times between monks and bishops about the appointment of priests to rural parishes in monastic estates, but since such parishes were few those disputes were rare.[31] More serious were monastic exemptions from payment of tithe. In 1103, for example, pope Paschal II exempted all the lands of the Mount Thabor monastery from tithe,[32] and although total exemptions were uncommon, partial exemptions became relatively frequent.[33]

But the bishops faced a more serious threat when the new orders of

[29] For example, the Benedictine monastery of Our Lady of Josaphat at Jerusalem had daughter-houses at Tiberias, Ch. Köhler, 'Chartes de l'Abbaye de Notre-Dame de la Vallée de Josaphat en Terre Sainte (1108–1291). – Analyses et extraits', *ROL* 7 (1899) pp 113–14, no 2; at Sidon, *ibid* p 124, no 14; at Sichem, *ibid* pp 156–7, no 48; at Antioch, *ibid* pp 172–3, no 64.

[30] Many of these monasteries received privileges similar to that which Paschal II granted to Santa Maria Latina, Jerusalem: 'Cimiterium quoque, quod vel in ipso monasterii claustro vel in ecclesiis ad ipsum pertinentibus habetur, omnino liberum esse decernimus, ut eorum, qui illic sepeliri deliberaverint, petitioni et extremi voluntati, nisi forte excommunicati sint, nullus obsistat.' ed W. Holtzmann, 'Papst-Kaiser-und Normannenurkunden aus Unteritalien', *QFIAB* 35 (1955) pp 50–3, no 1.

[31] For example, archbishop William of Nazareth disputed the right of the monks of Josaphat to control the parish church in the *casale* of Ligio which his predecessor had given them, Delaborde, pp 56–8, no 24.

[32] Jaffé 5948, Constable, pp 95–6.

[33] See, for example, the large number of grants of tithe confirmed to the monastery of Josaphat by Anastasius IV, Delaborde pp 63–7, no 28.

fighting monks were founded, the Templars in 1128, and the Hospitallers, who became militarised soon after. Both orders came to have their own chaplains and to receive from the holy see virtual rights of exemption from the ordinary, the Templars in 1139, the Hospitallers in 1154.[34] They established houses in many of the cities of the crusader states and their chapels, which possessed many papal privileges such as the right to say mass even during an interdict, attracted lay congregations. Moreover, the orders soon came to acquire large tracts of territory, by gift or by purchase, particularly in frontier districts, and this often led to disputes with the local bishop about his right to collect tithes in those areas or to exercise jurisdiction in chapels or parish churches which the orders owned. Although William of Tyre's account of the degree of exemption which the orders enjoyed is clearly much exaggerated,[35] it remains true that the powers and revenues of Latin bishops were much diminished as a result of the orders' growth. Take, for example, the case of Tortosa where in 1152 the castle and its dependencies were granted to the Templars. It was agreed that the bishop of Tortosa should control the churches of the city, but that churches elsewhere in the fief belonging to the order should be exempt from episcopal jurisidiction; that the demesne lands of the order should not pay tithe, but that the tithe on all other lands owned by the order should be divided with the bishop.[36] This was fairly typical of the compromises reached between bishops and members of both orders.

The power of the secular church was also threatened by the Italian maritime communes whose shipping gave the crusader states naval protection, kept open their lines of communication with the west and handled the bulk of their commerce. In return for their support these cities received important concessions in the Frankish east, which normally included the gift of quarters in some of the ports in which they might build churches for the use of their nationals. In the more important ports all three communes, the Genoese, Pisans and Venetians, had their own chapels. Although these chapels did not at first have parochial status, most of them later tried to obtain it, and

[34] The Templars in the bull *Omne Datum Optimum* of 1139. The Hospitallers' right to have brother priests and to become a completely exempt order was formally recognised in the bull *Christiane fidei religio* of 1154. [J.] Riley-Smith, [*The* [*Knights*] *of St John in Jerusalem and Cyprus, 1050–1310*] (London 1967) pp 235–6.

[35] WT bk 18 cap 6, *RHC Occ* 1, pp 826–7.

[36] J. Riley-Smith, 'The Templars and the castle of Tortosa in Syria: an unknown document concerning the acquisition of the fortress', *EHR* 84 (1969) pp 278–88.

also to gain total exemption from the authority of the local bishop.[37] Some of them succeeded in this ambition, so that when Jacques de Vitry went to Acre as bishop in 1216 he found that the Italian churches there did not acknowledge his jurisidiction at all, and their clergy even refused to allow him to preach in them.[38]

The problem of exempt churches was not peculiar to the crusader states but common to the whole of Latin Christendom. What was unique in the case of Frankish Syria was that during the twelfth century the secular clergy, who were few, came to be outnumbered by the monastic clergy, the chaplains of the military orders and the priests of the Italian communes, and that their powers and their financial resources were seriously eroded by the rights of partial or total exemption which those clergy enjoyed.

Nevertheless, before 1187 there were adequate resources to support the entire religious establishment of Frankish Syria, and although episcopal powers were curtailed by the exempt clergy they were not, in most cases, dangerously impaired. This changed after the battle of Hattin, for the Franks were then restricted to a narrow strip of coastal territory, with only intermittent control over parts of Galilee. The Frankish population was not greatly diminished, since refugees from Moslem-occupied territory came to live in the coastal cities. To meet this increase in population bishops created extra parishes in some towns.[39]

The secular church was hardest hit by this change in fortune, although in some ways it was its own worst enemy. In the thirteenth century only four of the fourteen dioceses of the kingdom of Jerusalem remained permanently in Christian hands.[40] Nevertheless, bishops continued to be appointed to twelve of the former sees and the patriarch of Jerusalem, together with seven other bishops whose cathedrals were in enemy hands, came to the new capital, Acre, with their

[37] The exemption of the Venetian churches at Acre and Tyre is attested in [*Urkunden zur älteren Handels- und Staatsgeschichte der Republik Venedig mit besonders Beziehung auf Byzanz und die Levante*, ed G. L. F.] Tafel and [G. M.] Thomas, *Fontes rerum Austriacarum*, Sectio 2, 12–14, 3 vols (Vienna 1856–7) 2 pp 445–8, nos 212, 213; that of the Pisan church of Acre in [G.] Müller, [*Documenti sulle relazioni delle città toscane coll 'Oriente cristiano e coi Turchi fino all' anno 1531*], *Documenti degli archivi toscani*, 3 (Florence 1879) pp 82–3, no 52.

[38] *Lettres* [*de Jacques de Vitry (1160/70–1240), évêque de Saint-Jean d'Acre*, ed R. B. C. Huygens] (Leiden 1960) pp 85–6, no 2.

[39] For example, two new parishes are named in Acre in 1200, Müller pp 82–3, no 52; and two in Antioch in 1227, Riant 1, p 145, no 11.

[40] Acre, Tyre, Caesaraea, Beirut.

households and their chapters of canons, and set up pro-cathedrals which were exempt from the authority of the bishop of the city.[41] They were always anxious to increase their often meagre revenues, drawn chiefly from endowments still in Christian hands, and were not above trying to collect tithes from their former parishioners who, like themselves, had sought refuge in Acre.[42] The secular church, therefore, had to support a hierarchy of almost pre-1187 size while its resources were only a fraction of what they had formerly been.

The situation was made worse because they faced increased competition for a share of those resources from the other groups of clergy. The monastic establishment grew in size after 1187, for all the many religious communities of Jerusalem set up houses at Acre after the third crusade[43] and during the thirteenth century new religious orders founded houses there and in some of the other coastal cities. The most important of these new orders, but by no means the only ones, were the Dominicans, the Franciscans and the Carmelites.[44] All these foundations attracted landed endowments together, often, with some part of the tithe which was thus lost to the secular church; and they also took Frankish laymen, and their legacies, away from the parish churches.[45]

The chapels belonging to the Italian maritime cities were virtually unaffected by the conquests of Saladin, since they were situated in ports most of which remained in crusader hands. As the volume of Mediterranean trade increased in the thirteenth century new groups of merchants, like the Provençals and the Anconitans, came to the Syrian ports and they too built chapels for their nationals,[46] so that the

[41] The patriarch of Jerusalem, the archbishop of Nazareth and the bishops of Bethlehem, Lydda, Hebron, Sebaste, Tiberias and Sidon.

[42] Innocent III, *Regesta, PL* 214–16 (1856) *an* I, no 516; *PL* 214, col 476.

[43] Our Lady of Josaphat, Our Lady of Sion, Mount of Olives, Santa Maria Latina, Templum Domini, Saint Anne's, Sainte Marie la Grande, Convent of Bethany, Saint Samuel's, and the hospital of Saint Lazarus.

[44] Carmelite church at Acre, [*Les Registres d'Alexandre IV,* ed C.] Bourel de la Roncière, *BEFAR*, 2 series, 2 vols (Paris 1902–31) no 3250. On the Franciscans, Golubovich 1, *passim.* References to the Dominicans in the crusader states in F. M. Abel, 'Le couvent des frères précheurs à Saint-Jean d'Acre', *Révue Biblique* 43 (Paris 1934) pp 265–84. Some of the more important of the minor houses at Acre were Sancta Trinitas Captivorum, Auvray no 4014; the Cistercian nuns of Saint Mary Magdalen's, *CGOH* no 1828; Saint Catherine's, E. Strehlke, *Tabulae Ordinis Theutonici* (Berlin 1869) pp 68–9, no 86; Saint Thomas of Canterbury, Bourel de la Roncière, no 1553.

[45] For example the many bequests listed in the will of Saliba, burgess of Acre, in 1264, *CGOH* no 3105.

[46] Anconitan church, S. Pauli, *Codice diplomatico del sacro militare ordine gerosolimitano oggi di Malta,* 2 vols (Lucca 1733–7) 1, pp 157–61; church of the Provençals, Tafel and Thomas,

authority of the secular clergy was correspondingly weakened. But the most serious threat to the authority of the bishops came from the military orders, which now included the Teutonic knights, founded after the third crusade, as well as the two older orders. During the thirteenth century they came to control between them most of the castles and much of the land of Frankish Syria, and this led to a further decline in episcopal patronage and revenue.[47]

When Jacques de Vitry came to Acre in 1216 he complained to friends in Paris that his new see was like a nine-headed monster.[48] This was, if anything, an understatement, for the ecclesiastical condition of Outremer at that time was one of chaos, tempered only by expensive, and often not very effective, appeals to Rome. This remained true until James Pantaleon, patriarch of Jerusalem, became pope Urban IV. Having personal experience of the situation, he attempted to remedy matters by uniting the see of Acre to the patriarchate of Jerusalem in 1262, so that the head of the Latin church in the holy land should have an adequate power-base,[49] and by giving the patriarch legatine powers over all the remaining crusader territories.[50] In theory at least the patriarch as legate could exercise authority in the pope's name over the exempt clergy as well as over his own suffragans; but a situation which had taken so long to develop would have taken time to put right and time was not on the patriarch's side, for within thirty years of this settlement the Mameluks had overrun all crusader territory.

The fact that the Latin church in Syria existed only for a ruling minority which lived almost exclusively in a few cities certainly brought about a collapse in episcopal authority, for the bishops had to compete in resources and spiritual influence with exempt groups of clergy who out-numbered them and who were vying for control of the same

---

3, p 32. The commune churches sometimes faced setbacks. Thus the Pisan church of Acre was deprived of its parochial status by pope Innocent IV in 1247, *Les Registres d'Innocent IV*, ed E. Berger, *BEFAR*, 2 series, 4 vols (Paris 1884–1921) no 2801.

[47] Bishops fought tenaciously for their rights, sometimes with success. Thus the compromise reached between the bishop of Acre and the Hospitallers about payment of dues and parochial rights in 1221, (*CGOH* no 1718), was re-negotiated in 1228 in the bishop's favour (*ibid* no 1911). On the other hand the archbishop of Nazareth in 1263 renounced all his episcopal rights over the Mount Thabor monastery and the lands which it owned in his diocese in favour of the Hospital, who had gained possession of it (*ibid* no 3054).

[48] *Lettres*, p 83, no 2.

[49] *Les Registres d'Urbain IV*, ed J. Guiraud, *BEFAR*, 2 series, 4 vols (Paris 1901–29) no 168.

[50] *Ibid* no 241.

limited number of souls and the same restricted amount of real estate. Reading the surviving sources, one can easily form the impression that the crusader clergy spent most of their time wrangling about who should have the largest slice of an ever-diminishing economic cake.

But such a negative assessment of their work would be distorted, for they achieved much that was of value. The orders of the Temple and the Hospital which, in their different ways, had a profound influence on the whole of Catholic Christendom, had their inception in Outremer and in their formative stages received much encouragement from the secular church there.[51] The crusader clergy were also responsible for building an impressive number of shrine churches as a visible expression of their veneration for the holy places,[52] while the extent of their work as patrons of a flourishing school of manuscript illumination is only now receiving full recognition.[53]

But their most remarkable achievement was to promote a spirit of religious tolerance in an age when that was rare. Although the union between Latin and Orthodox broke down in the thirteenth century, that was the result largely of political pressures generated by the fourth crusade rather than of any failure of consideration for the Orthodox on the part of the Latin hierarchy.[54] Moreover, the good relations which the Franks maintained with the other Christian confessions who lived among them produced positive results. For the Maronites, Jacobites and Armenians all entered voluntarily into union with the western church during the crusader period, although only the Maronite union outlasted the collapse of Frankish political power in Syria.[55] This achievement seems all the more remarkable

[51] Riley-Smith, *Knights* pp 32–59; WT bk 12 cap 7, *RHC Occ* 1, p 520 gives details of support for the early Templars.

[52] T. S. R. Boase, 'Ecclesiastical Art in the Crusader States in Palestine and Syria. A. Architecture and Sculpture', *A History of the Crusades,* ed K. M. Setton, 4 vols (Philadelphia 1955–) 4, ed H. W. Hazard, *The Art and Architecture of the Crusader States* (Wisconsin 1977) pp 69–116; B. Hamilton, 'Rebuilding Zion: the holy places of Jerusalem in the twelfth century', *SCH* 14 (1977) pp 105–116.

[53] H. Buchtal, *Miniature Painting in the Latin Kingdom of Jerusalem* (Oxford 1957); J. Folda, *Crusader Manuscript Illumination at Saint-Jean d'Acre, 1275–91* (Princeton 1975).

[54] There is some discussion of this in S. Runciman, *The Eastern Schism* (Oxford 1955) pp 112–17, but a fuller treatment of this subject is needed.

[55] The Maronites were reconciled in 1182, WT bk 22 cap 8, *RHC Occ* 1, pp 1076–7; the Jacobite union lasted from 1236 (see Gregory IX's bull, *Causam Conditoris Omnium,* Auvray no 3789), until 1263, Bar Hebraeus, *Chronicon,* cap 96, ed J. B. Abbeloos, T. J. Lamy, 2 vols (Louvain 1872–4) 1 cols 746–50. For the Armenian union, formally inaugurated in 1198, see B. Hamilton, 'The Armenian Church and the Papacy at the time of the Crusades', *Eastern Churches Review* 10 (1978) pp 61–87.

when it is considered how intolerant the Latin church in western Europe became of any deviation from Catholic norms in the course of the thirteenth century. It is arguable that the weakness of the Latin episcopate in Syria and the fact that much of their energy was directed into struggles with other groups of western clergy contributed in some measure towards their tolerance of eastern Christian confessions who constituted no kind of threat to the authority or the resources of the Frankish bishops.

University of Nottingham

A TRUTH UNIVERSALLY ACKNOWLEDGED

by EMMA MASON

'IT is a truth universally acknowledged that the practice of religion will be influenced by the social conditions prevailing in any given locality.' The debate on this statement is largely concentrated for present purposes into a consideration of activities between *c*1100 and *c*1250 in two distinctive societies: Westminster abbey and its environs and, in contrast, the city and diocese of Worcester. The essential function of Westminster abbey was, of course, intercessory, and while this role was shared with Worcester cathedral, the latter church had also a wide-ranging pastoral responsibility. In this sense, no exact equation can be made, yet the richness of the records which both churches accumulated presents adequate material for a valid comparison in other respects. It is not intended, and is, indeed, impossible to make an arbitrary definition of Westminster as town and Worcester as countryside. Elements of both were contained in Westminster and Worcester alike.

Westminster centred on an eminent and wealthy Benedictine abbey, under royal patronage, and from the latter part of Henry II's reign the administration of the realm was directed from the immediate vicinity. Tenants of the abbey included prominent and sophisticated *curiales*, both clerical and lay, while successful and articulate citizens of London, a few kilometres down the Thames, were also involved in transactions with the chapter, in a spiritual as well as in a tenurial capacity. There were considerable suburbs around the abbey, although the lands adjoining these in turn were rural.[1] Within the abbey precincts, artistic and scholarly activities of considerable significance were pursued, while haymaking and other agricultural occupations were in full swing barely a kilometre away. Westminster may be depicted as a sophisticated urban district but not as a town in the formal sense, even though it had its own reeve from the late twelfth century.[2]

[1] [Barbara] Harvey, ['Work and] Festa Ferianda [in Medieval England',] *JEH* 23 (1972) p 301.

[2] [H. G.] Richardson, 'William of Ely, [the king's treasurer (? 1195–1215)'], *TRHS* 4 series, 15 (1932) pp 84–5.

Worcester, in contrast, may be described as a bucolic city, and even today, it is little more than a market town clustered around a cathedral. The diocese covered a clearly defined geographical region—the lands of the old tribal kingdom of the Hwicce, comprising Worcestershire and Gloucestershire, but apart from their county towns, it contained no others of any real significance in the period under discussion. Worcester itself developed the institutions of urban government, with officials who became increasingly articulate, during the period under discussion,[3] but the surrounding countryside was governed in a much more conservative way. The bishop and chapter were among the leading landholders, and exercised jurisdiction over the triple hundred of Oswaldslaw, while the neighbouring Benedictine house of Evesham, also a major landholder, held a fourth hundred. Pershore abbey had been deprived of much of its property when Edward the Confessor made arrangements for the endowment of Westminster abbey,[4] but while both houses were prominent landholders, neither competed for jurisdictional influence in the shire to any great extent.

It was perhaps as well for them that they did not. The lay lords of the diocese included several old-established baronial families, all largely non-resident,[5] but also the Beauchamps of Elmley Castle, who were very much present. They controlled the shrievalty of Worcester intermittently in the twelfth century and almost constantly in the thirteenth, using their official powers to enhance their territorial position. The existence of the ecclesiastical franchises, and in particular that of Worcester, appeared as an obstacle to the family's ambitions, and they stopped at nothing to assert supremacy over these troublesome priests.[6] Royal intervention in the mid thirteenth century ensured the formal continuation of both franchises,[7] but the Beauchamps persisted in making piecemeal encroachments on the rights of the two houses.[8] Any evaluation of the conduct of Christian life in the diocese must be seen against this background of continual harrassment, not merely in

[3] [*The Cartulary of*] *Worcester* [*Cathedral Priory* (Register 1), ed R. R. Darlington] *P*[*ipe*] *R*[*oll*] *S*[*ociety*], ns 38 (1968) p xl.

[4] [Barbara] Harvey, *Westminster abbey* [*and its estates in the middle ages*] (Oxford 1977) p 73.

[5] R. H. Hilton, *A Medieval Society* (London 1966) p 41.

[6] See the introduction to my edition of [*The*] *Beauchamp* [*Cartulary*], *PRS*, ns, forthcoming.

[7] *Beauchamp*, nos 50, 58–60.

[8] [*The Register of Bishop Godfrey*] *Giffard*, [ed J. W. Willis Bund], 2, *Worcestershire Historical Society* 15 (Oxford 1902) p 75; BL Harley MS 3763, fol 168v.

time of civil war, when most houses suffered depredations by neighbouring magnates,[9] but also in what passed for a time of peace.

Social conditions were undoubtedly primitive in this respect, but not necessarily so in others. Following the establishment of the marcher fiefs in the later eleventh century, Worcestershire itself was largely immune from Welsh raiding. The cathedral's more remote estates in the marches might suffer from time to time,[10] but successive bishops could normally administer their diocese free from the alien intruders who hampered the activities of Gilbert Foliot as bishop of neighbouring Hereford.[11] Moreover, most of the bishops of Worcester in the period under discussion had been secular priests,[12] several of whom had gained administrative experience in one diocese or another, while some had served the royal government. Prominent among the latter were Simon (1125–50); Mauger (1199–1212); Walter de Grey (1214–15) and the forceful Walter de Cantilupe (1236–66).[13] Roger of Gloucester (1163–79) had the equally useful qualification of being a cousin of Henry II.

The bishop of Worcester resembled the abbot of Westminster in being the head of a Benedictine house, although the actual supervision of Worcester cathedral priory would normally be left to its prior. Few of the bishops themselves were Benedictines. Only Wulfstan (1062–95), just outside the period under consideration, and three short-reigning bishops within it—Henry de Soilli (1193–5); Randulf of Evesham (1213–14) and Silvester of Evesham (1216–18)—belonged to this order, while Baldwin (1180–5) was a Cistercian.[14] Monks would not normally regard themselves as being obliged to undertake pastoral work, except perhaps in respect of certain privileged individuals.[15] Many conscientious Benedictine abbots would no doubt have agreed with Samson of Bury that furthering the architectural glories of their houses ranked ahead even of sound estate management in their order of priorities.[16] In the eleventh century, Wulfstan had demonstrated

[9] [*The Letters and Charters of Gilbert*] *Foliot,* [ed A. Morey and C. N. L. Brooke] (Cambridge 1967) nos 2–3, 5, 22, 35.

[10] *Worcester,* pp xxxij–iij; nos 252, 256.

[11] *Foliot* nos 13, 65.

[12] *Worcester* p lv.

[13] Le Neve, 2, pp 99–101.

[14] *Ibid.*

[15] Marjorie Chibnall, 'Monks and Pastoral Work: a problem in Anglo-Norman History', *JEH* 18 (1967), p 168.

[16] [*The Chronicle of Jocelin of*] *Brakelond,* [transl and ed H. E. Butler] (London 1949) pp 47–8. In fairness it must be observed that early twelfth-century conciliar decrees debarred

that a monastic bishop could be a very effective pastor indeed,[17] but with the growth of administrative business in the twelfth century, a bishop of any description who gave much of his time to pastoral activities was a subject for comment. Prominent among this minority, however, were the Benedictines Herbert Losinga of Norwich[18] and Gundulf of Rochester.[19]

On the other hand, it is unrealistic to draw a hard and fast line between the theoretically exclusive spiritual life of the Benedictines and the consciously outgoing ethos of later orders such as the Augustinians or Franciscans. The interaction between the monks and the laity was in practice considerable. Both Worcester[20] and Westminster[21] had lay officials—stewards, butlers or even cooks—who with their families lived in close contact with the religious community. Such officers, often hereditary, were attached to most houses of any size, and made themselves conspicuous at Bury[22] and Norwich[23] among other places. Indeed, it was the wife of one such official who, on her return to Norwich cathedral priory from a pilgrimage to Compostella, prompted an important development in the new cult of St William,[24] an episode which illustrates the influence which the laity associated with a house might have on its conduct.

Westminster abbey, in the late twelfth century, included among its tenants in the immediate neighbourhood various craftsmen, such as painters. While much of their contact with the abbey was either on professional business or in tenurial transactions,[25] occasional donations, such as those of Rose the cushion-maker, show that they might also feel some community of identity with its religious aspirations.[26] No doubt other churches, monastic and secular alike, which had embarked

---

monks from pastoral activities – [C. N. L.] Brooke, 'The missionary at home: [the Church in the towns, 1000–1250'] *SCH* 6 (1970) p 82.

[17] *The Vita Wulfstani of William of Malmesbury*, ed R. R. Darlington, *CSer*, 3 ser, 40 (1928).

[18] [M.] Brett, [*The English Church under Henry I*] (Oxford 1975) p 117.

[19] R. A. L. Smith, *Collected Papers* (London 1947) pp 96–7.

[20] *Worcester* no 129.

[21] *Beauchamp* nos 190–92.

[22] *Brakelond* p 27.

[23] [M. D.] Anderson, [*A Saint at Stake: the strange death of William of Norwich, 1144*] (London 1964) pp 44–5.

[24] *Ibid* p 45.

[25] *Beauchamp* nos 183, 197.

[26] See my 'The Mauduits and their chamberlainship [of the Exchequer'], *BIHR*, 49 (1976) appendix 10, p 23; Westminster abbey muniment no 13845.

on major architectural or decorative programmes, were surrounded by a comparable group of laity. Normally they would occur in an urban setting, since they would naturally be attached to the more prosperous houses, around which towns had grown. Clerical source material, whether of regular or secular origin, is normally silent on the nature of the relationship between clergy and laity. Generally, it is touched upon, and even then only by implication, either in chronicles or letters, when tensions between the parties gave rise to administrative difficulties, or else when the writer of a biography wished to emphasise some remarkable quality in his subject. In particular, we know little of the extent to which urban laity in general had recourse to their cathedral or abbey church in this period. Episodes in the *vita* of St William of Norwich suggest that they swarmed around virtually at will, although here they were, of course, attracted by spectacular events, while a large proportion of the crowd may well have been lay servants—cooks and the like—who had business in the precincts in any case.[27] The monks at Bury thought it remarkable that their abbot should set up a pulpit and preach to the laity in the vernacular,[28] yet at Canterbury the citizens were evidently in the habit of slipping into the church of St Augustine's abbey for private prayer.[29]

Turning from the monks to the secular priests, we find an even closer interaction between cleric and laity. Despite the determined efforts of reformers to eradicate them,[30] married priests continued to function in considerable numbers throughout the twelfth century and perhaps beyond.[31] Their personal interests coincided to a large extent with those of their lay neighbours, creating an understanding of the problems of daily living and thereby increasing their effectiveness as pastors. We should expect their survival to be prolonged in rural districts rather than in more intensively supervised urban ones. In fact, however, attestations to charters issued in the late twelfth and early thirteenth centuries in town and countryside alike still include numbers of 'sons of priests',[32] while several married clergy played a respected role in Norwich in the mid twelfth century.[33] The exclusive ethos

[27] Anderson pp 45, 125.
[28] *Brakelond* p 40.
[29] W. Urry, *Canterbury under the Angevin Kings* (London 1967) p 165.
[30] [*Select Letters of Pope*] *Innocent III* [*concerning England (1198–1216)*, ed C. R. Cheney and W. H. Semple] (London 1955) no 26; *Foliot* no 264.
[31] [C. R.] Cheney, [*From Becket to Langton: English Church Government 1170–1213*] (Manchester 1956) pp 137–8.
[32] *Beauchamp* nos 187, 189, 209.
[33] Anderson pp 70–1.

and disciplinary austerities of the religious reformers are prominent in the ecclesiastical records of the time—naturally enough, since the whole point was to establish what had not previously been accepted. The innovations probably met with a strong passive resistance from the secular clergy, but it is only rarely that one of their number, such as Henry of Huntingdon, was able to voice his views for posterity.[34]

Occasionally the right of hereditary succession to benefices was openly conceded by the royal courts.[35] This concession to conservative opinion opens the wider question of how far in general the articulate and sophisticated higher clergy were obliged to give way on their reforming policies when confronted with resistance in the rural benefices to which they were translated. It is a debatable question whether they soldiered on regardless, fortified by the increasingly legalistic ethos of the period (certainly this is the impression one gains from the correspondence of men such as archbishop Theobald or Gilbert Foliot), or whether they tacitly admitted defeat in the face of entrenched customs, at least until people had become accustomed to the new ideals. The records document the former attitude, but for obvious reasons are generally silent on the latter. As translation became more commonplace, regional hostility towards an outsider might fuse with resentment at his innovations. This in turn could combine with the professional jealousy of less successful subordinates to create a situation which, if not explosive, was perhaps one of stalemate. That such a situation could arise within the cloister we know from the attitude of the locally recruited choir monks of Bury St Edmunds towards abbot Samson, whom malcontents among them designated as a 'barrator from Norfolk'.[36] When such an attitude was expressed in that comparatively well educated society, we might expect to find it intensified among the poorer secular clergy, perpetually obliged to take orders from a series of alien, careerist archdeacons and rural deans. Even rectors might be introduced from the court itself if the living was rich enough to tempt them. In Henry III's reign, the Mauduit chamberlains of the exchequer presented clerks who worked for them at Westminster to livings in the Midlands,[37] and reserved the benefice of Hanslope itself, the *caput* of their fief, for such eminent colleagues as Silvester of Everdon,

[34] A. G. Dyson, 'The Monastic Patronage of Bishop Alexander of Lincoln', *JEH*, 26 (1975) p 23.

[35] Cheney p 127.

[36] *Brakelond* p 42.

[37] *Rotuli Hugonis de Welles*, ed W. P. W. Phillimore and F. N. Davis, 2, *CYS*, 3 (1907) pp 70, 170.

Philip Lovel and Henry Wingham.[38] Such great men would normally be too busy elsewhere to spend much time imposing their views on their rustic subordinates and congregations, but Lovel was certainly a disruptive influence at Hanslope,[39] where he retired after his disgrace at court.[40]

Translations and presentations, made over a long distance at the prompting of clerical patrons, could nevertheless introduce new ideas and disciplinary practices to rural congregations. It is doubtful whether a lay patron was often prompted by such considerations. His chief concern was to provide a dignified status for a son or younger brother,[41] or else for a confidential clerk, who would continue to spend most of his time on estate administration, an expanding preoccupation of the thirteenth century. The clerk could, at the same time, keep an eye on his lord's interests in the village in question. In a parish where the patron was only one manorial lord among others, rights of advowson gave him an advantage over his rivals in this respect, while the clerk, in his pastoral capacity, was admirably placed to learn of personal situations which might affect the land market. In the twelfth century advowsons, along with other ecclesiastical sources of income, had formed a major proportion of donations to religious houses,[42] but this was not always true at a later date. In Yorkshire, for instance, not only did the donation of advowsons cease during much of the thirteenth century, but there was also a successful move by lay lords to recover some of those which had been granted at an earlier date. Patronage simultaneously became concentrated in the hands of the greater lords and rising curial families,[43] and whereas the lesser gentry might on occasion be prompted to consider the suitability of their nominee for their one and only parish, these greater personages, with their far-flung interests, could not be expected to do so.

Whatever the quality of the beneficed clergy, that of their

[38] *Rotuli Roberti Grosseteste,* ed F. N. Davis, *CYS,* 10 (1913) pp 224, 375; *Calendar of entries in the papal registers relating to Great Britain and Ireland: Papal Letters (1198–1492),* 1 (1893) p 366; *Rotuli Ricardi Gravesend,* ed F. N. Davis, *CYS,* 31 (1925) p xxiv.

[39] *Beauchamp* no 251.

[40] Matthew Paris, *Chronica Majora,* ed H. R. Luard, 5, *RS* (1880) p 731.

[41] *Beauchamp,* no 365. Determination to install his own candidate might even prompt a local lord to expel the current incumbent under threat of death – [*The Letters of John of*] *Salisbury,* [1 (*1153–1161*), ed W. J. Millor, H. E. Butler and C. N. L. Brooke] (London 1955) no 65.

[42] See my 'Timeo barones et donas ferentes', *SCH* 15 (1978) p 70.

[43] J. E. Newman, 'Greater and lesser landholders and parochial patronage: Yorkshire in the thirteenth century', *EHR,* 92 (1977) pp 280–308.

unbeneficed subordinates who actually undertook most of the pastoral work, seems to have been generally low, particularly in rural areas where they could not be kept under close supervision. Occasionally some exceptional misdemeanour would provoke an episcopal admonition, as when William of Northall, bishop of Worcester 1186–90, found it necessary to prohibit the singing of bawdy songs by clerics during mass.[44] The long term effectiveness of such injunctions may be questioned, given the absence of any rigorous procedures of selection or training.[45] Discipline in Worcestershire continued to be lax, particularly in the distinction between clerical and lay functions. A synodal statute of 1229 proclaimed that 'laymen are not to sit in the choir among the clergy, nor carry cross or candle in processions except as a matter of necessity,'[46] a concession no doubt due to the lack of a clerical infrastructure in the poorer rural parishes. It was all very well to debar laymen from standing in the chancel of a church during divine service, but the patron, and other members of the local hierarchy, would not expect to stand anywhere else. Eleven years later, as a concession to their no doubt forceful comments on this ruling, it was agreed that they alone might remain.[47]

Urban conditions were naturally somewhat different, partly of course because the gradations of society could not be asserted with equal strength in such matters. Ecclesiastical discipline should certainly have presented no problem in Worcester itself, for late in the eleventh century a jury of ancient men of the shire had declared that the cathedral was the only true church in the city, and the others, of which there were several, were subordinate to it.[48] The situation was even simpler in Westminster, where a church dedicated to St Margaret of Antioch was established immediately outside the abbey in the eleventh century to cater for the pastoral needs of the suburb's inhabitants. The boundaries of its parish enclosed a sizable part of what is now west-central London.[49] At the time, its extent created no pastoral difficulties, since much of the land was rural, but when the area became urbanized, some centuries later, there was a considerable delay before the greatly increased population was provided with further churches. Meanwhile, in the twelfth and thirteenth centuries,

[44] Cheney p 144.
[45] *Ibid* p 138.
[46] *Ibid* p 155.
[47] *Ibid* p 157.
[48] Brooke, 'The missionary at home', p 64.
[49] Harvey, *Westminster abbey*, pp 45–6.

the abbot expected all the laity of the parish to attend St Margaret's, although some of them had other ideas. When the centre of government was moved to Westminster, senior officials bought up houses in the suburb, and were not overjoyed at being required to attend the parish church along with their insignificant neighbours. In consideration of their rank and influence, the abbot occasionally allowed them a way out, at a price. Abbot William Postard, for instance, at some point between 1195 and 1200, acted on the petition and urging of the king's barons (of the exchequer) in granting the chamberlain Robert Mauduit licence to have a private chapel in his *curia* adjoining Longditch in Westminster. The existence of this chapel was not to damage the financial interests of the parish church; none of the parishioners was to be admitted, and Robert was to render an annual pension of two bezants to the high altar of the abbey. Churchings were to be allowed, in the presence of the parish priest, who would receive all the offerings, but no banns were to be called, and no weddings or churchings held which involved parishioners of St Margaret's. If any of Robert's household fell ill, confession, unction, communion and other rites were to be administered from St Margaret's, which would receive the dues, while during the absence from Westminster of Robert and his wife, the caretaker who had charge of their houses and *curia* was to hear the divine office in the parish church, and render his ecclesiastical dues there.[50]

Private chapels were licensed with increasing frequency in various dioceses from the thirteenth century onwards. In rural areas, they were sometimes granted on account of the distance from the parish church, or the infirmity of some member of the licensee's household,[51] but social exclusiveness also played its part. Robert Mauduit himself purchased another licence from the priory of St Mary Overy, Southwark, permitting him to have a chapel in his *curia* in Mitcham,[52] while his grandfather William Mauduit made different arrangements, but to the same effect, regarding their estates in Hanslope. The original parish church there was in the hamlet of Castle Thorpe, clustered around Hanslope castle. William Mauduit II, however, received permission from Alexander, bishop of Lincoln (1123–48) to establish a new parish church a few kilometres away in Hanslope itself. The parochial dues would be owed to the new

[50] See my 'The Mauduits and their chamberlainship', appendix 5, p 19.

[51] See my 'The [role of the] English parishioner, [1100–1500]', *JEH,* 27 (1976) p 22.

[52] *Beauchamp* no 205.

church,[53] a financial arrangement which contrasted with normal procedure when a second church was built within a parish. It was perhaps made in recognition of the fact that William had in effect converted the original parish church into a private chapel for himself and his household.

When laymen built new churches on their rural estates to meet the growing population of the twelfth and thirteenth centuries, they were often prompted by motives far removed from the pastoral needs of their tenants. Their chief interest was more likely to be in the tithes, burial dues and other offerings which would hopefully accrue to the new foundation. The diocesan bishop maintained that such a church was legally a dependent chapel. The bulk of the dues must be rendered to the mother church, which those who normally attended the chapel were required to seek out on specified major festivals of the year.[54] In 1122, for instance, bishop Theulf of Worcester ensured that the church of Ettington would receive an annual payment from the newly-founded church of Middleton. Here, however, he was dealing with a village of which the overlords were magnates remote both in residence and interests, and who did not object to their sub-tenants being bound to the agreement. At the same time he was taking no chances, and persuaded every notable of the district, both clerical and lay, to witness the agreement.[55] The internal colonisation of Worcestershire was still proceeding apace over a century later, when a new settlement was created near Birlingham, at Sheriff's Hay. The land here belonged to the hereditary sheriff, William de Beauchamp, who enterprisingly established a self-styled 'free chapel' at Wadborough, to which he directed that the laity of Sheriff's Hay should render their religious dues. This arrangement was contested by the abbot of Pershore, who successfully insisted that burials should take place in the cemetery of his church, thus vindicating his jurisdictional claims at least. On the other hand, the relative strength of the contenders was such that he was obliged to concede to William an equal share in heriots and bequests.[56]

Town life, responsive to much closer supervision by the clerical hierarchy, was not likely to accommodate *ad hoc* arrangements, whether devised by magnates or by lesser men. Innocent III, for instance, ordered

[53] *Ibid* no 168.
[54] See my 'The English parishioner', p 22.
[55] Brett p 129.
[56] *Beauchamp* no 65.

the closure of new chapels which had been founded in Northampton, since he maintained that these were detrimental to the financial interests of St Andrew's priory in older-established churches in the town.[57] His action was to be expected in an age which put legal rights before pastoral concerns. The interests and the wishes of the laity were steadily demoted in the period covered by this paper,[58] in contrast with an earlier age, when the laity had founded churches as and where they pleased. Lay assertiveness could, of course, go to extremes, as instanced by the numerous little neighbourhood churches founded within the City of London, and it is questionable whether all were equally effective from a pastoral point of view. It can be argued that proliferation to this extent represented neighbourhood or even racial loyalties, rather than religious aspiration.[59]

Just what were the aspirations of the laity is a moot point. We should expect to find a contrast between the beliefs and practices of a sophisticated urban population and those of the more remote shires. At Westminster abbey, the cult of the Blessed Virgin was promoted in the late twelfth century by prior Robert de Molesham.[60] Donations made to the abbey by solid citizens of London and bourgeois of Westminster at the turn of the century evince their faith in her merits as an intercessor,[61] a belief which they shared with the occasional aristocrat, such as Isabel Basset, the wife of the chamberlain Robert Mauduit.[62]

From the early twelfth century onwards, Westminster abbey offered a whole range of spiritual services to the laity in order to attract donations. The need for these might seem surprising in view of the well-known generosity shown towards the abbey by Edward the Confessor and Henry III. Intervening kings and their greater subjects were not particularly forthcoming however, and consequently the chapter was not very class-conscious in its attitude towards potential benefactors. Burial within the precincts of the abbey was one such option available from the early twelfth century, and the monks were surprisingly open-minded about whom they accepted. They did,

[57] *Innocent III* no 9.

[58] See my 'The English parishioner', pp 18–23.

[59] [C. N. L.] Brooke and [Gillian] Keir, [*London 800–1216: the shaping of a city*] (London 1975) pp 124–43.

[60] Harvey, *Westminster abbey*, p 39.

[61] Westminster abbey muniments, nos 17081, 17322, 17413; Westminster abbey domesday (muniment book 2), fol 546.

[62] See my 'The Mauduits and their chamberlainship', appendices 6–7, pp 20–1.

however, reserve certain parts of the church for aristocrats or distinguished officials, even though these people did not exactly overwhelm them with requests for this privilege.[63] Confraternity was also offered to benefactors from the early twelfth century. It did not automatically include burial within the abbey, but when the *confrater* died, a mass would be sung by every priest within the community; his name would be enrolled in the abbey's martyrology, and entered in the next mortuary brief that went out for a monk. It was presumed that *confratres* were French-speaking,[64] a social class which ranged upwards from the urban bourgeoisie. A third, and more expensive option available from the twelfth century was the anniversary celebrated regularly every year. The perpetual anniversary had to be endowed, although *ad hoc* payment might be made for a one-off celebration.[65] Evidence for laymen taking advantage of one or sometimes more of these options dates, with rare exceptions, from the late twelfth century onwards. Those who did so included leading citizens and merchants of London,[66] besides the chamberlain Robert Mauduit and his wife.[67] Other *curiales* and their families occasionally chose to link their spiritual fortunes with those of the crown,[68] but magnates rarely did. Westminster's prestige derived from its status as the coronation church,[69] rather than from its being the burial place of Edward the Confessor, whose cult was not popular outside court circles.[70]

Some of the most prestigious cults were established in quite small places. The extent to which they attracted the devotions and offerings of the laity depended less on their location than on the enterprise of their clerical custodians and the reputed merits of the relics in individual cases. Worcester possessed no outstanding authorized attraction before the early thirteenth century, when the cathedral church received two windfalls in quick succession. The first was the canonisation of bishop Wulfstan, belatedly achieved in 1203,[71] although he was already venerated in the region. Even the Beauchamp family set great store by

[63] Harvey, *Westminster abbey*, pp 37–8.
[64] *Ibid* pp 38–9.
[65] *Ibid* pp 39–40.
[66] *Ibid* pp 388–92.
[67] See my 'The Mauduits and their chamberlainship', appendices 8–9, pp 21–3.
[68] *Ibid* appendix 10, p 23.
[69] Brooke and Keir p 297.
[70] Harvey, *Westminster abbey*, p 43.
[71] Le Neve 2, p 99.

the *surcella* of Wulfstan which they possessed,[72] despite the fact that they were locked in hostilities with his successors.[73] The second windfall came in 1216, when the chapter, somewhat to their bemusement no doubt, were presented with the body of king John for burial.[74] In the unsophisticated countryside, the tombs of the most unlikely people could provide a focus for (admittedly somewhat dubious) cults, like that of Rosamund Clifford at Godstow.[75] King John was a non-starter even for a cult of this kind, but he was a profitable acquisition all the same, thanks to the donations which his descendants made in his memory.[76] Worcester was less business-like than Westminster in cashing in on its modicum of spiritual prestige, although grants by the burgesses of Worcester of small urban properties, which had begun in the late twelfth century, became more frequent from now on. The citizens of Worcester were increasingly inclined to specify that the revenues from their gifts should go towards particular 'good works'.[77] The chapter was a major landholder in the little city, but Worcester was not a 'bishop's town',[78] and responsible citizens may well have felt a personal commitment towards the betterment of its living conditions. Grants to Westminster were not normally earmarked in this way during the comparable period. This was in sharp contrast to practice in London, where charitable gifts to churches from the early twelfth century onwards were often designated for specific 'good works', both by individual citizens,[79] and by the royal family, prompted, perhaps by political considerations.[80] In any urban district, there was probably a correlation between the incidence of earmarked grants and the stage currently attained in the development of the institutions of self-government. Civic consciousness seems to have been the chief prompter of such donations, which were rarely made in rural districts in this period.

[72] *Giffard* 2, p 8.

[73] *Ibid* p 75.

[74] *Worcester* p xxiv.

[75] Anderson, pp 150–1. Writers in the twelfth century occasionally put into the mouths of their more cynical characters the opinion that where no cult existed, it must be created, by fair means or foul, and for what cities such as Winchester or Norwich received, they should be truly thankful – *The Chronicle of Richard of Devizes of the time of King Richard the First,* ed J. T. Appleby (London 1963) p 64; Anderson p 89.

[76] *Worcester,* nos 328, 330. The monks certainly held king John in esteem as a valued if unwitting benefactor. His tomb was lavishly endowed with candles, and the chapter enjoyed a pittance on his anniversary (*Ibid* no 332).

[77] *Ibid* nos 370, 372, 375.

[78] *Ibid* p xxxix.

[79] Brooke and Keir p 336. [80] *Ibid* p 315.

The religious beliefs of the rural laity of the Worcester diocese were necessarily inarticulate for the most part. The precariousness of an economy based on crops and livestock which were liable to sudden destruction would encourage the vast majority to maintain conscious religious beliefs of some kind, if not for philosophical reasons then at least in the hope of averting disaster.[81] The village church would be by far the most impressive building which most peasants had any occasion to frequent. Even in towns, stone buildings, other than churches, were a rarity well into the thirteenth century.[82] By no means all villages had even a manor house,[83] so that the visual impact of the village church was guaranteed, whatever the merits of its architecture. The sculpture of its tympanum, and the murals around its walls, however crude they were, would naturally seem imposing to people who saw no other art, and would thereby reinforce the message from the pulpit. Village life was primitive, harsh and precarious in the extreme, and the ritual of the liturgy, whatever the deficiencies in its celebration, would seem impressive, timeless and potent in contrast, offering a stable focus in an uncertain world.

The ratio of orthodox beliefs to unorthodox would no doubt vary according to time, place and circumstances. The survival of pagan fertility cults, lightly disguised under the trappings of orthodox religion, is understandable in an agrarian economy,[84] and modern man is in no position to deride, given the prevalence of superstition in the twentieth century among people of all shades of religious belief, agnosticism and atheism alike. One suspects that in the high middle ages many people simultaneously maintained both approved and unapproved beliefs, regardless of the illogicality of their position, but determined to find something to cling to. Most would no doubt assent to the basic propositions of the creed, although when it came to devotional practices, the conservatism of the peasantry was reflected

[81] Brett p 122.

[82] Richardson, 'William of Ely', p 60.

[83] In the twelfth century, the knightly class was stratified into a rich minority, whose members might each hold several manors, and a much poorer majority. Members of the latter group were scarcely better off than the more affluent peasants, and their status was gradually declining – Sally Harvey, 'The Knight and the Knight's Fee in England', *PP* 49 (1970) pp 3–43. The former group would clearly not have a residence on every one of their manors, while the latter would not be able to afford a house any more imposing than that of their rustic neighbours.

[84] Joan Evans, *Art in Medieval France* (Oxford 1948) pp 20–2. In England, survival of such cults is shown by carvings of the Green Man, found on the exterior wall of Ottery St Mary (Devon), for instance.

in a calendar of major feasts observed in the diocese of Worcester, which was published by bishop William of Blois (1218–36). Those which his flock observed seemed old-fashioned in comparison with a contemporary list of holy days kept by workmen in Westminster. Countrymen clung doggedly to the old ways, even though many of their cherished festivals fell during the peak of the harvest season. In contrast, townsmen, uprooted from their background, were more likely to accept the latest liturgical gradings published by the church hierarchy.[85]

The violence endemic in medieval society at all levels renders it questionable to what extent the laity correlated their beliefs with their actions. At the upper end of the social scale, Christian beliefs were seen as in no way incompatible with designs on church property if the heavy hand of royal government was relaxed, as in Stephen's reign. Attacks on the lands of religious houses occurred with great frequency in the west Midlands and the marches,[86] and a skirmish between a Beauchamp *posse* and that of abbot William de Andeville of Evesham was remarkable only because the abbot's troop won.[87] Similar attacks are recorded in many English dioceses in this reign,[88] but while calm returned following the accession of Henry II, and the more fortunate houses even recovered their property,[89] Worcestershire witnessed a continuing jurisdictional struggle between the rising lay power and the entrenched Benedictine houses. Yet even while it continued, the Beauchamps were simultaneously the benefactors of the cathedral priory,[90] and buried their dead there.[91]

An impact could undoubtedly be made on recalcitrant magnates by the artistic achievement of the local cathedral or monastery. Decorative schemes were, of course, primarily devised for didactic purposes, and although the philosophical and allegorical content might be above the heads of their lay persecutors, most churches also

[85] Harvey, 'Festa Ferianda', pp 291, 303, 307–8.

[86] *Foliot* nos 3, 22, 35, 77, 85.

[87] *Chronicon Abbatiae de Evesham,* ed W. D. Macray, *RS* (1863) p 100.

[88] A. Saltman, *Theobald archbishop of Canterbury* (London 1956) nos 109, 118. Lower down the social scale, lay behaviour even in time of peace could be equally violent. Disgruntled parishioners of Ranworth (Norfolk) bodily removed the church from its site (*ibid* no 129), while laymen in deepest Yorkshire killed a thief who had stolen their priest's vestments (*Salisbury* no 89).

[89] *ASC,* transl and ed Dorothy Whitelock, D. C. Douglas and Susie I. Tucker (London 1961) p 200.

[90] *Worcester* nos 338–9, 368; *Giffard* 2, p 8.

[91] Worcester Annals, *Annales Monastici,* ed H. R. Luard, 4, *RS* (1869) pp 382, 471, 528.

contained vivid imagery, in sculpture or murals, of the probable fate awaiting them. Westminster had less trouble from lay persecutors than most other churches, and its wealth and status undoubtedly made it a front runner in the artistic field. While the patronage of Henry III was the predominant contribution to its glories in the thirteenth century,[92] its earlier attainment was also considerable, especially under abbot Gilbert Crispin (1085–1117),[93] and artists continued to be employed there throughout the twelfth century.[94] Worcester's artistic achievement, although by no means negligible, was scarcely in the same class, while its literary output was undistinguished. An anonymous monk wrote a set of uninspired verses on the earliest bishops of the see, *c*1250,[95] and some remarkably earthy poems are found in a Worcester manuscript of the mid thirteenth century. Their material is largely derivative, but it is entirely thanks to their preservation at Worcester that they have survived at all, even though we may wonder what impact a bawdy poem such as *Dame Siriz and the Weeping Bitch* had on the monks.[96] Cultural influences were very far-reaching in this period, and Worcester's rural setting would not of itself account for its poor showing in comparison with Westminster. Relative wealth was naturally a major factor, but more important was the lack of such sophisticated and purposeful patronage as Westminster enjoyed.

It may be concluded that town congregations could be brought to a much more satisfactory state of belief and discipline than could their rural counterparts. To step outside the walls of a town was in effect to enter an older era. The *mores* of feudal society ensured that the actions of both priest and people were manipulated in the interests of their territorial lord, while their beliefs would not bear too close an examination. It was perhaps some consolation for reformers that town populations were being swelled by immigration from the countryside, since the fact that social conditions influenced the practice of religion was a truth universally acknowledged.

University of London
Birkbeck College

[92] A. Martindale, *Gothic Art* (London 1967) pp 101–2.
[93] Brooke and Keir p 305.
[94] *Beauchamp* nos 183, 197.
[95] *Worcester* no 470.
[96] *Medieval English Verse*, transl B. Stone (Harmondsworth 1964) pp 230–43. Such poems were, however, capable of allegorisation (*ibid* p 230).

SERMONS TO THE UPPER BOURGEOISIE BY A THIRTEENTH CENTURY FRANCISCAN

by D. L. D'AVRAY

'L'IMPLANTATION urbaine des orders mendiants a-t-elle eu une influence sur le type de piété et de spiritualité qu'ils proposaient?' This was one of the questions posed in the *Annales* programme of research on the friars and the towns,[1] and the recent study of mendicant spirituality by Rosenwein and Little[2] is an answer to more or less the same question. They conclude that within the period when the original ideal remained more or less intact, the preaching of the mendicants was one of a number of related responses to urban money-making.[3] This is an excellent and stimulating study, and one of the lines of research it should stimulate is the analysis of the mendicant sermons themselves, which have survived in great numbers.[4] A number of years spent with these sources has left me with the impression that the urban context can provide a non-trivial explanation for certain aspects only of the 'spirituality' of mendicant preaching, and that many of its distinctive features will have to be accounted for in other terms. Provided that we do not mistake the part for the whole, however, those elements of mendicant preaching which can be directly related to their urban environment—both economic and political—are worthy of attention in their own right, and it is with them that I am concerned here. The sermons which I will discuss illustrate the church's effort to adapt itself to the re-emergence of a bourgeoisie, after the long centuries during which its social context was predominantly rural.

[1] Jacques Le Goff, 'Apostolat mendiant et fait urbain dans la France médiévale', *Annales* 23 no 2 (1968) p 344.

[2] [Barbara H.] Rosenwein and [Lester K.] Little, ['Social Meaning in the Monastic and Mendicant Spiritualities'], *PP* 63 (May 1974) pp 4–32.

[3] *Ibid* p 5.

[4] Rosenwein and Little do not cite any mendicant sermons. The systematic study of medieval sermon manuscripts is entering a new phase, as [J. B.] Schneyer's [*Repertorium der lateinischen Sermones des Mittelalters für die Zeit von 1150–1350*], *Beiträge zur Geschichte der Philosophie und Theologie des Mitteralters* 43 (Münster, Westfalen, 1969–) nears completion.

The sermons are by Guibert[5] of Tournai, a Franciscan contemporary of Bonaventure and, like him, a Parisian master.[6] They are from his *ad status* collection, which contains sermons to different sorts and conditions of men, and other kinds of special sermons. The sermons are in Latin, but those which were addressed to laymen and women would have been delivered in the vernacular. They are 'model' sermons, designed to provide preachers with ready-made material. We need not assume that all the sermons would have been preached exactly as they stand: they may have been a sort of quarry. There is, for instance, a sermon to widows. It is unlikely that there were many congregations composed exclusively of widows, but a preacher could have used part or all of Guibert's model in a sermon with wider scope.

Guibert's *ad status* collection was widely copied[7] and remained in demand long enough to be printed in the fifteenth century and after.[8] For some reason, however, the sermons which I want to discuss—those to citizens engaged in public affairs, to citizens 'living in communes', and to merchants—dropped out of the tradition at some point and are not included in any of the early printed editions I have been able to see. I have therefore used a fairly good and early manuscript, which I would date from the script to the second half of the thirteenth century.[9] Incidentally, the omission of these sermons at a late point in the tradition does not prove that they were not frequently copied together with the rest of the work in the thirteenth and fourteenth centuries. In fact there is reason to think that they were: the collection was one of those which we know to have been reproduced by the rapid copy *pecia* system at Parish.[10] The sermons in question

[5] Or Gilbert, Guibertus, Gilbertus, etc.

[6] For the life and works of Guibert, see Gilberto di Tournai, *De Modo Addiscendi,* ed E. Bonifacio, Pubblicazioni del Pontificio Ateneo Salesiano, 1, *Testi e Studi sul Pensiero Medioevale* (Turin 1953) pp 7–56, and Benjamin de Troeyer, *Bio-Bibliographia Franciscana Neerlandica ante Saeculum XVI,* 1 Pars Biographica: Auctores editionum qui scripserunt ante saeculum XVI (Nieuwkoop 1974) pp 15–43.

[7] For a list of manuscripts see Schneyer, Heft 2, pp 306–7.

[8] There are exemplars, for instance, in the British Library and in the university libraries of Oxford and Cambridge: BL IB.49228 ('Impressit Iohannes de Westfalia'); 846.b.6 ('Venundantur Lugduni ab Stephano guenyard'). Cambridge U[niversity] L[ibrary] G* 15 38 ('Sumptibus . . . Stephani Gueynard. Impressum Lugduni per Magistrum Iohannem de Uingle. Anno domini Mcccccxi . . .'). Bodleian Library 8° T. 34 Th. ('Sumptibus . . . Iohannes petit') (Paris 1513); Inc. d. N3. 2 (Ioh. de Westfalia); Vet. E1 108 (Guenyard/Gueynard).

[9] BN MS lat 15943.

[10] H. Denifle and A. Chatelain, *Chartularium Universitatis Parisiensis,* 2, 1 (Paris 1891) no 642, p 109. For the *pecia* system in general see J. Destrez, *La Pecia dans les manuscrits universitaires du xiiie et du xive siècle* (Paris 1935).

are included in at least one manuscript with *pecia* indications, which implies that they were being copied fast and efficiently as part of the collection.[11]

It is partly because he was so influential that I have singled out Guibert of Tournai rather than Jacques of Vitry (who was not of course a friar). Jacques also wrote a collection of sermons in the *ad status* genre, and Guibert borrowed from it very freely indeed, but although he seems to have been much more original Jacques's collection was much less in demand.[12] If one may judge by the manuscript counts which have been made to date, Guibert's *ad status* collection was also somewhat more widely read than that of Humbert of Romans, though the gap is not so large.[13] Humbert's collection is as interesting as Guibert's, but they have already received some scholarly attention as a source for religious life in the towns,[14] so I will confine myself to Guibert.

I will also, as I mentioned, confine myself to a small group of his sermons: those which are fairly obviously and directly aimed at what one might call the upper bourgeoisie. The sermons to citizens engaged in public affairs and to citizens living in communes (*communiter viventes*), and the two sermons to merchants, form a fairly homogeneous group, because they seem to be directed at the same strata of urban society.

[11] The manuscript is Cambridge Peterhouse 200. The sermon to citizens engaged in public affairs (on the text 'Estote imitatores dei . . .') begins on fol 74vb. The sermon to citizens living in communes (text: 'Qui amat divitias fructum non capiet ex eis') begins on fol. 76va. The first of the two sermons to merchants (text: 'Negotiamini dum venio') begins fol. 79ra. On fol. 42^{r} is written: xvii pec'. Similarly, on fol. 35^{r}: xiiii pec'. (In referring to this manuscript I have throughout been giving the medieval foliation. This begins after fol 62 of the modern foliation, which ceases at that point.) Paris was not the only place where a *pecia* system operated, but the presence of Guibert's *ad status* collection on a Paris *pecia* list makes it likely that the Peterhouse manuscript was copied there.

[12] The evidence for this is the manuscript count – a reasonable yardstick when the differences are substantial enough. For the manuscripts of Jacques de Vitry's *ad status* collection, his *Sermones Vulgares*, see Schneyer, Heft 3, pp 220–1. Compare above note 7.

[13] For the manuscripts of Humbert of Romans' *De eruditione praedicatorum*, see Th. Kaeppeli, *Scriptores Ordinis Praedicatorum Medii Aevii*, 2 (1975) pp 287–8. I would however be less confident about the manuscript count as a guide to comparative popularity here, where the lists of manuscripts come from two different *Repertoria* and where the difference between the number of manuscripts is less striking.

[14] See two important articles by A. Murray: 'Piety and Impiety in Thirteenth-Century Italy', *SCH* 8 (1972) pp 83–106, esp pp 88 and 92–3; 'Religion Among the Poor in Thirteenth Century France: The Testimony of Humbert de Romans', *Traditio* 30 (1974) pp 285–324. In these valuable studies Murray is asking questions slightly different from (though if anything more important than) the ones I am putting to Guibert's *ad status* collection, but there is hardly space to cover Humbert's sermons as well in this paper.

A few other sermons might conceivably be included in the group, but it seemed better to treat a small number in some detail.

The first of the sermons to be considered is clearly meant for men possessing political and judicial power in cities: *cives reipublice vacantes*. Its text is 'Be ye followers (*imatatores*) of God, as most dear children' (Eph 5:1), and the starting point is the idea that these men must imitate God himself. In God is the supreme power, truth and goodness; therefore men of power and influence effectively imitate him if they resemble him by power, wisdom, and holiness.[15] The part of the sermon which deserves most attention, I think, is the section on the wisdom with which they ought to be 'conformed' to God.

One facet of the wisdom through which they should resemble God is the ability to pass judgment on others.[16] The subsection is an attack on the abuse of judicial power. Scriptural authority is marshalled against 'those who give crooked judgements and take bribes'.[17] As he continues he mixes quotations and comment: ' "Your princes are unfaithful" (Isa 1:23)—because they do not keep the contract of baptism, and do not renounce the pomps of Satan, but give themselves over to vanities—"accomplices of thieves"—as long as they consent to plundering by others, and nourish usurers and Jews in the territory under their authority to take part of the profit. Therefore we should beware lest we accept gifts from people who gather their riches at the expense of the poor, lest we be "accomplices of thieves" and it be said to us: "if you saw a thief, you ran with him" (Ps 49:18)'.[18] His remarks might equally well have been addressed to feudal or royal judges, a reminder that much of the traditional religious and moral theorising about kingship and lordship could be applied without difficulty to city government.

[15] 'In deo est summa potestas, veritas, et bonitas. Deum igitur magnates efficaciter imitantur, si ipsi in potentia, sapientia, et sanctitate ei conformantur', BN MS lat 15943 fol 123va.

[16] 'Sapientia eorum declaratur in tribus: . . . Secundo, ut sciant alios iudicare.' *Ibid* fol 124va.

[17] 'Unde de illis qui pervertunt iudicium et munera accipiunt dicitur, ii Petr. ii Maledictionis filii: derelinquentes viam rectam erraverunt, sequti viam Balaam.' *Ibid* fol 125ra.

[18] 'Ys. i. Principes tui infideles, quia pactum baptismi non servant, et pompis Sathane non abrenuntiant, sed vanitatibus vacant, socii furum, dum aliorum rapine consentiunt et foventes in terra sua usurarios et iudeos partem lucri accipiunt. Ideo debemus cavere ne ab illis accipiamus munera qui de lacrimis pauperum congregant divitias, ne simus socii furum et dicatur nobis [*cod.* vobis?]: Si videbas furem, currebas cum eo'. *Ibid.*

This part of the sermon contains some less predictable and more striking instances of the application of notions of Christian kingship to the men who ruled cities—men who would in many cases have held office through election rather than by hereditary right. The interesting part of the sermon from this point of view is the first subsection of the section on the 'wisdom' of city rulers.[19] The theme of this subsection is that the political élite of cities should 'know how to rule themselves'.[20] I will pass by the sidelights on religious practice—for instance, the intriguing complaint about men who 'break the church bell so that people will not come to Mass'[21]—their interest lies in a different context. My immediate concern is with what one might anachronistically call the political theory presented by the sermon.

Guibert had centuries of thought and theory on the nature of governmental authority behind him, but, in general, the concern of the theorists had been with Christian kingship. In the towns, which were of course (outside Italy at least) a relatively recent phenomenon, political authority could take very different forms. It has even been argued, by one of our most distinguished medievalists, that 'the government of the town was conducted entirely on the principle of the ascending theory'.[22] This sermon *ad cives reipublicae vacantes* shows that in the mind of one preacher at least hierocratic themes could be applied to urban self-government. If this is a paradox, Guibert did not see it.

It is interesting, for example, that Guibert introduces both Salomon[23] and Charlemagne, in a context which suggests that he is presenting them as models for the *magni burgenses*.[24] Furthermore, there is

[19] *Ibid* fol 124^{v} for this subsection.

[20] 'Primo ut sciant se ipsos regere.' *Ibid* fol 124va.

[21] 'Nunc vero quidam non solum verbum non audiunt, sed audientes derident et impediunt, et eos a predicatione avertunt in quantum possunt, sacrilegium committentes, sicut homines qui frangunt campanam ut homines non veniant ad missam'. *Ibid* fol 124vb. Urban anticlericalism?

[22] [W.] Ullmann, *A History of Political Thought in the Middle Ages* (London 1970) p 161. Compare Ullmann, *Principles of Government and Politics in the Middle Ages* (London 1961) pp 219–20.

[23] Compare Humbert of Romans, giving material for a sermon *Ad rectores, et officiales ciuitatis:* 'Sciendum ergo, quod in huiusmodi statu non sunt ponendi nisi sapientes. Vnde Salomon, propter regimen populi sibi imminens, specialiter petiit sapientiam a Domino.' *De Eruditione Praedicatorum,* bk 2, tract 1, 73, *Maxima Bibliotheca Veterum Patrum* 25 (Lyons 1677) p 492.

[24] '. . . quia corrupto cordis palato saporem spiritualem non sentiunt, non sicut Salomon, qui valde placuit deo, qui offerente deo quod peteret quicquid vellet, sapientiam petiit. iii. Reg. iii. Non sic Karolus magnus, qui faciebat [* * *] legi in mensa sua, ut anima eius non minus satiaretur cibis spiritualibus quam corpus carnalibus. Unde inexcusabiles sunt.

reason to think that they are not being cited simply as individuals who were pious in their personal lives, but also in their 'official' capacity as rulers. Shortly before the Salomon-Charlemagne passage, and after exhorting *rectores civitatum* to hear sermons, Guibert quotes or paraphrases the passage from Deuteronomy which, in the Revised Version, reads: 'And it shall be, when he sitteth upon the throne of his kingdom, that he shall write him a copy of this law in a book, out of *that which is* before the priests and Levites: and it shall be with him, and he shall read therein all the days of his life' (Deut 17: 18–19). Guibert uses the passage in the following manner: 'This is why it is laid down, in Deuteronomy 17, that the king should always have with him a *Deuteronomium*, so that he may guide himself in the law of God, and form his judgements according to it;'.[25] Then he switches from singular to plural, but with no break in the chain of ideas: if 'they' were as zealously devoted to the divine law and to hearing sermons as to idle amusements, then 'they would be able to rule themselves and others, and would know the will of God.'[26] The phrase 'themselves *and others*'[27] would seem to imply that Guibert is thinking of official as well as private life.

In these remarks on the passage from Deuteronomy Guibert is applying the same ideas in the same breath to both town officials and kings, for when he switches so suddenly to the plural the 'they' must be taken as applying to the *rectores civitatum*. It is clear that Guibert does not find the transition incongruous. The passage, and in fact the sermon as a whole suggest that the traditional Christian ideology of political authority could be transferred to the new context of the towns without any signs of strain.

Si enim equm [*sic*]vel pannum emere volunt diligenter conditiones inquirunt; si egrotant, medicum vocant; et, [*sic*] de statu anime sue utrum sint in statu salutis vel perditionis non curant; cum tamen nulla sint periculosiora vulnera quam occulta, cuiusmodi [*cod.* cui^us^] sunt peccata que committuntur ex ignorantia; et potest hic poni exemplum de pantera quam sequntur [*sic*] minuta animalia propter odorem occulta eorum vulnera et morbos curantem; sed draco toxicatus fugit in foveam, ne odor anticipet eum; sic predicatorem sequntur hodie pauperes propter salutem suam, sed magni [*cod.* magis?] burgenses presentientes odorem et toxicati veneno usure et aliorum peccatorum descendunt in tabernam.' BN MS lat 15943 fol 124$^{va/b}$ Guibert appears to see nothing odd in the transition from Salomon and Charlemagne to usurious urban magnates.

25 'Inde est quod precipiebatur xvii. deut., ut rex semper haberet secum deuteronomium, ut se ipsum in lege dei dirigeret, et secundum eam iudicia sua formaret. [*cod.* formaret sua *cum signis inversionis*]' *Ibid* fol 124va.

26 'Si autem ita studiosi essent in lege divina et in sermonibus audiendis sicut in scatis [*sic*] et aleis, se et alios regere possent, et voluntatem dei cognoscerent', *ibid.*

27 My italics.

Much of the sermon could apply to anyone with authority or power,[28] and indeed he illustrates points with references to Roman emperors,[29] and to abuses of power which, he implies, took place in the countryside rather than the towns.[30] In the beginning of the sermon, in particular, Guibert speaks in very general terms: without the rubric and some other evidence[31] it might be hard to tell that he was addressing himself specifically to an urban audience.

Nevertheless Guibert does show some awareness of the problems which are more particularly associated with city politics. He criticizes the internal strife and the rapid changes of policy which, he said, characterised the political life of the cities of his day.[32] (He was not far wrong: faction seems to have been the besetting sin of medieval as of ancient cities.)

The very fact that a sermon like this could be written shows that the established church was adjusting to the new urban political structures which had grown up alongside older forms of government (themselves evolving rapidly). By reapplying traditional notions of governmental authority to this new class of rulers (without altogether ignoring the distinctive character of city politics), it was an attempt to find a place for them in the church's scheme of things. He pays them the compliment of making God himself their model. Perhaps the aspect of this conclusion one should emphasise, however, is the apparent ease with

[28] For example, '. . . ut se amabiles bonis exhibeant . . .', *ibid* fol 123vb, and '. . . ut se a malis timeri faciant . . .', *ibid* fol 124ra.

[29] For example, 'Non talis Gayus Caligula qui desiderabat populum romanum unicam habere cervicem ut in omnes exerceret crudelitatis sue tyrannidem . . .'. *Ibid* fol 124.ra

[30] '. . . multi dicunt quando arguuntur quod vaccam pauperis agricole abstulerunt: "sufficiat rustico quod ei vitulum dimisi; non feci ei tantum mali quantum fecissem si voluissem."' *Ibid* fol 124rb. Of course, there were many places where towns controlled the surrounding countryside; and the great men of towns could also be landowners.

[31] The rubric shows that the sermon is addressed to *cives,* and in the sermon itself Guibert makes it clear that he is writing for *rectores civitatum* ('Vocat enim dominus istos rectores civitatum ut audiant predicationis verbum et sciant regere se ipsos.' *Ibid* fol 124va). In this context the natural meaning of *civitas* would have been 'city' or 'town'. The best evidence is the use of the words *civis* and *civitas* in a *Collectio de Scandalis Ecclesiae,* for its modern editor has argued that Guibert himself was almost certainly the author – [P. Autbertus] Stroick, 'Verfasser und Quellen der Collectio de Scandalis Ecclesiae (Reformschrift des Fr. Gilbert von Tournay O.F.M. zum II. Konzil von Lyon, 1274)', AFH, 23 (1930) pp 3–41, 273–99, 433–66; and Stroick's edition, 'Collectio de Scandalis Ecclesiae, Nova Editio', *AFH,* 24 (1931) pp 33–62, esp p 33: 'Eiusdem auctorem quasi certum habemus Gilbertum Tornacensem O.F.M.' The description of the evils to be found *in civitae* build up a picture of an urban environment. See *ibid* p 60.

[32] 'sed cives nostri temporis ut sibi invicem noceant super diversa statuta officia diversa faciunt facta puniunt, deinde convellunt et alia faciunt.' BN MS lat 15943 fol 125vb. The text is probably corrupt but the general sense seems clear.

which Guibert redirects this traditional ideology to the *cives reipublicae vacantes*.

The next sermon is probably directed at much the same sort of people, though it is concerned with a different aspect of their lives. The rubric is: *ad cives communiter viventes*, and the text: 'Qui amat divitias fructum non capiet ex eis.' (Eccles 5: 9). The rubric shows that the sermon was for an urban public, and as the choice of text suggests, Guibert's subject is wealth. It is a reasonable inference that the sermon is especially (though perhaps not solely) directed towards the class from which the *cives reipublicae vacantes* would have most often been recruited: the upper class of the cities.

Just as the previous sermon raised the question of ecclesiastical attitudes to political authority, this sermon raises the question of ecclesiastical attitudes to wealth. In the economic as well as the political sphere the rise of the towns had provoked thought about questions which were new so far as the middle ages were concerned. Society and the church had depended for centuries on landed property, and that kind of wealth, obviously enough, was considered to be legitimate. The wealth of the upper class of the towns was a somewhat different proposition. It is true that some wealthy men living in cities, especially Italian cities, would have owned land in the country outside, and that urban property, as well as trade, could be a source of wealth for urban magnates. Then of course there were men like lawyers and notaries who made a comfortable living by their professional skills. After all these qualifications, however, it remains true that the majority of rich men who lived in cities must have been engaged in some kind of trade or finance. The established church's attitude to this kind of wealth was inevitably more complicated than its attitude to land.[33] As a major force in the social and economic life of northern Europe, the wealthy urban class does not go back beyond the twelfth century, and its power and importance must have increased considerably during the lifetime of Guibert himself. What attitude was he, a Franciscan, to take to this urban wealth?

Much of the sermon reads like a forceful diatribe against riches.[34] *Relinqunt etiam insatiabilitatem in appetitu . . . Relinqunt etiam cecitatem*

[33] Compare J. Gilchrist, *The Church and Economic Activity in the Middle Ages* (London 1969) pp 51–2.

[34] The following passage gives a good idea of the tone of the greater part of the sermon: 'Relinqunt etiam insatiabilitatem in appetitu. Eccl. [*col b*] iiii. Unus est et secundum non habet, et tamen laborare non cessat, nec satiantur oculi eius divitiis. Insatiabilis enim est oculus cupidi; nichil enim potest animam replere nisi deus. Unde tanta est

in intellectu . . . etiam relinqunt sterilitatem in fructu . . .—Guibert is uncompromising. His analogies are forceful, to say the least: 'They labour by fair means and foul in order to have, not in order to make restitution, unless they do so at the end, when the bitterness of death is approaching, just as a blood-sucker, when it is full up, vomits out the blood . . .'.[35]

After his diatribe against material riches Guibert implicitly draws the contrast—perhaps inevitable—with the riches that are not of this world: spiritual riches, heavenly riches, and the riches that are above heaven, in God himself. In one passage the contrast is made explicit,[36] and the theme is the same: '. . . for temporal riches, like imaginary banquets, deceive those who eat them, and send them empty away.'[37]

Guibert, clearly, believes in harsh medicine. Nevertheless he does try to sugar the pill, and the short section at the beginning, in which he tries to show how a rich man may be a good man, is perhaps as interesting as the series of criticisms which follow. He is prepared to talk about virtues as well as vices.

It is legitimate to possess temporal riches, he says, when they are acquired without ill-doing, and he cites the example of Abraham, who was rich in gold and silver.[38] He lists other virtues a rich man must possess before he can regard his wealth as licit. He must remain humble, because wealth nourishes pride. He must use his riches as a pilgrim uses the road, and be like a poor man in the midst of riches; and, of course, he must give alms from his riches: they must be 'distributed with piety'. He continues, citing 2 Kings 19 (32), 'Berzellai offered food to the king, when he was staying in the camp: for he was very rich man.

---

anime capacitas quod non repletur modicis. Ipsa autem anima ymago est dei, et ideo maior est toto mundo, immo quanto magis repletur temporalibus [tanto] minus repletur deo, et ita semper remanet vacua. Res enim in se vanitatem habent, et ideo non replent. Res etiam sunt extra. Sitis autem est in anima. Fatuus autem esset esuriens qui se refectum diceret eo quod panem in archa tantum haberet. Propterea [*cod* P] aviditatis vitium semper tendit in infinitum, sicut ignis semper adureret si quis ei materiam apponeret. Seneca: Si vis divitem facere, non divitiis addendum, sed divitiis detrahendum. Relinqunt etiam cecitatem in intellectu. Obnubilant enim divitie intellectum divitis ita ut inter se et divitias non distinguit [*cod* distingunt], ita ut si domus eius comburitur, dicit se combustum.' BN MS lat 15943 fol $127^{va/b}$.

35 'Laborant enim per fas et nefas ut habeant, non ut restituant, nisi in fine, adveniente mortis amaritudine, sicut sangui – fol 128va – suga repleta evomit sanguinem superposito sale.' *Ibid* fol $128^{rb/va}$.

36 'Sunt etiam divitie celestes . . . Non sunt autem hee divitie quales mundane . . .' *Ibid* fol 129va.

37 'temporales enim sicut fantastice epule comedentes fallunt et inanes dimittunt.' *Ibid.*

38 Gen 13:2.

For now Christ sojourns (*peregrinatur*) among the poor as if in camp.'[39] He ends the section with a comforting quotation, softening the strictures which follow, to the effect that riches are a hindrance to virtue in bad men, but a help to it in good men.[40]

'Gold and silver make neither good men nor bad men: the use of them is good, and the abuse of them is bad', as he puts it near the beginning of the sermon. What follows, however, might seem to exclude the profits of a merchant, for Guibert goes on to say that 'Anxiety (for riches) is worse; profit (*questus*) is more base'.[41] Guibert may be quoting someone else—it is not quite his style—and there is nothing more explicit about merchants in this sermon. He saves his comments for the next two sermons, which are directly addressed to merchants.

In the second of these sermons it is made clear that the merchant's profits are in themselves licit. It is true that some kinds of trade are by their very nature immoral (Guibert gives usury and 'fornication'—by which he presumably means prostitution—as examples of such trades).[42] Again, some are immoral because of the nature of the thing bought or sold, as when people buy or sell things which are not needed for anything except sin.[43] Ordinary buying and selling, however, are only illicit when the disposition of those involved makes them so, that is, when they are motivated by avarice, or over-preoccupied with worldly cares.[44]

[39] 'Distribuuntur cum pietate. II. Reg. xix. Berzellai prebuit alimenta regi cum moraretur in castris. Fuit enim vir dives nimis. Nunc enim Christus peregrinatur in pauperibus velud in castris.' BN MS lat 15943 fol 126[va].

[40] 'Gregorius: Divitie sicut impedimenta sunt in improbis [sunt in improbis *cod.* sunt improb.] ita in bonis sunt adiumenta virtutis.' *Ibid* fol 126[va]. I have not traced the quotation.

[41] 'Aurum enim et argentum nec bonos nec malos faciunt, sed usus eorum bonus est, abusio mala. Sollicitudo [*cod* Sollicito?] peior. Questus turpior'. *Ibid* fol 126[rb].

[42] 'Quedam enim negotia ex sui natura sunt inhonesta et illicita, ut usura, fornicatio, et huiusmodi'. *Ibid* fol 133[ra].

[43] 'Aliquando est negȏtia 'tio' illicita ex natura rei que emitur vel venditur, ut si quis talia vendat vel emat que ad nullum usum humanum possunt esse necessaria preter quam ad peccatum, . . .' *Ibid.*

[44] 'quedam ex adiuncto, ut venditio et emptio: licet in se sint licite, tamen ex causa sunt illicite quando fiunt ex cupiditate, et quando animam involvunt nimia curarum anxietate . . .'. *Ibid.* Guibert makes a similar statement of principle later in the sermon: 'Non est simpliciter negotiatio dampnanda: sicut enim dicit Cassiodorus: Actus pessimus non res honesta dampnatur; sicut divitem legimus non introire regnum celorum, cum tamen Abraham, Iacob, Iob, David fuerint divites.' *Ibid* fol 133va. Compare J. Le Goff, 'Métier et profession d'après les manuels de confesseurs au moyen âge'. *Beiträge zum Berufsbewusstsein des mittelalterlichen Menschen,* ed P. Wilpert, *Miscellanea Mediaevalia,* 3 (Berlin 1964) pp 44–60, esp p 58.

The passage in which Guibert distinguishes between licit and illicit trade is one of the few places in the two sermons where he comes anywhere near to a technical analysis of economic morality. The greater part of both sermons is on a rather different level: that of allegory.

A single allegory extends over both sermons. Guibert gives the gist of it at the beginning of the first one: 'the good merchant is Christ and just men; the bad merchant is the devil and unjust men'.[45] The first sermon is mainly concerned with Christ and the just, leaving the devil and the 'devil's merchants' to the second.

From a literary point of view the sermons are not particularly impressive. Quite apart from the heavy dependence on Jacques de Vitry, Guibert switches too suddenly, for some tastes, from the allegorical to the literal level, and sometimes he seems to be distributing his material rather arbitrarily among the different sections. For all that, the sermons are not without interest. Indeed they provide confirmation from sermon evidence of one of the theses which Rosenwein and Little illustrate from other kinds of source: the idea that the language of the friars was 'heavily impregnated with a market place vocabulary'.[46]

Allegory is everywhere in medieval sermons, but it is unusual to find an allegory so carefully tailored to so specific an audience. Guibert is addressing merchants, but he is concerned with general as well as economic morality; by making trade itself the basis of the allegory, he is able to orientate the whole sermon (not only the parts which deal with 'business ethics') towards the special interests and preoccupations of this particular section of the laity. Notions and events with which their business life would have made them familiar are transposed to the sphere of general morality when the devil is compared to a usurer:

> . . . but that userer makes his loans without risk, since he has a good security (*vadium*), that is, the sinner's soul; and a good pledge (*plegium*): the justice of God; and a good chirograph, which we gave to him, written in the blood from our souls, when we sinned; with these things the devil is certain that unless the sinner should buy back his pledge before his death, that is, before the

[45] 'bonus negotiator Christus et viri iusti; malus negotiator dyabolus et viri iniusti.' BN MS lat 15943 fol 130ra.

[46] Rosenwein and Little p 23 (with further refs), and p 32: 'The friars negotiated the Gospel without using money, thus exercising commerce as truly Christian merchants.'

fair breaks up (*divisio nundinarum fiat*) and the shout of Hale! Hale! goes up, according to the custom of the French, his security will be (forfeited) in perpetuity. Finally, when he (the devil) has stripped his debtor of everything and left him naked, and he sees that he is unable to pay, then a gibbet or gallows is erected—just as in the fairs of this world—and there the sinner is hanged. Then he weeps in vain, because he has lost everything, and because he will not be able to go back to the city in which he could do business again.[47]

The technical terms and the allusions to the customs of the trade fairs are not accidental. Guibert (and Jacques de Vitry, whom he is following)[48] must have hoped to hold the attention and catch the imagination of merchants by this device.

The two sermons to merchants are not the only place where Guibert employs an allegory adapted to a particular status. In the sermons *Ad iudices et advocatos* he makes Christ an advocate, with God the Father the judge of the case, and the cross the *locus iuris*.[49] In the sermons to the merchants Christ is instead a merchant who sells the robe of his flesh, dyed with his blood, to buy back souls.[50] By calling Christ an *advocatus* when addressing lawyers, and a *bonus negotiator* when writing for merchants, he was presumably trying to help these different audiences feel that they could in some sense identify with Christ himself.

The allegory of commerce in the sermons was one way of trying to meet the mentality of the upper bourgeoisie half way. In general, the sermons I have all too briefly discussed strike one as a serious attempt to

[47] '. . . Secure autem accomodat ille usurarius, quia bonum vadium habet, scilicet peccatoris animam; et bonum plegium: dei iustitiam; et bonum cyrographum, quod ei scriptum dedimus de sanguine animarum nostrarum cum peccavimus; per que certus est dyabolus quod nisi vadium suum redimat peccator ante mortem suam, scilicet antequam divisio nundinarum fiat et clametur: "Hale! Hale!" secundum modum gallicorum vadium suum erit in perpetuum. Ultimo cum debitorem suum nudum spoliaverit et videat quod ille solvere non possit, sicut fit in nundinis [*cod* mundinis] seculi, gibetum sive patibulum erigitur et peccator ibi suspenditur. Tunc lacrimas inefficaces emittit, quod totum perdidit, et ad civitatem in qua iterato negotiari valeat redire non poterit.' BN MS lat 15943 fol 132$^{rb/va}$.

[48] Compare *Analecta Novissima: Spicilegii Solesmensis Altera Continuatio,* ed J. B. Pitra, 2, *Tusculana* (republ 1967 by the Gregg Press Ltd) p 432.

[49] 'Advocatus igitur noster [*cod* videtur] in hoc ministerio Christus. Iudex: pater deus; locus iuris: patibulum crucis; res postulata: ecclesia de gentibus conversa; nomen actionis: petitio hereditatis'. BN MS lat 15943 fol 91ra.

[50] 'Tandem scaraliticium mundissime carnis sue purpureo sanguine suo tinctum pro redimendis animabus nostris dedit.' *Ibid* fol 130ra.

provide the upper bourgeoisie with a spirituality, if the word may be used in a loose sense, adapted to their way of life. While the general tone of the sermons is admonitory, Guibert does allow for the possibility of a good rich man and a good merchant (even in a non-allegorical sense). He shows them what they should try to resemble: Abraham was rich in gold and silver; Christ is a 'good merchant'; the political rulers of the cities should imitate God, being conformed to him in power, wisdom, and holiness. The other side of the same coin is the doctrinal continuity: the stress on the dangers of wealth and commerce, and the application to city rulers of the traditional ideology of government. Guibert was a child of tradition as well as of his age.

University of London
University College

TOWN MICE AND COUNTRY MICE IN THE PROVINCE OF YORK 1317–40

by ROSALIND M. T. HILL

A few months after the end of the second world war a journalist, walking through the streets of devastated Hamburg, saw a girl come out of the basement of a bombed house. She was wearing a clean white tennis-dress and carrying a racquet, and as she picked her way through the piles of burnt-out rubble he pondered, as historians have often pondered before him, upon the remarkable capacity of people not only for surviving, but for continuing the ordinary pattern of their lives, in the most adverse circumstances. I have often remembered that girl in Hamburg as I worked my way through the letters of archbishop Melton's register with its record of the way in which the ordinary people of the north, the town and country mice of my title, survived and carried on their normal activities, and even re-built and extended their churches, in the midst of the troubles in which they found themselves.

Troublous the times certainly were. Apart from a respite of five years between 1328 and 1333 there were continuous wars between the English and the Scots, and much of the fighting and raiding took place on the English side of the border. One of Melton's first instructions from the pope was to try to bring the Scots to accept a truce—a charge in which he was completely unsuccessful.[1] In 1319 the forces which he raised to defend his province were routed at Myton in Swaledale, and the ravaging by Bruce's army, already disastrous for northern economy, was intensified. One after another the Yorkshire abbeys were compelled to appeal for a re-assessment of taxation upon grounds of ruined crops, burned buildings, cattle driven off and people killed or carried into captivity.[2] The same story came from the western deaneries.[3] By 1334 it was evident that every archdeaconry except Nottingham had its share of devastation,[4] and although the treaty of Northampton had

[1] R[egister of Archbishop William] M[elton], Borthwick Institute, York. Foliated twice, new foliation indicated as NF, fol 495^{v} (NF 623).

[2] *CYS* 70 (1977) pp 37, 58. Compare RM fol 517^{v} (NF 648).

[3] *Ibid* p 39.

[4] *Ibid* p 107.

given a brief respite it was clear that the rage of the Scots was breaking out again.[5] Moreover they were not the only source of trouble in the north. The Lancastrian rising of 1322 was put down in a battle fought at Boroughbridge; the wars against France in the reigns of Edward II and Edward III brought doubts as to the loyalty of alien clergy in the northern province,[6] and they brought also heavy and oppressive taxation. Edward III sent mandates for the raising of forces of men-at-arms and archers[7] from a countryside already strained by the defence of the northern borders. Nor was there any lack of internal feuding. Gilbert of Middleton distinguished himself by kidnapping two papal legates;[8] Lewis de Beaumont bishop of Durham was accused by the archbishop himself of trying to kill him rather than allow him to carry out a visitation of the peculiar of Allertonshire; the bishop of Carlisle, whose cathedral had already been burned by the Scots,[9] was assailed in his own city with 'blasphemous words, arrows and stones'.[10] For an archiepiscopal visitation to be carried out 'peacefully' was considered to be an event worthy of special record,[11] and what the enemy spared famine, fires and murrain were apt to account for.[12]

Yet life went on, even though the standard of public morality was assumed to have dropped to such an extent that the archbishop could claim that perjurers had become so common that it was likely that the earth would open and swallow them up after the example of Dathan and Abiram.[13] Clerics were occasionally accused of burglary, arson or homicide, but for the most part they succeeded in clearing themselves.[14] People went to church; in fact they spent a good deal of money on church-building. Throughout the province celebrations of the newly-instituted feast of Corpus Christi[15] were held in churches which the efforts of the faithful were trying to restore with even greater splendour. Indulgences for the fabric-funds of York, Ripon and Beverley were carefully drawn up and entrusted to properly

[5] RM fols 536^{v}–7 (NF 671–2).
[6] *Ibid* fol 518 (NF 650), fol 551^{v} (NF 688).
[7] *Ibid* fol 549^{v} (NF 686).
[8] *Historiae Dunelmensis Scriptores Tres,* ed J. Raine, *SS* 9 (1839) p 100.
[9] *CYS* 70 p 71.
[10] *Ibid* p 95.
[11] *Ibid* p 16.
[12] *Ibid* p 58.
[13] RM fol 534 (NF 669).
[14] *CYS* 70 pp 2, 25, 119, 57.
[15] RM fol 514 (NF 643).

accredited pardoners, among them, interestingly enough, being four Scotsmen.[16] (Apparently the Scottish reputation for thrifty business dealings was good enough to overcome any national prejudice which might have arisen over their employment.) Funds were raised for the sick in St Leonard's Hospital, York, on two separate occasions.[17] Nor did northern charity confine itself to the province. Others benefited as well,—Oxford University, at which Melton himself had studied,[18] the hospital of St Thomas the Martyr at Canterbury,[19] the hospitals of St Antony at Vienne[20] and San Spirito in Saxia at Rome.[21] The northern clergy might be, as they repeatedly claimed, too poor to pay their taxes (on one occasion they offered to pray for the king instead of giving him a subsidy[22]), but their parishioners were not too poor to spare contributions for good causes, and religious foundations flourished. The devastation of Amounderness does not seem to have had much effect upon the grammar-school at Preston[23] or the decision of the abbot and convent of St Mary's York to set up a chantry at Kendal.[24]

Even in the middle of the wars, archbishop Melton had to turn his mind from the pressing affairs of state to the tiresomeness of his flock. In 1324, the year when Edward II was committed to the war of Saint-Sardos and when a mission under the bishop of Winchester went to Avignon to urge that Bruce's excommunication be continued, Melton was dealing with a case referred to him by the archdeacon of Northumberland because of the *perhorrescentia* felt by Robert at the very thought of coming into court to answer the claims of his putative wife Agnes Taylor *propter potenciam dicte Agnetis*,[25] whom he evidently regarded as a menace as serious as a force of moss-troopers. Ten years later, when the people of the diocese should have been attuning their minds to the archbishop's summons to pray for the good success of the king's army against 'the furious attack and presumptuous rage of the Scots'[26] the citizens of York were, in fact,

[16] *Ibid* fols 518v–19 (NF 650–1).
[17] *Ibid* fol 536 (NF 671), fol 539 (NF 674).
[18] *Ibid* fol 512 (NF 640), fol 525 (NF 658).
[19] *Ibid* fol 544v (NF 680).
[20] *Ibid* fol 518v (NF 650).
[21] *Ibid* fol 529v (NF 664).
[22] *CYS* 70 p 77.
[23] *Ibid* p 34.
[24] *Ibid* p 49.
[25] RM fol 517 (NF 648).
[26] *CYS* 70 p 106.

being led astray by the preaching of a popular, and possibly rather mad, hermit called Henry of Staunton who was causing trouble by putting forward 'sacrilegious, perverse and schismatic doctrines, holding unlawful conventicles, and urging married women to forsake their husbands'.[27] Further trouble was from time to time caused by pardoners, who occasionally succumbed to the temptation to embezzle the funds[28] but more often seem to have erred through inadequacy of training ('they do not preach to edification but rather give incentives to sin') or excess of zeal ('they run about the diocese, ... usurping the office of preachers and teaching various errors and abuses').[29] Preaching in fact seems to have caused considerable trouble, not least in country parishes lying within a short distance of a town which housed a community of friars. The superior skill and training of the friars aroused the jealousy of local incumbents and led to reprisals. At Boroughbridge the Dominicans, at York the Austin Friars and at Doncaster the Franciscans had to be supported by the archbishop against rectors who were trying to prevent their parishioners from confessing to friars or listening to their sermons, despite the fact that such friars were known to be properly licensed.[30]

Occasionally papal or royal mandates came to trouble the little world of parish or priory. One's mind boggles at contemplating the reception, by the parishioners of Howden, Welton and Walkington, of the news that Lewis duke of Bavaria, falsely calling himself emperor, was henceforth to be shunned as an excommunicated person,[31] but the sentence of automatic excommunication for dealings with the Scots was a real enough problem, especially when it was incurred inadvertently, as it was by Simon Le Candeler and Clement Ende of Depe who found on returning from business in Scotland that their neighbours in Ravenser Odd would sell them no food.[32] Then there was the problem—a real one in a time of fairly extensive papal provision—of the foreign incumbent who might well be a spy. Edward II wrote to Melton in 1324 for a list of ecclesiastical aliens resident in the diocese, and followed up his letter with instructions that any who were not subjects of the count of Flanders should be subjected to a kind of internment, which entailed their removal from

[27] RM fol 539^{v} (NF 674).
[28] *CYS* 70 pp 16–17.
[29] RM fol 533 (NF 668).
[30] *Ibid* fol 541^{v} (NF 676*bis*).
[31] *CYS* 70 p 134.
[32] RM fol 511 (NF 639).

benefices situated near the sea or navigable rivers to 'rather remote parts', where they were to be supplied with eighteen pence a week for their rations and a yearly allowance of forty shillings for clothes and shoes.[33] The archbishop did not take this very seriously. He replied to the king's mandate to the effect that, since he did not believe any of his clergy to be enemy aliens, he had done nothing about it,[34] and he seems to have been similarly unimpressed by a mandate on the same subject issued in 1339 by Edward III[35]

Other unwilling country mice might be found among the ex-members of the order of Templars, now pensioned off in various small and remote religious houses. It seems to have been the fate of this unfortunate order that it could never, in the eyes of contemporaries, do anything right. It had been dissolved as a result of various charges including heresy, financial chicanery and homosexuality, but within a few years its ex-members were in trouble for their 'insolence and damnable presumption' in wanting to get married, or rather, as John XXII sourly observed, 'to enter into a state of concubinage'.[36] As men under religious vows they were not allowed this solace,—farmed out with other religious orders, they seem to have stayed until they were *senio confracti et ad laborem impotentes*,[37] their only interest being to petition the archbishop to keep the Hospitallers up to the mark in the matter of the regular payment of their annual pensions. Thomas Screche, ex-Templar, was still pursuing his weary round at Nostell as late as 1335.[38]

Like mice in the cornfield, under the threat of the reaper, the faithful went on with their daily activities regardless of the wrangling of statesmen and the trampling of armies. Their lives were a chronicle of small-beer for the most part, but it is on such humble foundations that the history of the medieval church is bound to rest.

University of London
Westfield College

[33] *Ibid.*
[34] *Ibid* fol 518 (NF 650).
[35] *Ibid* fol 551^{v} (NF 688).
[36] *Ibid* fol 505^{v} (NF 633).
[37] *Ibid* fol 506 (NF 634).
[38] *Ibid* fol 537^{v} (NF 672).

PRIESTS AND PATRONS IN THE FOURTEENTH-CENTURY DIOCESE OF CARLISLE

by R. K. ROSE

THERE were several possibilities open to a man entering the secular clergy in the later middle ages. Among these were careers as a royal, papal, or episcopal servant, as a teacher or scholar, or as the rector or vicar of a parish church. If he did not set his hopes high, he could join the ranks of the chaplains of his diocese, helping the incumbents of the parish churches with the administration of their benefices and with the cure of souls, serving chapels and perpetual chantries, and serving oratories in noble and gentry households. Whatever his ambitions and aspirations, however, the secular priest's situation depended entirely upon the charity and good will of those in a position to exercise patronage: family and friends, the beneficed clergy, the bishop and his *familia*, and the established, landed families of the area. And whether the possibilities became opportunities in the form of the patronage desired depended to a large extent upon the social position of the priest's family, the proper connections, and the extent of his education. These were the realities faced universally by the clergy of the universal church, but each region had its own particular system of patronage, varying with the needs and structure of society. As a case in point, the lives and success of the clergy of the northern English diocese of Carlisle, despite the mission and aims held in common with the clergy of the entire church, were dictated to a degree by the rural nature of the diocese and its location on the Anglo-Scottish border.

At the centre of the diocese was of course the city of Carlisle, which, besides the Augustinian cathedral church of St Mary, had a parish church dedicated to St Cuthbert and both a Dominican and a Franciscan friary. J. C. Russell estimated the city's population in 1377 to be about 1,017, the third smallest city in England, outranking only Rochester and Bath.[1] Besides Carlisle, only Appleby, the county town of Westmorland, which had two parish churches and a Carmelite

[1] [J. C.] Russell, [*British Medieval Population*] (Albuquerque 1948) p 142.

friary, and Penrith, which had besides its parish church an Augustinian friary, could have qualified as towns of any importance or size. The rest of the diocese was broken up into expansive parishes averaging about nineteen square miles in size, something not unusual in the less populous north of England.[2] Nor was the church of Carlisle particularly well endowed. As it was a late creation and vacant for nearly fifty years in the twelfth century, the episcopal see lacked the patrimony which other bishoprics had built up over several centuries. Of the religious houses, only the Cistercian abbey of Holmcultram, which, according to the taxation of pope Nicholas IV of 1291, took in about £80 more than the bishop himself, could claim any standard of wealth. The rest were little better off than the few wealthy benefices.[3] The Anglo-Scottish war and the resultant raids of Scots across the border helped to undermine an already sorry state, and the fourteenth century became one of ceaseless moanings on the part of the diocesan clergy over destruction of church property and loss of revenue. The new taxation of 1318 indicates the drastic reduction of the value of benefices, which must have created something of an employment problem for chaplains and clerks in the early part of the century when the raids were heaviest.[4]

The number of clergy required to staff the diocese was not inconsiderable. Including the cathedral, the nave of which served as the parish church of St Mary, there were ninety-four parishes in the diocese of Carlisle. By 1291, twenty-six of the ninety-four churches were appropriated to either the bishop or a religious house. By the end of the fourteenth century the number had risen to fifty-one, nearly all on the pretext of the losses incurred as a result of the war.[5] Seventeen of the appropriated churches seem never to have had perpetual vicarages ordained and were probably served by chaplains or regular canons, as was normally the case in seven of the appropriated

[2] [R.] Donaldson, 'Patronage and the Church: [A Study in the Social Structure of the Secular Clergy in the Diocese of Durham, 1311–1540]' (University of Edinburgh PhD thesis 1955) p 103.

[3] *Taxatio ecclesiastica Angliae et Walliae Auctoritate P. Nicholai IV circa A.D. 1291*, ed T. Astle, S. Aynscough, and J. Caley, Record Commissioners (London 1802) pp 318–20.

[4] *Ibid* pp 332–3; *Reg*[*ister of John de*] *Halton*, [*Bishop of Carlisle, A.D. 1292–1324*,] ed W. N. Thompson, 2 vols, *CYS* (1906–13) 2, pp 183–9. With the great drop in ecclesiastical income in the early years of the century, it must have been difficult for the incumbents of benefices extensively to employ chaplains and clerks.

[5] [C. M. L.] Bouch, *Prelates and People* [*of the Lake Counties: A History of the Diocese of Carlisle, 1133–1933*] (Kendal 1948) pp 471–3. The table illustrates the churches appropriated by 1291 and by 1535. Of those appropriated by 1535, only Thursby and Kirkland had not been appropriated in the fourteenth century.

churches with perpetual vicarages.[6] The churches of Aikton and Kirkbampton, curiously, had two rectors each, and the church of Arthuret, technically appropriated to Jedburgh abbey, had for a time both a rector and a perpetual vicar.[7] Therefore, throughout most of the century, forty-six rectories and thirty-four perpetual vicarages existed. Most churches, at least the eighty rectories and vicarages, seem to have had at least one chaplain or 'parish priest', and at least twenty outlying chapels were in existence in the fourteenth century.[8] Chantries not being considered, a conservative estimate of the number of priests needed to administer the sacraments in the parish churches and chapels is nearly two hundred. This is a figure not far off the totals rendered by the poll-taxes of 1377 and 1379, both of which would appear to be underestimations. The 1377 poll-tax gives account of two hundrd and thirty-two beneficed and unbeneficed clergy but includes some fifty religious among those beneficed, bringing the number down to about one hundred and eighty-two.[9] The account of 1379 lists seventy-seven incumbents of benefices and ninety-nine chaplains, making a total of one hundred and seventy-six.[10] Realistically, however, the number of secular priests in the diocese was clearly more than this.

It is no easy matter to establish the number of the clergy in the diocese at any given time beyond the estimates arising from the poll-taxes at the end of the century. Thus the demographic variations for the period that witnessed the onslaught of war and the arrival of the plague are rather elusive. However, an examination of the extant lists of ordinations for the years 1294–1324, 1332–47, and 1354–83 will help to provide an indication of the supply of priests at hand in the fourteenth century.[11] In the first of these periods, covering the

[6] [J. L.] Kirby, 'Two Tax Accounts [of the Diocese of Carlisle'], *Transactions of the Cumberland and Westmorland Antiquarian and Archaeological Society*, ns 52 (Kendal 1953) p 73.

[7] *Reg Halton*, 1, pp 226, 228, 262–3; 2, p 221; C[arlisle, Cumbria County] R[ecord] O[ffice], MS DRC 1/1, fols 219^{r}, 238^{v}, 239^{v}; DRC 2/1, fols 20^{v}, 23^{r}, 50^{r}, 56^{v}, 79^{r}, 136^{v}, 155^{r}, 158^{v}, 185^{r}; *Reg Halton*, 2, pp 28–9; CRO MS DRC 1/1, fols 219^{r}, 238^{v}, 239^{r}; DRC 2/1, fols 35^{r}, 46^{r}, 86^{r}; DRC 1/1, fols 137^{r}, 131^{v}, 132^{r}, 136^{v}, 186^{v}, 188^{r}, 232^{r}; DRC 2/1, fols 10^{v}, 11^{v}, 47^{v}, 88^{v}, 121^{v}, 155^{r}.

[8] Bouch, *Prelates and People*, pp 161–3. The table does not include the chapels of Bramery, Burton, and Solport. *Reg Halton*, 1, p 69; 2, p 190; CRO MS DRC 2/1, fols 46^{v}, 53^{v}.

[9] Russell pp 161–3.

[10] Kirby, 'Two Tax Accounts', pp 74–81.

[11] *Reg Halton*, 1, pp 11–12, 23–7, 37–9, 60, 107–9, 118, 132–4, 183–7, 200–1, 203, 211–3, 221–3, 229–31, 241–7, 249–50, 263–4, 268–70, 272–7, 279–82, 290–92, 304–9, 320, 330–1; 2, pp 24–7, 29–32, 68–70, 73–4, 77, 88–91, 135–8, 140–1, 155, 164, 167–9,

years of bishop John de Halton, during whose episcopate were the heaviest Scottish incursions into northern England, an average of between four and five men were being ordained priests each year. The average rose to between seven and eight during the episcopate of John de Kirkby, when the borders were politically and economically more stable than previously. The plague took an even worse toll of the recruitment of priests in the diocese than the years of continuous Scottish raiding, and in the decade following the first pestilence there was a sharp drop in the number of men ordained. Gilbert de Welton, who was bishop from 1353 to 1362, managed to ordain no more than an average of one priest annually. The decline cannot be explained entirely by the high death rate but may also be attributed to difficulties in obtaining the support of a patron, which was necessary in order to be ordained, and the better opportunities which were arising elsewhere. Indeed, a number of the clergy were leaving the diocese, as is evidenced by the unprecedented number of dimissory letters, which granted the right to ordination by another bishop, during Welton's episcopate.[12] In view of the number of vacancies of benefices which would have arisen as a result of the plague, there certainly must have been a recruitment crisis in the 1350s.

Because of the gap in the episcopal registers for the crucial years, it is impossible to ascertain, as A. H. Thompson did for the diocese of York,[13] exactly how many vacancies were due to death. At the beginning of the episcopate of bishop Welton, however, only twenty-one of the eighty rectories and vicarages were still in the hands of those who had held them in 1347.[14] Of course, of the remaining fifty-nine benefices which had fallen vacant in the intervening years, a certain number would have been due to resignation. In any case, the rate of

---

190–1, 201–2, 206–8, 212–13, 217–18, 226–30; CRO MS DRC 1/1, fols 122^{r}–4^{v}, 128^{v}–9^{r}, 149^{v}, 154^{r}, 157$^{r/v}$, 161^{v}–3^{r}, 165^{v}–7^{r}, 169^{v}–70^{r}, 176^{v}–7^{v}, 181^{v}–2^{r}, 189$^{r/v}$, 201^{v}, 203^{r}, 205^{v}–7^{v}, 209^{r}–10^{v}, 214^{r}, 224^{r}, 226^{v}–7^{r}, 232^{v}, 237^{r}–8^{r}, 240^{r}–2^{r}, 250^{r}–4^{v}; DRC 2/1, fols 70^{r}–1^{v}, 141^{r}–9^{v}. See table 1 below.

[12] Bishop Welton conceded twenty-five dimissory letters between 1354 and 1362, as compared with four conceded by bishop Kirkby and one by bishop Appelby. CRO MS DRC 2/1, fols 9^{v}, 19^{r}, 22^{v}, 33^{v}, 36^{r}, 37^{r}, 38^{r}, 41$^{r/v}$, 42^{v}, 43^{r}, 44^{v}, 45^{r}, 50^{v}, 51$^{r/v}$, 55^{r}, 58^{v}, 59^{v}, 66^{r}, 67^{v}, 68^{r}, 81^{v}.

[13] A. Hamilton Thompson, 'The pestilences of the fourteenth century in the diocese of York', *Archaeological Journal,* 2 ser, 21 (London 1914) pp 97–154.

[14] *Reg Halton*, 2, pp 116, 124, 223; CRO MS DRC 1/1, fols 124^{v}, 141^{r}, 143^{v}, 160^{v}, 162^{v}, 171^{r}, 175^{r}, 185^{v}, 186^{v}, 200^{v}, 203^{r}, 233^{r}, 234^{v}, 241^{r}, 242^{v}, 247^{r}, 252^{v}, 253^{v}; DRC 2/1, fols 10^{r}, 21^{r}, 23$^{r/v}$, 25^{v}, 30^{v}, 34^{v}, 35^{v}, 36^{r}, 41^{r}, 48^{r}, 51^{v}, 53^{v}, 57^{v}, 59^{r}, 79^{r}, 155^{v}; *Test*[*amenta*] *Karl*[*eolensia, 1353–1386*], ed R. S. Ferguson (Kendal 1893) pp 1–3, 112.

death in the diocese among the beneficed clergy in 1349 and 1350 was probably close to that of York, that is, about forty-four per cent. For the next wave of the plague in 1361 and 1362, the diocesan records show that about twenty-four per cent of the incumbents of benefices died, a figure almost twice the death rate in the diocese of York.[15] It appears that bishop Thomas de Appelby, who succeeded Welton in 1363, implemented a definite policy to alleviate this problem. Whereas his predecessors ordained men sporadically, sometimes not celebrating an ordination for over a year and many times outside the diocese, Appelby consistently held four or five small ordinations each year, all but one within the diocese. It would seem that he was making an effort to avail the diocese of as many priests as possible, and the average number of men ordained each year rose to four, which nears the figure for the first quarter of the century.

The supply of priests available in any diocese depended upon the smooth and efficient running of the patronage system. Unless he were of independent means, it was absolutely necessary for the hopeful cleric to find someone who was willing to provide him with a 'title', an annual stipend usually set at forty shillings while he was in minor orders and raised to five marks by the time he was ordained a priest. The purpose of the title was to keep the clerk awaiting higher orders or ecclesiastical preferment from becoming impoverished and a burden upon the bishop and his church. Each title was granted by charter, which was scrutinsed and approved by the official principal before the clerk could proceed to ordination. Moreover, he had to proclaim himself satisfied with the amount of the title and promise not to trouble the bishop with it.[16] The benefactors of titles represent a remarkable cross-section of society, ranging from such men as Peter the butcher of Carlisle to the bishop himself.[17]

It may be assumed that generally throughout England many of the titles came from the beneficed clergy, who would then employ the beneficiaries as parish clerks in a kind of apprenticeship. But this was extremely rare in the diocese of Carlisle, and in several of the few such cases the patron appears to have been acting as benefactor to a relative rather than as an employer.[18] In fact, the diocesan clergy as a whole supplied relatively few of the needed titles. Religious houses, which

[15] CRO MS DRC 2/1, fols 44^{v}, 45^{r}, 46^{r}, 48^{r}/^{v}, 51^{v}, 53^{r}/^{v}, 54^{v}, 55^{v}, 57^{v}, 58^{r}/^{v}, 59^{r}/^{v}.

[16] *Reg Halton*, 1, p 263; CRO MS DRC 1/1, fol 122^{r}.

[17] The analysis of titles is based upon the titles listed in the extant ordinations lists. See note 11 above.

[18] *Reg Halton*, 2, p 141; CRO MS DRC 1/1, fols 157^{v}, 224^{r}.

provided a great number of titles in other English dioceses, conceded few in the diocese of Carlisle. The priory of Carlisle granted only twelve known titles in the course of the century, and the combined efforts of Holmcultram abbey, Shap abbey, Lanercost priory, and Wetheral priory produced but another twelve, only seven of the total twenty-four having been granted after the plague years.[19] The number of titles granted under episcopal auspices was, as may be expected, somewhat higher, since the bishop was probably in need of new clerks at most times for the duties of diocesan administration. For most of the century, however, the bishop's patronage in the form of titles comprised a small minority of the total number granted. Only bishop Kirkby, whose episcopate covered the years 1332 to 1352, actively conceded titles to his *familia*, while bishop Halton at the beginning of the century and bishop Appelby at the end left it in the hands of the officers and clerks in their employ.[20]

When the general decline of revenues and the impoverishment of the benefices and religious houses are taken into consideration, it need not be surprising that the parish rectors and vicars and the monastic chapters consistently failed to concede any bulk of titles and that the names of laymen are so strongly represented as the benefactors of ordinands. Nevertheless, it must have been somewhat traditional for the layman of means to indulge in this kind of patronage. As we have seen, the number of men entering the priesthood was not especially low during the episcopate of John de Halton, when the financial problems of the clergy were particularly acute, but the lay population was already providing the majority of titles at that time. With the exception of the 1350s, the laity of the diocese provided about sixty per cent of the known titles in the course of the century.[21] Within this group, the landowning families supplied most of the titles.[22] Some of these men, though not a great many, had inherited the advowsons

[19] *Reg Halton*, 1, pp 25, 201, 207, 242, 292, 306; 2, pp 31, 112, 138, 141, 229; CRO MS DRC 1/1, fols 170^{r}, 203^{r}, 214^{r}, 254^{v}; DRC 2/1, fols 144$^{r/v}$, 145^{v}, 71^{r}.

[20] *Reg Halton*, 1, pp 107, 132, 273, 305, 223, 321, 231, 292, 331; 2, pp 27, 30, 32, 77, 90, 111, 141, 230; CRO MS DRC 1/1, fols 123^{v}, 162^{r}, 163^{r}, 170^{r}, 189^{r}, 250$^{r/v}$, 254^{v}; DRC 2/1, fols 141^{v}, 142^{r}, 143^{v}, 144^{v}, 145^{r}, 146$^{r/v}$, 148^{v}.

[21] For a discussion of the titles granted in the neighbouring diocese of Durham, see Donaldson, 'Patronage and the Church', pp 375–89. According to Donaldson's study, ten per cent of the clerks of the diocese of Durham received titles from ecclesiastical sources and eighty-five per cent from the laity in the period 1334–45. From 1353 to 1373, about thirty-six per cent were ecclesiastical and sixty per cent lay, and from 1416 to 1436, ninety-six per cent ecclesiastical, four per cent lay.

[22] *C*[*alendar of*] *I*[*nquisitions*] *P*[*ost*] *M*[*ortem*] (London 1904–) 2, p 269; 3, pp 53–5, 147, 186, 211–12, 447–50; 4, pp 88–9, 183–4, 191–2, 219, 331; 5, pp 100, 215, 297–307;

of churches. Aside from the more important families, there was a sizeable group of smaller landowners, mesne tenants, and probable inhabitants of the smaller towns and villages of the diocese. Whereas the greater landowners usually provided two or more titles during their lifetimes, the smaller landowners generally acted as patrons only once. Together, these two groups conceded between eighty per cent at the beginning of the century and nearly one hundred per cent at the end of all the titles provided by laymen.

Not all the lay patrons came from the countryside. In the first half of the century, just over twenty per cent of the titles provided by laymen came from townsmen, most of whom were citizens of Carlisle and its nearby villages. That most of them were simple tradesmen is betrayed by such surnames as *tenator*, *pistor*, *aurifabrus*, and *carnifex*, and their patronage was almost exclusively extended to those of the same locale, clerks from Carlisle, Stanwix, Grinsdale, and Crosby.[23] The patronymic surnames of the beneficiaries, such as *filius Johannis Carpentarii de Karliolo*, suggest the common class of the patron and his client, and that such men as Peter the butcher were granting titles to the sons of friends, associates, and, in many probable cases, relatives.[24] Most of the benefactors from Carlisle supported only one clerk in their lifetimes, but others, such as Robert Tibay and Robert de Grennesdale supplied as many as nine known titles, something few of the greater lords did.[25] This phenomenon is difficult to explain, unless perhaps the name of the individual was being used when, in reality, the titles granted were the charitable exercises of guilds and confraternities. Even the most pious townsman would have felt the pinch of paying up to twenty-five marks in titles every year, as Tibay certainly would have done in the early 1340s. Despite the war,

---

6, pp 4, 22–6, 60–1, 87, 89, 93, 143, 154–5, 166, 174, 200, 232–3, 363, 403, 417; 7, pp 153, 196–7, 243, 401, 403, 411–12, 419–21; 8, pp 24–5, 67, 105–7, 187, 279, 303, 370–2; 9, pp 30, 78–9, 94, 172–3, 229, 281, 304, 374–6, 382, 421–2; 10, pp 3, 5–6, 61, 133, 184–5, 424–6; 11, pp 87–8, 218–19, 245, 252, 255–6, 268, 317, 333–4, 341–3, 457; 12, pp 41, 148–9, 213, 284, 334–6, 354, 360–1, 421–3; 13, p 123; 14, pp 41, 118, 208; 15, pp 54, 112, 123, 165–6, 393; 16, pp 148, 324–5. I have in some cases been rather arbitrary in distinguishing between greater and lesser landowners, as it is not possible to determine the value of lands in *CIPM*. The lesser landowners indicated on table 2 below mostly held one manor or less, whereas the majority of the greater landowners were knights.

23 *Reg Halton*, 2, p 141; CRO MS DRC 1/1, fols 154r, 170r, 240v.

24 *Reg Halton*, 1, pp 201, 222; 2, pp 2, 141, 208; CRO MS DRC 1/1, fols 154r, 123v, 189r.

25 *Reg Halton*, 2, pp 89, 135, 212, 208; CRO MS DRC 1/1, fols 129r, 154r, 226v, 240v, 238r, 224r, 124r, 162r.

or perhaps because of it, a degree of prosperity in the city of Carlisle may be deduced from the active practice of patronage on the part of some of its citizens. In the wake of the plague, titles emanating from the towns nearly ceased completely. This took place in other sectors of society as well and helps to explain the lower number of men entering the priesthood at the end of the century.[26] The failure of the townsmen to concede any titles in the latter half of the century enhanced the position of the landed families as patrons, and the concession of titles was more than ever the domain of the countryside.

The reasons behind the enthusiasm of the laity in granting titles is not entirely clear. Ecclesiastical patrons could normally offer immediate employment to their clients as clerks or as chaplains. The greater lay patrons sought clerks to serve in their households, chaplains in their oratories, and priests to be presented to churches in their gift. There was probably no such *quid pro quo* arrangement on the part of the large group of lesser landowners and the townsmen concerning their beneficiaries, as these patrons were in a less obvious position to make demands upon their clients. There is a danger of exaggerating the impersonal character of the patronage practised by the laity. The patron knew his client, and certainly in most cases for the lesser landowners and townsmen, he was acting as benefactor to the son of a friend, a tenant, or a relative. Indeed, in nineteen instances the beneficiary carried a surname that would indicate that he originated from an area where his patron held land. In forty-three instances the patrons and their clients were related or shared the same surname, and there must have been many cases of the two having been related, but which are now impossible to ascertain.[27] Also, it was undoubtedly considered laudable and meritorious to the soul of the layman who gave aid to a man entering the church, and the lesser lay benefactors probably saw their actions more in the light of pious charity than in the light of patronage. The prayers the client might say for the soul of his benefactor were perhaps attractive to the lesser lay patron, and the support granted to the man entering the church by such patrons might be regarded as 'the poorer man's chantry'. Whatever his motives, the importance of the layman as grantor of titles ought not to be underestimated. By exercising this form of patronage, the laity

[26] See table 2 below.

[27] *CIPM*, 3, pp 147, 449; 5, pp 215, 299, 302; 6, p 166; 7, pp 243, 401, 475; 9, pp 94, 304, 375; 10, pp 61, 133; 11, pp 87, 245, 256; 15, p 112; 16, p 324; ordinations lists, see note 11 above.

was also exercising a kind of control over the church, for they were in effect recruiting a large part of the diocesan clergy by choosing whom they would favour with titles.

The relationship between patron and client was rarely binding or life-long. Generally, there was little correlation between the benefactor as patron of a title and as patron of a benefice. Of all the laymen who granted titles, only nineteen possessed advowsons of churches within the diocese. But of the forty-six titles granted between them, in only five known instances were the recipients of titles from one of these nineteen patrons also presented to a church in his gift.[28] Clearly, after being ordained priests, most men would have had to find new patrons, either the incumbents of parish churches who would employ them as chaplains, or those who would present them to benefices. However, the lay patron of a title probably did take pains to see that his clerk was satisfactorily placed. There are several examples of priests who had been conceded titles from the more influential families eventually being beneficed upon presentation by other important laymen to churches in their gift.[29] The bishop was the single most important patron of benefices within his diocese, having in his collation up to twenty-two livings of the eighty rectories and vicarages. As the bishops' granting of titles was motivated by a need for clerks to be recruited into episcopal service and diocesan administration, it is not surprising that the incidence of men both conceded titles and beneficed by the bishop is slightly higher. For instance, of the eight men granted titles by master John de Bowes, bishop Halton's official principal from 1294 to 1307, three were eventually collated to churches in the gift of the bishop.[30]

Once beneficed, the relationship of the incumbent with the patron of his church appears to have been dependent upon circumstances and the personalities involved. Because of the nature of the bishop's patronage, that is, as a means of support and reward for those in the episcopal service, the relationship was binding. The connections between the incumbent and his lay patron were somewhat different, but throughout the century a number of rectors were granted licences of non-residence by the bishop, specifically so that they might

[28] *Reg Halton*, 1, p 321; CRO MS DRC 1/1, fols 183^{v}, 208^{r}, 240^{v}, 189^{r}; DRC 2/1, fols 21^{v}, 145^{v}, 152^{r}; *Test Karl* p 77.

[29] CRO MS DRC 1/1, fols 154^{r}, 227^{r}; DRC 2/1, fols 30^{v}, 83^{r}.

[30] *Reg Halton*, 1, pp 200, 223, 291, 322; 2, pp 13–14, 30, 145.

be in attendance upon their patrons.[31] Richard de Askby, rector of Uldale, for instance, was almost continuously absent from his cure in the service of Sir Thomas de Lucy, the patron of his church.[32] William of York, rector of Bolton, did not receive licences to be in attendance upon the patron of his church, Alexander de Mowbray, but spent most of his eight years as rector in the service of the Nevills.[33] Generally, the relations of the lay patron and his beneficed clerk appear to have been rather informal. This is best illustrated by the increasing amount of 'permutation' of benefices as the century wore on. When two incumbents exchanged their benefices, they not only replaced each other as rector or vicar of their respective churches, but often, of course, exchanged patrons as well. The Crakanthorp patrons of the church of Newbiggin, for example, rarely presented to the benefice except under conditions of permutation.[34] The laity's acceptance of these facts indicates the looseness of their relationship with their presentees. Whereas families such as the Cliffords and the Lucys appear to have had a formal relationship with their presentees sometimes involving service, patrons such as the Crakanthorps did not.

A great many questions about the relationship of priests and patrons are left unanswered in this brief paper. However, the nature of patronage is evident. Carlisle should be noted as an essentially rural diocese, and because of this the secular clergy lived and operated under rural patronage. Only in the first half of the century did the merchants and tradesmen of the towns actively offer support in the form of titles to the clergy that served them. The poorly endowed religious houses seemingly could not afford to indulge in the patronage of young and budding clerics to any considerable extent. Rather, the recruitment of the clergy was left largely to the landowning laymen by virtue of the number of titles they granted. Most important, the system of patronage and the recruitment and availability of the clergy were certainly directly affected by both the war and the pestilences of the second half of the century. Just as the rural character of the diocese implied a certain structure of society which helped to determine the system of patronage, so the location of the diocese on the borders, and

[31] CRO MS DRC 1/1, fols 169^{v}; DRC 2/1, fols 20^{r}, 23^{v}, 33^{r}.

[32] *Ibid* DRC 2/1, fols 13^{r}, 19^{v}, 22^{r}, 33^{r}, 45^{r}, 78^{v}.

[33] *Ibid* DRC 2/1, fols 9^{v}, 20^{v}, 21^{r}, 23^{v}, 42^{r}.

[34] *Ibid* DRC 2/1, fols 152^{r}, 155^{v}.

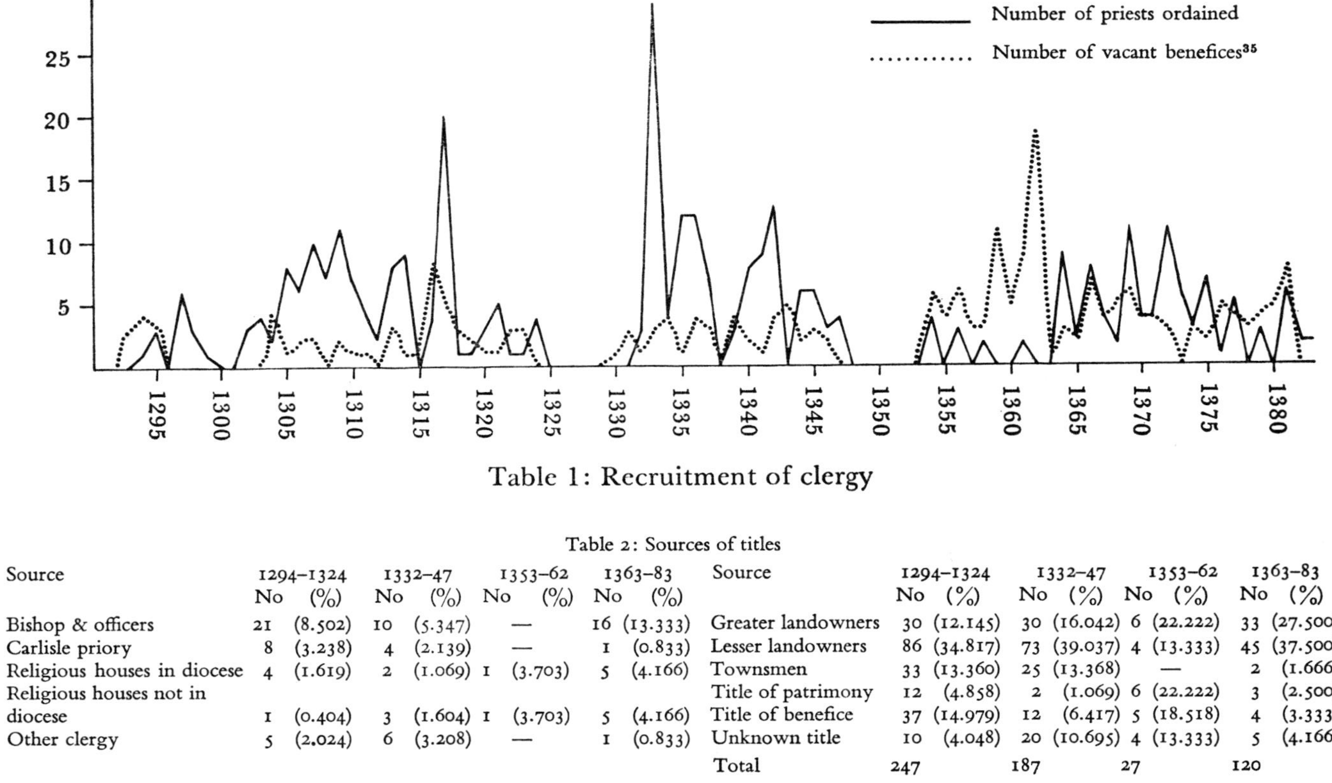

Table 1: Recruitment of clergy

Table 2: Sources of titles

Source	1294–1324		1332–47		1353–62		1363–83	
	No	(%)	No	(%)	No	(%)	No	(%)
Bishop & officers	21	(8.502)	10	(5.347)	—		16	(13.333)
Carlisle priory	8	(3.238)	4	(2.139)	—		1	(0.833)
Religious houses in diocese	4	(1.619)	2	(1.069)	1	(3.703)	5	(4.166)
Religious houses not in diocese	1	(0.404)	3	(1.604)	1	(3.703)	5	(4.166)
Other clergy	5	(2.024)	6	(3.208)	—		1	(0.833)

Source	1294–1324		1332–47		1353–62		1363–83	
	No	(%)	No	(%)	No	(%)	No	(%)
Greater landowners	30	(12.145)	30	(16.042)	6	(22.222)	33	(27.500)
Lesser landowners	86	(34.817)	73	(39.037)	4	(13.333)	45	(37.500)
Townsmen	33	(13.360)	25	(13.368)	—		2	(1.666)
Title of patrimony	12	(4.858)	2	(1.069)	6	(22.222)	3	(2.500)
Title of benefice	37	(14.979)	12	(6.417)	5	(18.518)	4	(3.333)
Unknown title	10	(4.048)	20	(10.695)	4	(13.333)	5	(4.166)
Total	247		187		27		120	

the incidence of plague, helped to undermine conditions that fostered that system.

University of Edinburgh

[35] Because of the incomplete episcopal registers, not all the vacancies of benefices are here indicated. It is not possible to determine the number of non-beneficed clergy who left the diocese or who died each year, so this line on the graph must not be interpreted as indicating the total number of new priests required each year but the number of those needed to fill benefices.

THE LATE BYZANTINE MONASTERY IN TOWN AND COUNTRYSIDE

by ANTHONY BRYER

IN this paper I want to look not only at the late Byzantine monastery in town and countryside, but how each category fared after the Turkish conquests, when towns became important again. By the late Byzantine monastery I mean one commonly established by a founder's *typikon*, and commonly enjoying *stavropegiac* rights of autonomy (especially from the thirteenth century). Material for the late Byzantine monastery is abundant enough both before and after the conquests, especially on Athos which is a special case. But it is comparatively less explored after the conquests. This is curious, for if it is true, as we are so often told, that it was the Orthodox church which kept alive the flame of *Hellenismos* during the dark centuries of the *Tourkokratia*, and if it is true that it is monasticism which is the peculiar guardian of Orthodoxy, and that monks are, in Theodore of Stoudion's words, 'the nerves and foundations of the Church',[1] the fate of the late Byzantine monastery should be an important field of study. I have adapted my approach to the nature of the bulk of the surviving evidence, which is economic. This may be like trying to write an account of a university's research on the basis of its finance department's records alone, but in times of a squeeze it may not be an unfair approach. A late Byzantine monk had to feast so as to fast.

I began my study by making a census of known Byzantine monasteries, within the twelfth-century borders. This has been done before. Beck worked on a corpus of a hundred and sixty monasteries, which Charanis brought up to two hundred and forty one.[2] Charanis reckoned that there might be about seven hundred recorded all told, less than a tenth of the actual total. By chance my list of monasteries came to exactly seven hundred, so I drew the line there, although it is clear that diligence would unearth up to one thousand. Charanis reckoned on a round hundred on Bithynian Olympos, but I have

[1] *Parva catechesis*, *PG* 99 (1860) col 393.

[2] Beck pp 200–29.

included only the forty six of which there is record.[3] There are many other factors for imbalance. Almost all the evidence is literary, not archaeological, and a monastery in Constantinople has more chance of being recorded than one in Cappadocia. Indeed of the three hundred and twenty-five monasteries recorded by Janin in and around the capital, less than forty have left any archaeological evidence, and of the scores of rock-cut monasteries of Cappadocia (happily outside the twelfth-century borders), not one has left a literary record.[4] The risk of duplication increases the more monasteries one counts. For example, can one postulate a continuous history of the Kyzikan monastery of Agros, well known from 787–826, less so in the tenth century, and again mentioned from 1272–1305, on the basis of an intervening but imprecise eleventh-century reference by Psellos; and is it the same Agros that was visited at Kurşunlu by archaeologists and travellers from 1892–1972?[5] Some monasteries become the *metochia* of others.

[3] [P.] Charanis, 'The Monk [as an element of Byzantine society]', *DOP* 25 (1971) pp 63–73. Charanis reckoned on an actual total of over seven thousand monastic establishments in the year 1000, but this calculation rests upon two suppositions which cannot be proved: that the population of the Empire was then about fifteen million and that about one per cent of it was monastic; nor is it clear how the figure of over seven thousand houses (with an average of twenty-one to twenty-two monks each) can be extrapolated from them. My census begins, as all must, with Janin (*GEEB*) of which only two volumes were published. On Constantinopolitan monasteries, see now [T. F.] Mathews, *The early churches of Constantinople: architecture and liturgy* (Pennsylvania 1971); the same's [*The Byzantine*] *churches* [*of Istanbul: a photographic survey*] (Pennsylvania 1976); and [W.] Müller-Wiener, *Bildlexikon* [*zur Topographie Istanbuls*] (Tübingen 1977). *GEEB* 2 was completed by J. Darrouzès and covers Bithynia, Hellespont Latros, Galesios, Trebizond, Athens and Thessalonike; its drawbacks are pointed out in a review by C. Mango, *BZ* 71 (1978) pp 113–16. For the Trebizond section, I have substituted figures of all Pontic monasteries from A. Bryer and D. Winfield, *The Byzantine monuments and topography of the Pontos* (Washington forthcoming); and have added monasteries with numerous amendments, from 'surveys' of varying degrees of inadequacy: of Athos in [D.] Papachryssanthou, [*Actes du*] *Prôtaton, Archives de l'Athos* 7 (Paris 1975) pp 86–93, and in [E. Amand de] Mendieta, [*Mount*] *Athos* [*: the garden of the Panaghia*] (Berlin/Amsterdam 1972); of the Meteora in D. M. Nicol, *Meteora: the rock monasteries of Thessaly* (London 1963); of the Morea in D. A. Zakythinos, *Le despotat grec de Morée* 2, *Vie et Institutions* (Athens 1953) pp 295–309; and of Cyprus in G. Hill, *A history of Cyprus* 1, *To the conquest by Richard Lion Heart* (Cambridge 1972); and R. Gunnis, *Historic Cyprus* (London 1956). For each area there is a pretence, however poorly justified, at a regional survey of monasteries, and I have resisted the temptation of selecting monasteries from 'unsurveyed' regions. So the seven hundred do not include such famous houses as the Nea Mone on Chios, St John on Patmos (or any Aegean island monastery), Holy Luke in Stiris, St John on Mt Menoikeon, or even the surburban monastery of Chortiates outside Thessalonike. *GEEB* 2 was, of course, published after Charanis, 'Monk'.

[4] *GEEB* 1, 3 p 4.

[5] *Ibid* 2 pp 195–9; C. Mango and I. Sevčenko, 'Some churches and monasteries on the southern shore of the sea of Marmara', *DOP* 27 (1973) pp 253–67.

Amoeba-like, they divide and combine. Yet I do not want to destroy the validity of my seven hundred. Nor because a monastery is remote is it necessarily more likely to be unrecorded. Byzantine holy men have not been bashful about recording their retreats from St Basil onwards—St Neophytos of Cyprus is a notorious example.[6]

My sample confirms the impression of Charanis: peaks of monastic foundation or activity in the fifth, sixth, ninth, eleventh, thirteenth and fourteenth centuries—nothing surprising in that.[7] It is obviously more difficult to establish how long most monasteries lived for. Charanis has worked on Janin's figures for the three hundred and twenty-five Constantinopolitan monasteries: of those only eighteen survived until the Fall, and of the cohort of ninety-two sixth-century monasteries in the capital only two reached the fifteenth century.[8] But I am surprised by the relative longevity of my seven hundred monasteries. Their total careers cover two thousand one hundred and seventy eight centuries, an average of over three centuries each. Here some refounded monasteries have probably been given a greater longevity than they deserve, but the average is surely offset by duplication and simply lack of record.

But for the purposes of this paper, the sample must be divided into urban and rural monasteries. Such definitions are peculiarly frustrating for the Byzantinist. With the exception of Constantinople, the Byzantine city is a concept which hardly survived the seventh century, and Constantinople is a special case. By the twelfth century it was already a head too large for the body of its empire. Yet the legal definition of a Byzantine city is that of the secular church: a *polis* was the seat of a bishop. But, to take an ancient city and venerable Byzantine bishopric, Lampsakos: that place had an early thirteenth-century adult male population of one hundred and sixty-three, one hundred and thirteen of whom were agriculturalists.[9] Yet

[6] C. Mango and E. J. W. Hawkins, 'The hermitage of St Neophytos and its wall paintings', *DOP* 20 (1966) pp 119–206; I. P. Tsiknopoullos, Ὁ ἅγιος Νεόφυτος καὶ ἡ ἱερα αὐτοῦ μονή (Paphos 1955); and the same's *The Encleistra and Saint Neophytos* (Nicosia 1965).

[7] Charanis, 'Monk' pp 65–8.

[8] *Ibid* p 65.

[9] M. Angold, *A Byzantine government in exile: government and society under the Laskarids of Nicaea (1204–1261)* (Oxford 1974) p 110; V. Laurent, *Le corpus des sceaux de l'empire byzantin*, 5, i (Paris 1963) pp 255–6. For the latest stage in the long discussion on the decline of the ancient city, see the review by A. Kazdan of C. Foss, *Byzantine and Turkish Sardis* (Harvard 1976) in Βυζαντινά (Thessalonike 1977) pp 478–84.

Athonite and Pontic villages were commonly larger than that.[10] Guesses for the population of late Byzantine Thessalonike range from twenty-five to forty thousand, but, as Palamas observed, its citizens melted away during harvest time.[11] Perhaps agriculture was even the principal industry of fourteenth-century Constantinople, which was one town and a series of villages set amid market gardens within the Theodosian walls.[12] At four to six thousand fourteenth-century Trebizond was perhaps less rural, for the Pontos was a land of small towns and large villages.[13] It was the Ottomans who restored urban life, recreating cities such as Bursa, Edirne and Istanbul, as the Selçuks and Danişmendids had Konya, Kayseri, Erzurum and Sivas before them. So I have rejected a legal definition for a late Byzantine city, but designate monasteries as urban if they lie in or around places whose walls were still maintained: Constantinople, Nikomedeia, Nicaea, Thessalonike, Mystra, Trebizond, Sinope, Kerasous, Rhizaion—but not the walled village of Athens. Of our seven hundred monasteries, four hundred and seventeen lie beneath such walls (three hundred and twenty-five in Constantinople). So it is easy to conclude that the average Byzantine monastery had moved from the desert to the city, and more particularly to The City. This did not make it necessarily less monastic. Indeed, it is difficult to conceive how the most influential of all Byzantine monasteries, the Stoudion, could have become so if it had not been in The City. Similarly major rural monasteries found it useful to maintain *metochia* or property in the capital: the Nea Mone of Chios, Pontic Soumela, or St Catherine's on Mt Sinai, which was to boast one of the most ornate Phanariot palaces as its unlikely outpost. The classic argument for the political advantages of a city monastery over the ascetic conveniences of a rural one comes in about 892, when Leo VI pressed his private holy man, the future patriarch Euthymios, to leave the country monastery of St Theodore for an

[10] On Athonite villages, see A. E. Laiou-Thomadakis, *Peasant society in the late Byzantine Empire: a social and demographic study* (Princeton 1977) pp 24–71; and on Pontic villages, see [N.] Beldiceanu, 'Biens [monastiques d'après un registre Ottoman de Trébizonde (1487): monastères de la Chrysoképhalos et du Pharos]', *REB* 35 (1977) pp 175–213.

[11] *Homilia XXIV, PG* 151 (1865) col 333; O. Tafrali, *Thessalonique au quatorzième siècle* (Paris 1913) pp 15–17; P. Charanis, 'A note on the population and cities of the Byzantine Empire in the thirteenth century', *The Joshua Starr Memorial Volume* (New York 1953) p141.

[12] *The travels of Ibn Battuta A.D. 1325–1354*, 2, trans H. A. R. Gibb (Cambridge 1962) p 508: 'Within the wall are about thirteen inhabited villages'.

[13] A. Bryer, 'The *Tourkokratia* in the Pontos: some problems and preliminary conclusions', *Neo-Hellenika* 1 (Amsterdam 1970) pp 36–41.

urban one nearer the palace. Euthymios protested weakly that 'as quiet a place is impossible to find in the city.' He took little persuading. Leo replied that 'it is not possible for you to live outside the city, when I am continually asking for you; I desire that the monastery which . . ., we have planned for you, should be in the city, near the sea-shore, so I may often be with you . . .' Euthymios's new monastery was unquestionably urban, for it was within the walls, but in fact it was 'the quietest, most pleasant of places',[14] near the Stoudion, and a good five kilometres from the Great Palace. Here Euthymios ostentatiously shut himself up for forty days after the consecration. It *was* possible to create a monastic desert in the city. Probably the most rigorous of fourteenth-century Pontic monasteries, and the one closest to the hesychast movement, was St Sabbas, where the athletes of God of the Nitrian desert still stare out of paintings in its uncomfortable cliffside caves. It was inhabited by recognised ascetics and was used as a penitentiary for disgraced Grand Komnenoi.[15] Yet St Sabbas is an unequivocally urban monastery, overlooking Trebizond's main market. By contrast I have classified the Athonite monasteries as rural, yet they represent a sort of monastic urbanism whose abbots and their own fleets were intimately linked to the politics and economy of Constantinople, which is not found within the walls of a city such as Trebizond. So by the fourteenth century, the distinction between town and country is almost meaningless. But so far as monasteries are concerned, it becomes clearer after the conquests.

Perhaps the distinction between town and country monasteries had been clearer in an earlier period, in the way in which they had been founded. On the whole the living holy man tended to be rural; the martyr of the past, small-town; and the lay patron, urban. The familiar tension between ascetic and patron is exemplified on an imperial level by Euthymios and Leo VI, Athanasios and Nikephoros II Phokas, Dionysios and Alexios III Komnenos. Martyrs could look after themselves, but some stations of the *Notitia Dignitatum* which became important for other reasons, had abundant patrons but were embarrassingly short of martyrs. Constantinople is the prime example,

[14] [A. M.] Vlasto, [*A History of the island of*] *Chios* [*A.D. 70–1822*] (London 1913) pp 117–20; [E. T.] Kyriakides, ['Ιστορία τῆς παρὰ τὴν Τραπεζοῦντα ἱερᾶς βασιλικῆς σταυροπηγιακῆς μονῆς τῆς . . .] Σουμελᾶ (Athens 1898) p 268; H. Sumner-Boyd and J. Freely, *Strolling through Istanbul: a guide to the city* (Istanbul 1972) pp 338–40; *Vita Euthymii patriarchae CP,* ed and trans P. Karlin-Hayter (Brussels 1970) pp 24–35.

[15] A. Bryer, 'Some Trapezuntine monastic obits (1368–1563)', *REB* 34 (1976) pp 129–31, 132.

but both Trebizond and Thessalonike probably had to import their patron saints too, while a late Byzantine place like Mystra had none at all. Late Byzantine monasticism is not short of holy men, but the lay patron becomes more emphatic. The late Byzantine monastery would commonly have been founded by a local ruler or lay dignitary, with lands, their dependent peasants (*paroikoi*), and a *typikon*. These were the new patrons of art, too, where Constantinople becomes only one of a series of centres. The new rulers, of Serbia or Trebizond, used monasteries to celebrate their dynastic obsessions: in wall paintings with royal group portraits more elaborate than any in the mosaics of the Hagia Sophia. Architecturally and socially, there is a parallel here with the west; this is the age of the chantry. Theologically, the parallel may be artificial: the Greeks at Florence were evidently unprepared for a clear-cut doctrine of purgatory.[16] But there is no doubt of a popular belief in the efficacy of prayers for the dead which goes with a sense of dynasty to provide a motive for the foundation of many late Byzantine monasteries. The Komnenoi had set the fashion in their massive family monastery of the Pantokrator, with its dynastic tombs, relics, hospital and immense income, cobbled ruthlessly together from other and older endowments.[17] Later *parekklesiai* for tombs of a founder and his family are features of the churches of Mystra, Arta, Trebizond and, especially Constantinople.[18] Fourteenth-century Constantinople was ruled not so much by the philosopher king as the philosopher prime minister: Nikephoros Choumnos, Theodore Metochites or Demetrios Kydones. The third turned Latin (and by his opposition to the Turk tried to demonstrate that it was still possible to be Greek)[19] but the first two Orthodox rivals, Choumnos and Metochites, took out an insurance for secure retirement and eternal commemoration by endowing monasteries whose monks they lectured and eventually joined. Choumnos died in 1327 as the monk Nathaniel in his monastery of the Saviour Philanthropenos (a dual house which took lady members of the family too), and Metochites died in 1332 as the monk Theoleptos

[16] J. Gill, *The Council of Florence* (Cambridge 1961) pp 120, 272; J. Meyendorff, *Byzantine theology: historical trends and doctrinal themes* (London/Oxford 1974) pp 220–1.

[17] *GEEB* 1.3 pp 529–38; [P.] Gautier, ['Le] typikon [du Christ Sauveur Pantocrator]', *REB* 32 (1974) pp 1–145. Six monasteries were engrossed by the new foundation.

[18] R. Krautheimer, *Early Christian and Byzantine architecture* (Harmondsworth 1965) pp 295–7, 309.

[19] R.-J. Loenertz, 'Démétrius Cydonès, 1: De la naissance à l'année 1373', *OCP* 36 (1970) pp 47–72; '2: de 1373 à 1375', *OCP* 37 (1971) pp 5–39.

in his monastery of the Saviour in Chora.[20] Choumnos's monastery does not survive, but Metochites's dazzling church still stands, as does the mortuary chapel of another rival, of the Glabas family, in the Pammakaristos monastery.[21] As an insurance policy, Metochites's investment paid off: his career and palace were ruined, but his monastery and library were spared and he died in his bed.

How large were these monasteries? The canonical minimum was three monks. I agree with Charanis's average of ten to twenty monks for most Byzantine monasteries, with a handful much larger and many rather smaller.[22] Later Venetian Cretan monasteries had an average of ten to eleven monks each.[23] After the Turkish conquests the average goes down: between three and four for the monasteries of the early Greek kingdom, but a new phenomenon is the rise of a few very large nunneries.[24] I cannot, unfortunately, establish any firm ratio of income, land and dependent peasants to monks. There are hints, not only in Prodromos's ballads, that some monks were not underfed.[25] In 1136 the staff of the Pantokrator enjoyed a diet of about three thousand, three hundred calories per diem, and their hospital patients two thousand, five hundred calories.[26] The FAO recommends two thousand four hundred calories per diem for modern Turkey. In 1054 the Great Lavra on Athos may have had seven hundred monks but it was down to five or six in 1623 (monastic populations fluctuate widely and

[20] *GEEB* 1.3 pp 541–53; J. Verpeaux, *Nicéphore Choumnos: homme d'état et humaniste byzantin (ca 1250/1255–1327)* (Paris 1959) pp 46, 48, 62, 67, 147; I. Sevčenko, 'Theodore Metochites, the Chora, and intellectual trends of his time', *The Kariye Djami*, ed P. A. Underwood, 4 (London 1975) pp 17–91; and I. Sevčenko, *Études sur la polémique entre Théodore Métochite et Nicéphore Choumnos* (Brussels 1962).

[21] The *parekklesion* has yet to be fully published. See Mathews, *Churches* pp 346–65; Müller-Weiner, *Bildlexikon* pp 132–5.

[22] Charanis, 'Monk', p 72.

[23] S. Xanthoudides, 'Η 'Ενετοκρατία 'εν Κρήτῃ καὶ οἱ κατὰ τῶν 'Ενετῶν ἀγῶνες τῶν Κρητῶν (Athens 1939) p 162.

[24] [C. A.] Frazee, [*The*] *Orthodox Church* [*and independent Greece 1821–1852*] (Cambridge 1969) p 120. The history of Byzantine and post-Byzantine nunneries has yet to be written. Nunneries seem always to be relatively few in number, but nuns increasingly numerous: St Theodora in Thessalonike had one hundred and fifty by 1669 and two nunneries on Chios two hundred and fifty in the eighteenth century: *GEEB* 2, p 375; Vlasto, *Chios* p 117. It is curious that the Armenian Church, in somewhat similar circumstances, did not develop nunneries: see H. F. B. Lynch, *Armenia: travels and studies* 1 (repr Beirut 1965) p 253.

[25] See A. Guillou, 'Production and profits in the Byzantine province of Italy (tenth to eleventh centuries): an expanding society', *DOP* 28 (1974) pp 91–2; A. Bryer, 'The first encounter with the West, A.D. 1050–1204', *Byzantium*, ed P. Whitting (Oxford 1971) p 107.

[26] Gautier, 'Typikon', p 19.

mysteriously). But economically its palmiest days must have been around 1321 when an incomplete census reveals that it had upwards of three thousand dependent peasants (*paroikoi*) on twenty thousand *modioi* of its land, which yielded over one thousand five hundred *nomismata*.[27] The trouble is that we do not know how many monks it had in 1321.

Let us take a provincial monastery of fair importance, perhaps in Charanis's ten to twenty monk category: the Pharos in Trebizond which had a chequered career from its foundation by grand duke John the Eunuch, a benefactor of Soumela monastery too, before 1344. But when John fell from power and was dispossessed, Soumela survived with its other endowments (although it needed imperial refoundation) while the Pharos was abandoned. It was not revived until after 1395, by imperial endowment then and in 1432; its last lands were settled in 1460 and they were all disposed of by the Ottomans between 1461 and 1465, after which nothing was heard of the Pharos until 1953 when its charters were published by Laurent. The second, imperial, endowments of the Pharos brought it property spread along two hundred and twenty-two kilometres of coastlands, with a *han* and workshops in town, three estates, a number of pastures and other holdings in fourteen *choria*, five *staseis* and twenty-four other places, together with artisans, more than sixty-five *paroikoi*, and one fisherman. There was an annual income of about 6,680 Trapezuntine aspers.[28] The Ottomans assessed the properties at thirty-five vineyards, five olive groves, two pastures, two nutgroves and two cultivated fields, yielding 5,456 Ottoman aspers.[29] By contrast the estates of the former monastery cathedral of the Chrysokephalos yielded 11,608 Ottoman aspers, and fourteenth-century imperial grants to Soumela included forty *paroikoi* and to Vazelon an income of about 3,757 Trapezuntine aspers.[30] What did endowments of this order mean in

[27] P. Lemerle, A. Guillou, N. Svoronos and D. Papachryssanthou, *Actes de Lavra 2, de 1204 à 1328, Archives de l'Athos* 8 (Paris 1977) pp 180–291. These figures exclude holdings at Gomatou and on Lemnos. I am grateful to Mrs Patricia Karlin-Hayter for her seminar on these Acts.

[28] V. Laurent, 'Deux chrysobulles inédits des empereurs de Trébizonde Alexis IV – Jean IV et David II', Ἀρχεῖον Πόντου [= *AP*] 18 (1953) pp 241–78; A. Bryer, *A cadaster of the great estates of the Empire of Trebizond* (Birmingham 1978).

[29] Beldiceanu, 'Biens', p 201.

[30] *Ibid* J. P. Fallmerayer, 'Original-Fragmente, Chroniken, Inschriften und anderes Material zur Geschichte des Kaiserthums Trapezunt', *ABAW* PhK abh 3 (Munich 1843) pp 91–100; [T.] Uspensky and [V.] Bénéchévitch, [*Actes de*] *Bazélon*. [*Matériaux pour servir à l'histoire de la propriété rurale et monastique à Byzance aux XIII-XIV siècles*] (Leningrad 1927) Act 106, taking fifteen aspers to the notional *nomisma*.

practice? In Byzantine times, the salaries of the Venetian *baili*'s staff ranged from 1,140–1,900 aspers a year each, Circassian girl slaves would fetch six to nine hundred aspers, and a horse from one hundred and fifty to four hundred aspers.[31] In 1292 the distinctly unmonastic diet of twenty-two Englishmen in Trebizond would, if they had managed to keep up their formidable consumption of food and drink, have amounted to about 1,730 aspers per head per year.[32] In Ottoman times, an annual income of four to five thousand aspers would support a *timariot*, equipped for campaign, with two attendants.[33]

Given a dozen monks, the Pharos endowment would have amounted to about five *paroikoi* and five hundred aspers a year to support one monk. This kind of scale seems about right for other Pontic monasteries but would give, for example, the fourteenth-century Lavra about six hundred monks. This is surely too many, but the Great Lavra in its prime was relatively much better endowed than any other Athonite house. It seems to have reached a point beyond where it was given because it had, and was able to add to its estates by natural momentum. We shall not know how the Lavra's numbers fluctuated with its endowments until the final volume of its Acts is published, if then. The late Byzantine donor was fully aware of a ratio between endowment and a number of monks which it could support: several *typika* allow for raising a fixed number if further endowments came. The cost-effectiveness of a monk obviously varied from place to place.

How did monasteries actually use their income? We can at least discount charity as a significant burden on the income of most late Byzantine monasteries. Philanthropy was not the business of a Byzantine monastery (and education even less so), although a surprising number of incidental monastic hospitals, almshouses, orphanages and soup kitchens existed. But no Pontic monastery is known to have devoted an asper to charitable purposes and it is difficult to see how Athonite ones could have done to any extent either: Lavra's obligation to look after sailors shipwrecked there cannot have been

[31] F. Thiriet, *Régestes des délibérations du Sénat de Vénise concernant la Romanie* 2 (Paris 1958) no 1008 of 22 March 1401 (where 190 aspers are taken to the *summo* or *sauma*); M. Bon, *Notaio in Venezia, Trebisonda e Tana (1403–1408)* (Venice 1963) pp 11–12, 16; [A.] Bryer, 'Greeks and Türkmens[: the Pontic exception]', *DOP* 29 (1975) pp 138–9.

[32] Figures extrapolated from accounts in Rot Pat, 19 Edw I, membrane 11, most accessible in C. Desimoni, 'I conti dell' ambasciata al Chan di Persia nel 1292', *Atti della Società Ligure di Storia Patria* 13 (Genoa 1884) pp 598–669.

[33] Beldiceanu, 'Biens', p 201.

heavy, while pilgrims were, on balance, a source of profit—although it is not until the nineteenth-century Soumela that we have the balance sheets to prove it.[34] But, although we have no figures for that either, it is also clear that the cost of building, and especially defending, a monastery and its *katholikon*, and of physical maintenance in the face of fires and attack, was by far the greatest burden upon a monastery after the annual one of keeping its monks alive. The insufficiently-endowed new monastery is a familiar late Byzantine phenomenon. Even the Great Lavra, always volatile in fortune, found itself in early difficulties with a ratio of eighty monks to thirty-two *paroikoi*; labour relations were acrimonious and the building of its church cost St Athanasios his life.[35] Something of the ratio between the foundation and running costs of a monastery can be seen in Alexios III's charter for Dionysiou on Athos of 1374. The grant for building the monastery is about nineteen thousand Trebizond aspers and for its annual maintenance one thousand aspers.[36] The annual grant, at least, is low by Pontic standards: Dionysiou was quick in searching for other sources of income and slow in getting up its *pyrgos* and aqueduct. But the proportion of about 19:1 may be right. As to how much monasteries actually saw of their endowments, there is an historic Byzantine distinction between the actual and required yield of a grant to a monastery which persisted until modern times.[37] But the late Byzantine monastery commonly enjoyed the *pronoia* of taxes which would otherwise have gone to the state and a sequence of tax exemptions which are a principal source for the existence of some impositions. For a man like Metochites, grant of land to his monastery was a kind of solution to his tax problems.

Donors count their aspers. They tend to give too little and what is often not quite theirs to give. The Grand Komnenoi, or more particularly Alexios III, did not start to endow monasteries on any scale until they had suppressed their major local rivals and confiscated their lands. These windfalls may have been, administratively, difficult to deal with unless they were returned to monasteries which local rivals had themselves once supported. The Grand Komnenoi crushed

[34] D. J. Constantelos, *Byzantine philanthropy and social welfare* (New Brunswick/New Jersey 1968) p 92.

[35] Papachryssanthou, *Prôtaton* pp 80–1.

[36] N. Oikonomides, *Actes de Dionysiou, Archives de l'Athos* 4 (Paris 1968) pp 50–61, 97–101, taking 190 aspers to the *soma:* see R. R. Milner-Gulland and A. Bryer, 'Two metropolitans of Trebizond in Russia', *AP* 27 (Athens 1965) p 24 n 5.

[37] Mendieta, *Athos* p 132.

a series of baronial families, including the Scholaris and Doranites, in the years 1342, 1344, 1345, 1349, 1350, 1352, 1354 and 1355. Their lands were confiscated. By 1361, when Grand Duke Niketas Scholaris, died, Alexios III was able to start redistributing lands. He refounded St Phokas, Kordyle, in 1362. In 1363 he suppressed the last great baronial conspiracy, confiscating the estates of Grand Logothete George Scholaris. In 1364 he refounded Soumela. By 1371 he could grant lands to his *emir candar*, the Grand Oikonomos George Doranites. In 1374 he went on to found Dionysiou, probably in 1376 to refound the Theoskepastos and probably in 1386 to endow Vazelon. The refoundation of the Pharos came soon after he died in 1390.[38]

Such hand-to-mouth endowments no doubt account for the extraordinarily scattered lands of a house like the Pharos. Monasteries commonly preferred their land en bloc, until, in the case of the concentration of Athonite lands in Macedonia, monasteries started competing with each other. The Pontic and Athonite monasteries may have stood in their own relatively remote deserts, but they overlooked the principal areas of agricultural surplus in both the Trapezuntine and Constantinopolitan states.

Three characteristics of the late Byzantine, especially Athonite, monastery, cannot be escaped. First, it is voracious in seeking lands, engorging lesser monasteries and in assembling immunities. Here the monastery is no different from a lay landowner; only in a stronger position. Second, it is determined to prevent its holdings slipping back into the hands of the state or of laymen. Third, there is the growth of anti-monastic opinion, more articulate than at any time since iconoclasm. These characteristics are well known, so I will illustrate them briefly:

First, Eustathios of Thessalonike describes, in terms only then becoming conventional, how late twelfth-century monks beguile the rich and threaten the poor to obtain their property, rejecting both when they had got what they had wanted: ' "Who are you, man; what is your power, and what is the profit derived from you?" And they threaten to deprive him of the little property which they had left him by common consent.'[39] The poor find themselves serfs on their own fields. Yet, even trying to read between the lines of the scores of

[38] Michael Panaretos, Περὶ τῶν Μεγάλων Κομνηνῶν, ed O. Lampsides (Athens 1958) pp 61–81; A. Bryer, 'The great estates of the Empire of Trebizond', *AP* 35 (Athens 1979) forthcoming.

[39] *De emendanda vita monachica, PG* 135 (1887) col 829. See [P.] Charanis, ['The monastic] properties [and the state in the Byzantine Empire]', *DOP* 4 (1948) pp 85–6.

pious preambles to the grants of their hereditary crofts by Pontic peasants to Vazelon, for the expiation of their sins and of those of their fathers, I cannot see that monastery as a real burden on its medieval peasants.[40] Their status was little changed, whether they paid dues to the monastery or state; they could still buy, sell, leave or inherit their crofts; their financial dues and labour services were slight; by giving it away, widows ensured the survival of a family farm; and the result was that Vazelon and its neighbouring monasteries preserved the social, cultural and economic cohesion of a group of Greek villages until this century. They also faithfully commemorated their small benefactors, which is exactly what their peasants had asked them to do. Perhaps, here as elsewhere, the Pontos is distinctive.

Second, the church was obdurate when called upon to disgorge its lands or properties in defence of the state. It is an old argument. The church could do no other than refuse; the emperor no other than to take. The last time the confrontation came on the old scale, in November 1367, was when John V Palaiologos wanted to settle soldiers on church land in Thrace, and a synod 'replied as if with one mouth that "neither their most holy lord, the ecumenical patriarch, nor his great and holy synod had the right to give any church property to any one, for the holy canons . . . prohibit it." ' They went on to say that ' "But if the holy emperor wishes to take them by his own power, to do with them what he has in mind, let him do so. He gave them to the church; let him take them if he wishes. . . . We ourselves will in no way do this, by our own will." '[41] The dilemma was not one-sided; at the turn of the century even the tiresomely ascetic and politically awkward patriarch Athanasios I had advocated the devotion of church lands to charity and monastic ones to the defence of the state.[42] Some monks, at least, would have shared the views of the so-called anti-Zealot Discourse, my third illustration:

> Is it terrible if, by taking a part of the goods dedicated to the monasteries, goods which are so plentiful, we feed some poor, provide for the priests and adorn the churches? That will cause them no harm, for that which remains suffices for their wants, and is not in contradiction with the thoughts of the original donors. . . .

[40] A. Bryer, 'Rural society in the Empire of Trebizond', *AP* 28 (1966) pp 152–60.

[41] *MM*, 1 pp 506–7; Charanis, 'Properties', 115; D. M. Nicol, *The last centuries of Byzantium 1261–1453* (London 1972) pp 280–1.

[42] See A.-M. M. Talbot, *The correspondence of Athanasius I* Patriarch (Washington 1975); and the same's 'The Patriarch Athanasius (1289–1293; 1303–9) and the Church', *DOP* 27 (1973) pp 11–28.

> Again, How is it not better if with this money we arm soldiers who will die for these churches, for these laws, for these walls, than if these same sums were spent in vain by monks and priests whose table and other needs are slight, for they stay at home, live in shelter and expose themselves to no danger? What injustices do we commit if we seek to rebuild ruined houses, care for fields and villages, and nourish those who are fighting for the freedom of these?[43]

It is obviously impossible to estimate what proportion of the lands of the late Byzantine empire were in ecclesiastical hands: for his rashness one scholar, who reckoned on a half, has been cited ever since.[44] But what is clear is that the flourishing of monasticism, which gave the late Byzantine state so much of its character, was made possible by the devotion of a substantial part of its receding resources. The state's control of what was left of its economy was also dwindling, at a time when its commitments were growing.

I want to turn now to what happened to urban and rural monasteries when they came under Turkish pressure and conquest. From the eleventh century, the first category of monasteries which suffered were the guardians of great shrines. A Byzantine's sense of *patrida*, his patriotism, was focused not on a universal empire which rejected local *patrida*, but upon what Turks call *memleket*: a home town or district, a birthplace the waters and water melons of which are sweeter than anywhere else in the world. In turn a town or district often derived, or created, its sense of identity from that of its patron saint. The old Roman *Notitia Dignitatum* was a network of army camps. It became a ghostly network of no less strategic importance for the coherence of early and middle Byzantine society: of pilgrim towns of soldier martyrs. To them were added patrons of every great city, beginning with the Theotokos of Constantinople. There was Nicholas of Myra, the Archangel of Chonai, the Wonderworker of Neocaesarea, Phokas of Sinope, the Forty of Sebasteia, the Tyro of Euchaita, Tryphon of Nicaea, Demetrios of Thessalonike (and Sirmium), John of Ephesos, Eustratios of Arauraka, and Eugenios of Trebizond. For some pilgrim towns, the saint sustained its very existence: employer of *paroikoi*, priests, monks and merchants, supernatural defender in times of trouble,

[43] P. Charanis, 'Internal strife in Byzantium during the fourteenth century', *B* 15 (1941) p 226; I. Sevčenko, 'Nicolas Cabasilas' "Anti-Zealot" discourse: a reinterpretation', *DOP* 11 (1957) pp 79–171, esp pp 93, 126, 159.

[44] A. Ferradou, *Des biens des monastères à Byzance* (Bordeaux 1896) p 165.

host to pilgrims and president of an annual fair on his feast day. Martyrs especially seem tactfully to have chosen the period either immediately after the harvest or before the spring sowing for their passion and subsequent commemorative fair. The feasts of the saints I have mentioned run from 6 September to 13 December, and from 20 January to 9 March.[45] Part of the pre-Ottoman Turkish success in breaking the local economies and sense of Orthodox *patrida* in Anatolia comes from the way that local shrines and their monasteries and lands were extinguished: Euchaita, Chonai, Sinope, Arauraka and Neocaesarea are examples. Once such a place has been wrecked, it is very difficult to revive: the annual *panegyris* of St Phokas recovered briefly, but the very site of Euchaita was in dispute until recently and Arauraka remains so.[46] Pre-Ottoman Turkish feelings about such awesome and alien places is summed up in the *Melikdanişmendnâme*. Among Christian heroes of that epic is one Metropid (evidently a metropolitan bishop, such as actually defended Chonai), and his son Gavras (Türkmens were evidently unaware of the canons on episcopal celibacy). The Türkmen hero is the Melik Danişmend. The point of contention is Neocaesarea. And, so far as epic tradition went, the key to Neocaesarea was the steep fortified monastery of its patron and evangelist, Gregory the Wonderworker. A Christian amazon called Efromiya turns Turk. Attractively disguised as a monk, she lures Gavras, captures the monastery of the Wonderworker, and lets the Melik in.[47] Not surprisingly, also, the process was repeated in most Anatolian towns where Turkish conquerors commonly converted the cathedral into an Ulu, or Fatih, Camii.

The Selçuks and Danişmendids did not choose such centres because they were monastic, but because they mattered. Nor did they have any obvious policy of discrimination against monasteries as such. In popular Islam, at least, there is tolerance, if not respect for the *rahib* and

[45] [S.] Vryonis, [Jr, *The*] *decline* [*of medieval Hellenism in Asia Minor and the process of Islamization from the eleventh through the fifteenth century*] (Berkeley/Los Angeles/London 1971) pp 10, 14–6, 20-2, 39–40, 16, 235, 279. On the patron of Constantinople, see now Averil Cameron, 'The Theotokos in sixth-century Constantinople. A city finds its symbol', *JTS* 29 (1978) 79–108.

[46] On Euchaita, see C. Mango and I. Sevčenko, 'Three inscriptions of the reigns of Anastasius I and Constantine V', *BZ* 65 (1972) pp 378–84; and on Arauraka, T. S. Brown, A. Bryer and D. Winfield, 'Cities of Heraclius', *Byzantine and Modern Greek Studies* 4 (1978) p 28.

[47] I. Mélikoff, *La geste de Melik Danişmend*, 1 (Paris 1960) pp 198–222; A. Bryer, 'A Byzantine family: the Gabrades, c979–c1653', *University of Birmingham Historical Journal* 12 (1970) pp 178–9.

endless curiosity about the *rahibe* and her *Kizlar Manastir*. In the thirteenth century Calal al-Din Rûmi taught in a Christian monastery and there are signs of monastic revival in Seljuk Cappadocia.[48] As late as 1379 the monks of Konya were in energetic contest with the secular church. It was the secular church which was the hardest hit.[49] It was not widely persecuted, but the shockingly swift evaporation of the established church of Anatolia after it had been deprived of most of its endowments is well known.[50]

Like Byzantine rulers, Turkish sultans used windfalls to make charitable endowments. This was fairly straightforward in the case of cathedral lands; they tended to go into *Evkaf*, equivalent Islamic charitable funds which supported a great range of social services, but not monks. The prime example is the establishment of the *vakif* of the Hagia Sophia in Constantinople, with its 3,395 properties in the city (including thirty beer houses and twenty-two sheep-head shops), which yielded a massive 718,421 Ottoman aspers.[51] Here there does not seem to have been a direct transfer of endowment from cathedral to mosque. But in Trebizond the correspondence is closer. Some of the Pharos lands passed into the hands of the *vakif* of Gülbahar, sultan Selim's Pontic mother, while the former monastic cathedral of the Chrysokephalos became the Fatih Camii, endowed with the Fatih *vakif*. This charity survives and may well incorporate property still being used for much the same purposes as its original Christian donors intended, to the benefit of their Muslim descendants.[52] In practical terms, the Byzantine legacy to the Ottomans was most of its monastic, ecclesiastical and imperial lands.

It is after the conquests that the distinction between urban and rural monasteries becomes significant, for the good reason that rural monasteries had a six times better chance of survival than urban ones. Of our seven hundred monasteries, I designated four hundred and seventeen as urban (three hundred and twenty-five in Constantinople), and two hundred and eighty-three as rural. On the eve of the con-

[48] S. Vryonis, 'Another note on the inscription of the church of St George of Beliserama', Βυζαντινά 9 (1977) pp 9–22.

[49] Vryonis, *Decline*, pp 334–5.

[50] A. H. Wächter, *Der Verfall des Griechenthums in Kleinasien im XIV. Jahrhundert* (Leipzig 1903).

[51] H. Inalcik, 'The policy of Mehmed II toward the Greek population of Istanbul and the Byzantine buildings of the City', *DOP* 23–4 (1969–70) p 243.

[52] M. T. Gökbilgin, 'XVI. yüzyil baslarında Trabzon livası ve dogu bölgesi', *Türk Tarih Kurumu Belleten* 26 (1962) pp 310–21.

quests eighty urban monasteries survived—eighteen in Constantinople But of those only twenty weathered the Fall, and only six survived until modern times. By contrast, of the two hundred and eighty-three rural monasteries, one hundred and fifty-eight existed on the eve of the conquests, ninety-one survived them and sixty-two were still flourishing in modern times. This disparity is partly explained by Ottoman laws of conquest.[53] If a walled town did not surrender on terms, and chose to resist, it was open to pillage and no title to property was recognised. And the late Byzantine urban monastery was also threatened by what seems to have been a deliberate fifteenth- and sixteenth-century Ottoman policy. The demographic problem facing Mehmed II was simply that there were still too few Muslims to go round, and of them, perhaps, there were too few Turkified Muslims. The Fatih secured his cities first. By repopulation, and using deportation (*sürgün*) as an instrument of state, he and his successors controlled their empire through its towns. Here the conversion of remaining Christians was relatively swift: first Islamization and two generations or so later, Turkification.[54] So the first centuries of the *Tourkokratia* saw the growth of Muslim cities as islands in a Christian sea. The trend was reversed in the nineteenth century, for the re-hellenization of Anatolia was a largely urban phenomenon.[55] The results were paradoxical, for if the secular church had to remain based on towns, its hierarchy had to be drawn largely from the rural monasteries—although the patriarchate itself fell increasingly into the hands of Phanariot lay managers.[56]

In the country, the brutal facts are that where a monastery was spared some of its lands it had a chance of survival, but where it was not, there was no hope. Deprived of their endowments, monasteries disappear very quickly. Given half a commercial chance, some monasteries flourished. St John on Patmos was patron of a successful

[53] H. Inalcik, 'Ottomam methods of conquest', *Studia Islamica* 2 (1954) pp 103–30.

[54] The process is described in detail in [H. W.] Lowry, [*The Ottoman Tahrir Defters as a source for urban demographic history: the case study of*] *Trabzon (ca. 1486–1583)* (Los Angeles 1977) (unpubl PhD dissertation). See also N. Beldiceanu, *Recherche sur la ville Ottomane au xve siècle* (Paris 1973).

[55] A. J. Toynbee, *The Western Question in Greece and Turkey* (London 1922) pp 122–44; M. Llewellyn Smith, *Ionian Vision: Greece in Asia Minor 1919–22* (London 1973) pp 21–34 concentrate on western Anatolia; for the re-hellenization of a Black Sea city, Samsun, see [A.] Bryer and [D.] Winfield, 'Nineteenth-century monuments [in the city and vilayet of Trebizond: architectural and historical notes,] Part 3', *AP* 30 (1970) pp 249–55.

[56] N. Iorga, *Byzance après Byzance* (Bucarest 1971) pp 84–129, 232–5.

merchant marine under Frankish protection.[57] All rural Pontic monasteries revived with a chance eighteenth-century silver-mining boom, when families like the Phytianos supplied both the mining concessionaries of Argyropolis (Gümüşhane) and the archbishops and abbots of Chaldia.[58] Even more significant were the massive endowments of Danubian and Phanariot princes from the sixteenth century. They were godsends to the monasteries of Athos and largely gave them their present aspect; only later could the hapless Romanians complain.

But generally, the effects of the Ottoman conquests, even the obscure but evidently favourable deal that Athos made in 1430, were to replace immunities with taxes and to reduce landholding and services.[59] The result was that, deprived of such high ratios of monk to dependent peasants and income as I have suggested, the surviving monasteries were almost bound to be in debt. It became the preoccupation of many. Ottoman monasteries were obsessed with the problem of raising money. This was, of course, equally true of the secular church. Like most Ottoman high offices, the patriarchate was in effect bought from the state by *peşkeş*.[60] The principal link between the swiftly changing patriarchs and their faithful was that the faithful had, eventually, to pay for the *peşkeş*. Even so, patriarchal debts rose from 100,769 piastres in 1730 to near one and a half million piastres by 1820.[61] Similarly the upkeep of a local church and its clergy fell upon

[57] P. Karlin-Hayter, 'Notes sur les archives de Patmos comme source pour la démographie et l'économie de l'île', *BF* 5 (1977) pp 189–215; *The Greek merchant marine (1453–1850)*, ed S. A. Papadopoulos (Athens 1972) pp 25, 30–2, 97, 177, 179, 233–5, 342, 363.

[58] Bryer and Winfield, 'Nineteenth-century monuments, Part 3', pp 324–49.

[59] There is no good history of Ottoman-Athonite relations. The arrangements of 1430 were a kind of relief from transitory Catalan, Serbian, Ottoman and Byzantine domination. See F. W. Hasluck, *Athos and its monasteries* (London 1924) pp 31–3; N. Oikonomidès, 'Le haradj dans l'empire byzantin du XVe siècle', *Actes du Ier Congrès international des études balkaniques et sud-est européennes III (Histoire)* (Sofia 1969) pp 681–8; P. K. Chrestou, 'Αθωνική Πολιτεία (Thessalonike 1963) pp 54–65; for a detailed description of the Lavra's finances under the Ottomans, see Alexander Lavriotes (Lazarides), Τὸ "Αγιον "Ορος μετὰ τὴν 'Οθωμανικὴν κατάκτησιν *EEBS* 32 (1963) pp 113–261; and for a number of useful articles, *Le millénaire du Mont Athos, 963–1963* 1 (Chevtogne 1963); 2 (Venice/Chevtogne 1965).

[60] [S.] Runciman, [*The*] *Great Church* [*in captivity: a study of the patriarchate of Constantinople from the eve of the Turkish conquest to the Greek war of independence*] (Cambridge 1968) pp 193–202; *Historia politica et patriarchica Constantinopoleos*, ed I. Bekker, *CSHByz* (1849) pp 3–204.

[61] Runciman, *Great Church* p 202. A not untypical European comment is in W. J. Grelot, *A late voyage to Constantinople . . .* (London 1683) pp 138–9: 'Since Vain-glory and

the faithful, and when in the sixteenth and seventeenth centuries the faithful were offering their faith to Islam, a fixed burden of dues and taxes fell upon fewer until a point of no return was reached and whole communities went over in a landslide.[62] Athos, which was paying seven hundred thousand aspers a year to the Porte by 1600, never seemed solvent.[63] The paradigm of monasticism became the beggar-monk, who could expect preferment to the chairmanship of his idiorrhythmic house if he returned triumphant with enough money to keep it in business. Institutions like the Holy Sepulchre were particularly well organised: their collectors arrived in Christian villages armed with lists of what each family had paid last time.[64] The beggar-monk is typified by the garrulous Dapontes, who left Athonite Xeropotamou on 22 May 1757, together with that monastery's relic

---

Simony became Masters of the Patriarchate, all these Prelates are constrain'd to reimburse the person, who to clamber over his Predecessor's head, gives never so much Money to the Grand Signor. Which is the reason, that whereas the Emperours formerly gave great Presents to the Patriarchs, to gain by their means the favour of the People under their Jurisdiction, they now receive vaster Sums from them; which daily increasing through the exorbitant Ambition of the Patriarchs, will soon enhance the price so high, that in a short time it will be a difficult thing for all *Greece* to raise the Sum demanded. In the space of two years that I stay'd at *Constantinople,* two different Patriarchs [probably Parthenios IV (1657–62, 1665–7, 1671, 1675–6, 1684–5) and Dionysios IV (1671–3, 1676–9, 1682–4, 1686–7, 1693–4)] gave for the Patriarchship, the one fifty, the other sixty thousand Crowns, as a Present to the Grand Signor. Considerable Sums for the *Caloyers,* who profess the Vow of Poverty, and ought to enjoy nothing of Propriety. Nevertheless when any of these Monks can meet with a rich Merchant, which will advance part of the Money, they propose their design to the Grand Signor [Mehmed IV (1648–87)], who fails not to grant the Title to him that gives most, and having received the Present, gives him the *Barat* or Grand Signor's Letters Patents, by vertue of which the old Patriarch is displac'd, and the new one settl'd in his room, with order to the *Greeks* to obey him, and to pay with all speed the Debts contracted, under the penalties of Bastinadoing, Confiscation, and shutting up their Churches. Which Order is presently sent to all the Archbishops and Metropolitans, who give immediate notice thereof to their Suffragans: who laying hold on the opportunity, tax the *Caloyers* and People under their Jurisdiction, the sum assess'd by the Patriarch, and something more, under pretence of Expences and Presents extraordinary.' The rivalry between Parthenios IV and Dionysios IV marked the nadir of patriarchal politics at a time when there were Greek and Armenian neo-martyrs after Mehmed IV's rebuff at Vienna in 1683: this is also the background of Anglican and non-juror overtures to the Orthodox church.

[62] Examples in Lowry, *Trabzon* pp 209–47.

[63] Mendieta, *Athos* p 113.

[64] N. A. Bees, 'Αφιερώματα καὶ λειτουργικαὶ συνδρομαὶ Τραπ3γουντίων καὶ ἄλλων Ποντίων ὑπὲρ τοῦ Παναγίου Τάφου κατ' ἀναγραφὰς 'ἱερολυμιτικοῦ κώδικος', *AP* 14 (1949) pp 124–60. The well-organised beggar-monk must be distinguished from the perennial wandering monk, of which a late example is in F. Halkin, 'Un ermite des Balkans au XIV siècle. La vie grecque inédite de Saint Romylos', *B* 31 (1961) p 134.

of the True Cross and two forged documents attesting its authenticity. He did not return until 11 September 1765, but with enough in the way of alms to rebuild Xeropotamou.[65]

Take the case of the three great monasteries of the Pontic interior: Vazelon, Peristera and Soumela. All held extensive properties in the three valleys they dominated before 1461, but managed to retain many thereafter: they were still controlling forty-six villages in this century. In *c*1529 the administrative district of these valleys was about eighty percent Christian. In *c*1920 it was about seventy-six percent Christian, when the Vazelon villages were still eighty-eight percent Greek and the Soumelan eighty-nine percent Greek.[66] Outside Athos, no other part of the Byzantine world remained quite so immune. But when your landlord is an abbot (and we will see that he is even more than that), you think twice about apostasy.

Soumela, which boasted forty *paroikoi* in 1364, was perhaps luckiest, for one of its Greek villagers gave birth to the future sultan Selim I and it had *firmans* or gifts from all sultans from Selim to Mustafa III.[67] Yet its seventeenth-century record is one of bickering over money and vicarates, settled by a covenant of reform in 1686.[68] Unlike Vazelon, it could not claim Peter the Great as a benefactor, but (as elsewhere) endowments came from the Danubian provinces in the eighteenth century and it particularly enjoyed the profits of the Chaldian mines. But they failed by the end of the century, and (as elsewhere) economic difficulties returned. By 1803 Soumela was 24,075 piastres in debt.[69] It had benefited from notable fund-raisers before: in 1747 its monk Meletios returned from a trip to Constantinople with 2,051 piastres in cash and goods.[70] But, with bankruptcy at the door, the entire monastery seems to have turned to begging. The monks Athanasios and Ioannikios set off for Smyrna and Bursa, and Euthymios and Timothy to Kayseri and Ankara in 1801; Jacob and Joasaph went to

[65] S. Binon, *Les origines légendaires et l'histoire de Xéropotamou et de Saint-Paul de l'Athos* (Louvain 1942) pp 158–68.

[66] Bryer, 'Greeks and Türkmens', p 121 and n 24; V. Cuinet, *La Turquie d'Asie,* 1 (Paris 1892) 1–129, when Vazelon held twenty villages, Soumela fifteen, and Peristera eleven.

[67] Kyriakides, Σουμελᾶ pp 79–90.

[68] *Ibid* pp 110–13; E. C. Colwell, *The four gospels of Karahisar,* 1 (Chicago 1936) p 52; Bryer [J.] Isaac and Winfield, 'Nineteenth-century monuments, Part 4', *AP* 32 (Athens 1972–3) pp 238–43.

[69] Uspensky and Bénéchévitch, *Bazélon* Act 188 of 1694; Kyriakides, Σουμελά pp 115–79; Bryer and Winfield, 'Nineteenth-century monuments, Part 3', *AP* 30 (1970) pp 270–98.

[70] Kyriakides, Σουμελᾶ pp 134–5. The goods ranged from a Moscow gospel and altar silver at 187 piastres, to an icon of the *Panagia* worth 25 piastres.

Amasya in 1802; Gregory to Wallachia in 1803; Gervasios, Athanasios and Jacob to Constantinople, and Eugenios to Wallachia in 1805; and Gregory to Bafra in 1808. By 1813 all debts were paid off.[71] Thereafter, judicious exploitation of Soumela's famous icon of the Panagia, believed to have been painted by St Luke, and good management, ensured the processing of thousands of pilgrims up the Soumela valley. Some were Muslims performing an unofficial *hac*, and rags of the Turkish sick still festoon Soumela's wrecked *aghiasma* today. The annual income of the monastery climbed from 38,735 piastres in 1840 to a record 414,262 piastres in 1904, but most abbots still had to make fund-raising trips through Anatolia, the Caucasus and Russia.[72]

A symptom of the monastic preoccupation with making ends meet, is that one of the principal Athonite disputes of the period 1754–1820 was a controversy over *kollyvades*. Briefly, donors could expect their names to be commemorated in lists which, in the more successful monasteries and *sketai*, achieved formidable length (in one *skete* twelve thousand had to be recited). Commemoration, with *kollyvades* bread, takes place on Saturdays. But Saturday was also the Athonite market day at its capital, Karyes. It was inappropriate to shift commemoration to a Sunday, to allow monks to go to market. It does

[71] Kyriakides, Σουμελᾶ pp 170–3; Chrysanthos of Trebizond and Athens (Philippides), 'Η 'Εκκλησία Τραπεζουντος', *AP* 4–5 (1933) pp 468–84.

[72] Accounts in Soumela MS 8, now in the Archaeological Museum, Ankara, from 1840–1905. Sample years show:

Year	Income	Expenditure
1840	38,735	39,952
1850	19,783	19,783
1860	43,736	56,109
1870	101,176	119,340
1880	77,918	79,044
1890	118,072	118,072
1900	241,095	241,095
1904	414,262	414,262
1905	153,805	153,805

Unfortunately there is no break-down of income and expenditure, except that the exceptionally high income for 1904 included 200,665 piastres from the abbot's fund-raising trip to Russia, while the largest expenditure that year was 133,869 on 'Various'. But Soumela MS 54 gives monthly accounts from June-December 1852, which reveals that by far the largest income and expenditure came in August (15 August, the Dormition, was Soumela's great festival). On Muslim pilgrims to Soumela, see Alfred Biliotti's despatch of 17 December 1877 in PRO FO 195/1141: 'It is also held in reverence by the Mussulmans many of whom, at least 500 yearly, go there in pilgrimage with important offerings in kind and money.'

not seem to have occurred to anyone to move the market to Thursday instead.[73]

A more serious effect was a breakdown of monastic discipline. We have seen that the average number of monks in a monastery was falling and it is difficult to see how monastic liturgies, let alone any coenobitic life, could be maintained with numbers which fell to three or four per house. Late Byzantine monasteries had successfully sought, through *stavropegiac* rights, a sort of institutional idiorrhythmy. The next stage, an idiorrhythmy of life *within* the institution, where monks omit vows of poverty and reduce those of obedience, may be a natural progression. Or perhaps the next stage is more of a consequence of the financial problems of the *Tourkokratia*. It is easy to be a poor monk in a rich house, but what happens when the house is poor? At any rate it is evident that idorrhythmy started spreading on Athos from the 1390s, before the Turks came, although its triumph came later.[74]

The baleful effects of the contraction of the economic basis of a monastery to make its financial survival a prime concern of its monks are all too obvious. The professional beggar-monk, the affluent committee elder in a poor monastery, and the steward of an ill-run Danubian estate, belong to a different institution from Theodore's Stoudion. They should not be compared. The late Byzantine monastery adapted itself to survive a new climate, and it survived.

There is a parallel here with what had happened to the Armenian church long before. Deprived of a state, the Armenian church became ruralised, its bishops retreating to monasteries which were safe because they were remote, and which became cultural and pilgrim centres, making up much of an Armenian national identity: the Nestorian church in Hakkari went one stage further by becoming, in effect, tribalised.[75] Like some Armenian monasteries, some Greek ones now felt that they should have schools—not so ambitious as Voulgaris's on Athos, but the cultural gloom of these centuries is often over-painted. A recent commentator on the Athonite libraries notes with scorn that the only one quarter of their eleven thousand manuscripts date from before 1500.[76] That says a deal for the activity of Athonite

[73] K. K. Papoulides, Τὸ κίνημα τῶν Κολλυβάδων (Athens 1971); L. Petit, 'La grande controverse des colyves', *EO* 2 (1899) pp 321–31.

[74] Mendieta, *Athos* pp 100–105, 107–8.

[75] There is still no critical work on Armenian monasticism and M. Ormanian, *The Church of Armenia* (London 1955) is no substitute. On the Nestorians of the Hakkari, see G. P. Badger, *The Nestorians and their rituals* (London 1852).

[76] Mendieta, *Athos* p 245.

scribes after 1500. Some rural Pontic monasteries had schools; that may have been out of step with the urban *Frontisteria*, with their touch of Danubian enlightenment, and they may have been teaching their physics from Aristotle and cosmology from Korydalleus until recently, but at least they were teaching, and some of the teaching was not undistinguished. The most remote of all Pontic monastic schools, at Goumera, sent a pupil straight out of the middle ages into a Leipzig doctorate by 1908.[77] So like the Armenian monasteries, the post-Byzantine ones should not be regarded as having a primarily monastic function: indeed some, like the Armenian ones, had none at all.

The three major Pontic monasteries, Vazelon, Peristera and Soumela, are comparable to the Armenian monastic church in another respect. Their abbots were, in effect, bishops. Until 1863 they enjoyed extraordinary and extra-diocesan exarchates in their valleys, and Soumela supplied vicars for Koloneia and bishops for Crimean Gotthia too. In parts of rural Pontos the secular church had become entirely monasticised. In 1863 the patriarchate tried to retrieve the situation by replacing the abbot-exarchs by a regular diocese, of Rhodopolis. Not surprisingly, the monks fought back, but so did their villagers, complaining that bishops cost even more than abbots. A compromise was reached in 1886.[78]

Did bishops cost more than abbots? When your abbot is not only your bishop, but your landlord, tax-collector and schoolmaster too, society is certainly preserved, but at a price of almost Tibetan proportions. The rural Greeks of the Pontos, locked in the past, led a life until this century at increasing variance with the urban Greeks of the coast. But the economic cost of maintaining a medieval monastery, with so much thrust upon it, might well have proved their undoing if the Turks had not stepped in in 1923. Take the case of a south Cretan valley, with about five hundred and fifty arable acres, which has been surveyed recently. In ancient and medieval times it may have supported up to thirty four small-holding families. But after the eleventh century it also had to support a monastery of the Hodegetria. By the seventeenth century (when three hundred and seventy six monasteries and about four thousand monks are claimed for Crete), the Hodegetria controlled the whole valley. No chance of conversion

77 Bryer, Isaac and Winfield, 'Nineteenth-century monuments, Part 4', *AP* 32 (1972–3) pp 190–8.

78 Kyriakides, Σουμελᾶ pp 204–59; another view is in Gervasios of Alexandroupolis (Sarasites), ''Επαρχία 'Ροδοπόλεως', *AP* 6 (1935) pp 68–85.

here, but the secular population declined. By 1881 the nine monks still had fifteen tenant families—a reasonable, if low, Byzantine ratio. But today there are only the monks left.[79] It is hardly surprising that the Romanians severely reduced the revenues of their absentee Athonite landlords when they got their chance in 1876.[80] It was one of the first things that the new Greek state had done. For the thanks of the new Greek state to the monasteries which had supposedly done so much to sustain *Hellenismos* through those long years of *Tourkokratia*, and which had actually provided so many revolutionary centres in 1821, were unexpected. In 1833-4, Georg von Maurer, the Thomas Cromwell of Greece, maintaining, as the Romanians were to do, that no modern state could afford to allow so much property to be held on medieval lines, dissolved no fewer than four hundred and twelve monasteries and confiscated their lands.[81] Today the town monastery, once the strength of the Byzantine church, is a thing of the past, and the country monastery, once the strength of the post-Byzantine church, hangs on as precariously as the winches which once swung pilgrims up into the Meteora. What the Turk had attempted, the Bavarian almost achieved—except, as always in the green countryside of Athos, where walled towns are monasteries; and they flourish anew.

University of Birmingham
Centre for Byzantine Studies

[79] D. Blackman and K. Branigan, 'An archaeological survey of the lower catchment of the Ayiofarango valley', *The Annual of the British School at Athens* 72 (1977) pp 77–80 and n 23 above.

[80] Mendieta, *Athos* p 132.

[81] Frazee, *Orthodox Church* pp 120, 125–7. The remaining two thousand or so monks were concentrated in a hundred and forty eight surviving monasteries. By 1840 there were one thousand six hundred and forty six monks in a hundred and twenty eight monasteries.

PENITENCE AND PEACE-MAKING IN CITY AND CONTADO: THE *BIANCHI* OF 1399

by DIANA M. WEBB

A MAJOR trend in the recent historiography of medieval and renaissance Italy has been towards the reassertion of the fundamental importance of the countryside and of agriculture.[1] This is not so much to deny the unique position occupied by the cities in Italian life as to remind us of some essential features of those cities and of the men who ruled them. Towns were more typically market centres for their localities than entrepôts of long-distance commerce; while many members of both the higher and the lower urban social strata carried with them throughout life a status ultimately derived from the status they or their forebears occupied or had occupied in rural life. Conversely, the members of, say, the Florentine urban patriciate around the year 1400 were almost to a man landlords in the surrounding countryside.[2] They were also of course the men who made the laws, levied taxation and generally controlled the government of the countryside as of the town. At every level of life we have to postulate an intimacy of relations between town and country which the conditions of modern urban life can make it an effort even to imagine.

If we are to look at religious life in the town and country of late medieval Italy in this light, it seems reasonable to suggest that as a preliminary to more specific questions we should ask how the distinction between the two was perceived by contemporaries and where we as historians can safely draw the dividing line. What follows is a very modest contribution to such an enquiry. It is proposed to look at an outbreak of religious excitement which flowed over the northern part of the peninsula in the year 1399, embracing both town and country. The sources are principally the chroniclers of Genoa,

[1] For a brief survey, see the preface to D. Waley, *The Italian City Republics* (2 ed London 1978), also pp 55–69. A major study is [P.] Jones, ['From Manor to Mezzadria'], *Florentine Studies*, ed N. Rubinstein (London 1968) pp 193–241.

[2] G. Brucker, *The Civic World of Early Renaissance Florence* (Princeton 1977) pp 31–4.

Bergamo, Lucca and Pistoia: not the only sources for the episode, but among the fullest. Naturally chronicles will not answer all the questions that we might ask about religious life and sentiment; but as the products of literate townsmen responding more or less spontaneously to the passage of events they can yield much valuable information, in this as in other contexts, about basic assumptions and mental categories.

In the summer of 1399 a wave of penitential processions, arising from causes still very imperfectly understood, spread from the Genoese riviera, ultimately perhaps from Piedmont, over much of northern and central Italy, merging indistinctly into the movement of penitents and pilgrims to Rome as the millennium approached.[3] The devotion, so many contemporaries believed, originated in a vision received by an agricultural labourer, in the Dauphiné as the Pistoiese notary Ser Luca Dominici has it, who was taking his midday snack in the fields. Here Christ appeared to him (although the labourer did not recognise him) and ordered him to throw three loaves into a nearby spring. At the spring he found a weeping woman, whom again he failed to identify as the Virgin Mary, and who tried to prevent him from carrying out Christ's instructions. In the end he managed to throw one of the loaves into the spring, at which the Virgin informed him that this meant that one-third of the world must perish. Exasperated by its sins, Christ intended to destroy mankind; and Mary urged the labourer to go *di città di città, e di castello in castello, e di villa in villa,* mobilising his fellow-men to avert this disaster by joining in processions robed in white and following instructions that she gave him.[4]

According to the Lucchese chronicler Giovanni Sercambi, who places this original vision in England, another rustic, in the region of Marseilles, received a complementary vision of an angel between the horns of his ox, holding a book which he said must be opened on the altar of St Peter's in Rome and which would prove to contain instructions for the future conduct of the church and mankind.[5]

[3] [G.] Tognetti, ['Sul moto dei bianchi del 1399]', *BISIMEAM,* 78, (1967) pp 205–343; E. Delaruelle, 'Les grandes processions de pénitents de 1349 et 1399', *Il movimento dei disciplinati nel settimo centenario dal suo inizio, (Perugia 1260)* (Perugia 1962) pp 109–45; A. Frugoni, 'La devozione dei bianchi del 1399', *Convegni del Centro di Studi sulla spiritualità medievale,* 3 (Todi 1962) pp 232–48.

[4] [Ser Luca] Dominici, [*Cronaca della Venuta dei Bianchi e della Moria, 1399–1400,* ed G. C. Gigliotti], *R*[*erum*] *P*[*istoriensium*] *S*[*criptores*], 1 (Pistoia 1933) pp 51–4.

[5] [Giovanni] Sercambi, [*Croniche,* ed S. Bongi], 3 vols, *F*[*onti per la S*[*toria d'*]*I*[*talia*], 19–21 (Rome 1892) 2, pp 302–3.

Let us for a moment leave aside the question of whether we should attach any particular significance to the role of the *contadini* in these episodes. Our sources frequently depict the devotion arriving at an urban centre after making an impact in the surrounding territory. It seems for example to have reached Genoa, its first major urban point of diffusion, from the neighbouring localities of Voltri, westward along the coast, and the valley of Polcevera. At Polcevera a principal characteristic of the whole movement became immediately apparent, for here *odiosissimae erant inimicitiae, quae subito sunt ad pacem redactae.* At Voltri there was a healing miracle, which moved the Genoese to no little fear and zeal towards God. On 5 July the inhabitants of the valley of Polcevera entered Genoa, accompanied by *qiudam nobiles et cives valentes cum eorum familiis qui tunc ruribus habitabant.* The devotion thus imported took hold in the city, sponsored by the archbishop, and two days later the men of Voltri entered Genoa in their turn, bearing with them a young boy who had been brought back almost from the dead. Peace-making among the citizens was stimulated by the spectacle of erstwhile enemies *de ruribus* going about the city linked together by a rope or girdle. The populace, clergy and confraternities of Genoa now took over, in great processions within the city and into the suburbs, and also in a reciprocal movement out into the surrounding territory. Here, as everywhere, the movement rapidly assumed the more familiar features of a pilgrimage, supported by the winning of indulgences. The Genoese embarked on a tour of the *templa urbis et rurium* and detachments of them went out from the city, first of all to Recco, south-eastwards along the coast, thus imparting the devotion to the eastern riviera, to places such as Chiavari and Rapallo, where again there were *acutissima odia.*[6]

We have already encountered one of the problems in interpreting our sources. The cities ruled their surrounding territories; they ruled subordinate urban communities as well as rural communes and mountain villages. The political distinction between city and subject territory cannot simply be equated with a distinction between town and country. The Genoese annalist Giorgio Stella is at least sometimes clear that he is speaking of the countryside and its inhabitants. The men of Polcevera certainly look like rustics, particularly when they are contrasted with the *nobiles et cives valentes* who accompanied them to Genoa, thus illustrating the social mix of the countryside and its close links with the city.

[6] [Giorgio] Stella, [*Annales Genuenses*], Muratori, 17 pt iii, pp 238–40.

Once the devotion was under way and rolling on from place to place it becomes strictly meaningless to speak of points of origin; but the chroniclers usually saw the movement as reaching their particular city from a particular place. It came to Bergamo, for example, from Soncino, some forty kilometres to the south, in the shape of a detachment of men and women from Soncino itself and from the *plebatus* of Soncino. Arriving at Bergamo, the penitents were provisioned by the citizens, six thousand of whom were present when one of the twelve priests of the *plebatus* who had accompanied the procession preached to great effect on the theme of peace-making among Christians and on the miracles that had occurred in several places. Thereupon once again the city took over: all the clergy, with the nobles, judges, doctors and other good men organised processions on successive days within Bergamo, going from one end of the city to the other and into the *burgi*, hearing many masses and much preaching from the mendicant friars. On 27 August the predictable movement out from the city itself took place, and the chronicler is gratifyingly particular about the variety of persons involved and their origins:

> . . . una maxima quantitas hominum et feminarum civitatis, burgorum et suburgorum et districtus Pergami, tam de montenariis omnium vallium pergamensium et de comunibus de plano Pergami in simul congregavit super monte de Farra . . . . . Et super dicto monte de Fara solemniter celebrate fuerunt multe misse.

The same site witnessed many peace-makings between the citizens; and on 28 August the *comitiva* with its processional banners began a series of excursions to surrounding areas, its itineraries punctuated by miracles and pacifications.[7] Perhaps the inhabitants of the places they visited saw themselves as receiving these benefits from the mother-city; but it is clear that Bergamo itself had received the devotion, at least immediately, from the small communes of the *plebatus* of Soncino, some way to the south of the city.

In Tuscany, it was from Sarzana, to the north-east, that the devotion spread to Pietrasanta and thence to Lucca and Pistoia, whose *brigate* in their turn penetrated as far as Florence, where the government received them with marked reserve, not to say suspicion. It is from the chroniclers of Lucca and Pistoia that we obtain our most detailed accounts of the nine-day processions conducted according to the

[7] *Chronicon Bergomense Guelpho-Ghibellinum,* Muratori, 16 pt 2, pp 94–8.

Virgin's original instructions, which took the participants out of their native cities for a tour of the surrounding localities. During this time they were bound neither to remove their white garments, nor to eat meat, nor to sleep in any walled place.[8] At Lucca and Pistoia, as also at Genoa and Bergamo, processions within the city were organised around the major churches to satisfy the aspirations of those inhabitants who for some reason could not embark on the nine-day excursion.

A modern commentator on the movement[9] has speculated as to whether the Virgin's command that the penitents on their circuit should sleep within no walled place should be interpreted as an attempt on the part of an urban populace to distance itself from its normal mores, adding the caution, however, that to be sure of this we would need to know that the movement was urban in origin. This is indeed uncertain, and the uncertainty goes further. Can it safely be asserted that the habit of sleeping within a protective circle of walls defines a population as truly 'urban' in character? The Virgin had urged the *contadino* to bear her message from *città in città*, from *castello in castello* and from *villa in villa*, thus neatly evoking both the topographical and the sociological variety of the landscape in which the devotion was going to unfold. Rural settlement in Tuscany had clearly had some 'urban' or quasi-urban features, even if now, by the end of the fourteenth century, there were signs of a greater degree of rural dispersal, of the desertion and depopulation of fortified villages and *castella*.[10] Furthermore, Sercambi's rendering of the Virgin's prohibition suggests that some at least interpreted it with important qualifications. The penitents must not sleep *in alcuna terra murata*, but this was provided that they could with safety remain outside; nor were they to sleep in the open air, nor in unmade beds, but in churches, on benches, on the ground or on straw.[11] Only with some reserve should we read into these conditions a rejection of the urban environment as such.

That certain non-urban localities carried religious associations not improbably reaching back to very ancient roots, and that not all the shrines and holy places that acted as magnets to the bands of white-clad penitents were located in the cities, is clear from the sources. We have seen how the populace of Bergamo and its environs

[8] Dominici pp 53–4; Sercambi pp 320–1.
[9] Tognetti p 227.
[10] Jones pp 232–4.
[11] Sercambi pp 320–1.

gathered to hear mass and make peace with one another on the *mons de Farra*. If in Tuscany the cathedral of Prato, with its possession of the Virgin's girdle, attracted crowds of pilgrims during these days of excitement,[12] so, if on a more modest scale, did the hilltop shrine of Santa Maria *a Ceuli*, at San Miniato, on the southern edge of the Val d'Arno, almost equidistant between Florence and Pisa.[13]

On a different level, it may well be that the *contadini* who received the visions from which popular belief derived the devotion were enacting a role which no urban dweller, however humble his standing, could so naturally have filled. The emblematic simplicity and humility of the rustic who received the first vision is enhanced by the uncertainty of his remote location: as a Florentine chronicler remarked, some placed the beginnings of the movement in Spain, others in Scotland, England or various parts of France.[14] Sercambi seems to be on the point of making this inner meaning explicit when he moralises *e poichè le signorie nè i prelati nè i savi non si muoveno, vuole la divina misericordia che in nelli huomini grossi et materiali si dimostri la sua potentia.*[15] It is clear however that he is generalising: the wrath of God is to be averted by a movement of penitence among the humble of the earth, and the essential distinction is between those who possess earthly wealth, power and wisdom and those who do not. The peasant would automatically come into the latter category, but so too would the mass of unenfranchised denizens of the cities, and there is nothing to suggest that Sercambi's allusion is not to this horizontal division rather than to any vertical division between the pure of the countryside and the impure of the towns. More hard-headed than Sercambi, Giorgio Stella reports that certain *rustici et viri simplices* of Provence, beholding (it is said) a divine miracle, initiated the processions; it is unclear whether he believes that their rustic simplicity made them suitable vessels for the divine message, or merely credulous dupes.[16]

Luca Dominici's narrative shows us instances of this temporary social reversal in operation, with the humble inspired to take spiritual initiatives. Not infrequently they were the humble of the countryside. Most striking of all was the little girl of ten or so, a swineherd from

[12] Dominici pp 60, 88.
[13] Sercambi pp 317, 363.
[14] [*Cronica volgare di*] *anonimo fiorentino* [*già attribuita a Piero di Giovanni Minerbetti*], Muratori, 27 pt 2, pp 240–1. Later, some believed that the original vision had been received by an Irish anchoress, Dominici pp 168–70.
[15] Sercambi p 291.
[16] Stella p 236.

the Val d'Elsa, whom Dominici describes simply as 'coarse' (*grossolana*). One day she received a vision of the Virgin who told her to ring the bells of the church of her *terra* and alert all those who had not gone in procession as *bianchi* to do so. The Virgin was prepared to back up the original vision with more, in order to convince the sceptical, and a fairy-tale touch is added: the *fanciulla* who had been coarse, rough and dirty all at once becomes delicate, beautiful and angelic, and embarks on her career as prophetess, leading the local populace to Santa Maria *a Ceuli*, with a *predicatore* by her side who spoke at her bidding, and displaying a miraculous knowledge of who had confessed and who had not.[17] When Dominici first heard of her she was being taken in triumph to Florence; later he describes in detail her ceremonial reception at Pistoia by all the clergy and the governing body of the city, amid scenes of great popular enthusiasm.[18]

Such visions, which at intervals refuelled the devotion, were not however confined to rustics. One of the most celebrated was granted to an emancipated slave-woman, by name Melica, in the household of Federigo Vivaldi of Genoa. At prayer in church one day she beheld Christ and Mary disputing over the fate of the world, and the Virgin urged her to exhort everyone to conduct a three-day fast to assuage her son's wrath. Melica did not manage to maintain a monopoly over her vision, which was obligingly repeated for her master and mistress when they came back to the church with her.[19] Nevertheless, the *fanciulla* of the Val d'Elsa, and the emancipated slave of Genoa both represented Sercambi's *grossi et materiali* in whom God had chosen to manifest his power.

It would be hard, then, to deduce from our sources more than the faintest, inconsistent hints that the countryside and its inhabitants were regarded as repositories of innocence and unspoilt spiritual values. What is made very clear is the fact that city and *contado* shared the same social and moral problems and were equally in need of the saving work of the *bianchi*. The enmities and hatreds which poisoned urban life spread over the surrounding countryside (if indeed that is the right way round to put it), not only because human nature is everywhere the same, but because the social network of town and country was continuous. In this context city and *contado* are frequently referred to as a unit. Recording the arrival of the devotion at Genoa,

[17] Dominici pp 182–4.
[18] *Ibid* pp 201–2.
[19] *Ibid* pp 125–7; Stella p 241.

Luca Dominici remarks *in verità Genova e il contado stava peggio che città di questo paese e uccidevansi come bestie.*[20] Giorgio Stella does not deny it, and it is he who underlines the short-lived effects of the movement, telling how soon afterwards a feud blew up in Bisagno, just north-west of the city, which rapidly communicated itself to Genoa.[21]

This was hardly a Genoese problem alone, however, as we have already seen at Bergamo. At Pistoia, on 16 August, inquiry was officially made throughout the city and *contado* to identify the groupings around which trouble normally organised itself: *per sapere tutte le brighe ci erano e facevansi scrivere e facevansi le paci: e tutto il di non si fece altro che acordi, paci e concordie per la città e contado.*[22] Both before and after 1399 the *contado* was a major theatre of warfare between the factions of Pistoia; Ser Luca's second chronicle is largely devoted to showing how Pistoia, weakened and threatened by these conflicts, finally slipped under the rule of Florence.[23] Preaching at Bergamo some eighteen years after the *bianchi*, Bernardino of Siena realised that he must address himself to the inhabitants of town and country alike, telling one of his first meagre audiences that he wanted them the following Sunday to bring with them all their *concives et convicaneos, rusticos et urbanos*; and after his introduction of the sacred monogram which was to replace the party insignia that he had seen on every door, we are told that *Nedum in civitate supradicta, verum etiam per diocesim eiusdem cessaverunt odia, inimicitia, partialitates et homicidia.*[24]

Everywhere the *bianchi* went peace-making was their major function, and the miracles worked by the crucifixes they carried before them were as often as not stimulated by the refusal of the stubborn to make peace. Not only was the *contado* as much in need of this initiative as the city, but it helped to supply it. *Brigate* from the *contado* continually arrived at Lucca and Pistoia to process through the city and visit its shrines, but all the while the *contado* was, so to speak, servicing itself.[25] On 31 August some nine hundred folk from

[20] Dominici p 55. [21] Stella p 242.

[22] Dominici p 73.

[23] [D.] Herlihy, [*Medieval and Renaissance Pistoia*] (New Haven 1967) p 210; [Ser Luca] Dominici, *Cronaca Seconda,* [ed Q. Santoli], *RPS* 3 (Pistoia 1937).

[24] 'Vie inédite de S. Bernardin de Sienne par un frère mineur, son contemporain', *An Bol,* 25 (1906) pp 316, 318.

[25] Dominici p 101: 'E voglio che tu sappi che tutto il nostro contado similmente faceva processione: quelli eran rimasi come noi vestiti di bianco con loro preti e con la loro croce; ogni comune per se e due comuni o cappelle insieme ordinatamente, di villa in villa cantando tutti la laude usata . . . tutti osservando come noi.'

S. Croce e da S. Maria in Monte e da Fucecchio e di quello paese arrived at Pistoia, toured the city in the normal way and proceeded towards the Valdinievole; they told Ser Luca that their crucifix had been performing many wonders, bringing about a difficult pacification at Montespertoli and healing a mute at San Casciano.[26]

The potency of the *bianchi* as peace-makers must sometimes have been that of strangers come thus unusually in peace and goodwill. The sudden increase in normal levels of interchange and mobility clearly had an unsettling effect on the emotions. When about a thousand *bianchi* set out from Lucca on 12 August, they gathered with them as they progressed adherents from the *contado*, so that on the following day there were two thousand five hundred penitents gathered together in the Valdinievole. Their passage left *le menti de paesani sospesi.* On 17 August the men of Borgo a Bugiano and the surrounding area struggled to bring to an end an old quarrel. Their frustrated prayers and tears were rewarded when the crucifix before which they stood jetted blood and the Virgin depicted on it turned to her son as if in enquiry. At this *quelli huomini e quelli mercanti* cried *misericordia* and made their peace.[27] The casual use of language which transforms the *paesani* of one sentence into *huomini* and *mercanti* may either confuse our understanding of the complexion of this society or, if taken at face value, confirm our impression of how deeply interpenetrated rural and urban, agricultural and mercantile, elements were in it. It may be partly because of their imprecise terminology that the chroniclers leave no very clear impression of any sense of distance between the ordinary townsman and his rural collaborators in the devotion; or it may be that this distinction bulked less large among their mental categories than the simple horizontal division between great and small. All observers were suitably impressed by the participation of the most distinguished citizens in the processions. Insofar as Coluccio Salutati, the humanist chancellor of Florence, commented on the social composition of the movement it was to point out that the three thousand Lucchese *bianchi* who first brought the devotion to Florence were *non viles quidem, sed urbis illius principes et notabiles mercatores.*[28]

Is it then a picture of simple unanimity and equality between town and country, sharing their temporary enthusiasm as they shared their

[26] *Ibid* p 112. [27] Sercambi pp 350–2.

[28] *Epistolario di Coluccio Salutati,* ed F. Novati, 4 vols, *FSI* 15–18 (Rome 1891–1911) 3, p 356.

problems? It would probably be going too far to say so without qualification. The cities possessed major churches and major relics; we have mentioned the Virgin's girdle at Prato. Throughout their long advance to political supremacy they had exploited their position as cult-centres. The eagerness with which bands of penitents from the *contado* came to pay their devotions at the churches of the mother-city seems to show how this simultaneous political and religious pre-eminence was accepted. An episode related by Luca Dominici shows how ambivalent, and yet enduring, these relationships could be. On 16 August ambassadors from Carmignano came to Pistoia to ask that their *brigata* be allowed to process behind the crucifix of Pistoia. When a few days later the *bianchi* of Pistoia entered Carmignano, however, they received few alms and little *aiuto*, and would have been in want but for what they brought with them. Desiring to return good for evil, they nonetheless brought about many pacifications there. Carmignano was in fact one of several communes that Pistoia had been compelled to hand over to Florence in 1329; in the thirteenth and early fourteenth centuries it was a substantial little township of upwards of twelve hundred people.[29]

On one level this political pre-eminence of the cities represented the domination of city over countryside, but it is not, as we have already indicated, a simple equation. As the process of state-building continued, cities came to rule over cities. The process can be well illustrated from the history of Pistoia itself in this period. In and after the year 1400, its population depleted perhaps by as much as half by the great plague which came in the wake of the *bianchi*, Pistoia fell completely under the dominion of Florence which had exercised a degree of control over it for much of the fourteenth century. Among the immediate consequences was the stipulation that every year Pistoia must send a *palio* worth a hundred florins to Florence on the feast of the Baptist, as Arezzo did.[30] The process worked the other way. Perceiving that Pistoia had lost the last vestiges of its independent power, the little commune of Serravalle, which numbered probably no more than two hundred and fifty persons in 1401, tried to refuse to send the customary *palio* to Pistoia for the feast of San Jacopo, and did so in the end only because the Florentine authorities wished it.[31]

[29] Dominici pp 73, 82; Herlihy pp 57, 65; Herlihy 'Plague, Population and Social Change in Rural Pistoia', *EcHR,* 2 ser, 18 (1965) p 230 n 1.

[30] Dominici, *Cronaca seconda,* p 63.

[31] *Ibid* p 160. For Serravalle's population, see Herlihy p 279.

In the latter instance an undeniably rural community had been subordinated to a city of modest size; in the former, that modest city had become subject to a city infinitely larger and more powerful. In either case political subjection was given similar symbolic forms of expression.

Mere narrative sources will not usually tell us how exactly we are to regard a given subject community: whether it is in every sense a rural settlement or whether it is of a size and character to be regarded as a centre, however modest, of urban life. Rarely is description so vivid as in Sercambi's apology for Montopoli, where a band of *bianchi* was terrorised by a cow run amok: *tal castello è solo una strada.*[32] Bearing this limitation in mind, we may still be justified in believing that the mode of subordination of which the chroniclers were most conscious was the political. Alone among them, the Florentine seems to hint at an economic element in the subjection of *contado* to city. He records how *brigate* of penitents came from the subject territories to Florence: there were two thousand or more from San Miniato and Empoli and those parts, a thousand or more from Volterra, and various numbers from Colle di Val d'Elsa, San Gimignano and elsewhere; all were given provisions, and it seemed to the chronicler that none of them seemed to remember that they had anything else to do.[33] It was after all a busy time of year, and we are reminded of the close concern of urban governments with the agricultural calendar when we read that on 10 September it was decreed at Pistoia that the *vendemmia* be postponed to 22 September so that the processions might be completed,[34] and that at Milan the duke gave a reluctant permission for processions to be held in the city, on condition that they did not go on beyond 5 September and obstruct the corn-harvest.[35]

The orderliness and beneficent effects of the *bianchi* were almost universally acknowledged. Our chosen sources have almost nothing to say about impostures, which seem to have occurred (or to have been detected) principally further south, in the papal states.[36] By way of contrast and postscript we may look at the hostile reaction evoked by a less orderly outburst of religious excitement, some twenty years after the *bianchi*, from a commentator of a different social and cultural

[32] Sercambi p 363.
[33] *Anonimo fiorentino* p 242: 'e di niuna cosa pareva che si ricordassono che a fare avessono.'
[34] Dominici pp 139–40.
[35] Tognetti pp 304–5.
[36] *Ibid* pp 282–91.

stamp from the chroniclers of 1399. In May 1419 the Dominican Manfredo da Vercelli entered Florence with a horde of followers of both sexes and all ages, who mostly originated from Lombardy. An eye-witness account was written, some time after Manfredo had been summoned to Rome at the end of 1423, by the Augustinian friar Andrea Biglia, who in 1419 was living in Florence.[37] The enhanced mobility of the *bianchi* had, in Manfredo's following, spilled over acceptable limits. In seeking to discover their motivation Biglia gleaned from some of them what may be a hint of confused anti-urban sentiment, fomented by Manfredo's apocalyptic preaching: with Antichrist imminent, he had told them, there was danger at home, but safety in the fields and in the mountains.[38] Confused they certainly must have been, as they had followed their leader to find themselves living ill-provided in one of the largest cities of Italy.

While it is clear that Manfredo's following was mixed in its social origins, Biglia chose at certain points to emphasise the predominance of rustics among them. It was not to be wondered at that Manfredo, unlearned though he was, should have attracted such a following, for they were mostly *agrestes*, by definition ignorant of high matters, such as one sees flocking in country places around those who go about making proclamations.[39] For Manfredo to draw peasants after him as he did footloose wives and widows (and their dowries) was to commit an injustice, for peasants were normally in debt to their lords, who were thus defrauded by their removal.[40]

Mingled here there seems to be some genuine observation of the facts of rural life, together with, one suspects, the influence of a topos. There is certainly no doubt of the burden of debt on the

[37] D. Webb, 'Andrea Biglia at Bologna: a humanist friar and the troubles of the church', *BIHR*, 39 (1976) pp 53–8, where Biglia's *Ammonitio ad fratrem Manfredum Vercellensem* is cited from Milan, Biblioteca Ambrosiana MS H. 117, fols 57^{v}–73^{v}. The work has been printed, with further discussion, by [R.] Rusconi, ['Fonti e Documenti su Manfredi da Vercelli O.P. ed il suo movimento penitenziale'], *AFP*, 47 (1977) pp 51–107.

[38] Rusconi, p 82: '. . . itaque nichil aliud iam curari oportere quam ut, relictis patriis sedibus, Christus quereretur, domi esse periculum, futuros in agris et in montibus securos.'

[39] *Ibid* p 78: 'Ego quidem non tanto opere admiror turbas et incultum et indoctum hominem secutas: facile enim intelligimus in huiuscemodi turbis ac vulgo rarissimum quemque inveniri, qui ingenio aut prudentia preditus sit, maximeque inter agrestes, quorum ad te concursus erat maior, ac ferme in illis terris quibus non magna inest harum rerum diligentia. Id enim sepe fieri vidimus etiam ad hos, qui passim per villas declamitant, incredibilem turbarum numerum convenire.'

[40] *Ibid* p 81: 'Siquidem in turba multi erant agricole, quos plurimum videmus dominorum suorum debitis oppressos, rem iniustissimam esse, ut illis suis creditis fraudarentur.'

peasantry in the early fifteenth century and Biglia's tone makes his patrician sympathies plain.[41] As academic, humanist and religious, he was also heir to a long tradition in which the word *rusticitas* had taken on meanings as much cultural as sociological. *Rusticitas* was virtually a synonym for ignorance, *sancta rusticitas* a mode of holiness which had both its opponents and its advocates. Biglia tended to be an opponent, as a treatise he wrote in 1431 on the origins and character of his order, which he saw as a unique fusion of the eremitical vocation with the intellectual life, makes plain.[42] There is a glancing reference in this treatise to what may be termed the obverse of the *rusticitas*-topos: the eulogy of the eremitical life in its setting of woods and wild beasts. Praising the hermitage of Lecceto near Siena in these terms, Biglia laments that his own lot is cast in the hurly-burly; but he adds, significantly, that for great talents (*magnis ingeniis*) the greatest opportunity for virtue and piety is afforded *in maioribus quoque et occupatioribus locis.*[43] There was at least a basic consistency in Biglia's aristocratic *urbanitas.*

Also in the year 1431, the humanist poet Maffeo Vegio[44] wrote a number of satirical epigrams under the title *Rusticalia.* Here, a step further up the scale of literary artifice from Biglia's writings, we find the *rusticitas*-topos full-blown. One epigram begins with Vegio musing *Non possum non mirari, gens incola ruris/ Cum nihil humani, nil sapitis fidei,/ Cur tantum veteres habitarent rura poetae.* The peasant laments the foulness of the weather and the failure of his crops, but his religious behaviour is such that it is no wonder he meets with disaster. His visits to the temple are rare, and he stays outside while the priest celebrates the mysteries; he gossips, jokes and fidgets; he considers it shameful to go to the temple on an empty stomach.[45] How much is there here of social observation, and how much of literary convention, gratifying to a certain social stratum?

Can we go so far as to suggest that actual contempt for the rustic, and a marked sense of distance from him, was a hallmark of the élite and the cultural mode of its expression an outgrowth from an élite

[41] Jones p 225.

[42] *Ad fratrem Ludovicum de ordinis nostri forma et propagatione,* ed R. Arbesmann, *Analecta Augustiniana,* 28 (Rome 1695) pp 186–218.

[43] *Ibid* pp 217–18.

[44] For Vegio's life and works see basically L. Raffaele, *Maffeo Vegio: elenco delle opere, scritti inediti* (Bologna 1909).

[45] *Carmina illustrium poetarum italorum,* ed G. G. Bottari, 11 vols (Florence 1719–26) 10, pp 318–20; also quoted by Raffaele pp 9–11.

classical tradition? Insofar as the humanists can be regarded as a group or as the collective mouthpiece of a group, there can be little doubt that they spoke for the urban patriciate and put their classicising talents at its service. A Sercambi or a Luca Dominici, while eagerly deferential to the best people and linked to them by partisan loyalties, did not occupy the same social or cultural stratum. Furthermore, as we have seen, in 1399 they were writing in praise and not in censure of the *bianchi*. The context would not have called for expressions of disdain. The chief value of these chronicles is not, therefore, that they enable us to argue, rashly and *ex silentio*, that their authors did not feel any sense of superiority as townsmen to their rural coevals. It is rather that they shed a spontaneous light on the relationship between town and country. The circumstances, in the summer of 1399, were unusual, but the relationships thus revealed were not, one feels, suddenly and artifically transformed, merely heightened and brought under the temporary scrutiny of history. If we are left with an impression of the fluidity and imprecision of these relationships, it is likely that we have gained rather than lost in our appreciation of the historical reality.

University of London
King's College

THE TOWN IN CHURCH HISTORY: GENERAL PRESUPPOSITIONS OF THE REFORMATION IN GERMANY

by BERND MOELLER

'THE German Reformation was an urban event.'—so A. G. Dickens wrote in his valuable and instructive book *The German nation and Martin Luther* (1974). In some directions this judgment may need qualification; nevertheless, it contains an essential element of truth. On any reckoning, put in a negative form, its truth is undeniable: the occurrence and the success of the reformation in Germany are inconceivable except in terms of the importance, and of the specific form, which urban life had attained in Germany at the end of the middle ages. No towns, no reformation; of this assertion we may be certain.

What, however, does this mean exactly and in detail? It is easy to understand why observations of this kind should fascinate so many of us nowadays. The encounter and the reciprocal inter-action of the two social entities, town and church, is a theme which has gripped me for a long time and engaged my attention particularly in relation to the study of the reformation. More generally, it has become one of the crucial questions in contemporary historical research concerned with the social presuppositions and the social effects of intellectual and religious developments.

I should like in this paper to elucidate the problem from the points of view of ecclesiastical history. That is to say, I shall try to see how the powerful attraction is to be understood, from the point of view of the church's history as a whole, which the reformation exercised on German towns and the strong influence of the urban environment in shaping the reformation. For this reason I shall take a very broad view. The theme of town and church is an ancient one, reaching back into the period of Christian origins. Seen in terms of ecclesiastical history, I think town and church form a conceptual pair.

For an understanding of this, it will be useful to begin with a glance

The generous assistance of the Goethe Institute Manchester, German Cultural Institute for Northern England, in the publication of this paper is gratefully acknowledged.

at the famous chapter on 'The town' in the posthumously published work *Wirtschaft und Gesellschaft* (1922) of the great sociologist and social historian Max Weber. Here we are given a systematic, and, we may say, classic portrayal of the distinctive qualities of this social structure. The town appears here as one of Weber's 'ideal types', as a specific form of association which came into being and developed in the European cultural milieu in antiquity as well as in the middle ages, in accordance with analogous laws of development. Here in the west the town, this distinctive structure, home of commerce and industry, became a *community*. It strove for autonomy, for 'liberty': its own law and jurisdiction, political independence and self-determination. Externally it closed itself off with walls and towers. It had the character of an association; that is to say, the communal relationships of the townsmen were organised. Both in antiquity and the middle ages, the town was an association constituted by a compact, in virtue of which the individual became incorporated into the community of the citizens by an oath or some other form of obligation. As a consequence he obtained privileges and incurred burdens. The corporation acted collectively. All this distinguished these ancient towns sharply from towns in other parts of the world: Weber spoke of the oriental type of town (*die orientalische Stadt*) and distinguished them from the towns familiar to us—groupings of men brought together more or less accidentally and living together more or less without communal obligations. This difference rests essentially on the different conditions of existence. For these ancient towns were—even though they fulfilled an essential function in contemporary society—special constructs, even, at times, foreign bodies. They were the natural places for money and for wealth, and the centres of culture. But they were also, in diverse ways and many circumstances, exposed to special threats: of fire and epidemic, of siege and conquest. In relation to the outside world exposed to perpetual danger, they were driven to relying on their internal cohesiveness. Their communal life was therefore buttressed by well thought-out and defined regulations, early constitutions, specific expressions of a communal morality and a distinctive form of religiosity. Towns, ancient and medieval, pre-Christian and Christian, had their own saints and special cults devoted to them. In the sphere of religion, as in other spheres, towns regarded themselves as special forms of association. Individual townsmen were required to enter into communal religious relationships. They prayed and sacrificed together, communal religious and moral attitudes were fostered. Towns were sacral communities and they were conscious—emphatically so—of being distinct as such not only from the world around them, but also from the generally current forms of religious life.

So much for Max Weber's socio-historical image. It is now over fifty years old, and no longer thought to be in all respects acceptable. The problem, for instance, of the relationship of town to country seems to us more complicated; and Weber's thesis seems more applicable, in the ancient world, to the Greek *polis* than to the Roman *civitas*. Nevertheless, taken as a whole that thesis still has much relevance for a modern observer and may still be instructive, especially for the church historian. We must note that Christianity was established and grew primarily—one is tempted to say exclusively—within an urban setting. At least from the moment that Christianity passed from a mode of existence, whose shape we are scarcely able to discern, of a charismatic movement of itinerant preachers in Palestine into the world of Hellenistic culture and from an Aramaic into a Greek-speaking world, its setting was urban. The main lines of the early church's development within the Roman empire, those we can discern and which lead towards the future, lie within an urban setting, that of the Hellenistic *polis*. St Paul's letters are directed to urban communities; early Christianity had its missionary achievements and became a mass-movement almost exclusively in towns. Christianity was attractive to towns, and towns were attractive to Christianity.

I will not here enter into the difficult questions about the reasons for this, but I will consider its consequences. The church's entry into the ancient *polis* and its settling there seems to be one of the conditions of the universal success and status achieved by Christianity. Epigrammatically we might say that it was in the cities that the cult of Jesus became a world-religion. For the towns were the centres of culture in antiquity, and Christianity was drawn into the culture of antiquity through finding its place in them and in becoming an urban phenomenon. In this way its spiritual energies were stimulated, and, in the end, it formed the structure which received and fostered ancient culture and assisted its further development. Christian theology—that is to say, the encounter of Christian beliefs with ancient philosophy and their clarification by this means—grew in the soil of the *polis* and linked intimately with it. Similarly, the church's administrative structure crystallised in antiquity around the towns. The bishop, who soon became the most important ecclesiastical official, was in antiquity something like the city-parish priest, much as he still is in Italy today. He had not yet become the superior of an ecclesiastical province as we later see him. Again, the offices of the presbyter and the deacon were from early on given an urban imprint. Scarcely any provision was made for the countryside; for the early church it hardly existed.

Let us now, leaping across the centuries, pass over the age of the collapse of the *polis* in late antiquity, over the beginnings of the expansion of Christianity from the town into the countryside in many areas of the empire, and turn our gaze on the western middle ages. That was the time when, if I may again speak in a somewhat epigrammatic manner, western Christendom took notice of the countryside, when, indeed, it received a rural mould and became countryfied. As is well known, from the point of view of the social historian the great divide between antiquity and middle ages lies here: in contrast with antiquity, medieval society was an agrarian one. Industrial production and money economy, long-distance trade and large-scale political organisation had collapsed, and with them, by and large, antique urban life vanished where it had once existed and was altogether absent in the lands newly brought into the orbit of western Christendom. The church became the vital link and the most crucial element in the continuity between antiquity and middle ages. It was, however, able to take on this role only because it was able to accommodate itself to the new conditions. The transformation had obvious consequences for church government: the bishop now became what he has remained ever since, the official in charge of an ecclesiastical circumscription; the priesthood in its modern sense was created, that is, the priest as charged with the pastoral care of Christians within a defined area of land. Here we have the 'parochial system'. Here lies the origin of a stratification among ecclesiastics which corresponds to the social stratification of feudal society. The medieval church became a church of the nobility (*Adelskirche*). The higher echelons of the hierarchy remained reserved for the aristocracy. Eventually the old monasteries came to occupy an important place, and to play an important part, within the ecclesiastical structure, as centres of devotion and piety, centres of aristocratic representation and at the same time places where an assurance of salvation was available. They replaced the towns as centres of ecclesiastical culture and education.

It was not only ecclesiastical administration, however, but the whole distinctive mentality of medieval Christendom, indeed medieval religion as a whole, that was decisively re-shaped by these changed social conditions. Medieval culture became what Curtius called a 'daughter-culture' of antiquity, with an overwhelmingly backward-looking historical self-awareness. This should be brought into relation with the fact that towns were ceasing to be centres of intellectual commerce, or were altogether lacking. Life was determined by an economy dominated by the rhythms of sowing and reaping rather than those of making; the cycles of nature rather than the future-oriented effort of producing provided the basic data of experience. We should see in this context the manifold nature-cults which found room within Christendom: the cults of holy places and holy objects, the prevalence of pilgrimages and processions, the cults of saints and relics. The varied expressions of the presence of God which moved into the centre of the church's activity and the piety of the faithful all belong to this setting: the crucial importance of the eucharist and the other sacraments for the spiritual life and the historical self-awareness of the middle ages; the increasing remoteness of the *Heilsgeschichte* which was a feature not only of popular piety but also made its mark on scholastic theology and on mysticism.

If my view is right, the emergence of a new urban life, originally in Italy from the tenth century and observable in northern Europe from the eleventh, brought about little or no specific change in the church thus articulated within the framework of a rural and feudally structured society. Now once more larger accumulations of people engaged in production and in more far-flung trading activity came into being. In these communes the arrangements and the notions of feudal society lost, in part, their hold. Their place was taken by constitutions based on communitarian conceptions; forms of living were renewed which had existed long ago, institutions of a venerated antiquity which had left their imprint on Christianity and on the church. This change, however, hardly entered the consciousness of the church in the central middle ages and exerted no influence either on its organisation or on its thought. In the earlier middle ages the church had been able to form the ideal of the Christian prince and of the Christian knight, that is to say, to sacralise, and in a sense, to Christianise, the main functions of feudal society. The new townsmen, however, did not receive a similar respectability. There was no idealisation, at any rate no clear idealisation, of Christian citizenship; and the profession of the leading form of urban society, commercial activity, remained more or less dubious in the light of the moral judgment of the church. So far as ecclesiastical administration is concerned nothing essential to the position of the bishop and the clergy was changed by the urban development. The bishops remained landowners, higher ecclesiastical office remained an aristocratic monopoly, monasteries remained rural. The parochial system was simply transplanted into the towns. Instead of boundary-lines, streets divided the parishes—as they still do; only rarely does one find any effort being made to devise any systematic urban ecclesiastical administration, and when one does, it is never based on theoretical considerations taking account of the characteristic features of the new social forms. In other words: the urban church of the central and later middle ages was not very well suited to the conditions and demands of the new social category of the town. The church provided urban saints and urban sanctuaries; but these, though they served as means of defining a communal identity, were no substitute for the provision of specific forms of pastoral care for the citizens. The holders of ecclesiastical office remained everywhere more or less clearly outside the body of the citizens. They were remote and alien to it, indeed, sometimes, hostile.

To be sure, this picture lost its clarity in the course of time. Since the thirteenth century there were types of ecclesiastical institution and of personnel which corresponded better with urban needs than did the established hierarchy. Such were the mendicant orders, the friars, and their convents. They had arisen during this period of vast urban expansion and they developed a characteristically urban orientation. Looked at from the point of view of the church's history, I think the reform movement which, in the early thirteenth century produced the Franciscans and the Dominicans, may be seen as the church's response to the rise of the new towns.

In some ways this had been anticipated by the dissenting movements of the twelfth century, especially those devoted to the cult of evangelical poverty. They were the predecessors of the mendicants and, if rightly seen, were based on the towns. Valdès, the father of the Waldensians, was a burgher of Lyon; the centre of gravity of the Waldensians lay in Northern Italy, the region at this time furthest advanced in urban development. What the Waldensians were in rebellion against was, primarily, the things which were distinctive of the feudal church: the importance given to wealth, authority and power in the church, the prominence given to the sacraments, the eclipse of the bible and the consciousness of the historical origins of

Christianity. In contrast to those of the older orders, the convents of the mendicants were established almost exclusively in towns. Current French research in urban history tends to go so far as to consider the existence of a mendicant convent in a place as justifying a claim for that place being considered a town. With their renunciation of property, their freely embraced poverty and their insistence on equality among the brethren, the friars offered the civic community a clear and relevant pattern of piety. Their readiness to become integrated in the civic community distinguished them from the parish clergy. Mendicant convents were conceived and used as communal property and they offered the citizens pastoral care in forms appropriate to the internal ordering of the commune. They preached to the whole town and administered penance and burial without respect for parish boundaries.

It is obviously not a matter for surprise that endless disputes arose in late medieval towns over the pastoral rights of the mendicants. Parish clergy and friars, as well as friars of different orders among themselves, quarrelled inconclusively for two hundred and fifty years over the question whether citizens had the right to withdraw from the ministry of the parochial clergy. What was at stake in this was, first and foremost, money: dues payable to the church, endowments and legacies. To go into too great detail would be wearisome—the upshot of the matter is clear enough: even with the mendicant orders the church did not succeed in establishing a harmonious pastoral ministry for the civic community.

All in all, urban ecclesiastical history in the later middle ages is a history of tensions. This is linked with the fact, sketched out earlier in this paper, that towns had the character of associations. This involved a certain exclusiveness of the citizen body and its striving to embrace within itself all the town's inhabitants. Thus a kind of conflict with the church's universality was generated. There was something intrinsically separatist about the communal movement. There was constant quarrelling in town councils about the bishops' right to intervene, about the rights of patronage, and thus about authority over parishes and parish clergy and about the extension or restriction of ecclesiastical jurisdiction. Corporations and councils tried to guard against attempts by the clergy to separate itself from the laity by claiming privileges such as immunity from taxes, jurisdiction and civic obligations. Town councils tried to control the administration of ecclesiastical and monastic property and to take over ecclesiastical functions which had civic consequences, such as schooling, provision for the poor and the sick, oversight of social morality.

But we should not misunderstand these attitudes and actions. There was no question of anti-clericalism or secularisation in anything like a modern sense. Hardly anybody doubted the efficacy of the church and the sacraments in mediating saving grace and the absolute necessity for them. Urban church history during the later middle ages, therefore, was marked by enormous works of pious benefaction and huge material support by the citizens for grandiose church-building, foundations, legacies. What was at stake was certainly not the saving power of church and priesthood, but their separateness. In our context we may sum it up in one phrase: their alienation from the town. The towns in the middle ages became increasingly what they had been in antiquity: centres of education and culture. The schools of the period, the universities, from the fifteenth century the printers, almost all who could read and write, authors and their public, lived in towns. The old rural monasteries were by-passed and the towns took their place as centres of education.

It was also in the towns that new ideas were conceived. It is true, I have some difficulties in fitting Wyclif and John Hus into the picture; but the *devotio moderna*, which laid the stress on personal piety as against sacrament and cult, had its centre in one of Europe's most urbanised areas, the Netherlands. Renaissance and humanism, the spread of a new vision of life also grew and flourished in an urban setting—Europe's other great area of urbanism, northern Italy. And as the most important elements of this development spread into the rest of Europe, France, England, the Netherlands and Germany, it was again urban societies, sodalities of educated townsmen, that provided the greater part of both the actors and the audience.

The social and intellectual élites to whom the ideas and attitudes of humanism appealed had no secularist or pagan inclinations. The humanists had no wish to shake the Christian foundations of western civilisation. On the contrary: genuine and powerful theological forces were given a new momentum. Lay tendencies did, however, come to the fore: active humanists were generally lay people. The humanist movement was, at least in Germany, fairly easily and simply integrated into urban life and took part in the polarisation of citizens against clergy and hierarchy which we have noted above. Concern about personal Christian conduct, about conscience, and serious attention to Christian moral teaching could be directed against the ecclesiastical system. Communal and humanistic attitudes could come together and reinforce each other; moral and intellectual arguments directed against the clergy again came into play. Here and there relations between clergy and laity came to be reversed: ecclesiastics, who in the earlier middle ages had been the guardians of education and culture, could now appear as uneducated and boorish—which is just what many of them were—in the eyes of men soaked in humanist culture.

Now I want, at last, to bring the reformation into closer focus. It will be evident that a fairly simple conclusion emerges naturally. The reformation in Germany, being substantially an urban movement, was also part of a centuries-old tradition. It could profit from centuries of disappointed expectations and disenchantment. Let this not be misunderstood, however: Luther's theological discovery which launched the movement was an event to which the social structure of the early sixteenth century town is hardly relevant. Moreover, movements such as the knights' rebellion and the peasants' revolt, though doubtless related to Luther's impact on the ecclesiastical and social order of the middle ages, were scarcely urban in character. If one asks what the most important result of the age of the reformation was for the political history of Germany, one would scarcely point to the evolution of urban life. Rather, it was the principality, the 'early modern state', that profited from the reform. We may say that Luther's initiative, his rejection of justification by works and the social consequence of that rejection, and his recovery of the church's original witness to Christ, had the unique power to touch all the social tensions of the time, to draw them into its orbit to transform them. This had an 'electrifying effect' (Oberman): all the tensions and conflicts of the age, between emperor and empire, princes and nobles, regions and towns, peasants and landlords, rich and poor, were touched by the new message. So were the tensions which lay within the cities and those within the church.

And yet, in a certain sense our slogan 'No towns, no reformation' remains true. The German towns were the social space in which the impulses originating from Luther were particularly felt and taken up. Above all, it was in the towns that Luther found the 'publicity' which gave him fame. Here it was that his cause became a mass movement. Far and away the greater part of the towns in the area of German-speaking Europe from Emden to Villach, from Reval to

Berne, fell under the spell of the reformation, either in passing or permanently. This holds above all for the greater communes with the power to determine their own destinies. Many and varied features of this development indicate that it was determined by the will of the majority of the townsmen and expressed their aspirations. And there was something even more significant: it was also in the towns that Luther found like-minded allies, who understood him and turned his cause into a comprehensive religious, intellectual and political movement; who, in short, made the 'reformation'. Luther's cause became the reformation in the towns.

To be sure, as we shall see more precisely, there were certain distortions and misunderstandings of Luther's original intentions. But compared with the deformations and misunderstandings by men such as Franz von Sickingen, or Thomas Münzer, and in the peasants' twelve articles, or in the ecclesiastical regime of the principalities, the urban reform movement presents a relatively unified picture. In such a comparison Zwingli and Bucer, Lazarus Spengler and Jakob Sturm, Jürgen Wullenwever and John Calvin must be reckoned genuine Lutherans.

In view of what I have said it should not be difficult to understand this development. Into it flowed everything that was virulent in the urban critique of the church. It came to comprise all the resistance—as we may now put it in shorthand form—to the shackling of the medieval church to the feudal order, and the difficulties of the church in creating forms of pastoral care appropriate to the social structure of the town, able to cater for its intellectual and spiritual needs. It is no accident that among Luther's adherents in the ranks of the urban clergy—which played a principal part in the spreading of his cause—the ordinary parochial clergy had, so far as I can see, relatively little importance. It was the friars and the so-called 'preachers' of the town churches who stood in the front ranks. These were the men who held benefices related to the whole citizen body, and for them a certain measure of education was a necessary qualification; preachers, *Prädikanten*, existed especially in Thuringia, Württemberg, upper Swabia and Switzerland. Moreover, the reformation wove into one skein all the various strands of urban ecclesiastical politics which had taken shape in the later middle ages, the attempt to gain control of and authority over ecclesiastical institutions and persons within the perimeter of the town and in accord with the communal unifications of all functions. Finally, Luther's polemic against immoral clergy and stupid monks found a peculiarly sympathetic audience in the towns.

In a sense, however, all this is external and formal. What is more important for us here are the urban conditions which were favourable to the content of Luther's teaching. In my view the crucial fact in this connection is that towns were the centres of education and culture, the places where people read and wrote and where there were books to be had. Luther's ideas were spread predominantly with the aid of the new printed book. The strongly flowing tide was reinforced by the suddenly swelling production of books in the German language. In response to the demand, within a very short time, they swamped the market: by the end of the year 1520 there was probably a copy of a work of Luther's for every German who could read; by the end of 1525 there was a copy of Luther's bible for a quarter or a third of all literate Germans. The number of copies of the writings of other protagonists of the reform must be counted in millions. All these books were produced in the towns, and most of them had their direct impact in the towns. A property of this new medium, the book, was its ability to transmit ideas in a relatively faithful and unadulterated form. Their author, thus, received a voice which could broadcast his words in a way not hitherto imaginable: a considerable difference between Luther's reform and the reform movements of, for example, Wyclif and Hus.

Finally we must note that the core of Luther's teaching contained elements which, beyond their relevance to the fundamentals of human living, could be especially illuminating and powerful for townsmen. Here it seems to me particularly important that the medieval dichotomy between clergy and laity was exposed to a penetrating attack which sprang from a fundamental belief: Luther's teaching on the 'priesthood of all believers'. This offered a new and apparently decisive argument in support of the old efforts to integrate the urban community and to do away with the clergy's privileged position. Moreover, townsmen's minds were peculiarly well attuned to Luther's preaching on the spiritual responsibility of the individual Christian, to his description of the spiritual relationship with God as a personal matter, and to his insistence on charity as the measure of man's correct posture in the world. And finally, it seems to me, it must have been clear to urban communities that the eucharist and the other sacraments were displaced from their central position in the church's life and its thought about salvation. With them had to vanish all nature-religion and cult of things and places. These elements of medieval religiosity had to yield the central place to preaching, faith and history. Some original themes of Christian belief were thus recovered.

All this could be clarified and elaborated in detail; but I will confine myself, finally, to a single point: these were the aspects and themes of reformation preaching which were given the highest relief and farthest development in the towns, and not only by Luther himself, who was a university professor in the first place and townsman in the second. I have in mind the theological teaching of the more 'urban' reformers in the strict sense, Zwingli, Bucer, Calvin and others, who took their point of departure from Luther precisely in laying all the stress on renewal of life through faith. They presented the ethics of the gospel as the ethics of a community and almost by-passed the sacraments as means of salvation. In all sorts of ways humanistic and urban themes were interwoven in such teaching. Corresponding forms of church-order were devised, all thought out and worked out on communal lines and converging on a unified urban church-order, with lay offices, synodal government, merging of the ecclesial and the civic communities.

Here I want to break off, without pursuing the problem of 'the town in church history' any further, into realms where the lines are less clear. At the close of the age of the reformation around the middle of the sixteenth century this problem took on a different dimension. This was the result of the fact that urban life was once more to fall away from its new state. The self-awareness and self-determination of the communes—not least in Germany—were in many ways restricted during the age of absolutism. Wealth moved out of cities and cities, specifically as civic communities, ceased to draw learning and culture to themselves. The boundaries of town and countryside became blurred. As a result protestantism did not become, in its further development, as did the ancient church, a specifically urban expression of Christianity. Least of all German protestantism: 'the pathos of freedom' which, according to Heimpel, originated in the reformation and received its religious basis in it, was to determine the political history of modern Germany far less than that of western Europe. That is to say, it came into its own far more in the lands where protestantism was introduced not through Luther but through Calvin and his urban reformation.

University of Göttingen

PAROCHIAL STRUCTURE AND THE DISSEMINATION OF PROTESTANTISM IN SIXTEENTH CENTURY ENGLAND: A TALE OF TWO CITIES

by CLAIRE CROSS

WHEN, after the abrupt changes in religion in the reigns of Henry VIII, Edward VI and Mary, Elizabethan protestants set about consolidating the protestant reformation they looked upon towns as one of the chief agencies for the conversion of the countryside. From the first moment of his appointment as lord president of the council in the north in 1572 that enthusiastic layman, the third earl of Huntingdon, made this assumption a guiding principle of his governorship. 'I do all I can to get good preachers planted in the market towns of this country', he told William Chaderton, bishop of Chester in 1584, adding with a characteristic note of realism, 'in which somewhat is already done, but much remaineth to be done.' Huntingdon's close associate and fellow worker in the north, archbishop Grindal, had earlier informed the queen in similar terms that 'the continual preaching of God's word in Halifax' in the 1560s had been responsible for the town's stalwart loyalty to the crown during the Rebellion of the Earls.[1] Yet both Grindal and Huntingdon knew very well from personal experience that towns in general and northern towns in particular had not by any means all accorded an automatic or unqualified welcome to protestantism. A comparison between York and Hull demonstrates forcefully how two towns in close geographical proximity could differ very considerably in their initial acceptance of protestantism and in the readiness of their ruling élites to further the propagation of protestant doctrines among the townspeople at large.[2] It also seems from the examples

[1] Cambridge University Library Add MS 17 fol 44; *The Remains of Edmund Grindal,* ed W. Nicholson, PS (1843) p 380.

[2] These generalisations on lay attitudes to religion are based on a study of some five hundred wills of Hull inhabitants made between 1520 and 1585 and registered in the probate registers now in the Bor[thwick] I[nstitute of] H[istorical] R[esearch, York], and on a sample of just over two hundred York wills proved in the York Dean and Chapter Court between 1530 and 1638, together with the wills of all York aldermen who held the office of mayor during the same period. The preambles of all York wills

of York and Hull that the structure of organised religion in the two towns, especially their parochial organisation, materially contributed in the one case to delaying, in the other to accelerating the whole-hearted commitment of influential sectors of the laity to the protestant cause.

Immediately before the reformation York, the ecclesiastical centre of the northern province, could without exaggeration be regarded as a church-dominated city, and the relatively recent decline in population to around eight thousand had served to accentuate this clerical ascendancy even more sharply. The minster with its archbishop, dean, thirty-six prebendaries, vicars choral, chantry priests and other staff constituted a quite separate ecclesiastical corporation within the walls: just outside stood the very rich Benedictine monastery of St Mary and elsewhere within the city there survived in differing degrees of vigour two much smaller Benedictine houses, a Gilbertine priory, a cell of Whitby abbey together with the important houses of the still popular four orders of friars. In addition to numerous maisons dieu, in St Leonard's the city also possessed one of the most lavishly endowed hospitals in the north of England. Yet what seems to have meant more to the citizens, to judge from expressions in their wills, than all these great religious institutions was the multiplicity of humble parish churches, about fifty at the beginning of the sixteenth century reduced to twenty-three by its end. Before the break with Rome York seems to have been affording a living to something in excess of six hundred regular and secular priests, and in the final analysis this abundance of clergy, the vast majority of whom proved not to be interested in religious reform, must have played a major part in perpetuating the city's religious conservatism.[3]

The contrast in formal ecclesiastical provision between York and Hull could scarcely have been more dramatic. Whereas the high number of tiny parishes indicated the very antiquity of York's development as a city, the paucity of religious institutions in Hull supplied evidence of its origins as a new town in the high middle ages. First planted by the abbey of Meaux in the late twelfth century

made between 1538 and 1553 have been analysed and tabulated in [D. M.] Palliser, *The Reformation in York [1534–1553]*, *Bor[thwick] P[aper]* 40, (York 1971). The spelling of all quotations has been modernised.

[3] Palliser, *The Reformation in York*, pp 1–4; Palliser, 'The Unions of Parishes in York 1547–1586', *YAJ* 46 (1974) pp 87–102; R. B. Dobson, 'The Foundation of Perpetual Chantries by the Citizens of York', *SCH*, 4 (1964) pp 22–38.

as an outlet for its woolcrop and that of other Yorkshire sheep farmers, Wyke upon Hull had become Kingston upon Hull in 1293 on its acquisition by Edward I. Although under royal patronage the town had grown rapidly into a thriving port in the high middle ages, it still in the sixteenth century had not gained formal ecclesiastical independence. Its main parish, Holy Trinity, continued as a chapelry of the much older settlement of Hessle, while its only other parish, St Mary's, in a similar way remained a dependency of North Ferriby. Only two orders of friars, the Dominicans and the Carmelites, had established themselves in Hull. The town's one monastery, the Charterhouse, had been founded outside its gates in 1378. Historians of Hull have been singularly reluctant to hazard a guess at its population, (and have only gone so far as to estimate that it may have approached six thousand in the mid seventeenth century) but it seems reasonable to propose that Hull at the very least was half, if not two thirds, the size of York in the sixteenth century. Because of its relative shortage of clergy, already in the medieval period richer inhabitants of Hull to a far greater extent than those in York had taken to self-help in order to secure adequate priestly ministrations. They had set up a series of chantries in Holy Trinity church, and by the early fifteenth century the twelve chantry priests there had formed a fraternity called 'the priests of the table'. Yet even when these twelve seculars are added to the numbers of friars and Carthusians the total of priests in Hull in the earlier part of the reign of Henry VIII can hardly have amounted to fifty compared with York's six hundred.[4]

On the whole the inhabitants of York and Hull seem to have lived in a state of religious quiescence in the early sixteenth century, though occasional cases of heresy occurred in both towns a little before the official Henrician reformation. In 1528 in York a 'Dutchman', named Johnson, appeared in the consistory court charged with denying the efficacy of prayers for the dead, confession to a priest and other practices of the church, but Johnson and the two sacramentarians, Valentine Freese and his wife, burnt for heresy on the Knavesmire some twelve years later, were all foreigners and their ideas seem to have had no lasting effect upon the natives of York. Perhaps more significantly, in Hull, again in 1528, Robert Robinson, a mariner, had been regaling his acquaintances with details of a Lutheran service he and other sailors had witnessed in Bremen: one member of his

[4] *VCH, York, the East Riding,* I (1969) pp 1–15, 76, 157, 287–92.

party in addition had obtained a copy of Tyndale's contraband translation of the new testament.[5] These seem, however, to have been very isolated incidents, and the general impression to emerge from a study of the wills of the inhabitants of both towns is one of contentment with late medieval religion. Most townspeople rich enough to do so asked for masses to be said for their souls after death. In 1530 in York Thomas Cookman of St Michael-le-Belfrey still felt it worthwhile to create an annual obit in St Lawrence's church; six years later his much more affluent fellow parishioner, Robert Fone, as well as ordering a most elaborate funeral to be attended by the priests of the important Corpus Christi guild, left bequests to St Mary's abbey and to the convent of Shap and hired a priest to sing for his soul for a year in the minster.[6] The sympathies of the more prosperous inhabitants of Hull inclined in exactly the same direction. The merchant, Thomas Huntingdon, who in 1527 wished to be buried in the north aisle of Holy Trinity near where he used to sit, founded obits at Pontefract and Hull and gave money for masses at the houses of the Dominicans and Carmelites: in 1527 also John Cokett sought burial in the Charterhouse at the same time arranging for a priest to pray for his soul for a year in his parish church of Holy Trinity. Others made donations to the fund for building the steeple and to other church works, requested a funeral with all the priests of the table and, in the case of alderman Robert Parker, stipulated that the priest chosen to pray for his soul for two years should be one who could sing and read well and so be in a position to assist in other services in the parish church.[7]

Despite their apparent satisfaction with the condition of their local church the inhabitants of York and Hull accepted the reformation changes of the 1530s without open manifestations of hostility. In neither town, however, does there seem to have been much explicit protestant preaching, and this absence of protestant instruction is mirrored in the wills. Of a sample of forty wills made in York between 1538 and 1546 all the testators without exception consigned their souls either to God, the Blessed Virgin and all the holy company of heaven, (the standard preamble) or, much more rarely, to God, asking the Virgin and the holy company of heaven to pray for them. In

[5] [A. G.] Dickens, *Lollards and Protestants in the Diocese of York 1509–1558* (London 1959) pp 16–52.

[6] BorIHR D[ean] and C[hapter] Will Reg 2 fol 185r (Cookman), fols 174v–5v (Fone).

[7] BorIHR Prob Reg 9 fol 382v (Huntingdon), fol 391r (Cokett), fol 448v (Baxter); Prob Reg 11 pt 1 fol 134v (Sparling), fol 51v (Parker).

Hull for the same period the picture varies only very slightly: there, out of seventy-five wills a mere four testators bequeathed their souls to God alone without seeking the intercession of the Virgin and the saints.

The dissolution first of the monasteries and then, perhaps even more importantly, of the chantries affected the two towns to a very different degree. York, because of its many parishes, retained a considerable number of dispossessed clergy, and indeed the parish clergy seem actually to have been augmented as pensioned former monks, friars and chantry priests availed themselves of city livings which before the reformation had sometimes been bereft of incumbents on account of their very small endowment. These not particularly well educated local clergy seem to have insulated their parishioners against the protestant winds of change which began to emanate from the minster on the arrival of Robert Holgate as archbishop in 1545. In contrast, Hull with the disappearance of the Carthusians, the friars and the chantry priests suffered a real decline in the number of its clergy who now seem to have been reduced to two or at the most three (if the non-resident vicars are included), in each of the two parishes. In effect, the town became something of a *tabula rasa* upon which new protestant doctrines could be inscribed. During the reign of Edward VI the governor of Hull, Sir Michael Stanhope, who had close ties with Somerset and the Edwardian court, and archbishop Holgate took full advantage of the ecclesiastical vacuum in the town. Under Holgate's protection the advanced Scottish protestant, John Rough, moved south to Hull and began a mission to the townspeople which lasted until the accession of Mary.[8] Some indication of the impact of his ministry can be glimpsed from the local wills: whereas in the Edwardian period nine testators still clung to a conservative preamble, commending their souls to God, the Virgin, and all the saints, no less than twenty-eight used a non-traditional form, bequeathing their souls to God alone. In the sample of York wills for the same five and a half years twenty-four remained traditional and only two used a formula which showed any bias towards protestantism.

The catholic restoration under Mary revealed further divergencies between the two towns. In York in the previous reign alongside two vicars choral and several (non-resident) prebendaries a mere two of the very many parish incumbents, Robert Cragges and Ralph Whiting, had availed themselves of the freedom to marry: in Hull a much higher

[8] *VCH York, the East Riding*, I, pp 90–4.

proportion of the parish clergy had ventured upon matrimony. Two, William Harland, an ex-regular, and William Utley, curate of St Mary's, agreed under pressure to set their wives aside, but a third, William Harper, chose to resign from the priesthood rather than be separated from his wife. A little evidence also exists for lay antipathy towards the re-imposition of catholicism in Hull. In Utley's church an attack took place on the reserved sacrament, although the ecclesiastical authorities never succeeded in apprehending the offenders. One alderman, Jobson, provoked comment by allying with the opposition to Mary in parliament, and there seems to have been some substance in the allegations a Hull merchant, William Flynton, brought before the council in the north to the intent that the mayor, the corporation and other townsmen were deliberately obstructing the government's policy.[9] While thirteen wills drawn up in Hull between the queen's accession and her death reverted to the traditional form of preamble, two seem to have used a protestant formula and no less than thirty-nine employed a neutral expression leaving the soul to 'God Almighty, to be accompanied with all his holy saints in heaven'. This phraseology does not appear at all among York wills which in the sample of thirteen with three exceptions returned to the full catholic preamble.

Although the royal visitation of 1559 resulted in much disruption at the minster when about half of the prebendaries were deprived for their refusal to conform to the religious settlement and replaced with committed protestants, it left the York civic clergy virtually untouched: the one city cleric, Henry More, who at first had scruples concerning the royal supremacy went on to become a conscientious protestant preaching minister.[10] Hull, on the other hand, again saw a considerably more violent reaction. Thomas Fugall, the vicar of Hessle and Hull, who had been absent, probably intentionally, from the royal visitation, lost his living two years later, having failed to clear himself of accusations of persecuting married clergy and protestant laypeople in Mary's reign. Some members of the corporation then seized the opportunity to invite Melchior Smith, already well known for his protestant opinions, to come from Boston to Hull to succeed

[9] Dickens, *The Marian Reaction in the Diocese of York: Part I, the Clergy, BorP* 11 (1957); *VCH York, the East Riding,* 1, pp 94–5.

[10] *The Royal Visitation of 1559,* ed C. J. Kitching, *SS* 187 (1975); J. C. H. Aveling, *Catholic Recusancy in the City of York 1558–1791,* Catholic Record Society, monograph series 2 (1970) pp 20–1.

him. As early as 1564 Smith was called before the high commission for not wearing vestments, an offence he repeated in 1566 at the height of the vestiarian controversy. A famous preacher, he continued as vicar of Hessle and Hull until 1591.[11]

Once more the wills of Hull townspeople confirm their growing adherence to protestantism. Of eighty-two wills proved during the first decade of Elizabeth's reign, five in the transitional year of 1559 referred to the Virgin Mary, forty were specifically protestant and the remainder neutral. The York sample yields a different and decidedly more conservative pattern: out of fourteen wills five made mention of the Virgin Mary, two were neutral, seven protestant. Even in the following decade when the balance decisively changed in York, four wills still called upon the Virgin, though seventeen were clearly protestant out of a total of twenty-eight. Of the hundred and thirty-six wills made in Hull between 1571 and 1584 almost twice as many were outspokenly protestant as were neutral.

Turning from mere numbers, which can never do more than give a very inadequate impression of changes in religious opinions, to actual statements of protestant piety, a sense of protestant commitment springs out from many Hull wills which is not nearly so prominent in the sample from York. York can produce few wills to parallel that which William Jackson of Hull wrote with his own hand as early as 1566. In a lengthy preamble he resigned his soul to 'God the Father, to God the Son, to God the Holy Ghost, three persons and one very God, having a sure and perfect faith that my soul shall ascend into heaven, and there to remain for evermore among the elect of God, by the shedding of Christ's blood, his pains and passion that he suffered for me, and all the elect of God, and by no merit or good works done by me or any other.' He then followed his confession of faith with a request to his executors to provide a funeral sermon 'if there be any preacher of God's gospel in the town at my burial.'[12] In the 1570s and onwards a whole series of wills called upon 'that immaculate lamb of God', or 'that most pure, unspotted and immaculate lamb', even upon 'the holy and precious heart blood of that immaculate lamb, our only saviour and redeemer Jesus Christ'.[13] Perhaps the sincerity of the devotion the new religion inspired among some Hull inhabitants

[11] *VCH York, the East Riding*, I pp 95–6.

[12] BorIHR Prob Reg 17 pt 2 fols 612^{v}–13^{r} (Jackson).

[13] BorIHR Prob Reg 19 pt 2 fols 729^{v}–30^{r} (Anderson); Prob Reg 21 pt 1 fol 45^{r}/^{v} (Maugham); Prob Reg 21 pt 2 fols 268^{r}–9^{r} (Dalton); Prob Reg 21 pt 1 fol 125^{r}/^{v} (Robinson) fols 125^{v}–6^{r} (Arnotson); Prob Reg 22 pt 1 fol 204^{r}/^{v} (Rand), fols 26^{r}–7^{r}

can best be gauged from the will a tailor, Henry Speed, composed in November 1577 when he was sick in body, 'but wholly sound and perfect in faith towards my God'. 'With my mouth and heart', he declared '[I] do confess my faith, and like a faithful soldier do fight under the banner of my lord Jesus Christ, who is the head and grand captain, that hath overcome hell, death and damnation for me and all mankind, and died that we might live through him. To him, therefore, I commit my soul.'[14]

Only one of these Hull wills mentioned 'Mr Smith the preacher', though there is frequent reference to Simon Pinder, 'our curate', and this suggests that Melchior Smith in fact spent little time in Hull away from Hessle.[15] The wills, however, quickly reflect the coming of the lecturer to the town. In 1560 the corporation had made overtures to pay for a preacher, but nothing resulted from this until 1573 when Grindal entered into an agreement with the corporation and the vicar for the foundation of a lectureship at Holy Trinity with the very considerable fee of £40 a year. Griffith Briskin became the first holder of the post in 1573 and remained in office until 1598. A Cambridge graduate and fellow of Trinity, Briskin was summoned several times before the high commission for nonconformity and perhaps partly on this account seems rapidly to have won the admiration of some of the leading inhabitants.[16] In 1583 Thomas Chapman, a ship's carpenter, requested 'Mr Briskin, our preacher' and Mr Stephen Prustwood to bestow 20s 'unto such as they shall think to be of the household of faith'. Frequently from about 1580 townspeople left gifts to Briskin, often on the understanding that he would preach their funeral sermon: Thomas Chapman's wealthy brother, James, even bequeathed his 'friend, Mr Briskin' a tenement in Hull, providing at the same time for a substantial course of sermons to be delivered in the town of Whitby and its hinterland not yet blessed with the evangelical preaching Hull enjoyed.[17]

(Stotte), fol 123^{v} (Prattie), fol 193^{r}/^{v} (Waghen), fols 88^{v}–9^{r} (Webster); Prob Reg 22 pt 2 fols 360^{r}–1^{v} (Chapman); Prob Reg 23 pt 1 fol 239^{r}–40^{r} (Clarkson).

[14] BorIHR Prob Reg 21 pt 1 fol 90^{v} (Speed).

[15] BorIHR Prob Reg 17 pt 1 fol 142^{r} (Alrede).

[16] [R. A.] Marchant, *The Puritans and the Church Courts* [*in the Diocese of York 1560–1642*], (London 1960) p 234.

[17] BorIHR Prob Reg 22 pt 2 fol 414^{r}/^{v} (T. Chapman); Prob Reg 22 pt 1 fol 147^{r}/^{v} (Foxley), fols 241^{v}–2^{r} (Lodge), fol 253^{r} (Best); Prob Reg 22 pt 2 fols 360^{r}–1^{v} (J. Chapman), fols 479^{r}–80^{v} (Empson); Prob Reg 23 pt 1 fols 239^{r}–40^{r} (Clarkson).

Parochial structure and the dissemination of protestantism

While the preambles of some York wills in the first half of Elizabeth's reign show a definite commitment to protestantism, not one testator in the sample studied laid out money for protestant preaching. The York civic authorities seem to have been more than content to leave sermons to the discretion of the minster dignitaries while they themselves continued to frequent their parish churches served by clergy unfitted to preach. Catholicism lingered in aldermanic circles well into the 1580s and in the previous decade one or two mayors had been rumoured to be protecting catholic recusants. To remedy what to him appeared a scandalous state of affairs, the earl of Huntingdon tried to persuade the corporation to assume more responsibility for civic religion, a responsibility which by force of circumstances the chief inhabitants of Hull had shouldered years before. In 1579 he wrote to the mayor and corporation suggesting that they should create the office of town preacher. A reply came promptly back that York ought not to be equated with Newcastle or Hull which did not have a cathedral or bishop, or preachers unless they themselves set them up. The city fathers would willingly go to the minster to hear sermons, but they did not think it necessary to be at further charges to pay for a preacher. Undeterred by this lack of enthusiasm, Huntingdon persisted in his undertaking, and in 1580 the corporation gave way. After an unsuccessful nomination, in 1585 Richard Harwood accepted the post of city lecturer, and as Briskin had earlier done in Hull, gradually attracted the active support of some of the leading citizens.[18] In 1597 Robert Askwith, a former mayor, led the way and commissioned Harwood to deliver his funeral sermon; two years later one of his colleagues, Christopher Beckwith, did the same.[19] In the early seventeenth century the city governors for the first time began to give indications of a yet more positive allegiance to protestantism by taking measures to improve the income of their local clergy in order to obtain a preaching ministry in the city parishes, a movement which developed further in the 1630s in opposition to the Laudian regime at the minster.[20] By the accession of

[18] York City Library Housebook 1577–80 fols 189, 230; Housebook 1580–5 fol 184.

[19] BorIHR Prob Reg 27 pt 1 fol 25^{r}/^{v} (Askwith); Prob Reg 27 pt 2 fol 722^{r}/^{v} (Beckwith)

[20] BorIHR Prob Reg 34 pt 1 fols 170^{v}–2^{r} (Robinson); Prob Reg 36 pt 1 fols 115^{r}–16^{v} (Hall); Prob Reg 38 pt 1 fols 238^{v}–40^{r}, (Moseley); Prob Reg 39 pt 2 fols 533^{v}–4^{r} (Robinson); Prob Reg 41 pt 1 fols 447^{v}–9^{v} (Agar); Prob Reg 42 pt 1 fols 109^{r}–10^{v} (Micklethwaite); Prob Reg 42 pt 2 fols 375^{v}–6^{r} (Greenbury); Marchant, *The Puritans and the Church Courts*, pp 52–106.

Charles I members of York corporation were revealing the sort of positive preference for protestantism which a sizeable minority of Hull inhabitants had displayed from at least the beginning of Elizabeth's reign.

Very different factors influenced the speed of the adoption of protestantism in York and Hull in the sixteenth century. The reason most commonly adduced for the rapid reception of protestantism in Hull, its commercial connections with the continent, does not seem to be of compelling force in this context since York merchants had almost as close trading links with foreign protestant states as their Hull counterparts. The explanation for the divergent attitudes to protestantism seems to lie rather in the formal ecclesiastical structure of the towns. Even in the late medieval period some Hull townsmen had attempted to improve the inadequate supply of priests caused largely by the dependent status of the two town parishes. Benefiting from their numerous (though ill-endowed) parishes, York citizens had not needed to take such vigorous action. Only after they had been persuaded to found a civic lectureship, and so had tardily assumed some responsibility for religion within the city, did the opinions of members of York's governing class significantly alter. Signs of this change were beginning to appear in the last decade of the sixteenth century: just before he died at the King's Manor in December 1595 they must have given the earl of Huntingdon reason to hope that at last the aldermen were in process of transforming York into being what Hull had long become, a city set on a hill.

University of York

CHURCH AND CHAPELRY IN SIXTEENTH-CENTURY ENGLAND

by CHRISTOPHER KITCHING

THE church has always experienced great difficulty in ministering to those dwelling in the remotest parts of its parishes. In this paper I shall look briefly at how the sixteenth century church coped with the problem, and attempt to answer two questions: what facilities for worship were available in outlying districts, and what was the impact of the reformation changes upon them?

Chapels abounded in England on the eve of the reformation. It is hardly an exaggeration to say that wherever he lived a parishioner could, without an unreasonably arduous journey, reach a place where mass was sung or said. Quite apart from matters of spiritual and moral discipline, it was important for very practical reasons that he should be able to get quickly to church. Disaster could take hold in villages and townships if the entire population had set off on a long hike to a remote parish church and was unlikely to return for some hours. Moreover, the length of the hike determined the extent of the diversion of labour from other pursuits, notably in the fields at harvest time: indeed, this was to influence government rulings on the number of saints' days to be observed by the laity.[1]

Past generations had seen the inconveniences of living distant from the church, and had built and maintained chapels to supplement the services offered there. And chapels of ease were still being built, and and consecrated by bishops, in the early sixteenth century, especially in areas of rapidly expanding population.[2] Their users—and we are not talking only of the halt and infirm—were to become vociferous in their defence when they smelt a threat to genuinely parochial chapels in the crown's policy of confiscating the buildings and endowments of institutions supposedly founded with narrower aims, such as free chapels and chantries.

1 *Lincoln Diocese Documents 1450–1544*, ed A. Clark, *EETS* 149 (1914) pp 217–18.

2 For examples of consecrations see [*Registrum Ricardi Mayew*, ed A. T. Bannister], *CYS* 27 (1921) p 232: Yellintre, and [*Registra Caroli Bothe, Edwardi Foxe et Edmundi Bonner*,] *CYS* 28 (1921) p 100: Norbury. See also [C.] Haigh, [*Reformation and Society in Tudor Lancashire*] (Cambridge 1975) pp 31, 66.

In the Fens, at Whaplode Drove (five miles from the nearest parish church) and Gedney Fen End (seven miles), the inhabitants had their own chapels, and represented to the chantry commissioners in the 1540s that if they all went off simultaneously to the mother church there would be nobody to raise the alarm when the banks needed strengthening or property rescuing from flood waters.[3] Or to take an urban example, the townsmen of Liverpool defended their chapel of ease—for the township had not yet achieved parochial status—on the grounds of the 'great concourse of strangers both by land and sea' in their 'haven town': no doubt wishing to stress their loyal xenophobia as much as the size of their floating population.[4] Their point was more forcefully put by the men of Weymouth, who argued that if they all went to their parish church at Wyke the harbour would be left a sitting target for foreign invasion.[5]

These perhaps extreme examples demonstrate the need for chapels of ease. And in the minds of the users, the cases differed only in degree from those of chapels in hundreds of other townships and hamlets. It seemed to be in everyone's interest that parochial chapels be kept alive, and Bancroft was to hit the nail on the head when he observed that parishioners would 'grudge in their hearts to be driven to go five or six miles to the church both winter and summer', adding, 'I have known great suits in law for the maintenance of a chapel of ease within half a mile of the parish church'.[6]

Distance was a relative concept. For the aged, even a quarter of a mile was a great trek. A mile in rugged upland country was quite a different thing, even to a parishioner in the flower of youth, from the same distance on level ground, and since the population of upland parishes, especially in the north, had tended to be both sparse and widely scattered, chapels were needed to cater for mere handfuls of people in circumstances where the responsibilities and financial obligations of full parochial status would have been inappropriate. Then take the case of the parishioner who lived only a stonesthrow from his parish church but was utterly unable to get there at certain seasons because of the flooding of an intervening stream or river, or in some areas the high tide. Some chapels were therefore needed

[3] 'The Chantry Certificates for Lincoln and Lincolnshire', ed C. W. Foster and A. Hamilton Thompson, *AASRP* 37 (1950) pp 33–4.

[4] [*A History of the Chantries within the County Palatine of Lancaster,* ed F. R.] Raines, *Chetham Society* 59 (1862) p 83.

[5] PRO Augmentation Office, Particulars for Grant E 318/1420.

[6] *Tracts ascribed to Richard Bancroft,* ed A. Peel (Cambridge 1953) pp 92–3.

seasonally. So it is clear that we cannot measure the usefulness of church plant purely in terms of the number of people it catered for or the distance from the parish church.

Chapels of ease, properly so called, where a priest attended to administer the sacraments, or such of them as any arrangement with the mother church might permit, had come into being by donation or legacy, by subscription raised among the parishioners themselves, or by extension from more limited uses such as free chapels, private oratories or chantries.[7] Free chapels had originally been exempt from parochial, though not generally episcopal,[8] control, founded by landlords including the crown for the benefit of themselves, their households and tenants. But by the mid sixteenth century many of the so called 'free chapels' had in effect become parochial, serving a much wider public. The same was true of many endowed chantry chapels; in fact the founders had often intended that their chantry priest serve the inhabitants as well as praying for souls departed. A multiplicity of buildings privately endowed, and independent, or semi-independent of parochial resources and jurisidiction, however, was to pose a threat to reformers intent on suppressing the observances of the old church. Only by establishing the extent of parochial use of such buildings could the courts and administrators at the time (or can the modern historian) be sure of their worthiness to continue. Vernacular usage of words and phrases such as 'church' and 'chapel', 'chapel of ease' and 'free chapel' was notoriously loose, and the returns of parishioners entered in the chantry certificates can be unreliable as a guide to the real significance of a building. Where parochial use was not sufficiently demonstrated, plant and endowments were to be liable to confiscation in the mid-century reforms.

The creation of any sort of chapel threatened the integrity of the parish, not only as a worshipping community but also as a viable economic unit. The parish clergy still had to be supported and the mother church maintained. Demands for tithes, offerings, fees or other income to support a chapel would reduce the funds available for the mother church to draw on. Moreover, the attendance of parish clergy at the chapel might stir up resentment among those who worshipped at the church.[9] Friction was therefore all too common

[7] For a study of the origins of chapelries in Lincolnshire see Dorothy M. Owen, *Church and Society in Medieval Lincolnshire* (Lincoln 1971) cap 1.

[8] This was strongly contested. See J. H. Denton, *English Royal Free Chapels 1100–1300* (Manchester 1970) pp 8–9.

[9] As at Carleton in Husthwaite: P. Heath, *English Parish Clergy* (London 1969) p 5.

between chapel and mother church, though we have to tread carefully when probing what constituted normal healthy relations simply because the surviving documentation is largely a product of their breakdown. The church courts had long echoed with disputes between parish clergy and chapel-goers. Diocesan archives had come in useful when a perplexed official endeavoured to settle a blazing argument over the appointment, attendance or remuneration of the clergy, the maintenance of buildings or the frequency and timing of chapel services: all potential flashpoints.[10] For one way of ironing out differences had been by approach to the bishop for a formally registered 'ordination', itemising the obligations of all parties.[11] Yet not all ordinations were honoured, and there were many more instances where no written agreement was entered into at all. Therefore no general code of conduct can be discerned. Local circumstances were all important.

The most common working arrangement, and the one which caused least trouble if respected by all parties, was for chapel-goers to be equally liable with other parishioners to pay tithes and offerings to the parish priest and to contribute an agreed proportion to the maintenance of the mother church, whilst being additionally responsible for the fabric of their chapel. In return, the parish priest committed himself to taking certain services in the chapel, or finding a deputy to do so.

In practice, as might be expected, the failure of chapel-goers to pay their share of the maintenance costs of the mother church figures largely in church court records. Maintenance of any church building was a burden at any time; maintenance of two, especially if the chapel happened to need major repairs,[12] might be well nigh impossible. Some chapelries managed to achieve exemption from such an obligation to the mother church.[13] To maintain their own building, chapel-goers resorted to the same fund-raising activities familiar at parochial level, including church ales, the renting out of cattle,[14] bequests, and rates levied upon freeholders of the

[10] *The Registers of Oliver King . . . and Hadrian de Castello,* ed H. Maxwell-Lyte, *S[omerset] R[ecord] S[ociety]* 54 (Taunton 1939) p 106: Batheaston; *CYS* 27 p 211: Shrawardine.

[11] [R. A. R.] Hartridge, [*A History of Vicarages in the Middle Ages*] (Cambridge 1930).

[12] [A. P. Moore, 'Proceedings of the Ecclesiastical Courts in the Archdeaconry of Leicester, 1516–35'], *AASRP* 28 (1905–6) p 123: Quarndon etc.

[13] As in Whalley: [J. E. W.] Wallis, [*A History of the Church in Blackburnshire*] (1932) p 99.

[14] As at Newton in Prestbury: [PRO Court of Augmentations Decrees and Orders,] E 315/105 fol 145.

chapelry.[15] Finances and discipline were controlled by chapel wardens elected for the purpose.

Numerous other complications might bedevil the working relationship. For example, if it were not the parish priest who served the chapel, it could be necessary to record what stipend or other form of remuneration the appointed chaplain was to receive.[16] It was normal for the parish priest to continue receiving the small tithes and offerings, but there were many exceptions: to take just one, at Stanford in Bromyard by 1518 the chapel-goers were administering their own tithes and oblations and paying their own chaplain.[17] In some chapelries the inhabitants were left to find their own priest even if it was the vicar who paid him, as at Wibtoft in Claybrooke in the reign of Mary.[18]

There was usually a prohibition on the holding of burials, and sometimes also of baptisms and marriages, in a chapel of ease, principally to preserve the parish priest's right to fees. Yet this rule too had long been overthrown in some chapelries which had acquired quasi-parochial status, like Didsbury in Manchester where burials had been allowed since 1352, to prevent the carriage of plague-ridden corpses into the town.[19] At Filton in 1527 we find the vicar of Keynsham, some three miles away, permitting the chapel-goers to bury their own dead because the road was frequently flooded or muddy.[20] The hardships of mourners in parishes where the rules had not been waived are readily apparent.

Apart from visits to the mother church for baptisms, marriages and burials, chapel-goers were expected to pay courtesy visits also at specified seasons: at the very least once a year, for example on the feast of dedication,[21] to make their offerings and pay their dues. The obligation might even extend to all major feasts.[22] In return, they had

[15] As at Denton in Manchester: J. Booker, *A History of the Ancient Chapel of Denton*, *Chetham Society* 37 (1855) p 51.

[16] Hartridge p 54: Aylesbury; p 58: Helperthorpe in Weaverthorpe.

[17] *CYS* 27 pp 154–5.

[18] *AASRP* 28 pp 123–4; but in 1516–17 the vicar had contributed 5 marks to the stipend: *ibid* p 131.

[19] J. Booker, *A History of the Ancient Chapels of Didsbury and Chorlton*, *Chetham Society* 42 (1857) p 13; compare Samlesbury in Walton: Wallis p 85.

[20] *The Registers of Thomas Wolsey . . . John Clerke . . . William Knyght . . . and Gilbert Bourne*, ed H. Maxwell-Lyte, *SRS* 55 (1940) p 74.

[21] [*Visitations in the Diocese of Lincoln, 1517–31*, ed A. Hamilton Thompson], *LRS* 33 (1940) p xliv.

[22] PRO Exchequer KR Ecclesiastical Documents, E 135/5/18: Sevenhampton in Highworth.

services in their own chapel. How regularly they chose to attend must remain largely a matter for speculation, but the theoretical frequency of the services offered may sometimes be documented. For a chapel in regular use before the reformation a common standard was to have mass said (or sung) on Sundays and all feast days and perhaps on Wednesdays and Fridays. In 1518 at Stanford in Bromyard there was 'mass and all other sacraments as necessary' on Sundays and principal feasts, whilst on every feast day from Christmas to epiphany and in easter and whitsun weeks mattins preceded mass and vespers immediately followed it, presumably largely for the priests convenience.[23] The residents of Stow cum Birthorpe protested to their bishop in 1519 when they found their chapel services reduced to Sundays only, and requested the restoration of their Wednesday and Friday celebrations.[24] At Burnley in Whalley the chantry commissioners were to note that 'the inhabitants thereof doth use to celebrate mass there *but three times* in the week'; this in a parish where 'three hundred people daily' are said to have attended mass at another chapel at Padiham.[25] At Horsey in Bridgwater, by contrast, the chapel was only being visited on a Sunday, by the parish curate,[26] whilst in the remote chapel at Laman in Talland services were offered only on six principal feasts in the year.[27] It would be interesting to discover whether the provision of chapel service was a *sine qua non* for attendance by the inhabitants at public worship.

The field-work has not yet been done which would enable us to quantify the impact of the reformation changes on parochial chapels, but some outlines of the principal effects are discernible. The dissolution of the monasteries, for example, led to the abandonment or demolition of some dependent or appropriated chapels, notably those intended for the monastic household and guests.[28] Parochial chapels which happened to be served by monks, or financed by the monasteries, were cushioned against the dissolution because the obligation to pay the priest's stipend was passed on to the new impropriator. Where this was the crown, the continuing payments

[23] *CYS* 27 pp 154–5; compare Priorsdean in *Registra Stephani Gardiner et Johannis Poynet*, ed H. Chitty, *CYS* 37 (1930) p 52.

[24] *LRS* 33 p 56.

[25] Raines pp 148, 143.

[26] [*The Survey and Rental of the Chantries . . . in the County of Somerset*, ed E. Green,] *SRS* 2 (1888) p 57.

[27] [*Documents towards a History of the Reformation in Cornwall*, ed L. S.] Snell (Exeter 1953) p 48. Compare Middleton in Ditton: *CYS* 28 p 248.

[28] For example the chapel of Saint Andrew in Saint Albans: E 315/105 fol 142.

may to some extent be traced through the Ministers' and Receivers' Accounts of the court of Augmentations.[29]

The proscription of shrines and pilgrimages led to the abandonment of further specialised chapels, which had in some cases been used only for one or two festivals per year. Rarely did anyone claim that these were needed for parochial use. The chantry commissioners were to note in passing a great number of ruined and abandoned chapels which had either fallen victim to such crown policy, or become redundant through shifts in population or the prohibitive cost of upkeep. In many parishes there was too much ecclesiastical plant of this kind, even for the needs of the old church when we consider maintenance and staffing costs in relation to resources available. When non-parochial chapels came under the crown's eye, many parishioners actually rejoiced to be rid of the burden, or the eye-sore as the case might be, and actively sought the materials for other purposes.[30] The whole question of the maintenance of expensive buildings on limited resources was reviewed by parliament at the same time as the chantries and free chapels came under attack, and in a little noted act[31] parishes were enabled to close one building in cases where two parishes had their churches less than a mile apart, or where an individual parish had a chapel less than a mile from the mother church, if one of the two was unable to raise £6 per year for its priest. Such closure was to be subject to the approval of the ordinary and the patron, and in the case of towns, the corporation. Closures then as now were bound to provoke local resentment, but they might be necessary for the greater good of the continuing church. It looks as if the last Henrician parliament was trying to come to terms with some of the economic problems of the church, and it looks as though a mile was regarded as a not unreasonable distance for a parishioner to have to travel to attend services.

The chantry acts of 1545 and 1547 added free chapels and chantry chapels to the list of condemned endowments. Here and there 'chapels' were quickly demolished or deprived of their lead and other fittings on the instruction of local crown officials zealous in the protestant cause or simply greedy for spoil. But were they indisputably parochial chapels? And if they were, was there no other accessible place of worship? Were they needed for the services of a reformed

[29] PRO, SC6 and LR2.

[30] Snell p 12: Botreaux Castle; *SRS* 2 p 88: Yatton.

[31] 37 Henry VIII cap 1.

church? These are some of the questions which still await detailed consideration, and which might profitably be asked again even for some of the localities where detailed studies have already been made.

Parliament's attack was confined to institutions that were badly administered (1545) or 'superstitious' (1547). Section 15 of the Edwardian act[32] expressly denied any designs on any 'chapel made or ordained for the ease of people dwelling distant from the parish church'. Unfortunately, it then added, 'or such like chapel where no more lands or tenements than the churchyard or a little house or close doth belong or pertain'. Pondering later legal judgements it becomes clear that this second clause was designed to safeguard premises that were technically free chapels but now used as parochial chapels: no more was intended than that any independent endowments should be removed, to render them properly subject to the parish. But the clause introduced an element of ambiguity and suggested to some that even chapels of ease, if they had any endowment, were subject to destruction.

Since it was the court of augmentations which settled most of the problems arising from the acts, it is instructive to note that there were only fifteen cases in that court's decree and order book for the whole of Edward VI's reign in which it was necessary to rule on the status of a building claimed to be a chapel of ease.[33] Of course, other cases were settled out of court, heard in other courts like Star Chamber,[34] or occasionally determined prematurely by the blow of the hammer before they could ever be brought to court, but this modest amount of litigation hardly suggests that many chapel-goers were discomfited by the legislation. Moreover, the courts vigorously denied any narrow interpretation of the ambiguous clause of the act just cited. Endowments of chantries, obits and the like within a chapel of ease were confiscated just as they would have been for a parish church, yet the chapel building itself, if genuinely serving a parochial purpose, was to remain inviolate.[35] This could mean a hiatus of several years before services were fully resumed, pending the rethinking of parish finances and strategy, as was apparently true even in one of the cases which did come to a successful result in the court of augmentations,

[32] 1 Edward VI cap 14.

[33] E 315/105.

[34] [PRO Star Chamber Proceedings,] STAC 4/7/2: Saint James chapel in Sutton, Lincs; STAC 4/6/2 and 4/6/34: Catcott chapel in Moorlynch; STAC 4/3/8: chapelries in Sleaford.

[35] E 315/105 fol 177^{v}: Stainburn; fol 184^{v}: Egleston; fol 193^{v}: Catcott.

concerning the chapel of Oakwood, which was unusual in serving the outlying districts of no fewer than six parishes whose churches were anything up to six miles away: Abinger, Ewhurst, Rudgwick, Ockley, Warnham and Wotton, the latter being Oakwood's mother church.[36]

It should be stressed that when parishioners disagreed with the official interpretation of their chapel's status there were ways and means of making their views known. The courts and the local officers of augmentations were generally amenable to acts of local solidarity and a reprieve might be earned or bought, whether by tipping the crown surveyor as at Yokefleet and Buckton in East Yorkshire,[37] by buying back a chapel which, alas, had been confiscated, as in several Lancashire parishes,[38] or by defiantly holding services in the porch of a locked chapel, as did the residents of Catcott in Moorlynch, whilst the prospective new owner rode past with a loaded shotgun, later claiming for the court's benefit that he was merely out bird-shooting.[39] Happily, he served a term in prison for knocking down the chapel despite a Star Chamber decree upholding an earlier court of augmentations ruling that it was to stand, and the chapel was rebuilt. Had there been any country-wide unrest we might have expected many more cases of this kind.

Haigh has shown that in Lancashire the great majority of chapels were quite ignored by the chantry commissioners, though along with the parish churches they were to suffer depredations at the hands of the commissioners for church goods.[40] Many of those whose endowments were confiscated in that county also seem to have been able to continue to function, and only a handful are known to have been destroyed.

Dickens has suggested that the Seamer rising in 1549 was in part fired by the closure of free chapels. It may be so, though Foxe, on whose initial account of the event he is largely dependent, says nothing of this.[41] Even if it were true, would it demonstrate that the chapels were really needed for authorised public worship? Or does it merely show a natural attachment to the old forms of service?

[36] *Ibid* fol 231; W. C. Richardson, *A History of the Court of Augmentations* (Baton Rouge 1961) p 293.
[37] [Humberside Record Office, Beverley], DDCC 139/65.
[38] Haigh p 149; compare J. E. Oxley, *The Reformation in Essex* (Manchester 1965) pp 159–60.
[39] See note 34.
[40] Haigh p 148.
[41] [A. G.] Dickens, 'Some popular reactions to the Edwardian Reformation in Yorkshire', *YAJ* 34 (1939) p 151.

Dickens has also drawn attention to the supposed excesses of an augmentations official, John Maynard, in Oxfordshire.[42] Yes, he pulled down chapels: but most of them were unquestionably the sort of deadwood we have already met: in decay or abandoned.[43] Serious charges were to be brought against the surveyor for the East Riding, John Bellow, in the reign of Mary.[44] Yes, he too ordered the destruction of several buildings, and made the most of the lead, bells and movable goods without rendering full account. For his peculation he was to serve a prison term.[45] But the allegations of outright destruction cannot all be accepted at face value. Holderness was not big enough for both Bellow and Sir John Constable, the deputy steward of the crown honour, who brought the charges against him; the two men had been engaged in litigious combat for years and had publicly threatened to murder each other.[46] The charges were preferred comfortably after the supposed crimes had been committed, and in a reign more favourable to anyone trying to demonstrate that the threatened buildings were needed for the form of public worship then authorised. The chapels at Fordon and Speeton which were supposed to have been destroyed are still gracing the countryside, whilst others such as those at Pockthorpe and Towthorpe served tiny, and dwindling, populations. That at Wansford was evidently destroyed not by Bellow but by its own patron, the earl of Lennox.[47] This is already a considerable hole in the case for the prosecution, though Bellow was clearly a rogue, and I do not wish to suggest that all chapelries were fairly treated.

There was undeniably scope for confusion and misjudgement, which was sometimes exploited for gain. Furthermore, chantry priests had certainly helped serve the cure in parishes where the removal of their endowment must have terminated their employment unless the inhabitants paid something to the parish to enable them to continue, or unless the crown recognised their usefulness and paid them a stipend, as in many cases it did. But it seems to me that chapels of ease came out of the reformation remarkably unscathed, and certainly not

[42] Dickens, *The English Reformation* (London 1964) p 213.

[43] *The Chantry Certificates* [for Oxfordshire], ed Rose Graham, *Oxfordshire Record Society* 1 (1919) p xvi.

[44] For fragments of the story see DDCC 139/65; *APC 1554–6* pp 271–2, 276 and sources in note 45.

[45] *APC 1556–7* pp 49, 62 and PRO Exchequer KR Church Goods, E 117/14/118(1).

[46] STAC 4/9/10 and 4/10/11.

[47] PRO Auditors of Land Revenue, an auditor's notebook: LR 9/27.

victimised in comparison with parish churches, whose endowments were equally under attack. The church plant which survived the dissolutions fell not far short of requirements for the forms of worship and levels of attendance demanded by the prayer books and acts of uniformity respectively. The loss of endowments was partially offset by the fact that, with the mass officially abolished the new routine of worship necessitated fewer clergy.

The parish as a unit for enforcing social, moral and religious discipline, was potentially strengthened by the abolition of so many independent endowments. The church courts in the later sixteenth century still endeavoured to enforce attendance, and to prevent parishioners crossing the bounds into other parishes whose churches happened to be nearer than their own. It was still in everyone's interest, then, that chapels of ease be kept up. The alternative was declining attendance at public worship, and with the church courts' spiritual censures carrying ever less weight apathy quickly set in where the authorities themselves were lukewarm and unconcerned for their flock. Henry Daynes of Redenhall cockily proclaimed, shortly before his excommunication by the bishop of Norwich in 1597, that he saved himself a hundred miles' walk a year by not going to church, whilst John More, who lived in Yarmouth parish but nearer to Gorleston church protested that he was 'too fat and corpulent' to set off for Yarmouth.[48]

Nevertheless, a strong indicator that distance was no obstacle to the devout is the number of parishioners who happily walked or rode miles to hear a good sermon, even in a neighbouring parish;[49] and where a chapelry was seriously neglected by the parish clergy the rules had to be ignored by those who wished to attend services. A group of puritan preachers in Lancashire in the 1590s noted among many other enormities in the church the following: 'The chapels of ease, which are three times as many as the parish churches and more, are utterly destitute of curates, many of them supplied with lewd men, and some bare readers. By means whereof most of the people refrain their parish church under pretence of their chapels, and having no service at their chapels come not at all, but many grow into utter atheism and barbarism, many enjoy full security in Popery and all popish

[48] *Bishop Redman's Visitation, 1597*, ed J. F. Williams, *Norfolk Record Society* 18 (Norwich 1946) pp 107, 124.

[49] [P.] Collinson, [*The Elizabethan Puritan Movement*] (London 1967) pp 374, 376.

practices'.[50] Even allowing for the *parti pris*, the observation is important. In these conditions it was virtually impossible to enforce church attendance. Moreover, it is very doubtful whether any significant broadening of the pastoral ministry in distant parts of the parishes resulted anywhere in the country from the reformation changes. It was difficult enough to find well trained men to serve the parish churches under Elizabeth, let alone the chapels of ease. In the main the chapelries were served by 'stipendiaries' in a new, respectable sense of the word: paid by the crown, the parish or the impropriator; or they were served merely by readers.[51] The small chapelries were neglected, even by puritan preachers who tended rather to concentrate on the market towns and draw crowds there,[52] and who saw in the larger chapelries, where the population had begun to outstrip that of the mother township in recent decades—such as Liverpool and Toxteth in Walton, or Sunderland in Bishop Wearmouth[53]—an opportunity for mission, while the church of England by law established stuck grimly to its obsolescent parish boundaries.

Public Record Office

[50] H. T. Crofton, *A History of the Ancient Chapel of Stretford*, 1, *Chetham Society*, ns 42 (1899) p 60.

[51] See, for example, a survey of all churches and chapels in the diocese of Exeter in the 1570s: PRO E 135/11/4.

[52] [W. J.] Sheils, ['Religion in Provincial Towns: Innovation and Tradition]', *Church and Society in England, Henry VIII to James I*, ed Felicity Heal and Rosemary O'Day (London 1977) p 161; Collinson p 168.

[53] Sheils pp 161, 172; M. James, *Family, Lineage and Civil Society* (Oxford 1974) pp 133–5.

FACTIONALISM IN TOWN AND COUNTRYSIDE: THE SIGNIFICANCE OF PURITANISM AND ARMINIANISM

by ANTHONY FLETCHER

FACTIONALISM in the local communities of Stuart England is a many-sided subject which has hardly been investigated. I am concerned in this paper primarily with the religious ingredient in local factionalism and in particular with a series of incidents of sustained hostility between clergy and laity, most of which occurred in the decade before the civil war. In every case conflict arose because clergymen were more or less assertively at odds either with deeply embedded custom and tradition or with strongly held views among the laity of their town or village. The intention is to consider the patterns of conflict that lie behind these incidents and to relate these patterns to the structures of rural and urban communities.

Villagers discontented with their clergy were likely to appeal to the secular courts. Angry over the failure of their minister, Nathaniel Lancaster, and their curate, John Jones, to perform customary rituals, some of the parishioners of Tarporley in Cheshire petitioned the Bench in January 1643. The clash at Tarporley was between traditionalism and radical puritanism: 'many orders and customs which we have had in former times we have now taken from us', wrote one of the petitioners John Walley. He enumerated twenty 'defaults', including the surplice, the cross in baptism, communion for the sick, the liturgy on saints days and Christmas Day, the rogationtide procession and 'fetching of the dead at the church gate'. For at least two years, it seems, use of the prayer book had been totally abandoned by Lancaster and Jones.[1] Moreover Sir Thomas Aston had told the house of lords, in December 1641, that Jones derided reading of the prayer book as 'worse than the mumbling of the mass upon beads' and insisted that those who did read it merely sent souls to Hell.[2]

The communion rails had been removed at Tarporley and the stained glass in the church windows had been replaced by plain glass

[1] Cheshire R[ecord] O[ffice], MS QJF 71/4/23–4, QSOB 9a, fol 87.

[2] [BL] Add MS 36913, fol 136; R. C. Richardson, *Puritanism in North West England* (Manchester 1972) p 40; [J. S.] Morrill, *Cheshire [1630–1660]* (Oxford 1974) p 35.

paid for by the parish. All in all the harshness of the campaign mounted by Lancaster and Jones to change the form of worship there had caused deep offence. More specifically it had set the puritan ministry at variance with a group of older parishioners. Lancaster and Jones excluded these men from communion since they would not be 'catechised by a catechism of their own invention not expressed in the book of common prayer'. Their determination in return to cling to the old ways is illustrated by the rough passage Lancaster received when he tried to stop them tolling the passing bell for a villager one Sunday after evening prayer. In the brawl the constable and the minister apparently 'thrust and pushed' each other up and down the church.[3]

The ideological content of the conflict at Tarporley is crystal clear: Lancaster subsequently became chaplain to the parliamentary army in Cheshire, and Jones, as we have seen, was a bitter enemy of that obsessive defender of bishops and the prayer book Sir Thomas Aston.[4] The unwillingness of the puritan clergy to suffer those who did not reach their lofty standards sets them beside some of the Elizabethan clergy of Essex and Kent.[5] Yet in the country as a whole, between the accession of Elizabeth and the civil war, confrontation showing this degree of vehemence between radical ministers and conservative parishioners was probably relatively rare.

Of course parish conflicts did not invariably represent fundamental differences in approach to worship. A prolonged struggle between minister and people in the Essex village of Little Wenden during the 1580s, for instance, was apparently based partly on the minister's slackness in performing his duties and partly on the contentious ways of John Feltwell, who distracted him from his spiritual office by persistent suits at law. In this instance the minister's omissions seem to have been due to oversight and forgetfulness rather than principle and the churchwardens' reports arose simply from a sense of responsibility to their neighbours.[6] The acrimonious quarrel between Henry Kent, vicar of Selsey, and some of his congregation, expressed in petitions by both sides to the Sussex quarter sessions between 1640 and 1642, seems at first sight also to be based entirely on personal

[3] Cheshire RO, MS QJF 71/4/23–4.

[4] Morrill, *Cheshire*, pp 45–56, 102, 165.

[5] [P.] Collinson, [*The*] *Elizabethan Puritan Movement* (London 1967) pp 348–9.

[6] F. G. Emmison, *Elizabethan Life: Morals and the Church Courts* (Chelmsford 1973) pp 200–1.

antagonisms. Kent was such a disagreeable individual that the chief parishioners could not stomach his ministry. Indeed, one of them told the chancellor of the diocese that he and his friends would remove him from the vicarage or remove themselves. Kent refused to read the burial service for some of the poor of the parish and rode off leaving women waiting to be churched. But it was not so much his defaults that enraged the village as his quarrelsome and ungodly behaviour, which included railing sermons and alehouse drinking and card playing. Kent was 'a very bold audacious and impudent spirit', it was alleged, in an extensive schedule of articles against him presented to the county Bench. He had struck and beaten several people of the parish and those who attempted to dissuade him from his 'lewd courses of life' he excluded from the sacrament. Above all he was a man of obscene and reviling words, as the sixth article explained:

> He is a man who without any cause at all given him hath, with a very loud extended voice, called many of the chiefest of his parishioners and others of honest and good conversation all to naught and amongst other things hath called them base cheating knaves and their wives base stinking hussies and to some others he hath said they were damned persons to the pit of hell, and many other reviling words he hath often used not fit for a Christian to speak or utter, to the great afrightment and fear of several people especially women.[7]

To be fair to Kent, the leader of his antagonists had for several years given as good as he got. The vicar's charges against Thomas Woodland included numerous instances of violent language and a series of attempts to disrupt his conduct of parish worship. Early in 1641 Woodland had gone so far as to ambush Kent as he rode to church with his wife behind him: 'the devil take the priest', said Woodland, 'and struck the minister's horse in the head and caused his wife to fall down'.[8]

Beneath the horseplay, obscenity and irreverence there was more to the Selsey quarrel than a clash of personalities. The choleric Henry Kent may look an unlikely exemplar of Arminianism, but he was plainly a man who found the sacerdotalism of Laud and his associates appealing, and who intended to do everything he could to heighten the prestige of his priestly office. Thus, when a number of

[7] West Sussex R[ecord] O[ffice], Sessions Rolls 42/50, 46/5; [A. J.] Fletcher, [*A*] *County Community* [*in Peace and War*] (London 1975) p 161.

[8] West Sussex RO, Sessions Rolls 43/63.

people were assembled for a service on St Luke's day in 1640, he refused to proceed until the parish clerk, who was a mile away at the time, had been summoned to put on his surplice for him. He was also fond of quoting the powers he believed he had been given by the new canons of 1640. Kent was furious when William Walliston told him that the canons were of no force and offered to call in the witness of the neighbouring JP, Sir Thomas Bowyer. He had Walliston made overseer of the poor out of spite and, visiting him at his home, called him a 'bankrupt and beggarly knave'.[9]

The Selsey altercations are important because they present in a dramatised form a pattern of conflict at the parish level which was probably repeated in a good many places during the 1630s. At Selsey, there seems to have been something of a puritan tradition to deepen the quarrel: Kent derided 'rascals and runigates that would go out of the parish to hear a sermon at another place'.[10] But the enforcement of Arminianism was provocative even where no more than a moderate protestantism was the established creed. Each time Robert Dove, the vicar of Ilsington in Devon, turned the communion table altarwise, the people turned it back again. By 1640 he had thoroughly alienated the parish. He preached that 'who so puts on his hat in the church, service or no service, he will punish him'; he read half the service at the altar, 'so that the people hear him not but say they have lost the vicar'; and he tried to insist that none should receive the sacrament at the altar till they had first made an oblation there.[11]

When the opportunity came, with the long parliament's establishment of its committee for scandalous ministers, to seek redress against Arminian innovators, the petitions of villagers up and down the country crowded in to Westminster. According to Sir Simonds D'Ewes, the committee received around nine hundred petitions between December 1640 and the following spring.[12] How many of these petitions reflected sustained local conflict between Arminian clergy and their parishioners of the kind we find at Selsey and Ilsington it is hard to say. One case is well documented: at Cottenham in Cambridgeshire the atmosphere of village society was so poisoned by the attempts of an Arminian incumbent to swing a puritan parish into line that the quarrel still went on when he returned

[9] *Ibid*, Sessions Rolls 42/50, 46/6.
[10] *Ibid*, Sessions Rolls 46/5.
[11] *The Buller Papers*, ed R. N. Worth (privately printed 1895) p 33.
[12] E. Dering, *A Collection of Speeches* (1642) p 43; BL Harley MS 165, fol 1021r.

to the living at the restoration. John Manby was rector of Cottenham from 1635 to 1643, when he was sequestrated, and his wife and five small children were thrown into the street.[13] Long after, his youngest daughter wrote about the animosity the family encountered when Manby was restored seventeen years later: 'the very children were so full of hatred, taking it from their parents, that if I and my sister straggled out on a holiday to see them play they would leave off and not company with us'. At play time at the village school one day she was viciously attacked: 'some boys pretended to espy a wonder . . . and I running among the rest to see, a boy, son to an adversary, took up a fork and thrust the tines into my head a little above my forehead; the scars I have yet to be seen'[14].

The lay-clerical conflicts discussed so far in this paper were essentially small scale, held within the bounds of intimate and introverted communities. Although, as the petitions used in this account show, attempts were sometimes made to seek outside support, they were basically vendettas expressed through direct and informal action and words. When clergy and laity were at odds in market towns there were greater opportunities for sizeable factions to mobilise. Divisions already present on personal and economic grounds might take on a more distinct form through religious controversy. There was therefore a tendency for religious dissonance to become more public and more intense.

Two cases, sharply contrasting in content, will illustrate this point. Robert Abbott's experience at Cranbrook in Kent, where there was a radical tradition going back to the 1570s, shows how, in the millennial atmosphere of 1641, a group of confident men could drive a minister to desperation.[15] In this case, the minister had done nothing to alienate his parishioners. He was energetic, studious, charitable and a regular preacher. He had done everything he could to satisfy a populous and demanding town. He was 'not so straitlaced but (as is well known) I can pray without book upon any occasion', he told Sir Edward Dering in a letter about his plight. Indeed he favoured reform of the prayer book and wished 'with all my heart that the way of our church were so smooth in all things that every tender foot could walk comfortably over it'. Yet because he could not in conscience abandon the prayer

[13] A. G. Matthews, *Walker Revised* (Oxford 1948) pp 83–4.

[14] Cited in M. Spufford, *Contrasting Communities* (Cambridge 1974) p 316.

[15] [P.] Clark, *English Provincial Society* [*from the Reformation to the Revolution*] (Hassocks 1977) pp 76, 165, 169, 364, 386.

book until parliament had ruled on the matter he suffered 'disaffections, discouragements and misreports'. In July 1641, Abbott was warned to expect a deputation of forty parishioners to persuade him to abandon the liturgy altogether, else they would cease to attend the parish church: 'the common prayer book doth so stink that none will please but one that is for down, down', he reported. Abbott's antagonists were 'the middle sort of the parish', men with independence of mind and means. He was in despair at losing the heart of his congregation. Later in 1641, the radical laity talked of forcing a lecturer on him of their own opinions, as the commons' order of 8 September allowing parishioners to set up weekly lectureships encouraged them to do. 'To have my conscience, credit and pains trampled on after twenty-four years', wrote this embattled puritan moderate, 'is an hard task to say no more'.[16]

The problems encountered by John Tombes as minister of Leominster were the obverse of those faced by Abbott. He was up against the conservatism and superstition of a region where puritan evangelistic efforts had found stony ground since Elizabeth's reign.[17] It was in nearby Shropshire that Richard Baxter's father was scorned for his opposition to dancing round the maypole and for his Sunday bible reading.[18] But there was also a very much more prominent personal element in the clash at Leominster than in the one at Cranbrook. Tombes's formidable opponent was Walter Brabazon, a local JP sympathetic to Laud's policies, who used his control of the churchwardenship to have the communion table turned altarwise. Brabazon systematically hindered Tombes's efforts to reform the ungodly, by protecting a servant whom he had licensed to keep an alehouse and bowling alley, for instance, and by persuading the bishop to absolve a dissolute youth who had been drunk at communion.[19] By early 1642 Leominster was utterly polarised. Tombes, it was reported, was 'hated and set against by a great number of superstitious people'. One of them, a tanner much favoured by Brabazon, declared that he and his friends had 'brought four muskets to kill puritans' and that he would not perform his duties of watch and ward if he thought it would do the puritans any good. 'I doubt not',

[16] BL Stowe MS 184, fols 27ʳ, 28ʳ, 43ᵛ, 44ʳ, 47ʳ; D. Hirst, 'The Defection of Sir Edward Dering 1640–1', *HJ* 15 (1972) pp 202, 206.

[17] C. Haigh, 'Puritan Evangelism in the Reign of Elizabeth I', *EHR*, 42 (1977) pp 30–58.

[18] R. Baxter, *Autobiography*, ed N. H. Keeble (London 1974) pp 4–6.

[19] BL, Loan MS 29/121/172. I am most grateful to Mrs Jacqueline Levey for letting me use a transcript she has made of this manuscript. See also BL, Loan MS 29/172, fol 344.

wrote the sheriff in an account of the state of the town to Sir Robert Harley, 'but if the times would serve they would show as little favour to those that they call puritans as any English or Irish papist would do'.[20]

Personal confrontation and defiance, the incidents at Cranbrook and Leominster suggest, were as characteristic of religious disputes in market towns as in villages. The urban and rural disputes were not essentially different in kind. Whether there were more cases of a radical incumbent falling out with a traditionalist congregation, as at Leominster, or of a radical group of laity finding fault with their minister, as at Cranbrook, is hard to say until research on more of the country has been done. But it would not be surprising if the Cranbrook model turned out to be the more common of the two. The urban environment, which was often more open to outside influences and more conducive to independent thought than the village one, seems almost to have prompted disagreement and division among the puritan laity. Inevitably, the clergy were drawn in to their theological and liturgical quarrels. Collinson has suggested that the gradual disintegration of religious harmony was virtually inherent in the assimilation of the primary protestant doctrines by local communities. He found the process at work in Essex villages but it was probably more commonly found in towns.[21] In Elizabethan Northampton, Sheils has found 'puritans of widely differing views among all levels of society'.[22] In Cromwellian Rye, I have argued elsewhere, the quest for the millennium, entangled with the personal strivings and animosities of a declining port, produced bitterness and factional strife.[23]

Finally, cathedral cities: there, a distinct pattern of conflict emerged in the 1630s which deserves particular treatment. It can be detected with slight variations at Canterbury, Chichester, Gloucester, Salisbury, Worcester and York; very likely it was present elsewhere as well. In each case, the puritan merchant oligarchy, or a puritan clique among the merchant families, were at enmity with the Arminian inhabitants of the close. In most cases, the close occupied a considerable part of

[20] *Ibid* 29/173, fols 106^{v}, 208^{v}.

[21] Collinson, *Elizabeth Puritan Movement*, pp 372–82; P. Collinson, *The Godly: Aspects of Popular Protestantism in Elizabethan England* (Papers presented to the Past and Present Conference on Popular Religion, 1966) p 3.

[22] W. J. Sheils *The Puritans in the Diocese of Peterborough 1558–1610*, Northamptonshire Record Society, 30 (1979) pp 119–27.

[23] Fletcher, *County Community*, pp 117–20.

the intramural area and enjoyed complete immunity from the city's jurisdiction. The economic and legal privileges of an often non-resident chapter of prebendaries were usually glaringly provocative. In some cases, such as at Chichester, deliberate measures of insulation, like the building of a high wall and restrictions on the vicars choral becoming involved in the trading life of the city, were practised. These circumstances made it predictable that the triumph of Arminianism in the cathedrals would bring long standing resentment into the open.[24] In the first place the jurisdictional struggle often became intensified. Thus, at Chichester in 1635 the mayor tried unsuccessfully to impose heavy ship money contributions on the close.[25] At Salisbury, the bishop and cathedral chapter vigorously disputed, and eventually reversed, the city's new charter of 1630 confirming its independence from episcopal jurisdiction.[26]

But it was the issues of faith which went deepest and caused most emotion. In a speech in the house of commons in June 1641, Thomas Pury, an alderman of Gloucester, told colleagues of the neglect of the gospel in his own city. Not only did the canons fail to preach; worse still they prevented outsiders from occupying the cathedral pulpit. Pury wanted parliament to order the dean and chapter to allow Sunday afternoon sermons.[27] In at least two cases the Arminians had in fact tried to interrupt well established traditions of preaching within the cathedral precincts. At Canterbury, sermons were removed from the chapter house to the cathedral proper in about 1635; at Worcester, on the arrival of a new dean, Christopher Potter, in 1637, the venue for sermons sponsored by the city was changed from the west end of the nave to the choir. The intention was the same in both cases: to bring to an end undisciplined and unseemly crowding around the preacher and to ensure that citizens—and above all the corporation—sat through the whole elaborate cathedral liturgy. Potter explained to archbishop Laud what he found on his appointment as dean: 'on Sunday mornings, before sermon, during the choral service, some walked and talked in the nave, others gathered their auditors about them in seats and read to them some English divinity, so

[24] *Ibid* p 235; C. Cross, 'Achieving the Millenium: the Church in York during the Commonwealth', *SCH* 4 (1967) pp 122–34.

[25] Fletcher, *County Community*, pp 235–6.

[26] P. Slack, 'Religious Protest and Urban Authority: the Case of Henry Sherfield, Iconoclast, 1633', *SCH* 9 (1972) pp 297–8.

[27] A. J. Fletcher, 'Concern for Renewal in the Root and Branch Debates of 1641', *SCH* 14 (1977) pp 282–3.

loudly as that the singers in the choir were much disturbed by them'.[28]

In the tense atmosphere of cathedral cities during the 1630s both parties were on the defensive, sensitive to anything that could be interpreted as a slight to their dignity, status or prestige. Symbolism was all important in the power struggle of those years. Puritan merchants answered Arminian ceremonial with the ritual of their mayoral and aldermanic offices. Thus an old argument about the carrying of maces in the close at Chichester was revived in 1636, after the mayor ostentatiously had a new great mace carried before him when he attended cathedral services.[29] The most delicate question of all in several cities was seating. One of the reasons for moving the sermons at Canterbury was that the seating arrangements in the chapter house were thought to give undue prominence to lay dignitaries.[30] There was a major row at York in 1633, with the corporation boycotting services altogether for a time, when archdeacon Wickham occupied a stall in the minster higher than that of the lord mayor.[31] At Worcester as well, seating was at the heart of the conflict: a massive scaffolding of seats, entirely covering the tomb of one bishop of the see and reaching the bottom of the west window, had been erected by degrees during the previous decades: 'there the senators and their wives sat in more pomp and state than in their guildhall', dean Potter told Laud with the utmost scorn.[32]

The social and political circumstances of cathedral cities were certainly propitious for the development of full scale religious factionalism. A struggle between city and close could absorb personal energies and focus ideological rivalries. Arminian clergy needed little prompting to appeal to higher authorities. Corporations may not have been over scrupulous about using intimidation in reply and they sought the best legal advice they could get. Whether the setting was a small village community like Cottenham, or a cathedral city, the basic issues at stake between puritans and Arminians were the same. But where the laity came face to face with the power houses of the Arminian movement the conduct of the struggle was bound to be much more formal. When the factional conflicts of cathedral cities

[28] Clarke, *English Provincial Society*, p 363; *Cal SPD 1636–7*, pp 359–60, 390–1, 495; *Cal SPD 1639–40*, pp 79–80, 106–7.
[29] Fletcher, *County Community*, p 237.
[30] Clark, *English Provincial Society*, p 363.
[31] *SCH* 4 (1967) pp 128–9.
[32] *Cal SPD 1639–40*, p 106.

became the subject of privy council hearings, they contributed to the national controversy over Laud's religious policies.

Yet the petty squabbling which was so characteristic of village conflicts could break through the factional pattern, even in the august surroundings of a cathedral close. The Worcester documentation provides a picturesque example of this. Bishop Thornborough was so successful at inflaming lay hatred of his own special enemy in the chapter, Mr Tomkins, that a party of schoolboys mobbed Tomkins 'coming out of choir service as he was doing his adoration to God'. His attempt to reprove their insolence by boxing one of them on the ear was quickly the talk of the city and the boy's father planned to sue him for striking his son on consecrated ground.[33]

That forays into the archives should easily turn up dramatic instances of religious controversy, such as those discussed in this paper, need occasion no surprise. Recent research has made us aware of the divisive potentialities of both puritanism and Arminianism and has deepened our understanding of their essential dichotomy.[34] The importance of religious issues in seventeenth-century factionalism is evident. But the interpretation advanced here of the patterns of factional dispute in town and countryside must remain tentative until much more of the work that is waiting to be done on local communities has been completed.[35]

University of Sheffield

[33] *Cal SPD 1636–7*, p 391.

[34] N. R. N. Tyacke, 'Puritanism, Arminianism and Counter-Revolution', *The Origins of the English Civil War*, ed C. S. R. Russell (London 1973) pp 119–43.

[35] I am grateful to my wife and to Mark Greengrass for their comments on a draft of this paper.

THOMAS FULLER AS ROYALIST COUNTRY PARSON DURING THE INTERREGNUM

by W. B. PATTERSON

ALTHOUGH Thomas Fuller, the church historian, spent the first year of the civil war in London, where he articulated from the pulpit a political point of view consonant with that of the parliamentary peace party, there can be little doubt that his allegiance was with the king in that struggle.[1] In the late summer of 1643 Fuller left London for the royalist capital at Oxford and before the end of the year entered the service of Lord Hopton as a chaplain in the royal army. During the latter stages of the civil war he resided in Exeter, where he served as chaplain to the infant princess Henrietta Anne, and where he enjoyed close relations with members of the court circle there.[2] Fuller left the royalist community in Exeter only when the city itself surrendered in 1646, two months before the fall of Oxford. Because of these activities and because of a series of plainspoken books and pamphlets during the years of religious and political conflict, Fuller was widely known as an adherent of the royalist cause, albeit never as militant or as uncritical a partisan as many others in the king's camp. Yet Fuller managed to carry out a public ministry in the stormy years following the surrender at Exeter, and was the incumbent, successively, of two parishes in the countryside

[1] Fuller's political opinions, which revolved about the need for negotiations between the king and parliament, were expressed in print in *A Fast Sermon Preached on Innocents Day* (London 1642), *A Sermon Preached at the Collegiat Church of S. Peter in Westminster, on the 27. of March, Being the Day of His Majesties Inauguration* (London 1643), *A Sermon of Reformation, Preached at the Church of the Savoy Last Fast Day, July 27, 1643* (London 1643), and in *A Petition of the Citie of Westminster, and the Parishes of Saint Clement Danes, and Saint Martin in the Fields* (London 1643), which bore Fuller's name. See also [*The*] *Life of* [*that Reverend Divine, and Learned Historian, Dr*] *Thomas Fuller* (London 1661) p 16, where Fuller's sermons at the Savoy chapel are described as 'exhortations to peace'. For the activities and views of the parliamentary peace party in the opening months of the war, see J. H. Hexter, *The Reign of King Pym* (Cambridge, Massachusetts 1941) pp 3–98.

[2] Fuller, *Truth Maintained, or Positions Delivered in a Sermon at the Savoy, Since Traduced for Dangerous, Now Asserted for Sound and Safe* (Oxford 1643); Epistle to Master John Saltmarsh; *Life of Thomas Fuller*, pp 24–5, 33; Fuller, *Good Thoughts in Bad Times* (Exeter 1645), dedication to Lady Dalkeith, head of the princess's household.

near London in the 1650s. His was not the more usual case of an incumbent hanging on to his living through an era of ecclesiastical change; by his royalist service Fuller lost the benefices he had enjoyed in the years just prior to the war. He had, rather, to find a new place in an apparently hostile ecclesiastical system. His career is thus of interest in showing how that system worked and what accommodations a former royalist chaplain had to make to exercise his vocation in a period which church historians are now beginning to examine in detail and on the local level.[3] It also provides a glimpse of the pastoral ministry in town and country in this 'time of troubles'.

The terms of the surrender itself provide a clue as to how it was that Fuller was able to serve the altered church of the post-war years without acting in violation of the principles for which he stood. Exeter had held out long and honourably against the siege of the parliamentarian troops in the west, and when its capitulation finally came, on 13 April 1646, Sir Thomas Fairfax granted generous terms to Sir John Berkeley, the royal governor, and the royalist community there. The governor, lords, clergymen, gentlemen, military officers, and common soldiers were allowed to leave with full armament and baggage and to proceed, under convoy, to Oxford, or to return home, after being disarmed. Those who submitted themselves to 'reasonable and moderate composition for their estates' were, with the exception of certain persons already named by parliament, to be pardoned for their actions in the civil war.[4] Furthermore, 'no Oath, Covenant, Protestation, or Subscription (relating thereunto)' was to be imposed upon 'any person whatsoever' covered by the articles.[5] Fuller was not, as a result, required to subscribe to the solemn league and covenant, which he had left London at least partly to escape in the summer of 1643.[6] By 1 June 1646 Fuller was back in London, where he petitioned

[3] See [Claire] Cross, 'The Church in England, 1646–60', *The Interregnum: The Quest for Settlement, 1646–60*, ed G. E. Aylmer (London 1972) pp 99–120, and *Church and People*, [*1450–1660: The Triumph of the Laity in the English Church*] (Hassocks, Sussex 1976), pp 199–221; and [Robert S.] Paul, *The Lord Protector:* [*Religion and Politics in the Life of Oliver Cromwell*] (London 1955) pp 251–95, 324–33. For a vivid picture of the religious groups which sprang up outside the framework of the national church in the Cromwellian era, see *Association Records of the Particular Baptists of England, Wales and Ireland to 1660*, ed B. R. White, 3 pts (London 1971–4).

[4] *A True Copy of the Articles* [*Agreed on at the Surrender of Exeter; Examined, Perused, and Signed by His Excellency Sir Thomas Fairfax, with a Punctuall Relation of the Setlement and Condition of That City by His Excellency*] (London 1646) pp 6, 9.

[5] *A True Copy of the Articles* pp 12–13.

[6] Fuller, [*The*] *Church History of Britain:* [*From the Birth of Jesus Christ untill the Year M.DC.XLVIII*] (London 1655) bk 11 pp 206–7.

the committee charged with dealing with 'delinquents', sitting at Goldsmiths' Hall, to effect his composition, according to the terms agreed to at Exeter.[7]

The next several years were, nevertheless, filled with difficulties. Fuller's living at Broadwindsor, Dorset, had been sequestered and the parliamentary committee for Dorset had, only a few months before, appointed another incumbent to officiate and to enjoy the glebe lands and emoluments of the parish.[8] The Savoy chapel, London, where Fuller had served as lecturer, was now under the care of a member of the Westminster assembly.[9] Fuller's prebend at Salisbury cathedral had long since been appropriated by parliament. Though the Dorset committee had directed that one fifth of the income of Fuller's sequestered benefice be paid to maintain Fuller's young son, this was not an income which would provide for much except bare essentials.[10] Lands in Dorset belonging to Fuller were still under sequestration in March 1647.[11] After first taking refuge at the lodgings of John Williams, his London publisher, Fuller obtained a chamber at Sion College in July 1646. By May 1648, however, he was so far behind in paying his rent that the governing board threatened to put an attachment on his chamber.[12] Probably only the hospitality of friends—Lord Montagu, Sir John Danvers, and Thomas Morton, the deprived bishop of Durham—enabled Fuller to survive in the straitened circumstances in which he found himself.[13]

[7] PRO MS S.P. 23/G.85/1022, request for composition by Thomas Fuller, received 1 June 1646. According to the Exeter articles composition was not to exceed two years' value of a man's real estate, plus a proportion of his personal property. No record seems to remain, however, of Fuller's real and personal property or of the sum levied against him by the committee.

[8] [*The*] *Minute Books* [*of the Dorset Standing Committee, 23rd Sept., 1646 to 8th May, 1650*, ed Charles H. Mayo] (Exeter 1902) pp xxxvi, 23.

[9] *Life of Thomas Fuller* p 36; article on John Bond in [A. G.] Matthews, *Calamy Revised:* [*Being a Revision of Edmund Calamy's Account of the Ministers and Others Ejected and Silenced, 1660–2*] (Oxford 1934) p 63.

[10] BM Add MSS 8845, Book of the Committee for Sequestrations in the County of Dorset, 1645–7, fol 34 (order dated October 1645).

[11] *Minute Books* p 222.

[12] London, Sion college MS Court-Register from 3 May 1631 to 14 April 1716, pp 84, 103–4. For Fuller's association with Sion college see [E. E.] Pearce, *Sion College* [*and Library*] (Cambridge 1913) pp 95, 241. Fuller's residence at The Crown in Saint Paul's churchyard, the place of business of the bookseller and publisher John Williams, is indicated in his petition for composition.

[13] For these associations see Fuller, *The Cause and Cure of a Wounded Conscience* (London 1647), dedication dated at Boughton, home of Edward, second baron Montagu, a contemporary of Fuller's at Sidney Sussex college, Cambridge, sig A4; Fuller, [*A*]

During these years Fuller was eager to resume his pastoral career, a wish poignantly expressed in the preface to a work of political allegory published in 1646. There he wrote of his longing to 'bee restored to the open Exercise of my profession, on termes consisting with my Conscience, (which welcome Minute, I doe heartily wish, and humbly wait for; and will greedily listen to the least whisper sounding thereunto)'.[14] He resisted, however, any suggestion that he conduct the kind of *sub rosa* anglican services in his private lodgings which the diarist John Evelyn so often attended.[15] Writing of this practice in 1647, Fuller said: 'Some perchance would perswade me, to have the Pulpit carried after me, along with me to my private Lodgings, but hitherto I have refrained from such exercises, as subject to offence, hoping in due time to bee brought backe to the Pulpit.'[16] Beginning in this year Fuller found pulpits becoming available to him once again. In 1647 he was paid £1-6-8 for four sermons delivered at Saint Clement's church, Eastcheap,[17] and in the same year he preached twice at Saint Dunstan's, East, also in London. Thereafter he continued to preach occasional sermons at Saint Clement's for the next several years.[18]

In 1648 Fuller's wish to be restored to the regular practice of his vocation was finally fulfilled. This was made possible by the exercise of lay patronage, a practice the ecclesiastical legislation of the long parliament had not put in jeopardy. Fuller's benefactor was James Hay, second earl of Carlisle, whose house was adjacent to the ancient abbey church in the town of Waltham-Holy-Cross, Essex, some twelve

---

Sermon of Assurance, [*Fourteen Yeares Agoe Preached in Cambridge, Since in Other Places, Now by the Importunity of Friends Exposed to Publike View*] (London 1647), Dedicatory Epistle to Danvers, sig A2–A3; Fuller, *A Sermon of Contentment* (London 1648) Dedicatory Epistle to Danvers, sig A3^{v}–A4; Fuller, *The History of the Worthies of England* (London 1662) pp 229–30.

[14] Fuller, *Andronicus, or, The Unfortunate Politician, Shewing, Sin Slowly Punished, Right Surely Rescued* (London 1646), sig A3. The plight of royalist clergy in this era is discussed in Paul H. Hardacre, *The Royalists during the Puritan Revolution* (The Hague 1956) esp pp 39–51.

[15] *The Diary of John Evelyn*, ed E. S. de Beer (London 1959) pp 327, 332, 335, 355, 372–3, 375, 377, 388.

[16] Fuller, *Sermon of Assurance*, sig A4^{v}.

[17] London, Guildhall Library MS 977/1, Saint Clement's, Eastcheap, Churchwardens' Accounts, 1636–1740, p 58.

[18] Sermons at Saint Clement's and Saint Dunstan's, East, are cited in John Spencer, ΚΑΙΝΑ ΚΑΙ ΠΑΛΑΙΑ: *Things New and Old, or, A Store-house of Similies, Sentences, Allegories, Apophthegms, Adagies, Apologues, Divine, Morall, Politicall* (London 1658) pp 14, 29, 72, 128, 141, 143, 146, 148, 153, 230–1, 234–6, 256, 473, 603.

miles from the centre of London. The earl's father, the first earl of Carlisle, had been a prominent member of the court during the reign of James I and the early years of the reign of Charles I, and had served on a number of diplomatic missions, including that which king James had sent to Germany in an effort to avert the thirty years' war. The first earl had been a lavish entertainer, running up enormous debts by the time he passed on his estate and his title to his son in 1636. The second earl had taken the royalist side at the beginning of the civil war, as might have been expected, but had transferred his allegiance to parliament in March 1643. He had, nevertheless, a reputation for showing generosity to the loyalist clergy.[19] On the earl's appointment, Fuller began to serve as 'perpetual curate' of Waltham abbey beginning in late 1648.[20] There he received the not inconsiderable stipend of £100 a year, the result of a substantial augmentation made to the living by the earl's maternal grandfather, Edward Denny, earl of Norwich, in 1637.[21]

The churchwardens' accounts at Waltham reveal that the parish disbursed a large number of gifts to relieve those in need, especially those who had suffered loss and dislocation because of the civil war. 'To 2 poore Wemon that came from Ireland with children', reads one entry in 1648, suggesting that the exodus of protestants ruined by the civil war in that country was continuing. 'To a poore man his Wife & Children being in all 19 persons', reads another.[22] It is evident that Fuller took a personal interest in these charitable benefactions, especially when the person needing assistance was a fellow clergyman. Towards the end of 1648, the accounts show that a donation was made 'to a poore minister sent to me by M^r^ ffullers derection'. In 1649 another was made 'to Mr Higgons a poore distressed minister at M^r^ ffuller his request'. Again, in 1650, assistance was 'given to M^r^

[19] S. R. Gardiner, life of James Hay, first earl of Carlisle, *DNB*, 25, pp 265–7; Bulstrode Whitelocke, *Memorials of the English Affairs from the Beginning of the Reign of Charles the First to the Happy Restoration of King Charles the Second*, 4 vols (Oxford 1853) 1, pp 245, 430; [David] Lloyd, *Memoires [of the Lives, Actions, Sufferings & Deaths of Those Noble, Reverend, and Excellent Personages]* (London 1668) p 676.

[20] William Winters, 'Notices of the Ministers of the Church of Waltham Holy Cross', *TRHS* 8 (1880) pp 370, 374.

[21] BM Lansdowne MS 459, Register of churchlivings of seventeen counties, *c*1650, fols 116^v^–17; Chelmsford, Essex County Record Office MS D/DQt 122, copy of the will of the earl of Norwich; Fuller, [*The*] *History of Waltham-Abby [in Essex, Founded by King Harold]* (London 1655), published with the *Church History of Britain*, p 20.

[22] Chelmsford, Essex County Record Office MS D/P75/5/1, Waltham Holy Cross, Churchwardens' Accounts, 1624–70, fol 141^v^.

Tho: Addams Minister at the request of M^r ffuller'.[23] There are some half a dozen other entries which mention Fuller as having recommended ministers for relief, and over a dozen more which show that ministers in the same necessitous condition in which Fuller himself had so recently found himself were given relief during his tenure at Waltham abbey. These accounts point to the serious social problem created by the sequestration of substantial numbers of livings served by loyalist clergymen.[24] They also help to confirm the view expressed by Fuller's anonymous seventeenth-century biographer, that he had abundantly exercised the 'grace of charity' to ministers 'distrest and ruined' by the ecclesiastical policies of the 1640s and 50s.[25]

Not long after Fuller settled in Waltham, his performance underwent an official scrutiny. On 8 June 1649 parliament passed an ordinance requiring a parochial inquisition of the country to ascertain the financial and spiritual state of the various parishes.[26] In the following year, on 9 September, the commissioners for Essex met at Chipping Ongar to hear witnesses from parishes in the hundreds of Ongar, Harlow, and Waltham. The report drawn up concerning Waltham abbey stated that the cure was being supplied by a Mr Fuller, who is described as 'an able godly preaching minister'.[27] Fuller, it seems, had passed with flying colours. His own writings testify that he formed many lasting friendships with members of the parish and suggest that he won a secure place in their affections.[28] In describing

[23] Chelmsford, Essex County Record Office MS D/P75/5/1, fols 141^v, 147, 155^v.

[24] The evidence for the dislocation of royalist clergymen is given in detail in John Walker, *An Attempt towards Recovering an Account of the Numbers and Sufferings of the Clergy of the Church of England, Heads of Colleges, Fellows, Scholars, &c. Who Were Sequester'd, Harrass'd, &c. in the Late Times of the Grand Rebellion* (London 1714) and [A. G.] Matthews, *Walker Revised: [Being a Revision of John Walker's Sufferings of the Clergy during the Grand Rebellion, 1642–60]* (Oxford 1948). See also Cross, *Church and People,* pp 203–4. If, as Matthews's figures suggest, as much as one third of the parishes in England had an incumbent removed by sequestration in the period indicated, the problem of unemployed ministers must have been continuing and severe.

[25] *Life of Thomas Fuller* p 44.

[26] Harold Smith, *The Ecclesiastical History of Essex under the Long Parliament and Commonwealth* (Colchester 1932) pp 234–5.

[27] London, Lambeth Palace Library MS Cod 909, Survey of Church Lands Anno 1649, E, vol 8, pp 1–4, 67–8.

[28] The dedications in Fuller's *A Pisgah-Sight of Palestine and the Confines Thereof, with the History of the Old and New Testament Acted Thereon* (London 1650) and *Church History of Britain* include many residents of Waltham. His *The Infants Advocate; Of Circumcision on Jewish Children and Baptisme on Christian Children* (London 1653), is dedicated 'To the Right Worshipfull, Edward Palmer, Henry Wollaston, and Matthew Gilly, Esquires; John Vavasor, Francis Bointon, Gent. with all the rest of my Loving Parishioners in Waltham Holy-Cross' (sig B1).

Waltham abbey in 1655 Fuller wrote that the best feature of the church was that 'on Lords-dayes generally it is filled with a great and attentive Congregation'.[29]

On political issues Fuller was circumspect and determinedly pacific during his years at Waltham abbey. His loyalty to the memory of the king was nevertheless evident within a short time of Charles I's execution in January 1649. In November of that year Fuller published a sermon entitled 'The Just Mans Funeral' in which, without mentioning the regicide specifically, he wrestled with the question of why God would allow a righteous man to perish while the wicked continued to flourish. Fuller's plea for a remembrance of the deceased, containing an allusion to another king, made his reference reasonably clear: 'Yea as in the case of Josiah his death, let there be an *Anniversarie of Mourning* kept in remembrance thereof.'[30] Yet before the end of the protectorate of Oliver Cromwell, Fuller had recognised qualities in the government of the interregnum which deserved respect and admiration. In a sermon preached in 1656 before a judge of the assizes, Fuller declared that whatever doubts might be entertained about the government it had warded off many evils and had, in particular, kept the peace at home. In terms which breathed a heartfelt prayer of thanks, he compared England with Germany, where a civil war had also recently torn the fabric of society:

> Our happiness will appear the greater, if we consider the state of forreign countries, divided from us no less in condition, then by the sea; look upon high Germany which ever Prometheus like hath a cruell eagle feeding upon her entrailes: Is this the civil law, wherein nothing stands good but *violenta possessio*, and *firma ejectio*? where souldiers keep Term all the year long, and scarce make a short vacation in the dead depth of winter? whilest thus the continent is drowned with woes, our happy island is dry; the waves rage round about us, but thanks be to God none runne over us; wee are more safe under our vines, then our neighbours in their castles.[31]

Fuller stayed on at Waltham abbey through the commonwealth period and most of the protectorate, leaving early in 1658. There is no

[29] Fuller, *History of Waltham-Abbey*, p 6.

[30] Fuller, *The Just Mans Funeral, Lately Delivered in a Sermon at Chelsey, before Several Persons of Honour and Worship* (London 1649) p 23.

[31] Fuller, *Strange Justice* (London 1656), part of a collection of Fuller's sermons entitled *The Best Name on Earth, Together with Severall Other Sermons Lately Preached at S. Brides, and in Other Places* (London 1657) p 43.

certain evidence as to why he severed what appears to have been a happy and profitable association. It may be, however, that a change in his patron's attitude towards him led Fuller to seek another position. Thomas Woodcock, the incumbent of Saint Andrew Undershaft, London, until his ejection in 1662, related a story suggesting that Fuller, always a witty writer and conversationalist, offended his patron by a jest at the expense of the countess of Carlisle. 'Dr Thomas ffuller', he said, 'was reading a witty paper of verses upon a Scold to my Lord of Carlile: my lord said I must have copy of these; the D^r^ replyed, what need that, my lord, you have the Originall: which true, and biteing jest lost him my Lord's favour ever after.'[32]

Whatever the reason for Fuller's leaving, he had evidently begun to solicit for another post by about 1657. Robert South, the *Terrae-filius* at the Oxford act in 1657, after lacerating Fuller as a representative of Cambridge scholarship, added: 'This one thing remains worthy of note, that when recently the position of Sub-Librarian [of the Bodleian] was vacant, he supplicated our university through letters that she take him upon herself; but the university declined, and did not admit him as Librarian, for this reason, that he should not inflict his writings upon the Library'.[33] Not long after being turned down at Oxford, however, Fuller received another benefice through the exercise of lay patronage, this one at Cranford, Middlesex, a small agricultural community twelve miles to the west of London, a living in the gift of the Berkeley family.

Fuller's presentation was made by George Berkeley in February 1658.[34] This was evidently the eighth baron of Berkeley, who had sat in the long parliament in the early 1640s and had subsequently worked for a peaceful accommodation with the king until he was imprisoned for disloyalty to the government in about 1647. But it was the younger George Berkeley, the successor to his father's title in August 1658, who was Fuller's special friend and benefactor. The royalist historian David Lloyd said that this member of an illustrious family 'hath been as bountiful to the Church of England, and its suffering Members of late (witness Doctor Pearson, Doctor Fuller, &c) as his Honourable Ancestors were to the same Church and its devout

[32] ['Extracts from the Papers of Thomas Woodcock (Ob. 1695)', ed G. C.] Moore Smith, *The Camden Miscellany* 11 (1907) p 80.

[33] Robert Southey, *Commonplace Book,* ed J. W. Warter (London 1850) second edition, p 305.

[34] London, Lambeth Palace Library MS 998, certificates of the commissioners for approbation of public preachers (1657) p 203.

Members formerly; when there were twelve Abbies of their erection'.[35] Fuller had known Berkeley since at least 1653, when he had dedicated a published sermon to the 'Sole son and Heir' of Lord Berkeley, and by 1655 the younger Berkeley seems to have become Fuller's major literary patron. Fuller referred to him in that year as 'the paramount Mecaenas of my Studies'.[36] Berkeley, who had been an undergraduate at Christ Church, Oxford, evidently shared a good many interests with Fuller, especially in history and religion. In 1667 Berkeley was to publish a work entitled *Historical Applications and Occasional Meditations*, whose very title recalled several of Fuller's writings. It went through four editions and earned a graceful tribute from the poet Edmund Waller.[37] No doubt Fuller saw a good deal of his literary and ecclesiastical patron. The rectory, called Cranford Moat House, which had been built by the Berkeleys, stood quite near the church, which was itself just next to the manor house in which Lord Berkeley lived.[38]

Fuller's appointment as rector of Saint Dunstan's church, Cranford, which carried a stipend of £80 a year, along with fifteen acres of glebe land, brought him under the surveillance of the authorities of the Cromwellian church. In March 1654 'Commissioners for Approbation of Publique Preachers' had been authorised by ordinance to pass on all ecclesiastical appointments made on or after 25 March of that year. Every new appointee was required to appear in person before the commissioners, or 'Triers' as they came to be called, and to provide testimonials from three persons of good repute, including one from a minister settled in some cure. In an ordinance of September 1654 it was further stated that no minister who had ever been sequestered

[35] Lloyd, *Memoires*, p 128.

[36] See Fuller's *Perfection and Peace, Delivered in a Sermon Preached in the Chappel of the Right Worshipful Sir Robert Cook at Dyrdans* (London 1653) sig A2, and *Church History of Britain*, bk 2, p 142; bk 9, pp 47–50.

[37] See the lives of George Berkeley (1601–58) and of his son George (1628–98) by James McMullen Rigg in the *DNB*, 4, pp 346–8. Fuller's own *Good Thoughts in Bad Times, Consisting of Personall Meditations, Scripture Observations, Historicall Applications, Mixt Contemplations* (Exeter 1645) and *Good Thoughts in Worse Times, Consisting of Personall Meditations, Scripture Observations, Meditations on the Times, Meditations on All Kinds of Prayers, Occasionall Meditations* (London 1647) were among the most popular books he wrote.

[38] Fuller, *The Appeal of Iniured Innocence, unto the Religious, Learned and Ingenuous Reader in a Controversie betwixt the Animadvertor Dr Peter Heylyn and the Author Thomas Fuller* (London 1659), dedication to Lord Berkeley, sig A2. For a description of the church see Nikolaus Pevsner, *The Buildings of England: Middlesex* (Harmondsworth 1951) pp 38–9.

was to be approved without the consent of the lord protector and the council.[39]

It was probably in connection with this last provision as well as with his approaching appearance before the Triers that Fuller applied to John Howe, domestic chaplain to Oliver Cromwell, for his advice and assistance. According to Edmund Calamy, Howe's biographer, this moderate puritan, a follower of the Cambridge Platonists, was never known 'to be backward to assist any of the Royalists or Episcopalians in Distress, if they were but Persons of real merit'. 'Among the rest that apply'd to him', wrote Calamy,

> the celebrated Dr. Thomas Fuller, who is so well known by his punning Writings, was one. That Gentleman, who was generally upon the merry Pin, being to take his turn before these Triers, of whom he had a very formidable Notion, thus accosted Mr. Howe, when he apply'd to him for Advice. Sir, said he, you may observe I am a pretty corpulent Man, and I am to go thro a Passage that is very strait, I beg you would be so kind as to give me a shove, and help me thro. He freely gave him his Advice, and he promised to follow it; and when he appeared before them, and they propos'd to him the usual Question, Whether he had ever had any Experience of a Work of Grace upon his Heart? he gave this in for Answer, that he could appeal to the Searcher of Hearts, that he made Conscience of his very Thoughts; with which Answer they were satisfy'd, as indeed they well might.[40]

The question was evidently intended to disclose whether Fuller had experienced God's redeeming grace in the way many of the independents and baptists represented on the commission understood this process. Thomas Woodcock reported Fuller's answer somewhat more fully, relating that Fuller added: 'certainly to keep up to closet [*sic*] duty and retain God in our minds with delight are the true marks of inward vital religion.'[41]

Certificates in support of Fuller's fitness as a minister were filed by five persons: John Fuller, William Bates, Fulke Bellers,

[39] [*Acts and Ordinances of the Interregnum, 1642–60*, ed C. H.] Firth and [R. S.] Rait, 3 vols (London 1911) 2, pp 855–8, 1025–6, 1459–62. For the composition of the commission, see Matthews, *Calamy Revised*, p lxx.

[40] *The Works of the Late Reverend and Learned John Howe, M.A., Sometime Fellow of Magdalen College, Oxon.*, ed Edmund Calamy, 2 vols (London 1724), 'The Life of Mr John Howe', 1, p 7. See also the life of Howe by Alexander Gordon in the *DNB*, 28, pp 85–8.

[41] Moore Smith p 70. That the question asked Fuller was commonly asked by the commissioners is suggested by Paul, *The Lord Protector*, pp 324–5.

John Wells, and Thomas Case.[42] Four of these men were members of the London clergy during the 1650s. John Fuller had been rector of Saint Martin's, Ironmonger Lane; Bates was vicar of Saint Dunstan's in the West; Wells was vicar of Saint Olave, Jewry; and Case was rector of Saint Giles in the Fields. Two had served in positions of responsibility in the ecclesiastical agencies of the interregnum. Wells had been scribe of the London provincial assembly, a part of the presbyterian system of church government authorised in 1646, but never fully realised in the country at large. Bates had been assistant to the Middlesex commission for ejecting scandalous ministers, a part of the system instituted by the creation of the Triers to regulate the appointment and retention of ministers receiving livings within the national church. Case had been a prominent preacher before the long parliament in 1641–7, and a member of the Westminster assembly. He had sought, though unsuccessfully, to become one of the Triers a few years before.[43] Altogether, this would seem to have been very solid support. The commissioners acted in Fuller's favour, admitting him as rector of Cranford on 3 March 1658.[44]

The degree of acceptance Fuller enjoyed among the ministers of London during the 1650s must have owed a good deal to his continuing association with Sion College. This institution, which contained among its facilities lodgings, a dining hall, and a respectable library, had been founded in 1623 by Thomas White, a prebendary of Saint Paul's cathedral, for the use of the London clergy. Despite Fuller's difficulty in paying his bills there in the late 1640s, he continued to use the facilities of the college in the 1650s, becoming, in fact, an occasional resident, beginning in 1654. It was in his chamber in Sion College that Fuller wrote the preface to his great *Church History of Britain*, published in 1655. In the late 1640s and in the 1650s Sion College seems to have been a favourite gathering place for ministers of a presbyterian persuasion. It was here, in 1647 and afterwards, that the provincial assembly of London held its meetings.[45]

If Fuller's association with Sion College suggests an affinity between

[42] London, Lambeth Palace Library MS 998, p 203.

[43] Matthews, *Calamy Revised*, pp 35–6, 104–5, 215, 519; A. B. Groshart on William Bates, *DNB*, 3, pp 399–400; J. E. Bailey on Thomas Case, *DNB*, 9, pp 264–7; Thompson Cooper on John Wells, *DNB*, 60, pp 229–30; John F. Wilson, *Pulpit in Parliament: Puritanism during the English Civil Wars, 1640–8* (Princeton 1969) pp 47, 77, 113.

[44] London, Lambeth Palace Library MS 998, p 203.

[45] Pearce, *Sion College*, pp 1–38, 110–26; Fuller, *Church History of Britain*, To the Reader, sig a4.

his religious outlook and that of presbyterians, so does the form of service he seems to have used during the interregnum. Fuller's contemporary biographer described the form of worship used by Fuller only in general terms:

> A Constant form of prayer he used, as in his Family, so in his publique Ministry; onely varying or adding upon speciall occasions, as occurrences intervening required, because not only hesitation (which the good Doctor for all his strength of Memory, and invention, was afraid of before so awful a presence as the Majesty of Heaven) was in prayer more offensive than other discourse; but because such excursions in that Duty, in the Extempore way, were become the Idol of the Multitude.[46]

Even from this description it is evident that Fuller did not rely upon extemporaneous prayer, as did many other ministers during the commonwealth and protectorate periods. On the other hand, there is no indication here or elsewhere that he used the book of common prayer, which was forbidden by law.[47] At least a part of his 'Constant form of prayer' seems, however, to be contained in a volume published in 1659 under the title *Pulpit Sparks or Choice Forms of Prayer*.[48] Here a prayer used by 'Mr. Tho. Fuller' is printed, along with prayers by thirteen other ministers.

Fuller's prayer is long and comprehensive, covering fifteen pages in this duodecimo volume.[49] It began with a confession of sin in both general and specific terms, using the ten commandments as the basis for self-examination. After the confession, Fuller asked God's blessing upon the 'Church scattered far and wide over the face of the whole Earth', and upon the temporal rulers. He then asked for God's blessing upon the sermon which was to follow:

> Be present with us and President amongst us, at this time in the hearing and handling of thy holy Word; Lord let not the manifold corruptions and the more imperfections of thy servant hinder the operation of thy word, but give me to speak it plainly to every capacity, methodically to every member, effectually to every conscience that shall be here present, so that it may sink

[46] *Life of Thomas Fuller* p 81.

[47] Firth and Rait 1, pp 582–3.

[48] *Pulpit Sparks* [*or Choice Forms of Prayer, by Several Reverend and Godly Divines, Used by Them, Both before and after Sermon*, ed Thomas Reeve] (London 1659) – copy in the library of Trinity College, Cambridge.

[49] *Ibid* pp 156–71.

> in all our hearts, and bring forth fruit in the amendment of all our lives and conversations.[50]

The prayer concluded with the Lord's Prayer. In form, this prayer was in general accordance with the pattern of the Sunday service as prescribed in the *Directory for the Public Worship of God*, prepared by the Westminster assembly of divines, and issued on the authority of parliament in 1645.[51] If the rest of the service which Fuller followed conformed to the provisions of the *Directory*, then it would also have included, in addition to the 'Publique Prayer before the Sermon', an opening prayer, a psalm, and an old testament and a new testament lesson. After the sermon would have come another prayer, a psalm, and a blessing. On those Sundays when the Lord's Supper was celebrated, this service would follow the morning sermon and prayer.[52] There is no way of knowing how often Fuller celebrated the Lord's Supper, though early in his ministry he had urged frequency of communion, and had stressed that the church of England required communicants to receive the sacrament at least three times a year.[53]

The evidence of Fuller's practice in ecclesiastical matters in the 1650s throws light upon his own *credo* on church polity, declared in the midst of a controversy in which he was engaged in 1654 over discipline, the ministry, and the use of the Lord's Prayer. In his *Triple Reconciler*, Fuller stated:

> Not to dissemble in the sight of God and man. I do ingenuously protest, that I affect the Episcopal Government (as it was constituted in its self, abating some corruptions which time hath contracted) best of any other, as conceiving it most consonant to the word of God, and practice of the Primitive Church. But seeing it hath pleased God to set by Episcopacie for the present, (whether or no *animo resumendi* to him alone is known) far be it from me to close with such, whom I confess I love the worse; those Practicers of so much libertie in the Church, that it tendeth directly to confusion, and whose disorderly Order deserves not the name of any Discipline. But I know that Religion and learning hath flourished under the Presbyterian Government in France, Germanie, the Low-countreys. I know many worthy Champions

[50] *Ibid* pp 169–71.

[51] Firth and Rait 1, pp 583–607. See also Horton Davies, *The Worship of the English Puritans* (Westminster 1948) pp 127–33.

[52] Firth and Rait 1, pp 585–96.

[53] Fuller, *Ioseph's Party-Coloured Coat* (London 1640) pp 58–9.

> of the Truth, bred and brought up under the same. I know the most learned and moderate English Divines (though Episcopal in their callings and judgements) have allowed the Reformed Churches under the discipline for sound and perfect in all essentials necessarie to salvation. If therefore denied my first desire to live under that Church-Government I best affected, I will contentedly conform to the Presbyterian Government, and endeavour to deport my self quietly and comfortably under the same.[54]

Fuller evidently found the jumble of sects which the liberty allowed by Cromwell had fostered to be alarming and a danger to the integrity of the church. Presbyterian government, on the other hand, offered the promise of order and stability. Further, no less an authority than archbishop James Ussher had defended the validity of ordination in the reformed churches.[55] While waiting, therefore, for the restoration of episcopacy, without, he hoped, the corruptions of recent times, Fuller was content to pursue his ministry at the parish level, following the provisions established by parliament, on the recommendation of the Westminster assembly, in 1645–6. Fuller was exceptional among his clerical brethren for his homiletical, literary, and scholarly gifts. But in his attitude towards the ecclesiastical changes of the interregnum he may have been very typical of the incumbents of those two out of three parishes in England in which there was no change by sequestration from the beginning of the civil war to the year of the restoration.[56]

Davidson College
North Carolina

[54] Fuller, *A Triple Reconciler, Stating the Controversies, Whether Ministers Have an Exclusive Power of Communicants from the Sacrament; Any Persons Unordained May Lawfully Preach; The Lords Prayer Ought Not To Be Used by All Christians* (London 1654) pp 34–6.

[55] See Nicholas Bernard, *The Judgement of the Late Archbishop of Armagh, and Primate of Ireland: 1. Of the Extent of Christs Death, and Satisfaction, &c.; 2. Of the Sabbath and Observation of the Lords Day; 3. Of the Ordination in Other Reformed Churches* (London 1657) pp 122–40. Also Norman Sykes, *Old Priest and New Presbyter* (Cambridge 1956) pp 85–117.

[56] Compare Matthews, *Walker Revised*, pp v, xiii, xvii; Cross, *Church and People*, pp 203–6. See also I. M. Green, *The Re-establishment of the Church of England, 1660–3* (Oxford 1978) pp 9, 177, 235, and *passim*, where the close relations between moderate anglicans and presbyterians at the time of the restoration are stressed.

'A PRACTICE OF A VERY HURTFUL TENDENCY'

by W. M. JACOB

THE church of England in the eighteenth century has been bitterly criticised by succeeding generations for what the high Victorian church of England regarded as two cardinal sins, firstly non-residence of the clergy on their cures and secondly, and consequently, lack of pastoral care. However, generalisations are misleading and especially these generalisations which are largely based on the evidence of opponents of the established church in the early nineteenth century and on standards of pastoral care of one man to one parish, however small the parish, that were only achieved for a period of sixty or seventy years during the later nineteenth century. How misleading these generalisations are becomes apparent when the evidence for non residence and for standards of pastoral care is examined more closely. The object of this paper is to demonstrate that from the evidence of one particular county a clear pattern of clerical residence emerges that is not entirely incompatible with contemporary expectations of pastoral care.

As Sykes has pointed out the 'clergy ministered to the needs of the age according to the expectations of the age'.[1] In general, pastoral care was seen in terms of Sunday duty and the occasional offices, preaching, catechism, visitation of the sick, good works and charitable acts but this was no mean standard if interpreted in the light of Gilbert Burnet's preface to his third edition of *A Discourse on the Pastoral Care* (1712) in which he recommends that clergy should 'preach catechetical sermons lasting fifteen minutes in the afternoon. Visit the sick diligently not waiting till you are sent for'. He further recommends an hour or two of ordinary visiting two or three times a week.[2] This was a work which had enormous currency during the century being one of five works adopted by SPCK as the standard books for those in or contemplating holy orders.

Although the general public in the eighteenth century seemed to have conceived of the clergyman's role only in terms of the performance

[1] *Johnson's England,* ed A. S. Turberville, 2 vols (London 1933) 1 p 33.

[2] Quoted in W. K. Lowther Clarke, *Eighteenth Century Piety* (London 1944) p 22.

of public worship, and it is clear that occasional offices normally took place in the interval between morning and evening prayer on a Sunday so that it was possible for a priest to get away with only being in his parish on Sundays the general assumption of eighteenth-century 'manner books' (hand books written for the instruction of young clergymen) like Burnet, expects much more of a priest than this. Such manner books saw the Sunday sermon as the most important single event of the week which called for the clergyman's greatest effort and for a considerable amount of preparation; for the facility to preach every Sunday, especially in a largely illiterate society gave to the clerical profession and to the individual clergyman a great deal of power and in the eighteenth century it was widely recognised that part of the power of the clergy resulted from their weekly opportunity to disseminate views and opinions with the sanction of divine authority. The manner books expected the clergyman to be sufficiently acquainted with his parishioners to make his sermons comprehensible to them. It was envisaged that the clergyman should divide his time between his study and visiting and both these activities were seen as focusing the central teaching opportunity of the week, the sermon.[3] Catechising was also seen as an integral part of Sunday duty. Thomas Bray, in fact, saw pastoral care largely in terms of education believing that the children and youth must be taught and led through the catechism and led to communion and to true devotion.[4]

Although many of the manner books insist on the duty of a clergyman to visit his flock this does not seem to have happened to any considerable extent and the public expectation did not require of the parish priest more pastoral visiting than was involved in the visitation of the sick; although Woodforde, if he may be taken as typical, was assiduous in visiting and praying with the sick and dying, and was even prepared when requested to administer the sacrament to the dying.[5] Further it needs to be borne in mind that in relatively small pre-industrial communities where churchgoing was still a majority practice, visiting was much less necessary than it became in the nineteenth century in order to exercise some means of pastoral oversight.

There were further though subsidiary areas in which a parish

[3] For a very detailed analysis of the clergyman's role based on an examination of eighteenth-century manner books see A. J. Russell, *A Sociological Analysis of the Clergyman's Role with special reference to its development in the early nineteenth century* Oxford DPhil thesis (1970) to which this section is much indebted.

[4] H. P. Thompson, *Thomas Bray* (London 1954) p 109.

[5] [*The Diary of a Country Parson,* ed J.] Beresford, 5 vols (London 1926–31) 1 p 221.

priest was expected to exercise pastoral care; for the good parish priest like rather surprisingly, Sydney Smith as rector of Foston in the East Riding never thought of his formal duties as the whole of his pastoral responsibility: he saw himself as village doctor and comforter and was greatly concerned for the welfare of the poor.[6] And this is also perhaps the most admirable aspect of Woodforde's long ministry at Weston Longueville, for as C. R. Cragg observes 'Woodforde was always accessible to the humbler members of his parish'.[7] He not only entertained his genteel and aristocratic neighbours including the premier baronet of England, he also welcomed the poor of the parish to his table. In addition to distributing charity himself the parish priest was also expected to maintain the parochial charitable trusts and especially to control education through endowed and charity schools, although the evidence is not at all clear as to the extent to which the parish priests were in general responsible for the high survival rate of parochial charities.

If the contemporary standard of pastoral care was seen then in these terms as carrying out Sunday duty which included reading morning and evening prayer together with such occasional offices as were required, preaching at least one sermon and catechising the young and visiting at least the sick and dying and succouring the poor and impotent of the parish both spiritually and materially, due consideration must be given as to whether at least some degree of success might not be possible here which would not be incompatible with residence outside, but in the vicinity of the parish.

Because there is little documentary evidence of pastoral activity other than Sunday duty, apart from the rare survival of clerical diaries, the bulk of the evidence must depend upon a consideration of answers to bishops' inquiries made prior to visitations. An examination of the answers to Wake's visitation inquiries for the archdeaconries of Lincoln and Stow in 1706 gives the impression that non residence did not necessarily mean that a parish was poorly served, for often parishes with a non resident incumbent had divine service twice on Sundays, perhaps because one hundred and forty-seven of the three hundred and sixty-two non resident incumbents lived within four miles of their parish.[8] It is clear that non residence has to be divided into a number of categories. There were those clergy like Samuel

[6] A. Bell, *Sydney Smith, Rector of Foston 1806–29* (York 1972) p 13.
[7] *Man versus Society in Eighteenth Century England,* ed C. J. Clifford (London 1968) p 62.
[8] *Speculum Dioceseos Lincolniensis 1705–23,* ed R. E. G. Cole, *LRS* 4 (1912).

Kerrich, vicar of Dersingham in Norfolk who had no vicarage house and so was technically non resident even though he lived in his own house in the parish.[9] There were others who for one reason or another did not live in their parishes but resided in the vicinity. How common this is in Wiltshire is shown by Ransome who says 'Of two hundred and thirty-two parishes making returns only ninety were served by a resident incumbent but thirty-nine more were served by a resident curate so that a little over half were served by resident clergy. Eighty parishes were served by an incumbent or curate living not more than five miles away and no parish was served by clergy living more than ten miles away'.[10] There seems to be a similar though less clear pattern in Oxfordshire where in the answers to the visitation inquiries of 1778 although only sixty-five benefices have a resident incumbent and one hundred have non resident incumbents, of the parishes with non resident incumbents thirty-three have incumbents 'living in the vicinity' and twenty-seven have a resident curate.[11] In Oxfordshire, however, one special factor affecting non residence was the presence of the university. Woodforde makes this clear when he notes in his diary for 14 January 1776 'Scarce ever was known so deep a snow as at present . . . No Curates could go to their Churches today'.[12] In Devon the picture is the same: in the replies to the visitation inquiries of 1779, whilst two hundred and thirty-one incumbents in Devon were resident in their parishes and one hundred and fifty-nine were non resident, thirty-three of the one hundred and fifty-nine lived in 'adjoining parishes' and fifty-six had a resident stipendiary curate.[13]

Now it is those incumbents or curates who live in adjoining parishes who need to be considered more closely because if they can, in general, be seen as carrying out their pastoral duties reasonably satisfactorily this reduces very considerably the impact of non residence. One of the first difficulties is deciding what was meant by an adjoining parish. It seems unlikely that the standard literary example of Tylney in Northanger Abbey, for whom Jane Austen does not think it too much that he should ride twenty miles from his family

[9] *Memoirs of a Royal Chaplain*, ed A. Hartshorne (London 1905) p 42.

[10] *Wiltshire Returns to the Bishop's Visitation Queries 1783*, ed M. Ransome, *Wiltshire Record Society* 27 (Devizes 1971) p 9.

[11] [D.] McClatchey, [*Oxfordshire Clergy 1777–1869*] (Oxford 1960) p 28.

[12] Beresford 1 p 173.

[13] A. Warne, *Church and Society in Devon in the Eighteenth Century*, Leeds PhD thesis (1963) p 62.

seat to his parish to do Sunday duty should be taken as typical, although Woodforde's diary reveals clearly how mobile clergy were in doing Sunday duty over a range of seven or eight miles.

That non residence was not considered improper if it was possible to do the Sunday duty is made clear in a letter of Humphrey Prideaux 'I have resigned the living of [Saham] . . . I could not persuade myselfe to take the wages of a minister where I intend never [more] to do the work . . . nothing seems to me more unjust, then that the maintenance appointed to God's worship should goe to such as never attend it; and on this account I have on many occasions, especially when I am Archdeacon, discouraged non residence . . .'[14] but he accepted instead the living of Trowse, about three miles from Norwich which he could serve personally whilst still living in the Close. A similar example is that of the Revd Jonathon Wrench, rector of Metton in Norfolk who, after a very complicated exchange of livings with his ageing father, was unwilling to live in Metton and asked leave of the patron to come over from Aylsham, a neighbouring market town to take the Sunday services. Ashe Windham of Folbrigg, the patron, objected but a mutual friend the Revd Patrick St Clair interceded on Wrench's behalf 'They have lett the house and gleabs . . . reserving the Parlour and Parlour chamber to their own use, and the young man propos'd being there two or three days in the week; but I told him, if he came every Saturday night and lay there, I believ'd you would be satisfied . . . this will be more than legal Residence, and answer all the ends of the promise of Residence made by the old man.'[15]

Both these examples are of interest because they are examples of clergy serving rural parishes from a base in a neighbouring town and this practice, though the evidence is very circumstantial in the first half of the century seems to have been very common in Norfolk at least, and the evidence is sufficiently obvious later in the century for the practice to attract episcopal censure by Lewis Bagot in his primary visitation charge when he observes 'The first object for a Parochial Minister is to reside with his flock as constantly as may be, to watch over them incessantly as a good and faithful shepherd . . . Of late years a practice hath been growing in many parts of the Kingdom (and no where doth it prevail more than in this Diocese) of a very hurtful tendency. I mean the resort of the clergy to the most considerable

[14] HMC 5 Report pt 1 p 374, *Letter to Mr Richard Coffin* (8 October 1694).
[15] [R. W.] Ketton-Cremer, [*Country Neighbourhood*] (London 1951) p 117.

neighbouring Town.'[16] At Blakeney, then a port, on the north Norfolk coast in the 1720s the Revd Christopher Seaman, vicar of Wiveton and the Revd Samuel Thornton vicar of Saxlingham were living, and journeyed inland to their parishes to do Sunday duty and their successors in office both continued to live in Blakeney whilst serving their parishes into the 1750s.[17] John Tailleure who held a very complicated succession of parishes around Cromer in the 1730s lodged in Aylsham with Mrs Athill, a widow whom his neighbour St Clair notes 'hath four brisk daughters', the eldest of whom, to St Clair's disgust he marries, for 'The family is wretchedly poor, and a great many sons and daughters.'[18] At the bishop's visitation of 1735 Dr James of Swannington and Mr Cory of Hackford are both presented for non residence and for living at Norwich,[19] although Swannington at least is within easy riding range of Norwich. Further evidence of surrounding country parishes being served from a nearby town comes from the diary of Joseph Charles, vicar of Wighton, who notes 'Some short account of Curacies which I have taken and of Sequestrations which I have had since my coming to Wells.

April 25 1755	Agreed with the Revd Mr Robert Fountain to serve the cure of Wells during his absence £1-1s per week
April 1755	Undertook to serve Mr Smithson at Burnham Thorpe. [He died on November 2nd 1755]
December 24 1755	Received of the Revd Mr Nelson £6 for the Instrument of Sequestration and Service up to December 4th
February 22 1756	Agreed with Mr Nelson to serve Norton once a fortnight in the morning for £10 per annum

1758	Sequestrator of Burnham Overy
1758	Sequestrator of Langham April 16th till Michaelmass
1762	Sequestrator of Warham All Saints 15th February-18th April
	Curate of Holkham February-December

[16] *A Charge delivered to the Clergy at the Primary Visitation of Lewis Lord Bishop of Norwich* (Norwich 1784) pp 10–11.

[17] [C. L. S.] Linnell, [*Some East Anglian Clergy*] (London 1961) p 101.

[18] Ketton-Cremer p 206.

[19] Norwich, N[orfolk and] N[orwich] R[ecord] O[ffice], N[orwich] D[iocesan] R[ecords] VIS 16 *Comperta Book for Visitation of 1735*.

1775 Sequestrator of Holkham April 30th-June 17th
Curate of Holkham June-October
1777 Curate of Warham 18th June-26th August
Rector having broken his arm'.[20]

However, Charles's ministry at Wells next the Sea was not all plain sailing: in 1747 the churchwardens and thirty-nine other inhabitants had petitioned the chancellor of the diocese against the rector's being 'too Often and too much with Strong Liquors' and against Mr Charles's reading of prayers and omission of the prayer for parliament, conduct of baptisms and funerals, a failure to read prayers after announcing them on Wednesday in holy week and to administer the sacrament on Easter Sunday.[21] One wonders how objective this petition was and in what way it relates to an action as a result of the visitation of 1735, as a result of which the 'Church wardens [of Wells next the Sea] are admonished to take down the Singers Seats built without Authority and certify the same under the Minister or Curate's hands by Christmas next and further admonished to take care that only Common psalm singing be in the Church for the future'.[22] In such cases it always has to be borne in mind how extremely vulnerable the clergy were to disgruntled parishioners if they failed to observe all the rubrics and canons.[23]

As a result of the answers to the visitation inquiries of 1777 (which is the first occasion such a questionnaire was issued in the diocese) the position becomes clearer because article 6 inquires 'Do you constantly reside upon your Cure, and in the House belonging to it? If not, where, and at what Distance? And how long in each Year are you absent? And what is the Reason of such Absence? And have you a licensed Curate residing in the Parish, or at what Distance from it? . . .' Unfortunately the answers only survive for seven out of twenty-six deaneries, that is for one hundred and seventy-three out of approximately six hundred and eighty-five parishes in the county of Norfolk in the diocese of Norwich. Out of those parishes one hundred and three had non resident incumbents, although seventy-four

[20] Norwich, NNRO MS 11927 a and b 34D *Diary of the Revd Joseph Charles.*

[21] Norwich, NNRO, NDR, SUN 16 *A petition by the Churchwardens and Inhabitants of Wells to the Chancellor* (April 1747).

[22] Norwich, NNRO, NDR VIS 16 *Comperta Book for Visitation* of 1735.

[23] McClatchey p 31 quotes Addington's speech on behalf of the clerical residence bill in 1802 'The attention of the House was not so much called to compel the residence of the clergy as to prevent them from being persecuted by informers' (*Hansard* 36, cols 472, 885).

had resident curates (of whom forty-eight served another cure), and of the rest (twenty-nine) sixteen who did not have resident curates noted their place of residence as a market town in the vicinity of their parish.[24]

As a result of Bagot's queries before his primary visitation in 1784 the picture is much more clearly filled in and one can see why he reacted so sharply in his charge. The information sought by article 6 of the 1777 queries is now under two headings: article 6 'Do you constantly reside upon your Cure, and in the House belonging to it? If not, where and at what Distance do you reside? How long in each Year are you usually absent? And what is the Reason of such Absence? Have you more Benefices than one? Do you serve any Church besides your own?' and article 7 'Have you a licensed Curate residing in your Parish? or what Distance from it . . .' An analysis of the five hundred and seventy-nine surviving returns for Norfolk shows that only one hundred and twenty-eight incumbents were resident on their benefices although two hundred and eighty-five of the rest had curates (of whom two hundred and twenty-three served other cures as well). As a result the general impression is of a very poor state of affairs with only twenty-two per cent of the incumbents resident and with a great deal of pluralism. However, a closer examination of the returns reveals that of the non resident incumbents fifty-three lived in towns within easy reach of their parishes, and that if pluralism is taken into account one hundred and thirteen parishes were served by these fifty-three incumbents, none of whom had resident curates, and if one takes into account clergy who had curates resident in their benefices there were a further forty (that is a total of ninety-three) living in towns within easy reach of their parishes, and that one hundred and seventy-three parishes were served either by a resident curate or by an incumbent or curate who lived in a town within easy reach of the parish.[25] This, although not good by standards that expect the ministrations of one man to one parish, is still a great deal better than first appears and is perhaps very similar to the situation that pertains after the Pastoral Measures 1968 in the Norwich diocese.

Bagot, however, seems to have been determined to end this 'practice . . . of a very hurtful tendency' and he used a court of audience which he had instituted on his coming into the diocese to bring some of the recalcitrant clergy to heel, and presumably he hoped that their example

[24] Norwich, NNRO, NDR VIS 26 and 27 *Visitation Queries 1777*.
[25] Norwich, NNRO, NDR VIS 28, 29, 30 *Visitation Queries 1784*.

would act as a tonic to others. On 20 September 1783 George William Lemon, vicar of East Walton, rector of Gayton Thorpe and perpetual curate of Mundham and Seething was cited for non residence. It transpired that he lived in Norwich and served as curate the parishes of Framingham Earl, Framingham Pigott and Bixley. He was admonished to give up his curacies and to reside at East Walton and to do duty there and at Gayton Thorpe himself. On 29 January 1786 Isaac Horsley, vicar of Briston, vicar of Antingham St Mary and curate of Felmingham and Bacton was cited for non residence as he resided in the neighbouring town of North Walsham. It was claimed that he had been warned by the bishop in 1784 that he might only hold two cures and therefore must give up two but that he had not done so. He was admonished to reside at Briston and to do duty there himself.[26] However, Bagot's activities seem to have had a fairly small impact on the pattern of non residence because an examination of the replies to the queries put out by Henry Bathurst before his primary visitation in 1806 shows an only slightly different picture. Out of the six hundred and eighty-five parishes for which returns survive still only one hundred and sixty-five have resident incumbents (a seven per cent improvement on 1784), of the non residents three hundred and thirty-six have curates (of whom two hundred and fifty-nine also serve other cures) but still forty-one of the non resident incumbents without curates live in nearby towns and serve ninety parishes in the neighbourhood of the towns.[27] This suggests that Bagot had little success in altering a long established and generally acceptable pattern of pastoral ministry.

It is also worth considering some of the reasons for the practice and why it might not be entirely unacceptable. One obvious reason is the general shortage and frequent inadequacy of parsonage houses during most of the century. During the century there seems to have been a steady improvement in land values and consequently of benefice income but this increase often had to be husbanded over a long period to provide sufficient surplus to finance the building of a parsonage

[26] Norwich, NNRO, NDR SUN 16 *Act Book of the Court of Audience of the Rt Revd Lewis Lord Bishop of Norwich.*

[27] Norwich, NNRO, NDR VIS 40, 42, 44 *Visitation Queries 1806.* If these figures are compared with figures obtained from the return made to the house of commons in 1805 (NNRO NRM 1) the 1805 figures are found to be much lower, that is, only twenty-two of the non-resident incumbents without curates live in nearby towns and serve thirty parishes in the neighbourhood. There is unlikely to have been such a marked change in such a short period of time which suggests that the accuracy of the *Returns for Non Residence* should be questioned.

house fit for a gentleman. This seems to have become generally possible only towards the end of the century. As Ward has noted, as a result of enclosure and tithe commutation clergy in many rural parishes acquired considerable land holdings and enabled them to move out of the village centre to a grander house.[28] Chesher has noted a similar pattern in Cornwall observing that in the late eighteenth and early nineteenth centuries there is an altogether new type of parsonage house. The change was more than structural: it was the culmination of a process which was as important socially as it was architecturally. The parson was going up in the world and having been provided for centuries with a house little better than the farm-houses of his better off yeoman parishioners, his status now required a gentleman's residence.[29] The register of mortgages made under Gilbert's Act of 1777 for building and repairing parsonage houses shows that a similar pattern was apparent in Norfolk, twenty-four houses being built or rebuilt in the period 1779 to 1807.[30] Meanwhile the incumbents seem to have taken the easy way out and have bought or rented houses in neighbouring small towns which they perhaps saw as a safer financial venture than investing their income on property which they would be unable to pass on to their widows or children.

A further and very important factor was the attraction that the social life of either a city like Norwich or even a small market town offered. For a man who had received a little of the benefits of life in a Cambridge college, even at the lowest social level, as most of the Norfolk clergy had, life in a remote village without any opportunity for polite social or intellectual intercourse must have been a daunting prospect. Even Woodforde with his busy social round confides to his diary: 'When Bill [his nephew] goes away I shall have no one to converse with—quite without a Friend'.[31] So the attraction of life amongst the merchant classes of a town must have been very great. Norwich, still the third city of the kingdom, was a very lively social centre[32] and even the small market towns had their assemblies,

[28] W. R. Ward, 'The Tithe Question in England in the Early Nineteenth Century', *JEH* 16 (1965) p 72.

[29] *Calendar of Cornish Glebe Terriers 1673–1735*, ed R. Potts, Devon and Cornwall Record Society, ns 19 (Torquay 1974) p 19.

[30] Norwich, NNRO, NDR PHM 1 *A Register of Mortgages made under an Act to Promote the Residence of the Parochial Clergy 17 Geo III.*

[31] Beresford 1 p 231.

[32] For a description of the social attractions of Norwich see T. Fawcett, *The Culture of*

theatres and balls as well as very popular race meetings at Holt and Swaffham.

Education of children, as well as society for oneself and one's wife seem also to have been a factor. In Norfolk many of the market towns had free schools where clergy sons might receive a classical education and a number of these schools had closed scholarships to either Corpus Christi or Gonville and Caius Colleges Cambridge which must have been an attraction to fathers who had high hopes for their sons, and the advertisements in the county newspapers show that there were a large number of schools in these towns in which daughters might learn the social graces. St Clair in writing to Ashe Windham on Wrench's behalf shows this as an explicit reason for non residence. 'The old Gentleman will write to you himself and plead on his daughter-in-law's behalf, and the poor children's, for whose education it is absolutely necessary that they should go to Aylsham'.[33] The clergy themselves also had a personal interest in education for to own a school or to teach in a free school was a highly respectable means of supplementing a meagre income. Martin Routh's father, Peter Routh was master of the free school at Beccles whilst serving his parish at South Elmham St Margaret for many years.[34] The mastership of North Walsham school was endowed with the living of Horsey and in 1784 the master also served Knapton and Paston, the usher of North Walsham school served Edingthorpe, the master of the free school at King's Lynn served East Walton and Gayton Thorpe, the master of Thetford free school served Santon and the master of Brandon free school served Mundford, West Tofts and Downham Parva.[35]

It also needs to be borne in mind that what the parishes may have lost by the lack of a resident incumbent they may have gained by the stimulus he received from his wider social life. Early in the century the promoters of the SPCK had advocated oppportunities for clergy to meet together to discuss matters of common interest and this had been taken up by the evangelicals; as Davies points out 'the increased efficiency and usefulness of each of the clergy within his own parish by these mutual exchanges of ideas and opinions was the prime cause

---

Later Georgian Norwich: a conflict of evidence, University of East Anglia Bulletin, ns 5 no 4 (Norwich 1972) pp 1–14.

[33] Ketton-Cremer p 117.

[34] Linnell p 88.

[35] Norwich, NNRO, NDR VIS 28 *Visitation Queries 1784.*

of the [clerical] club's formation.'[36] It does not seem improbable to conjecture that the few clergy living as neighbours in country towns may not have encouraged each other to minister and preach in their country parishes.

Nor does it seem necessary to assume that parishes served in such a way were neglected either materially or spiritually. Although the evidence is slender there does not seem to be any clear correlation between such parishes and churches noted in archdeacons' visitation books as being at all neglected and, if Joseph Charles is at all representative, he took a very close interest in his parish of Wighton though he lived at Wells. He inquired closely into how an endowment left for a school had been lost by the bankruptcy of the trustees and he also records his attempt to secure an augmentation by Queen Anne's bounty of the living by £200 to match his own gift of land to the value of £200 but because of the dilatoriness of the secretary to Queen Anne's bounty the deal fell through.[37]

It would seem quite clear therefore that towns did make an impact on the pattern of residence in their localities, that there was a tendency for clergy to congregate in them and if these towns were clerical strongholds like Oxford or to a lesser extent Norwich[38] the impact could be very considerable. It is also clear that, setting aside the thorny question of pluralism (and it must be remembered that for a county like Norfolk the population of some of these parishes even in the 1801 census was very small) it was not necessary that such a system should detract from the standard of pastoral care expected by the age, or even by the charge in the ordinal of the book of common prayer, that it was not in fact dissimilar to the pattern of large parishes and chapelries to be found in medieval Hampshire in the Meon Valley and until the mid-nineteenth century in the West Riding of Yorkshire. Although the practice might not have been desirable in an ideal situation, bearing in mind the points that have been made and especially the meagreness of many of the livings in question from the point of view of both population and income, it was not so hurtful as bishop Bagot implied.

Salisbury and Wells Theological College

[36] G. C. B. Davies, *Truro Clerical Club 1750–60*, *Church Quarterly Review* 145 (London 1947–8) p 83.

[37] Norwich NNRO MS 11927 a and b 34D *Diary of the Revd Joseph Charles*.

[38] Sixteen of the incumbents without curates who served parishes in the locality in 1784 lived in Norwich and five of them also held city parishes.

PERPETUAL CURACIES IN EIGHTEENTH CENTURY SOUTH WALES

by JOHN R. GUY

IN 1715 the governors of Queen Anne's Bounty promoted a bill in parliament 'for making more effectual her late Majesty's gracious intentions for augmenting the maintenance of the poor clergy'.[1] Section four of this statute declared that the bounty had been 'intended to extend not only to parsons and vicars who come in by presentation or collation, institution and induction; but likewise to such ministers who come in by donation, or are only stipendiary preachers or curates'.

These classes of livings, donatives and impropriate or appropriate curacies, were quite extensive. In the six rural deaneries of the diocese of Llandaff, for example, there were forty-two livings out of a total of one hundred and eighty in these categories—some twenty-four per cent. Clearly if the bounty benefactions had not been made available to these classes of livings, a high proportion of needy parishes would have been excluded, for it is generally accepted that donatives and curacies upon impropriation were amongst the poorest livings. In 1737 the anonymous author of a pamphlet entitled *Some Considerations upon Pluralities, Non-Residence and Salaries of Curates*[2] admitted that 'The Churches of many Parishes, whose whole Tythes are in the hands of Lay Impropriators, have either no fixt Maintenance at all, or a very insufficient one'.[3] The commission of enquiry set up by bishop John Tyler of Llandaff in 1718 'to Inform ourselves of ye true and clear improv'd yearly value of Every Benefice'[4] certainly gives evidence of this in south Wales. For example, the curate of St John the Baptist in Llantrisant was paid 'by voluntary contributions'[5] and at Penterry the curate received two pounds from the appropriator.[6]

[1] Queen Anne's Bounty Act. 1 George I, c.10 (1715).
[2] *Some Considerations upon Pluralities, Non-Residence, and Salaries of Curates* (London 1737).
[3] *Ibid* p 25.
[4] Aberystwyth, N[ational] L[ibrary of] W[ales] MS LL/Bounty/139–40, 145–6, 148, 150, 153–4.
[5] NLW MS LL/Bounty/145.
[6] NLW MS LL/Bounty/150.

As a general rule, curates upon impropriations received a salary the equivalent of between one quarter and one third of the rectorial tithe. Some impropriators were more generous. Lord Mansel paid the curate of Margam a salary of forty pounds 'plus lodgings and food at the house'[7] (the curate was his domestic chaplain) and in several other of his parishes the curate received about one-third of the tithe as a salary from his lordship. Other impropriators were less generous. The curate of Llandevaud was supposed to receive four pounds from the prebendary of Warthacwm in Llandaff, but in 1718 no salary had been paid for six years. The commissioners reported that as a result there had been no service for six years, and the church was in ruins.[8]

Obviously there was a pressing need for the augmentation of the income in such cases as these, though whether the somewhat haphazard lottery system of the Queen Anne's Bounty was the best way of achieving it is open to debate. Samuel Smith, lecturer of St Alban's, Wood Street saw the problem when, preaching before the 'Trustees for Establishing the Colony of Georgia in America' in 1731, he said 'There are Numbers of Parochial Cures, whose mean Endowment the Revenues of the Corporation can't in a long Course of Years by the best Management, be enlarg'd to augment'.[9] As far as Llandaff was concerned, there was much truth in his judgement. By 1771, the curacy of Llandevaud mentioned earlier had been augmented to ten pounds, a rise of two hundred and fifty per cent, but this was still the equivalent only of the wages of a 'tolerably expert husbandman' or agricultural labourer in the area at the time.[10]

Very few of the Llandaff impropriate curacies attracted benefactions to Queen Anne's Bounty during the century, which the corporation would then meet by an equivalent augmentation, but most of those benefactions were from the impropriators themselves. Lord Mansel in 1743 gave lands worth two hundred pounds to the curacy of Briton Ferry, and the reverend Miles Bassett the vicarial tithes and a rent-charge of three pounds a year to the curacy of Bonvilston in 1764. Both were met by an equivalent augmentation from the bounty.[11]

[7] NLW MS LL/Bounty/140.

[8] NLW MS LL/Bounty/150.

[9] *Sermon before the Trustees for Establishing the Colony of Georgia in America and the Associates of the late Rev Dr Thomas Bray by Samuel Smith, LLB, Lecturer of St Alban's, Wood Street, 1730–1* (London 1733).

[10] D. J. Davies, *The economic history of south Wales prior to 1800* (Cardiff 1933) pp 146–7.

[11] [Christopher] Hodgson, [*An Account of the Augmentation of Small Livings by the Governors of the Bounty of Queen Anne*] (London 1826) pp 164, 179.

However, with livings as poor as the Llandaff impropriate curacies, the augmentations of the bounty would never be adequate to provide a realistic living wage for a resident incumbent. The only solution would be the return to the parishes of the impropriated tithes—a most unlikely event. As early as 1550 Thomas Lever had seen that the vested interests of the gentry, ecclesiastical corporations and capitular bodies would all stand in the way of reform. As Christopher Hill commented 'though on paper the economic problems of the church could easily have been solved by the restoration of impropriations, in practice cure was less simple than diagnosis'.[12]

Related to this problem of inadequate income was that of the absence or insufficiency of parsonage houses. Addressing his clergy in 1802, bishop Richard Watson of Llandaff linked the two very clearly. 'To enforce the residence of the Clergy without giving them, in a thousand, in many thousand instances, a competence to live on, or an house to put their heads in, is, in my mind, beginning the business at the wrong end'.[13] The impropriate curacies—indeed, the majority of livings in his diocese—fell far short of Watson's definition of a 'competence' which he had spelt out as early as 1783 in his *Letter to the Archbishop*: 'Whether we suppose an officiating minister to have £120 or £150 a year, it is a sum not much to be envied him. Apothecaries and Attornies, in very moderate practice, make as much by their respective professions . . .'[14] In many cases the income of curates upon impropriations still fell short of the 'Act for the better Maintenance of Curates' of 1714[15], which provided for allowances for licensed assistant curates of not less than twenty pounds and not more than fifty. In relation to parsonage houses, the situation in these parishes was well nigh hopeless. Not one possessed a place of residence for its minister. In forty-one of the forty-two there was no house at all, and in the sole exception, Peterston Wentloog, the glebe house was in ruins.[16] Unless the impropriator or appropriator was prepared voluntarily to provide a residence house, then the chances of there being a resident minister were remote. The incumbent simply was not in a financial position to

[12] Christopher Hill, *Economic Problems of the Church* (Oxford 1956, Panther ed 1971) pp 138–9, 149, 153.

[13] Richard Watson, *A Charge to the Clergy of Llandaff at the Visitation of 1802* (London 1803) pp 22–3.

[14] Richard Watson, *Letter to the Archbishop of Canterbury* (London 1783) p 28.

[15] 13 Anne, c. 11.

[16] NLW MS LL/PB/1, ['Particulars of Benefices 1771–1812, "Bishop Barrington's Book" '].

build or acquire a suitable house, even after the passing of the 'Gilbert Acts' of 1777 and 1781, which enabled him to raise money for a parsonage by mortgaging the income of the benefice. They were of no help in such poor parishes as these.[17] Thus in the majority of cases, such parishes were condemned to service by clergy resident elsewhere. In 1771, for example, only four had a resident incumbent, and of these one was also patron, impropriator and lord of the manor. All possessed other livings.

It has to be said that the absence of a resident parson in many of these parishes was not too serious a spiritual deprivation. In the earlier part of the eighteenth century all were in the rural areas of the diocese, and though as the century advanced some were affected by industrialisation, most remained as country parishes with small populations. Even today only sixteen of these forty-two parishes have resident incumbents. Of those for which some estimate of population is possible, the majority were below three hundred. Penterry contained only four families in 1763.[18] Yet in several cases the absence of a resident minister or of adequate provision for one was to the detriment of the church. Parishes such as Margam (two hundred and twenty-nine families in 1763), Bedwellty (three-hundred and fifty) or Newchurch (one hundred and fifty) were quite heavily populated by south Walian standards at this time, yet none possessed a parsonage house and none an income of more than forty-four pounds a year. Of the parish of Newchurch there is this almost contemporary record: 'The stated service of the parish church was never performed more frequently than once a fortnight, and six weeks were often allowed to pass away without the attendance of a clergyman'.[19]

Impropriate curacies were affected by another provision of section four of the 1715 Queen Anne's Bounty Act, namely that 'all chapelries or curacies augmented by the Governors would be thenceforth perpetual cures and benefices.' Savidge has this as meaning that 'their ministers to be in law bodies politic and corporate and their succession to be perpetual. No impropriator, patron, rector or vicar of a mother church may obtain any kind of profit from such augmentation, but

[17] 'An Act to promote the Residence of the Parochial Clergy, by making Provision for the more speedy and effectual building, rebuilding, repairing or purchasing Houses, and other necessary Buildings and Tenements, for the Use of their Benefices', 17 George III, c.53.
'An Act to explain and amend an Act . . .', 21 George III, c.66.

[18] NLW MS LL/QA/2, Visitation Queries and Answers. 1763.

[19] Sir Thomas Phillips, *The Life of James Davies, a Village Schoolmaster* (London 1852) p 28.

on the other hand, they must continue always to pay to the ministers concerned "such annual and other pensions, salaries and allowances which by ancient customs or otherwise, of right and not of bounty", ought to be by them respectively paid and allowed before the benefices were augmented'.[20] The purpose of this provision section four of the act itself makes clear. 'In many places it would be in the power of the impropriator, donor, parson or vicar to withdraw the allowance now or heretofor paid to the curate or minister serving the cure . . . and the maintenance of the curate or minister would thus be sunk instead of being augmented'.

This provision gave to the ministers of such benefices, as soon as an augmentation had been made, the security that they had hitherto not possessed. They were now 'perpetual curates' who could not be removed at the whim of the impropriator, whereas previously as often unlicensed ministers their tenure had been very uncertain. They were now assured of the income, however small, previously allowed 'by ancient customs or otherwise' plus that from the bounty augmentation. Thus the curate of Merthyr Mawr after that benefice was first augmented by lot in 1761 was guaranteed his tenure and his salary after his appointment by the sinecure rector, the archdeacon of Llandaff.

There were, however, several unlooked-for problems created by the bounty legislation. Its effect upon the impropriators in south Wales, with very few exceptions, was to freeze the stipend of the perpetual curate from this source. Thus in 1771 the compiler of the parish terrier of Merthyr Mawr, ten years after the first augmentation of that living, could write 'the salary of the Curate always and ever was £13-6-8d. yearly'.[21] Not until 1786 did this particular living receive a benefaction, and then not from its patron and appropriator, the archdeacon of Llandaff.[22]

A second problem was that under the provisions of the 1715 act chapelries became eligible for augmentation and their ministers perpetual curates thereafter. Further, the incumbent of the mother church was debarred from profiting from the augmentation. In the diocese of Llandaff the effect of this was to create a whole new group

[20] Alan Savidge, *The foundation and early years of Queen Anne's Bounty* (London 1955) pp 61–2.

[21] Glamorgan County Record Office MS D/D Cl 1/90–104, Leases of Merthyr Mawr Church and tithes, etc. 1738–*c*1801.

[22] Hodgson p 194.

of inadequately endowed 'perpetual curacies' and once the augmentation had been accepted for these former chapelries the original incumbent of the parish church was prevented from serving them in person and obliged to appoint curates for them. As the century progressed and augmentations by lot were received, the ancient chapelries within such widespread parishes as Llantrisant in Glamorgan and Llanover in Gwent became perpetual curacies, with only the right of patronage left with the incumbent of the mother church. In the former, the chapelry of Aberdare was first augmented in 1772,[23] and a perpetual curacy established—but worth only twenty-eight pounds a year and possessing no parsonage.[24] Instead of reducing the number of livings which could not support a resident minister, in the Llandaff diocese the 1715 act increased the number.

Again, an unlooked-for effect of this bounty legislation was to provide further opportunities for plurality and non-residence. As Phillimore expressed it, for legal purposes 'a perpetual curacy is not an ecclesiastical benefice [and] was under the old law tenable with any other benefice'.[25] Such livings did not come within the provisions of the principal post-reformation statute regulating plurality.[26] The legal position was this: 'canon law and statutory rules are construed strictly against the legislators, so that any given case not clearly within the scope of the canon or statute would be considered exempt from them'.[27] Further, not being for legal purposes ecclesiastical benefices, it is doubtful whether the provisions of the same statute regulating non-residence could be enforced either.[28] In any case, want or insufficiency of the parsonage house was regarded as a valid reason for the granting of a licence of non-residence by the diocesan bishop, and as has been seen, most of the perpetual curacies in south Wales fell within this category.

When bishop Shute Barrington completed his survey of his diocese after his primary visitation in 1771,[29] the pattern for the perpetual curacies was evident. In only four cases did the incumbent reside,

[23] *Ibid.* Contained in the alphabetical list, pp 334–42.

[24] NLW MS LL/PB/1.

[25] Robert Phillimore, *The Ecclesiastical Law of the Church of England,* ed W. G. F. Phillimore and C. F. Jemmett, 1 (London 1895) p 240.

[26] 21 Henry VIII, c.13, sec.9.

[27] The legal opinion of Mr Timothy Briden, Gray's Inn. I am grateful to the revd chancellor E. Garth Moore for providing me with this.

[28] 21 Henry VIII, c.13, sec.15.

[29] NLW MS LL/PB/1. See also LL/QA/4–5.

though in another twenty-six he served his cure in person. In fourteen instances, the perpetual curate was himself employing a curate to discharge the duties of his living. In these cases, in all but one instance there was a profit margin for the incumbent. For example, the perpetual curacy of Michaelston-super-Avon was worth thirty pounds, the serving curate received fourteen; that of Llanfair Discoed was worth fifteen, the serving curate received seven. So the incumbents, all pluralists, were without prejudice to their other preferments receiving modest but useful augmentations of their income for no extra work, but to do so were employing usually unlicensed curates at grossly substandard wages, and thus violating the spirit if not the letter of the bounty governors' intentions. The wages paid to the curates being insufficient to support them, in their turn they themselves are revealed as non-residents or pluralists or both. Edward Thomas, serving Llanfair Discoed for seven pounds, also served the adjacent curacy of Caerwent for fifteen, as well as his own living of Caldicot, worth thirty-five. He possessed another benefice at the other end of the diocese worth sixty, where he himself employed a curate for fifteen. In this complex manner, he brought his gross income to one hundred and seventeen pounds, and his net to just over the one hundred, which was still what his subsequent diocesan bishop Watson considered below the minimum 'competence' upon which to live. The career of Edward Thomas can be used to exemplify something else. Because almost without exception the perpetual curates held other local benefices they cannot be distinguished as a class in isolation from the other diocesan clergy in social origin or academic attainment.

On balance, in South Wales the creation of perpetual curacies created more problems than it solved. At the end of the eighteenth century almost all were still too poor to support a resident incumbent, few had anywhere for him to live, and because of their anomalous legal position they gave further opportunity for the exploitation of an already far from satisfactory system.

Wolvesnewton
Gwent

WHEN CITY SPEAKS FOR COUNTY: THE EMERGENCE OF THE TOWN AS A FOCUS FOR RELIGIOUS ACTIVITY IN THE NINETEENTH CENTURY

by ALAN ROGERS

THE theme of this paper is an attempt to establish when the town emerged as a focal point for religious activity for a set district in the nineteenth century. I have some hesitations in setting about the task, for we are dealing here with attitudes, with what the French call *l'histoire des mentalités*, and it is not at all clear that all the evidence exists. I propose, however, to use three examples—circuit records from the Louth area of Lincolnshire, diaries (again from Lincolnshire), and a rather briefer case-study of Saint Mary's church, Nottingham. Apart from the last, it may be agreed that these particular instances are not typical of Victorian England—that the towns are small and not industrialised, unlike Bradford or Bristol; and that the area is large and diversified unlike a county like Leicestershire where almost all roads lead to the county town. Nevertheless, both the enquiry and the range of evidence can be justified; and the conclusion—that the town emerged as a focal point for religious activities later than for other more secular functions—may be applicable to other areas.

Let us be quite clear what it is that we are and that we are not talking about. I am not suggesting that there was no difference in quality between the religious life of town and country in the early years of the nineteenth century or that they had little interaction. Contemporaries themselves saw a clear difference: the Reverend John Rashdall who served as curate in Orby (Lincs) in 1833–5 wrote of his new incumbent: 'a good man certainly, and better fitted for a Village than a Town'.[1] The size of church and chapel (both the congregation and the building), the quality of the ministry, the relationship with qualified professional clergy and the range of services (in all senses of the word) available to the town laity, and probably even the quality of lay leadership—all these were markedly different from those in rural

[1] Oxford Bodleian MS Eng misc e 351. I must acknowledge with deep gratitude the help of the following: D. N. Robinson (Louth), D. G. Stuart and J. H. Briggs (Keele).

areas, and they grew more pronounced, not less, as the century progressed. Many towns like Louth were religious 'centres' in a different sense; the number of full-time clergy who resided in Louth (that 'nest of rooks') in preference to living within call of their cures was noted with disapproval frequently throughout the first half of the century.[2] But it is not the differences between town and country that is the subject of this paper.

Nor are we so concerned with the fact that titularly the town frequently stood at the head of any church grouping at this time. The two earliest methodist circuits known to north Lincolnshire were centred on Grimsby and Epworth; but thereafter virtually all the circuits in Lincolnshire were named after a town (Gainsborough, Horncastle, Boston (temporarily), Spalding, Louth (established in 1799), Lincoln, Spilsby, Grantham and so on), although Barrow-on-Humber also features in this early list. In the re-organisation after the reform movement of 1849–50, the circuits were again named after twelve towns.[3] The salaried ministers usually resided at these urban 'centres'. But this probably reflects a ministerial set of attitudes rather than the view of the more average Wesleyan supporter; it represents an urban view of the church to start with, just as the life-style of the minister set him apart especially from his rural followers.

My concern rather is with the village and its interest in the town, not vice versa. Town and country in the first half of the nineteenth century were separate, distinct; and the enquiry I wish to pursue is when (if ever) did the rural resident come to regard the town as a natural focus for special religious events or indeed for normal religious 'servicing' functions (if I may abuse a word in this context!). When did the town church or chapel come to regard itself as the dominant partner, the leader and spokesman for the more rural congregations round it?

My first set of evidence is drawn from the records of Louth Wesleyan circuit (the largest of the Lincolnshire circuits) and especially circuit preaching plans. A study of these reveals some surprising features.[4] In

[2] [J.] Obelkevich, [*Religion and Rural Society*] (Oxford 1976) pp 116–17, 119, 191. Obelkevich's important study of the Louth area is the basis of all further study, but he omits the town from his examination of rural religion.

[3] W. Leary, *Wesleyan Circuits in Lincolnshire* (privately printed).

[4] L[incolnshire] A[rchives] O[ffice], Louth Circuit records.

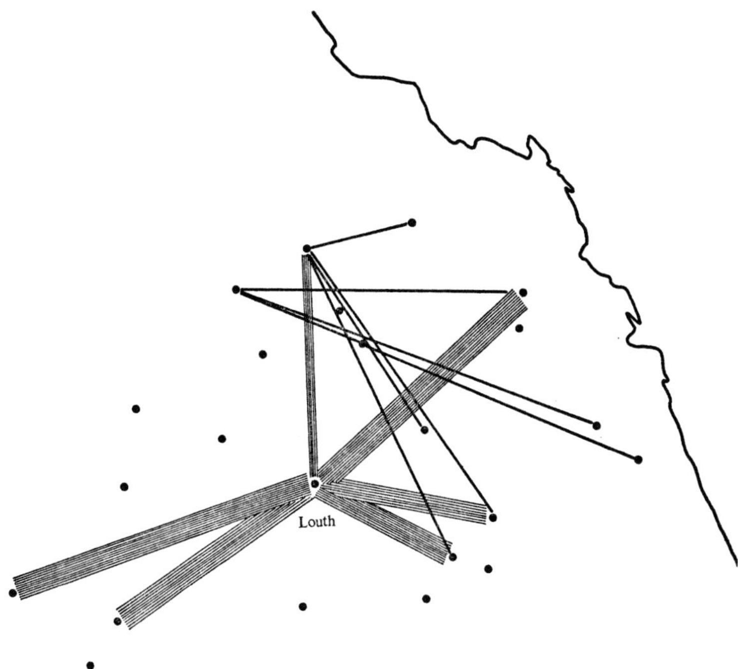

FIG. 1A. Sketch map of Louth circuit (Wesleyan) based on the circuit preaching plan of 1819. The journeys made by the full-time ministers from Louth to local societies are indicated by multiple lines. The preaching networks of two of the twenty-three local preachers who served the rural societies are also shown: Thomas Storr of Fulstow and George Rose of Ludborough.

the early years of the century the salaried ministers preached in very few of the rural chapels of the circuit. In 1818, the ministers conducted Sunday worship with only seven societies, and in 1819 with only six societies, leaving nineteen others without their presence (Fig 1A). What is more, their relations with these select centres were intensive; in 1815, a salaried minister took half of all the services in six societies and *all* the services in a further two; but seven others saw them not at all. For many years, the ministers monopolised the Louth pulpit to the almost complete exclusion of laymen; and their duties extended to only a limited number of other centres. The members of most of the rural societies did not see their minister for Sunday worship from one year's end to the next; they depended on local preachers. Some half of these lay leaders came from Louth, but many of the more active came from centres outside Louth. Michael Burman of North Somercotes, for instance, and Thomas Storr labourer of Fulstow, both preached during the second six months of 1819 to six societies of the circuit, George Easting of Legbourn shoemaker in four. Not all the local preachers on the plan can be identified, unfortunately; but at least one of the rurally based (Waterman) preached to no less than ten societies. The implication of this is that it was not the town *per se* which was the focal point, but the residence of activists in the movement, and that there could be more than one such centre in each circuit. This came to be recognised somewhat later, in that ministers of the circuit lived for short periods in North Somercotes and in Grimoldby.

Louth circuit may in this have been untypical, but a glance at other circuits suggests that it was not. In Grimsby for instance in 1822, the ministers preached in eleven of the twenty-two places in the plan, in most of them taking all or most of the services: Grimsby, Caistor and Cleethorpes being towns (albeit small) expected and obtained the services of the professionals; so did Scartho, Laceby and Grasby where the morning service was always taken by a minister. Another five places saw one of the ministers once, the rest not at all. The same pattern is revealed by an examination of other focal events. Baptism[5] was held infrequently and very rarely on a Sunday, but it was as likely to be in one of the village 'centres' as in a town. Services of holy communion of course occurred only where the minister served, but more frequently (comparatively) in villages than in towns. In 1815, Louth had three services in the six-month plan period, Marshchapel and Grainthorpe, and Saltfleet and North Somercotes (both united societies) four times each. Two love feasts were held at Louth, two at Carlton and one at three other (rural) centres; so that even if the injunction which appears on the Sheffield New Connexion (1809–10) plan was honoured later and elsewhere without explicit mention: 'no preaching at those places within six miles of Sheffield on Love-feast days',[6] it would in the Louth circuit apply as much to rural areas as to towns. Even quarterly meetings were held in Carlton as often as in Louth.

What is thus clear is that in Louth circuit in the early nineteenth century there were several centres at which the ministers preached,

[5] LAO Louth Circuit, Register of Baptisms.

[6] For this information and other material on the Louth circuit, I owe thanks to W. Leary of Lincoln whose collection of circuit plans has proved most useful.

administered the sacraments, conducted love feasts and held quarterly meetings—places as small as Legbourn, Carlton, Saltfleetby, North Somercotes and Benniworth; and it is to these centres that their attentions were restricted. The laity outside these centres of course had contact with their ministers, especially through their quarterly renewal of membership tickets, but Sunday worship led by the minister was confined to some six centres. Why they should have existed is not clear. It is not a matter of chapel building, for fifteen of the twenty-two places in the circuit had built chapels before 1819. It is possible that these six favoured chapels were among the earliest preaching centres in the circuit and may thus have inherited a status above the other newer societies. But this can hardly be the full explanation, for there were other early preaching centres (such as Grainthorpe where a chapel had been erected as early as 1790) not so honoured.

By the 1840s, the picture had moderated slightly. The Horncastle 'glory' (the New Year's love feast) emerged in the 1840s as a major event in the calendar; and in 1835, at the opening of the new Louth chapel by Jabez Bunting, the circuit plan announced: 'usual preaching in other parts of the circuit will be dispensed with' (4 October 1835). But these were still rare.[7] By 1844 however ministers preached in thirty-eight out of the forty-nine places listed on the plan, and rarely more than four times in the quarter. Nevertheless, preachers from Saltfleet, Reston and Legbourn preached in fourteen, fourteen and eleven places in the circuit respectively. While Louth was still distinctive in its style of religious life, there are few signs that it was the centre to which all the chapels in the circuit looked. By 1866, (Fig 1B) however, only six very small societies did not appear on the full-time ministers' preaching plan; the centrality of Louth had thus been considerably strengthened. At the same time came the spreading of the sacraments and other special services more widely throughout the circuit; by 1837, love feasts were held in twenty-two villages and holy communion in eighteen villages. Nevertheless the central role of Louth was now clear. Both occasional services and organisational meetings came to be centred in the town—the missionary prayer meetings, prayer leaders' meetings and circuit committees, all held monthly. A covenant service appears at Louth (after the break) in 1855, and spreads by 1883 to five places in the circuit. Gradually the role of Louth becomes predominant. 'A Public Meeting for Prayer and Humiliation before

[7] The same instruction is given on the Lincoln plan for 1835 on the occasion of the opening of the 'Big Wesley' there.

FIG. 1B. Sketchmap of Louth circuit (Wesleyan) in 1886, drawn from preaching plan. The thick lines represent the preaching journeys from Louth of the full-time ministers. The preaching network of one of the fifty-three local preachers who served the circuit is also shown. It will be noted that very few of the local chapels did not receive a preaching visit from a full-time minister by 1886.

God will be held . . . in the Vestry of Eastgate Chapel [Louth]; and it is earnestly Requested that similar Meetings be held, where practicable, throughout the Circuit' (Friday 28 June 1861) gives way to 'In connection with the Quarterly Meeting there will be a Christmas Tree and Sale of Goods to pay off the Circuit debt. . . . The Friends throughout the Circuit are entreated to help this effort to the utmost of their ability' (1883). Louth comes to command the attention of the rest of the circuit. It is from this year that the 'festival and aggregate' meeting appears, with a visit by the president of Conference; but even then other services are scheduled, even in nearby chapels. From 1884, a circuit convention is held in Louth: 'The attendance was large and the proceedings were very hopeful for the future of Methodism in the circuit'. As changes in the administration of Wesleyanism on a national scale emphasised the role of the circuit (such as the assessment from Conference for the Children's Fund), so the town chapel assumed the role of focus and leader of the village chapels. By 1886, there were held there in three months a local preachers' convention (17–18 January), a circuit festival (17 February), a Band of Hope festival (1 March), the trustees' yearly meeting (9 March), a home missionary anniversary (14–15 March) and a quarterly meeting (26 March). The town had arrived.

The evidence of Wesleyan circuit records suggests that in part of Lincolnshire, at least, the focal functions of town chapels did not reach maturity until the 1870s or 1880s. And this is in striking contrast to other areas of social concern. The town for instance was the dominant partner and focus for the new Poor Law unions as early as the 1840s. Louth was at the centre of a union covering eighty-eight villages, and its workhouse contained inmates drawn from a large proportion of those villages, while the collection of the poor rate provided a regular reminder of the centrality of the town. Such groupings were not unusual, although Louth was by far the largest in the county; both Stamford and Bourne unions in south Lincolnshire covered thirty-seven villages each. Again, the quarter sessions, the parliamentary elections and the continuing hundred organisation all emphasised the role of the town, apart from the more obvious centrality of trading functions.

Such evidence as may be adduced from the rather impersonal circuit records suggests that the town emerged late on the religious scene as a focus for a rural region. The evidence may of course be partial; it may reflect changes in the information recorded in the preaching plans more than changes in patterns of behaviour. But it is important to remember that such records will reflect the views of the centre more than the views of the villages, and as such they will tend to over-emphasise rather than under-emphasise the role of the urban community. Indeed, this bias was felt from the 1850s onwards; in an attempt to match the bishops' efforts to remove the anglican clergy from the towns where they had congregated into the villages by means of the so-called 'vicarage movement' of the 1830s and 1840s among other things, there were calls to establish Wesleyan ministers in rural areas;[8] but since these came from the more 'urbanised' elements in the denomination, they were unsuccessful. Nevertheless, they point

[8] Obelkevich pp 185, 215.

clearly to contemporary appreciation of the dichotomy between town and country which had not been bridged.

Is there any evidence which will reveal more truly the attitudes of country dwellers to the town at the centre of their region? My second strand looks at a number of journals or diaries of persons living in rural areas: the enquiry is simple—on what occasions did they visit the towns and for what purpose? The collection used here covers both anglican and methodist, clergy and lay, and ranges in date from the late eighteenth century to the last years of the nineteenth century. The fact that they reveal all the preoccupations of their writers, more often secular than religious, enhances their value.

Thomas Edman[9] was an early Wesleyan preacher and pioneer, whose preaching book relates his daily journeys in the Grimsby, Louth and Gainsborough areas between 1795 and 1819, before he moved off to Norwich. A very human picture emerges of a somewhat naive young man, on occasion surprised at being followed by young women (and at least twice causing local scandals by his innocence) and liable to bouts of despair: 'I am going to give over travelling', he writes at the end of one particularly tiring tour. His work was almost entirely rural in character; he visited Lincoln to bank money left to him by his father, and Horncastle for its fair. All the religious functions he attended were in the villages. 'Yesterday was our Quarter-Day at Barrow—Love Feast' he recorded; and other quarter days and love feasts were held at Ferriby, Grainthorpe and Tealby ('my two fellow labourers are at odds', perhaps over the Kilham agitation) as well as at Louth ('the Love was a Solemn Good time in deed'), while a district meeting was held at that centre of rural methodism, Raithby. The situation is clearly revealed by the national fasts: 'Yesterday was a National Fast. I spake in the Morning at Whitton and Last Night at Alkborough—But I did not offer to Meddle with anything of a Political nature'. Later national fasts were held at Great Cotes and Stallingborough, both small villages in north Lincolnshire. The town does not emerge with any particular major role, other than business, in Edman's diary.

William Allison's[10] memoirs are more tedious than Edman's

[9] LAO, Louth Circuit records.
[10] *Ibid.*

journal. He was a weaver from Theddlethorpe and his jottings, which cover his whole life's span, 1782 to 1854, reveal him as introspective, self-doubting and only semi-literate. His whole life centred round his own chapel: 'if It had Not a been For Class meetings and Lovefeasts and Fellshipmeetings my Saul would got on very badly i Should Found it very Hard Woark To get on at all'. He refused to become class leader at first (1828) but later (1837) accepted. His book is, as he himself tells us, the chronicle of his soul, begun in earnest in 1836 after his son was taken fatally ill while he was away from home preaching at Mablethorpe; he wrote up every Sunday what spiritual progress he had made since the last entry.

Allison went out of Theddlethorpe virtually only for religious functions. He went to Burgh for family reasons, but apart from this it is preachings and love feasts which drew him away from home. None of these was to a town; love feasts at Strubby, Trusthorpe and Huttoft and preachers at Mablethorpe attracted him: 'many good testimonies' were given at Strubby in August 1841. What is clear also is that his own chapel's functions attracted visitors from neighbouring villages: a revival in September 1842, a love feast in 1846 ('never saw so many people'), another in October 1848 ('did three hours pas away'). In June 1846, 'had our Scool Feast—and a wonderfull Compene of People we had—it was soposed there was Five Hunderred People Yong and ould the Collection was To amound of £13.6s. . . . We had Elven preachers'. Louth did not appear to impinge on his little world.

This was perhaps to be expected with the various branches of methodism, with its strong rural base ('the country villages which . . . are its principal strongholds', as bishop Jackson expressed it in 1864),[11] and its traditions of open-air preachings and camp meetings. What of the church of England, more used to visitations held in town churches? It is of course possible that such visitations might well set the rural people against the town rather than encourage recognition of its central role. The evidence is that the town was no more a centre for the anglicans than for the methodists. Two diaries help us here, both written by clergy.

The Reverend F. C. Massingberd was a member of a local gentry family, rector of Ormsby and Driby, two small villages in the south Lincolnshire wolds. His diary,[12] which covers effectively the years 1826

[11] T. W. Mossman, 'The Church in Lincolnshire', *Union Review* 3 (Lincoln 1865).

[12] LAO, Mass 8/1.

to 1841, opens with a fancy dress ball at Derby and this remains its tone throughout. He is an excellent example of that urbanised cultured clergyman depicted by bishop Jackson: 'whose tastes and sphere of action seem to lie . . . in the library, the drawing room, and the garden, if not in the ball-room, at the card-table, and in the hunting field', who swept the board at urban flower shows and read Tory papers in the Lincoln news-room.[13] He travelled extensively, almost hectically—'all on seemingly necessary business' as he put it—much of it on family affairs; there was a marked decline in his itineration after he got married in 1831, but he still travelled. Social events like races, stuff balls and dinners took him to towns and villages indiscriminately—to Lincoln, to Horncastle ('evening spent as usual playing whist with CBM')[14]; dinner at Harrington, Theddlethorpe and Anderby: the fair at Horncastle, a booksale at Spilsby, the cricket club at Louth, shooting on the marshes at Skegness, races at Lincoln. Business took him to Alford (to buy canal shares), voting to Lincoln and 'the Shipwreck Society' to Spilsby and Skegness. He was kept busy after his appointment as a JP ('there being apprehensions of fire and disturbance in consequence of the general discontent . . . much occupied with investigations about incendiary fires', 1831); all the sessions and magistrates' meetings were held in the neighbouring towns. A few of his visits were for religious purposes; a meeting at Louth in 1836 concerning tithe commutation, the visitation at Horncastle, and the diocesan education board (which he joined in 1838) at Lincoln—but these were often combined with other functions. At easter 1827 he went to Lincoln for a fancy dress ball, the installation of bishop Kaye and family affairs; in 1836, he combined the assizes and the education board. He preached away from home too, at Horncastle (for the dispensary 1828) and Lincoln (the Friendly Society sermon and for the county hospital 1829), though sermons did not come easily to him. But these—and his lectures—were almost as frequently in villages like Humberstone and Tetford as in towns. The religious life of Massingberd's wolds centred as much on the missionary meeting at Navenby, the revival at Calceby and indeed the 'Religious Society' in his own rural parish ('it seems to me to be a possible means of bringing back the universal people to the Church') as on the CMS meeting in Spilsby (1840). In the years from 1826 until he left for Rome (on a visit, that

[13] Obelkevich pp 125–7.
[14] The reverend Clement Madeley, vicar of Horncastle.

is), he only once went to a town for anything that resembled a religious regional meeting.

John Rashdall's diary[15] is different. After all, he was a poor curate in Orby, 1833–5, before he moved to Devon, rather than a rich gentleman-vicar. He was more moved by religious sentiment, having listened to Charles Simeon while at Cambridge, and his sympathies lay with the methodists. At first, not too serious-minded ('six weeks spent there [in London] between Idleness and Gaiety'; 'dined with the bishop [of Lincoln at Buckden]—sumptuous dinner—venison—all kinds of wine, etc—large establishment—handsome plate etc'), he seems to have undergone a conversion. Certainly the tone of his diary changes: after a visit to Horncastle fair, he wrote: 'it will I hope be the last that I shall attend'. His staple was culture and religion: a friend of 'Fred Tennyson' and habitué at Somersby, he also regularly attended bible meetings and methodist services.

He too travelled from Orby a lot in his two years—to Boston on business and family matters; to Louth for a masonic meeting, the fair and a concert; to Skegness for a holiday ('very idle'); to Lincoln for the hustings. He preached too—in Spilsby, Wainfleet and a number of villages. He went out hunting, shooting, riding and making social calls. He went to Spilsby for the visitation, but apart from that most of his urban religious visits were incidental, like Massingberd's. Passing through Boston, he 'heard Fox—Baptist Minister, Partney, preach, not as an Evangelist, as he says, but as a servant among the Brethren'; and on another occasion in Boston 'went to the Methodist chapel to hear Mr [that is, Dr Robert] Newton of Manchester'. Again, he went to Sunday service in the cathedral at Lincoln on his way through the town. A few 'central-type' meetings occur in the pages of the diary of this energetic curate: a 'grand Meeting at the Chapter House, Lincoln: Bishop in the chair: it was certainly a failure'; a sermon at Spilsby by 'Jones, Missionary of London Society at Madagascar for 14 years'; a bible meeting at Boston. But these too were often village centred; bible meetings at Wainfleet, Bolingbroke and Burgh ('went to Bible Meeting at Burgh, my first speech on such an occasion'), a visiting preacher at Partney ('heard Harris, Independent Minister at Alford in Partney chapel') and at Skendleby ('heard Wilson at Skendleby preach flowery language'). The town has not yet come to occupy a special role.

[15] Bodl MS Eng misc e 351: transcript in LAO Misc Don 125.

What of the laity? Henry Winn, parish clerk of Fulletby, teacher and grocer, provides an example.[16] His diary is somewhat later, 1845 to 1846, but the picture is much the same. Both Wesleyan and anglican, he too travelled much, but there is no record that he ever went to a town for a church function. He went to Horncastle for the market, fair and entertainment ('a small but good collection of wild beasts was in the town, and their excellent brass band enlivened the market'); he was sworn in there as a constable, attended a booksale, a temperance festival ('in Baptist Chapel because Wesleyan chapel not allowed him—no procession or music') and lectures ('The friends of temperance, education and civil and religious liberty all alive anticipating a rich intellectual treat next week, as H. Vincent an eloquent and popular lecturer is engaged to lecture on these subjects for four evenings' . . . 'the attendance was good'). He went to markets at Alford, Spilsby and Louth, and for business reasons to Louth, Boston and Spilsby. But he went to villages for the same range of functions: to Skegness for the Life Boats Regatta, to Tetford for a sale, a sick club anniversary and committee ('the West Ashby Church singers were in attendance, which was quite a treat'), to Belchford teetotal festival ('a large company'), and to Gayton le Marsh and Greetham for social and business purposes. It is clear that he and his rural contemporaries were as used to assemble in villages for large meetings as in towns. 'The Wesleyans had their annual missionary meeting in our village', he wrote of the circuit anniversary in 1846; and the Sunday School anniversary attracted visitors from outside of Fulletby.

The fact that these diarists—more likely to have been associated with urban culture than most of their neighbours—do not reveal signs of the regular focal meeting being held more often in towns than elsewhere is significant. It can be seen to make sense of other evidence. An anglican choir festival could still attract ten neighbouring villages to tiny Holton-le-Beckering in 1864 (population one hundred and eighty-five). Early in the nineteenth century, anglican confirmations (hitherto held in towns) were moved into the villages as part of the attempt to capture the population there. In 1851, the bishop of Lincoln held confirmations in thirty-one places[17]—all the major towns (eleven) and twenty villages in the northern half of the diocese. Nor were the villages short on confirmands. While Alford produced two hundred and three and Brigg had one hundred and forty-one, Ulceby had one

[16] LAO, Winn 1/1; see Obelkevich p 335.
[17] LAO, Mass 9/2.

FIG. 2. Diagram to show the number of confirmands in various urban and rural centres in north Lincolnshire in 1851, in relation to the size of the town or village. *Above:* the centres of confirmation have been arranged in order of population size (expressed in thousands), ranging from Lincoln (17,536) to Ormsby (261). *Below:* is shown the number of confirmands for each place (expressed in hundreds).

hundred and twenty-three, Owston one hundred and sixty-three and Scotter (a methodist stronghold if there ever were one) no less than one hundred and fifty. South Somercotes provided almost as many as Barton on Humber. As late as this, the towns had no clear predominance.

All this confirms fragmentary information elsewhere. It was at a meeting in Rauceby (Lincolnshire) rather than in a town that the first steps were taken to establish the Church Missionary Society. The chapel at Olney in north Buckinghamshire retained its prestige well into the nineteenth century, while the Baptist Missionary Society emerged from Moulton, near Northampton. The Northamptonshire Home Mission Society was founded in 1840 at Kislingbury (Northants), and within the area under discussion, the Ecclesiological Society began in the villages and only with difficulty spread to the towns.[18] Examples of such rural initiative could be multiplied.

Does the situation change later in the century? Two further journals help. The first is that of Cornelius Stovin[19] of Binbrook. A junior member of a well-known Lincolnshire farming family, he was also related to prominent early methodists like the Riggalls. His journal, commenced after a visit to Ireland, covers the years 1871–6 and reveals Cornelius as deeply—almost tediously—religious:

> In strolling as a pedestrian from Sotby last Tuesday night I saw a light in the window of one of our tenements. I concluded it was Coney waiting, but on approaching discovered that it was Smith who with his wife were bowed at their family altar, and she was very loudly and earnestly praying and he responding. The clock had struck eleven when these delightful voices of devotion reached my ear. I am deeply impressed with the guidance of God. I have seldom passed such a day of contrast in my own individual experience. The day has a heavenly winding up though at the fair I was brought in close contact with what was earthly, sensual and devilish. A larger amount of annoyance and distraction from without during the day than usual, while in the early morning and later eve my soul never seemed more high toned by glowing

[18] C. Hole, *Early History of the Church Missionary Society* (London 1896); [J. W. F.] Hill, *Victorian Lincoln* (Cambridge 1974) pp 175–6; Hill, 'Early days of a society', *Lincolnshire History and Archaeology* (Lincoln 1966) pp 57–63. I owe the information on Kislingbury to my student S. E. Payler.

[19] I owe the transcript to Miss Jean Stovin who is editing the diary under my supervision; the analysis is mine but I am most grateful to Miss Stovin for her comments. The diary is in private possession.

> thoughts of divine spirituality. My soul has great strength of wing for lofty contemplation.

Stovin was part of the Free Methodist movement and as such was in the Market Rasen circuit and in the Grimsby district. Class leader, local preacher, chapel trustee, district delegate to national conferences, he missed no opportunity to improve his knowledge and his piety, or to commit his new insights to writing in the form of papers, journals or letters. While staying with relatives, he visited the Bodleian Library, and he bought newspapers and books of sermons. Like many of his contemporaries, he was obsessed with health matters, his own or his family, frequently adapting the latest fad for a short time. When a visiting preacher revealed that he wore no braces, Stovin gladly threw away his, wondering why it was that he had been so long in bondage to such restrictive articles of clothing!

The diaries reveal a pattern of travel common to most middle rank tenant farmers of his day—mainly for business and partly for family reasons. Fairs at Horncastle, Alford, Louth, Market Rasen, Caistor and Partney claim his time. Of sales, those 'centres where the peasantry . . . met for gossip', he wrote: 'we have in our own neighbourhood abundant opportunities of posting ourselves in this kind of intelligence.' Louth was his main centre—for shopping, schooling for his son, the reading room and mechanics institute library: 'you have here at Louth a little temple of literature'. A member of the board of guardians, his duties regularly took him to that town, and so did his rent day and occasional lectures. He went to London for the agricultural show, and with his family to Woodhall Spa and Matlock in search of health.

But the majority of his journeyings were made for religious events—preaching engagements in the villages, quarterly meetings at Market Rasen and district meetings at Grimsby attended by representatives and office holders. He visited the new Louth Eastgate chapel on several occasions for special anniversaries and for the more regular Sunday services, and preached there—it was clearly regarded in the 1870s as some sort of central point for the region around. His own circuit held aggregates and circuit missionary meetings at Market Rasen, usually in the town hall. Local chapel events, such as the re-opening of Muckton chapel, the anniversary at Ludborough or South Reston, and the stone-laying ceremony at South Somercotes attracted support from other chapels including Louth; but the main circuit events like the 'reception' service were held in the town of Market Rasen. In 1874, at the circuit aggregate tea meeting, 'several representatives from the rural societies gave addresses of about five or ten minutes in length.' 'A large and enthusiastic congregation' attended the service in 1872; 'a very enthusiastic meeting' was held in Grimsby in 1873—most of them characterised by an ecumenical spirit which even then must have been remarkable. What is clear is that by the time this diary was composed, circuit events were normally centred in the town—although large gatherings aimed to bring in both cash and conversions still took place in village centres, many of which he chaired.

George Bird, the final diarist in this study, comes from Corby Glen in south Lincolnshire. A wheelwright and undertaker in his father's small business, he started his diary in 1865 at the age of fifteen, and volumes survive up to 1883.[20] It is one of the most valuable and vivid of all pictures of rural life, for brief entries of the doings of himself, of his family and of the village were made each day of the year. His work took him frequently into the villages around Corby, and to Bourne and especially Grantham for the market and the bank.

He and his family were more than usually devout, although his own interest in piety seems to have fallen off as time went on. They went to church and to chapel regularly including special weekday services and even to the Roman church whenever the bishop came to Corby. Occasionally his 'polite' susceptibilities were offended by a primitive methodist camp meeting: 'was very disappointed with the speaking and the clapping of hands, seemed to be altogether out of place in a place of worship' (28 March 1871); but on the whole his taste was more for services (especially preachings) than for churchmanship. His father was churchwarden as well as parish constable in Corby. Perhaps it was this which led to the entry: 'Father and I went to Church in the morning, we took possession of a fresh Pew, like it better than the old one'; although pews could on occasion cause embarrassment: on a visit to nearby Burton chapel, 'we turned in a pew when Mr Hutchinson no doubt wishing to show what little authority vested in him, gave us plainly to understand, we were in the wrong pew, as it was a paid sitting, so we were obliged to get into another, not customary to turn strangers out of a pew in a place of worship, but from "an Ass we can expect nothing but a Bray". I set it down to the poor fellow's ignorance; this is politeness in the nineteenth century.'

Two things facilitated his travelling—the railway which passed through Corby and which enabled him to make excursions to

[20] A few years are missing. The diary is in private possession; a transcript has been made by my student John Liddie.

Liverpool, Manchester (Belle Vue Gardens) and London as well as to nearer places like Nottingham and Cleethorpes ('the breeze is so bracing'); and secondly the bicycle. The arrival of the 'velocipede' in the village in 1870 caused a stir, and George Bird was the second to try it out and indeed to acquire one. It was these two means of travel which enabled him to visit relatives and friends in Rotherham, Nottingham, Southwell, Waltham (Leicestershire) and Leicester regularly and spend most Christmases away from home, to go to agricultural shows at Boston, Spalding, Grantham and, further away, at Doncaster and Liverpool, to attend the working men's exhibition and Goose fair at Nottingham, and to go to Grantham for the races, the gala, the circus, the theatre, for a special pre-Christmas sale of jewelry and even just for a ride on the omnibuses.

In all of this, religious functions came to play a larger part. Sometimes it was incidental; while at Southwell he went to the minster, while at Nottingham to the Roman catholic church ('saw a vast deal of ceremony amounting to mimicry, I thought'). But other occasions were specifically for religious functions, especially his cycle ride in 1870 to Melton Mowbray to hear Spurgeon preach in a tent in aid of the erection of a baptist chapel in that town: 'I went over to Waltham . . . to hear Mr Spurgeon at Melton . . . a great quantity of people there . . . 10,000 people supposed to be present at both services'. Much of this activity was still village based: the bible society meeting and chapel anniversary in Corby matching the confirmations at the anglican (two hundred and two candidates) and Roman churches; the Burton chapel opening anniversary; special preachers at Swinstead and elsewhere, all commanding his attention. Reports such as 'the place full', 'the Church was full', 'the place was crowded, supposed to be a good way on for 300 there', indicate that these were 'regional' meetings. At Burton it was said, 'they came from the Grantham school, about a score of them', and in 1874, on a visit to Nottinghamshire, he wrote: 'I went to church and chapel along with my cousins, hundreds of people at Oxton from neighbouring towns, being the feast' (12 July 1874). If there is a suspicion that 'club feasts' were as important as those of the chapels and churches, there is also for the first time a clear sense of the importance of the towns. But one point must be made: when his father attended Grantham as churchwarden for the visitation, this was felt to be no more than a routine business call, not a religious 'event': 'Father went to Grantham to be present at the Church, it being the Archdeacon's visitation day' (26 October 1868).

The evidence so far reviewed suggests a growing centralisation and concentration on the town, albeit in a rather slow process. Bird's world came to centre on the Wesleyan guild meeting at Grantham. Parallels can be seen elsewhere. The primitive methodists, although they do not seem to have done well in some market towns until quite late, were nevertheless often tied to the urban community by their system of licensing; and their large investment (comparatively speaking) in buildings which may be seen as conferring prestige on their church was probably a compensation for this poor performance. Certainly they came rather early to concentrate their special services in the towns. Thus Scotter of 1829 (where the Conference once met) and Springthorpe of 1845 (a fifty-eight day revival in a village of not much more than two hundred) gave way to Gainsborough, Grimsby, Horncastle and Louth. The Roman catholics, with the restoration of the hierarchy in the 1850s, came to stress the role of the urban centre. There were of course in places contrary movements. In Leicestershire the congregationalists and in Nottinghamshire the baptists moved out from town chapels into the countryside, preaching and encouraging the rural chapels; but in the case of the baptists, new associations formed during the century also strengthened the role of the town.[21] Other movements like the Pleasant Sunday Afternoons (an urban venture) and even the friendly societies increased the domination of the town. In one respect, as Stovin with his reference to the 'peasantry' shows, it was part of the attack on peasant culture, but there was more to it than that. Gay[22] has suggested that rural methodism became a financial liability from the 1870s, ever more dependent on the town chapels, but this would seem to be an oversimplification. Stovin certainly bewailed the load of debts which weighed down many rural chapels, but he gives no hint that the town chapels helped to support the villages; it was rather the wealthier members of the village congregation who helped to stem the rising tide of debt. Nevertheless changes in methodism, by which the emphasis moved from the circuit (1830s) to the district (1850s) and then to the national structures (1870s), as

[21] Obelkevich pp 226–27, 237, 245, 256. For Leicestershire, I owe the information to D. M. Thompson; for Nottinghamshire, see D. Bebbington, *History of a Nottingham Baptist Church* (Nottingham 1977).

[22] J. D. Gay, *Geography of Religion in England* (London 1971) p 163.

witnessed by (for instance) the increased numbers of collections centrally directed, together with the various schisms and reform movements from 1849, all contributed to the trend. Troubles with individual trusts encouraged ministers to tighten their hold on village chapels both before and after the agitation of 1849[23].

The evidence from journals may however reveal merely the whims and activities of their writers; or it may reflect the growing organisation and centralisation of circuits, or even the increasing numbers of special events in both countryside and town which increased facilities of travelling made easier for large numbers to attend. Certainly rural events continued to attract large attendances even from the towns: Saxilby in 1860 and 1861 drew Lincoln folk by the train load, and Heapham in 1872 was attended by visitors from Lincoln, Gainsborough and Brigg. Star preachers in both town and country continued to appeal; but gradually they came to see the towns as their main sphere of action.[24]

Was there really any substantial change in practice and attitude? A final investigation suggests that there was. My third line of enquiry is into certain trends in the church of England in the nineteenth century. Among these, the emergence of rural deaneries would seem at first sight to be relevant to our enquiry. This is a neglected field still and there is no space for a full examination here. I want to make two simple points. The first is that these rural deaneries do not always seem to have been urban-based, nor did they establish a single focal point for the area, and the second is that until the end of the century they seem to have been singularly ineffective. The example of Stamford (Lincolnshire), although unusual, is nevertheless revealing.[25] The office of dean of Stamford was an ancient one, preserved because its holder had duties in relation to Browne's hospital in the town. The office was usually held by some dignitary (the archdeacon of Huntingdon, of Lincoln, or of Bedford, or the rector of Great Casterton or of King's Cliffe). On the revival of rural deaneries in Lincoln diocese by bishop

[23] I owe this suggestion to R. W. Ambler of Hull University, to whom I am grateful for general comments on this paper.

[24] Obelkevich pp 205, 213.

[25] J. P. Hoskins. 'The Dean of Stamford', *Lincolnshire Architectural and Archaeological Society Reports and Papers* 3 (Lincoln 1945) pp 18–35.

Kaye between 1836 and 1842,[26] the post was attached to the antique deanship, the holder of whom was generally an absentee. A controversy in the 1860s over the nature of the deanship (which led one dean to subscribe himself 'Dean of Stamford (Peculiar)') led eventually to the appointment of a second dean, a 'rural dean', based on one or other of the town's churches; but it was not until 1884 that a chapter emerged and not until 1910 that Stamford became regularly the central point of the deanery.

It was then not the revival of deaneries in the middle of the century but other changes later on which helped forward the recognition of the town as a centre for a given region. Among those changes was the decline of the sense of parochial responsibility in towns consequent upon the struggles of church parties over ritual and patronage. The marquess of Exeter was intermittently concerned to secure a balance of churchmanship (avoiding both extremes) in his six churches in Stamford, and thus endowed each of them with an urban more than a parochial role.

My last example comes from Nottingham. There were three ancient parishes in the town, Saint Nicholas and Saint Peter, both very small and surviving with few changes throughout the nineteenth century, and Saint Mary's in which lay all the town's unenclosed fields and most of the urban area. The parochial population of Saint Mary's thus rose from twenty seven thousand in 1811 to more than seventy thousand in 1831. Studies of the early part of the century do not show Saint Mary's as occupying any 'regional' role.[27] Two new churches were built in the huge parish between 1806 and 1844, one on an extra-parochial plot and the other on newly enclosed land, both part of an evangelical opposition movement to the original parish church. After 1844, as the new allotments became built up, the parish was sub-divided time and again. The area left to Saint Mary's grew smaller and smaller; and as town centre re-development proceeded from the 1860s, its parochial population dropped. When canon Francis Morse entered his new parish in 1864, he wrote:[28] 'three new Churches . . . had just been opened, and three swarms from the old hive, including

[26] They were not in existence when William Dansey published the first edition of his *Horae Decanicae Rurales* in 1835, but they had been revived by the time of the second edition, 1844.

[27] J. C. Weller, *Say to the Wind* (Nottingham c1959).

[28] A. Rogers, 'Religion in Nottingham in the nineteenth century', *Town and Village*, ed J. F. Phillips (Nottingham 1972) pp 48–9; first annual report (1863–4) of Saint Mary's church, N[ottinghamshire] C[entral] L[ibrary], Local Collection.

Sunday-school Teachers, Missionary Collectors and other active members of the congregation, had gone to occupy them. Almost all the wealthier houses had been cut off from the District. The Congregation remaining at the Mother Church was small, and the streets left in connection with it composed almost entirely of warehouses and poor . . . the parish had been reduced from 17,000 to 6,000 . . .'. But against this, as its parochial role declined, so its 'regional' role as well as its 'civic' role rose. About 1848, the Reverend J. W. Brooks had issued an appeal for money commencing with the words: 'The Church of St Mary, Nottingham, is the Mother Church of the Town and County . . .', but this note was rare until the 1870s. Thereafter canon Morse never tired of asserting that 'St Mary's by its position has became very much the church of the poor of the parish and yet it is in no inconsiderable degree the church of the town and the church of the county, on all public occasions'. Gradually the roles became reversed: 'St Mary's, it should be remembered, has two distinct offices. In the first place, it is the principal Church in the Town, the greater part of which was once its Parish, and in the next place, it has still a district of its own, though inhabited almost entirely by poor' (1879). Part of this ecclesiastical aggrandisement was designed to secure Saint Mary's church as the cathedral of the eventual new diocese. A booklet in 1874 opened with the words: 'From every point of view whence the great town of Nottingham can be seen as a whole, the Tower of this Church constitutes its crowning feature, and a stranger might well imagine it to be a Cathedral. Whether it ever will serve as high a purpose time alone can determine; but this is at least possible; and if required for such a use, it stands ready for the reception of its future Bishop without further adornment, or the addition of any accessories'; and again in 1878, canon Morse, comparing the church with 'a good many Cathedrals and Leeds Parish Church', wrote: 'Frequented as it is by persons of all classes, from all its old Parish, it seems its office to provide something like a Cathedral Service becoming so important a town. This is aimed at, and, I believe, attained'.

But not all of this revised status grew from ecclesiastical in-fighting; the church came to be used for many 'central-type' functions. In May 1869 and again in 1882, the bishop of Lincoln addressed some fourteen hundred church workers from all the churches in the town, and in the 1870s Saint Mary's was used for the consecration of the first (but not the second) suffragan bishop of Nottingham. In October 1871, the Church Congress met there, and again in 1897. In 1877 when deaneries were established in the archdeaconry of Nottingham, Saint Mary's church was made the centre of the Nottingham deanery with an honorary canonry for its incumbent, and a 'chapter house of sufficient size for meetings of the clergy' was built between 1883 and 1888.[29]

The failure of the church to be selected as the cathedral of the new diocese in 1883 did not deter its vicar: 'The people of Nottingham have not done much for the Bishopric of Southwell . . . [it is to be hoped they will] make the principal Church of their town worthy of being the chief church—if not the Cathedral—of the new Diocese.' In 1884, its patronage was transferred by order in council from private hands (Lord Manvers) to the new bishop of Southwell in exchange for rural Edwinstowe, a recognition of its special position. Although its role was not firmly established until the end of the century (in July 1887, the Southwell diocesan board of education distributed its prizes in the archdeaconry of Nottingham in the university buildings rather than in Saint Mary's), it continued to rise in ecclesiastical status. With the closure of its burial grounds (the last interment was in 1889) Saint Mary's ceased to have serious parochial pretensions. The incumbent came to be known as 'vicar of Nottingham' by customary usage, and offertories for non-parochial purposes became more frequent, including collections for other churches in the neighbourhood. Gatherings for members of the region's football clubs (1898) and especially the erection in 1902–5 of a whole series of war memorials (following hard on the heels of 'regional' services with their 'great manifestations of patriotism which it [the Boer war] has called forth') reveal most clearly its regional character: apart from regimental brasses and plaques, three windows were set in the church, designed by C. H. Kempe (1837–1907) and donated by the duke of Portland, in memory not just of those from the parish but of all the Nottinghamshire men of the regular army who fell in the South African war. From 1902, great 'central' services for royal or national events became even more common, some three or four every year. But even then the process was slow; and it was not until the first world war that Saint Mary's church came to be recognised as possessing a role for the area around the centre; its war memorial of 1918 consists of a cross with the numbers of all Nottinghamshire fallen, village by village, although

[29] *London Gazette* 27 September 1877; NCL, Local Collection Box L 24; annual reports, Saint Mary's church, 1863–1914.

most of the villages erected their own memorials as well.[30] The city had come to speak for the county.

My theme has been one concerning attitudes; and I have suggested that people in rural areas came to look to the town as a focal point in religion only late in the nineteenth century, surprisingly late in fact. All three lines of enquiry indicate the same pattern. I must finish by offering a few suggestions as to why this should have happened.

It is not just a matter of the size of buildings, that in towns alone were gradually built the churches and chapels capable of housing large congregations. The size of the town buildings expressed the growing self-consciousness of the urban congregations, the difference between town and country; but the buildings were not put up to serve regional needs. That town congregations did become more self-conscious is clear: in King's Lynn, all the nonconformist chapels moved from back lanes and courtyards to street frontages on main roads by the 1830s.[31] Such moves reflected the views of the urban congregation rather than the district; and it was the town hall at Market Rasen and the tent at Melton Mowbray rather than the new chapels which attracted the rural crowds. What the buildings do suggest is an attempt particularly by the Wesleyans to import urban culture into the villages—an attempt as unsuccessful as it was quickly abandoned.

George Bird's experience suggests that improved travel facilities were probably more important than buildings. Nevertheless, it is easy to over-rate the direct importance of the railway and the bicycle. The railway in Louth (for a short period after 1848 on the London line) no doubt helped to establish its centrality; trainloads came into its two junctions, from Donington into Louth West and from Mablethorpe into Louth East, and trains enabled Spurgeon and the president of Conference to visit areas hitherto remote and to preach to rail-head crowds. But such facilities did not materially affect men like Winn or Stovin, nor most of the villagers around Louth; for them the normal mode of transport well into this century was the horse, the pony and

[30] A. Stapleton, *The Churches and Monasteries of Old and New Nottingham* (Nottingham 1903) p 29; J. C. F. Hood, *An Account of St Mary's Church, Nottingham* (Nottingham 1910) pp 31, 59–61; *Nottingham Journal* 4 July 1887; Nottinghamshire Record Office, PR (St Mary's) 2077; PR 6238 fols 470–77; PR 9730–36; *St Mary's Church, Nottingham, its past and present history* (no author) (Nottingham 1874).

[31] A. Rogers, *Approaches to Local History* (London 1977) pp 136–9.

trap or feet. The improvements in the rural roads early in the nineteenth century may have been much more influential, but the effects were probably shortlived: studies of local carriers suggest that these services fell off from the 1870s for reasons which cannot yet be determined. Again, horses and traps were available only to prosperous shopkeepers and farmers. For most, visits to mass meetings in the towns meant long walks over poorly made roads.

It is probable that other changes in the town—and especially in its image—were more influential; and here the railways did play a part. The range of goods and services available in the town was, of course, greatly increased as time went on, and the town came to represent 'urban culture'. Stovin, for example, did not distinguish between the religious and the secular occasions which drew him to the town; the stimulus of a circuit gathering in Louth was much the same for him as a day in the reading room there. It was the town and what it stood for which attracted. Such a change in the urban image developed as the century progressed, and no doubt contributed to the town's attraction. But this at the same time led to some resistance, an assertion of local independence, an insistence on the validity of 'rural culture'.[32] Stovin also treasured rural-based activities.

These secular tensions were reflected in the churches as the century progressed. The early 'evangelistic' period in each of the churches, as has recently been shown,[33] led to a greater reliance on local initiatives and independence; the rural chapels were busy converting their neighbours. Later however as the churches passed into their 'denominational phase' with more emphasis placed on the cultivation of the 'interior' rather than the 'exterior' constituency, the churches turned in on their own organisations. Probably in this lies the true explanation of what can be seen to be happening. Early in the century, during a period of rapid growth, the rural chapels were in the front line of the advances being made. As such they claimed and were accorded independence and equality of status with their urban counterparts, however different they may have been from each other. But later there was a greater concentration on the families of members, on fostering common identities rather than engaging with the 'world'. It is of course easy to exaggerate; a great deal continued to happen in

[32] A. M. Everitt, *The Pattern of Rural Dissent; the nineteenth century* (Leicester 1972) suggests social and economic reasons for differing patterns of rural independence.

[33] A. D. Gilbert, *Religion and Society in Industrial England* (London 1976); R. Currie, A. Gilbert and L. Horsley, *Churches and Churchgoers* (Oxford 1977) pp 5–9.

the countryside even when organisation had become more urbanised and bureaucratised. But the trends seem to be clear, and they became strongest towards the end of the century.

Associated with these changes would seem to be the growing control of the professionals in running the churches from the 1850s, and it was their influence, looking to the towns for servicing, which led in the end to the great evangelistic campaigns of the later nineteenth century like Spurgeon's being urban-based unlike the movements of the early part of the century. The growing class consciousness of different groups in rural areas made these trends acceptable. Wesleyan farmers went to Louth for holy communion as well as to meet other Wesleyan farmers and traders. The local community was losing its coherence; the horizontal links which bound the village to the town became stronger at the expense of the vertical community bonds. Stovin perhaps in this as before reveals these tendencies most clearly. Still jealous of the autonomy of the village chapel, he resented interference or dominance by the professional circuit minister (especially when he disliked them or felt they were not up to their job!). On the other hand, he was attracted to the great town occasions of aggregates and conferences, and found more intellectual 'meat' in the contacts he made at them. The tension was still muted; he drew equal but differing satisfaction from the village chapels and from 'town' occasions. It was later, as rural societies began to close and the rural community declined, especially in the great agricultural depression, that the tensions became more apparent.

And behind all this there are changes in theological understanding. Perhaps here, in the religious sphere as in the secular, is another example of the well established clash between the autonomy of the local on the one hand and growing concepts of association, co-operation and union on the other. For what, after all, is the church? Is it a local congregation of believers or is it a wider fellowship of disciplined groups? It may be that what we are seeing is an attempt to come to terms with some of these issues.

University of Nottingham

THE VICTORIAN TOWN PARISH: RURAL VISION AND URBAN MISSION

by DAVID E. H. MOLE

WHEN leading churchmen and statesmen cast around for ways of restoring the health of English society at the end of the eighteenth century, the theme to which they constantly returned was the renewal of the parish. The parish was the basic social unit in church and state, small enough to be conceived in terms of personal relationships. On the principle that, if you look after the pennies, the pounds will look after themselves, it seemed obvious that if you could make the parish a healthy harmonious unit, then the life of the nation as a whole would become healthy and harmonious. Ideally the parish was a large family, with the squire as its father and the incumbent as its spiritual father. Southey wrote in the *Quarterly Review* in 1820:

> Every parish being in itself a little commonwealth, it is easy to conceive that before manufactures were introduced, or where they do not exist, a parish, where the minister and the parochial officers did their duty with activity and zeal, might be almost as well ordered as a private family.[1]

Southey was not suggesting that every parish actually was well ordered, but that it might become so where everyone involved did his duty. Notice, however, the qualification which he inserted: 'before manufactures were introduced, or where they do not exist.' His ideal parish was a traditional rural parish: the presence of manufactures was a disturbance. But in the nineteenth century parishes were being increasingly disturbed by manufactures. The disturbance was most noticeable in the new towns where large populations were gathered together, with all the problems which followed. The urban parish was largely a new phenomenon, in which the traditional parochial structures were strained to breaking point. In the large towns it was difficult to develop human relationships when so many inhabitants were incomers. The factory system encouraged impersonal relationships and large numbers. The classes became separated from one another: they

[1] *Quarterly Review* 23 (1820) p 564, quoted by [Geoffrey] Best, [*Temporal Pillars*] (Cambridge 1964) p 165.

lived in different parts of the town, out of sight of one another. Unemployment and poverty were common and their causes were often unknown. Social amenities were rare—too few schools, too few churches, too little fresh air or open space. Among the respectable classes there developed a fear of the urban mob, angry and sullen. How could an area like that become 'a little commonwealth'?

The answer of churchmen in the nineteenth century was the creation of the urban parish. Divide the parishes of the large towns into small manageable units, sufficiently compact for the parson to establish pastoral contact with his parishioners. Bishop Blomfield originally hoped for one clergyman for every thousand parishioners, though when he launched his metropolitan churches fund he had to limit his objective to one for every three thousand.[2] Each group of urban streets was to be considered like a village, with its church and incumbent acting as the centre and the agent for social renewal. The concept of the urban parish was thus paradoxically based on the ideal of the rural parish. The rural parish was the norm, and the town was at this stage still thought of as an unnatural growth on the face of the countryside.

This attitude was encouraged by the fact that during the eighteenth century the beneficed clergy had come to take as their ideal the life of the country gentleman. Even those who held office in large towns (either as urban incumbents or as canons of cathedrals) liked to retire to the countryside for part of the year. It was the country parish, rather than the town parish, which was the ideal sphere for clerical labours.[3] Even when the growing importance of the towns in the nineteenth century combined with new ideals of priestly vocation to enhance the importance of the leading city parishes, there was still the feeling that real life could only be lived in the countryside, a feeling which was encouraged by the social and physical evils of the towns and by the romantic view of rural life which was so strong in Victorian culture.

We are thus faced with the paradox that even those pioneers who are most famous as the founders of the Victorian urban parish still thought of the rural parish as the norm to which the urban parish should be brought to approximate. When Thomas Chalmers of Glasgow published the prospectus of his work on *The Christian and Civic Economy of Large Towns,* the first matter to be dealt with in the

[2] [Desmond] Bowen, [*The Idea of the Victorian Church*] (Montreal 1968) pp 20, 24.

[3] Best pp 68–9.

first volume was to be 'The Advantage and Possibility of Assimilating a Town to a Country Parish'. Similarly, W. F. Hook of Leeds, considering the best training for a young clergyman, decided 'without hesitation that the very worst training a man can have is that which he receives if appointed early in life to a town parish. The strong pastoral feeling is generated in the country, and I attribute what little success I have had entirely to my country breeding.'[4]

The subdivision of parishes was not the only possible answer. There were others. In its inability to provide a comprehensive solution to the problem, the eighteenth century had groped its way pragmatically to a different answer. The eighteenth century's answer to problems was to supplement the old rather than to reform it. Thus the outdated and inadequate local government of the urbanised parish had been supplemented by special commissions empowered by local acts of parliament to fulfil what was needed. The old parochial officers continued alongside the new commissioners. In a similar way the ecclesiastical system was left virtually untouched: only a few extra parishes were created by the expensive and troublesome machinery of special acts of parliament. The spiritual requirements of the new towns were more usually met by the building of proprietary chapels and chapels of ease. These chapels were built by private subscription and maintained by pew rents. They were as easy to erect as dissenting chapels and apparently did not even need consecreation. They appeared all over the place to meet the needs of new populations. The extra church accommodation was thus found without the trouble of upsetting the entrenched system, and the clergyman was encouraged in his duties by the need to keep up the pew rents. This piecemeal approach to the problem might distress tidy and logical minds, but it satisfied the cautious pragmatism of the English temperament.

In the end, however, it would not do. It could not cope with the sheer weight of the problem. The proprietary chapel could function only in areas where a substantial and respectable congregation could be found to support its minister and to repay its loans. It could not function in missionary areas where only the poor lived, the poor who paid little or no pew rents, and who needed to be coaxed into attendance anyway. Moreover, under the existing legal system it could only provide part of what a normal congregation would need: it could not be used for weddings or funerals, and it had no pastoral district. It

[4] [W. R. W.] Stephens, [*Life and Letters of Walter Farquhar Hook*] (London new ed 1880)p 47.

had no real place in the parochial system. For that reason, the reformers who wanted church and nation to be renewed through the regenerated parish swept the proprietary chapel to one side. When bishop Blomfield arrived in London in 1828, he made it known that he would not allow any more proprietary chapels to be opened in his diocese.

Another possible answer to the new situation was the increase of clergymen without any new buildings or parishes. In the eighteenth century the church of Scotland had met the expansion of population by increasing the number of ministers serving in the existing churches, which thus became collegiate.[5] In the early nineteenth century some English town parishes had several curates assisting the incumbent, though in many cases these were also curates of chapels within the parish. This method did not satisfy the reformers: the incomes of the extra ministers were always at risk, and the demand for new parishes was too strong to resist. Only in the second half of the nineteenth century was the idea taken up again with any enthusiasm.

The first movement in church building reflected rural ideals only imperfectly. When parliament turned its attention to the problem after Waterloo, it thought in terms not of intimacy but of greatness. In thanksgiving for victory it voted a million pounds to provide extra churches in needy areas. The act of 1818 called for 'proper accommodation for the largest number of persons at the least expense', and the church building commissioners tried at first to provide it by erecting very large church buildings, each seating two thousand or so people, in the hope of solving the shortage quickly and effectively. These churches were in appearance and character definitely urban and not rural, but they tended to be costly, and many people said that they were too large for the minister's voice to carry throughout the building. In the 1830s the commissioners turned towards smaller and cheaper buildings.

None of these attempted solutions satisfied those reformers whose ideal was the small country parish. Each urban parish could only become 'a little commonwealth . . . almost as well ordered as a private family' if it was sufficiently intimate and if it was properly brought under the care of its pastor. Herein lay the chief thrust of the movement which created the Victorian town parish—the subdivision of overlarge parishes and the provision of adequate pastoral oversight.

The main problem of urban society was its size. The first step must therefore be the subdivision into small manageable parishes. The

[5] [J. H. S.] Burleigh, [*A Church History of Scotland*] (London 1960) p 319.

church building acts, from 1818 onwards, created machinery for bringing this about. The difficulties of making new parishes were at first so many that the clergy of Birmingham got together in 1829 and made a gentlemen's agreement, dividing the parish into unofficial pastoral districts and making each incumbent responsible for the area near his own church or chapel. But this was purely informal, and it did not alter the hard facts of legal boundaries and parochial rights.[6] Several acts of parliament were needed before it became relatively easy to create new parishes, but in the early years of Victoria's reign most cities had their church extension schemes, of which perhaps the most famous was bishop Blomfield's metropolitan churches scheme of 1836. The aim was to erect parish churches in strategic places and to endow them sufficiently for a clergyman to begin work in each one. It was assumed that church and parson together would gather round them all the uplifting and civilising agencies which would transform disaffected regions of dirt and ignorance into communities of Christianity and good order.

The classic example of the subdivision of one huge parish is that of Leeds, where W. F. Hook in 1841 was faced with a parish of 152,000, comprising eleven townships, and including among its twenty-one Anglican chapels eighteen perpetual curacies without cure of souls. There were three proprietary chapels, from which the poor were virtually excluded. The burden of providing the services of baptism, marriage and burial for this huge population fell mainly on the old parish church, where the body of clergy had little hope of establishing proper personal contact with more than a small proportion of the people who came. Hook decided to divide the parish, and to that end he arranged for the Leeds vicarage act of 1844. By 1851 the old parish had been divided into seventeen parishes, all of them endowed and with their own incumbents, while the clergy had increased from twenty-five to sixty.[7]

The creation of smaller parishes was only the first step. The new parish still needed to be made an effective unit of pastoral oversight. Even with smaller parishes, it was impossible for the incumbent to know everyone in his parish. To make sure that everyone was cared for, he had to turn to the laity for help. Hence the emergence of schemes for organised parish visiting.

At Clapham in 1799, John Venn (rector 1792–1813) and friends set

[6] *Aris's Birmingham Gazette*, 23 November 1829.

[7] Stephens pp 380–4, 463–4.

up a parochial 'Society for Bettering the Condition of the Poor'. The society consisted of more than thirty members, who met monthly 'to drink tea together in each other's houses' and to execute the business of the society. The parish was divided into eight districts, each with its own treasurer and two or three other visitors who met regularly to determine what aid should be given, and in what form, to those who needed it. Each visitor undertook the care of eight or ten families in order to attain 'the familiarity of a small village'. The society even undertook the vaccination of the whole parish in 1800.[8]

In Scotland Thomas Chalmers created a system which provided spiritual oversight and poor relief in a highly organised manner. Chalmers was a strong advocate of church extension and the renewal of parish life in accordance with what he called 'the Principle of Locality'. His work in St John's parish in Glasgow was meant to be a demonstration of what could and should be done. He persuaded the city fathers to create a new parish with a population of about ten thousand, and it was there that from 1819 to 1823 he established his system. He divided the parish into twenty-five districts, each of four hundred or so people, and assigned a church elder to each district, charging him with the spiritual oversight of all the inhabitants who were not effectively connected with a dissenting church. In each area there were one or more Sunday schools, staffed by voluntary teachers, and a deacon whose duty it was to take note of the material needs of the people, and to help the needy to help themselves, carefully refraining from giving them too much charity for fear of pauperising them. The scheme was famous largely because of its method of dealing with poor relief. Chalmers himself believed that it provided a good example to England in this matter, and he travelled into the southern kingdom to speak on behalf of the proper use of the parochial system in established churches.[9]

His scheme could not be transferred to the English parish without change, but his influence south of the border was immense, particularly among evangelicals. J. B. Sumner when bishop of Chester took up the idea of visiting schemes with enthusiasm, because they enabled an incumbent to keep a large parish 'really under pastoral superintendence'. In his first charge as bishop of Chester in 1829 he suggested that carefully chosen laymen might assist by 'visiting and examining

[8] Michael Hennell, *John Venn and the Clapham Sect* (London 1958) pp 141–6.

[9] Burleigh pp 320–1; L. J. Saunders, *Scottish Democracy 1815–40* (Edinburgh 1950) pp 213–16.

the schools, reading and praying with the infirm and aged, by consoling the fatherless and widows in their afflictions.' Each visitor in his district was to encourage parents to send their children to Sunday school, and to report to parents on the behaviour of their children; he was to sell bibles and prayer books, to point out the advantages of savings banks and charitable institutions, to provide necessary relief in cases of sickness, and at such times especially to be watchful for any signs of religious feeling, so as to minister to the soul as well as to the body. Each visitor would thus get to know the people of his area, and would report back to the incumbent.[10]

Such schemes enabled the pastor to get to know his parish in a way which otherwise would have been impossible for him. In the villages there had been great emphasis upon the virtue of charitable giving to the poor and needy. Everyone knew which families were in need: their circumstances were well known, as also were their characters and habits. In the new towns rich and poor no longer had the personal contact which had been natural in rural society, and it was difficult to give help where it was most needed and in the most suitable manner. The visiting scheme was meant to restore the personal contact and to provide the requisite knowledge in such a way that discriminating charity might be given. The conditions of rural society were therefore created as far as was practicable in the midst of urban society. In a speech in 1822 Chalmers spoke of the effects of proper pastoral care upon an area of 'putrid alleys' and 'loathsome hovels':

> The pastor who lives and who labours there will soon be regaled by the greetings of a home-walk, and will soon surround himself with the breath and the blandness of a village economy.[11]

Visiting schemes were only one aspect of the well organised Victorian parish. There were many others. There were schools—Sunday schools to teach people the faith, and sometimes also reading and writing; infant schools and day schools for the children; evening classes for young men and women, giving elementary instruction in the three Rs, plus book-keeping for the men and housekeeping for the women. There were schemes to render social first aid, like soup kitchens in times of depression. There were savings clubs, clothing clubs and sick clubs. There were local branches of missionary societies. And there

[10] R. S. Dell, 'Social and Economic Theories and Pastoral Concerns of a Victorian Archbishop', *JEH* 16 (1965) p 203.

[11] Thomas Chalmers, *Speech delivered on 24 May 1822 before the General Assembly of the Church of Scotland*, p 14.

were bible classes and weeknight lectures. Under the revitalised parish system, each church was expected to provide for its immediate area a centre for charitable work, education and culture, bringing light and refreshment into the lives of the working classes.

In order to provide all that was expected of him, the pastor needed the help of his laity, not only paid agents but also voluntary workers. The ideal rural parish was cared for by resident parson and squire, benevolently superintending the lives of parishioners. Who was the urban equivalent of the squire? In most cases there was none, though churchmen continually look around for one. It might perhaps be a leading manufacturer, whose wealth and influence might be drawn into the service of the parish. 'There would be a link of sympathy and bond of union, which is not now felt, if the factory boy saw his employer taking an active interest and personal part in the Sunday-school,' remarked the *Christian Observer* in April 1859.[12] Sometimes the leading employer was a company or a government department: not much could be expected of them. The nearest equivalent to a squire in an urban parish was usually a composite one—the middling and professional classes acting together to provide the charitable and paternal role which none of them could fulfil individually. But what was to happen in a one-class parish, where none of the parishioners was in a position to take on this role of benevolence, where the clergyman found himself the only professional man, the only man of education and of assured means?

Social teaching also looked back to rural society, to the encouragement of traditional virtues—the responsibility of the poor to be patient and of the rich to be charitable. Anglican social protest, when it occurred, tended to be tory-radical, the championing of an idealised rural past against the industrial present. Too often it was unrealistic, a tilting at windmills, but it did make a protest on behalf of humanity against the inhumanity of such things as child labour and the new poor law.

In the new towns early Victorian Britain was faced with problems which it had never met before on such a scale. There were no precedents for dealing with them, and even the basic facts of urban society were imperfectly known. It is therefore hardly surprising if at first people turned for answers to the sort of society which they knew well—rural society—and used rural ideals for their mission to the urban society which they did not understand. As time went on,

[12] *Christian Observer* (1859) p 238.

however, it became increasingly clear that this would not do. Urban society must be interpreted on its own terms. In the 1840s and 1850s clergymen were prominent among those who were speaking and writing about urban social conditions with a knowledge that few people in the professional classes shared. 'The condition of the towns' became a burning issue in early Victorian society, and the alleged 'heathenism' of the towns was one of the themes in the discussion of the report of the 1851 census of attendance at religious worship. In 1851 for the first time more than half of the inhabitants of Great Britain lived in towns. A select committee of the house of lords was appointed—'to inquire into the Deficiency of Means of Spiritual Instruction, and Places of Divine Worship, in the Metropolis, and in other Populous Districts in England and Wales,' though its report in 1858 was attacked by the *Christian Observer* in February 1859 as too timid. Suggestions were put forward for novel means of furthering the church's mission to urban society. Bishop Fraser of Manchester in 1872 was one of the first to advocate a team ministry, a 'body of mission-clergy' to assist in the Christian mission to make better the life of the poor.[13] It was clear that flexibility and originality were required rather than the wholesale application of traditional forms. The rural ideal for the urban parish had broken under strain. The incumbent could not fulfil the old ideal of pastoral oversight, for however hard he worked there were still important things undone. 'A clergyman,' said one of them, 'attends upon the sick and dying; visits, in his ministerial capacity, the members of his congregation; superintends his schools. This is all he does, and (with little exceptions not worth noticing) this is all he can do.'[14] The incumbent was the king pin of parochial organisation: the careful arrangements to ensure that the activities of the laity did not threaten his position as chief pastor of the parish also ensured that all the demands of the age were laid ultimately at his door. He was so busy being the incumbent that he had no time or energy left for the ordinary concerns of his parishioners. By the 1860s it was becoming increasingly clear that most clergymen did not understand the new urban culture, and in the absence of understanding they resorted to denunciation.

In society in general more positive attitudes towards cities had developed, notably among nonconformists, who were more at home

[13] James Fraser, *Charge Delivered at his Primary Visitation* (1872) p 77, quoted by Bowen p 275.

[14] Thomas Nunns, *A Letter to the Right Hon Lord Ashley* (Birmingham 1842) p 52.

in them than churchmen were. In his book, *The Age of Great Cities, or, modern society viewed in its relation to intelligence, morals and religion* (1843), the congregationalist minister Robert Vaughan saw cities as centres of civilisation, though even he was as concerned as everyone else with what he saw to be the great problems of city life. The undenominational liberal preacher George Dawson of Birmingham in the middle of the century portrayed the great city as the place where men in community might create new standards of civilised life, fit to rival the cities of renaissance Italy. Even Hook of Leeds, in the warm afterglow of a public dinner at the mechanics institute in 1857, told his audience that morally the towns were better than the country.[15]

By 1870 it was becoming clear that the cities needed a new type of parson, theologically and pastorally trained to work in the new urban culture. 'We have a morbid horror of being *vulgar,*' J. C. Miller of Birmingham told the church pastoral-aid society in 1854. 'Our ministers have not been trained for a work among "the common people"; and "the common people" have soon discerned their want of adaptation to their wants and tastes.' Curates arrived in an urban parish fresh from the university without any special training, quite ignorant of the ways of the people to whom they were called to minister. The result, said Miller, was that the common people felt more at home under the local preacher than under the graduate of Oxford or Cambridge.[16]

Meanwhile, the urban parish had become even less like the rural parish than ever. It was in the towns that the distinction between civil and ecclesiastical parishes became clearest. Rural parishes usually operated as units of both civil and ecclesiastical government. The new urban parishes were usually only ecclesiastical. The filling and consequent closure of urban churchyards led to the provision of municipal cemeteries. Insistence on keeping the consecrated church holy sent public meetings into civic halls. Church rates were rarely levied in urban parishes after the 1840s. The parochial system remained in principle, but in practice the parish church was regarded more and more as a private association with its own property, dependent upon its own members and supporters for its continuing life. The 'congregational principle', so long denounced, had made increasing inroads upon urban parochial life, and the partisan policies of ritualists and evangelicals were to encourage it still further. The urban parish might

[15] C. J. Stranks, *Dean Hook* (London 1954) p 105.
[16] J. C. Miller, *The Church of the People* (London 1855) p 14.

well have its little commonwealth, as well ordered as a private family, but it achieved it only at the expense of being separate from the general life of the community around it.

By 1870 the rural ideal for urban mission was weakened beyond recall. Did an urban ideal take its place? Or did other controlling ideals appear which were applicable to both urban and rural society? The power of rural parishes lingered on for a long time. As late as 1958 it was said that sixty-five per cent of the 14,332 Anglican parishes were still rural, in a nation which was overwhelmingly urban.[17] Twenty years later, the movement of reorganisation has spread from the towns to the countryside: where today is the traditional rural parish?

The College of the Ascension
Selly Oak Colleges.

[17] Bowen p 242 n 3.

THOMAS CHAMBERLAIN—A FORGOTTEN TRACTARIAN

by PETER G. COBB

THOMAS Chamberlain, vicar of St Thomas's Oxford for fifty years (1842–92), has fallen into undeserved obscurity. Except for a very brief memoir, written by Algernon Barrington Simeon just after his death, and a section in Thomas Squires' history of the parish[1] which is largely based on it, there is no account of his life and work. Yet in many ways his was the model tractarian parish. The *Ecclesiologist* acknowledged it as 'an example of correct ritualism'[2] whilst a local evangelical regarded it as 'the headquarters of the ultra devotees of the Pusey party'.[3] The restoration and furnishing of the parish church were the epitome of tractarian ambitions. Chamberlain himself, with his energy and reserve, was regarded as an archetypal parish priest. Felicia Skene, 'a person of strong feelings and decided opinions',[4] so admired him that she not only came to live in the parish to work for him, but also used him as the basis for her portrait of the dedicated clergyman, Mr Chesterfield, in one of her novels, *S. Albans's, or the Prisoners of Hope*.[5] Even his sartorial habits were imitated, a sure sign of the regard in which he was held. One young man, about to be ordained to a title at St Alban's, Holborn, wrote to his sister that he had been to Oxford to be measured by a certain tailor for his first clerical suit. 'He makes things for Mr Chamberlain and his curates, so I think I am pretty sure of having mine correct.'[6]

It is not known who or what primarily influenced Chamberlain to join the tractarians. Born of a clerical family in Warwickshire, he had completed his formal education at Westminster and Christ Church before the Oxford movement began. He was a Student of the House with rooms in college until 1869 but does not seem to have been on close terms with Pusey who lived near him. However, he lived in Oxford, working in the parish of Cowley, throughout the early

1 [*In West Oxford*, ed T. W.] Squires (London/Oxford 1928).
2 *Ecclesiologist* 14 (London 1853) p 305 n 1.
3 [Peter] Maurice, *Postscript* [*to the Popery of Oxford*] (London 1851) p 22.
4 E. C. Richards, *Felicia Skene. A Memoir* (London 1902) p 123.
5 Margaret M. Maison, *Search Your Soul, Eustace* (London 1961) p 51.
6 Mother Kate [Warburton], *Old Soho Days and Other Memories* (London 1906) p 164.

crucial years of the catholic revival. He was not, in fact, an extreme party man. He refused to commit his vote to Isaac Williams in the election for the professorship of poetry[7] and he resigned from the Association for the Promotion of the Unity of Christendom in 1858 because it was too pro-Roman.[8] When Samuel Wilberforce, newly installed as bishop in 1845, demoted him from being rural dean on the ground that he was a party man, his curate, Alexander Forbes, later bishop of Brechin, twitted him: 'It serves you right, Chamberlain, for you never have been a party man, and you ought to have been one.'[9] Opposition made him more aggressive. He joined the English Church Union[10] and was one of the first members of the secret ritualist society, the society of the Holy Cross,[11] acting as host to its first retreat conference in 1856.[12]

From the beginning of his ministry at St Thomas's, he seems to have been convinced of the importance of restoring and refurnishing the church. He very carefully thought out—or at least subsequently justified—all the changes he made in the furnishing, decorating and reordering of the church. A paper he gave in 1852 to the Oxford architectural society, of which he was a leading member, 'On some principles to be observed in ornamenting churches', is particularly illuminating in this respect.[13] He also published a small book, *The Chancel: an appeal for its proper use,* in 1856.

His first object was to enlarge the church which was far too small for the population of the parish. He did this by adding a new north aisle in 1846,[14] although it involved demolishing a sixteenth-century chantry. He planned to add another aisle in 1865 but had to abandon the idea due to what he called the 'red tapism' of the diocesan church building society.[15] He took advantage of the enlargement of the

[7] [Oxford], P[usey] H[ouse] MSS Thomas Chamberlain to E. B. Pusey, November 1841. The Pusey House material in this essay is used by kind permission of the governors of Pusey House.

[8] [H. R. T.] Brandreth, [*Dr Lee of Lambeth*] (London 1951) pp 91–2.

[9] [A. B.] Simeon, [*A Short Memoir of the Rev Thomas Chamberlain M.A.*] (London 1892) p 18.

[10] *The Ritualistic Conspiracy* (London 1877) p 8.

[11] J. Embry, *The Catholic Movement and the Society of the Holy Cross* (London 1931) pp 18–49.

[12] [H. P.] Liddon, [*Life of Edward Bouverie Pusey*], ed J. O. Johnston and R. J. Wilson (4 ed London 1894) 3 p 378.

[13] *Ecclesiologist* 13 (London 1852) pp 101–8.

[14] *Ibid* 7 (1847) p 117.

[15] Oxford, Bodleian, MSS, Oxford diocesan papers d 796 fol 177; Top Oxon c 104 fols 200–18.

church to rearrange the pews so that they all faced east, lowering their height and removing their doors where he could, and to restore the pulpit, shorn of the clerk's desk, to the position near the chancel arch from which his predecessor had moved it only a few years before. Previously the 'motley group of high pews of all sizes' as he later called them, had 'converged to the pulpit' halfway down the south side of the nave.[16] This reordering of the church, which effected 'an extraordinary alteration . . . in its interior aspect'[17] was made in the teeth of fierce opposition which necessitated the arbitration of the bishop in person.[18] As Chamberlain had gone through the due processes of obtaining a faculty, the bishop upheld him but he was not able to dislodge one family from the chancel (although he reduced them to benches) or to remove the western gallery.[19] In spite of the fact that the cost was borne by private individuals, half of it, £500, by a single person (thought to be Alexander Forbes)[20] the parish took its revenge at a vestry meeting the following year by reducing the parish rate, usually 2d or 3d in the pound, to a farthing. Another vestry meeting snubbed Chamberlain personally by passing a vote of thanks to the church wardens, one of whom he had dismissed, 'for their upright discharge of the Office and especially for the correct and straight forward manner in which they treated the attempts of the Reverend T. Chamberlain in October last to remove the Pews in the Church against the desire of the Parishioners.'[21]

The object of Chamberlain's reordering of the church was to shift the focal point from the pulpit to the altar. He stated the principle quite clearly in his book on the use of the chancel: 'The altar in every church should be made to arrest and fix the eye of the beholder and to this everything should point.'[22] It should be of a decent size and vested to enhance its dignity: 'The altar should never be less than six feet long, and raised on a separate platform or footpace and three feet six high. Its vestments too, should be as rich as we can any way provide.'[23] Eventually he installed a handsome stone altar, ten feet

[16] [T.] Chamberlain, *Memoir* [*of the Church of S. Thomas the Martyr in Oxford*] (Oxford/London 1871) p 6.

[17] *E*[*nglish*] *Ch*[*urchman*] (London) 24 December 1846.

[18] *ECh* 22 October 1846.

[19] *Ecclesiologist* 7 (1847) p 118.

[20] Squires pp 17–18.

[21] Oxford, St Thomas's Church, Vestry Book 16 July 1847, 6 April 1847.

[22] p 12.

[23] *Ibid* p 17.

long,[24] but at this early date he had to content himself with vesting a communion table. He got his cousin, Marian Hughes, who was later to help him found a sisterhood in the parish, to make a frontal 'from Pugin's pattern'.[25] Later he varied the frontals, following the Roman cycle of liturgical colours.[26] All this no doubt irritated some in the parish as a 'liberal and handsome present of a Crimson Cloth and Cushions for the Communion Table' had been made only a few years before.[27] He further drew attention to the altar by fencing it with sanctuary rails 'from Mr Butterfield's design, solid with piercings of geometrical design'.[28]

Not content with this, Chamberlain had by 1853 acted on the axiom stated in his paper the previous year, that 'the whole east end demands enrichment'.[29] As the *Ecclesiologist* enthusiastically reported, 'Some colour has been boldly and effectively introduced in an arcade which serves as reredos'[30] and stained glass inserted in four of the five chancel windows. The central light of the east window had a representation of the crucifixion, which Chamberlain thought 'as a general rule' should always occupy that position.[31] In the three small windows, each of a single light, were represented St Thomas of Canterbury and St Nicholas, the joint patrons of the church, and St Frideswide, the patron saint of Oxford, witnessing by their subordinate position to the communion of saints in the members rather than in the head, according to Chamberlain.[32]

By 1871 he must have felt that he had basically completed his restoration and refurnishing of the church because he published in that year a short *Memoir of the Church of S. Thomas the Martyr in Oxford* giving an account of his achievement. This reveals that since 1853 he had removed the western gallery, resited the font under the tower and paved the church throughout with encaustic tiles. In all this he had the help and advice of William Butterfield and G. E. Street, the diocesan architect. What was most striking visually was the painting of the walls and roofs of both nave and chancel 'chiefly after designs

[24] Maurice, *The Ritualism of Oxford Popery* (London 1866) p 8; Chamberlain, *Memoir* p 6.
[25] PH MSS, Marian Hughes' Diaries, 1, August 1846, Summer 1847.
[26] *Ecclesiologist* 13 (1852) p 105; *The Churchman's Diary*, ed T. Chamberlain (London 1851).
[27] Vestry Book 2 April 1839.
[28] *Ecclesiologist* 14 (1853) p 304. They have since been replaced.
[29] *Ibid* 13 (1852) p 105.
[30] *Ibid* 14 (1853) p 304.
[31] *Ibid* 13 (1852) p 107.
[32] *Ibid* p 108.

by Mr C. E. Kempe'.[33] There is a photograph of the church in *c*1875, which shows the effect.[34] Even the transverse beams are decorated and inscribed with Latin texts. Ten of the church's fourteen windows were filled with stained glass, mostly by O'Connor and Clayton and Bell. The filling of the rest of the windows was completed before Chamberlain's death.

Chamberlain lavished all this care on the building only because it was the setting for the worship of God and it is to this which we must now turn. Unfortunately the parish has not preserved any register of services and there are no visitation returns between 1838 and 1854. In 1838 Chamberlain's predecessor reported to the bishop that morning and evening prayer were said on Sundays at eleven and three but on no other days except Christmas Day and Good Friday, and that 'the Sacrament of the Lord's Supper' was administered once a month. From the beginning of his incumbency apparently Chamberlain instituted 'the daily service', the public recitation of morning and evening prayer. Certainly the *Ecclesiologist* in 1847 commented that even during the building of the north aisle, 'there was no occasion for intermitting the daily matins'.[35] Chamberlain was quite clear that the offices should be choral and that the proper place for the choir was the chancel. Surprisingly he had no objection to girls being in the choir although he thought 'for their own sakes' they should be out of sight.[36] He seems to have achieved his objects by 1853, by which time the benches of the recalcitrant family who had insisted on retaining their place in the chancel had been ousted by stalls for the clergy and 'Mr Street had added subsellae and desks for the chorister boys'. The *Ecclesiologist* commented, 'The services of this church are very vigorously and efficiently performed, the music being almost entirely Gregorian, and a large voluntary choir being in operation.'[37] In later years matins was sung daily at 11.15 and evensong at 7.30. Antiphons were introduced before the psalms and canticles.[38] Chamberlain himself compiled a hymn book[39] which was still in use as late as 1875. *Hymns Ancient and Modern* had taken its place by 1890.[40] The choristers were recruited

[33] Chamberlain, *Memoir* p 7.
[34] Squires plate 7.
[35] p 117.
[36] Chamberlain, *The Chancel* pp 13, 19–20.
[37] *Ecclesiologist* 14 (1853) pp 304, 305n.
[38] Squires p 22.
[39] *Hymns used at the Church of S. Thomas the Martyr, Oxford* (London 1866); also, *Hymns, chiefly for the Minor Festivals* (London 1863).
[40] Oxford, Bodleian MS Oxford diocesan papers, visitation returns.

from the boys at the parish schools and from among the undergraduates. Simeon describes how he and a friend joined the choir in *c*1867 and 'were arrayed, to my great astonishment, in surplice and cassock, which in those days were novelties'.[41] Chamberlain was scornful of the church orchestra, 'the vagaries of the bassoon, and clarinet and fiddle'[42] so common a feature of Anglican worship in the early nineteenth century, but St Thomas's had already advanced to a barrel organ before he arrived. The vestry meeting opposed its disposal but eventually agreed to its replacement by 'a new finger Organ',[43] which Chamberlain sited rather curiously in the chancel between the choir stalls and the sanctuary, believing it to be the best place.[44] The congregation for these daily offices was, one suspects, largely conscripted. The boys from St Edward's school and the girls from St Anne's school, both founded by Chamberlain, were taken to them.[45] Felicia Skene may well have been drawing on her knowledge of the parish when she rather ingenuously describes the heroine of one of her novels persuading all the female apprentices in her father's business to go to daily service.[46] On the other hand, one of the curates remembered that 'a cowman employed at the Ox Pens Farm was frequently at Evensong, and often fell asleep from weariness, as his working day lasted from 4 a.m. to 6 p.m.; the smell of his boots kept everyone at a distance.'[47]

Important though the daily office was, for Chamberlain 'the celebration of the Holy Eucharist [was] the central act of Christian worship'.[48] As he explained in his notes in *The Churchman's Diary* for 1851, 'The celebration of the Holy Sacrament is the principal act of Christian worship, inasmuch as it calls directly into action the office of our great High-Priest, not only to present our prayers to the Father, but to plead anew the merits of His own adorable Sacrifice.'[49] We may surmise that with these views Chamberlain would institute a weekly celebration of the eucharist as soon as he could. The first evidence we have of it is in 1854 when he declares in his visitation

[41] Quoted by [R. D.] Hill, [*A History of St Edward's School*] (privately printed 1962) p 18.
[42] Chamberlain, *The Chancel* p 23.
[43] Vestry Book 12 August 1852, 11 December 1856.
[44] Chamberlain, *The Chancel* p 23; Squires plate 7
[45] Hill p 13.
[46] *S. Alban's, or The Prisoners of Hope* (London 1853) p 309.
[47] W. H. Smithe, quoted by Squires p 22.
[48] Chamberlain, *The Chancel* p 17.
[49] p 3.

return that he celebrates holy communion on every Sunday alternately at eight and twelve and also in the week on festivals and Wednesdays, 'never less than twice in the Week'.[50] This seems to have been the pattern for the next twenty years except that by 1869 he was celebrating at least three times in the week. From 1875 there was a eucharist at eight every Sunday but the later sung celebration, at 12.30 by this time, was still only on the first and third Sundays of the month. In spite of the greater emphasis on the eucharist the average number of communicants on an ordinary Sunday showed no increase over the whole period for which we have figures. It hovered between forty and fifty.[51]

The ceremonial of the eucharist at St Thomas's was causing adverse comment as early as 1851. Coloured stoles were worn by the assistant clergy and a strangely adapted MA hood by the celebrant. The three officiating ministers were 'grouped most histrionically' the principal one taking his stand with his back to the congregation while the other two, at some distance on each side, 'continue[d] kneeling on the ground, so that our simple Protestant service has all the appearance of the Romish office of the Mass.'[52] On Whitsunday 1854 Chamberlain, egged on by his curates, wore a chasuble, of Gothic shape, for the first time. He had been preparing for it for some years. 'Slowly but surely he increased the MA hood which he reserved for Celebrations until it assumed the size and character of a chasuble.'[53] One of the curates described the process in a letter to Ollard.[54] A white chasuble was introduced the following Christmas and a violet one in lent 1855. He adds interestingly that, 'No green was worn in my time [1853–6] nor did we ever wear a proper alb . . . or girdle, or maniple or amice.' There is a remarkable window in the church however, erected in 1860,[55] which shows in the lower central light a priest fully vested and elevating the chalice, before an altar with two lights and a crucifix.

[50] *Bishop Wilberforce's Visitation Returns for the Archdeaconry of Oxford in the Year 1854*, transcribed and edited E. P. Baker, Oxfordshire Record Society (Banbury 1954) p 117.

[51] The visitation returns give the following figures – 1854 *c*40; 1857 *c*35; 1860 40; 1866 *c*50; 1869 *c*40; 1872 40–50. There are no comparable figures in the later returns.

[52] Maurice, *Postscript* pp 22–3. Compare the picture of the celebration at the Margaret Chapel, London, in 1851, reproduced in [S. L.] Ollard [*A Short History of the Oxford Movement*] (London 1932).

[53] *Church Times* (London) 29 January 1892.

[54] PH MSS, Ollard Papers, Thomas Russell to S. L. Ollard 27 August 1906, published in Squires p 20 n 4. The adapted MA hood must be the origin of the popular story that the first chasuble worn at St Thomas's was made out of two MA hoods sewn together by Marian Hughes.

[55] *The Builder* (London) 13 October 1860 p 661; *Guardian* (London) 24 October 1860.

This presumably reflects the later practice of the vicar as it certainly reflects his theology.[56] This was the first chasuble worn in post-reformation Oxford, though not in the whole country.[57] He is a very close second for the first use of incense in England, at ascensiontide 1855.[58]

Chamberlain was certainly a very knowledgeable liturgiologist. His notes in *The Churchman's Diary,* which he edited anonymously from its beginning in 1846,[59] contain much information about church customs and give very practical rules about the coincidence of feasts, the closed seasons for weddings, floral decorations and fasting. It was this diary, 'that well known, correct and most useful publication', which John Purchas acknowledged to be the basis of his *Directorium Anglicanum,* published in 1858. Purchas also included his name in his list of the 'eminent ritualists' who corrected the book.[60] Brandreth believes he was influenced by F. G. Lee, who was responsible for the second edition of the *Directorium,*[61] but the influence is more likely to have been the other way. Chamberlain was never as extreme as Lee. Even his opponents recognised that he concentrated on the essentials 'without those gairish adjuncts . . . to be found in more precocious districts.'[62] He has therefore a good claim to be regarded as the 'father of ritualism'.

Besides being an antiquary and liturgiologist, Chamberlain was also an active writer and editor. He wrote a number of simple biblical commentaries[63] and short dogmatic works[64] as well as contributing a

[56] The rest of the window shows the Lamb of God on the heavenly altar adored by St Thomas and St Frideswide amongst others. In *The Chancel* (p 15), Chamberlain wrote, 'The true object of Christian worship . . . is nothing less than this – the joining with angels and archangels, and all the company of heaven, in adoration of the Lamb slain before the foundation of the world . . . and receiving to ourselves the benefits of that Passion.' He also wrote of 'the heavenly mansions, of which the chancel . . . where is offered the sacrifice of the Holy Eucharist, is the acknowledged, but of course, inadequate type.' [*Ecclesiologist*] 13 (1852) p 103.

[57] R. D. Middleton, *Magdalen Studies* (London 1936) pp 233–4 gives an instance in 1841. See also Ollard p 172.

[58] See n 54 above. The relevant passage is omitted in Squires. It is said to have been used at St Mary Magdalene's, Munster Square, London on Christmas Eve 1854. See Ollard p 178.

[59] Apart from internal evidence, it is explicitly attributed to him by his curate, W. H. Smithe. See Squires p 25.

[60] *Directorium Anglicanum,* ed John Purchas (London 1858) p xxiii.

[61] Brandreth p 164.

[62] Maurice, *Postscript to the Ritualism of Oxford Popery* (London 1867) p 75.

[63] *The Seven Ages of the Church* (London 1856); *The Acts of the Apostles* (London 1856); *The Epistle to the Romans* (London 1870).

[64] *A Guide to the Eucharist* (London 1858); *The Doctrine of the Sacraments* (London 1882).

stream of articles and reviews to various church papers. He edited, at various times, *The Ecclesiastic,* a theological review whose contributors included E. A. Freeman, A. J. Beresford Hope, J. M. Neale, R. I. Wilberforce, W. J. Irons and R. F. Littledale, *The Churchman's Companion,* a monthly magazine, and the *Oxford University Herald.* Moreover he was literary adviser to Burns, the chief tractarian publisher (who eventually seceded to Rome) and later to Masters who took his place. For Burns he edited the *Englishman's Library* which included novels by William Gresley and F. E. Paget, historical works by William Palmer, R. I. Wilberforce and F. C. Massingberd and some devotional and educational literature. All this work had to be fitted into a busy parochial life. One of his curates recalled, 'I have heard how he would come down from Christ Church to the eight o'clock service on weekdays with a bundle of printer's proofs under his arm, to be looked over whilst he ate his breakfast in the old vicarage.'[65]

The impression may have been given of a narrow, ecclesiastically minded priest and scholar but this would be an injustice to Chamberlain. He deliberately selected St Thomas's as the sphere of his work because it was one of the poorest parishes in Oxford and had been sadly neglected by many of the Students of Christ Church who had been its vicars before him. The baptism registers show that the inhabitants were working class almost to a man—coopers, engineers, wheelwrights, shoemakers, gardeners, bakers, plasterers, saddlers, boatmen, boatbuilders, carpenters, printers, railwaymen, servants, or just plain labourers. But poverty was perhaps the least of its problems. When Chamberlain first went there, 'almost every other house in the centre of the parish was a house of ill-fame. Policemen durst not enter some of the courts.'[66] It was 'the haunt of thieves and harlots.'[67]

Overcrowding, illiteracy and moral degradation were the chief problems of the parish. Housing was something which Chamberlain never tried to tackle. His only concern was to provide seating in church, sufficient and free for the poor. We have seen how he enlarged St Thomas's, but he also built one church, St Frideswide's (consecrated 10 April 1872) and allowed another, St Barnabas's to be built (consecrated 19 October 1869), the one to accommodate the growing population, mostly railwaymen,[68] in the west of the parish and the

[65] W. H. Smithe quoted by Squires p 25.

[66] See n 53 above.

[67] Simeon p 8.

[68] The GWR station was opened in 1852, the LNWR in 1851.

other to accommodate the workmen at the new university printing works in the north. Under his predecessor a curious floating chapel[69] had been provided for the needs of the canal bargemen, and when it sank in 1868, Chamberlain built a small chapel-school room, St Nicholas, to replace it.[70] Indirectly the overcrowding may have helped him recover from the extreme unpopularity which his innovations had earned him. The outbreaks of cholera in Oxford in 1848 and 1854 affected St Thomas's parish particularly badly because of the housing conditions. Simeon claimed

> The Vicar was always to the front, working night and day with the doctors, comforting the sick and dying. . . . There is no doubt that it increased his influence immensely among the people. . . . From those times may be dated many friendships that lasted unto death. . . . The best of the parishioners were won, and unworthy suspicions were lulled.[71]

One feels slightly suspicious that Simeon may be exaggerating because of the failure of Dr Acland to mention the heroism of Chamberlain in his comprehensive report on the 1854 outbreak when he explicitly names various clergymen for their part.[72]

Education was a concern near to Chamberlain's heart. He became secretary to the diocesan board of education in 1839 and served on it for several years. In his own parish he founded various educational establishments, St Anne's School for the daughters of gentlemen, St Scholastica's for the training of school mistresses, which eventually became a school for older girls, the Osney House school for boys, which, under his curate Thomas Russell, was 'hopelessly mismanaged'[73] and went bankrupt after three years, and finally St Edward's school which has survived to the present. This last was opened in 1863 with only two pupils, but its numbers increased rapidly and, when its premises became too dilapidated, its enterprising new head, A. B. Simeon, moved it to its present site outside the parish against Chamberlain's initial opposition.[74]

As for the moral degradation, Chamberlain's first ploy was 'to appeal to the strong arm of the law' to close the brothels in his parish,

[69] See Squires plate 91.
[70] Now the shop of Oxford's bed specialists!
[71] Simeon pp 18–19.
[72] H. W. Ackland *Memoir on the Cholera at Oxford in the year 1854* (London 1856) p 98.
[73] A. B. Simeon quoted by Hill p 5.
[74] Hill p 21.

or at least to force them to move elsewhere.[75] There were various penitentiaries in Oxford to shelter and reform the victims but in September 1866 he opened a 'Home for Young Women and Servants' which was partly to house fallen girls who for some reason could not go to such institutions, and partly to protect those in particular moral danger. It dealt with thirty four cases in its first year and forty two in its second.[76] This seems to have evolved into what became known as the St Thomas industrial home and orphanage, dealing with younger girls. In 1885 its conspectus claimed nearly eighty were 'receiving such a bringing up as is likely to make them good and useful women'.

In all this work, Chamberlain was helped by curates, rarely fewer than three at any one time, by voluntary helpers such as the redoubtable Felicia Skene whose own home was a refuge for girls in danger and who even visited the city prison, and, above all, by the sisterhood of St Thomas.

This sisterhood was one of the first Anglican religious communities, preceded only by the Park Village sisterhood, the Devonport sisters and the community of St Mary the Virgin at Wantage. Chamberlain did not originally envisage a sisterhood but a more general institution. In 1843 an article entitled 'The Revival of Conventual Institutions' prompted him to tell its author, 'the necessity of this step is what I am now more than ever confirmed in,'[77] but the letter goes on to outline a plan similar to one he had already propounded in the *Christian Remembrancer*.[78]

> The form which, it appears to me, would be most feasible, *as a beginning*. is that some individual or individuals of property should open a large House, into which to receive persons of any kind who are willing to give themselves to piety and study—some to prepare themselves as Missionaries—one or more to keep School—some to read—some to do the work of a Deacon.

In August 1844, however, during a visit to the home of his uncle, the vicar of Shenington, he was told by his cousin, Marian Rebecca Hughes, of her intention of joining a sisterhood.[79] She had in fact already taken vows, the first woman in the church of England to do

[75] Simeon p 16.

[76] *Second Yearly Report of the Home for Young Women and Servants.* There is a copy in the Bodleian, G.A.Oxon b 153(R) p 64.

[77] Oxford, Bodleian MS Don d 120 fols 101–2, Chamberlain to Francis Kilvert 1843.

[78] *Christian Remembrancer* 3 (London 1852) pp 231–43.

[79] PH MSS, Marian Hughes' Diaries, 1. All the unidentified quotations in the following paragraphs are from this source.

so since the reformation,[80] but felt bound by her responsibility for her elderly parents to stay at home for the time being. Chamberlain seems to have done nothing about it then but by 1848 the idea of starting a sisterhood had taken hold of him. In June, visiting his cousin again, 'he talked to [her] of the want of Sisters in Oxford and wondered what could be done', and by November he was 'very anxious' to have sisters in his parish.

In 1849 more definite steps were taken. The death of her father and the approaching marriage of her brother (who had succeeded him in the living) freed Marian Hughes to come to Oxford, and the curate, J. L. Patterson, provided the money to buy a house opposite Worcester College where a beginning might be made. Chamberlain cast round to find others to join her. He introduced her to Felicia Skene who was then living at Leamington with her parents. Although they talked over a sisterhood and 'she was very loving . . . and much influenced by T. Chamberlain', she was not, Marian Hughes shrewdly observed, 'called to a Community life'. In spite of this, and in spite of Patterson's defection to Rome,[81] Marian Hughes, together with her mother, moved into Rewley House, so called 'in memory of the old Oxford Abbey which at first we had hoped to have, or rather a house built upon the old remains'.[82] She then 'wrote to the Bishop of Oxford for his sanction to form a Sisterhood of Mercy in his Diocese and received a kind letter giving a most full permission to do so on Dec. 11th.' A personal interview followed on 23 December at Christ Church in which 'the Bishop spoke most kindly to me and gave me his blessing upon the proposed work.' It will be seen that the initiative was taken by Marian Hughes, who was under the spiritual direction of Dr Pusey, and in this lay the seeds of discord.

In January, whilst Felicia Skene was staying at Rewley House, 'Mr Chamberlain proposed our having one evening in St Thomas Church a little meeting of prayer for the beginning of a Sisterhood of Charity.' It was at this meeting presumably that the *Instrument of Foundation of the Sisterhood of St Thomas of Canterbury*, a copy of which has been found among Marian Hughes' papers, was laid on the altar.[83] The main object of the community is declared to be 'the care of the poor

[80] Liddon 3 p 10. Her own diary entry is quoted by A. M. Allchin, *The Silent Rebellion* (London 1958) pp 59–60.

[81] He later became bishop of Emmaus. *Church Times* 29 January 1892.

[82] The land was purchased by the NW Railway Co.

[83] There is a draft dated S Agnes (either 21 or 28 January), but the fair copy is dated S Agatha (5 February). The discovery of these documents and the supporting evidence

in the parish of St Thomas' under the direction of Chamberlain with Dr Pusey as 'Spiritual Father'. It is signed by Marian Hughes, who describes herself as 'sister of Charity', and by Esther Sophia Chambers, 'Postulant', and witnessed by Thomas Chamberlain, his curate Robinson Thornton, and Miss Skene. Esther Chambers was the sister of J. D. Chambers, a high church barrister who had been associated with the founding of the Park Village sisterhood, and of Catherine Chambers who was one of the founder members of the Devonport sisters.[84] She found that the way lent was kept was too hard for her and left, but others took her place. Pusey sent Helen Ind, who had already tried her vocation with the Park Village sisters, but she also gave up after six months. Two others are known to us from Marian Hughes's diaries, Catherine Fraser, who was a relative of Miss Skene and bishop Forbes, and Augusta Landon.[85]

Conflict soon developed over who was to have ultimate control over the community. It was brought to a head over the form of profession to be used by Catherine Fraser. Chamberlain saw no reason for not using the form Marian Hughes had herself used even though it had not the bishop's sanction. Pusey and Marian Hughes thought this wrong. As the latter wrote in her diary: 'This brought out Mr Chamberlain's intentions of the Sisterhood being entirely under his care. This not having been my intention it seemed impossible to go on together.' In October they agreed to part company and on 4 November 1850 Marian Hughes left Rewley House and in time started her own community, 'the Society of the Holy and Undivided Trinity'.

Information about the St Thomas's sisters is tantalisingly meagre. Sister Catherine apparently stayed with Chamberlain,[86] and was presumably the first professed sister in 1852. Another sister was professed in 1853 and three more in 1857, one of them being the later

---

of the diary prove wrong the foundation date of 1847 given by A. Cameron, *History of Religious Communities in the Church of England* (London 1918) and often repeated.

[84] T. J. Williams and A. W. Campbell, *The Park Village Sisterhood* (London 1965) pp 61–2.

[85] Maurice thought there were 'about seven Sisters' as well as the mother in residence in 1850. Maurice, *Postscript* p 22.

[86] PH MSS, draft letter from Marian Hughes to bishop Wilberforce (in Pusey's handwriting): 'A difficulty . . . about the internal arrangements and guidance of the sisterhood has compelled me to resign all connection with it and I now only remain for a time, until Mr Chamberlain and S. Catherine can make arrangements for carrying on the work.' Catherine Fraser evidently did not join SHUT as P. F. Anson states in *Call of the Cloister*, 2 ed, rev A. W. Campbell (London 1964) p 292.

mother Beatrice.[87] The number had grown to eight by 1861.[88] Their main work was visiting the poor in the parish, but to this was added teaching. They took over St Anne's school and started St Scholastica's. They also ran the 'Home for Young Women and Servants' and eventually took on the diocesan penitentiary at Basingstoke. By 1873 they were strong enough to respond to the appeal of bishop Webb of Bloemfontain for help in starting a community in his diocese in South Africa.[89]

All was not well, however. In an undated entry in the second volume of Marian Hughes' diary, probably referring to 1876 or 1877, we read, 'At 12 S. Isabel of Rewley came to talk about S. Anne's School being incorporated with us. . . . She seems one who would help us in our work for Christ. Probably she and 4 of those sisters who left with the Mother may join us from St Thomas's.' The difficulty seems to have been the autocratic ways of Chamberlain himself. This at least was Pusey's confidential opinion a few years later. In 1880, thinking that Chamberlain was in difficulty about the future direction of his sisterhood, he persuaded mother Marian to write to her cousin and propose the union of the St Thomas's sisterhood with her society. He was determined, however, that Chamberlain should never be in a position to take over the united community.

> His is the smaller society but the difficulty is—what you cannot tell him—himself. His is a mind which will rule, wherever he is. I thought he was virtually giving up his Society but he has good health and strength, and while he lives and takes part in the affairs of his sisters, I should think [it] hopeless.[90]

Not surprisingly the proposed union came to nothing.

This autocratic temperament was Chamberlain's great weakness. He could inspire loyalty but rarely affection. There were some exceptions. Miss Skene worked with him for over forty years. One of his curates stayed for thirty. But even he, in his memorial sermon, betrayed the general opinion of him when he said that he had 'a greater love for men's souls than many, I know, have been wont to believe'.[91] Simeon, recalling his first meeting with him, said, 'He was a stern looking man,

[87] *Osney. A Half Yearly Paper of the Sisterhood of S. Thomas the Martyr, Oxford* June 1892 pp 2–3. Most of the information in this paragraph comes from this paper. A very few numbers of it survive in the Bodleian.
[88] *Letters of John Mason Neale*, selected and edited by his daughter (London 1910) p 337.
[89] Anson pp 287–8.
[90] PH MSS, E. B. Pusey to M. R. Hughes, 2 April 1880.
[91] *Guardian* 3 February 1892.

peculiarly devoid of sympathy,' and, speaking of the resiting of St Edward's school, he commented, 'He was very unintelligible at that time to me. . . . It was difficult, almost impossible to deal with him.'[92] Even more damning is a letter among Pusey's papers from a woman who wanted to make her confession to him: 'I should say, too, that two years since, I saw Mr Chamberlain at St Thomas's for [confession] but it gave me *no relief, none at all* . . . I did not like his manner at all—he discomforted me more than I can describe and made me feel very nervous'.[93] Chamberlain achieved a great deal in the parish of St Thomas and, indirectly by his example and writings, in the church at large but it was this flaw in his temperament which led to his being virtually forgotten.

Pusey House
Oxford.

[92] Quoted by Hill pp 18, 21.
[93] PH MSS, Annie Parker to E. B. Pusey 14 March 1863.

URBAN CHURCH ATTENDANCE AND THE USE OF STATISTICAL EVIDENCE, 1850–1900

by NIGEL YATES

OVER the last two decades historians of the Victorian church have been paying an increasing amount of attention to the various forms of statistical evidence which are available for the period. There are in fact three major categories of such evidence. Firstly there are the membership figures and other statistics published by churches and meant for external consumption; many of these have now been brought together in a useful compendium.[1] Then there are the returns of the first (and last) national religious census, held in 1851, and of various local censuses, especially those taken for several large and medium-sized towns in 1881; these were also made public either in summary or detail depending on the nature of the census. Finally there are the statistics compiled by churches at various levels purely for their own use, but now open to public inspection in record offices: Anglican visitation returns and service registers, those records of nonconformist churches that yield such valuable information about membership and communicant figures and the numbers of Sunday scholars. Not all of these statistics have been used with an equal degree of enthusiasm, and very few studies have made effective use of all three. The aim of this paper is to look in some detail at the uses to which they have been put so far and to indicate some other uses to which they might be put in the future.

It is not my intention to say very much about the use of those official statistics published by the churches themselves, though they have been interpreted as showing a remarkable recovery in the fortunes of the church of England between 1830 and 1914, and a comparable collapse by all the major nonconformist churches.[2] There are, however, considerable difficulties in the use of these statistics. In the case of most

[1] [R.] Currie, [A.] Gilbert and [L.] Horsley, [*Churches and Churchgoers*] (Oxford 1977).

[2] A. D. Gilbert, *Religion and Society in Industrial England* (London 1976) esp pp 23–48, 125–43. Parts of Gilbert's thesis have been constructively criticised in a review by H. Macleod, 'Recent Studies in Victorian Religious History', *Victorian Studies* 21 (London 1978) pp 245–55.

nonconformist churches they relate to membership, which is not the same thing as the number of worshippers; it could even be that membership of a particular chapel might increase at the same time as actual attendances were declining, or vice versa, so the figures could easily be misleading. In the case of the church of England it is difficult to base much on such statistics as the number of confirmations or easter communicants, since neither are reasonable criteria of Anglican commitment.

Compared with these statistics the evidence of religious censuses is perhaps more informative, though they are not simple sources to use and require very careful analysis. Very much more use has been made of the 1851 national census[3] than of the later local censuses,[4] although in the main the returns of the latter are much more reliable, and hardly any comparisons between censuses have been made for those towns for which the information is available.[5] Some of the uses to which these census returns have been put is perhaps questionable. There has been a general desire to establish a national pattern of Victorian churchgoing, a religious geography of England, though it is quite clear from the evidence that there were significant variations in the total number of churchgoers, and in the respective strengths of the particular denominations, not merely from one region to another, but within a region itself, and often between two adjacent towns or villages. Attempts have been made to compare levels of churchgoing in areas of different social standing within large towns, but there are considerable difficulties in doing this, since it cannot be supposed that all those who attended particular churches or chapels lived in the parish or the immediate catchment area; indeed many churches and chapels must have had for various reasons such as the standard of preaching, music or ritual, substantially eclectic congregations.

Two areas in which census returns can be of particular use are in estimating how full Victorian churches were, and in comparing the

[3] [K. S.] Inglis, ['Patterns of Religious Worship in 1851'], *JEH* 11 (1960) pp 74–86, substantially modified and usefully reorientated by D. M. Thompson, 'The 1851 Religious Census: Problems and Possibilities', *Victorian Studies* 11 (1967) pp 87–97.

[4] An exception is [H.] Macleod, ['Class, Community and Region: The Religious Geography of Nineteenth-Century England'], *Sociological Year Book of Religion in Britain* 6, ed M. Hill (London 1973) pp 29–72.

[5] There is a rather superficial analysis of the 1851 and 1881 returns for Sheffield in [E. R.] Wickham, [*Church and People in an Industrial Society*] (London 1957) pp 108–10, 147–50, 275–80, and an exceptionally confusing one of the 1851 returns with an interesting series of three local censuses for 1881, 1891 and 1902 in [R. B.] Walker, ['Religious Changes in Liverpool in the Nineteenth Century'], *JEH* 19 (1968) pp 195–211.

relative strengths of denominations and churches in particular towns for which more than one set of figures is available. There was a general feeling of unease among Victorian churchmen as to the inadequacy of the number of sittings to cater for the population, and in many towns during the second half of the nineteenth century the provision of additional accommodation more or less kept up with, and in some places was even in excess of, the growth in population. Yet the evidence is, contrary to modern popular rumour, that most churches were very far from full; new churches were being built in many cases for potential rather than actual congregations, and for potential congregations that never materialised. If we look at the 1851 census returns for central Leeds,[6] only at four churches, two Anglican and two Roman catholic, were more than seventy per cent of the available sittings occupied at all the main services; at the other end of the scale less than thirty per cent of the available sittings were occupied at each service in two Anglican churches and one independent chapel, and at the Inghamite chapel a grand total of twenty eight adults and nineteen scholars, divided between three services, occupied two hundred seats. An analysis of the 1851 returns for many areas, both urban and rural, and of later local censuses reveals a similar inability to fill churches to anywhere near capacity throughout England.

Unfortunately, Leeds is not one of those places for which it is easy to compare church attendances at different points of the nineteenth century, but there are a substantial number of towns, of very different social types, for which such comparisons are indeed possible. For the purpose of this paper I have looked in some detail at the returns for four towns where censuses were held in 1881—Hull, Portsmouth, Sheffield and Southampton—and compared these returns with those of the 1851 national census.[7] As has been noted elsewhere, there is a good deal of variation in both the national and local census returns. The Hull figures for 1851 exclude the number of attendants at two Anglican churches and one baptist chapel, as this information was omitted from the returns. The Anglican returns for Portsmouth in

[6] PRO, HO 129/501.

[7] See the appendix to this paper for a summary of the evidence. In the case of Sheffield this is based on the figures published by Wickham. For Hull there is an accurate summary of the 1851 returns in *VCH Yorkshire: East Riding* 1 p 316 , and of those of the local census in *Eastern Counties Herald*, 8 December 1881. For Southampton I used the summary of the 1851 returns and the details of the local census published in *Hampshire Independent*, 10 December 1881. The figures for Portsmouth have been calculated from the original returns for 1851 in PRO, HO 129/96 and those of the local census published in *Portsmouth Times*, 21 December 1881.

1851 are also defective; there is no return at all for Portsmouth parish church, at another the incumbent declined to make one and the attendances are approximate guesses by the registrar, and for two others there are two returns each which give substantially conflicting attendance figures. It should also be noted that the 1851 figures used in this paper for Sheffield and Southampton include Sunday scholars whereas those for Hull and Portsmouth do not; none of the 1881 figures include Sunday scholars, but those for Southampton contain attendances for practically all services, including early celebrations at Anglican churches which had them, with the exception of the evening service at the Catholic apostolic church, where the enumerator was refused admission on the grounds that he was late. The inclusion of Sunday scholars in the 1851 summaries, and at some churches no separate figures were given for adult attendances,[8] is generally thought to have exaggerated nonconformist attendances, though at Portsmouth the difference was very marginal and at Leeds, where nonconformists substantially outnumbered Anglicans, the church of England attracted 46.5% of the Sunday scholars compared with 32.4% of the adult attendants.

It must therefore be emphasised that any calculations based on any type of religious census return ought to be regarded as approximate and the margin of error may be quite wide. Nevertheless if one looks at the respective gains and losses of the major religious groupings within the four towns between 1851 and 1881, there are some interesting trends. In terms of numbers, of course, nearly everybody gained, simply because of the rapid rise in the population over the thirty years, though in Portsmouth there was a significant drop in the actual number of both baptist and independent or congregationalist attendances. In terms of the proportion of the population in church, though this is notoriously difficult to calculate, there may have been a more significant decline than has sometimes been suggested,[9] and this decline seems to have been universal, though it was more severe in some places than others. In Hull and Sheffield, as also at Bolton, Bristol and Coventry, it seems not to have been very great. At Portsmouth and Southampton the decline seems to have been more marked, though it was much greater still in Ipswich, Leicester, Northampton, Nottingham and Warrington.[10] The fluctuations, sometimes very pronounced, in

[8] For example Waterlooville, PRO, HO 129/111.

[9] [W. O.] Chadwick, [*The Victorian Church*] (London 1966–70) 2 p 229.

[10] Compare the indices of attendance for these and some other towns published for 1851

denominational strengths or weaknesses are summarised in table 1, and amplified in the appendix to this paper.

Table 1: Comparative changes in attendances for major denominational groupings between 1851 and 1881.

	Hull	*Portsmouth*	*Sheffield*	*Southampton*
Church of England	−9.9	+15.5	+4.4	−2.0
Congregationalists	−3.2	−14.4	−1.5	−6.8
Baptists	−1.1	−6.6	−1.7	+2.8
Methodists	−3.4	+1.9	−2.2	−3.9
Roman Catholics	−0.5	+0.6	−2.8	−2.4
Others	+18.1	+3.0	+3.8	+12.3

Of the four towns, the most religiously stable was clearly Sheffield, except for the divisions within methodism where the Wesleyans seemed to have lost heavily to the other branches of methodism, a process which can be seen in reverse at Bradford, Hull and Nottingham.[11] The Hull and Southampton results are remarkably similar, with both showing a substantial shift from the major denominations to either undenominational missions or the salvation army. The Portsmouth result is remarkable, with an enormous shift to the church of England at the expense of the baptists and congregationalists. What, however, is quite clear is that it is exceedingly difficult to detect general trends, either nationally or regionally, in the growth or decline of denominations except perhaps for the decline of congregationalism and the growth of new sects and missions.

The improvement in the position of the church of England between 1851 and 1881 at Portsmouth and Sheffield seems to have been paralleled at Bradford and Wolverhampton, both towns where the church of England was the underdog in 1851. The dramatic change in the fortunes of the church of England at Portsmouth brought the town into the same general religious group as Bath, Bristol and Southampton. In all these three towns the church of England was by far the largest religious grouping in 1881, though in all three it had suffered

by Inglis pp 80–5, and for 1881 by Macleod pp 46–7; the lowest drop (0.9 percentage points) was at Coventry, the highest (27.8 percentage points) at Warrington.

[11] This and other comparisons below are based on the figures published by Inglis and Macleod, see above.

a slight decline in its position since 1851.[12] Unlike Southampton, however, though like Portsmouth, there had been significant gains by Wesleyan methodists at Bath and Bristol, as there had also at Bolton and Leicester; the Wesleyan collapse at Sheffield is partly repeated at Bradford and Nottingham, where the increase in numbers fell well short of the average increase for all denominations, despite gains from the other methodist churches.[13] The significant drop in the Anglican proportion of attendances at Hull seems to have been paralleled at Liverpool,[14] though there appears to have been some improvement in the Anglican position there between 1881 and a later census in 1902.

Apart from the church of England and, to a greater or lesser extent, the baptists, congregationalists and methodists, most other denominations were very weak in most Victorian towns, but the variety of religious worship available was considerable, and it grew between 1851 and 1881. What is perhaps surprising is the weakness of Roman catholicism outside the main centres of Irish immigration; in Sheffield and Southampton there seems to have been a serious drop in the proportion of Roman catholic to total attendances, though it looks as if, as at Liverpool, attendances may have been underestimated. In Portsmouth, where the returns counted both morning masses, there was a marginal increase in the proportion of attendants. In Hull a marked feature of the 1881 attendances was the strength of the newly founded salvation army, but it was much weaker in Sheffield and Southampton and had still to establish itself in Portsmouth. By 1851 both quakers and unitarians were insignificant numerically in most towns, though their political and social influence was much greater than their numbers, which were further eroded as the century progressed.

In comparing attendances in 1881, or other local censuses, with those in 1851, it is also important to compare the number of sittings

[12] For Bristol see Chadwick 2 p 229. There is some useful material on Bristol churchgoing in J. H. S. Kent, 'The Role of Religion in the Cultural Structure of the Later Victorian City', *TRHS* 5 series 23 (1973) pp 153–73.

[13] R. B. Walker, 'The Growth of Wesleyan Methodism in Victorian England and Wales', *JEH* 24 (1973) pp 267–84.

[14] 1851: Church of England 40.7 Nonconformist 26.8 Roman Catholic 32.5.
1881: Church of England 29.5 Nonconformist 36.5 Roman Catholic 34.0.
Figures calculated from Inglis and Macleod, see above, with adaptation of the latter to the criteria of the former. But see also Walker p 211, who demonstrates that the 1881 census seriously underestimated the number of Roman catholic attendances; this would make the Anglican collapse look worse, the nonconformist improvement smaller and the Roman catholic improvement larger.

available, as has been done in the appendix to this paper. This is for two reasons; firstly one can see whether particular churches or groups of churches were better or worse attended from one census to another. Table 2 suggests that the very different patterns that one can discern between two towns in a similar social grouping or within the same geographical region are in fact repeated between different churches of the same denomination in the same town.

Table 2: Percentage of sittings occupied at morning and evening services in selected Portsmouth churches, 1851 and 1881.

	1851		1881		
	Morning	*Evening*	*Morning*	*Evening*	*Overall Change*
Church of England					
St Mary, Portsea	29.6	27.3	69.4	99.6	+56.0
St George, Portsea	26.1	31.9	27.4	30.2	−0.2
St John, Portsea	56.2	81.2	28.2	37.8	−35.7
Wesleyan methodist					
Arundel Street	55.3	62.4	59.9	80.3	+11.2
Green Row	43.9	48.2	33.1	24.6	−17.2
Congregationalist					
Buckland	43.9	61.6	59.0	77.1	+15.2
King Street	76.6	80.2	11.5	11.7	−66.8
Baptist					
Kent Street	53.9	59.5	34.0	41.0	−19.2
St Thomas Street	6.9	10.0	20.0	17.1	+10.1

In some cases the fluctuations can be explained to some extent by social changes in the area between the dates of the censuses, in others by a change of minister or ritual observance which had altered the size and character of the congregation. But in many cases the cause is not clear, and the sometimes startling changes over a short period are a further warning to those who are too eager to see general patterns in urban churchgoing. The second reason for a comparison of sittings available is to examine how far increases or decreases in the proportion of attendances relate to increases or decreases in the proportion of accommodation. If one looks at the statistics for Hull, Portsmouth, Sheffield and Southampton, then it is clear that in many cases changes in attendance proportions are not related to those for sittings. In the case of the church of England in Sheffield the proportion of sittings fell substantially between 1851 and 1881, but there was a marginal increase in the proportion of attendances; at Portsmouth the increase in the proportion of Anglican attendances was much greater, and at Southampton the decrease much less steep, than the respective increase and decrease in the proportion of sittings. In Hull and Sheffield the proportion of methodist attendances fell whilst the proportion of sittings increased, and at Sheffield the congregationalists suffered the same fate. Clearly denominational increase or decrease in the proportion of its attendances from one period to another cannot necessarily be ascribed to the ability or inability of a denomination to provide adequate sittings for potential worshippers.

Despite the problems raised by the evidence, the use of the different types of census material available is an essential aid to our understanding of religion at the grass roots in the Victorian period. But where it is impossible, as it is very often, to make comparisons between different periods because of the lack of local census material, then the ecclesiastical historian must make use of the third type of statistical material identified at the beginning of this paper. Indeed he should make use of it in any case because it is a valuable supplementary source in its own right of which comparatively little use has so far been made. Some use has been made of Anglican visitation returns, and as a result of their use for groups of parishes in Cheshire,[15] Oxfordshire and Yorkshire,[16] it has been suggested that there was a spectacular decline in the number of Anglican communicants between the mid-eighteenth and the mid-nineteenth centuries, and a substantial increase thereafter. There is, however, a danger that the use of this source, which in many areas is only available periodically, with long gaps in between, may be misleading; there is also the additional problem that an incumbent's return of the number of communicants to his bishop or archdeacon may not be accurate. An alternative check on Anglican communicant figures can be made from a study of such parish documents as sacrament money books, which only occasionally survive, and service registers, which survive in much greater quantity, especially for urban areas, from the mid-nineteenth century. The evidence of the surviving sacrament money book for the small town parish of Havant appears to contradict the evidence of such visitation returns as have so far been examined, for there appears to have been a continuous steady increase

[15] R. B. Walker, 'Religious Changes in Cheshire 1750–1850', *JEH* 17 (1966) pp 77–94.
[16] Currie, Gilbert and Horsley pp 22–3.

in the number of communicants, despite little change in the number of celebrations, between 1779 and 1848.[17] Table 3 gives details of the number of whitsun communicants in three groups of urban Anglican parishes for the last three decades of the nineteenth century, chosen not on a random basis but including all those parishes in the respective towns for which service registers survive.[18]

Table 3: Whitsun communicants in selected Anglican churches in Gosport, Portsmouth and Southampton 1870–1900

	1870	*1880*	*1890*	*1900*
Gosport:				
Christ Church	—	82	151	168
St John, Forton	54	—	118	207
Portsmouth				
St Mary, Portsea	—	325	415	599
St Luke, Southsea	—	41	52	98
St Simon, Southsea	75	112	171	263
Southampton:				
St Mary	69	174	276	314
St Michael	—	40	61	87
St Peter	—	66	95	218
Millbrook	—	85	109	79

Eight out of nine parishes had a substantial increase in the number of communicants at whitsun, the figures being based on an average over three years so as to prevent any distortions caused by freak years. How much this adds to recent theories about the growing popularity of the church of England in the second half of the nineteenth century is a difficult issue, but such a substantial increase over a comparatively short period, in churches which represent most shades of Anglican theological opinion and liturgical practice, is difficult to explain entirely in terms of population growth or changing views among Anglicans about the importance of receiving the sacrament. If one is going to analyse changes in communicant figures, and one would like to see much more use of this type of evidence for both urban and rural communities, then the use of figures for whitsun communions is

[17] P[ortsmouth] C[ity] R[ecord] O[ffice], CHU 38/2A/1.

[18] PCRO, CHU 3/1F/1–3, CHU 16/1D/1–3, CHU 25/1C/1–4, CHU 50/1D/1–5, CHU 52/1E/1–3; Southampton City Record Office, PR 5/2/1/1–2, PR 7/1/19–21 and 29, PR 10/2/1–3, PR 23/2/1–3.

probably the least misleading; ordinary Sunday communion figures fluctuate from week to week because it was not normal to communicate weekly, and both easter and Christmas figures included many who were not regular attendants at Anglican services. It would certainly be interesting to see how consistent this pattern of seemingly improved Anglican communicant figures really was in national terms.

Certainly no consistent pattern can be seen from the limited amount of work that has been done at the local level, largely in unpublished theses, on the membership and communicant figures of nonconformist churches. The success or failure of a particular chapel depended very much on the preaching or pastoral ability of the minister, or the financial acumen of the trustees, or the political complexion of the membership. There is good evidence to suppose that similar factors, though perhaps to a lesser extent, also determined the growth or decline of Anglican congregations. The only religious bodies with a guaranteed following were the Jews and, in towns with a large Irish population, the Roman catholics. Everybody else was in competition with each other in their efforts to retain and preferably to increase, their congregations.

My aim in this paper has been to examine the various forms of statistical evidence that have been used, are being used or ought to be used by historians of the Victorian church, with particular reference to the problems of urban church attendance. My conclusions are twofold. Firstly I believe that it is right that this type of evidence should be exploited to the full, and that those types that have only been used in a very limited way, particularly the records of individual churches, should be put to much greater use in the future. The great value that the records in this category have over published statistics or census returns is that they were, in most cases, not designed for any sort of public consumption and they are as a result the most accurate type of statistical evidence available. Their drawback is that they exist in such quantity, and that they therefore cannot be used very effectively in the national context until they have been used for primarily local or regional studies in different parts of the country. Secondly, however, despite the value of statistical evidence, I think there are great dangers in trying to use it in a national context to see clear patterns where no such clear patterns exist. That is not to say that there are no patterns to be seen; in certain respects there are, but they have to be very carefully expressed and substantial qualifications attached. Again the need for more detailed studies at a local or regional level has to be reiterated. In the present state of our knowledge I suspect that it is far too early to compile a satisfactory 'religious geography of nineteenth century England' or to analyse accurately the 'patterns of religious worship'. As I have tried to show in this paper the variations that existed between regions, between localities in the same region, between districts or churches in the same locality, are so great that the overall picture is very much more complicated than has sometimes been imagined, and even the more sensible attempt to compare areas of similar social structure in different towns, would need to be qualified by what I have said about the difficulties in determining religious catchment areas.

City Records Office
Portsmouth

Appendix: Tables showing the proportion of sittings and attendances by denominations in Hull, Portsmouth, Sheffield and Southampton, 1851 and 1881

	% *Sittings*		% *Attendances*	
	1851	*1881*	*1851*	*1881*
Hull				
Church of England	36.2	26.9	31.9	22.0
Methodists	35.6	40.8	42.1	38.7
Congregationalists	12.8	9.6	9.6	6.4
Baptists	2.9	1.8	2.4	1.3
Presbyterians	1.6	3.5	0.5	3.0
Salvation Army	—	8.1	—	18.2
Roman Catholics	1.7	1.8	4.3	3.8
Others	9.2	7.5	9.2	6.6
Methodist Divisions				
Wesleyans	21.2	18.7	19.3	20.0
Primitives	7.3	17.0	12.9	15.2
Independents	1.7	—	3.4	—
New Connexion	2.8	4.0	2.1	2.3
Wesleyan Reformers	2.6	—	4.4	—
United Free Church	—	1.1	—	1.2

	% Sittings		% Attendances	
	1851	*1881*	*1851*	*1881*
Portsmouth				
Church of England	41.1	48.1	43.5	59.0
Methodists	16.1	20.4	14.5	16.4
Congregationalists	19.8	10.6	20.9	6.5
Baptists	16.9	12.3	16.6	10.0
Presbyterians	—	1.3	—	1.3
Roman Catholics	2.7	1.4	2.4	3.0
Others	3.4	5.9	2.1	3.8
Methodist Divisions				
Wesleyans	12.5	14.1	11.0	12.1
Primitives	1.1	3.0	0.7	1.6
Bible Christians	2.5	3.3	2.8	2.7

	% Sittings		% Attendances	
	1851	*1881*	*1851*	*1881*
Sheffield				
Church of England	44.5	33.8	34.3	38.7
Methodists	31.9	42.4	36.3	34.1
Congregationalists	10.1	11.3	10.5	9.0
Baptists	5.0	3.3	5.4	3.7
Presbyterians	—	0.6	—	0.5
Salvation Army	—	2.9	—	4.7
Roman Catholics	2.1	2.8	9.2	6.4
Others	6.4	2.9	4.3	2.9
Methodist Divisions				
Wesleyans	23.7	15.5	24.3	13.6
Primitives	2.3	9.2	5.8	6.3
New Connexion	4.4	5.5	5.0	3.1
Wesleyan Association	1.5	—	0.9	—
Wesleyan Reformers	—	3.8	0.3	2.9
United Free Church	—	8.4	—	8.2

	% Sittings		% Attendances	
	1851	*1881*	*1851*	*1881*
Southampton				
Church of England	58.1	45.3	54.8	52.8
Methodists	9.2	9.0	10.7	6.8
Congregationalists	14.2	12.6	18.3	11.5
Baptists	5.1	10.3	4.3	7.1
Presbyterians	—	2.6	—	2.4
Salvation Army	—	1.8	—	2.9
Roman Catholics	1.7	1.8	3.8	1.4
Others	11.7	16.6	8.1	15.1
Methodist Divisions				
Wesleyans	6.1	4.8	6.2	3.5
Primitives	1.5	1.3	3.0	2.1
Bible Christians	1.6	2.9	1.5	1.2

BETWEEN TOWN AND COUNTRYSIDE: CONTRASTING PATTERNS OF CHURCHGOING IN THE EARLY VICTORIAN BLACK COUNTRY

by GEOFFREY ROBSON

DISRAELI's romantic novel Sybil deliberately and vividly contrasts the two nations of its subtitle. Only Egremont, the aristocratic hero, attempts to cross the impassible gulf between them when, in the guise of Mr Franklin, he lives for a while in Mowedale alongside the catholic Gerards. Ironically he has only two contacts with the poor. He visits an honest handloom weaver in the company of Mr St Lys, the saintly tractarian vicar of Mowbray, and a model factory set in a garden village, the creation of a paternalistic aristocrat. It is left to the Owenite Stephen Morley, rather than the admirer of the ancient catholic faith, to penetrate the hideous mining area from which the hell-cats eventually emerge to burn Mowbray castle. Here the absence of religion is made explicit in the description of Wodgate where 'no church . . . has yet raised its spire . . . and even the conventicle scarcely dares show its humble front in some obscure corner.'[1] So, unrestrained by established religion and hardly touched by dissent, the brutalised colliers and ironworkers are suited to the violent, plundering role they fulfil in the final chapters of the book. They form a dark contrast to the noble and restrained workforce of aristocratic Mowbray a little further north.

In his life of Disraeli Blake recognises the historical accuracy of the scenes portrayed in Sybil, derived as they were, without acknowledgement, from the parliamentary blue books especially the children's employment and midland mining commissions of 1842.[2] Wodgate, in fact, can be identified with Willenhall which, although it had less than a quarter of the population of nearby Wolverhampton, so horrified the children's employment commissioner that he devoted an equal amount of space to each on the ground that 'there is no place which

[1] [B.] Disraeli, *Sybil* (London 1845) bk 3 cap 4.

[2] R. Blake, *Disraeli* (London 1966) p 212. S. M. Smith, 'Willenhall and Wodgate: Disraeli's use of blue book evidence.' *Review of English studies*, ns 13 (Oxford 1962) pp 368–84.

bears any resemblance to Willenhall; nor do I know of any place elsewhere which resembles it.'[3] Disraeli had his own ideological reasons for excluding religion from the colliery district. In respect of Wodgate he was curiously accurate, but in giving an irreligious character to the rest of the Black Country in the 1840s he was singularly wide of the mark. Instead of the irreligion of the colliers contrasting with the piety of the aristocratic estates in the surrounding countryside the opposite is nearer the truth. The Black Country is revealed by the 1851 census of religious worship to be an anomaly. It appears as the one area of the country where industrialisation and urbanisation, far from diminishing church attendance, actually improved it. The contrast between high rural and low urban church attendance was evident to all in 1851 and Mann, in his introduction to the published report, ascribed it to those very characteristics which Disraeli had portrayed. 'But our modern populous towns,—erected more for business than for residence—mere aggregates of offices and workshops and overcrowded dwellings of the subordinate agents of industry,—are inhabited by none whose means permit them to reside elsewhere . . . the masses, therefore, of our large and growing towns—connected by no sympathetic tie with those by fortune placed above them—form a world apart, a nation by themselves; divided almost as effectually from the rest as if they spoke another language or inhabited another land.'[4]

It has been left to scholars possessed of electronic calculators to analyse the specific quality of the contrast. Inglis seemed to confirm Mann's hypothesis that industrialisation was the key factor in explaining the poor church attendance record of the urban areas.[5] But a closer comparison between urban and rural church attendance carried out by McLeod shows that with few exceptions every town which exceeded Inglis's average for urban church attendance (49%) was surrounded by a rural hinterland where church attendance was even higher.[6] Bristol was one of only two towns with over a hundred thousand inhabitants and higher than average attendance (56.7), but it drew its immigrant population from Gloucestershire, Somerset and

[3] [R. H.] Horne, [*Second report of the children's employment commission*], P[*arliamentary*] P[*apers*] 13 (London 1843) section Q p 38.

[4] [H.] Mann, [*Report on the census of religious worship 1851*], *PP* 89 (London 1853) p cxxviii.

[5] K. S. Inglis, 'Patterns of religious worship in 1851', *JEH* 11.1 (April 1960) p 82.

[6] D. H. McLeod, 'Class, community and religion,' *A Sociological Yearbook of religion in Britain* 6 (London 1973) pp 39–43.

Wilts where church attendance averaged well above 68%.[7] This seems to suggest that many rural labourers maintained their connection with the churches when they moved to the town. The one exception for large towns is Wolverhampton. With over a hundred thousand population its index of attendance is 53.08 whereas the surrounding rural area of Staffordshire averages only 49.62. The case of Dudley (population 37,692) is more complicated because of the crazy political geography of the Black Country. Although a part of Worcestershire it was surrounded on all sides by Staffordshire. Nevertheless the index of attendance is even higher than Wolverhampton at 55.32 whilst rural Worcestershire, though better at church attendance than Staffordshire, only has an average of 54. Thus even the published figures show the Black Country to be unduly religious for an industrialised urban area.[8] A study of the original returns produces only one modification of the picture.[9] The published statistics for Wolverhampton are based on the parliamentary borough which, in 1851, included the nearby iron town of Bilston and the industrialised villages of Sedgley, Willenhall and Wednesfield. Sedgley and Bilston had between them a higher population than Wolverhampton itself and a much higher figure for church attendance. The exclusion of four duplicate Wesleyan returns for Sedgley still gives it an index of over 70% whilst Bilston, at 58.69, is considerably higher than Wolverhampton which is thus reduced to 42.2. Not only are these figures higher than anywhere in rural Staffordshire but even higher church attendances are recorded elsewhere in the Black Country, the highest being Rowley Regis (Staffordshire) at 79.44. Its Worcestershire neighbour Halesowen reaches 68.46. Only Evesham (69.36) in rural Worcestershire exceeds this figure and most other parts of the county fall far below it. The local origins of the working population of the Black Country are confirmed by the 1851 census where over 85% of them give their place of birth within the counties of Staffordshire, Worcestershire, Warwickshire and Salop. Only in Wolverhampton and Walsall are there significant Irish minorities of just over 4% in each case.[10]

The pattern of higher than average church attendance in the Black Country is broken by Willenhall, the Wodgate of Disraeli's Sybil.

[7] *Ibid* p 40.

[8] Mann pp cclxxii, 69–78.

[9] PRO Home Office papers HO129 Subsequent calculations for Black Country townships are based on these figures.

[10] *Census of Great Britain 1851*, tables on ages, civil condition, occupations and birthplace of the people. *PP* 88 part 1 (London 1854) pp 523–4.

Here a mere 40% attended church or chapel compared with nearly 59% just over a mile down the road at Bilston. The contrast between Rowley Regis and Willenhall, the top and bottom of the church attendance table, was reinforced by the character of their respective clergy. Despite Disraeli's distortions both had ancient parish churches of medieval origin. At Rowley a crown appointment ensured the incumbency of a zealous evangelical. For the first forty years of the nineteenth century George Barrs, a protégé of Simeon, ministered faithfully on a stipend of forty pounds a year, preaching twice each Sunday, teaching the catechism in lent and devoting the sermon on the second Sunday of each month to a denunciation of the pope as anti-Christ.[11] By contrast the antics of the drunken William Moreton, incumbent of Willenhall from 1789, caused the living to be vested in trustees who were to pay off his debts of over six thousand pounds and give him a salary of a hundred pounds a year 'payable weekly but in case of his being arrested for any debt not disclosed to the Trustees a deduction is to be made thereout to pay the person officiating for him'.[12] This continued from 1814 to Moreton's death in 1834. Previous attempts dating back to 1801 had failed to recover the debts he had contracted despite holding a living worth at least three hundred pounds a year.[13] Yet this contrast was not adequately reflected in the church attendance statistics. In Rowley the church of England attracted 24.22% of the population compared to only 15.59 in Willenhall. But although Willenhall, with its greater population, had only three fifths of the church attendance of Rowley the established church obtained 38% of the worshippers. Other factors, apart from the character of their clergy must have been at work.

Barrs himself, for all his evangelical zeal, had a poor opinion of his parishioners:

> Such is the degraded and grovelling condition into which many of the nailers are sunk, that, during the late war, when wages were high, those who could just make a miserable living by earning two shillings per day, would not earn another two pence,

[11] F. W. G. Barrs, *Four Sermons by the late Reverend George Barrs* (2 ed Birmingham 1879) p xxiv.

[12] L[ichfield] J[oint] R[ecord] O[ffice] MS, [Wolverhampton consistory court papers] P Wol/A/8.

[13] N. W. Tildesley, 'William Moreton of Willenhall,' *Historical collections, Staffordshire*, 4 series 6 (Stafford 1970) pp 171–85.
Report of the royal commission on ecclesiastical revenues, *PP* 22 (London 1835) p 507.

when they might, by no great exertion, have earned twice two shillings per day . . . many from their very youth contract habits of idleness and prodigality and these are a certain and fruitful source of rags and wretchedness. Since that national pest the 'Beer Act' came into operation in 1830 their manners have become more dissolute; their morals more corrupt; their habits more idle and unthrifty and of course neither their personal appearance, nor their domestic comfort has much improved.[14]

This low opinion was reciprocated, at least by some, whom Barrs accused of wilfully blocking, through greed and sectarian animosity, his plan to rebuild the decayed parish church, 'Certain individuals, calling themselves churchmen, with a view to make a larger church unnecessary, actually solicited the Wesleyan methodists to build a meeting house in the parish.'[15] Divine retribution had fallen on these malcontents but despite such warnings the dissenting character of the parish increased so that by 1851 the non-Anglican proportion of the worshippers was nearly 70%, most of whom were methodists. This was not unusual. Elsewhere in the Black Country the methodist percentage was even higher than at Rowley Regis and its progress was not restrained by the ardent toryism of all but one of the resident clergy.

Whereas in Birmingham strong minded Wesleyan superintendents kept any radically inclined laymen in check the opposite seems to have occurred in the Black Country.[16] The demand for democratic rights in conference during the Warrenite controversy in 1835 enabled the Wesleyan association to carve itself a sizeable empire out of Wesleyanism between Dudley and Stourbridge. The political overtones of the conflict are revealed in Elijah Morgan's despairing letter of 1836 to Jabez Bunting. After recounting the chapels lost to the Stourbridge circuit he concludes 'I hope no objection will be made to my leaving this circuit, my health has suffered, my spirits greatly sunk and my character blasted far and near; we are called thieves, robbers, Conference Devils and that which is worse than all others in the ears of the people *tories.*'[17] Three years earlier a similar complaint was

[14] Smethwick central library MS, Rowley Regis parish records 9/6, G. Barrs manuscript notes on the history of Rowley Regis undated but probably 1834.

[15] *Ibid.*

[16] Compare Manchester John Rylands library MS, Methodist Church Archives, diary of James Rogers 26 March 1795, J. Waterhouse to T. Lessey 25 May 1834, J. Waterhouse to J. Bunting 31 March 1835.

[17] *Ibid* E. Morgan to J. Bunting 18 July 1836.

addressed to Thomas Jackson from Dudley by William France. He recounts the successful numerical and financial position of the circuit but declares 'that I have given them notice to quit at the conference. My reasons you shall have. In the first place I have all along been grieved of heart, among all pleasure I felt at our prosperity, at the miserable radical politics I am obliged to hear from day to day.' He concludes that two previous superintendents quit Dudley as soon as they could for the same reason.[18] Only in West Bromwich was it possible for a Wesleyan to say 'Our people here are generally Conservative, indeed to such an extent that they are suspected as a political party by Radicals. I regret this because if they confound us with any political party it will limit our influence and usefulness.'[19]

Mere political radicalism was not enough to ensure methodist success. Its preaching style and evangelistic methods gave methodism distinct advantages among Black Country folk which were not readily appreciated in better educated circles. As far back as 1797 Samuel Bradburn noted 'I preached last night at Cherry Street and after the blessing some *godly booby* gave out a hymn and began a noisy meeting. I stopped in the vestry a while and perceived that very few of the people remained. Take no notice of them and they will die of themselves. They are chiefly *young* and *low* people. Our best friends disapprove of them.'[20] But this was in Birmingham. Black Country Wesleyanism was not so inhospitable to noise. Joseph Entwistle junior spent a year in the Dudley circuit in 1829–30. On new year's eve he held a watch-night service at Tipton. 'After I had preached the celebrated R. Griffiths gave an exhortation. He scraped his throat so unmercifully that it was with great difficulty that I could understand two-thirds of what he said. He quite destroys the distinctiveness of his utterance by . . . an overstrained effort to speak immoderately loud. What I could understand was simple and appropriate but I could discover no indications of a mind at all above the ordinary standard. I hear that he reads little else but his Bible and Baxter's saints rest and always preaches on the joys of heaven and the torments of hell. Perhaps this may account for his popularity.'[21]

If Black Country Wesleyanism was thus addicted to noisy hell-fire preaching primitive methodism was unlikely to be more restrained.

[18] *Ibid* W. France to T. Jackson 6 April 1833.
[19] *Ibid* R. Leake to J. E. Coulson 29 September 1838.
[20] *Ibid* correspondence of S. Bradburn 30 August 1797.
[21] *Ibid* journal of J. Entwistle junior 31 December 1829.

The impact of the primitives came through their capacity to put intense pressure on one industrial settlement for a week at a time, bombarding its inhabitants with processions, camp meetings and a sustained series of emotional salvation meetings. The latter seem to have originated as a tactic in the Dudley area in November 1839. On this occasion twelve preachers were appointed to one chapel on a specific Sunday. Processions and open air preaching took place through the village before morning, afternoon and evening services which were themselves a series of ten minute addresses punctuated by prayers and singing and followed at night by two simultaneous prayer meetings in different parts of the chapel.[22] Such was its impetus that it enabled the primitives to dominate the place for the rest of the week. After describing such an occasion at Brierley Hill on Sunday 23 February 1840 the report continued

> About eight-o-clock the praying companies took their stations in the gallery and below—seventeen professed to find liberty in the gallery, and fifteen below. This was on the Sunday.
>
> Monday night we held a meeting to gather them in, and four more got converted; and it was moved seconded and carried to have another salvation meeting on the Tuesday night, in place of the regular preaching. When the time came we platformed it again and thirty seven more got converted.
>
> Wednesday night prayer meeting; thirty more professed to obtain pardon.
>
> Thursday night class meeting (Mr Southall's). It could not be led—Twenty more stepped into liberty.
>
> Friday night Mr Fisher's class could not be led—Above twenty more rejoiced in the Lord. Halleluia. This was such a week as was never known in this country before.[23]

Such excitement was a welcome break from the weary round of exploitation which was the normal lot of the working population. The midland miner's strike of 1842 created national alarm because chartist orators captured the ear of the miners in both north and south Staffordshire. But the resulting enquiry revealed appalling working conditions in the Black Country. The miners had no check on their long hours. They were not paid for clearing stone from the workings. When paid they were often cheated by the middlemen, called butties, who both employed them and ran the beer and tommy shops where

[22] Primitive Methodist Magazine (London 1840) pp 226–8.
[23] *Ibid* p 261.

their fortnightly earnings had to be spent.[24] One other group of workers was generally acknowledged to be even more grossly exploited than the miners. The domestic nailers got their iron rod on credit from warehousemen called foggers who subsequently bought, at a heavy discount, the finished products on which the whole family had laboured day and night.[25] In both industries the work pattern enabled men and women to take time off on their own initiative and a series of salvation meetings could well provide a suitable opportunity. Some of the converts would follow the recognised pattern of becoming leaders not only in the chapel but also among their fellow workers. The two did not always go happily together. In 1852 the Brierley Hill primitive methodist local preachers resolved 'that brother Southall, Halesowen, have no appointments next quarter and that he be recommended to withdraw from the position he holds with the nailers.'[26] Thomas Tancred, who conducted the midland mining commission, was most impressed by the evidence given against the butty system by a Wesleyan called Hughes who did not exaggerate the piety of his fellow miners. Asked if there were many pits about West Bromwich in which there were daily prayers he replied laconically 'I fear not, pits that have praying companies in them are as few as parish churches.'[27]

The impression given to outside observers was that the ironworkers, unlike the miners and nailers, were not so susceptible to high pressure evangelism.[28] Yet their grievances were equally serious. Bilston, where there were hardly any nailers, had almost as many ironworkers as miners.[29] It was also the headquarters of truck payments which dominated the local iron trade. As far back as 1822 the privates and NCOs of the Bilston troop of the Staffordshire yoemanry threatened open revolt if the lord lieutenant imposed a 'Tommy-man' on them as an officer.[30] The churches in Bilston were opposed to truck, with the church of England taking an impressive lead. William Leigh, the perpetual curate, took the initiative in getting a private member's

[24] [T.] Tancred, [*First report of the midland mining commission*] *PP* 13 (London 1843) *passim*.
[25] Horne Q p 77.
[26] S[tourbridge] M[ethodist] C[hurch] MS, B[rierley] H[ill Circuit] Q[uarterly] M[eeting] M[inutes] 27 September 1852.
[27] Tancred appendix p 21.
[28] Horne q p 53.
[29] *Population of England and Wales occupation abstract*, *PP* 27 (London 1844) pp 166–75.
[30] S[tafford] R[ecord] O[ffice] MS, [Hatherton papers] D260/M/F/5/27/52, E. J. Littleton to W. Leigh 23 November 1822.

bill outlawing truck passed through parliament. When it came to enforcement, however, he was the only magistrate who would hear cases against the ironmasters so that blatant contempt of the law became normal at Bilston.[31] In two other respects Leigh forms a contrast with Anglicans like Barrs and Moreton. He was the only liberal among the local clergy, acting as election agent for Lord Hatherton and complaining bitterly about his situation. In 1835 he sent him a list of the members of the new conservative association with the remark 'also observe that there are eleven clergymen putting themselves forward and yet if I only raise my voice when called upon, even on the dissolution of parliament, I am instantly attacked for interfering in politics. Can anything be more unfair and unreasonable than this? In fact a Tory parson may do anything with impunity and a clergyman of liberal opinions must, to satisfy the Conservatives, be hanged, drawn and quartered at their pleasure.'[32] After the cholera epidemic of 1832 he launched a national subscription to build a school for the orphans which did not endear him to his successor. The school was undenominational, belonging to the town not the church, but its size and quality prevented a national school being established under Anglican control.[33] Leigh's successor, Horatio Fletcher, who complained of this to Tancred, was less worthy of the working man's respect. He refused to take part in politics or become a magistrate.[34] This was just as well for in 1862 he was exposed for defrauding the Bilston savings bank, of which he had become secretary, treasurer and actuary, of £8,840.[35] The memory of Leigh rather than the ministry of Fletcher may have assisted the church of England to attract a slightly larger proportion of the churchgoers of Bilston in 1851 than of Rowley Regis.[36] On the other hand the incidence of cholera would appear to be a more immediate cause. Bilston had the highest mortality rate in the country in 1832 and was little better in 1849.

The virulence of cholera was one thing which clearly differentiated the Black Country from Birmingham on the one side and rural Staffordshire and Worcestershire on the other. While the epidemics were at their height they were accompanied by impressive outbreaks of piety, especially among the miners. 'Occasionally . . . as many as

[31] Horne Q p 68.
[32] SRO MS D260/M/F/5/27/10 Letter 88.
[33] Tancred appendix p 88.
[34] *Wolverhampton Chronicle* 1 June 1836.
[35] P. H. J. H. Gosden, *Self Help* (London 1973) pp 234–44.
[36] Bilston 31.06%, Rowley Regis 30.48%.

one or two hundred colliers would assemble, and in one instance as many as seven hundred; and after singing a hymn, would remain on their knees for nearly an hour at a time, following the prayers of one of their local preachers (usually one of their own body), and lamenting aloud their own sinful lives, specifying their own particular failings, such as spending so much of their money in drink, and giving so little of it to their wives and families, and resolving to amend. But within a fortnight of the disappearance of the cholera these meetings began visibly to decline; . . . about six weeks after . . . many of them had been abandoned'.[37]

It would be tempting to explain the difference in religious observance between the Black Country and its neighbours on this basis alone, especially as it was noted by contemporary observers. The Brierley Hill primitive methodist circuit, reporting a fall in membership in 1851, stated 'the principle cause of the decrease is owing to persons withdrawing from us since the colara.'[38] But when specific areas are compared there seems to be no clear relationship between the incidence of cholera and the percentage of churchgoers. No doubt fear of cholera did not necessarily match the actual incidence of the disease but it seems strange at first sight that although Bilston still has the highest mortality in the Black Country Willenhall comes second and Rowley Regis last, only fourteen deaths being recorded at Rowley and three hundred and sixty two at Willenhall.[39] The random effect of cholera on churchgoing can be revealed by comparing Sedgley with Wednesbury. Each had the same number of deaths from cholera in 1849 (203). In 1851 Sedgley had twice the population of Wednesbury and 70% of them went to church, or rather chapel. At Wednesbury, despite a mortality rate more than double that of Sedgley, only 57% attended church or chapel. Needless to say a cholera mortality of only fourteen fails to explain a church attendance of almost 80% at Rowley Regis. Fear of cholera did influence churchgoing. Methodist membership statistics reveal huge short term gains in many areas visited by the disease. Bilston Wesleyans gained over a hundred members in 1849 only to lose them again in 1850.[40] But the pattern is not repeated in Willenhall. There the high mortality from cholera produced, at most,

[37] *Report on the state of the population in the mining districts*, *PP* 23 (London 1850) p 24.

[38] SMC MS BHQMM 24 March 1851.

[39] F. W. Hackwood, *Sedgley Researches* (Dudley 1898) p 99. N. W. Tildesley *History of Willenhall* (Willenhall 1951) p 124.

[40] Wolverhampton reference library MS, Wolverhampton methodist archives 10, Darlington street circuit schedule book 1843–53.

thirty new Wesleyan members. This only raised the membership total ten above the level of the previous year, so that the impact of cholera, though noticeable, cannot be described as striking.[41]

Cholera was not the only thing which Willenhall shared with Bilston, their ecclesiastical constitution was identical. The deanery of Wolverhampton, an extra episcopal peculiar belonging to the deanery of Windsor, included the chapelries of Bilston and Willenhall. To avoid having to pay for resident clergy in these two places the dean had offered the townspeople the right to elect their own curate so long as they provided for him. All householders were entitled to vote, and contested elections with vigorous placard warfare took place. Endowments of land increased their value as mining rights came to be exploited so that Willenhall was 'supposed to be worth some £1,400 a year' and Bilston had £600 a year clear income before adding mineral revenues in 1842.[42] Had Disraeli's description of Wodgate kept to all the facts he would not have needed to lament the separation of church and people. 'The church deserted the people and from that moment the church has been in danger and the people degraded' claims Mr St Lys in Sybil.[43] Disraeli looked to enlightened aristocratic patronage to ensure a supply of faithful pastors for the poor. The rough and tumble of an election where the patronage was in the hands of a degraded people would have appeared worse to him than the fictional absence of the church from Wodgate altogether.

Outside influence of another kind was certainly present. The local ironmasters had an obvious interest in the results of clergy elections at Bilston. In 1813 five candidates came forward. William Leigh, the eventual winner, claimed to have been a curate in the town for five years but proctor Robinson asserted that he was a relative of the leading ironmaster, the Wesleyan Fereday. 'When you consider what his situation is amongst you whose Industry and Enterprise have diffused so many comforts around you, you must allow I am resting any claims to your support on a foundation not inferior to that of any other candidate.'[44] This sort of pressure aroused Slatter, another candidate, to reply with a vigorous appeal: 'I believe there is scarcely one poor man but would (conscientiously) give his Vote to Mr

[41] Willenhall methodist church MS, notes at the front of the register of collections, Willenhall Wesleyan chapel. Membership figures are: March 1848, 217; December 1848, 200; December 1849, 226; December 1850, 212.

[42] F. W. Hackwood, *Annals of Willenhall* (Wolverhampton 1908) p 103; Tancred p 87.

[43] Disraeli, *Sybil*, bk 2 cap 5.

[44] LJRO MS P Wol 11/A.

Slatter. . . . If then, poor people, your inclinations lead towards him, let not anyone by threats or otherwise turn them;—if your Landlords and Employers threaten you, consider that at this crisis you are called on in a contest of Rich and Poor and Violence and Oppression'.[45]

Fereday's influence was not enough for his son-in-law Robinson who came third on the first day of the poll. Slatter and Crockett shared fourth place with only three votes each and subsequently withdrew. Crockett's cause had not been helped by the intervention of Moreton of Willenhall. Two days before the poll Crocket read prayers and was expected to preach at Bilston but Moreton ascended the pulpit, 'very tipsy' according to an eyewitness:

> . . . he began to viciferate like someone addressing a population from an Hustings at an Election. . . . 'I hope you that have my interest will use it in behalf of my worthy friend Mr Cockett. I know his family and friends. I know nothing of him. He is a Christian and I am a Christian. Mark the expression. What care I for the magistrates, smacking his finger, I don't value the magistrates *that.*' He then said something about the Bishop and the Dean of Windsor. . . . The church then became in confusion, many leaving. He then spoke very loud saying 'I know I am not beloved by all. . . .'[46]

Crocket's attempt to calm the confusion came too late. Leigh was always ahead and when, after two days, he had polled 856 against 607 for Thomas Pearson the other candidate, Robinson also withdrew. His 125 votes were then added to Leigh and Pearson gave up the contest.[47]

In the 1836 election the candidates were quickly reduced to two; Fletcher, who had been Leigh's curate for six years, and Fisk from nearby Darlaston. Brawls between Fletcher and Fisk partisans took place and the Wolverhampton chronicle summed it up on 10 February 'This election did not end until Friday evening, when, after five days of polling, the number of votes was declared to be Fletcher 1,784, Fisk 1,339, a majority of 445. Therefore for a whole week the greater portion of the population neglected their avocations. The expenses are estimated at five thousand pounds. The validity of the election is likely to be disputed like that of Willenhall.'[48]

[45] *Ibid.*
[46] *Ibid.*
[47] *Ibid.*
[48] *Wolverhampton Chronicle* 10 February 1836.

That election, held the previous year, was also a victory for the resident curate, George Fisher, who had served out the last two and a half of Moreton's declining years. The churchwardens preferred an older man, John Howells from neighbouring Tipton and four other candidates presented lengthy testimonials to the public.[49] Among the lively placards which resulted the most significant was that of G. B. Thorneycroft, the dominant ironmaster of the locality. He arranged that his candidate, Robert Robinson, should conduct services at Willenhall a fortnight before the poll. Compared to the intervention of Fereday at Bilston, however, his approach to the Willenhall electors was positively obsequious. 'There is no man in your town who, after the Election has terminated, will be wicked enough to inflict an injury upon you for having done what, in your conscience, you believed to be your paramount duty. If, on mature consideration, you should decide in favour of my respected friend Mr Robinson, I shall feel grateful for your support, but if you should find any other of the candidates better qualified to do good to you and your fellow parishioners, I say, in God's name, support him by every lawful means in your power'.[50]

When Disraeli portrayed the Wodgate locksmiths as proud aristocrats of labour he was echoing the sentiments of the children's employment commission. Served by a collection of half starved and ill-treated apprentices the Willenhall man worked up to twenty hours a day standing at the vice. He competed against his fellow locksmiths and his need of ready cash enabled the factors, or warehousemen, to demand discounts of up to ninety per cent on the finished article which was often sold at the cost of the iron. He religiously observed saint Monday and often saint Tuesday too. He lived in a clean but bare, unfurnished, ill ventilated hovel overlooking his private dung heap which his family would defend against outside intruders.[51] This fiercely independent labour force, rather than any other feature, seems to distinguish Willenhall from the rest of the Black Country. Even though ecclesiastical democracy of a sort existed Willenhall folk were less loyal to the church of England than those at Bilston. Even though cholera mortality was almost as high as Bilston's church attendance was very low. The extreme poverty of the workforce and their long

[49] MS photocopies of original broadsheets in the possession of N. W. Tildesley, Willenhall.

[50] *Ibid.*

[51] Horne Q pp 39–49, 54–7.

hours of labour are comparable to those of the nailers of Sedgley and Rowley Regis but attempts at mass evangelism signally failed to produce similar effects. Again and again the local primitive methodists, whose headquarters lay only a mile away at Darlaston, attempted camp meetings and salvation meetings at Willenhall. They all failed.[52] Their cause only became secure in 1847 when a dissident Wesleyan group, calling themselves the teetotal church, was officially received into membership 'upon the rules of our conference and upon no other conditions.'[53] Perhaps the only dependence from which Willenhall men felt some need of salvation was dependence on drink.[54] In 1837 the warehouse owners threatened to refuse locks from any locksmith who did not vote tory. This was as ineffective as the tory provision of three or four dinners a week for Willenhall voters.[55] Radicalism prevailed in politics without needing either the support or the vehicle of religion. The noble virtues of independence and self respect which Disraeli sought in the countryside seem to have developed in the town, but at the expense of that religious devotion which could still be found where the worker was openly exploited and his dignity persistently denied.

Westhill College
Birmingham

[52] Walsall reference library MS, Darlaston primitive methodist circuit quarterly meeting minutes 1–5, 1 July 1824 and *passim*; G. Robson, 'Why Willenhall?', *Bulletin of the Wesley Historical Society*, West Midlands Branch (Birmingham) 3.1 (1976) p 3.

[53] J. Rowley, 'The Willenhall teetotal methodists', *ibid* p 9.

[54] Horne Q p 54 'There are not above a dozen butchers in the town and their business is by no means extensive, while there are between fifty and sixty retail brewers and public houses.'

[55] *Birmingham Journal* 30 September 1837.

THE CITY, THE COUNTRYSIDE AND THE SOCIAL GOSPEL IN LATE VICTORIAN NONCONFORMITY

by D. W. BEBBINGTON

THE late nineteenth-century city posed problems for English nonconformists. The country was rapidly being urbanised. By 1881 over one third of the people lived in cities with a population of more than one hundred thousand.[1] The most urbanised areas gave rise to the greatest worry of all the churches: large numbers there were failing to attend services. The religious census of 1851 had already shown that the largest towns were the places where there were the fewest worshippers, although nonconformists gained some crumbs of comfort from the knowledge that nonconformist attendances were greater than those of the church of England.[2] Unofficial surveys in the 1880s revealed no improvement.[3] Instead, although few were immediately conscious of it, in that decade the membership of all the main evangelical nonconformist denominations began to fall relative to population.[4] And it was always the same social group that was most conspicuously unreached: the lower working classes, the bottom of the social pyramid. In poor neighbourhoods church attendance was lowest. In Bethnal Green at the turn of the twentieth century, for instance, only 6.8% of the adult population attended chapel, and only 13.3% went to any place of worship.[5] Consequently nonconformists, like Anglicans, were troubled by the weakness of their appeal.

In 1883 the secretary of the London congregational union, Andrew Mearns, published an analysis of the problem in the capital. He urged more intensive evangelism as many had done before him. But his booklet, *The Bitter Cry of Outcast London*, also broke new ground by relating the issue of non-attendance to the urban environment.

[1] G. F. A. Best, *Mid-Victorian Britain, 1851–1875* (London 1971) p 7.

[2] K. S. Inglis, 'Patterns of Religious Worship in 1851', *JEH* 11 (1960) pp 80–4.

[3] For example in Sheffield. E. R. Wickham, *Church and People in an Industrial City* (London 1957) p 148.

[4] A. D. Gilbert, *Religion and Society in Industrial England: church, chapel and social change, 1740–1914* (London 1976) p 39.

[5] Hugh McLeod, *Class and Religion in the Late Victorian City* (London 1974) pp 300, 303.

Thousands in central London, he showed, lived in the 'fever dens'[6] of the slums. Public health, a major preoccupation of earlier decades, was not however his central concern. The great obstacle to religious influences, he contended, was the appalling state of overcrowding. The honest and the depraved were thrown together. 'That people condemned to exist under such conditions take to drink and fall into sin is surely a matter for little surprise.'[7] Mearns was drawing attention to an evil that had been exacerbated over the previous three decades. Between 1851 and 1881 the population of London had increased by almost a million and a half; in the same period only about one hundred and eighty thousand houses had been built, and most of those were for the comfortably off rather than for labourers.[8] The consequence was a growth of overcrowding, especially in the areas nearer the central workplaces. W. T. Stead, a devout if unorthodox son of a congregationalist manse, sensationalised Mearns's evidence in his newspaper *The Pall Mall Gazette* so fervently that the force of public opinion led to the setting up of a royal commission on the housing of the working classes chaired by the prince of Wales.[9] *The Bitter Cry* therefore opened a new chapter in public policy over housing.

The booklet stirred the churches particularly deeply. In response to the congregationalist appeal the nonconformist public began to take a wider interest in the condition of the cities and especially London. The problem, at least for the more advanced thinkers, was not now solely how to bring the working classes under the sound of the gospel; it was also how to deal with the conditions that inhibited their response to the gospel. Mearns had pinned on two issues bound up with overcrowding that were to excite continuing concern among late Victorian nonconformists. One was the threat to the home. Without privacy, slum-dwellers could not create a family atmosphere and incest could hardly be avoided.[10] The other was sheer poverty. The increasing competition for somewhere to live among the badly paid pushed up rents so that, as Mearns put it, 'Dives makes a richer harvest out of their misery'.[11] In the decade after Mearns wrote two other dimensions

[6] [Andrew] Mearns, [*The*] *Bitter Cry* [*of Outcast London*, ed A. S. Wohl] (Leicester 1970) p 69.
[7] *Ibid* p 60.
[8] [A. S.] Wohl, [*The*] *Eternal Slum*[*: housing and social policy in Victorian London*] (London 1977) p 22.
[9] Mearns, *Bitter Cry* pp 81–8, 33.
[10] *Ibid* p 61.
[11] *Ibid* p 69.

of the urban problem crystallised in the minds of commentators in the churches, as elsewhere: social tension and industrial relations. Already in 1883 the London baptist association resolved that the state of affairs described in *The Bitter Cry* 'is a source of danger to the well-being of the community and a grave peril to the state'.[12] The riots by dock and building workers of February 1886 that included the overturning of carriages in Hyde Park and the clearing of a meeting from Trafalgar Square on 'bloody Sunday' in November 1887 increased such fears.[13] Guinness Rogers, a leading congregationalist divine with strong tendencies to social conservatism, wrote in 1890 that ministers must 'discourage anything like a war of classes . . .'.[14] It was increasingly recognised that social tension normally arose from industrial relations. The London dock strike of 1889 in particular led nonconformists to perceive that there was a need for greater harmony in industry. The example of cardinal Manning, who was chiefly responsible for the eventual settlement of the strike, made nonconformists ponder the potential role of the churches in reconciliation.[15] Nonconformist leaders seldom if ever isolated the casual labour system as a root cause of London's problem in the 1880s,[16] but many of them did begin to see the urban crisis in its complexity as their own legitimate concern.

What then were the chapels to do about it? There were those who believed that the answer lay in redoubling the temperance campaign. If the working classes spent less on drink, it was commonly held, they would have more with which to pay rents for better homes and obtain other benefits.[17] The more adventurous urged, especially in the wake of the dock strike, that nonconformist ministers should show their sympathy for the workers in labour disputes by offering their services as arbitrators. Andrew Mearns, for instance, took the initiative in settling two threatened disputes by the coal porters and the stokers before 1889 was out.[18] More remarkable because entailing a break with normal nonconformist leanings towards *laissez-faire* were calls for the state to do something about the problem. They began in *The Bitter*

[12] *The Daily News* 29 November 1883 quoted by Wohl, *Eternal Slum* p 218.

[13] [G. S.] Jones, *Outcast London*[*: a study in the relationship between classes in Victorian society*] (Oxford 1971) pp 290–6.

[14] J. G. Rogers, *The Congregational Review* (London) January 1890 p 97.

[15] [*The*] *C*[*hristian*] *W*[*orld*] (London) 19 September 1889 p 721.

[16] As has been done by Jones, *Outcast London*.

[17] For example [H. P.] Hughes, [*The*] *Philanthropy of God*[*: described and illustrated in a series of sermons*] (London 1890) p 279.

[18] *CW* 12 December 1889 p 984.

Cry itself[19] and gathered momentum in the 1890s. Using the vote to encourage public promotion of social reforms seemed the key to progress. Whether temperance, industrial arbitration or increased state action were taken up, religion confronted with the problems of urban living was being broadened. A baptist lay social investigator put it like this: 'That gospel which does not concern itself with man's body, mind, and environment, as well as his soul, is a contradiction in terms. . . . If we cannot make our politics part of our religion, we have no right to cast even a vote. . . . If cleaner streets, better housing, sweeter homes do not come within the scope of our aim, neither will those who are convinced that they have a right to these things come within the shadow of our places of worship'.[20] A Christian appeal to city-dwellers must embrace their aspirations. So the social gospel was born.

If the social gospel was a response to the problem of the city, part of its content was given by the countryside. The root of the urban malaise as perceived in *The Bitter Cry*, overcrowding, found its obvious remedy in settling people in the wide open spaces. Rural cottages would guarantee the integrity of family life. Poverty would be alleviated if there were plots of ground where men could grow their own food. Even social tension and industrial disputes would abate under the healthful influence of fresh air and green trees. Such ideas were remarkably widespread among the nonconformist leaders who were proponents of the social gospel. 'Back to the Land!' was a common cry—and was even the title of a book published in 1893 by an active free churchman.[21] An alternative solution was to remodel cities on rural lines. The countryside offered a panacea—but why was this so?

First there was the influence of what may be called romantic ruralism, the idealisation of country living found in William Morris and John Ruskin. The hard-headed social gospeller John Clifford, minister of Westbourne Park baptist church, Paddington, could be carried away in a sermon by an idyllic rural vision: 'The landscape of the farm is full of Divine feeling, and rich in suggestions that inspire calm and quicken industry. It throbs with the tender heart of God. It is alive. In its simple and steady processes it reveals the Father's care for His child, and invites him to steady and healthful toil in obedience

[19] Mearns, *Bitter Cry* p 69.

[20] *The Religious Life of London*, ed Richard Mudie-Smith (London 1904) p 13.

[21] Harold Moore, *Back to the Land* (London 1893). See W. J. Rowland, 'Some Free Church Pioneers of Social Reform', [*The*] *C*[*ongregational*] *Q*[*uarterly*] (London) 35 (1957) p 143.

to its laws. . . .'[22] The vogue of romantic poetry was at its height, encouraged in congregationalism especially by chapel Browning clubs, so that Wordsworthian panentheism could readily steal into nonconformist thought. God could perhaps be found more readily in the countryside. Men on the fringe of nonconformity were drawn into the heart of circles where such thinking was dominant. Bruce Wallace, for example, who had transferred from presbyterianism to congregationalism because of dissatisfaction with the Westminster confession, left the regular ministry in 1885 to publicise a variety of schemes for returning men to the soil. He was the first to print in England the American Edward Bellamy's utopian novel *Looking Backward* in 1889, but was more affected by William Morris's advocacy of small semi-agricultural settlements in his critique of Bellamy called *News from Nowhere* (1891). Wallace became the chief English advocate of Tolstoyan communities.[23] Yet it was not only the fringe that was affected. John Clifford, after the death of C. H. Spurgeon in 1892, was undoubtedly the most eminent of baptist ministers. Romantic ruralism encouraged nonconformists generally, but more particularly the city-dwellers among them, to think of the countryside as a beneficent influence in itself.

Secondly the vogue of rural redress for urban ills was strengthened by the social Darwinism of the day. This, the dominant current of social theory, flowed less from Darwin than from Herbert Spencer, with his teaching that human society was organically developing towards perfection.[24] One side of social Darwinism that became deeply imbued in the nation was belief in the survival of the fittest, and particularly belief in the survival of the fittest nation. Benjamin Kidd's *Social Evolution* (1894), one of the chief expositions of this view, was applauded by Hugh Price Hughes, the social gospel leader among the Wesleyans.[25] But more widespread among nonconformists was another side of social Darwinism, the belief that, just as nature adapts to suit its environment, so human beings are moulded by their surroundings. It followed that the manipulation of the environment

[22] John Clifford, *The Gospel of Gladness and its meaning for us* (Edinburgh 1912) p 74.

[23] W. R. Hughes, 'Bruce Wallace and "Brotherhood"', *CQ* 15 (1937) p 469. [P. d'A. Jones] [*The*] *Christian Socialist Revival* [*1877–1914: religion, class, and social conscience in Late-Victorian England*] (Princeton 1968) pp 335 *et seq.*

[24] J. W. Burrow, *Evolution and Society: a study in Victorian social theory* (Cambridge 1966) p 114.

[25] J. H. S. Kent, 'Hugh Price Hughes and the Nonconformist Conscience', *Essays in Modern English Church History in Memory of Norman Sykes*, ed G. V. Bennett and J. D. Walsh (London 1966) p 197.

permitted men to improve their fellows. John Scott Lidgett, who on the death in 1901 of Hugh Price Hughes took up his mantle as the Wesleyan leader of advanced thought, wrote that God's purpose embraces 'the handling of our earthly environment so that it may be made increasingly the instrument of bringing about . . . individual and social perfecting'.[26] Such environmentalism jarred sharply with the conviction of evangelical nonconformists that the gospel alone can create a true change of heart. Clifford, for instance, warned against attributing too much power to transform human life to the environment, for according to Jesus 'the inward is chief'.[27] Yet Clifford with many others began to see an urban setting, and especially overcrowding, as a bad spiritual influence over man.[28] It was an obstacle to the gospel. Further, nonconformists were beginning to claim an interest in man's physical welfare, and there was apparent evidence that urban conditions damaged health. Healthy policemen, Hughes noted, came from small country towns.[29] Hence cities should be given an infusion of rural influences—by opening them to fresh air, by setting up parks and, as Hughes put it with typical hyperbole, 'by planting trees in all directions'.[30] In accordance with the precepts of social Darwinism, the environment must be changed.

A third source of rural remedies was the United States. Several prominent nonconformists were fascinated by the proposals of Henry George, the American author of *Progress and Poverty* (1880), for solving the problems of modern civilisation. George argued that the rents charged by greedy landowners determined the rate of wages and profits in the rest of the economy. There was therefore a conflict of interest between landowners on the one hand and capitalists, urban workers and rural labourers on the other—who in addition were being cheated of their natural right to land ownership. George's remedy was a 100% tax on what the landlords received in rent. That would be sufficient for all government needs, and so there would be only a single tax.[31] The wealth of the countryside could be used to eliminate urban problems. George's second lecturing tour of England in 1884 provoked Guinness Rogers into denouncing him as a 'reckless agitator, who has come for the purpose of disturbing the peace of a nation to which he

[26] J. S. Lidgett, *Reminiscences* (London [1928]) p 93.
[27] John Clifford, *God's Greater Britain: letters and addresses* (London 1899) p 164.
[28] John Clifford, 'The Housing of the Poor', *Free Church Yearbook* (London) 1902 p 35.
[29] Hughes, *Philanthropy of God* p 277.
[30] *Ibid* p 279.
[31] Henry George, *Progress and Poverty* (London 1880).

does not belong . . .'.[32] Bruce Wallace, however, was a fervent advocate of George's ideas in the early 1880s, and it was this issue that led him on into other rural schemes.[33] A more important convert came at the end of the decade, when Albert Spicer, a member of the paper manufacturing family, shortly afterwards an MP and one of congregationalism's leading laymen, began to advocate George's panacea. As treasurer of the London congregational union, Spicer knew the conditions that gave rise to *The Bitter Cry* and was attracted to the single tax precisely because he saw it as a solution to the problem of urban poverty.[34] Other congregationalist MPs like W. P. Byles and Richard Winfrey, both proprietors of provincial newspapers, also took up the cause.[35] Clifford, who was a member of the Fabians, did not stop short of land nationalisation,[36] but most nonconformists who took up the land question preferred a position like George's that was more consonant with traditional nonconformist individualism and anti-landlordism. The wealth of the rural rich seemed enough to deal with the troubles of the urban poor.

Fourthly there was the example of German labour colonies set up under church auspices in the countryside. Pastor von Bodelschwingh was responsible for beginning the first in 1883 for the sake of any who needed work. Ten years later there were twenty-two.[37] The growth was largely due to subsidies from the state, which was eager to be seen to help the unemployed in the face of socialist criticisms.[38] Although there were British government blue books on such continental schemes, the chief medium for the transmission of the idea to England was J. B. Paton, principal of the Nottingham congregational training institute. Annual visits to Germany opened his eyes to a variety of projects that the churches could undertake on behalf of the deprived.[39] He was described as walking the London streets, his pockets bulging with schemes for bringing about the new Jerusalem.[40] In the 1890s his

[32] *The Congregationalist* (London) April 1884 p 34.

[33] Jones, *Christian Socialist Revival* p 336.

[34] *The British Weekly* (London) 4 November 1897 p 48.

[35] A. J. Peacock, 'Land Reform, 1880–1919: a study of the activities of the English Land Restoration League and the Land Nationalisation Society', Southampton MA thesis 1971 pp 104n, 147.

[36] *CW* 20 January 1898 p 9.

[37] Julie Sutter, *A Colony of Mercy: or social Christianity at work* (London 1893) p 147.

[38] [José] Harris, *Unemployment* [*and Politics: a study in English social policy*] (Oxford 1972) p 118.

[39] [James] Marchant, *J. B. Paton*[*, MA, DD: ecclesiastical and social pioneer*] (London 1909) pp 114–16.

[40] J. S. Lidgett, *My Guided Life* (London 1936) p 102.

foremost dream was the imitation of the German rural colonies in order to transform the urban unemployed 'under healthful conditions' into an efficient workforce.[41] A Christian council of social service, of which Paton was the leading spirit, eventually launched a farm colony at Lingfield in Surrey in 1898 and took over another at Starnthwaite in Westmorland two years later.[42] It seems to have been difficult to persuade working men to travel to these centres and live under what Paton called 'wise and kindly discipline',[43] so that the colonies rapidly became training establishments for the mentally or physically disabled, specialising in care for epileptic children.[44] Without state assistance the prospect of providing extensive work for the victims of the city labour market was a distant one.

A fifth stimulus to considering how the countryside could alleviate urban problems was, perhaps strangely, the declining state of nonconformity in the countryside. As early as 1876 Clifford drew attention to the difficulties of village chapels: 'Letter after letter has come to hand assuring me that the struggle for existence is becoming more keen, because men and women are becoming more scarce'.[45] He attributed the problem to the replacement of men by machines that led to migration to the towns and emigration abroad. Those most likely to leave were those who 'in fidelity to conscience join the conventicle in the village back street'.[46] Underlying the departure of the people was the depression of arable farming that marked the last three decades of the nineteenth century.[47] Agriculture, especially in the nonconformist heartland of East Anglia, was afflicted by low wages. Meanwhile farmers were deserting nonconformity, often because of the radicalism among their labourers that it seemed to fuel. It was said in 1891 that whereas not many years before two-thirds of the land of the parish of Coggeshall in Essex was represented by its owner or tenant in the congregationalist chapel, in that year only one farmer was a member.[48] The decay of support among farmers often meant the decay of the cause. The countryside, and especially the village

[41] [J. B.] Paton, 'Labour [for the Unemployed upon the Land', *Co-operative Labour upon the Land*, ed J. A. Hobson] (London 1895) p 81.

[42] Marchant, *J. B. Paton* pp 164–5.

[43] Paton, 'Labour' p 81.

[44] Marchant, *J. B. Paton* pp 164–5.

[45] John Clifford, *Religious Life in the Rural Districts of England* (London 1876) p 6.

[46] *Ibid.*

[47] T. W. Fletcher, 'The Great Depression of English Agriculture, 1873–96', *EcHR* 13 (1960–1).

[48] *CW* 26 November 1891 p 966.

chapel, was underpopulated. What better than to transfer the surplus labour of the cities back into the countryside? This would solve at a stroke the problems of both. The leading advocate of this solution was again Paton, although he had been anticipated by others including the unitarian Henry Solly.[49] More than once Paton urged on the congregational union the desirability of increasing the number of small farmers, with a view, as he declared, to reviving rural churches.[50] His aim was to 'restore in all our country districts the yeoman peasantry who made England great in the centuries that are past'.[51] A small group inspired by Paton did establish a colony of 'yeomen' at Purleigh in Essex in 1897, but it lasted only two years.[52] This scheme seemed even more visionary than that for labour colonies, and nothing further seems to have come of his project.

These five factors, but more especially the widespread currents of romantic ruralism and social Darwinism, kept the potential of the countryside to the fore in the nonconformist social gospel. Furthermore, some resulting rural palliatives had far more impact than Paton's proposals. There was, first of all, Booth's scheme of social salvation arising from his book *In Darkest England and the Way Out* (1890). The project originated not simply in the mind of the general of the salvation army. Most of the book was in fact ghost-written for Booth by W. T. Stead, the publicist of *The Bitter Cry* who had remained near the centre of the social gospel movement in nonconformity.[53] The idea was that the salvation army should administer three sets of colonies—in the city, in the countryside and overseas. The poorest 'submerged tenth' of the population would be drawn into the army's urban relief agencies. They would then be transferred for rehabilitation to the farm colony before eventual settlement in the colony overseas. The healthful influences of the countryside were therefore central to the plan. Booth—or Stead—contrasts the homeless of the towns, 'sleeping in the streets or in the fever-haunted lodging-houses, or living huddled up in a single room, and toiling twelve and fourteen hours in a sweater's den' with the rescued, 'living in comparative comfort in well-warmed and ventilated houses, situated in the open country, with abundance of good, healthy food.'[54] A farm colony

[49] Henry Solly, *Industrial Villages* (London 1884) p 3.
[50] *CW* 14 October 1897 p 6. Marchant, *J. B. Paton* pp 169–74.
[51] Marchant, *J. B. Paton* p 172.
[52] Jones, *Christian Socialist Revival* p 316.
[53] Frederic White, *The Life of W. T. Stead* (London 1925) 2, p 12.
[54] General Booth, *In Darkest England and the Way Out* (London 1890) p 264.

was duly created at Hadleigh in Essex, designed by Harold Moore, the author of *Back to the Land.*[55] It combined stock and poultry farming and market gardening (which were unprofitable) with brick-making from the clay on the site (which turned out to be profitable).[56] Between two and three hundred men were involved at a time.[57] The 'Darkest England' scheme, despite chaotic finances,[58] was a project that caught the public imagination, and so drew attention to the beginnings of the salvation army's tradition of social relief work with *éclat.*

Another major initiative that emerged from the nonconformist social gospel was the wave of manufacturers' planned suburbs of the turn of the twentieth century. Best known are W. H. Lever's Port Sunlight at Bebington in Cheshire and George Cadbury's Bournville in Birmingham, but there were also others like Joseph Hartley's Aintree housing for his jam workers and Joseph Rowntree's New Earswick scheme near York that was inspired by Bournville. Hartley was at the centre of primitive methodism, becoming vice-president of conference in 1892 and president in 1909.[59] Lever (later Lord Lever-hulme), though never a church member in congregationalism, subscribed liberally to congregationalist funds, built four congregationalist chapels and persuaded the congregationalist churches of his native Bolton to federate.[60] Cadbury was a quaker who saw himself as a free churchman,[61] and Rowntree probably followed his elder brother in doing the same.[62] All had moved their factories into the countryside at an earlier date—Cadbury in 1879, Hartley in 1886, Lever in 1889 and Rowntree in 1890.[63] Their object was to liberate their workers from the blight of city life. The housing schemes were a further step in the same direction. Natural surroundings were scrupulously respected. In the planning of Bournville there was special emphasis on the preservation of existing trees, on a low housing density and on

[55] Harris, *Unemployment* p 131.

[56] W. H. Hunt, 'An Interesting Industrial Experiment', *The Westminster Review* (London) 154 (1900) p 293.

[57] *Ibid* p 292.

[58] Harris, *Unemployment* p 131.

[59] [A. S.] Peake, [*The Life of Sir William*] *Hartley* (London 1926) pp 93, 97.

[60] [Viscount Leverhulme, *Viscount*] *Leverhulme* (London 1927) pp 224, 253 *et seq.*

[61] [A. G.] Gardiner, [*Life of George*] *Cadbury* (London 1923) p 120.

[62] Phebe Doncaster, *John Stephenson Rowntree: his life and work* (London 1908) p 240.

[63] Gardiner, *Cadbury* p 35. Peake, *Hartley* p 24. C. H. Wilson, *The History of Unilever: a study in economic growth and social change* 1 (London 1970) p 37. Asa Briggs, *Social Thought and Social Action: a study of the work of Seebohm Rowntree, 1871–1954* (London 1961) p 10.

houses occupying no more than one quarter of their sites.[64] Lever made an even more significant advance at Port Sunlight by breaking away from the 'block and corridor' patterns of nineteenth-century working-class housing in order to let the roads follow the contours.[65] In such surroundings, Lever declared at the cutting of the first sod in 1888, his workers would be able 'to know more about the science of life than they can in a back slum'.[66] Cadbury believed explicitly that 'coming into touch with nature brings men into closer touch with nature's God'.[67] The planned suburbs are a monument to the social gospel of the day.

The final and the most important development to be generated in the atmosphere of the nonconformist social gospel was the garden city movement. Its progenitor was Ebenezer Howard, and his plans were sketched in *To-morrow: a peaceful path to real reform* published in 1898. Like other nonconformists, Howard was influenced by Henry George and Edward Bellamy, and liberal nonconformity was the setting for the evolution of his scheme. He was reared in congregationalism. He became for three months secretary to Joseph Parker, minister of the city temple, who felt the bumps on Howard's head and announced that he should be a preacher.[68] In the late 1870s Howard was in America, where, remarkably, he was a founder of the Ebenezer congregational church in Howard county, Nebraska.[69] He moved to Chicago, where discussions with a sceptical quaker led him to new views about the relation of 'material conditions' to 'the spiritual elements of our nature'.[70] He returned to England far from orthodox. Howard nevertheless attended Rectory Road congregational church, London, whose minister, C. Fleming Williams, was a leading social gospeller and an alderman on the LCC with a special concern for slum housing.[71] Howard's book germinated in the soil of Fleming Williams' circle, whose visionary tone it well reflects: 'Yes, the key to the problem of how to restore the people to the land—that beautiful land of ours, with its canopy of sky, the air that blows upon it, the sun that warms

[64] W. L. Creese, *The Search for Environment: the garden city and after* (New Haven 1966) pp 108–10.
[65] *Ibid* p 188.
[66] *Leverhulme* p 49.
[67] Gardiner, *Cadbury* p 171.
[68] [Dugald] Macfadyen, [*Sir Ebenezer*] *Howard* [*and the Town Planning Movement*] (Manchester 1933) p 3.
[69] *Ibid* p 9.
[70] *Ibid* p 10.
[71] *Ibid* p 13. *The Congregational Year Book* (London) 1938 p 674.

it, the rain and dew that moisten it—the very embodiment of the Divine love for man—is indeed a *Master-key*, for it is the key to a portal through which, even when scarce ajar, will be seen to pour a flood of light on the problems of intemperance, of excessive toil, of restless anxiety, of grinding poverty—the true limits of Governmental interference, ay, and even the relations of man to the Supreme Power'.[72] The kernel of the message was that there must be a fusion of the social advantages of the city with the natural advantages of the countryside to create 'garden cities'. Their magnetism would draw people from the overcrowded cities back into rural surroundings. In December 1898 Howard was still humbly propagating his ideas in a magic lantern lecture at Rectory Road church,[73] but before long a garden city association was formed and began to gather momentum. With Bruce Wallace as his secretary, Howard arranged for the first two annual conferences of the association to be held at Bournville and Port Sunlight.[74] Soon a site was found and the first garden city was declared open at Letchworth in 1903. The garden city tradition, with its enduring influence over government new towns policy and town and country planning worldwide, was the greatest single fruit of nonconformist ruralism.

With the inspiration of the 'Darkest England' scheme, Bournville and Port Sunlight and the garden cities to its credit, the social gospel managed to make an impression on the problems of the city by drawing remedies from the countryside. This body of thinking was not solely nonconformist, for canon Samuel Barnett shared many of the same attitudes and was partly responsible for their incorporation in Hampstead Garden Suburb.[75] Nor was it solely Christian in origin, for secular trends of thought had much to do with its emergence. Yet it was part of an ambitious programme that showed the nonconformist conscience at its best—in trying to achieve, as Hugh Price Hughes once put it, 'the gradual reconstruction of a Christian society'.[76]

University of Stirling

[72] Ebenezer Howard, *To-morrow: a peaceful path to real reform* (London 1898) p 5.
[73] Macfadyen, *Howard* p 22.
[74] *Ibid* p 38. Jones, *Christian Socialist Revival* p 338.
[75] See Mrs Barnett, *Canon Barnett: his life, work and friends* (London 1918).
[76] H. P. Hughes, *Essential Christianity: a series of explanatory sermons* (London 1894) p 169.

CHURCH EXTENSION IN TOWN AND COUNTRYSIDE IN LATER NINETEENTH-CENTURY LEICESTERSHIRE

by DAVID M. THOMPSON

STUDIES of nineteenth-century urban religion have often been conducted with very little reference to the surrounding countryside. Even Obelkevich in his stimulating study of rural religion in Lincolnshire suggested that there, 'In the Church of England, though the ideal and model of the village parish church continued to inspire town churchmen, towns and villages largely remained in separate compartments. Only through Methodism did the towns have much effect on village religious life. . . . The circuit, the key unit of Methodist organization, brought preachers and people from towns and villages into regular contact with each other and made it possible for the financial and human resources of the town chapels to contribute to the life of the outlying village chapels'.[1] But the methodist exception is significant, not so much in a denominational sense (although the methodist form of organisation was in theory the best for this purpose) but because it is an example of a situation in which the money and men available in any one particular place were not sufficient to carry out what the church concerned wished to do there. It was therefore necessary to tap the resources of other places to help. In large towns such as Manchester, Leeds and Birmingham, and in some of the smaller industrial towns as well, the necessary resources often had to be found within the town or not at all; and to that extent the study of urban religion on its own is understandable. But in many parts of the country rural evangelism was felt to be as urgent a priority as urban evangelism. The church of England sought to overcome the consequences of rural neglect; and all nonconformists, not only methodists, attempted to involve town members in the life of country chapels. Thus in less exclusively industrial parts of the country than Lancashire, the West Riding of Yorkshire and the Black Country, a genuine conflict of priorities between town and countryside could arise. When money had to be raised to support new churches and their

[1] James Obelkevich, *Religion and Rural Society* (Oxford 1976) pp 5–6.

ministers, or to maintain or improve the position of existing churches and their ministers, and when, as was almost invariably the case, the money available was less than what was felt to be required, a new range of questions arose with implications for the rural-urban relationship in the churches.[2] Moreover, as the organisations which had to take decisions in such cases usually included representatives of both urban and rural interests, they were bound to take up a position on the relationship of rural and urban priorities.

The significance of the countryside has been recognised by historians in so far as it was the former home of the many migrants to the towns, whose spiritual welfare constituted the major challenge of the age. This was also the contemporary view. But the reciprocal nature of even this relationship has not always been realised. Bishop Magee of Peterborough made this point in Leicester in 1869: 'This new population that comes in by so many hundreds and thousands a year, represents not only the successful labours of religion in the country, but all the evils and all the defects of country work. If there has been a neglected parish . . . and if there comes from that place an immigration into the town of Leicester . . . we must feel that the town of Leicester is deeply interested in the spiritual work of the county. And then *as the inhabitants of the town return into the country villages*, we ought both clergy and laity to feel interested in the spiritual condition of this town of Leicester. The whole blood of the diocese is ever circulating through this great town, and according to the condition of this heart of the county, will be the spiritual condition, more or less, of our country parishes'.[3] It was expected, for example, that many of those who went into service would eventually return to the country. The later nineteenth century was the period when this circulatory migration pattern gave way to straightforward rural depopulation, but much work still remains to be done on the chronology of this, and indeed on the question of whether the circulatory pattern ever completely died out. So long as it remained, the kind of argument advanced by bishop Magee had some force, and it is wrong to make a clear separation between the study of urban and rural religion. Leicestershire has been chosen for this study because it is a particularly clear example of the way these attitudes affected the policy of church extension. The town

[2] Stephen Yeo has rightly observed that the concern with 'numbers unlimited' and buildings was not the only choice open to the churches, but that does not affect the argument here: [*Religion and Voluntary Organisations in Crisis*] (London 1976) pp 69–74, 154–5.

[3] *Leicester Journal*, 21 May 1869 (italics mine).

of Leicester, which developed rapidly as an industrial centre after 1860, was strongly nonconformist: yet the attention of nonconformist bodies was fixed firmly on the countryside, even though there were voices pressing for a more concerted urban policy from the 1870s. The countryside provided the centre of strength for the church of England, and so the urban church extension needed could only be provided at its expense. On each side financial difficulties sharply exposed the conflict of priorities.

The church of England built nearly twenty new churches in Leicestershire (outside Leicester) in the nineteenth century, and most of these were built before 1851.[4] The subdivision of parishes commissioners in 1851 named three places in the county in their list of six hundred new churches needed: by contrast they named four in Leicester itself.[5] Only two of the county churches were ever built—at Whitwick and Loughborough. In 1851, following the initiative of the reverend J. P. Marriott of Cotesbach (who was, it may be noted, a rural incumbent) a county church extension fund was launched. Two new churches were built in Leicester, supported by this fund, in the next ten years: St John's, completed in 1854, and St Andrew's, completed in 1862. The church at Earl Shilton in the county also received help from the fund, which raised nearly £9,000 in five years.[6]

In 1864 the new bishop of Peterborough, Dr Francis Jeune, appointed a committee to enquire into the spiritual wants of the archdeaconry, an action which was supported by the Leicester clerical association when it discussed church extension on 4 April.[7] On 1 February 1865 a public meeting was held in the County Rooms, Leicester, at which an association for church extension in the archdeaconry was formed, with the bishop of Peterborough as president, and most of the county nobility and gentry as vice-presidents. Subscriptions were invited with the option of spreading them over eight years. This was described by a later writer, the reverend W. G. Whittingham, as 'the first call to a *united* effort for Church Extension in the Archdeaconry'.[8] Three sites

[4] Four of these were in the towns of Loughborough, Hinckley and Ashby de la Zouch.

[5] *Return of 600 New Churches needed:* Parliamentary Papers, H.C. (1852–3) 78, p 46.

[6] [W. G.] Whittingham, [*Church Extension in the Archdeaconry of Leicester*] (privately printed nd) p 4.

[7] Leicester Clerical Association Minutes, 4 April 1864: L[eicester] M[useum], 27D 64/A/1.

[8] L[eicester] A[rchdeaconry] C[hurch] E[xtension] A[ssociation] Min[ute]s 1, pp 3–8; LM Misc 184/4; Whittingham, p 4.

in Leicester were quickly selected as priorities. The association also adopted the existing project of St Matthew's, which had been begun by the old fund, but ran into problems when the contractor went bankrupt. With considerable reluctance an extra grant was made and the church was consecrated on 1 May 1867. It was the first 'free and open' church in Leicester, and was nicknamed 'the poor man's cathedral'.[9]

To begin the first church of their own the committee decided to borrow money against the security of subscriptions promised but not yet paid, and they approved a grant of £6,000, even though they only had £1,600 in the bank. The treasurer declined to sign cheques for the proposed loan, and so three members of the committee were authorised to sign cheques up to £4,000, whilst the other members guaranteed that the three would not be held liable for more than their individual shares as members of the committee in the event of mishap.[10] Such were the hazards of financing church extension. To stimulate further giving one of the three, W. Perry Herrick, made the first of what was to be a series of offers: he offered £500 if the committee could raise £3,500. At the 1868 annual meeting they still needed another £1,100 and the reverend J. N. Bennie of St Mary's said that in view of 'the immense amount of prosperity which was indicated by the building of so many handsome dwellings' he hoped that some of the wealthy men in the town would make up the sum; 'they had received such handsome support from the noblemen and gentlemen of the county that he thought the town ought now to come forward and raise this £1,100 (Hear, hear)'.[11] It is not clear how far this appeal was successful. St Luke's church was opened on 29 December 1868, and the committee decided to build the two other churches planned in 1865 and to find sites for two more. The annual meeting of 1869 was therefore very much a fund-raising occasion, and the relative obligations of town and country were once again a prominent theme. Dr W. C. Magee had just become bishop of Peterborough and he set the tone with a rousing speech. £25,000 was needed: he said that he had just come from a part of Ireland where £34,000 had been raised in five years, and £12,000 in six months for a cathedral: was it too much to ask the town and county of Leicester to raise £25,000 in four

[9] Report of LACEA annual meeting 1867 in the *Leicester Advertiser:* LACEA Mins 1, pp 66–7.
[10] LACEA Mins 1, pp 64–5, 74–8.
[11] Report in *Leicester Journal:* LACEA Mins 1, p 90.

or five years? He continued: 'I am quite aware that sometimes there is a feeling in counties that the town should help itself, and the country parishes should help themselves, and that it is not quite fair to call upon the country to help the town. If you are quite free from that jealousy in the town and county of Leicester, all I can say is you are a very exceptional county and town.' But he went on to argue, in the passage quoted earlier, that migration created a mutual relationship between town and country and he heartily commended the idea of an annual collection for the spiritual needs of Leicester to every parish in Leicestershire and Rutland.

The bishop won many 'hear, hears' for his remarks, but the Duke of Rutland was cheered when he said that 'anxious as he felt the county were to support the town and subscribe to the building of these new churches in the town, he could not but help thinking that they would still further perhaps increase their zeal if, as this was an archdiaconal association, some small portion of the funds that were raised should be given to some of the difficult parishes in the county'. The reverend T. H. Jones of St Matthew's put the claims of the town on the diocese in a different way: 'There was no town in the diocese, no little village where there were not some resident who had some connection with the town of Leicester. Either they had relatives living in the town or they had friends among its operatives, or they had business relations with the town, and although their first claim was upon the manufacturers and traders and owners of property in Leicester, yet he felt they had a claim upon every village and every town in the diocese.' Albert Pell, MP referred to the need of other increasing towns in the county, which were only villages a few years before: but W. U. Heygate declared that 'It was in the towns that the battle of the church had to be fought. . . . They had not lost sight of the country, but . . . they, as business-like men, looked to see where spiritual destitution existed to the largest extent, and although there were many places in the county where they should like to see churches, there was no place which would bear the slightest comparison with Leicester'. A sum of £3,625 was contributed at that meeting, but over 80% of that came from the county nobility and gentry: £1,000 each was given by earl Howe and W. P. Herrick.[12] In June 1869 Mr Herrick offered on behalf of his sister and himself to undertake the entire building of one of the churches, St Mark's, in lieu of his subscription, provided that the committee would build the second simultaneously, an offer which was

[12] *Leicester Journal*, 21 May 1869.

taken up with 'most grateful thanks'.[13] The two churches were completed by the summer of 1872.

The discussion in 1869 has been recounted at some length because it provided the fullest rehearsal of the arguments on both sides. The events of the later 1870s saw the words of the doubtful county gentry and nobility turned into action. By this time too the most notable county supporters of urban church extension, earl Howe and W. P. Herrick, were dead. In November 1872 the church extension association annual meeting heard that the original three churches planned by the committee were now complete, and that the balance in hand was barely £750. The reverend J. N. Bennie pointed out that the eight-year subscriptions given in 1865 had now come to an end, but that if giving were renewed work could be extended to the county.[14] The ploy does not seem to have carried conviction, and in any case the additional two churches planned in 1869 were both in Leicester.

Both caused problems. St Peter's was built as a memorial to earl Howe on land given by a local man, Joseph Harris of Westcotes. Urgency was given to the project by a chance to gain an endowment of £165 per annum from the ecclesiastical commissioners, if the building were completed by 1 January 1874. The Howe memorial committee gave £3,000 but the association's balance in June 1873 did not even contain enough to meet the £1,500 already promised and a further £2,300 was needed to complete the work.[15] After a strike had held up work the church was consecrated on 16 April 1874 in an unfinished state, with £2,000 still needed to pay for its completion. W. P. Herrick offered another gift of £1,000 if the other £1,000 could be raised by subscription, and the final payment was made in January 1875.[16]

The bishop of Peterborough had held out the hope of assistance to churches in the county in 1873. In 1874 archdeacon Fearon of Loughborough said that some jealousy was felt by the principal inhabitants of the county that their needs had not been considered enough. Five new churches in Leicester had been completed in the last ten years and St Leonard's, the next project, could in his view be met by private subscriptions. He hoped that the society would now turn to the needs

[13] LACEA Mins 1, pp 129–30.
[14] Report in *Leicester Advertiser:* LACEA Mins 1, p 177.
[15] *Leicester Journal,* 13 June 1873.
[16] *Leicester Journal,* 24 April 1874; LACEA Mins 2, pp 9–12, 20; LM Misc 184/6.

of the county. Nevertheless the 1875 annual meeting saw archdeacon Fearon moving the opening of a new subscription list for St Leonard's, and dean MacDonnell saying that £3,000 was needed for Leicester before work could be done in the county.[17] This time, however, the bluff was called. The foundation stone of St Leonard's was laid on 4 July 1876 by Mr W. Thompson, a local manufacturer who had contributed to the building fund—an action publicly praised by W. U. Heygate as recognition by an employer of his responsibility to those who worked for him. But at the annual meeting of the association which followed in the afternoon, it had to be reported that scarcely anything had been received during the year and the contractor was threatening to remove the scaffolding if the money was not obtained by the end of the year. W. P. Herrick had died during the year and so was not available to make an incentive offer. The bishop of Peterborough, who had indicated in his charge of 1875 that he thought the spiritual needs of the town had been fairly overtaken for the present,[18] said that it would be a disgrace to Leicester if St Leonard's could not be completed for the want of £3,000: in Leeds £100,000 was to be raised and £60,000 was subscribed at once. He made it clear that he thought the people of the county had done their share.[19] But it was all to no effect. When the church was consecrated on 6 November 1877 there was a deficit of £550 on the building fund, and by March 1878 it had risen to £1,450. An offer by the committee to meet half the cost if the vicar and churchwardens would raise the rest was not taken up.[20] An appeal to the leading churchmen of the county 'was not successful in eliciting much response in any quarter'.[21] Eventually in July 1878 it was decided to borrow £1,200 from Pares' Bank at 5%: no further projects were planned until this was repaid and the debt and accumulated interest of £200 was finally cleared in February 1881.[22] It is clear that the main reason for the association's financial difficulties was the virtual refusal in the county to support any more Leicester projects. It is interesting to note that the very years when St Leonard's was running into trouble, 1877–8, were the years when Holy Trinity, Loughborough was built. The site was given by Edward

[17] *Leicester Journal,* 11 June 1875.

[18] W. C. Magee, *A Charge delivered to the Clergy and Churchwardens of the Diocese of Peterborough at his Second Visitation, October 1875* (London 1875) p 7.

[19] *Leicester Journal,* 7 July 1876.

[20] *Leicester Journal,* 9 November 1877; LACEA Mins 2, pp 30, 33, 35–6.

[21] LACEA Mins 2, pp 37–8.

[22] *Ibid* pp 39–43, 51.

Warner, and most of the money was raised by private subscription.[23] Archdeacon Fearon may not have won the argument as far as the policy of the church extension association committee was concerned: but Loughborough's church was paid for before Leicester's. The fifteen years from 1865 to 1880 therefore illustrate both the extent of the support which the country was prepared to give to the town, and the conditions on which that support was given.

Among nonconformists the circuit system in methodism provided an institutional link between countryside and town, as has been mentioned. The very formal nature of circuit records makes it difficult to detect the kind of tensions observed in the church of England. Evidence for this has to be indirect. Such tensions were in any case less likely to be found if the churches were doing well. Thus the primitive methodists expanded more rapidly than any other methodist group in Leicestershire in the second half of the nineteenth century. But in the county many of the new chapels built replaced older meeting rooms. In Leicester itself new chapels were built at Curzon Street and St Nicholas Street, and two other chapels were purchased from the congregationalists and general baptists.[24] The Wesleyans were much less energetic and the 1850s were a time of slow recovery from the *Fly Sheet* controversy. The success of a home mission established in a working-class area in 1860 encouraged the Bishop Street circuit to build a new chapel: but care was taken to devise a scheme whereby the appeal for funds for the new chapel was associated with a reduction of the Bishop Street chapel debt. The records imply that the Bishop Street trustees were fearful lest the new chapel attract support from their own.[25] A scheme for building three new chapels was rejected as impracticable in 1870, but within the next three years land was bought and three new chapels begun. Again care was taken that the

[23] W. G. D. Fletcher, *Historical Handbook to Loughborough* (Loughborough 1881) pp 26–7; Church Commissioners' Benefice Files, no 56235, letters 15752 (27 October 1877), 13885 (16 October 1878).

[24] J. Petty, *History of the Primitive Methodist Connexion* (3 ed London 1864) pp 495–6; [H. B.] Kendall, [*The Origin and History of the Primitive Methodist Church*] (London nd) 1, p 334.

[25] Leicester Wesleyan Circuit Q[uarterly] M[eeting] Min[ute]s 1, pp 17–18; Bishop Street Chapel Trustees' Minutes 1, pp 348–9; 2, pp 10, 12, 13, 15–16: all at Bishop Street methodist church.

appeal for funds here (which raised £8,000 including the proceeds of the sale of an old chapel) included a project for Bishop Street—this time new schools.[26] Rivalry in methodism therefore was not so much between town and country as between older and newer town chapels.

The older dissent pursued a more active policy in the countryside. At the same time as the church of England was beginning to tackle the problems of the town, the Leicestershire congregational association was launching an elaborate campaign of rural evangelism. In 1834 soon after its formation committees were appointed to 'devise, if practicable, means for the introduction of the preaching of the gospel into such villages as are most destitute'.[27] The result of this was the support, in association with the congregational home missionary society, of three itinerant ministers from 1838 to 1858. In March 1860 the reverend T. Mays of Ashby de la Zouch suggested that lay evangelists, under the direction of a minister, might be employed and he drew attention to the spiritual destitution around Ashby and Market Bosworth.[28] In November the executive committee expressed its willingness to cooperate with the home missionary society 'in the new efforts which they propose to make for more effectively evangelizing the neglected rural districts of England', and two evangelists were employed.[29] Two years later Samuel Morley, the energetic treasurer of the home missionary society, offered the association £50 per annum for three years if it would guarantee to double its income. The challenge was taken up and between 1863 and 1866 five new evangelistic districts were formed, so that by 1867 there was work in some eighty villages with an average Sunday attendance of around 1,900.[30] This was not achieved without considerable cost. In 1866 the executive committee resolved 'That believing the town of Leicester to have done more than its fair share in raising contributions hitherto they would urge upon the General Committee the pressing necessity for taking means to arouse friends in the County to a deeper sense of their responsibility and a greater effort to sustain the Association by subscription'.[31] The

[26] Leicester Wesleyan Circuit QM Mins, 1, pp 85, 88, 95, 97, 106–9, 112–13, 123–5, 126–7, 129.

[27] L[eicestershire and Rutland] C[ongregational] U[nion] Min[ute]s 1, pp 19–20; Leic[e]s[tershire] C[ounty] R[ecords] O[ffice] N/C/MB/1.

[28] L[eicestershire and Rutland] C[ongregational] U[nion] Exec[utive Committee] Min[ute]s 1, pp 47–8; Leics CRO N/C/MB/2.

[29] LCU Exec Mins 1, pp 51–2.

[30] LCU Mins 1, pp 213–14, 222, 230–1; LCU Exec Mins 1, pp 75–7, 79–80, 87–9.

[31] LCU Exec Mins 1, pp 107–8.

resolution is almost a mirror image of the complaints soon to be made in Anglican circles about the town. It was these financial difficulties, which did not ease in the 1870s, which prevented further expansion. As the evangelists were failing to produce self-supporting congregations, they threatened to be a permanent liability on the association. Eventually the system was changed: in 1882 examinations for evangelists were introduced and in effect efforts were made to develop them into regular ministers.[32] The former mission stations became independent churches, or died.

The particular baptists considered appointing evangelists between 1869 and 1872, but did nothing because of lack of money. In 1871 John Bennett, a leading baptist layman, told the secretary of the Leicestershire congregational union that 'the Baptist Association as far as aggressive effort is concerned is in a sleep which I am afraid knows no awaking'.[33] From 1879 to 1894 the association employed an evangelist in the Arnesby district, which demonstrated a continuing commitment to the countryside.[34]

But there were other nonconformists who thought that this attention to the countryside was mistaken. In 1869 the reverend J. J. Goadby, minister of Dover Street general baptist church, Leicester, criticised attempts to start home missionary stations in sparsely populated neighbourhoods: contentment with village centres, he said, 'has been a fatal bar to anything like solid and continuous expansion'.[35] More sharply the reverend S. T. Williams, minister of London Road congregational church, Leicester, criticised the Leicestershire congregational union in 1872 for spending too much effort on the county. He thought it was a strange inconsistency 'to care with eagerness for the evangelisation of scattered hundreds, and to be comparatively heedless of the spiritual welfare of dense thousands, exposed to far greater temptations and more demoralising influences'. He estimated that five new churches were needed in Leicester to bring the level of provision of places of worship back to that of 1851 and said that one ought to be built by congregationalists; and he compared the religious provision in Oakham, Melton Mowbray and Hinckley with three parts of Leicester of comparable size where there was no congregationalist activity at all. He too referred to rural migration to the towns, and

[32] LCU Mins 2, p 176: Leics CRO N/C/MB/8.

[33] LCU Stationing Committee Minutes p 21; Leics CRO N/C/MB/15.

[34] L[eicestershire] B[aptist] A[ssociation] Min[ute]s 3, pp 41–2, 247; in possession of the East Midlands baptist association.

[35] *The General Baptist Year Book, 1869* (London 1869–): Association Letter p 15.

like bishop Magee argued that this was 'a strong reason why the county should *just now* help us'.[36] His suggestions were taken up, and a programme of action for Leicester was worked out in the autumn of 1872. £1,000 was raised to build a mission in Sanvey Gate and the new buildings were opened for worship on 7 June 1874. But £600 was still needed and it was October 1875 before the debt was cleared after a special appeal to the country churches.[37] The other two projects were less successful, and both ran into financial difficulties. The property at Willow Street had to be sold in 1879 after five years' precarious existence; and the Humberstone Road church had to mortgage an outstanding debt of £600 in 1882 with the three leading town congregational churches accepting responsibility for interest repayments for the first five years. The mission building committee was wound up in 1884.[38] Clearly the congregationalists shared the Anglicans' problems over finance, though the country resources they had to draw on were not so great. But they were also still considering the rural areas. In 1875 a subcommittee reported on the possibilities of making Burbage the centre of an evangelistic district as follows: 'The population of Burbage was 2,000, the Wesleyan chapel supplied by local preachers from Hinckley was thinly attended and . . . at the Primitive Methodist chapel only about 11 or 12 persons were in the habit of attending. Around Burbage were six villages, all within a radius of three miles, and in the whole of this district there was no resident dissenting minister.' The executive committee accepted the recommendation to make Burbage the centre of a new district.[39]

Three main conclusions emerge from this study. The first is the persistence of nonconformist concern for rural areas. For a long time the aim was simply to establish a presence. In 1859 the *Wesleyan Methodist Magazine* described south-east Leicestershire as follows: 'Here are 30 villages, with populations from 100 to 1,000 each—and in another direction there are nearly 20 villages more—in which *there is no Methodism*. . . . In some few places there is a Dissenting cause,

[36] S. T. Williams, *Our Duty in relation to the Moral and Religious Needs of Leicester* (Leicester 1872) pp 5, 8: LCU Mins 1, p 344.

[37] LCU M[ission] B[uilding] C[ommittee] Min[ute]s pp 23–33, 54–6: Leics CRO N/C/MB/16.

[38] LCU MBC Mins pp 77–8, 108–9, 116.

[39] LCU Exec Mins 2, pp 79–80; Leics CRO N/C/MB/3.

generally speaking but feeble; and the bulk of the villages are in the hands of careless Churchmen or Puseyites'.[40] The attitude here was typical, and the remarks of the congregationalist subcommittee on Burbage previously quoted show the same assumptions fifteen years later. Even the idea of cooperation, or rather non-competition, between the nonconformist denominations was slow to develop, although in 1873 the Leicestershire congregational union sought an understanding between themselves, the general baptists and the primitive methodists as to which body would start a cause at Stoney Stanton because of the new stoneworks there. The initiative was actually taken by the owner of the works, and the general baptists were given the responsibility.[41]

Nonconformist attitudes to rural areas were complicated by the subtle change that was taking place in the position of village churches themselves. There had always been difficulties in village work; but it is not easy to spot the point at which establishment hostility gives way to more serious economic changes as the root cause. Thus in 1876 John Bennett, as moderator of the Leicestershire baptist association, criticised the ignorance in many town churches about rural conditions. Many village churches, he said, 'as far as practical sympathy and counsel from many of our church members are concerned might nearly as well be in Madagascar or Ceylon as within 15 miles of our doors'.[42] Bennett believed that the established church was losing its hold upon the affection and allegiance of Christian men in villages and small towns, and this provided an opportunity for nonconformity. The reverend John Clifford expounded a similar theme in an address to the baptist union assembly in 1876, when he urged the necessity of not neglecting villages but taking advantage of the opportunities they offered and interesting town churches in them.[43] It is necessary to appreciate the seriousness with which this positive view was put forward right up to the onset of the agricultural depression; and also to appreciate how long it took people to realise that this was no tjust a temporary depression but a more fundamental change in the economic relationship of town and country. In such circumstances it took a strong mind to plead for the towns as the reverend S. T. Williams did in 1872—particularly if support for urban church

[40] *Wesleyan Methodist Magazine* (London 1859) p 371.
[41] LCU Mins 2, pp 43–4.
[42] *Report of the Leicestershire Baptist Association, 1876* (Leicester 1876) pp 6–7, 9–10.
[43] *Baptist Handbook 1877* (London 1877) pp 105–21.

extension looked like depriving struggling rural churches of the means of survival. H. B. Kendall, writing at the beginning of this century, illustrates a common attitude when he said of primitive methodism, 'Formerly the temptation was to neglect the towns in favour of the villages; now the temptation is to abandon the villages and concentrate on the towns'.[44]

The second conclusion concerns the church of England. In general the only places where the church of England needed to build new churches were the towns. There was a significant need for the restoration of churches in rural areas, but that was a different problem. The cost of urban church extension also included parsonages and schools, as well as the 'invisible' cost of endowment. Between 1860 and 1885 the number of churches in Leicester increased from nine to nineteen, and over £110,000 was spent on new church buildings alone. £45,000 of this went on the two churches entirely built at private expense.[45] By comparison with some larger towns Leicester's need for new churches was modest. Though it was stressed in appeals for money that the established church, unlike nonconformity, had a duty to build where the poor were, rather than in the richer suburbs, it is doubtful whether it could be argued in Leicester, as Ward did for Manchester, that 'the Church's own pastoral efficiency was being sacrificed to its uneconomic claims as an establishment'.[46] Despite these modest needs, and the added incentive of destroying the reputation of Leicester as the metropolis of dissent, it proved impossible to sustain rural support for church extension in the town. After an initial flush of enthusiasm in the late 1860s and early 1870s that feeling was replaced by resentment at the failure of the town to do more. Moreover, since so much of the financial support came from a few nobility and gentry, it might be questioned whether the significant fact is that these men lived in the countryside or that they were men with a wider awareness of what was going on in the nation as a whole.

The question of awareness is linked to the last conclusion, which may well be the most significant. These developments indicate the end of an era in which either town or country could manage on their own. After the state declined to give direct financial support to the established church in the early nineteenth century, the church of England found that, like the non-established churches, it had to raise the money for

[44] Kendall 1, p 298.
[45] *Church of England Year Book, 1887* (London 1887) p 48.
[46] W. R. Ward, 'The Cost of Establishment', *SCH* 3 (1966) p 286.

further development itself. There was little difference in the pattern of organisation between the archdeaconry church extension association and the Leicestershire congregational union or the Leicestershire baptist association. Like other voluntary societies they had to be organised in such a way as to maximise contributions: and ultimately that meant that the policy pursued had to be acceptable to the subscribers, otherwise the funds dried up. It is ironical that the established church should provide the starkest example of this in the case of St Leonard's.

These organisations also exercised significant supervisory powers, regardless of the formal polity of the denominations concerned. Bunting's reforms had formally written such powers into methodist connexional discipline: but both the congregational and baptist associations in Leicestershire took direct control of churches which were financially dependent upon them. Dependent churches in the congregational association could not vote on the distribution of the association's funds.[47] The baptist association actually acquired the nucleus of an evangelism fund as the result of the sale of the Sparrow Hill church, Loughborough, in 1888 which they had had to prop up for years.[48] In the church of England such powers were not exercised by the church extension association, but they were exercised by the ecclesiastical commissioners, whose role in determining what was and was not possible in church policy increased steadily. Not the least of these various powers was an insistence on denominational exclusiveness. When the Leicestershire congregational union applied to the home missionary society for a grant for the Sanvey Gate mission in 1874, one of the reasons they were unsuccessful was that the premises were held on an open trust.[49] National church organisation was gaining in influence at the expense of the local and the significance of this was to transcend the significance of older differences between town and countryside.[50] In Leicestershire churches, therefore, the interplay between town and countryside was rather greater than some studies have suggested: what perhaps needs further examination is why and how some churchmen had a wider awareness of the tasks of the church than others.

University of Cambridge
Fitzwilliam College

[47] LCU Mins 1, p 143.
[48] LBA Mins 3, pp 338, 342.
[49] LCU MBC Mins pp 27, 48–9.
[50] Yeo pp 296–308.

IDEALS IN URBAN MISSION: EPISCOPALIANS IN TWENTIETH CENTURY GLASGOW

by GAVIN WHITE

AT THE beginning of this century Glasgow was romantic. It was a successful city, and it was growing rapidly. The 1901 census had shown that Scottish cities were growing faster than English, and Glasgow had increased by fifteen per cent in ten years.[1]

Much of this increase came from England, and from urban England at that. The bishop of Glasgow and Galloway said of his flock in 1901, 'I can never find a west of Scotland man who is a hereditary episcopalian. The church seems to have been wiped away just as a man wipes a dish, and turns it upside down'. Instead they had migrants who 'have come bringing no money with them, requiring us to provide religious ministrations for them. We have done our best.'[2] It was estimated that there were fifty thousand episcopalians and Anglicans in Glasgow, of whom only fourteen thousand were known to the clergy. In 1894 a census of four areas rated episcopalians at six per cent of the population, and another census in Govan at ten per cent. In a famous speech to the representative church council of 1901, Anthony Mitchell admitted 'a feeling of dejection' at the size of the problem, though he added that nowhere else would missionary work find 'a readier return'. The bishop substantiated this, saying that Glasgow people were 'not hostile to religion . . . many of them are thirsting after it', as shown by the crowds attracted by street preachers.[3] The rural dioceses in Scotland were asked to support the work as their migrants were in Glasgow, though in fact these were probably not a significant number.

When A. E. Campbell became bishop in 1904 he had three aims. These were to reduce the burden of debt on existing congregations, to develop work from strong centres, and to stir up missionary interest. 'Had the Glasgow problem come before me at an earlier stage, I should have built ten great churches holding from a thousand to

[1] *Reports on the Schemes of the Church of Scotland* (Edinburgh 1902) p 275.

[2] *Scottish Guardian* (Edinburgh) 18 October 1901 p 663.

[3] *Ibid.*

fifteen hundred people, or, at any rate, parts of them, and to each would have been attached a staff of at least three men. As it is, we have some thirty places of worship, some of which are mere rabbit hutches, and a number of priests starving in solitude on a hundred and fifty pounds a year.'[4] Few were actually paid so little, but Campbell had spent his formative years in the south when the subdivision of large parishes had been tried and found wanting. The new ideal in his youth was to have teams of curates under vicars of such superior abilities that not enough of them would have been available for a larger number of parishes.[5] This policy, with its emphasis on natural leaders and on team spirit, probably stemmed from social Darwinism and the public school ethos. Campbell was on stronger ground when he tried to abolish ancient differences between funds of incumbencies and funds for missions, but the resultant joint boards soon lost any sense of missionary responsibility. He also felt that he could not attract the right sort of clergy to his diocese,[6] though it is hard to know what sort of clergy he considered to be right. In 1910 there were thirty clergy in the city of whom thirteen were graduates of Scottish universities, ten were graduates of English universities, and one was an Irish graduate. Twenty of the thirty had been ordained in Scotland.[7] These proportions would seem to have been ideal, and Campbell was clearly not dependent on disaffected or unwanted clergy from the south.

Later generations were to remember Campbell as a great missionary bishop, but in fact his influence was severely limited. Of the ten great centres around which he planned development, he saw his hopes realised in only one such new centre.[8] In other areas extension continued through the spontaneous and unregulated creation of missions in shop-fronts or huts wherever there seemed to be a demand. These new missions were almost invariably begun by local clergy and congregations with local resources and only became the concern of the diocese when they ran into debt.

The first world war interrupted a programme of intermittent expansion and it also interrupted a million shilling fund which was

[4] [*The Right Rev. Archibald Ean Campbell D.D.: A Memoir,* ed G. T. S.] Farquhar (Edinburgh 1924) p 114.

[5] K. S. Inglis, *Churches and the Working Classes in Victorian England* (London 1963) p 27; *The Times* 6 August 1883 p 7.

[6] Farquhar p 134.

[7] *Year Book of the Episcopal Church in Scotland* (Edinburgh 1910).

[8] *St Margaret's Magazine* (Glasgow) 13 no 5, May 1921 p 74.

bringing in new money at a satisfactory rate. The new money, however, was used to re-finance old debts and not to build new churches.[9] And a temporary but ominous decline in numbers was rather casually attributed to the absence of some clergy on war service.[10] Yet Glasgow diocese was doing better financially than other Scottish dioceses in the war years, and this may have led Glasgow to block financial re-organisation of the episcopal church. Instead of new financial schemes the Glasgow men promoted a recurrent will-of-the-wisp in the shape of a separate rural diocese of Galloway in order to give the city of Glasgow the full attention of one bishop.[11] Throughout this period the emphasis was on numbers of clergy and on episcopal oversight rather than on the shifting trends of popular thought. And throughout this period the rural end of the diocese was considered to be a distraction from urban reality.

When Campbell died in 1922 he was succeeded by E. T. S. Reid whose ideals were said to be identical. His first aim was to prevent free-lance extension on small sites incapable of holding more than a hut. Instead he would raise the money first and only then build halls for worship. These would be given to congregations free of debt, and the congregations would then finance their own permanent churches and rectories. Twenty-two districts were selected, but only six could be actually developed, and under this programme only four halls were actually built.[12] Raising the money proved to be very difficult, and the decade was more marked by the improvement or embellishment of existing churches than by the building of new ones. Moreover, the cold wind of statistical decline was now blowing upon the episcopal church in Glasgow. Givings were also failing, though in this respect it was argued that working-class congregations were holding up better than middle-class.[13] If true, this might have been due to working-class episcopalians being largely English, and thus somewhat isolated from secular ideas while in Scotland, while the middle-class episcopalians tended to be more Scottish.

A steady decline in numbers could be observed in London from about 1885, but for Glasgow episcopalians it did not begin until about 1920. Probably this difference was due partly to a flow of new

[9] [*Report of the*] *Council* [*of the Diocese of Glasgow and Galloway*] 3 February 1915.
[10] *Ibid* 8 February 1916.
[11] *Ibid* 4 February 1919.
[12] *Ibid* 6 February 1924, 3 February 1926, 8 February 1928.
[13] *Ibid* 6 February 1924, 3 February 1926.

immigrants to compensate for internal decline and partly to church-going together with other Victorian customs having continued much longer in Scotland than in England. In 1900 the diocese claimed 38,538 adherents and by 1920 these had risen to 55,816 but fell to 48,037 by 1930.[14] The rural factor in these figures may be discounted as most episcopalians were urban in occupation even if they lived in the country. Numbers have declined steadily ever since, save for the temporary rise in the early 1950s experienced by almost every church. That rise, which some say was created by Billy Graham but which more probably created the success of Billy Graham, was, oddly enough, experienced by the Glasgow episcopalians in the late 1940s instead of five years later. By 1970 the number of adherents was only 28,950 and the decline has since continued steadily.[15] Church of Scotland figures show the staying power to be expected from a much larger body and its rate of decline has been slower, though that decline also started around 1921. Figures for Glasgow presbytery are only to be had from the union of 1929, but they show a decline parallel to the national figures, though steeper, and with the same rise in the early 1950s followed by a sharp drop wiping out the gains.[16] Scottish baptists show a similar decline to that of the episcopalians, as might have been expected, though their rise was in the early 1950s and not in the late 1940s.[17] Roman catholic decline in Glasgow only dates from 1961, and national Roman catholic decline only from 1973.[18] These varied figures would seem to indicate that whatever was happening to the episcopal church could not be blamed on internal factors which were not present in other churches.

But episcopalians did not blame the decline on any factors at all. They denied its existence, and it must be admitted that the reality of the decline was obscured by other circumstances. As the eucharist became the main service in more and more congregations, non-communicants found their position untenable. They either became communicants or they left. There was no longer a place for the infrequent worshipper with an eighteenth-century doctrine of Sunday school morality, though it is quite possible that the changes in worship were themselves caused by such people becoming extinct.

[14] Farquhar p 101; *Council* 6 and 7 February 1962.
[15] *Council* 2 February 1971.
[16] *Church of Scotland Reports to the General Assembly with the Legislative Acts* (Edinburgh 1976).
[17] *Baptist Union of Scotland Yearbook* (Glasgow 1900–75).
[18] *Catholic Directory for Scotland* (Edinburgh 1976).

Whichever was cause and whichever was effect, the resulting statistics showed numbers of adherents falling and numbers of communicants rising, though the rise could not account for anything like the numbers of adherents who were lost. Faced with this situation, observers rightly noted that the adherent figure was notoriously unreliable as a guide to true numbers. It was overlooked that it was not unreliable as a guide to longterm trends. All that was believed was the communicant rise which continued until 1940, declined slightly until 1945, then rose slightly before going steadily downhill.[19]

Yet signs of trouble were not totally disregarded. As early as 1926 bishop Reid felt obliged to state that there was no foundation to rumours that his extension fund campaign was already finished. He added that he had hoped for fifty thousand pounds for the first stage of his programme, but had only received twenty thousand.[20] By 1930 he was obliged to agree to the building of one hall without having all the money in hand, thereby abandoning, however reluctantly, his policy of debt-free construction.[21] Dissatisfaction was particularly expressed by John McBain, rector of Christ Church in the east end, who urged division of the diocese in familiar terms and in 1929 attributed stagnation to 'want of interest and vital energy'.[22] This was one of the earlier expressions of the doctrine that evangelism waxed or waned according to churchly vitality rather than the felt needs of men and women. McBain's next suggestion was that the diocesan council should meet four times a year instead of once, thereby involving the laity more often if not more deeply. He was supported by canon E. J. Petrie who argued that 'matters could not be worse, as far as interest was concerned'.[23] The experiment was tried, accomplished nothing except extreme aggravation, and came to an end. By 1931 McBain was also arguing that 'the most effective and economical mission work can be done by increasing the manpower in existing populous centres, rather than in opening new missions'.[24] This was partly the old ideal of bishop Campbell, but as presented by McBain it was also an appeal to the diocese not to desert the working-class and retreat to the suburbs. He was himself a labour party councillor and his parish of Christ Church with its missions had

[19] *Council* 9 February 1949.

[20] *St Margaret's Magazine* 18 no 9 September 1926 p 110.

[21] *Council* 5 February 1930.

[22] *Ibid* 4 June 1929.

[23] *Ibid.*

[24] *Ibid* 4 February 1931.

sixteen bedrooms in its clergy house, though some of these were occupied by settlement workers. Its thriving anglo-catholic congregation mounted rogationtide processions amongst the factories and tenements led by choir, crucifix, and bagpipes.[25] Yet McBain was to be faced with slum clearance and re-settlement in new housing areas to which the episcopal church could scarcely penetrate. And, despite Petrie's prediction that things could not be worse, they did become worse.

Before his retirement in 1952, bishop How noted that his predecessors had opened fifty churches in as many years. 'Then we come to the past thirteen to fourteen years, and I can only record the planting of one new mission'. In fact that planting soon wilted. 'At first sight', continued the bishop, 'it may seem somewhat discouraging'. Nonetheless he felt that there had been 'a truly amazing record of consolidation . . . though the loosely attached are dropping away, the devotion of our staunch members is deepening . . . I believe I can foresee a really great forward movement with the right man to lead'.[26] It is easy to dismiss this as wishful thinking, yet the prevailing ecclesiology of the decade favoured closely-knit Christian communities in a pagan environment which was to be encouraged if it did not actually exist. How was only expressing the wisdom of his day, and although most congregations were weaker than before there were admittedly others which had gone from strength to strength during his episcopate.

Yet an increasing number of congregations had either faded away to nothing or had simply collapsed despite quite large numbers. In 1953 these closures were attributed to a shortage of clergy rather than of people, and in the following year this same reason was given for the closure of no less than three churches.[27] At each annual diocesan council the synod clerk read out the diminishing numbers, and year by year it was argued that the figures did not mean very much. When comment was made, it was to the effect that 'if church membership has numerically decreased, the quality of churchmanship has definitely improved'.[28] This last assumption was based on an increase in acts of communion, but in 1959 a new synod clerk made a unique attempt to face the facts and attributed this increase to nothing more basic

[25] Canon R. Bisset, letter of 26 January 1978.
[26] *Council* 11 and 12 February 1952.
[27] *Ibid* 9 and 10 February 1953, 8 and 9 February 1954.
[28] *Ibid* 12 and 13 February 1959.

than 'changed modes of worship'. He employed graphs to demonstrate that there had been a 'a noticeable decline' over the past fifty years, partly through what he called 'social conditions', and he added that the difficulties of home mission work 'were not fully grasped or understood'.[29] This frankness was shortlived. In the following year there was yet another synod clerk, and two years later he was observing that 'what we might lose in quantity we would make up in quality'.[30] Once again it should be noted that this owed much to the prevailing ideology of the day, but it must be added that there were precedents for giving unwelcome statistics a kind interpretation even before there was an ideology to justify the practice. When bishop Campbell had noted a marked dip in baptismal figures for his diocese as far back as 1906, he had joyfully proclaimed that this meant his clergy were being more careful not to baptise indiscriminately.[31]

That episcopalians in Glasgow have been declining numerically for half a century does not mean that they have failed. They did provide churches for those who would use them. Most of those churches have now disappeared. Saint David's, Saint Barnabas's, Saint Luke's, Saint Columba's, Saint Andrew's, Saint John's, Saint Paul's, Saint Saviour's, Saint Peter's, Saint Mark's, Saint Michael's, Saint Cuthbert's, Saint Christopher's, Saint Patrick's, Saint Faith's, Saint Philip's, Saint Margaret and Saint Mungo's, all these are gone. Christ Church remains, a gaunt improbability in a waste of desolation, and so do the churches of suburban Glasgow. But most of the inner churches have died with their neighbourhoods.

There are lessons to be drawn from this experience. Around the turn of the century it had been argued that episcopalians should devote resources to Glasgow as there were openings there, and the parochial nature of expansion meant that resources went where openings were to be found. But forty years later none of the leaders were looking for openings. They were asking themselves if they had a sufficiently missionary spirit, as if this would have drawn in others who had very little choice in the matter. This being the case, statistics were not of much interest, and statistics of other churches were of no interest at all. In retrospect it would have been more useful for the would-be missionaries to have studied their unchurched neighbours more and themselves less, and had they done so they might have discovered

[29] *Ibid* 4 and 5 February 1959.
[30] *Ibid* 7 and 8 February 1961.
[31] *Scottish Chronicle* (Edinburgh) 9 February 1906 p 85.

some opening or at least a point of contact. But it is probable that they would have found no point of contact anyway.

This probability derives from the relationship between bishop and clergy. Any clergyman tends to be independent, but when a clergyman is both Scottish and episcopalian he becomes absolutely ungovernable. In the period under review the bishop was treated with great respect. He was either English or anglicised, he had been trained to lead, and he was regarded as a link with the higher social classes and sometimes with theological scholarship. But, just because he was these things, he was not expected to be of much use in the practical business of running a parish. Furthermore, it was an accepted practice for Scots to let the English leaders make the speeches while the real decisions were made by the Scots in private. We have already seen that bishop Campbell laid down one policy while some of his clergy cheerfully followed another, and to some extent this was true of his predecessor. We may therefore assume that whatever any bishop said, some of his clergy were probably doing the opposite. In mission work we know that McBain was one such, but there do seem to have been others, even if none of them was so rash as to propose missions to the countryside. Yet they do not seem to have made any significant breakthrough. Had they done so, it is quite possible that official policy would have immediately changed course. And this, of course, raises another problem. We do not know whether the official policy of rejoicing in declining adherents prevented positive action, or whether the impossibility of positive action led to an official policy of rejoicing in the inevitable. But this is not surprising. Whatever the area or the period, when church historians deal with the interaction of church and society they do not know and cannot know very much.

University of Glasgow

URBAN PROBLEMS AND RURAL SOLUTIONS: DRINK AND DISESTABLISHMENT IN THE FIRST WORLD WAR

by STUART MEWS

OVER ten years ago Brian Harrison drew attention to certain inadequately explored areas 'where Marx's classes still make their appearance but are overlain by the more lasting dichotomies of traditionalist versus radical, provincial versus Londoner, town-dweller versus countryman, intellectual versus the mass, Anglican versus Nonconformist, male versus female'.[1] This paper does not isolate the urban-rural dichotomy which for most of the twentieth century has chiefly acquired a separate social significance only in and through the romantic speculations of intellectuals,[2] but assumes its importance as one of several factors in interaction with each other which have divided and sometimes united societies and segments of societies along horizontal rather than vertical lines. Two areas which demand that complex analysis, sensitive to social and cultural cross-pressures, proposed by Harrison, are leisure (an area in which he has himself practised with distinction what he has preached) and secularisation. This paper considers one aspect of each of these, namely drink and disestablishment, as they impinged upon each other in a very specific episode in 1915.

Drink and disestablishment are two topics which raised issues and were the subject of agitations generally recognised as important for an understanding of nineteenth century Britain but usually regarded as at most of only marginal significance in the twentieth.[3] Yet though

[1] Brian Harrison, 'Religion and Recreation in Nineteenth Century England', *PP* 38 (December 1967) p 98.

[2] I would not go quite so far as a former colleague in arguing that the rural peasant 'became socially acceptable only through the romantic speculations of nineteenth century German intellectuals', Bryan S. Turner, *Weber and Islam* (London 1974) p 95, but for a discussion of some of the difficulties in the use of this and other similar dichotomies see Stuart Mews, 'Community as a Sociological Concept', *The Christian Community*, ed Laurence Bright (London 1971) pp 1–40.

[3] D. A. Hamer, *The Politics of Electoral Pressure. A Study in the History of Victorian Reform Agitations* (Hassocks 1977); *Pressure from Without in Early Victorian England*, ed P. Hollis (London 1974).

the power of their electoral appeal was steadily diminishing in society as a whole, the drink and disestablishment questions retained a special prominence in the often out-moded social and political ideologies of religious institutions, institutions which like the British army were frequently found to be fighting the wars of the present with the weapons of the past. It was true that profound changes of attitude were taking place in the minds of younger Christian leaders but when Harold Anson lived in Manchester between 1910 and 1919 he found that 'Church circles were scarcely interested in any other cause except the disestablishment of the Church in Wales, and the maintaining of Anglican rate-supported schools', to which he later added as a third cause for concern: opposition to licensing restrictions. Churchmen did dislike drunkenness, Anson noted, 'but they believed in the public house':

> Generally speaking they distrusted the man who did not like his glass of ale. The pious Lancashire churchman regarded his glass of ale and a reasonable liking for the public house, as a safeguard against the fanaticism and dishonesty of which he accused his Nonconformist neighbours.[4]

Manchester, as Ward and Clarke have demonstrated,[5] was a rather special place, but its enthusiasms were not unique and could erupt in the most unlikely places at the most unexpected times. One of the most remarkable of such effusions, and one of the least understood, was the re-emergence at roughly the same time, of the drink and disestablishment questions shortly after the beginning of the first world war.

'For reasons that are still obscure', Morgan has observed,[6] the chancellor of the exchequer David Lloyd George in the spring of 1915 announced his determination to settle the drink question by the nationalisation of all public houses. Lloyd George's intentions were as baffling to his contemporaries as they remain to modern historians. Why should the most prominent member of the government after the prime minister of a nation fighting the most ferocious war in its history devote months of his energies to the apparently lost cause of temperance reform? Asquith at the time thought the scheme an indication of his colleague's lack of 'perspective and judgment'; to

[4] Harold Anson, *Looking Forward* (London 1938) pp 129, 181.

[5] W. R. Ward, *Religion and Society in England 1790–1850* (London 1972); Peter F. Clarke, *Lancashire and the New Liberalism* (Cambridge 1971).

[6] Kenneth O. Morgan, *Lloyd George* (London 1974) p 84.

Max Aitken (later Lord Beaverbrook) it was 'a strange vagary . . . somewhat rash and quixotic'. 'When a cabinet minister says drink is a greater danger than the armies of Germany', wrote a unionist opponent, 'one almost wonders whether he was sober or merely hysterical.'[7] Insobriety was not however, the personal weakness most readily associated with Lloyd George and though his solution to the drink question may, as Asquith insisted, have oscillated between 'two poles of absurdity',[8] his resolve to push forward this particular issue was not as eccentric as some of his contemporaries seemed to think. It was in fact a political manoeuvre designed primarily as a response to something rather more than a little local difficulty which threatened his position amongst his ever fickle supporters, the nonconformists of Wales. It was an attempt to maintain the support of an increasingly rural religious sub-culture by adopting its participants' solution to what appeared to be a serious urban problem.

When war was declared in 1914 it created a sense of national unity which was hailed with relief by those social pessimists who had viewed with alarm the turbulence of the immediate pre-war period.[9] But the social and spiritual solidarity of August 1914 was superficial. Within months every pressure group and school of thought was re-deploying its arguments and putting its own programme forward as an essential ingredient for victory or as the only appropriate response to the challenge of the wartime situation. On the whole the new circumstances favoured the reactionaries rather than the radicals. Although Lord Halifax, the Anglo-Catholic leader, accused teetotallers 'for whom he had a strong aversion' of exploiting the war 'in the interests of their pernicious fad',[10] it cannot be said that they made the best of their opportunity. The production of new and topical arguments to justify old conclusions did not impress when they rested on contradictory interpretations of wartime events. Why had the German troops advanced with such efficiency and manifested such amazing resilience? Because, suggested bishop Welldon, they had not been allowed to incapacitate themselves through strong drink. Why had the Germans committed such atrocities in Belgium? Because, said

[7] H. H. Asquith–Venetia Stanley 31 March 1915 quoted in [Cameron] Hazlehurst [*Politicians At War*] (London 1971) p 211; [Lord] Beaverbrook, [*Politicians and the War*] (London 1928) pp 71, 74; Hatfield [Quickswood] MS Qui 19/34 Arthur Elliot–Lord Hugh Cecil 8 April 1915.

[8] H. H. Asquith–Venetia Stanley 31 March 1915 quoted Hazlehurst p 211.

[9] *Manchester Diocesan Magazine* September 1914.

[10] [J. G.] Lockhart, [*Viscount Halifax 1885–1934*, 2] (London 1936) p 237.

bishop Hicks, they had 'unlimited opportunities for getting themselves drunk.'[11]

Edward Lee Hicks, bishop of Lincoln, was president of the Church of England Temperance Society. When he raised the question of drink at the first bishops' meeting after the outbreak of war 'a general silence followed'. Only two bishops supported him and he felt keenly his isolation: 'I feel always out of my element here at Lambeth: an "outsider" . . . I fear I am thought a bore or a bear, or a bounder'.[12] Certainly the archbishop of Canterbury Randall Davidson, was very wary of seeming to break the wartime truce on controversial matters by pushing for a radical measure of temperance legislation, though he was prepared to warn against the treating of soldiers which had produced some unsavoury incidents and to urge voluntary acts of abstinence for the duration of the war.[13] In October 1914 he had initially declined a request from the bishop of Croydon, an old teetotal stalwart, to preside over a gathering of the temperance clans, planned on inter-denominational lines. When Croydon had taken this rebuff as a personal insult and deplored the 'general lack of earnestness and enthusiasm' in the church of England, the archbishop reconsidered but his obvious lukewarmness was more typical of Anglican attitudes than the fervour of his zealous suffragan.[14] What turned the tables in favour of the temperance lobby was the gradual accession of support for some of their objectives from the least likely quarter, the right-wing die-hards.

The war provided an opportunity for those forces of reaction which had formerly been on the defensive to attempt to reimpose their control of society.[15] Those who had felt threatened by the pre-war self-assertiveness of the women's movement and the labour movement found the new situation particularly favourable. Women were an easy target. Did not the war prove that the full privileges of citizenship should only be granted to those who were able to answer their country's call to fight, and possibly die, in her defence? One leading Anglo-Catholic, H. F. B. Mackay, vicar of All Saints, Margaret Street,

[11] *Alliance News* February 1915 p 29; March 1915 p 47.

[12] MS Diary of E. L. Hicks 21 October 1914 p 291.

[13] [G. K. A.] Bell, [*Randall T. Davidson,* 2] (London 1935) p 748.

[14] [Lambeth Palace Library] Davidson MS: H. H. Pereira–R. T. Davidson 20 September, 6, 10 October 1914; R. T. Davidson–H. H. Pereira 6 October, 12 November 1914. Part of Davidson's reluctance stemmed from a desire not to compromise the 'dual basis' of the CETS by association with bodies officially committed to prohibition.

[15] [Samuel] Hynes, [*The Edwardian Turn of Mind*] (Princeton N.J. 1968) p 13.

had gone even further and had come close to suggesting that the war itself was a divine retribution for the increasing rejection by women of their traditional role.[16]

The image of womanhood which the clergy most liked to invoke in the early years of the war was of a creature weak either in body or will. The bishop of London in his highly successful recruiting appeals often played upon the chivalrous instincts of his hearers by portraying the angel of the home, physically weak but spiritually sensitive who relied upon male protection to stand between her and the marauding Hun.[17] The obverse of this highly idealised picture was the alternative image of the working class feckless woman, who could neither manage her money nor adequately look after her home. Canon E. A. Burroughs, later bishop of Ripon, deplored the 'heedlessly liberal scale' of the separation allowances that had made many women, in his words, 'wealthy and idle who have never been anything but industrious and poor':

> 'Eighteen shillings a week, and no husband? Why it's heaven!' And 'heaven' for such people is too often hard by the public-house; largely because the latter is the normal receptacle of spare cash and they have few other ideas of spending. And then their home goes to ruin, and the children run wild unchecked by the disciplinary influences which even a not very edifying male parent radiates.[18]

'It sounds horrid to say it, but the fact is that the women dependents of our soldiers are getting more money than they can wisely handle', remarked the archbishop of Canterbury. 'Money is pouring into their homes', exclaimed the bishop of London, and reminded his audience of women church workers that many wives were getting their husbands' entire earnings for the first time. Anxious about their husbands, with money in their purses and the public houses open in the mornings, the bishop of London was not surprised that many were drinking excessively.[19] But canon Burroughs would not accept even these extenuating circumstances. He claimed that when social

[16] *Church Union Gazette* (London) October 1914 p 294. Mackay had long been obsessed by 'that contemptuous young woman': F. B. Mackay, *The Religion of the Englishman* (London 1911) pp 14, 25.

[17] A. F. Winnington Ingram, *A Call To Arms* (London 1914) p 7.

[18] [E. A.] Burroughs, [*The Valley of Decision*] (London 1916) p 151. Even the normally enlightened Peter Green of Salford believed that out of every 1/– received in separation allowances, 3d found its way to the public house: *Challenge* 6 November 1914.

[19] Bell p 747; A. F. Winnington Ingram, *A Day of God* (London 1914) pp 62, 82.

workers asked what the husband would think if he returned to find his wife drunk, 'the wife's reply is not infrequently that "she wouldn't mind if he never came back".'[20] Speakers at a Roman Catholic League of the Cross meeting in Notting Hill had no doubt that drunkenness amongst women had increased, while monsignor W. F. Brown, rector of St Anne's, Vauxhall, demanded the total exclusion of women from public houses. Licensees in London did agree to a request from the metropolitan police commissioner to bar women before 11 30 am, but the monsignor's request was regarded as highly insulting not just by the predictable Mrs Pankhurst's WSPU but also by catholic supporters of the women's movement.[21] Sylvia Pankhurst insisted that newspaper moralising had simply prompted the police into greater diligence in making arrests with the consequence that the increase in convictions for female drunkenness was artificially inflated.[22] This contention was supported by the investigations of the NSPCC. Their inspectors reported in January 1915 that one hundred and twenty two of their branches had found that female drunkenness had decreased since the outbreak of war; in twenty six there had been an increase, but in twelve of these the situation was returning to normal. The society concluded that the charge made against soldiers' wives was 'a great slander'.[23]

Nevertheless the clergy, with very few exceptions,[24] were only too willing to believe the worst of working class women, and to maintain mental assumptions about female weakness of will which were to reach epic proportions of credulity in the totally bogus 'war babies' scandal of April 1915. In the earlier agitation about drunkenness nonconformists and Roman Catholics had expressed concern chiefly about the way in which the women chose to spend their money, but Anglican indignation was aroused particularly by the amount of money paid and the ease with which it was obtained. In fact the rates paid to soldiers' dependents had not changed since the Boer war but those with no other source of income could apply for supplementation to either the Soldiers' and Sailors' Families Association or the National Relief Fund. The latter was accused of 'setting out to destroy the very

[20] Burroughs p 152.

[21] *London Catholic Herald* 31 October, 14, 28 November 1914. On Brown see W. F. Brown, *Through Windows of Memory* (London 1946).

[22] B. Sylvia Pankhurst, *The Home Front* (London 1932) p 101.

[23] *G[lasgow] H[erald]* 11 January 1915.

[24] According to Edwyn Barclay, the clergy of south London believed the charge 'much exaggerated', *Challenge* 25 December 1914.

basis of Christian marriage' because it gave the same allowances to both married dependents and those whom Violet Markham called the 'unmarried wives' of soldiers.[25] The archbishop of Canterbury had urged the government to put a stop to this scandal but Lloyd George and his secretary-mistress Frances Stevenson thought his attitude 'a piece of blatant hypocrisy'.[26] Lloyd George consulted two leading free churchmen, the baptist J. H. Shakespeare and R. J. Campbell of the City Temple, both of whom he found 'very reasonable'. Further support came from the new Anglican paper *The Challenge* edited by Tissington Tatlow, secretary of the SCM, which held that 'the day is passed when the Church could insist on sacramental tests'.[27] But with the expansion of the army the problems became too great to be left to the charities and in framing the naval and war pensions act of November 1915 the government did follow the archbishop's advice and prescribed different ways of meeting the needs of the two groups of women dependents.[28]

If drunken women were letting their husbands down, drunken workers were letting the rest of the country down. When nine thousand engineers on the Clyde went on unofficial strike for more pay in February 1915, it was the signal for a generalised attack on working class irresponsibility.[29] At Bangor Lloyd George addressed a Sunday afternoon meeting of black-coated citizens 'most of whom had probably spent the morning in the tabernacles of dissent'.[30] In a speech rapturously received in free church circles, he asserted that 'drink is doing more damage in this war than all the German submarines put together' and specifically linked bad time-keeping and bad workmanship to over-indulgence in alcohol.

In fact the report which he later commissioned stated that no significant increase in drinking had occurred on the Clyde since the war began.[31] Why then did Lloyd George believe that it had? Two days before making the Bangor speech the chancellor had discussed

[25] Violet Markham, *Return Passage* (London 1953) p 148.
[26] Bell p 750; [*Lloyd George: A Diary by Frances Stevenson*, ed A. J. P.] Taylor (London 1971) p 6.
[27] *Challenge* 11 December 1914.
[28] Bell p 750.
[29] Walter Kendall, *The Revolutionary Movement in Britain 1900–21* (London 1969) cap 7 'Clydeside in Wartime'; [R. K.] Middlemas, [*The Clydesiders: A Left-Wing Struggle for Parliamentary Power*] (London 1965).
[30] *Manchester Guardian* 1 March 1915.
[31] *Report of the Committee on Bad Time Keeping,* Parliamentary Papers 1914–16, LV 220 p 3, 24.

what he should say with Dr Alexander Whyte, the distinguished minister of Free St George's, Edinburgh and principal of New College.[32] It seems likely that he was the source of Lloyd George's information. Dr and Mrs Whyte were in London for a few days and spent most of their time, as Mrs Whyte put it, 'in an attempt to get a little forward with our drink difficulties in Scotland',[33] Their son was liberal MP for Perth and parliamentary private secretary to the first lord of the admiralty Winston Churchill, who was at that time member for Dundee. They thus had access to the highest political and ecclesiastical circles and were evidently lobbying vociferously on behalf of the demands of the Scottish temperance movement.

This movement had been reinforced enormously by the experiences of war. As in England, concern had been aroused by the treating of soldiers and the alleged dissipations of soldiers' wives.[34] Glasgow provided the driving power of the movement, and looked naturally for help to the conservative leader Andrew Bonar Law, himself formerly a Glasgow iron-merchant, the son of a presbyterian manse, and a teetotaller. Frank Knight, minister of Hillhead united free church appealed to both Law and his predecessor A. J. Balfour in December 1914.[35] In January 1915 Sir Joseph Maclay, a Glasgow shipowner, urged Bonar Law to assure the government that drastic measures would not be opposed. Maclay pointed to the breadth of support for action in Scotland: all the parties and all the churches wanted wartime prohibition. Amongst the recent converts he mentioned Norman Maclean, minister of the wealthy and fashionable Park church ('and you know that that Church is not famed for Temperance').[36] Norman Maclean was a romantic highlander, florid and fervent in both the pulpit and the press. In an article in *The Scotsman*, re-published in his book *The Great Discovery*, he deplored the insufficient steps being taken to protect the homes of 'the men who are baring their breasts to the arrows, standing between us and death':

> When they come back, war-worn, to what will they return? To homes in which the fires are extinguished, the candles burnt down to the socket; the cupboards bare, the children famished and

[32] *Daily News* 1 March 1915; G. F. Barbour, *The Life of Alexander Whyte, D.D.* (London 1925) p 573.

[33] SCM A[rchives] (consulted at Annandale) Jane Whyte–T. Tatlow 17 March 1915.

[34] On soldiers see the discussion of Lord Tullibardine's letter to members of the Perth UF presbytery about the Scottish Horse, *GH* 7 January 1915.

[35] BM Bonar Law MS 35/4/42 G. A. F. Knight–A. Bonar Law 16 December 1914.

[36] *Ibid* 36/1/17 J. P. Maclay–A. Bonar Law 12 January 1915.

neglected? Is that to be the guerdon of their sacrifice; is it for that that they have gone down into hell? Surely it cannot be for that! A wave has passed over us, raising us to the realisation of the higher values of things. Words live for us now which were dead yesterday. A beam of light has fallen into the chamber of imagery, and the word *Temperance* has risen from the couch on which it lay dying, and it claims us for its own. Through it we can make the world know that we are worth fighting for – worth that the young, the strong, and the brave should take everything they hold dear – their ideals, their love, their little children unborn – and throw them into the trench, and there give themselves and their dreams to death for us. We must see to it that we are worthy of the sacrifice.[37]

Of the strength of feeling in Scotland as a whole, and Glasgow in particular, there were many manifestations. Prohibition was even advocated at a meeting of the Glasgow Catholic Socialist Society in January 1915 (though not all the members agreed)[38] and in February the reverend Colin M. Gibbs persuaded the Glasgow parish council to ask the government for stronger restrictions to protect women. A week later speeches by Knight and professor J. W. Gregory advocating wartime prohibition were published as a pamphlet and reached a large circulation. The *Spectator* saw the pamphlet as evidence of the great movement of opinion in Scotland and expressed sympathy.[39] On 22 February while the Clyde strike was still solid, a large meeting for wartime prohibition was held in the Merchants' Hall, Glasgow, and decided to send deputations to the prime minister and leader of the opposition. The meeting was a gathering of the business and academic communities, presided over by a retired professor of civil engineering, and attended by prominent shipowners and shipbuilders. A letter was read from Alexander Gracie, chairman of Fairfields shipbuilding company which complained of excessive drinking by his workers.[40] A fortnight later the secretary of the Scottish temperance league stirred the pot further by remarking:

[37] N. Maclean, *The Great Discovery* (Glasgow 1915) pp 148 *seq.* For another example of how Maclean's rhetoric could outrun his judgement see [Stuart] Mews, 'Kikuyu and Edinburgh [: the interaction of attitudes to two conferences'], *SCH* 7 (1971) pp 345–59.

[38] *Scottish Prohibitionist* 2 January 1915. On the society see Middlemas pp 36–40; Patrick J. Doyle, 'Religion, Politics and the Catholic Working Class', *New Blackfriars,* May 1973 pp 218–25.

[39] J. W. Gregory and G. A. Frank Knight, *A Plea for Prohibition during the War* (Glasgow 1915); *Spectator* 13 February 1915.

[40] *GH* 23 February 1915.

> In the widespread agitation for increased wages being waged in the shipbuilding industry, I sometimes wonder if either master or men have fully realized the great economic waste being caused by indulgence in strong drink.[41]

On the same day the distinguished Glasgow theologian James Denney informed Robertson Nicoll, editor of the *British Weekly* that a memorial to the prime minister to stop the sale of distilled liquors in Scotland during the war 'is having extraordinary support. Everyone to whom it is submitted seems willing to sign it – especially employers of labour, irrespective of party connections'.[42] The Scottish press reported all these developments and Mrs White was hardly divulging any secrets when she told Tissington Tatlow shortly after her visit to London and her husband's chat with Lloyd George, 'privately we hear that the reports from some of the ship-building yards in the West are so bad that there is bound to be action'.[43]

Despite the chancellor's bold words at Bangor, which built up the hopes of the temperance lobby, he was to take no action whatever for several weeks. When he did move it was in such a flurry of frenetic activity that some explanation apart from the earnest petitions of a slightly panicky Scottish bourgeoisie is required. The true explanation requires a shift of scene: from urban Glasgow with all the social problems and political unrest of the modern metropolis to rural Wales with its more traditional and possibly more vicious ecclesiastical and political divisions.

On 9 March 1915 the government had introduced into the house of lords without notice or consultation with its supporters, a bill to delay the disestablishment and disendowment of the Welsh church until six months after the end of the war.[44] It had passed through all its stages in a single day and on the very next day was brought before the commons. But for the pressure of government business, the Welsh church disestablishment act, the goal of a generation of nonconformist political effort would in the space of forty eight hours have been placed in jeopardy. For the bill aroused in Welsh nonconformist minds the great fear that if the election which had to be held immediately after the war were to install a conservative government

[41] *Ibid* 8 March 1915.

[42] J. Denney–W. R. Nicoll 8 March 1915, *Letters of Principal James Denney to W. Robertson Nicoll 1893–1917*, ed W. R. Nicoll (London 1920) p 245.

[43] SCMA J. Whyte–T. Tatlow 17 March 1915.

[44] [P. M. H.] Bell, *Disestablishment* [*in Ireland and Wales*] (London 1969) p 300.

in office, there would be nothing to prevent it from repealing an act which had not even begun to take effect.

Welsh disestablishment was the greatest nonconformist legislative victorv of the twentieth century but was little enough return for the energy and enthusiasm devoted to the liberal cause by free churchmen.[45] Now even this triumph looked as if it might be snatched away and changing circumstances suggested that any ground lost now would be unlikely to be re-captured later. In Wales despite the revival of 1904–5, itself a defensive reaction to the threat of alien cultural forces,[46] the chapels were increasingly conscious of declining power, especially in the industrial areas of the south. In the nineteenth century nonconformity had been 'the most important link between rural and industrial Wales',[47] but the depopulation of the rural areas and the movement into the mining valleys of workers from England, Scotland, and Ireland destroyed the shared values of town and country.[48] Welsh-speaking nonconformity was being turned into a rural religion with a set of traditional values which seemed out of place in the modern world.

In his autobiography Goronwy Rees – aged six in 1915 – has described the Aberystwyth of his boyhood. It was a small country town with an astonishing number of chapels and churches: 'On my way to school every day I passed a Salem, a Shiloh, a Tabernacle, a Bethel, and a Moriah; it was like taking a walk through the Middle East'. His father was a Calvinistic methodist minister 'and this made him a person of considerable importance in the town':

> Ours was a theocratic society, ruled by priests and elders; they formed a sort of unofficial Sanhedrin which exercised an absolute dictatorship over the morals and behaviour of the town.[49]

In the smug, claustrophobic society of small towns like Aberystwyth disestablishment mattered. It had been achieved in the very nick of time. It was the last act before the curtain finally fell on a world which we have lost.

The outbreak of war in 1914 provided a further challenge both to

[45] On free church disillusionment with politics: Stuart Mews, 'Puritanicalism, Sport and Race: A Symbolic Crusade of 1911', *SCH* 8 (1971) pp 303–31; Stephen Koss, *Nonconformity in Modern British Politics* (London 1975) cap 5.

[46] C. R. Williams, 'The Welsh Religious Revival 1904–5', *British Journal of Sociology* 3 (London 1952) p 242.

[47] David Williams, *A History of Modern Wales* (London 1950) p 246.

[48] J. Vyrnwy Morgan, *The War and Wales* (London 1916) p 282.

[49] Goronwy Rees, *A Bundle of Sensations* (London 1960) pp 19 *seq*.

nonconformist assumptions about human nature and to nonconformist claims in Wales. The chief justification for disestablishment was the overwhelming numerical preponderance of chapel-goers over church-goers. The records of enlistments in the army, however, suggested either that the figures presented in the royal commission had been fudged or that nonconformists were not pulling their weight in the defence of their country.[50] Robert Graves claimed that the reason Welsh-speakers were such rarities in the Royal Welch Regiment was because 'the chapels held soldiering to be sinful, and in Merioneth, the chapels had the last word. Prayers were offered for me by the chapels not because of the physical dangers I would run in France, but because of the moral dangers threatening me at home'.[51] Whatever the truth of these claims and impressions, the war created a situation in which the standing of the established church was enormously enhanced, while Welsh nonconformity could too easily be made to look mean, petty and unpatriotic. Moreover these same pressures were simultaneously undermining English support for Welsh nonconformist claims. 'What seems now to be desired', commented the Anglican *Guardian* of English nonconformity, 'is not so much the disestablishment of one communion, but the equal establishment of all'. Though free churchmen would not admit it, 'the war is only one of the links which have bound them more and more closely to the state'.[52]

The schizoid nature of the free church mind at this time was well illustrated when its national council met in Manchester on the day after the introduction of the bill. It was bitterly denounced, mainly by speakers from Wales, but this demonstration of wrath had to be cut short so that the delegates could get to the cathedral in time for an ecumenical service arranged for them by the dean. In Cambridge T. R. Glover, fellow of St John's and a baptist stalwart, felt 'upset' at the government's 'surrender . . . after all that has been done'.[53] But Robertson Nicoll was 'furious' at what he saw as a 'betrayal of the Dissenters'. His *British Weekly* noting the 'general amazement and consternation' called for 'unrelenting opposition'.[54] On this occasion

[50] The official statistics of religious affiliation in the 38th division from Wales in August 1916 were 63% church of England, 32% nonconformist, 6% Roman catholic. For the difficulties this caused in the provision of chaplains see Stuart Mews, 'Religion and English Society in the First World War' (unpubl Cambridge PhD thesis 1973) pp 196–9.

[51] Robert Graves, *Goodbye To All That* (London 1966) pp 70 *seq*.

[52] *Guardian* 25 March 1915.

[53] Diary of T. R. Glover (courtesy of Miss A. Glover) 10 March 1915.

[54] [*Lord*] *Riddell's* [*War*] *Diary* [*1914–18*] (London 1933) 10 March 1915 p 68; *B*[*ritish*] *W*[*eekly*] 11 March 1915.

Lloyd George's 'usual intuition . . . seems to have failed him', divined Beriah Evans, a journalist once editor of one of the chancellor's Welsh papers but increasingly distrustful of his former master's commitment to Welsh national interests. 'This was the last straw', Evans wrote, 'it overstrained the patience of even the submissive Welsh members'. In response to a great wave of resentment which swept through Welsh nonconformity, the Welsh parliamentary party 'for once took a bold and determined stand against Mr Lloyd George and the government'.[55]

When the bill came up again in the commons on 15 March Lloyd George tried to talk his old colleagues round. Once again the business was badly mismanaged. Immediately preceding it on the order paper was a naval bill sent down from the house of lords. Unfortunately it included an amendment moved by the archbishop of Canterbury to make it illegal for a sailor's marriage to take place in a nonconformist chapel if the banns had been read in an Anglican church. At the very mention of the archbishop's name 'loud ironic cheers arose' and the debate had to be hastily adjourned. After this unpromising beginning the house turned its attention to the Welsh church bill. Lord Robert Cecil spoke 'gently as a cooing dove', noted the *Daily News*, but any eirenic atmosphere created was soon dispelled when Ormsby Gore began taunting Sir Alfred Mond, the German-Jewish member for Swansea: 'What has this representative of Welsh nonconformity done for the British army?'[56] Now the fat was in the fire and the house witnessed 'a strange, almost grotesque revival of the Welsh Church controversy in the midst of war.'[57] Even Lloyd George with all his debating skill failed to make any impression. 'At one point his voice broke under stress of his emotions', reported the *British Weekly* 'and he claimed the indulgence of the House on the ground that the matter vitally affected him as he counted the good opinion of his native country Wales more than anybody in the whole world'.[58] 'Went for the Welsh MPs' he wrote home to his wife, 'They are a poor lot of hounds. They thoroughly misrepresent the Bill. It is a *very* small

[55] [Beriah] Evans, [*The Life Romance of Lloyd George*] (London nd-1915?) pp 124, 123. Eight years earlier Lloyd George had written in the margin of a letter to Robertson Nicoll: '"B" is the jobbing journalist I refer to in my interview as a manufacturer of revolt copy – his full name is Beriah G. Evans', National Library of Scotland MS 5666 D. Lloyd George–W. R. Nicoll 6 October 1907; Kenneth O. Morgan, *Wales in British Politics 1868–1922* (Cardiff 1970) p 102 n.

[56] *Daily News* 16 March 1915.

[57] Bell, *Disestablishment* p 300.

[58] *BW* 18 March 1915.

concession for the sake of Unity'.[59] One of Lloyd George's colleagues claimed that the general feeling of the house was that this was 'one of the pluckiest speeches' he had ever made,[60] but it did not persuade the Welsh members and the virulence of their opposition caused Asquith to defer the vote and promise a further debate. Nor did Lloyd George convince the leaders of the disestablishment movement outside the house. 'What a gas-bag speech George made on Monday night!' wrote John Massie, president of the Liberation Society and congregational minister, formerly a Mansfield college tutor and briefly a liberal MP. Massie was thoroughly disenchanted with Lloyd George. Behind the postponement proposal he saw the sinister hand of the church tories who, he claimed, had already persuaded Sir Henry Lunn ('the self-advertising Lunn') to petition for the removal of the disendowment clauses. 'George's trapping of the P.M. is just enabling the Robert Cecil lot to step back for a final leap'.[61]

The Robert Cecil 'lot' did indeed want to take the final leap and repeal the act in its entirety but Massie's reading of the situation was an oversimplification. On the church side there were three significant groups which did not always pull together. There were the English bishops, the bishops in Wales, and those Anglicans in parliament who had a special interest in this particular cause. Unlike the other two groups, the church tories were conscious of both the ecclesiastical *and* political dimensions of the question. They wanted not only to save the Welsh church but also to bring down the liberal government, and they knew that in some areas it was still possible to work up a politically advantageous agitation on the theme of church defence. Archbishop Lang had been immensely impressed by the great demonstration against the Welsh church bill held in York in the summer of 1913. The minster had been crowded from end to end and afterwards the market place packed with what is said to have been 'the largest crowd seen there for more than a generation'.[62] In 1914 a report on liberal electoral prospects in the Howdenshire division of the east riding of Yorkshire stated that the country clergy were exerting themselves to 'poison the minds' of their flocks. In several villages it was reported

[59] D.–M. Lloyd George 15 March 1915, *Lloyd George Family Letters 1885–1936*, ed Kenneth O. Morgan (Cardiff/London 1973) p 176.

[60] [Christopher] Addison, [*Four and a Half Years*, 1] (London 1934) p 70.

[61] N[ational] L[ibrary of] W[ales] Griffith MS 468 J. Massie–E. Griffith 19 March 1915.

[62] [Hickleton,] Halifax MS A4.259 C. G. Lang–Lord Halifax 26 June 1913.

that 'our vicar says' that the liberals were killing religion in Wales 'and shutting up all the churches'.[63]

Once the bill had been passed, some English bishops like Edward Talbot of Winchester, were prepared to accept it but wanted to work for minor adjustments to enable the new body to function efficiently, but the Welsh bishops encouraged by the church tories to believe that total repeal was just around the corner, were reluctant to acquiesce or compromise.[64] Bishop Talbot had been dissuaded from writing to *The Times* in October 1914 by Lord Robert Cecil but he did write privately to Lloyd George about the financial difficulties which would be caused by the gradual removal of the church's pre-1662 endowments at a time when wartime conditions made it impossible to build up a capital fund to take their place. In all his dealings about the Welsh church Talbot stressed the need to overcome the divisions of the past. He told Lord Hugh Cecil that he was 'not just after pickings for the Church' but wanted to demonstrate the new temper arising through co-operation in the war'. Though a strict high churchman Talbot was an enthusiast for the ideal of church unity, a conviction which had been strengthened by his connections with the student Christian movement and the Edinburgh missionary conference of 1910. In January 1915 he did write to *The Times* along these lines and was supported by the veteran nonconformist minister Arnold Thomas of Bristol.[65] Meanwhile Sir Henry Lunn, a prominent Wesleyan who supported disestablishment but not disendowment, had offered to organise a petition of English nonconformists if the Cecils and their friends would help to defray the costs. The Cecils were not over-enthusiastic and sent him off to the ECU office where he was told that it was 'quite impossible to raise £200 just now from any rich man in the Church of England'. Lunn persevered and winkled out enough small subscriptions to proceed. The duke of Devonshire contributed £25 but expressed his doubts to Lord Hugh Cecil about whether the rest of the bill would be repealed if disendowment was deleted.[66]

[63] [House of Lords Library] Lloyd George MS: 'Report on Howdenshire Division' 12 May 1914. See also *Newcastle Daily Journal* 24 March 1914.

[64] Halifax MS A4.267 Lord Salisbury–Lord Halifax 15 August 1914.

[65] Bodleian Selborne MS 90/11 Lord Robert Cecil–Lord Selborne 18 August 1914; Lloyd George MS C/11/2/4 E. S. Talbot–D. Lloyd George 18 August 1914; Hatfield MS Qui 18/161 E. S. Talbot–Lord Hugh Cecil 30 December 1914; Mews, 'Kikuyu and Edinburgh' pp 348 *seq; Times* 12 January 1915.

[66] Hatfield MS Qui 18/129 Sir H. Lunn–Lord H. Cecil 4 December, Qui 18/150 Lunn–Cecil 17 December; Qui 18/153 Lunn–Cecil 25 December 1914; Qui 18/159 Duke

To head off this possibility and take advantage of the more favourable climate created by Lunn's petition, the duke proposed in the house of lords on 9 January 1915 that the act as a whole should be postponed until the end of the war. Government ministers met the unionist leaders and agreed that if the duke would withdraw his bill, they would introduce their own. The government's bill was based on a memorandum submitted to Asquith by the home secretary Reginald McKenna. He later explained to the Welsh nonconformist members when they complained about the lack of consultation that it had never occurred to him that the prime minister would act so quickly, but his critics noted that 'there is no question that McKenna has behaved very cryptically' and 'his anger was not impressive'.[67]

Lloyd George blamed McKenna for muddling the business but there was a widespread belief in Wales that the chancellor must have known what was going on. Even such an old friend as John Williams of Brynsiencyn, the greatest Welsh preacher of the day, who had stood by Lloyd George during the Marconi scandal, now described the bill (in Welsh) as 'an inexcusable betrayal of Wales'; Lloyd George would have to produce something better than another soothing speech at the pavilion (his usual stamping ground in his constituency) to explain away this treachery.[68] The executive of the Welsh national liberal association was due to meet at Llandrindod Wells on 30 March and there was no doubt about the main item on the agenda. Of course Lloyd George had been in hot water before, but this time it had reached boiling point. Could he escape unscathed yet again? 'I earnestly hope that George will not bamboozle the Welsh Party', wrote John Massie none too confidently. 'He will play low down to do it. But we trust you to stand to your guns'.[69]

In the breathing space between the commons debate on 15 March and the Welsh executive on 30 March Lloyd George worked ferociously. Supporters of the government pointed out that there was one

---

of Devonshire–Lord H. Cecil 28 December 1914. See also Sir Henry S. Lunn, *Chapters From My Life* (London 1918) cap 22.

[67] Davidson MS, 'Memorandum on the Welsh Church Question', 1918; A. G. Edwards, Archbishop of Wales, *Memories* (London 1927) cap 13; Eluned E. Owen, *The Later Life of Bishop Owen. A Son of Wales* (Llandyssul 1961) cap 21; Sir Almeric Fitzroy, *Memoirs* 2 (London nd) pp 586, 590.

[68] In fact Lloyd George denied any knowledge of what had been happening: *The Political Diaries of C. P. Scott 1911–28*, ed Trevor Wilson (London 1970) p 119; *Holyhead Mail* 8 August 1913; Griffith MS 503: John Williams–Ellis Griffith 17 March 1915.

[69] Griffith MS 468 J. Massie–E. Griffith 19 March 1915.

issue which outran the disestablishment question in the chapel-dominated communities of nonconformist Wales – the drink question: 'I feel that if you can see your way to take strong action in regard to the licensing question, really recognising the advanced condition of opinion in Wales', advised one Liberal MP, 'you would do a great deal to create an atmosphere in which the Church controversy would dwindle greatly alike in difficulty and acrimony'.[70] Tackling the drink question would not only salve the nonconformist conscience but might also be a means of vindicating the honour of nonconformist Wales. Speakers at Welsh recruiting rallies were trying hard to sell a new image of the army. 'The Army was a profession they could now adopt with dignity', said Sir Edward Pryse at Aberystwyth in 1914; 'it was composed of gallant young men, and the old vice of drunkenness had been done away with practically, and the bulk of the men were now teetotallers'.[71] If Lloyd George could give substance to that illusion he could yet be the saviour of Wales.

The temperance card was clearly the one to play, but Lloyd George rightly sensed that words alone were not enough. In the field of temperance reform no proposals were practicable which were not acceptable to the trades unions. On 17 March he took advantage of a meeting with union representatives to secure their agreement for new restrictions if two conditions were met: there had to be sufficient evidence to justify the proposals, and they should be applied equally to all classes. Having got so far, the chancellor's next task was to outline proposals, manufacture the evidence to justify them, and to awaken public opinion in support of them.

On the same day that Lloyd George was coaxing the trades unionists into accepting further controls on drink Mrs Jane Whyte was once again busily lobbying on behalf of the Scottish temperance movement. She wrote to Tissington Tatlow passing on a complaint she had several times heard in Scotland: 'why does the Church of England do nothing?' She also persuaded J. H. Oldham, secretary of the continuation committee of the Edinburgh missionary conference of 1910 to approach the bishop of Winchester. He told Talbot that when the prime minister had received the petition for prohibition from Glasgow he had said that firm action needed the strong backing of public opinion. Oldham had been shown a letter from the government chief whip forecasting bold measures from Lloyd George 'if he feels that

[70] NLW E. T. John MS, E. T. John–R. McKenna 22 March 1915.

[71] Newspaper cutting in Griffith MS 149.

public opinion will support him'. Two moulders of public opinion in the tory press, J. L. Garvin and Lord Northcliffe, were prepared to support a popular agitation if it once got underway. Unfortunately 'the Liberal press has been very half-hearted in its support of what Lloyd George said, and . . . it is not possible for the Tory press under these circumstances to initiate a campaign.' It was obvious from Lloyd George's trades union meeting the previous day that the government was angling for the support of labour. 'I cannot help thinking, however, that knowledge that the Church was with them would greatly strengthen their hands.' Tatlow also wrote to Talbot to reinforce Oldham's plea but it fell on stony ground. The bishop of Winchester had been staying with the archbishop of Canterbury and learned that he had already discussed the matter with the prime minister. Asquith had characteristically assured him that there was no need to rouse public opinion. But then Asquith never did pay much attention to popular outbursts, and was even less likely to be influenced by a storm got up in favour of proposals which he felt were radically unsound. Oldham had wanted to avoid resurrecting the old teetotal versus anti-teetotal arguments by resting his case solely on the claims of national efficiency. But Davidson and Talbot 'felt rather strongly that it is not the Church's special business to urge restrictions in the interests of war materials.' Moreover they agreed with Asquith that general measures which did not take into account local circumstances were unwise. But this was just the opposite of Oldham's opinion. Limitations only on munition areas implied a slur on the men involved. Why should not the west-end clubs accept the same limitations? 'After all this is a national affair. We don't want to pillory certain sections of the population but to submit to an act of national discipline'. This was also the view of William Temple, who was always rigorous on moral questions: he favoured total wartime prohibition as an act of national self-sacrifice. But though the archbishop was ready for personal self-sacrifice, he was not willing to advocate sacrifice by government decree. Nor did he take to Tatlow's suggestion that an interdenominational meeting should be called at Lambeth on the same lines as those called at the beginning of the war to thrash the matter out.[72]

Asquith, Davidson and Talbot were right to be sceptical of the breadth and spontaneity of the demands for new temperance legislation. In his private diary, Sir J. Herbert Lewis, a liberal and free church

[72] SCMA J. Whyte–T. Tatlow 17 March 1915; J. H. Oldham–T. Tatlow 18 March 1915; T. Tatlow–E. S. Talbot 22 March 1915; E. S. Talbot–T. Tatlow 26 March 1915.

MP, and lifelong disciple of Lloyd George, let the cat out of the bag about his master's methods. 'In his own astute way he worked up interviews and a press agitation to obtain the necessary driving power'. The grand climax came on 29 March, the very eve of the Llandrindod meeting, when a deputation of the shipbuilding employer's federation met the chancellor ('probably at his own instigation' noted Lewis) and requested total wartime prohibition 'We are fighting Germany, Austria and Drink', thundered Lloyd George in a speech which every member of the Welsh executive could read on the morning of their meeting, 'and, as far as I can see, the greatest of these deadly foes is Drink'.[73] The conversion of the shipbuilders to prohibition was impressive enough, but the chancellor had an even bigger rabbit yet to pull out of the hat.

On the same day that he met the shipbuilding employers, Lloyd George had earlier had an audience with king George V. According to the royal biographer Harold Nicolson, he had 'bustled into the King's audience room, his little arms swinging with excitement, his eyes flashing flame, his lower lip protruding with scorn of those who drank'.[74] In the Bangor speech the chancellor had held up the example of czar Nicholas. He had been told that the royal example had been a major influence in making the prohibition of vodka acceptable in Russia. Now he told king George that 'it would be much easier to apply coercive measures if he took the lead by announcing that he proposed to be a total abstainer during the War'. 'He was impressed', Lloyd George reported to his uncle, adding later, 'whilst I have been engaged all day on this gigantic problem I suppose my Welsh teetotal friends are engaged in nagging at me in Rhyl. God help the country that is under their care'.[75]

Immediately after the shipbuilders had departed the chancellor sent an account of the meeting to Buckingham palace in which he stressed that the situation was deteriorating and that any remedy must apply to all classes of the community: 'it was most important that the workmen should not imagine that drink was to be forbidden them whilst the rich were to be permitted still to indulge'.[76] Lord Stamfordham replied immediately on the king's behalf:

[73] [NLW J. H.] Lewis [MS 231], Diary of 23 October 1915; 30 March 1915. Hazlehurst p 212; *Times* 30 March 1915.

[74] Sir Harold Nicholson, *King George the Fifth. His Life and Reign* (London 1952) p 261.

[75] William George, *My Brother and I* (London 1958) p 249.

[76] R[oyal] A[rchives] GV Q762/12 D. Lloyd George–Lord Stamfordham 29 March 1915.

> I am to add that if it be deemed advisable the king will be prepared to set the example by giving up all alcoholic liquors himself and issuing orders against its consumption in the Royal Household, so that no difference shall be made so far as His Majesty is concerned between the treatment of rich and poor in this question.[77]

Lloyd George read the king's letter to the cabinet and according to his reply to the palace 'they felt that if the King took the lead in the matter the nation would follow him'.[78] However the prime minister did not share this optimistic assessment: 'the country will not stand prohibition', he insisted, 'it isn't feasible'. Frances Stevenson suggested the real reason was that he himself was not prepared 'to give up his wine and whisky'. Later that day he sent for the chancellor and said, 'About that King thing – I would not play that card yet if I were you'. Lloyd George then explained that even under prohibition it would always be possible to get alcoholic drinks with a doctor's certificate. This seemed to lift a burden from the prime minister's mind and he gave his permission for the king's letter to be sent to the press.[79]

The king's pledge, as it came to be known was the high point of Lloyd George's campaign. It horrified the archbishop of Canterbury. Randall Davidson's career owed much to the patronage of the court. As dean of Windsor he had put that career at some risk in an attempt to save queen Victoria from looking ridiculous when he opposed the publication of a further volume of her highland diaries. The possibility of her grandson now being made into a laughing-stock troubled the archbishop deeply. He was also somewhat embarrassed. Lloyd George was asking the heads of the professions, the bar, medicine and the church, to follow the king's lead and urge their colleagues and subordinates to join them. But the archbishop of Canterbury had already ruled out such action. Shortly after the Bangor speech, a suggestion had been made in *The Times* by Sir Edward Clarke, president of the national church league, and a former conservative law officer, that the Anglican clergy should make a great united act of patriotic self-denial by pledging themselves to wartime abstinence. The proposal was applauded by the bishops of Croydon and Durham but briskly denounced by the dean of Durham, Hensley Henson, as both irrational and ineffective. The idea had been similarly dismissed

[77] RA GV Q712/14 Lord Stamfordham–D. Lloyd George 30 March 1915.
[78] RA GV Q762/15 D. Lloyd George–Lord Stamfordham 30 March 1915.
[79] Taylor p 39.

by the archbishop because 'the fact of every bishop, priest, and deacon in the country becoming a teetotaller would not in the smallest degree impress the popular imagination.'[80] How, then, would he react to the king's request? His difficulty was enhanced by a profound conviction that the king had been both misled and misunderstood. The royal message was conditional – '*if* it be deemed advisable' – and was intended to demonstrate that the king would personally share any restrictions imposed by the government upon his subjects. But the message was being interpreted to mean that the king had already given up alcohol which he had not. To avoid the possibility of accusations of hypocrisy, the king now gave orders that no alcoholic drinks were to be served in the royal household. At Windsor castle the servants decorated the cellar-door with black crepe.[81] Two former prime ministers Rosebery and Balfour, both thought that the king had been disgracefully treated and the archbishop tried to shield him from further exploitation. The archbishop was not very receptive to the idea that the king should be invited to attend temperance meetings and that further declarations in favour of prohibition should be issued from Buckingham palace. The king's secretary thanked him for suggesting that 'no notice' be taken of the bishop of Willesden's letter.[82] But in response to a request from the king, Davidson did try to issue an appeal signed by the leaders of all the churches, though cardinal Bourne took some time before he agreed to add his name.

The secretary of the free church council, F. B. Meyer, wrote to ministers suggesting a king's pledge Sunday on which they could urge their congregations to follow the royal lead, but in at least one Lancashire town this was regarded as quite superfluous: 'We should be wasting our effort inasmuch as the vast majority of our folk are pledged abstainers already'. The *Tablet* testified to Roman catholic scepticism about the pledge.

> A professor in the seclusion of the Athenaeum, may give up his accustomed pint of claret, and a clergyman in his lonely parsonage may deny himself his glass of whisky-and-water, but in what possible way can these changes serve for an example to the workmen on the Clyde?

[80] RA GV Q762/19 D. Lloyd George–Lord Stamfordham 1 April 1915; Davidson MS G. K. A. Bell–R. T. Davidson 1 April 1915; Lord Stamfordham–R. T. Davidson 6 April 1915; *Times* 5, 6, 8, 19 March 1915; *Guardian* 25 March 1915.

[81] [Durham Chapter Library MS, Diary of H. H.] Henson 29 April 1915.

[82] Davidson MS R. T. Davidson–C. F. Harford 10 April; *ibid* Lord Stamfordham–R. T. Davidson 1 April 1915.

There seemed to be too little connection between the suggested privation and the public example.[83]

That was precisely the view of Hensley Henson. 'This is a strange proceeding', he observed when he read of the king's pledge, 'and creates a situation of some difficulty for the loyal subject who dissents from the royal example':

> What ought the Dean of Durham to do? All that loyalty rightly demands he must take the lead in doing, but does a self-respecting loyalty require him to admit the governing lead of the King's example within his own house? Does not his duty rather require him publicly to differentiate loyalty from such servility? And is not the consideration the more cogent in his case since the King is the author of 'preferment', and any demonstration of independence on his part may affect adversely the Royal mind?

Two days later Henson records: 'We drank champagne in spite of the King's example'.[84]

A fortnight later Henson was in London to be invested as grand chaplain of a masonic order. He spent some time at the Athenaeum where he found everyone drinking wine, and bumped into Lord Halifax, a long-standing opponent on almost every conceivable ecclesiastical question. But on this matter they were united; indeed Halifax was quite adamant: '*I* shall not give up my beer – It ought never to have got the encouragement it has from the archbishop of Canterbury'. Halifax could not, however, control the tables of his hosts. The warden of Keble, to his delight, continued to serve alcohol but archbishop Lang offered lemonade and archbishop Davidson could only manage water. On his next visit to Lambeth palace Halifax took with him a secret supply of whisky, and after retiring to his bedroom for the night began a small drinking-party with a fellow guest. All was in full swing when a knock on the door revealed an embarrassed archbishop seeking a few final words with his equally embarrassed noble guest.[85]

In the week before the king made his decision Lloyd George was attempting to represent the Welsh church postponement bill to his fellow country-men as a bargaining counter which could be used to prise temperance reform from an unwilling tory party. John Williams

[83] *Burnley News* 24 April 1915, but for a more optimistic assessment see E. K. H. Jordan *Free Church Unity* (London 1956) p 147; *Tablet* 10 April 1915.

[84] Henson 6 April 1915.

[85] *Ibid* 29 April 1915; Halifax MS A.40214 Lord Halifax–H. W. Hill 7 April 1915; Lockhart pp 237–8.

of Brynsiencyn was invited to 11 Downing Street on 24 March and told that a new licensing bill could be got through because the brewers could no longer count on conservative support. But he was warned, if the Welsh postponement measure were to be withdrawn, the tories would say ' "Very well, have things your own way, but you give way to your friends, we must give way to our friends" and goodbye to the best chance of carrying Temperance reform we have had in our generation.'[86] It was this argument which Herbert Lewis presented at the Llandrindod Wells meeting on Lloyd George's behalf. It is a measure of the force of what Beriah Evans called 'such subterranean rumblings as portended an earthquake' that despite the Welsh wizard's earnest attempts to shift the scenery of the political stage, a decision was taken to oppose the postponement bill, a decision which was to result in July in its withdrawal.[87]

The decision was as much a vote of no confidence in Lloyd George as a revolt against the government. It was now even more vital for the chancellor to put his own personal stamp on some major measure of liquor control if his rocking throne in Wales was to be steadied. In his view the refusal of the house of commons to follow the royal gesture by closing its bars doomed the voluntary approach and some form of state intervention was unavoidable.

Lloyd George called the bishop of Lincoln to the treasury on 12 April and outlined to him a drastic solution. He wanted to nationalise the pubs and breweries and to prohibit altogether the sale of spirits.[88] He believed that he could carry this plan through parliament because he had the acquiescence of the brewers and the conservative leaders. Unfortunately he had not taken sufficient account of the sectarian divisions of the temperance movement and of the absolute refusal of some of its most influential leaders to countenance state purchase in any shape or form. The bishop of Lincoln, when mesmerised by Lloyd George had seen state purchase as a step towards the obtaining of local veto, but his friends in the United Kingdom Alliance soon convinced him that he was mistaken and should come out in opposition.

The UKA has been described as 'essentially a protesting body' which 'conceived of prohibition in millenial terms'.[89] The tenacity with which

[86] Lewis 24 March 1915.

[87] Evans p 220; Lewis 30 March 1915; Bell, *Disestablishment* p 301.

[88] Hicks 12 April 1915.

[89] Brian Harrison, *Drink and the Victorians. The Temperance Question In England 1815–72* (London 1971) pp 375, 372.

the more extreme wing of the temperance movement held to its single-minded and narrow objectives, together with their defective political sense, made it unlikely that they would accept any half-measures; indeed they were likely to be more hostile to temperance plans which diverged from their own pet schemes.

'A powerful section of temperance advocates were up in arms against the abhorrent suggestion that the State should sully its soul by becoming the manufacturer and distributor of alcoholic poison', recalled Lloyd George. 'The conscience of the devotee is an eccentric thing and argument never converts but only exasperates a true believer. The resistance of this section grew.'[90] Leaflets headed 'Lloyd George, Publican' were produced by some teetotal fanatics, and something of the flavour of the UKA's political style can be ascertained from its secretary, G. B. Wilson's address, to the free church council in the summer of 1915. Even if state purchase were to halve the consumption of drink it must be resisted. Under nationalisation 'it will be your hands that . . . pass the drink into the hands of your brother or sister trembling with eager unholy excitement for the deadly draught. . . . All these ruined souls will be *your* servants for whom you must answer to Almighty God!' To accept such a scheme would be to abandon hope just when 'the promised land lies before us.'[91]

The churches were divided in their attitude. When rumours were still flying about the nature of the proposals to be put to parliament Anglican opinion seemed to veer towards state purchase which was supported by the convocation of York. Free church opinion, however, was fragmented and the council's general committee could only produce an anaemic resolution which avoided favouring any particular scheme. The president of the free church council, Sir Joseph Compton Rickett, a liberal MP and congregationalist layman, was bitterly criticised for making several speeches in favour of nationalisation and against prohibition. The president of the UKA Leif Jones, a liberal MP also and son of a Welsh congregational minister, was horrified to observe the free church president turning 'from advocating the disestablishment and disendowment of the church in order to preach to the country the establishment and endowment of the liquor trade'.[92]

[90] [D.] Lloyd George, [*War Memoirs*, 1] (London 1934) p 197.

[91] Quoted in Norman Longmate, *The Water Drinkers* (London 1968) p 267.

[92] *Manchester Guardian* 22, 29 April 1915; F. A. Iremonger, *William Temple* (London 1948) p 179; national free church council minutes of general committee no 9, 11 June 1915; Leif Jones, *Why Leave the Straight Road? A Warning to Temperance Reformers* (London 1915) p 3.

The determination of the UKA to campaign actively against Lloyd George's plan provided Asquith with good grounds for killing it. The UKA secretary claimed that the announcement of the movement's opposition at a crucial moment in the cabinet discussion was a major factor in the abandonment of the scheme: 'they threatened the most extreme action in the House of Commons', noted Herbert Lewis. According to Lloyd George the prime minister 'feared serious trouble inside the party.'[93] But though Asquith was justified in refusing to proceed with controversial legislation in wartime, he had serious practical objections to the scheme. He was disturbed by the heavy cost involved and disliked the opportunities for corruption which would be opened up by such a vast extension of state ownership and patronage. Nor was he convinced by Lloyd George of the necessity for such drastic action. When the archbishop of Canterbury had discussed the matter with him in March, the prime minister had asked for further evidence. This the archbishop had gone to some lengths to collect by writing to clergymen in industrial centres, ports and garrison towns. Most were in favour of some additional restrictions but there were sufficient exceptions to raise doubts about wholesale measures. The bishop of Sheffield, for example, considered 'the attitude of the Sheffield Armament men is beyond all praise' and was opposed to further action. F. O. T. Hawkes, vicar of Aldershot suggested only bringing forward closing time by one hour, adding 'there is not a great deal of drunkenness now'.[94]

The proposals which Asquith and his cabinet eventually allowed Lloyd George to put before the commons fell far short of the original plan. On 24 April 1915 the chancellor proposed an amendment to the defence of the realm act which would set up a central control board to regulate entirely the supply of alcohol in munition-making areas. By the end of 1916 the whole country apart from a few rural areas had passed under its supervision. In most places the board instituted the shortest drinking hours ever known, made treating illegal, diluted the strength of spirits, and began the great 'Carlisle experiment' in which the state purchase plan was put into operation in an area of fifty square miles. Despite the doubts of both friends and foes of the temperance cause, the total consumption of absolute alcohol in Great Britain

[93] George B. Wilson, *Looking Back* (London 1944) p 17; Lewis 23 October 1915; Lloyd George p 198.

[94] Lloyd George MS C/6/11/38 R. T. Davidson–H. H. Asquith 30 March 1915.

dropped from eighty nine million gallons in 1914 to thirty seven million in 1918.[95]

The first world war had three long years yet to run, and at various times calls were heard for further action to restrict the manufacture and sale of drink, particularly in 1917 when there was a severe shortage of grain and sugar. By that time, however, Lloyd George had gone off the subject. He always insisted that it was in 1915 that the golden opportunity for a final solution had presented itself and been lost. According to Robertson Nicoll, he blamed the nonconformists, presumably because most of the members of the UKA were nonconformists. The UKA secretary blamed the churches in general for not coming out whole-heartedly for total prohibition. The bishop of Lincoln blamed Asquith. 'What a touchstone the "Drink" question is!' observed bishop Hicks. For him it was the decisive factor in weighing the worth of national leaders. 'Asquith will not give up his liquor', he told C. P. Scott, 'this is the bottom of it', but Lloyd George 'is the biggest and best man of them all'.[96] This conclusion was also beginning to dawn on some of the unionist leaders. Lloyd George's attack on his supporters in the commons over the Welsh church and his consultations with the opposition in March created such a favourable impression that Lord Beaverbrook believed that 'the "Drink" problem smoothed the way towards Coalition'.[97] It did not, however, smooth the way for Lloyd George in Wales. In October 1915 Herbert Lewis noted that when Lloyd George's name had been mentioned at the Liverpool meetings of the North Wales temperance association 'there was not the faintest breath of applause and the same was the case at a meeting . . . at Llanelly'. Lewis did not attribute his hero's fall from grace directly to the events of the spring, he knew that 'at temperance meetings people think about other things than temperance'. In Liverpool there had been Welsh liberals who hated Lord Northcliffe and drew their own conclusions from his newly developed friendship with Lloyd George 'Lloyd George's old supporters think a man is

[95] Henry Carter, *The Control of the Drink Trade. A Contribution to National Efficiency 1915–17* (London 1918); Michael E. Rose, 'The Success of Social Reform? The Central Control Board (Liquor Traffic) 1915-21', *War and Society*, ed M. R. D. Foot (London 1973) pp 71–84.

[96] W. R. Nicoll–J. D. Jones 22 October 1915 quoted in J. D. Jones, *Three Score Years and Ten* (London 1940) pp 232 *seq;* G. B. Wilson, *Nationalisation of the Liquor Trade. Ought the Churches to Advocate it?* (London 1915) p 6; BM Scott MS 50908/82 E. L. Hicks–C. P. Scott 7 May 1915.

[97] Beaverbrook p 74.

known by the company he keeps, and they don't like the company'.[98]

In analysing this episode it is important not to be so overwhelmed by the larger than life personalities that we ignore the social realities of the situation. Lloyd George was only able to manipulate events by playing upon the very real fears, anxieties and frustrations of an influential section of the British people. The precariousness of existence, so often commented upon by Edwardian social pessimists now found concrete reinforcement in the failure of the British armies to defeat the Germans.[99] The Bangor speech had forged the link between the threat from without and the threat from within. At a time when some explanation was required for national failure, the focus on drink provided a framework through which the wider crisis could be perceived and acted upon. The drink agitation should not be isolated as an amusing, quixotic interlude but seen as one of a series of moral panics which swept British society both before and during the first world war. As such it should be viewed both historically and laterally. In fact it had two histories. The first would locate it in a succession of moral reform crusades; the second would associate it with a much wider and more ferocious right wing reaction which in Edwardian times had been manifest in the anti-aliens campaign, the naval scare, Lord Roberts' call for conscription, and the quest for national efficiency.[100] In the 1915 campaign the moral authoritarianism of the temperance movement merged with the political authoritarianism of the right-wing diehards for whom the so-called drink problem was only one element in a wider ideological crusade to mobilise British society against both the internal and external enemy. The desire to deprive women and workers of drink was part of an attempt to put the clock back, to clean up Britain, to make England worth fighting for, to make England worthy of victory.

[98] Lewis 23 October 1915.

[99] For a thorough discussion of Edwardian social pessimism see Hynes *passim*. David Newsome, 'The Assault on Mammon: Charles Gore and John Neville Figgis', *JEH* 17, 2 (1966) pp 227–41. For an example see Neville S. Talbot, 'The Modern Situation', *Foundations. A Statement of Christian Belief in Terms of Modern Thought*, ed B. H. Streeter (London 1912) cap 1.

[100] On moral panics see Stanley Cohen, *Folk Devils and Moral Panics* (London 1972). Cohen's work has been brilliantly utilised by Stuart Hall, 'Racism and Reaction', *Five Views of Multi-Racial Britain* (London 1978). In this section of my paper the influence of Hall's talk will be obvious. For Edwardian social panics: Bernard Gainer, *The Alien Invasion* (London 1972); Stuart Mews, 'Religion and Conscription 1906–16' (paper delivered to the conference of the Commission Internationale d'histoire Ecclésiastique Comparée at the university of Uppsala, 1977).

Finally, it should be mentioned that there was one man who after this incident could never forget and could never forgive Lloyd George. King George V, ostensibly left high and literally dry for the duration of the war, for the rest of his life nursed a grievance. On 1 April 1922, the seventh anniversary of the announcement of the king's pledge, he moaned not for the first time about it to Hensley Henson, now bishop of Durham. But on this occasion he revealed to Henson that he had in fact continued to drink his normal amount 'under doctor's orders' but had had to do so privately and been unable to offer drink to his guests.[101] So even the king can not be absolved from that 'humbug and hypocrisy' which Lloyd George himself admitted 'saturated' the drink question. As well he might, for on 30 April 1915 he had admitted to one of his colleagues that he believed the shortages of ships and shells were primarily due to government mismanagement. 'The idea that slackness and drink, which some people talk so much about, are the chief causes of delay, is mostly fudge'.[102]

University of Lancaster

[101] Henson 1 April 1922.
[102] *Riddell's diary* 10 April 1915 p 74; Addison p 73.

ABBREVIATIONS

AASRP	*Associated Archaeological Societies Reports and Papers*
AAWG	*Abhandlungen der Akademie* [*Gesellschaft* to 1942] *der Wissenschaften zu Göttingen*, (Göttingen 1843–)
AAWL	*Abhandlungen der Akademie der Wissenschaften und der Literatur* (Mainz 1950–)
ABAW	*Abhandlungen der Bayerischen Akademie der Wissenchaften* (Munich 1835–)
Abh	Abhundlung
Abt	Abteilung
ACO	*Acta Conciliorum Oecumenicorum*, ed E. Schwartz (Berlin/Leipzig 1914–40)
ACW	*Ancient Christian Writers*, ed J. Quasten and J. C. Plumpe (Westminster, Maryland/London 1946–)
ADAW	*Abhandlungen der Deutschen* [till 1944 *Preussischen*] *Akademie der Wissenschaften zu Berlin* (Berlin 1815–)
AF	*Analecta Franciscana*, 10 vols (Quaracchi 1885–1941)
AFH	*Archivum Franciscanum Historicum* (Quaracchi/Rome 1908–)
AFP	*Archivum Fratrum Praedicatorum* (Rome 1931–)
AHP	*Archivum historiae pontificae* (Rome 1963–)
AHR	*American Historical Review* (New York 1895–)
AKG	*Archiv für Kulturgeschichte* (Leipzig/Münster/Cologne 1903–)
AKZ	*Arbeiten zur kirchlichen Zeitgeschichte*
ALKG	H. Denifle and F. Ehrle, *Archiv für Literatur- und Kirchengeschichte des Mittelalters*, 7 vols (Berlin/Freiburg 1885–1900)
Altaner	B. Altaner, *Patrologie: Leben, Schriften und Lehre der Kirchenväter* (5 ed Freiburg 1958)
AM	L. Wadding, *Annales Minorum*, 8 vols (Rome 1625–54); 2 ed, 25 vols (Rome 1731–1886); 3 ed, vol 1– , (Quaracchi 1931–)
An Bol	*Analecta Bollandiana* (Brussels 1882–)
Annales	*Annales: Economies, Sociétés, Civilisations* (Paris 1946–)
Ant	*Antonianum* (Rome 1926–)
APC	*Proceedings and Ordinances of the Privy Council 1386–1542*, ed Sir Harris Nicolas, 7 vols (London 1834–7)
—	*Acts of the Privy Council of England 1542–1629*, 44 vols (London 1890–1958)
—	*Acts of the Privy Council of England, Colonial Series* (*1613–1783*) 5 vols (London 1908–12)
AR	*Archivum Romanicum* (Geneva/Florence 1917–41)
ARG	*Archiv für Reformationsgeschichte* (Berlin/Leipzig/Gütersloh 1903–)
ASAW	*Abhandhungen der Sächischen Akademie* [*Gesellschaft* to 1920] *der Wissenschaften zu Leipzig* (Leipzig 1850–)
ASB	*Acta Sanctorum Bollandiana* (Brussels etc 1643–)
ASC	*Anglo Saxon Chronicle*
ASI	*Archivio storico Italiano* (Florence 1842–)
ASL	*Archivio storico Lombardo*, 1–62 (Milan 1874–1935); ns 1–10 (Milan 1936–47)
ASOC	*Analecta Sacri Ordinis Cisterciensis* [*Analecta Cisterciensia* since 1965] (Rome 1945–)

ABBREVIATIONS

ASOSB	*Acta Sanctorum Ordinis Sancti Benedicti*, ed. L' D'Achery and J. Mabillon (Paris 1668–1701)
ASP	*Archivio della Società* [*Deputazione* from 1935] *Romana di Storia Patria* (Rome 1878–1934, 1935–)
ASR	*Archives de Sociologie des Religions* (Paris 1956–)
AV	Authorised Version
AV	*Archivio Veneto* (Venice 1871–): [1891–1921, *Nuovo Archivio Veneto*; 1922–6, *Archivio Veneto-Tridentino*]
B	*Byzantion* (Paris/Boston/Brussels 1924–)
Bale, *Catalogus*	John Bale, *Scriptorum Illustrium Maioris Brytanniae Catalogus*, 2 parts (Basel 1557, 1559)
Bale, *Index*	John Bale, *Index Britanniae Scriptorum*, ed R. L. Poole and M. Bateson (Oxford 1902) *Anecdota Oxoniensia*, medieval and modern series 9
Bale, *Summarium*	John Bale, *Illustrium Maioris Britanniae Scriptorum Summarium* (Ipswich 1548, reissued Wesel 1549)
BEC	*Bibliothèque de l'Ecole des Chartes* (Paris 1839–)
Beck	H-G Beck, *Kirche und theologische Literatur im byzantinischen Reich* (Munich 1959)
BEFAR	*Bibliothèque des écoles francaises d'Athènes et Rome* (Paris 1876–)
BEHE	*Bibliothèque de l'Ecole des Hautes Etudes: Sciences Philologiques et Historiques* (Paris 1869–)
Bernard	E. Bernard, *Catalogi Librorum Manuscriptorum Angliae et Hiberniae* (Oxford 1697)
BF	*Byzantinische Forschungen* (Amsterdam 1966–)
BHG	*Bibliotheca Hagiographica Graeca*, ed F. Halkin, 3 vols+1 (3 ed Brussels 1957, 1969)
BHI	*Bibliotheca historica Italica*, ed A. Ceruti, 4 vols (Milan 1876–85), 2 series, 3 vols (Milan 1901–33)
BHL	*Bibliotheca Hagiographica Latina*, 2 vols+1 (Brussels 1898–1901, 1911)
BHR	*Bibliothèque d'Humanisme et Renaissance* (Paris/Geneva 1941–)
Bibl Ref	*Bibliography of the Reform 1450–1648, relating to the United Kingdom and Ireland*, ed Derek Baker for 1955–70 (Oxford 1975)
BIHR	*Bulletin of the Institute of Historical Research* (London 1923–)
BISIMEAM	*Bullettino dell'istituto storico italiano per il medio evo e archivio muratoriano* (Rome 1886–)
BJRL	*Bulletin of the John Rylands Library* (Manchester 1903–)
BL	British Library, London
BM	British Museum, London
BN	Bibliothèque Nationale, Paris
Bouquet	M. Bouquet, *Recueil des historiens des Gaules et de la France. Rerum gallicarum et francicarum scriptores*, 24 vols (Paris 1738–1904); new ed L. Delisle, 1–19 (Paris 1868–80)
BQR	*British Quarterly Review* (London 1845–86)
Broadmead Records	*The Records of a Church of Christ, meeting in Broadmead, Bristol 1640–87*, HKS (London 1848)
BS	*Byzantinoslavica* (Prague 1929–)
Bucer, *Deutsche Schriften*	*Martin Bucers Deutsche Schriften*, ed R. Stupperich and others (Gütersloh/Paris 1960–)
Bucer, *Opera Latina*	*Martini Buceri Opera Latina*, ed F. Wendel and others (Paris/Gütersloh 1955–)

ABBREVIATIONS

Bull Franc	*Bullarium Franciscanum*, vols 1–4 ed J. H. Sbaralea (Rome 1759–68) vols 5–7 ed C. Eubel (Rome 1898–1904), new series vols 1–3 ed U. Höntemann and J. M. Pou y Marti (Quaracchi 1929–49)
BZ	*Byzantinische Zeitschrift* (Leipzig 1892–)
CA	*Cahiers Archéologiques. Fin de L'Antiquité et Moyen-âge* (Paris 1945–)
CaF	*Cahiers de Fanjeaux* (Toulouse 1966–)
CAH	*Cambridge Ancient History* (Cambridge 1923–39)
CalRev	Calumy Revised, ed A. G. Mathews (Oxford 1934)
CalLP	*Calendar of the Letters and Papers (Foreign and Domestic) of the Reign of Henry VIII*, 21 vols in 35 parts (London 1864–1932)
CalSPD	*Calendar of State Papers: Domestic* (London 1856–)
CalSPF	*Calendar of State Papers: Foreign*, 28 vols (London 1861–1950)
Calvin, *Opera*	*Ioannis Calvini Opera Quae Supersunt Omnia*, ed G. Baum and others *Corpus Reformatorum*, 59 vols (Brunswick/Berlin 1863–1900)
Canivez	J. M. Canivez, *Statuta capitulorum generalium ordinis cisterciensis ab anno 1116 ad annum 1786*, 8 vols (Louvain 1933–41)
Cardwell, *Documentary Annals*	*Documentary Annals of the Reformed Church of England*, ed E. Cardwell, 2 vols (Oxford 1839)
Cardwell, *Synodalia*	*Synodalia*, ed E. Cardwell, 2 vols (Oxford 1842)
CC	*Corpus Christianorum* (Turnholt 1952–)
CF	*Classical Folia*, [*Folia 1946–59*] (New York 1960–)
CGOH	*Cartulaire Générale de l'Ordre des Hospitaliers de St.-Jean de Jerusalem (1100–1310)*, ed J. Delaville Le Roulx, 4 vols (Paris 1894–1906)
CH	*Church History* (New York/Chicago 1932–)
CHB	*Cambridge History of the Bible*
CHistS	*Church History Society* (London 1886–92)
CHJ	*Cambridge Historical Journal* (Cambridge 1925–57)
CIG	*Corpus Inscriptionum Graecarum*, ed A. Boeckh, J. Franz, E. Curtius, A. Kirchhoff, 4 vols (Berlin 1825–77)
CIL	*Corpus Inscriptionum Latinarum* (Berlin 1863–)
Cîteaux	*Cîteaux: Commentarii Cisterciensis* (Westmalle 1950–)
CMH	*Cambridge Medieval History*
CModH	*Cambridge Modern History*
COCR	*Collectanea Ordinis Cisterciensium Reformatorum* (Rome/Westmalle 1934–)
COD	*Conciliorum oecumenicorum decreta* (3 ed Bologna 1973)
Coll Franc	*Collectanea Franciscana* (Assisi/Rome 1931–)
CR	*Corpus Reformatorum*, ed C. G. Bretschneider and others (Halle etc. 1834–)
CS	*Cartularium Saxonicum*, ed W. de G. Birch, 3 vols (London 1885–93)
CSCO	*Corpus Scriptorum Christianorum Orientalium* (Paris 1903–)
CSEL	*Corpus Scriptorum Ecclesiasticorum Latinorum* (Vienna 1866–)
CSer	*Camden Series* (London 1838–)
CSHByz	*Corpus Scriptorum Historiae Byzantinae* (Bonn 1828–97)
CYS	*Canterbury and York Society* (London 1907–)
DA	*Deutsches Archiv für* [*Geschichte*, –Weimar 1937–43] *die Erforschung des Mittelalters* (Cologne/Graz 1950–)

DACL	*Dictionnaire d'Archéologie chrétienne et de Liturgie*, ed F. Cabrol and H. Leclercq (Paris 1924–)
DDC	*Dictionnaire de Droit Canonique*, ed R. Naz (Paris 1935–)
DHGE	*Dictionnaire d'Histoire et de Géographie ecclésiastiques*, ed A. Baudrillart and others (Paris 1912–)
DNB	*Dictionary of National Biography* (London 1885–)
DOP	*Dumbarton Oaks Papers* (Cambridge, Mass., 1941–)
DR	F. Dölger, *Regesten der Kaiserurkunden des oströmischen Reiches (Corpus der griechischen Urkunden des Mittelalters und der neuern Zeit*, Reihe A, Abt I), 5 vols: 1 (565–1025); 2 (1025–1204); 3 (1204–1282); 4 (1282–1341); 5 (1341–1543) (Munich/Berlin 1924–65)
DRev	*Downside Review* (London 1880–)
DSAM	*Dictionnaire de Spiritualité, Ascétique et Mystique*, ed M. Viller (Paris 1932–)
DTC	*Dictionnaire de Théologie Catholique*, ed A. Vacant, E. Mangenot, E. Amann, 15 vols (Paris 1903–50)
EcHR	*Economic History Review* (London 1927–)
EEBS	Ἐπετηρὶς Ἑταιρείας Βυζαντινῶν Σπουδῶν (Athens 1924–)
EETS	*Early English Text Society*
EF	*Etudes Franciscaines* (Paris 1899–1938, ns 1950–)
EHD	*English Historical Documents* (London 1953–)
EHR	*English Historical Review* (London 1886–)
Ehrhard	A. Ehrhard, *Uberlieferung und Bestand der hagiographischen und homiletischen Literatur der griechischen Kirche von den Anfängen bis zum Ende des 16. Jh*, 3 vols in 4, *TU* 50–2 (=4 series 5–7) 11 parts (Leipzig 1936–52)
Emden (O)	A. B. Emden, *A Biographical Register of the University of Oxford to 1500*, 3 vols (London 1957–9); *1500–40* (1974)
Emden (C)	A. B. Emden, *A Biographical Register of the University of Cambridge to 1500* (London 1963)
EO	*Echos d'Orient* (Constantinople/Paris 1897–1942)
ET	English translation
EYC	*Early Yorkshire Charters*, ed W. Farrer and C. T. Clay, 12 vols (Edinburgh/Wakefield 1914–65)
FGH	*Die Fragmente der griechischen Historiker*, ed F. Jacoby (Berlin 1926–30)
FM	*Histoire de l'église depuis les origines jusqu'à nos jours*, ed A. Fliche and V. Martin (Paris 1935–)
Foedera	*Foedera, conventiones, litterae et cuiuscunque generis acta publica inter reges Angliae et alios quosvis imperatores, reges, pontifices, principes vel communitates*, ed T. Rymer and R. Sanderson, 20 vols (London 1704–35), 3 ed G. Holmes, 10 vols (The Hague 1739–45), re-ed 7 vols (London 1816–69)
Franc Stud	*Franciscan Studies* (St Bonaventure, New York 1924–, ns 1941–)
Fredericq	P. Fredericq, *Corpus documentorum inquisitionis haereticae pravitatis Neerlandicae*, 3 vols (Ghent 1889–93)
FStn	*Franzikanische Studien* (Münster/Werl 1914–)
GalC	*Gallia Christiana*, 16 vols (Paris 1715–1865)
Gangraena	T. Edwards, *Gangraena*, 3 parts (London 1646)
GCS	*Die griechischen christlichen Schriftsteller der erste drei Jahrhunderte* (Leipzig 1897–)
Gee and Hardy	*Documents illustrative of English Church History* ed H. Gee and W. J. Hardy (London 1896)

GEEB	R. Janin, *La géographie ecclésiastique de l'empire byzantin*;
CEM	1, *Le siège de Constantinople et le patriarcat oecumenique*, pt 3 *Les églises et les monastères* (Paris 1953);
EMGCB	2, *Les églises et les monastères des grands centres byzantins* (Paris 1975) (series discontinued)
Golubovich	Girolamo Golubovich, *Biblioteca bio-bibliografica della Terra Santa e dell' oriente francescano:* series 1, *Annali*, 5 vols (Quaracchi 1906–23) series 2, *Documenti* 14 vols (Quaracchi 1921–33) series 3, *Documenti* (Quaracchi 1928–) series 4, *Studi*, ed M. Roncaglia (Cairo 1954–)
Grumel, *Regestes*	V. Grumel, *Les Regestes des Actes du Patriarcat de Constantinople*, 1: *Les Actes des Patriarches*, I: 381–715; II: 715–1043; III: 1043–1206 (Socii Assumptionistae Chalcedonenses, 1931, 1936, 1947)
Grundmann	H. Grundmann, *Religiöse Bewegungen im Mittelalter* (Berlin 1935, 2 ed Darmstadt 1970)
Guignard	P. Guignard, *Les monuments primitifs de la règle cistercienne* (Dijon 1878)
HBS	*Henry Bradshaw Society* (London/Canterbury 1891–)
HE	*Historia Ecclesiastica*
HistSt	*Historical Studies* (Melbourne 1940–)
HJ	*Historical Journal* (Cambridge 1958–)
HJch	*Historisches Jarhbuch der Görres Gesellschaft* (Cologne 1880–, Munich 1950–)
JKS	Hanserd Knollys Society (London 1847–)
HL	C. J. Hefele and H. Leclercq, *Histore des Conciles*, 10 vols (Paris 1907–35)
HMC	Historical Manuscripts Commission
Holzapfel, *Handbuch*	H. Holzapfel, *Handbuch der Geschichte des Franziskanerordens* (Freiburg 1908)
Hooker, *Works*	*The Works of . . . Mr. Richard Hooker*, ed J. Keble, 7 ed rev R. W. Church and F. Paget, 3 vols (Oxford 1888)
Houedene	*Chronica Magistri Rogeri de Houedene*, ed W. Stubbs, 4 vols, *RS* 51 (London 1868–71)
HRH	*The Heads of Religious Houses, England and Wales, 940–1216*, ed D. Knowles, C. N. L. Brooke, V. C. M. London (Cambridge 1972)
HS	*Hispania sacra* (Madrid 1948–)
HTR	*Harvard Theological Review* (New York/Cambridge, Mass., 1908–)
HZ	*Historische Zeitschrift* (Munich 1859–)
IER	*Irish Ecclesiastical Record* (Dublin 1864–)
IGLS	*Inscriptions greques et latines de la Syrie*, ed L. Jalabert, R. Mouterde and others, 7 vols (Paris 1929–70) in progress
IR	*Innes Review* (Glasgow 1950–)
JAC	*Jahrbuch für Antike und Christentum* (Münster-im-Westfalen 1958–)
Jaffé	*Regesta Pontificum Romanorum ab condita ecclesia ad a. 1198*, 2 ed S. Lowenfeld, F. Kaltenbrunner, P. Ewald, 2 vols (Berlin 1885–8, repr Graz 1958)
JBS	*Journal of British Studies* (Hartford, Conn., 1961–)
JEH	*Journal of Ecclesiastical History* (London 1950–)

JFHS	*Journal of the Friends Historical Society* (London/Philadelphia 1903–)
JHI	*Journal of the History of Ideas* (London 1940–)
JHSChW	*Journal of the Historical Society of the Church in Wales* (Cardiff 1947–)
JIntH	*Journal of Interdisciplinary History* (Cambridge, Mass., 1970–)
JLW	*Jahrbuch für Liturgiewissenschaft* (Münster-im-Westfalen 1921–41)
JMH	*Journal of Modern History* (Chicago 1929–)
JMedH	*Journal of Medieval History* (Amsterdam 1975–)
JRA	*Journal of Religion in Africa* (Leiden 1967–)
JRH	*Journal of Religious History* (Sydney 1960–)
JRS	*Journal of Roman Studies* (London 1910–)
JRSAI	*Journal of the Royal Society of Antiquaries of Ireland* (Dublin 1871–)
JSArch	*Journal of the Society of Archivists* (London 1955–)
JTS	*Journal of Theological Studies* (London 1899–)
Kemble	*Codex Diplomaticus Aevi Saxonici*, ed J. M. Kemble (London 1839–48)
Knowles, *MO*	David Knowles, *The Monastic Order in England, 943–1216* (2 ed Cambridge 1963)
Knowles, *RO*	, *The Religious Orders in England*, 3 vols (Cambridge 1948–59)
Knox, *Works*	*The Works of John Knox*, ed D. Laing, Bannatyne Club/Wodrow Society, 6 vols (Edinburgh 1846–64)
Laurent, *Regestes*	V. Laurent, *Les Registes des Actes du Patriarcat de Constantinople*, 1: *Les Actes des Patriarches*, IV: *Les Regestes de 1208 à 1309* (Paris 1971)
Le Neve	John Le Neve, *Fasti Ecclesiae Anglicanae 1066–1300*, rev and exp Diana E. Greenway, 1, St Pauls (London 1968); 2, Monastic Cathedrals (1971) *Fasti Ecclesiae Anglicanae 1300–1541* rev and exp H. P. F. King, J. M. Horn, B. Jones, 12 vols (London 1962–7) *Fasti Ecclesiae Anglicanae 1541–1857* rev and exp J. M. Horn, D. M. Smith, 1, St Pauls (1969); 2, Chichester (1971); 3, Canterbury, Rochester, Winchester (1974); 4, York (1975)
Lloyd, *Formularies of faith*	*Formularies of Faith Put Forth by Authority during the Reign of Henry VIII*, ed C. Lloyd (Oxford 1825)
LRS	*Lincoln Record Society*
LQR	*Law Quarterly Review* (London 1885–)
LThK	*Lexicon für Theologie und Kirche*, ed J. Höfer and K. Rahnes (2 ed Freiburg-im-Breisgau 1957–)
LW	*Luther's Works*, ed J. Pelikan and H. T. Lehman, American edition (St. Louis/Philadelphia, 1955–)
MA	*Monasticon Anglicanum*, ed R. Dodsworth and W. Dugdale, 3 vols (London 1655–73); new ed J. Caley, H. Ellis, B. Bandinel, 6 vols in 8 (London 1817–30)
Mansi	J. D. Mansi, *Sacrorum conciliorum nova et amplissima collectio*, 31 vols (Florence/Venice 1757–98); new impression and continuation, ed L. Petit and J. B. Martin, 60 vols (Paris 1899–1927)
Martène and Durand	E. Martène and U. Durand, *Veterum Scriptorum et Monumentorum Historicorum, Dogmaticorum, Moralium Amplissima Collectio*,

Collectio	9 vols (Paris 1729)
Thesaurus	*Thesaurus Novus Anedotorum*, 5 vols (Paris 1717)
Voyage	*Voyage Litteraire de Deux Religieux Benedictins de la Congregation de Saint Maur*, 2 vols (Paris 1717, 1724)
MedA	*Medium Aevum* (Oxford 1932–)
Mendola	*Atti della Settimana di Studio, 1959–* (Milan 1962–)
MF	*Miscellanea Francescana* (Foligno/Rome 1886–)
MGH	*Monumenta Germaniae Historica inde ab a.c. 500 usque ad a. 1500*, ed G. H. Pertz and others (Berlin, Hanover 1826–)
AA	*Auctores Antiquissimi*
Ant	*Antiquitates*
Briefe	*Epistolae 2: Die Briefe der Deutschen Kaiserzeit*
Cap	*Leges 2: Leges in Quart 2: Capitularia regum Francorum*
CM	*Chronica Minora* 1–3 (=*AA* 9, 11, 13) ed Th. Mommsen (1892 1894, 1898 repr 1961)
Conc	*Leges 2: Leges in Quart 3: Concilia*
Const	4: *Constitutiones et acta publica imperatorum et regum*
DC	*Deutsche Chroniken*
Dip	*Diplomata in folio*
Epp	*Epistolae 1 in Quart*
Epp Sel	4: *Epistolae Selectae*
FIG	*Leges 3: Fontes Iuris Germanici Antique*, new series
FIGUS	4: , *in usum scholarum*
Form	2: *Leges in Quart 5: Formulae Merovingici et Karolini Aevi*
GPR	*Gesta Pontificum Romanorum*
Leges	*Leges in folio*
Lib	*Libelli de lite*
LM	*Ant 3: Libri Memoriales*
LNG	*Leges 2: Leges in Quart 1: Leges nationum Germanicarum*
Necr	Ant 2: *Necrologia Germaniae*
Poet	1: *Poetae Latini Medii Aevi*
Quellen	*Quellen zur Geistesgeschichte des Mittelalters*
Schriften	*Schriften der Monumenta Germaniae Historica*
SRG	*Scriptores rerum germanicarum in usum scholarum*
SRG ns	, new series
SRL	*Scriptores rerum langobardicarum et italicarum*
SRM	*Scriptores rerum merovingicarum*
SS	*Scriptores*
SSM	*Staatschriften des späteren Mittelalters*
MIOG	*Mitteilungen des Instituts für österreichische Geschichtsforschung* (Graz/Cologne 1880–)
MM	F. Miklosich and J. Müller, *Acta et Diplomata Graeca medii aevi sacra et profana*, 6 vols (Vienna 1860–90)
Moorman, *History*	J. R. H. Moorman, *A History of the Franciscan Order from its origins to the year 1517* (Oxford 1968)
More, *Works*	*The Complete Works of St Thomas More*, ed R. S. Sylvester and others Yale edition (New Haven/London 1963–)
Moyen Age	*Le moyen âge. Revue d'histoire et de philologie* (Paris 1888–)
MRHEW	David Knowles and R. N. Hadcock, *Medieval Religious Houses, England and Wales* (2 ed London 1971)
MRHI	A. Gwynn and R. N. Hadcock, *Medieval Religious Houses, Ireland* (London 1970)

MRHS	Ian B. Cowan and David E. Easson, *Medieval Religious Houses, Scotland* (2 ed London 1976)
MS	Manuscript
MStn	*Mittelalterliche Studien* (Stuttgart 1966–)
Muratori	L. A. Muratori, *Rerum italicarum scriptores*, 25 vols (Milan 1723–51); new ed G. Carducci and V. Fiorini, 34 vols in 109 fasc (Città di Castello/Bologna 1900–)
NCE	*New Catholic Encyclopedia*, 15 vols (New York 1967)
NCModH	*New Cambridge Modern History*, 14 vols (Cambridge 1957–70)
nd	no date
NEB	*New English Bible*
NF	Neue Folge
NH	*Northern History* (Leeds 1966–)
ns	new series
NS	New Style
Numen	*Numen: International Review for the History of Religions* (Leiden 1954–)
OCP	*Orientalia Christiana Periodica* (Rome 1935–)
ODCC	*Oxford Dictionary of the Christian Church*, ed F. L. Cross (Oxford 1957), 2 ed with E. A. Livingstone (1974)
OED	*Oxford English Dictionary*
OMT	*Oxford Medieval Texts*
OS	Old Style
OHS	*Oxford Historical Society*
PBA	*Proceedings of the British Academy*
PG	*Patrologia Graeca*, ed J. P. Migne, 161 vols (Paris 1857–66)
PhK	Philosophisch-historische Klasse
PL	*Patrologia Latina*, ed J. P. Migne, 217+4 index vols (Paris 1841–64)
Plummer, *Bede*	*Venerabilis Baedae Opera Historica*, ed C. Plummer (Oxford 1896)
PO	*Patrologia Orientalis*, ed J. Graffin and F. Nau (Paris 1903–)
Potthast	*Regesta Pontificum Romanorum inde ab a. post Christum natum 1198 ad a. 1304*, ed A. Potthast, 2 vols (1874–5 repr Graz 1957)
PP	*Past and Present* (London 1952–)
PPTS	*Palestine Pilgrims' Text Society*, 13 vols and index (London 1896–1907)
PRIA	*Proceedings of the Royal Irish Academy* (Dublin 1836–)
PRO	Public Record Office
PS	Parker Society (Cambridge 1841–55)
PW	*Paulys Realencyklopädie der klassischen Altertumswissenschaft*, new ed G. Wissowa and W. Kroll (Stuttgart 1893–)
QFIAB	*Quellen und Forschungen aus italienischen Archiven und Bibliotheken* (Rome 1897–)
RAC	*Reallexikon für Antike und Christentum*, ed T. Klauser (Stuttgart 1941)
RB	*Revue Bénédictine* (Maredsous 1884–)
RE	*Realencyclopädie für protestantische Theologie*, ed A. Hauck, 24 vols (3 ed Leipzig, 1896–1913)
REB	*Revue des Etudes Byzantines* (Bucharest/Paris 1946–)
RecS	Record Series
RGG	*Die Religion in Geschichte und Gegenwart*, 6 vols (Tübingen 1927–32)
RH	*Revue historique* (Paris 1876–)

RHC,	*Recueil des Historiens des Croisades*, ed Académie des Inscriptions et Belles-Lettres (Paris 1841–1906)
Arm	*Historiens Arméniens*, 2 vols (1869–1906)
Grecs	*Historiens Grecs*, 2 vols (1875–81)
Lois	*Lois. Les Assises de Jérusalem*, 2 vols (1841–3)
Occ	*Historiens Occidentaux*, 5 vols (1844–95)
Or	*Historiens Orientaux*, 5 vols (1872–1906)
RHD	*Revue d'histoire du droit* (Haarlem, Gronigen 1923–)
RHDFE	*Revue historique du droit français et étranger* (Paris 1922–)
RHE	*Revue d'Histoire Ecclésiastique* (Louvain 1900–)
RHEF	*Revue d'Histoire de l'Eglise de France* (Paris 1910–)
RHR	*Revue de l'Histoire des Religions* (Paris 1880–)
RR	*Regesta Regum Anglo-Normannorum*, ed H. W. C. Davis, H. A. Cronne, Charles Johnson, R. H. C. Davis, 4 vols (Oxford 1913–69)
RS	*Rerum Brittanicarum Medii Aevi Scriptores*, 99 vols (London 1858–1911). *Rolls Series*
RSCI	*Rivista di storia della chiesa in Italia* (Rome 1947–)
RSR	*Revue des sciences religieuses* (Strasbourg 1921–)
RStI	*Rivista storica italiana* (Naples 1884–)
RTAM	*Recherches de théologie ancienne et médiévale* (Louvain 1929–)
RV	Revised Version
Sitz	*Sitzungsberichte*
SA	*Studia Anselmiana* (Roma 1933–)
sa	*sub anno*
SBAW	*Sitzungsberichte der bayerischen Akademie der Wissenschaften*, PhK (Munich 1871–)
SCH	*Studies in Church History* (London 1964–)
ScHR	*Scottish Historical Review* (Edinburgh/Glasgow 1904–)
SCR	*Sources chrétiennes*, ed H. de Lubac and J. Daniélou (Paris 1941–)
SF	*Studi Francescani* (Florence 1914–)
SGra	*Studia Gratiana*, ed J. Forchielli and A. M. Stickler (Bologna 1953–)
SGre	*Studi Gregoriani*, ed G. Borino, 7 vols (Rome 1947–61)
SMon	*Studia Monastica* (Montserrat, Barcelona 1959–)
Speculum	*Speculum, A Journal of Medieval Studies* (Cambridge, Mass. 1926–)
SpicFr	*Spicilegium Friburgense* (Freiburg 1957–)
SS	*Surtees Society* (Durham 1835–)
SSSpoleto	*Settimane di Studio sull'alto medioevo*, 1952– , Centro Italiano di studi sull'alto medioevo, Spoleto 1954–)
STC	*A Short-Title Catalogue of Books Printed in England, Scotland and Ireland and of English Books Printed Abroad 1475–1640*, ed A. W. Pollard and G. R. Redgrave (London 1926, repr 1946, 1950)
Strype, *Annals*	John Strype, *Annals of the Reformation and Establishment of Religion . . .during Queen Elizabeth's Happy Reign*, 4 vols in 7 (Oxford 1824)
Strype, *Cranmer*	John Strype, *Memorials of . . .Thomas Cranmer*, 2 vols (Oxford 1840)
Strype, *Grindal*	John Strype, *The History of the Life and Acts of . . . Edmund Grindal* (Oxford 1821)

Strype, *Memorials*	John Strype, *Ecclesiastical Memorials, Relating Chiefly to Religion, and the Reformation of it . . . under King Henry VIII, King Edward VI and Queen Mary I*, 3 vols in 6 (Oxford 1822)
Strype, *Parker*	John Strype, *The Life and Acts of Matthew Parker*, 3 vols (Oxford 1821)
Strype, *Whitgift*	John Strype, *The Life and Acts of John Whitgift*, 3 vols (Oxford 1822)
sub hag	*subsidia hagiographica*
sv	*sub voce*
SVRG	*Schriften des Vereins für Reformationsgeschichte* (Halle/Leipzig/Gütersloh 1883–)
TCBiblS	*Transactions of the Cambridge Bibliographical Society* (Cambridge 1949–)
Tchalenko	G. Tchalenko, *Villages antiques de la Syrie du Nord*, 3 vols (Paris 1953–8)
THSCym	*Transactions of the Historical Society of Cymmrodorion* (London 1822–)
TRHS	*Transactions of the Royal Historical Society* (London 1871–)
TU	*Texte und Untersuchungen zur Geschichte der altchristlichen Literatur* (Leipzig/Berlin 1882–)
VCH	*Victoria County History* (London 1900–)
VHM	G. Tiraboschi, *Vetera Humiliatorum Monumenta*, 3 vols. (Milan 1766–8)
Vivarium	*Vivarium: An International Journal for the Philosophy and Intellectual Life of the Middle Ages and Renaissance* (Assen 1963–)
VV	*Vizantijskij Vremennik* 1–25 (St Petersburg 1894–1927), ns 1 (26) (Leningrad 1947–)
WA	*D. Martin Luthers Werke*, ed J. C. F. Knaake (Weimar 1883–) [*Weimarer Ausgabe*]
WA Br	*Briefwechsel*
WA DB	*Deutsche Bibel*
WA TR	*Tischreden*
WelHR	*Welsh History Review* (Cardiff 1960–)
Wharton	H. Wharton, *Anglia Sacra*, 2 parts (London 1691)
Whitelock, *Wills*	*Anglo-Saxon wills*, ed D. Whitlock (Cambridge 1930)
Wilkins	*Concilia Magnae Britanniae et Hiberniae A.D. 446–1717*, 4 vols, ed D. Wilkins (London 1737)
YAJ	*Yorkshire Archaeological Journal* (London/Leeds 1870–)
Zanoni	L. Zanoni, *Gli Umiliati nei loro rapporti con l'eresia, l'industria della lana ed i communi nei secoli xii e xiii, Biblioteca Historica Italica*, 2 series, 2 (Milan 1911)
ZKG	*Zeitschrift für Kirchengeschichte* (Gotha/Stuttgart 1878–)
ZOG	*Zeitschrift für osteuropäische Geschichte* (Berlin 1911–35) = *Kyrios* (Berlin 1936–)
ZRG	*Zeitschrift der Savigny-Stiftung für Rechtsgeschichte* (Weimar)
GAbt	*Germanistische Abteilung* (1863–)
KAbt	*Kanonistische Abteilung* (1911–)
RAbt	*Romanistische Abteilung* (1880–)
ZRGG	*Zeitschrift für Religions- und Geistesgeschichte* (Marburg 1948–)
Zwingli, *Werke*	*Huldreich Zwinglis Sämmtliche Werke*, ed E. Egli and others, *CR* (Berlin/Leipzig/Zurich 1905–)